THE COUNCIL OF THE EUROPEAN UNION

The Council of the European Union
(3rd edition)

by

MARTIN WESTLAKE and DAVID GALLOWAY

with Toon Digneffe

JOHN HARPER
PUBLISHING

The Council of the European Union
3rd edition

Published by John Harper Publishing
27 Palace Gates Road
London N22 7BW, United Kingdom.
Telephone: +44 (0) 20 8881 4774
E-mail: jhpublish@aol.com

First edition 1995
2nd edition 1999
3rd edition 2004
ISBN 0–9536278–8–8

Typeset in 10/11pt Palatino

Printed and Bound in Great Britain by the Cromwell Press

CONTENTS

PART 1: INTRODUCING THE COUNCIL

PART 2: THE COUNCIL IN ITS DIFFERENT GUISES

PART 3: THE EUROPEAN COUNCIL AND INTERGOVERNMENTAL CONFERENCES

PART 4: PREPARING THE COUNCIL

PART 5: NEGOTIATING AND BARGAINING IN THE COUNCIL

PART 6: LEADERSHIP AND CONTINUITY IN THE COUNCIL

PART 7: LOOKING TO THE FUTURE

APPENDICES

LIST OF BOXES

LIST OF TABLES

LIST OF FIGURES

was previously secretary of the Commission's task force on German unification, head of training for the Commission's External Service, advisor on ESDP and NATO and Commission representative in the G8 and EU Council Terrorism working groups. Before joining the Commission, he was lecturer in politics at the Sorbonne and head of European training at the UK Civil Service College. He has published widely on European affairs and is the editor of *The European Commission*, also published by John Harper Publishing.

Foreword by Javier Solana

Secretary-General of the Council of the European Union
High Representative for the common foreign and security policy

If press coverage were to be believed, Europe is in some sort of permanent crisis. It is true that 'crises' are frequent and that European integration is a daily struggle. Critics of the integration process are quick to single out these difficulties to make their point. But if one adopts a historical perspective, the successes of the critics seem ephemeral at best. The simple truth is that Europe has always progressed and, looking back over the past fifty years, that progress has been phenomenal. Even twenty years ago, the single market existed only on paper, economic and monetary union was a pipe dream and European-level foreign policy was limited to the gesture politics of the former European Political Cooperation. Today, we have a vast single market. The euro is in the pocket of most Europeans. The European Union has absorbed ten new member states, with more to come soon.

After the rejection by the French Assemblée Nationale in 1954 of the draft Treaty for a European Defence Community, European integration took a decisive step towards the economic and the functional. To my mind, the Single European Act, with its single market objective, and the Maastricht Treaty's provisions on the achievement of an economic and monetary union crowned this approach. It was an approach sometimes characterised as a sort of 'inverted federalism' – it left outside Community competence all matters which, in a federation or even a confederation, would be done at central level; in particular, economic and foreign policy. But Maastricht also marked the point of departure for a new approach towards a more political Europe; a Europe which had decided to give itself a genuine foreign policy and a Europe which began to cooperate in such traditionally sensitive areas as justice and home affairs.

Why did Europe opt for this more political approach? The first reason must surely be that such political motives were always there, waiting in the wings. The 'founding fathers' of the European Union always had political integration as their final objective. The choice of a more economic and functional approach was dictated by circumstances, but there was no doubt in their minds about the final aim. The second reason can be found in the geo-political changes that occurred in the late 1980s. It was against the backdrop of impending German unification that Chancellor Kohl and President Mitterrand proposed, in April 1990, to add an intergovernmental conference on political union to the existing intergovernmental conference on economic and monetary union. The third reason resides in the development of the European Community itself. Creating the single market and a single currency presupposed a high degree of solidarity among the member states, and logically that solidarity would be reflected externally, as it had been for a long time in the commercial field. Moreover, the sheer size and power of this emerging economic and commercial entity had in any case transformed it into a serious player on the international stage. The fourth reason is that other countries themselves increasingly began to view the European Union as a political entity.

The Maastricht Treaty put in place the foundations for establishing a common foreign and security policy which could also give rise to a common defence policy. This sort of laboured incrementalism may seem frustrating, but it is a method that has proved its worth and is well adapted to Europe's inherent complexity. A great deal of reluctance and opposition, some bureaucratic and coroporatist, had to be overcome to put the new pillar in place, with progress only possible through the Union's supranational institutions by innovating new approaches alongside the Community method. The eruption of the Balkans crisis showed that the new policy was far from ready, but it also demonstrated graphically why such a common policy was vitally necessary. It was in large part due to that common realisation that the post that I currently occupy was created by the 1997 Amsterdam Treaty.

Thus, despite undeniable setbacks, progress continues to be made towards the political objectives I have described above. What makes such progress possible? My answer would be that, in an increasingly broad range of policy areas, the governments of the Union's sovereign states have been – to borrow a phrase from the earlier stages of economic and monetary union – 'learning by doing'. The institution where this extraordinary experiment has been taking place is the Council of the European Union. There are many reasons for Europeans to be proud of the ingenuity of the design of the Union's institutions: the world's only trans-national directly-elected Parliament; the revolutionary autonomy of the European Commission and its role in the 'Community method'; the common acceptance of the jurisdiction of the European Court of Justice. Perhaps the most extraordinary and ingenious of them all is the Council.

This book, which I warmly commend, describes in an accessible way how the Council has evolved and how it really works. It brings together a range of intellectual and academic talent, but all of its contributors are also, in one way or another, practitioners. It is therefore a work of considerable authority.

Over the years, the Council has had many detractors. It has all too frequently been portrayed as the 'bad guy' of European integration, the breach where national sovereignty swarms back into the pure citadel of the Community method. In reality, the Council was always, from the outset, an integral part of the Community method, which could best be described as a symbiotic mutual dependency for, if the Council could not act without a Commission proposal, the Commission's proposal could not be implemented without Council consent. This remained true once the European Parliament began to develop its powers of democratic oversight and participation in the legislative process. The Maastricht Treaty further consolidated the central role of the Council. It created new (some would say more 'intergovernmental') ways of doing business. But that business was still done in the supranational framework of the Council. It is more than time, then, for the Council to cast off its 'bad guy' image. I welcome the third edition of this excellent guide to an institution that deserves to be better known and which I think, without exaggeration, has played a vital role in making the European Union what it is. This book shows how.

Brussels, October 2004

Introduction

The first edition of this book was published in 1995. A slightly revised update was published in 1999, taking account of the changes resulting from the Amsterdam Treaty. The introductions to both previous editions made what seem in retrospect to have been vain predictions that, with regard to the Council, nothing very radical was likely to change in the near future. In fact, an awful lot of major change has occurred over the past five years: the emerging role of high representative for the CFSP; the integration of new military structures; regular meetings of EU defence ministers; the advent of ten new members; six substantial revisions of the Council's rules of procedure; and the entry into force of yet another new treaty in 2003, to mention but a handful. Consequently, this edition has been completely rewritten.

The Nice Intergovernmental Conference was billed as the occasion when the fifteen heads of state or government would prepare the European Union and its institutions for the largest wave of enlargement the EU had ever experienced. However, the Nice IGC was more concerned with issues of power than issues of efficiency, and redistributing power inside the Union, like redistributing money, is always a particularly fraught exercise. While each new treaty represents a further step forward in shaping the Union into its own constitutional mould, the assessment made by many commentators in the immediate aftermath Nice IGC was less than flattering. But, as with preceding IGCs, a dispassionate reappraisal in the fullness of time will almost certainly cast the Treaty of Nice in a more nuanced light.

Subsequent to Nice, a convention was established to deal with questions relating to the balance of powers between the Union and the member states, and between the Union's institutions. The outcome was a single, coherent constitutional text for the European Union. The convention delivered its draft text in June 2003, and an intergovernmental conference was convened in the latter part of the same year. The IGC reached agreement in June 2004, and the process of ratification has now begun. As André Gillissen puts it in chapter 21, this book has therefore been written 'in the shadow of the IGC'. The various changes which will occur if and when the draft constitutional treaty has been ratified by the twenty-five member states are discussed at various points in the book.

In the meantime, the wave of enlargement for which Nice was supposed to prepare the Union has come to pass. As Gillissen describes in chapter 21, the Council adopted a two-pronged approach to face up to the impending operational challenge that such a massive enlargement would necessarily create. In the first place, there were changes at the constitutional level (Nice, the convention, the IGC). In the second place, and at a more pragmatic level, there were reforms that could be undertaken without recourse to constitutional mechanisms. At various European Councils (Helsinki, Seville, Brussels) heads of state or government have sought to adapt the Council and the European Council's basic working methods. At a more modest, but equally effective, level, the Council's preparatory bodies have undergone major reforms and adjustments. All of those changes, and their consequences, are set out in this book.

In the context of change and enlargement, reference must also be made to the impact of the preceding enlargement in 1995. One of the most significant consequences, following on from the 'near misses' in the Danish and French referendums on the Maastricht Treaty, was a new and sustained emphasis on openness and transparency, including a very liberal access to documents regime. Martin Bauer gives a comprehensive overview of these measures in chapter 20. These changes also had major (and happy) consequences for the editors of this book. The first edition was pretty much the first major study of the Council in the English language. As such, there was great emphasis on providing as much information and documentation as possible, mainly in the form of annexes. Thanks to the Council's policy of openness and the extraordinary potential offered by the internet and computers, comprehensive provision of basic documentation is no longer necessary, for the Council is now the proud possessor of a user-friendly and generous website (http://www.consilium.eu.int). The provision of so much information on the web has meant that far more space could be dedicated in this edition to more analytical studies of the way the Council works and has evolved.

Such studies are necessary because, largely independently of all the changes described above, the Council and its various formations and bodies have been steadily evolving in step with the developments, political and other, which have been occurring in the European Union. These range – to take just some of the more significant – from agricultural and fisheries reform (Paul Culley, chapter 7), through the creation and increasing importance of the Eurogroup (Sixten Korkman, chapter 5.1), through the consolidated role of the Justice and Home Affairs Council (Hans G. Nilsson, chapter 6), to the emergence of a common foreign and security policy and a European security and defence policy (Paul Reiderman and Toon Digneffe, chapters 4.2 and 4.3). All of these changes have had knock-on effects on the way member states coordinate their policy and negotiate towards their desired ends (David Spence, chapters 15 and 17).

Two important chapters in the first and second editions, on the Council and the Commission and on the Council and parliaments, have disappeared from this edition, but not the material they contained. The editors decided simply that it would be better for Council-Commission and Council-parliament relations to be covered at appropriate places in the analytical texts.

We would like to extend our appreciation to all of those who contributed to this book, thus sharing their considerable expertise with a broader audience. All the authors involved in this study, who have contributed entirely in a personal capacity, are agreed that the Council of the European Union should be better known and better understood. For a long time the Council was characterised as the villain of the piece. Such a characterisation is no longer possible; the Council is, as it has in fact always been, a vital supranational institution intimately involved in the process that has made the European Union what it is today.

Our thanks go to Anna Skulavikova for having efficiently compiled the index.

The editors are grateful to our publisher, John Harper, for his patience and understanding. As usual, any errors of fact or judgement lie squarely on our shoulders.

Martin Westlake and David Galloway
Brussels, October 2004

Abbreviations used in the text

ACP	Africa, Caribbean and Pacific (countries)
AFSJ	Area of Freedom, Security and Justice
BEPGs	Broad Economic Policy Guidelines
CAP	Common Agriculture Policy
CATS	Article 36 committee (Comité de l'article trente-six)
CDPC	Eur opean Committee on Crime Problems
CELAD	European anti-drug committee (Comité européen de lutte anti-drogue)
CELEX	Data base on European legislation
CEPOL	European Police College (network of training colleges for senior police officers)
CFP	Common Fisheries Policy
CFSP	Common Foreign and Security Policy
CHOD	Chiefs of Defence
CIREFI	Centre for Information, Discussion and Exchange on the Crossing of Frontiers and Immigration
Civcom	Committee for civilian aspects of crisis management
CJTF	Combined Joint Task Forces
COCOR	Comité de Co-ordination (forerunner of Coreper)
COLLEVAL	Collective evaluation working group
COMIX	Mixed committee procedure
Coreper	Comité des représentants permanents (permanent representatives committee)
COREU	An encoded correspondence network between foreign ministries and the European Commission (from: correspondance européenne)
DG	Directorate-General
EAGGF	European Agricultural Guidance and Guarantee Fund
EC	European Community
ECAP	European Capability Action Plan
ECB	European Central Bank
ECHR	European Convention on Human Rights
Ecofin	Economic and Financial Affairs Council
ECSC	European Coal and Steel Community
EDP	Excessive Deficit Procedure
EFC	Economic and Financial Committee
EEC	European Economic Community
EFTA	European Free Trade Association
EIB	European Investment Bank
EJN	European Judicial Network
EMU	Economic and Monetary Union
EP	European Parliament
EPC	European Political Cooperation / Economic Policy Committee
ESCB	European System of Central Banks
ESDI	European Security and Defence Identity
ESDP	European Security and Defence Policy
EU	European Union
EUMC	European Union Military Committee
EUMS	European Union Military Staff

EUPM	European Union Police Mission
Euratom	European Atomic Energy Community
FCO	Foreign and Commonwealth Office
FIU	Financial Intelligence Units
FSAP	Financial Services Action Plan
FSC	Financial Services Committee
GAC	General Affairs Council
GAERC	General Affairs and External Relations Council
GATT	General Agreement on Tariffs and Trade
GHD	Horizontal working party on drugs
GNI	Gross national income
IGC	Intergovernmental Conference
IIA	Interinstitutional Agreement
IMF	International Monetary Fund
JHA	Justice and Home Affairs
KIP	Key issues paper
MAGS	Mutual assistance between customs authorities
MDG	Multi-disciplinary group on organised crime
MEP	Member of the European Parliament
Milreps	Military representatives
NATO	North Atlantic Treaty Organisation
NCBs	National central banks
NSA	National security authority
OECD	Organisation for Economic Cooperation and Development
OLAF	European Anti-Fraud Office (Office européen de lutte anti-fraude)
OSCE	Organisation for Security and Cooperation in Europe
OMC	Open method of coordination
PPEWU	Policy Planning and Early Warning Unit
PSC	Political and Security Committee
QMV	Qualified majority vote/voting
SAB	Supplementary and Amending Budget
SCA	Special Committee for Agriculture
SCH-EVAL	Schengen evaluation group
SCIFA	Strategic Committee on Immigration, Frontiers and Asylum
SGCI	Secretariat générale pour la coordination interministérielle des affaires économiques européennes
SGP	Stability and Growth Pact
SIS	Schengen Information System
SITCEN	Joint Situation Centre
SOFA	Status of forces agreement
TACs	Total allowable catches
TEC	Treaty establishing the European Community
TENs	Trans-European Networks
TEU	Treaty on European Union
UKREP	United Kingdom Permament Representation to the European Union
WEU	Western European Union
WP	Working Party
WTO	World Trade Organisation

This and following pages – some of Marc Schober's takes on the EU and the Council

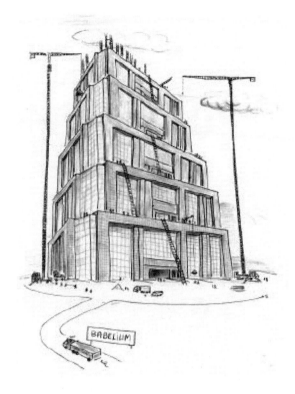

DOSSIER TRES DELICAT

WHEN THE UNION WILL HAVE 35 MEMBER STATES

"LE COREPER I EST COMPOSÉ
DE PERSONNES TRES INTELLIGENTES!"
(citation de son Président)

PART 1: INTRODUCING THE COUNCIL

'On 12 July, the Heads of Delegation met together once more. "I have to admit," I said, "that there was a gap in our original draft, which Spierenburg and Suetens have suggested ways of filling. We can now distinguish two types of problem: those which the Treaty, by a collective decision of our national Parliaments, will expressly entrust to the High Authority; and those which will spill over into the responsibility of Governments, and in which Governments should be empowered to intervene, provided that they act collectively. In such circumstances, well defined in advance, the High Authority and the Governments could hold joint meetings. We have just made a great step forward." We had: the Council of Ministers of the European Community had just been born.'

Jean Monnet, *Memoirs*, Collins, London, 1978

The purpose of this book is to provide a general introduction to the Council, going beyond a straightforward description of what it does, and analysing the altogether more interesting questions of *why and how it does it*. Many of the subjects covered could have been treated in greater depth; for many, a substantial body of academic literature is available. But in a book such as this the main objective is to provide a sufficiently comprehensive picture of the institution to give the reader a 'feel' for its *raison d'être* and modes of behaviour, without descending into a tedious compendium of detail of little interest except to policy specialists or procedure wonks.

However, enough internal anatomy has been dissected and exposed in the following pages to explain the outward appearance and actions of this fundamental component of the EU's structures. In doing so, the subsequent chapters convey some of the sense of wonderment felt by the editors and authors about the Council; that it works as it does, despite its imperfections and shortcomings, is still something of a feat. An underlying thread and shared concern, however, is that the Council has now reached a stage in its existence where, despite the many recent attempts at reform described in the book, challenging questions remain about its ability to deliver in a Union of thirty or more members. The answer, as chapter 21 explains, is far from a foregone conclusion.

Chapter 1: What is the Council?

Emerging from anonymity

The Council of the European Union is the second of four European institutions whose origins lie in the 1951 Treaty of Paris, which established the European Coal and Steel Community. The Council of Ministers – as it is more usually termed[1] – is, along with the European Commission and the European Parliament, one of the European Union's policy-making institutions. It is the most powerful of the three; no important policy or legislative decision in the Union can be taken without the Council's agreement. Understanding the nature of the European Union therefore pre-supposes a thorough understanding of the Council, how it works and its place and role in the Union's institutional system. Yet, for most of its existence the Council has been little known and still less understood.

Indeed, it is only in the past fifteen years that the Council has started to become better known. There are many reasons for the Council's previously low profile. Academics traditionally regarded it as the poor relation to the European Commission and the European Parliament; the latter – rightly portrayed as revolutionary supranational institutions – were perceived as being much more innovative in terms of European integration, whereas the less well understood Council was generally regarded as being an 'intergovernmental' (and therefore relatively uninteresting) mechanism.

For most of its existence, the Council has been largely unknown to the general public. Until recently, its secretariat and meeting rooms were located in anonymous buildings. Television usually preferred the European Commission's more recognisable Berlaymont headquarters as a backdrop to correspondents' reports on the latest events in Brussels. Ministers would be filmed going into, and coming out of, Council meetings, but the attendant national media were, understandably, more interested in their 'own' ministers' pronouncements than about the institution in which they had been working. The Brussels-based journalists accredited to the European institutions saw the Council mainly as an inhospitable building where they had to wait for lengthy periods for ministers to emerge for interviews. The journalists, and their editors, were only interested in the Council when the ministers were in town. There was very little interest in the Council's Brussels-based permanent structures – the preparatory committees and its general secretariat – which have always underpinned its higher-profile political face.

The Council tended to make the headlines only when engaged in one of its regular 'marathon' sessions on the Common Agriculture Policy (CAP) (see chapter 7). Even then, the institution's existence was barely acknowledged. Ministers emerging dishevelled from an all-night negotiating session would be all too eager to claim 'positive' decisions as a national and personal triumph, while the blame for politically awkward outcomes was most often placed on the shoulders of 'Brussels' (that is, the European Union in general, and more often than not the European Commission in particular).

Since the early 1990s there has been increasing public awareness of, and academic interest in, the Council in its own right. There are a number of reasons for this. Cumulatively, the Maastricht (Treaty on European Union, TEU), Amsterdam and Nice treaties, in force from 1993, 1999 and 2003 respectively, transformed the Council, extending the scope and the nature of its powers and turning it into a far more complex and politically visible institution. One of those changes was the transformation of the Council's secretary-general into the European Union's high representative for foreign and security policy, the Union's foreign policy supremo. The dynamic role played by the first such secretary-general, Javier Solana (a former Spanish foreign minister and NATO secretary-general), did much to put the Council more firmly 'on the map'. The 1992 Edinburgh European Council began a process of greater openness and transparency in all of the European Union's institutions, and the Council very rapidly introduced measures – such as those regarding access to documents – which encouraged journalists and academics to look more closely at the institution (see chapter 20). This trend towards greater openness was consolidated by the arrival of the new Nordic member states in 1995.

As the 1990s progressed, academics and journalists became more interested in the Council. The pace of policy developments accelerated, and their nature changed. Whilst initially exciting media attention, the '1992' target for the creation of a single market seemed to dissolve into a largely technocratic exercise. The same could not be said of the Maastricht Treaty's aims to create a single currency and a common foreign and security policy, nor of the foundations it laid for cooperation in the equally sensitive areas of justice and home affairs (see chapters 4, 5 and 6). The Brussels-based media became far more aware of the Council. In addition to the developments described above, this was perhaps in part also due to the Council's 1995 move to a new headquarters building (see chapter 2) which included a state-of-the-art press room and deliberately provided a secure location for interviews and photographs of arriving and departing ministers.

There are twenty-five national public opinions in the European Union. Inevitably, politicians and the national media tend to portray EU policy and law making in terms of the domestic political arena. Nevertheless, the Council has over the years proved to be an effective forum for reconciling and resolving differences between governments with very different national interests, histories, political hues and complexions, cultural heritages, negotiating styles and personalities. Like many policy- or law-making institutions in modern liberal democracies, the Council has, to achieve this, evolved highly sophisticated structures. This sophistication reflects the fact that the European Union is a complex and still-developing political system that cuts across virtually every area of public policy. In many areas, the Union passes laws and takes decisions that have legal effect in all member states and have a direct impact on citizens. This sets the Union aside from other groupings of states. Member governments, with the backing of national parliaments, have voluntarily pooled sovereign powers in carefully circumscribed areas and created institutions and procedures through which these collectively shared powers are exercised. Before the Second World War, national sovereignty was deemed indivisible. Cooperation between sovereign states took place largely on the basis of shifting power bloc alliances for territorial or dynastic ends. Endowing the Union with a unique and carefully crafted institutional structure, in which power is deliberately dispersed and tempered with numerous checks and balances, has undoubtedly been one of the key factors in its success.

The Council has its own unique place in this structure. As the Union's reach has extended in line with the ever-expanding powers conferred by successive treaties, the Council's tasks have also grown and developed. Within its evolving formal structures, it has developed its own informal traditions, rules, customs and working practices to remain what it has always been – a negotiating machine geared to taking decisions. However, the machine is complex and the Council is riven with dichotomies and apparent contradictions stemming from the Union's institutional design. This book details the mechanics of the machine and considers its inner workings. In so doing, it expands upon the themes and issues touched upon in this chapter and takes a forward-looking view about the Council's ability to rise to the twofold challenge of enlargement and the evolution of the Union's structures under the new constitutional treaty.

The origins of the Council

As oil has been to Europe since the 1960s, so coal was to Europe before then. By geological quirk, much of Europe's coal lay beneath the battle-scarred plain of Alsace, on the political fault line between France and Germany, and in the neighbouring valleys of the Saar, the Moselle and the Rhine. The coalfields and the rivers and the huge coke and steel plants that grew up beside them were not only a source of economic tension, but also the potential backbone of Europe's war machines. The late 1940s saw a number of ideas floated about how this structural tension could be reduced. Most of these foresaw some sort of cooperative management of the French and German coal and steel industries. Jean Monnet, a far-sighted and well-connected French businessman, took such ideas to their logical conclusion: France and Germany should relinquish all national sovereignty over their coal and steel production and pool it in a supranational and entirely autonomous organization, a High Authority. This was the essence of Robert Schuman's 1950 declaration, and it touched at the heart of the nation state, for there was to be no place for governments in the High Authority.

Monnet and Schuman, wary of their proposal becoming bogged down in diplomatic negotiations, sought prior agreement on the principle of the supranational and autonomous High Authority. Britain could not accept the principle, but in 1950 the representatives of Italy, the three Benelux countries and France and Germany – countries so recently at war among themselves – sat down to negotiate a revolutionary treaty. From the beginning,

however, is often described as a sui generis subject of international law. While the current treaty represents a new stage in the process of creating 'an ever closer union among the peoples of Europe' (article 1 TEU) and the draft constitution foresees a union 'reflecting the will of the citizens and States of Europe to build a common future' (article 1 of the constitutional treaty), neither enshrines the principle of equality between member states (a basic principle underlying intergovernmental organisations). The constitution is founded rather on the principle of equal treatment of, and non-discrimination between, member states and citizens in the application of EU law; member states are 'equal before the Constitution' (article I-5 of the constitutional treaty). It is true that member states are 'masters' of the treaties in equal measure, and that in the Council, the vote of each of its members holds equal weight and power when decisions are taken by unanimity, simple majority or reinforced majority.[4] Yet the Union also explicitly recognises differences in economic, political and demographic size in the way in which member states' 'presence' is reflected in its policy-making institutions, including the Council (see chapter 14).

Often misleadingly portrayed as the 'intergovernmental' component of the European Union's novel institutional blend, the Council is first and foremost a *supranational* institution. It is the primary decision-making body established by the treaties and acts as a collective body when defending its interests vis-à-vis the other EU institutions or the Union's interests to the outside world. It is an institution in a Union governed by the rule of law, with its own prerogatives under the treaties. In many cases it takes decisions

Box 1.1: *The Council – national and supranational*

The Council's dichotomy was recognised from its very inception and was neatly encapsulated in the words of Konrad Adenauer, the German Chancellor, who presided over the very first meeting of the Council held in Luxembourg on 8-10 September 1952:

"With today's inaugural meeting of the Council of Ministers, five months after the High Authority itself began work, the second Community institution has come into being. It is a massive undertaking, and one laden with responsibilities. The Council is the Community's 'federative' body; this means that it has a dual task under the treaty:

It will act as a Community body, acting for this supranational organisation which is vested with its own sovereign rights and now stands apart alongside the Member States. As a Community body, the Council of Ministers plays a major role in regulating and administering sovereign rights which Member States have voluntarily shed and transferred to the Community...

The Council also has another task; it does not merely represent the Community's interest in the areas of sovereignty which have been ceded; it also represents the interests of individual Member States in the areas of competence which they retain...

The Council is located at a point where two forms of sovereignty overlap – one supranational, the other national. It must strive, impartially, to preserve the Community's general interest as well as the interests of individual Member States by seeking compromises which give both parties their due." (Council, 1952).

by a majority or a qualified majority of its members. At the same time it is the forum in which the interests of member state governments are legitimately articulated and arbitrated in the Union's decision-making process. It is composed of members who are representatives of their governments at ministerial level authorised to commit their government (see chapter 3). Although intergovernmental in composition, it is therefore misleading to describe it as an 'intergovernmental' institution. It is at one and the same time supranational and national in character.

Legislature and executive

One of the difficulties in conveying how the EU works is that its political system does not readily fit the systemic mould with which people in western liberal democracies are generally familiar. This mould is typically based on a Montesquieu-inspired separation of powers between a legislature, executive and judiciary. Parliament legislates under the political leadership of an accountable executive, which initiates and implements policy. Institutions and citizens are subject to the judicial control of the courts. More often than not, political leadership of the executive is exercised in a visible and personal form by a president or prime minister. If the electorate is dissatisfied with its political leadership, it can 'chuck the scoundrels out' of office at the next elections.

Although the Union's institutions perform similar functions to those carried out by national institutions, those functions are not separated in the same way. The design is so novel that portraying the working of the Union's main institutions by drawing direct analogies with institutional equivalents in a national context only serves to cloud understanding of the way in which the institutions operate (with the possible exception of the Court of Justice). Approaching the Union in this way is arguably at least in part responsible for nurturing the misconception that it is evolving towards some national institutional model and classic separation of powers – a so-called European superstate. However, while the European Union is not a state in any accepted sense (nor will it be even when the new constitutional treaty enters into force), it already possesses many of the attributes of a federal regime. Under the existing treaties, certain powers are conferred on the 'federal' (i.e., EU) level and are exercised by common institutions whose existence is distinct from that of the member states. The Union enacts laws that are binding on citizens in all member states. The ultimate judicial authority for matters falling within the scope of the treaties is the European Court of Justice.

The Union's institutions are based on a separation of interests rather than a separation of powers. The European Parliament represents the popular interest – bringing together the directly elected representatives of the peoples of the member states. The Commission represents the general interest of the Union. To enable it to fulfil this role and ensure legitimacy, commissioners are entirely independent of national governments and the other EU institutions, and the institution operates on a collegiate basis. The Council is the forum where the interests of the Union's democratically elected governments can be legitimately advanced and defended.

It is apparent from the above that the Union does not have a 'legislature' as such. It has a legislative process in which all three policy making institutions (the Commission, the Council and the European Parliament) play a role. In certain areas, the Council wields ultimate legislative power, with the Parliament acting in an advisory role. Over the years, the debate has focused on the extent to which the Council's legislative power should be shared with the Parliament and whether the Parliament should have the final say on budgetary matters. The so-called 'co-decision' powers of the Parliament have been extended with successive treaty changes, including in the new constitutional treaty, extending the logic embarked on under the Single European Act in 1986 and the Maastricht Treaty signed in 1992. Thus, in most policy areas for which the EU has legislative responsibilities, the Council now co-legislates with the European Parliament. In this sense, the Council can, at least in part, be likened to a kind of upper chamber, albeit one with real powers to shape the outcome of the legislative process.

The task of a political executive is to provide leadership. It is at the core of any system, and the executive is expected to play a vital role in policy initiation and policy-shaping, crisis management and policy implementation; in short, it is expected to 'govern'. As seen above, executive power in the Union is shared between the Council, the Council presidency, the Commission and the European Council (the quarterly meetings of heads of state or government of the EU – see chapter 9). Leadership in the EU is consequently far more complex. Leadership of the college of commissioners is vested in its president, who is appointed for a period of five years by the Council and the European Parliament. The Council and the European Council have a presidency which, until now, has rotated every six months among each member state in turn (and will continue to do so at least until the end of 2006). The Council secretary-general and high representative for the CFSP is also expected to fulfil certain leadership roles. In the Council and the European Council, it is the presidency which is expected to provide leadership and drive forward work during each six-month stewardship (see chapter 18). Arguably, dispersal of power has been one of the important factors in rendering the system politically acceptable.

One of the main issues at the centre of discussions during the 2003/2004 IGC was how executive power in the EU could be strengthened and organised against the background of a more heterogeneous union resulting from enlargement. Part of the problem was that the issue of strengthening the European Union's executive function was viewed as an ideological battleground between many proponents of an 'integrationist' agenda (who saw the Commission evolving into some form of EU government), and advocates of 'intergovernmentalism' (who felt that the EU's core executive and political leadership functions should lie mainly in the hands of member state governments). Thus, the debate in the Convention and IGC about the role of the future permanent president of the European Council was portrayed as a struggle for ascendancy between 'integrationists', who were reluctant to see any weakening of the Commission's executive role, and advocates of a strengthened executive power in the Council.

Both views reflected a certain 'ideological' stance about the Union's development. Those views were balanced by another distinct view, that of what could be termed the 'realists'. Their line of argument was that, given that the EU represented an important tier of government whose decisions affected people in their day-to-day lives, the system had above all to function properly. The basic question for them was, therefore, how to strengthen the EU's executive function in order to meet the expectations placed in the EU by its citizens. This presupposed an analysis of what the Union needed to do, and how it could deliver the expectations that had been placed in it by the general public in a way which would be – and would be perceived as being – legitimate, acceptable and accountable. From this point of view, arguably, part of the Council's weakness in recent years reflects weaknesses found in the Commission.

Having a single institution fulfilling a dual legislative and government-type function has not been without complications. While a legislative institution would naturally be transparent and open, the opposite would normally be true of a governmental/cabinet type body, in which ministers typically need 'space to reflect' and reach a collective view out of the public spotlight. In most member states, cabinet meetings are not public. This fundamental duality explains many of the difficulties the Council has encountered, particularly since the early 1990s, in the face of claims that it did not afford sufficient transparency in its proceedings and access to its documents when acting in legislative mode (see chapter 20). A further complicating factor was that the treaties which preceded the constitution did not provide any clear definition of what constituted a legislative act. Pity the poor official struggling on the one hand to implement rules on public access to documents and televising legislative discussions, while at the same time having to apply stringent regulations on professional secrecy and managing classified documents!

One institution, different guises

In legal terms, the Council is a single institution; there is only one 'Council'. Over the years, however, and as the range of work covered by the Union has expanded, the Council has met in many different 'formations' of ministers, depending on the particular policy areas concerned. While such regular meetings of ministers from different policy sectors has undoubtedly been effective in 'socialising' them, and the national administrations working to them, into the structures and workings of the Union, the practice has inevitably led to compartmentalisation of policy issues which, in turn, has to some extent allowed vested corporatist interests to flourish and at times worked against policy consistency across different sectors.

Until recently, the Council met in twenty-one different formations. However following successive reforms in 1999 and 2002 (Council 1999b and 2002c), and in order to obviate the difficulties mentioned above, the number of formations has been scaled back. The Council currently meets in nine different formations depending on the bulk of the subject matter being discussed (see introduction to part 2). Because the Council is a single legal entity, any Council formation may formally adopt a Council act or decision. As will be seen, this frequently happens under the non-discussion part of the agenda (so-called 'A' items) (see chapter 3). Put another way, a Council act or decision has exactly the same status, no matter which particular Council formation adopts it.

Negotiating conflict and cooperation

The Council is in essence an extremely sophisticated negotiating and decision-making machine. In some respects it is quite remarkable that twenty-five governments of different political complexions, anchored in very different political systems with diverse national interests and with ministers of different personalities can reach agreement on such a vast array of policy issues. The apparent complexities of the system are a reflection not only of the range and detail of policy that the Council grapples with, but also the degree of sophistication of the Union's polity, in which the Council and the European Council assume a central position. This process of negotiation is also shaped by the interaction of the Council and its members with the other two main policy-making institutions – the Commission and the Parliament.

While considerable political importance has been attached to the formal rules under which the Council takes decisions (see chapter 14), in actual fact negotiation and negotiating styles are determined as much by the various informal conventions, practices and working methods that have evolved over the years. Through all of these mechanisms, member state governments seek to shape policy outcomes to render them more politically presentable and acceptable for their national parliaments and electorates. At first sight, this would seem to suggest that negotiating participants in the Council are engaged in zero-sum games, whereby each participant seeks to maximise national advantage, necessarily at the expense of the others.

However, while seeking acceptable political outcomes from a purely national perspective is certainly a feature of the system (even though determining the national interest is not as self-evident as it sounds – see chapter 15), the negotiating process is as much characterised by cooperation to secure particular outcomes as by conflict between opposing positions. The reasons for this are varied and complex. First, all governments have an overriding interest in ensuring that the system functions, and will frequently subsume misgivings on certain second order points to the overall need to achieve a decision, even if that decision is, in the view of the individual government concerned, a less than perfect one. Thus, in a sense, it is in the national interest to preserve the system, and all governments recognise this.

Second, all governments understand the need to accommodate any genuine political difficulties which their peers might encounter. Governments are usually willing to engage in serious attempts to address such real political concerns, since all acknowledge that they may on occasion find themselves in a minority position and be confronted by a similar need for understanding to be shown. There is thus a strong drive to find consensus – even where majority voting could be employed to push a decision through. Third, the Council is increasingly obliged to negotiate collectively with the European Parliament on legislation, or with third states or organisations in the Union's external relations. Again, through such experiences governments have learnt that cooperation to reach collective views can also secure more favourable outcomes for individual member states (indeed, some would argue that, through the co-decision procedure, the European Parliament itself has become 'socialised' into understanding the political difficulties that individual governments sometimes encounter).

Fourth, there is the phenomenon found among many national negotiators who may more easily share a common general understanding of the issues at stake and the likely realistic endgame of negotiation, even when this might be at odds with the positions being taken in national capitals in the process of internal coordination. (This is more commonly described as 'going native'!) These observations underline the fact that the Council is a far more complex and sophisticated body than might at first be supposed.

Chapters 13, 14 and 15 analyse various aspects of the negotiating process by considering not only the formal rules, but also the structures within which negotiations and bargaining take place below the level of the Council, how a national negotiator typically operates within and beyond these structures, and how the process is designed to resolve inter-state conflicts. Chapter 16 considers a case study of a major 'package' negotiation in the Council. Chapter 19 describes how this process is guided by the Council secretariat, the permanent staff supporting the institution, which has evolved from being a logistics provider, amanuensis and purveyor of legal advice to become a political secretariat supporting a political figure at its head and increasingly involved in planning and implementing civilian and military crisis management operations in third countries.

Not to be confused with...

A potential stumbling block in understanding the Council of Ministers is the frankly confusing terminology used within the treaties. The existence outside the European Union of other bodies with similar-sounding names is also a potential pitfall. Two bodies in particular are easily and frequently confused with the Council of (Ministers of) the European Union.

The first such body is the *European Council*. The European Council is an integral part of the European Union's structures. Its composition and role are set out in article 4 of the TEU. The European Council is the meeting of the Union's heads of state or government and the president of the Commission. Meetings take place every three months, in Brussels. It is the Union's supreme political authority, although it remains 'above' the EU's institutional structure, since its decisions are for the most part not legally binding but political in character. The development, role and nature of the European Council, as well as its organic relationship with the Council, are discussed in detail in chapter 9.

The second such body is the Strasbourg-based *Council of Europe*. This organisation has nothing to do with the European Union. The Council of Europe was founded in 1948 and now consists of 45 member states stretching far to the East, including the Russian Federation. The Council of Europe consists of a committee of ministers and a parliamentary assembly, serviced by a general secretariat. Its basic method is intergovernmental, negotiations taking place in the committee of ministers, which is formally composed of foreign ministers but who are normally represented by specially accredited ambassadors. Its basic instrument is the convention which, in classic diplomatic style, is negotiated, initialled, signed and then implemented by a number, but not necessarily all, of its member states. One of the earliest and most important of these conventions is the European Convention on Human Rights (ECHR). Another of the Council of Europe's institutions, the

European Court of Human Rights, also based in Strasbourg, interprets and applies the Convention. (It should not, as is often the case in the media, be confused with or mistaken for the European Union's Luxembourg-based Court of Justice.)

The European Union's evolving constitutional topography

In the past, the propensity for the European Union's structure to confuse was due in no small part to the organic and incremental way in which it evolved, primarily through the negotiation of treaties, each amending or supplementing previous such treaties. One of the major aims of the European Convention's work (and that of the subsequent IGC) was to replace these confused (and confusing) structures with a single, coherent constitutional treaty. This new treaty may go a long way toward achieving this objective, thereby greatly facilitating understanding of the European Union's structures, processes and institutions. Nevertheless, it is important to consider, if only briefly, the European Union's previous topography, since parts of this study will inevitably refer to past structures and terminology.

The earliest incarnation of the European Union, the European Coal and Steel Community (ECSC), came into being with the signing of the Treaty of Paris on 18 April 1951. A second Community, the European Economic Community (EEC), and a third, the European Atomic Energy Community (commonly abbreviated to 'Euratom'), came into being with the signing of the Rome Treaties on 25 March 1957. From the outset, the three communities shared a Common Assembly (which began to call itself 'European Parliament' in 1962), but there were separate ministerial Councils and Commissions (or the High Authority in the case of the ECSC). These were merged into a single Council and a single Commission by the 1965 Merger Treaty (which entered into force in 1967).

Between 1967 and 1985 a number of treaties were signed, amending the provisions of the existing treaties in areas such as budgetary procedure, or introducing direct elections, but the basic architecture and methodology remained largely unchanged. A foundation stone of that methodology was the European Commission's sole right of initiative. In virtually all policy areas, the Council was only able to decide on the basis of a Commission proposal, and the Commission could withdraw its proposals at any stage. Subject to certain variations, the Council was obliged to consult the European Parliament (as seen above, in many policy areas the Parliament now co-legislates together with the Council), and all of its acts were subject to the jurisdiction of the Court of Justice. Taken together, these conditions were commonly referred to as 'the Community method'.

The 1986 Single European Act introduced a new policy area, European cooperation in the sphere of foreign policy (commonly known at the time as European political cooperation or 'EPC'), which lay beyond the traditional Community method. Seen as a nascent foreign policy, EPC was to be conducted between the foreign affairs ministers of the 'High Contracting Parties'. Nevertheless, the EPC provisions were inserted as a new title in the EEC Treaty.

The Maastricht Treaty took matters a step further. The new treaty, entitled 'Treaty on European Union', was divided into seven titles. The first title consisted of common provisions, including the creation of a European Union, to be served by a single institutional framework (though the institutions had different roles and powers, depending on which title they were acting under). The second, third and fourth titles respectively amended the 1957 EEC Treaty, the 1951 ECSC Treaty and the 1957 Euratom Treaty. The second title included provisions leading to the creation of economic and monetary union (EMU). Title Five was devoted to provisions on a common foreign and security policy, and the sixth title was devoted to cooperation in the fields of justice and home affairs. The seventh title contained general and final provisions.

It should be noted that the so-called 'Community method' described above was confined to titles II and III. Within the EMU provisions of title II, new sui generis procedures and institutions were foreseen (including, for example, an independent European Central Bank) which fell outside the Community method (see chapter 5). The Council's traditional relationship with the Commission was limited only to those areas where the Community method applied. Elsewhere, it could play a more important and autonomous role as policy initiator and coordinator. As described above, it was these developments, among others, which led to increased academic and media interest in the Council as an institution in its own right.

During the Maastricht Treaty negotiations, it became common to refer to the 'pillar structure', as opposed to the 'tree structure'. Proponents of the tree structure saw the European Union evolving organically through a gradual extension of the Community method. The French government, a proponent of a more 'intergovernmental' approach, resurrected the term 'pillar' from proposals made in the early 1960s (Teasdale, 1995). According to the pillar structure, the European Union would be built on several pillars. One pillar was the Community method. The second and third pillars would use hybrid and more 'intergovernmental' methods in foreign and security policy and justice and home affairs, both considered to be bastions of national sovereignty. Although these terms never had formal status and were not used in any legal text, it is still common to refer to foreign and security policy and cooperation in police and criminal justice matters as the 'second' and 'third' pillars respectively.

The treaties (as they still tended to be collectively known) were further amended by the Amsterdam and Nice treaties. The Amsterdam Treaty contained a number of significant measures, including the reduction and simplification of decision-making procedures, an extension of qualified majority voting in the Council, and provisions for so-called 'enhanced cooperation', but it was seen more as 'fine-tuning' and 'bedding down' of existing provisions than as a radical departure. The Nice Treaty, on the other hand, which came into force in 2003, was supposed to mark the completion of the structural renovations deemed necessary by the Union to allow more members to be accommodated after enlargement. It was commonly recognised that the simultaneous arrival of ten new member states would put immense and perhaps unsustainable pressure on the Union's existing structures and working methods. The Nice intergovernmental conference had deliberately sidestepped a number of fundamental issues. There was also a growing recognition that the IGC method in itself, with its arcane and secretive working methods, its distance and lack of transparency, was becoming discredited. At the same time, it was clear that further constitutional discussions were required, given the fact that during negotiations on the Nice Treaty, European leaders were vying with one another in offering a flurry of new constitutional blueprints for the Union.

Because of these considerations, the 15 December 2001 Laeken European Council decided to convene a Convention bringing together representatives of parliaments (national and European) as well as of member state governments, and representatives and observers from the other EU institutions and bodies and from the candidate countries. The mandate of the Convention, which began its work on 1 March 2002, was to prepare the work of a further IGC by addressing the democratic challenge facing Europe, Europe's new role in a steadily globalising world, and the expectations of Europe's citizens. Through a draft constitutional treaty, the Convention was expected to propose a better division and definition of competences in the Union, to simplify the Union's instruments, and to provide more democracy, transparency and efficiency.

The Convention's final text – a draft European Constitution (18 July 2003), albeit still in the form of a treaty – was generally recognised to have achieved a significant number, though not quite all, of its initial aims. Against the odds, a general consensus on all of the main issues had been maintained, giving the text considerable authority. At the subsequent IGC, which opened in Rome on 4 October 2003, the danger of unravelling the general consensus package was recognised by all sides. At the same time, member state governments, together with those of some of the acceding countries, had made it plain that they could not accept certain aspects of the consensus package.

While agreement on the draft constitutional treaty was reached at the meeting of the intergovernmental conference at the level of heads of state or government in June 2004, the outcome of the ratification procedure – which is likely to take at least two and a half years – is uncertain. This process takes place against the background of enlargement on 1 May 2004, the possible conclusion of accession negotiations with Bulgaria and Romania at the end of 2004 and their accession in 2007, decisions on Turkey's accession and internal political wrangling on the Union's new financial framework beyond 2006.

Whatever the outcome, the Council will remain at the centre of EU decision-making; much of what is set out in this book will remain valid. Various chapters in this book assess more generally the changes which might affect the Council under the new constitutional treaty, analysing the potential impact of the institutional innovations, in particular those relating to the rotating Council presidency, the transformation of the secretary-general/high representative (along with the commissioner for external relations) into a single minister for foreign affairs and the creation of a full-time president of the European Council.

Chapter 2: Where it meets and what it speaks

Although it may seem curious to begin with nuts and bolts logistics before considering what the Council actually does, its buildings – like those of any institution or organisation – project a certain public image that reveals something of the spirit and 'character' of the institution and its organisational logic. In particular, the politics of language in a multinational and multicultural institution such as the Council – where the medium of communication is as much a political issue as the message itself – has had a significant impact on the design requirements of its buildings. The Council's headquarters building in the rue de la Loi in Brussels is a rather austere pink marble-clad building which has all the charm and style of a building designed by committee – which it was. Its somewhat forbidding exterior (often uncharitably described as 'Ceausescu-like') perhaps symbolised more the nature of the Council twenty years ago, but hardly projects today's image of an open and transparent legislative institution. Inside, however, it is functional and businesslike.

Where it meets

The Council

Where the Council meets is laid down in the treaty. The protocol on the location of the seats of the institutions annexed to the Treaty of Amsterdam establishes the seat of the Council in Brussels and stipulates that during the months of April, June and October, the Council shall hold its meetings in Luxembourg. This protocol simply codifies previous decisions[1] and established practice, for the Council has always met regularly in Brussels, except for April, June and October, when meetings were held in Luxembourg (which is where the very first Council meeting took place on 8-10 September 1952). Meetings in Brussels currently take place in the Justus Lipsius (Consilium) building (see below). In Luxembourg, they take place in a special meeting complex located near the other Community buildings (of the European Commission, European Parliament, and European Court of Justice) on the Kirchberg Plateau. In 2003, extensive work began on enlarging and refurbishing the complex. The work, which is expected to last four years, was so extensive that the Council was obliged temporarily to meet in a specifically designated part of the Luxembourg International Fair (Foires Internationales du Luxembourg).

There are exceptions to the Brussels-Luxembourg general rule. In the past some Council meetings were held in Strasbourg, generally in the context of the budgetary procedure and particularly in the case of (budgetary) conciliation procedures with the European Parliament. A second exception involves extraordinary meetings of the Council elsewhere in the world, normally, but not necessarily, linked to the European Union's external relations. For example, on 21 September 1992 the Council met in New York. The matters discussed were all European (the result of the French referendum on the Maastricht Treaty, continued turbulence in the European Monetary System), but the British presidency decided to take advantage of the presence in New York of the EU's foreign affairs ministers (there for the opening session of the United Nations General Assembly) to hold a 'crisis meeting'. A similar crisis meeting took place in Oslo, where NATO ministers happened to be meeting, after the 2 June 1992 'no' result in the first Danish referendum on the Maastricht Treaty. More recent sessions of the Council convened outside Europe include the Council sessions in Cancun, Mexico, in September 2003, Doha in November 2001 and Seattle in December 1999, in the margins of the WTO trade negotiations. A Council meeting was convened in Rio de Janeiro in June 1999 in the margins of the EU-Latin America-Caribbean summit. Occasionally, ministerial coordination meetings (rather than formally convened Councils) are also held in the margins of international meetings where EU ministers are present. A third exception is the informal meetings of ministers which are held in the country holding the six-month rotating presidency.

Coreper, working parties, the general secretariat

Both Coreper II and Coreper I (the Council's senior preparatory body – see chapter 11) invariably meet in Brussels. Thus, unlike their ministerial peers, permanent representatives are not obliged to meet in Luxembourg in certain months of the year, although they usually accompany their ministers to meetings there. Council working parties also meet in Brussels as a rule, although there can be exceptions. For example, the article 133 committee may occasionally meet in Geneva in the margins of World Trade Organisation negotiations. The general affairs group, which handles routine business with the European Parliament, usually meets in Strasbourg once a month.

Although the general secretariat of the ECSC's Special Council of Ministers was initially based in Luxembourg, those parts involved in the preparation of the Rome treaties moved to Brussels in 1955. In 1958, a single general secretariat of the two new Councils and the old ECSC Council was established in Brussels, where it has remained to this day. Staff of the general secretariat follow Council to wherever it meets.

The Council's buildings

After originally occupying premises in rue Ravenstein in Brussels' city centre until 1971, the Council's general secretariat was located from 1971 until 1995 in the Charlemagne building, which had previously belonged to the Commission (as it does again now). During that 1971-1995 period, virtually all Brussels-based Council and Coreper meetings took place in this building. The Charlemagne's relatively small size put the Council under increasing pressure of space throughout the 1980s. Parts of the general secretariat were moved to rented office buildings elsewhere in Brussels, and annexes were built to provide more space for meetings. As the need for meetings inexorably increased, the lack of adequate meeting space put the Council under increasing practical pressure. The decision was taken to commission a new building which could house the Council and all of its general secretariat under one roof. Work began in 1988, and the bulk of the building was completed in 1994. Coreper met there for the first time on 24 May 1995, and the General Affairs Council 'baptised' the building on 29 May 1995 at the Council's 1,847th meeting.

The new building, clad in pink marble and tinted glass, was also situated on the rue de la Loi, opposite the Berlaymont building, on a site that had stood empty for many years. The €450 million split-level building is built on a slope. Several floors lower than the old Charlemagne building, it sprawls away down the slope to the rue Belliard, beyond which lies the home of the European Parliament. The building's formal name is the 'consilium', the Latin term for the Council; this is also the institution's telex address, and the name that appears on the building's foundation stone. However, a decision was later taken to call the building 'Justus Lipsius'.[2]

No sooner had construction work begun than the Berlin wall fell, triggering a chain of events that were to result in the Maastricht Treaty and the 1995 enlargement. The Maastricht Treaty created new tasks and roles for the Council so that, even had no enlargement taken place, more office space would have been needed. But enlargement created additional needs. The Council meeting rooms had to be adjusted to accommodate additional interpreting facilities, and in some cases could only fit in one of the two new languages (Finnish and Swedish). Additional staff were recruited. In the shorter-term, all this meant that the Council had to seek additional office space in addition to the consilium building, and the disgruntled Swedish and Finnish translators found themselves isolated in a separate building (Frère Orban).

The Amsterdam Treaty agreed in 1997 extended and consolidated the Council's role and powers, further squeezing limited space. Moreover, by 1997 it had become clear that the countries of Central and Eastern Europe, though so recently under the Soviet yoke, would soon become member states, with all that such a major enlargement would entail in terms of additional officials, Council members and working languages. Even before the 2004 enlargement, pressure on the Council's new building spaces had increased to such an extent that the Council's location was again becoming fragmented. As the Union's embryonic foreign and security policy developed, in particular with the creation and expansion of the EU's military staff, the politico-military structures had to be housed in a separate building secured against espionage. The result was an 'outpost' in avenue Kortenberg, within walking distance of the main Justus Lipsius building, but distinctly separate.

The Nice Treaty signed in 2001 provided that, by 2002, at least one European Council meeting per presidency would be held in Brussels, and ultimately all European Council meetings would be held in the Belgian capital. Since the Italian presidency in the latter half of 2003, all European

Council meetings have taken place in Brussels. At first the Belgian authorities considered creating a new, specific complex for European Council meetings, but a pragmatism born out of immediate requirements prevailed and, almost by default, it was decided that European Council meetings would be held in the Justus Lipsius building, with inevitable overspill of staff. Thus, by 2002 it had become abundantly clear that the Council required at least one more major building, and planning began. By 2003, on the eve of enlargement, the resulting plans had been finalised. A first step was to adapt and enlarge the existing Justus Lipsius building, primarily by adapting some of the existing meeting rooms, adding a floor, extending the press centre and by glassing over the central courtyard. This work, which got under way in 2003, was expected to be completed by 2005.

Two new buildings were also envisaged. The first is an entirely new building, dubbed the 'Lex' building. This is currently being built on a demolition site immediately adjacent to the Residence Palace on the rue de la Loi. Building work is expected to continue until the end of 2006. The second, offered by the Belgian authorities and accepted by the European Council in March 2004, is an adapted wing of an existing building, the Residence Palace, which stands next to the Justus Lipsius building on the rue de la Loi. This is an historic building subject to various protection orders, and so it was necessary to apply for special authorisation to carry out the renovation work. This work should be completed by the end of 2010.

In the meantime, there has been a distinct atmosphere of 'making do'. In particular, temporary office space has been rented in two further buildings at some distance from the Justus Lipsius to house services until such time as the Lex and Residence Palace buildings are ready for occupation. The hope is that once both of these projects are completed, the entire Council secretariat and conference facilities will at last be located in a single site! However, with further expansion of the Union expected in 2007 and new tasks continuing to be foisted on the Council structure, this is far from certain. The fact that the Council's need for buildings has constantly outgrown planned office requirements is a telling indicator of the pace of change in the Council over the past decade.

Geneva and New York

Since 1973 the Council has had a small permanent liaison office in Geneva, housed within the Centre International des Conférences (CICG), to assist it in its work, principally with the General Agreement on Tariffs and Trade (GATT - now the World Trade Organisation, WTO), as well as the other Geneva-based international organisations. As with the Council's Brussels buildings, the 2004 enlargement and the requirement for larger meeting rooms prompted the move to a new, specially-adapted building on a site known as the 'Grand Pré'. This new building, in which the Commission's Geneva delegation is also housed, was expected to be operational by the end of 2004.

In 1995 the Council established a permanent liaison office in New York (on United Nations Plaza). This office was set up to give technical support to the presidency and the other permanent delegations of member states of the European Union mainly for the implementation of the common foreign and security policy related to United Nations activities. Once again, the consequences of the 2004 enlargement, combined with modern security requirements, militated in favour of a move to larger and more appropriate premises. A suitable building was found in E 41st Street, and the new premises, which are shared by the European Commission's New York delegation, became operational in mid-2004.

What it speaks: languages in the Council

Coping with linguistic diversity

One of the Union's hallmarks – and assets – is its linguistic diversity, part of Europe's rich cultural fabric. No other international organisation or grouping of states operates with as many official languages as the European Union – twenty since 1 May 2004, with the prospect of that number increasing further with future enlargements. This means that, at every formal Council session, all legislative and policy texts to be debated or agreed by the Council must exist in twenty languages[3]. In addition, simultaneous interpreting from and into twenty languages is provided (involving a total of 380 linguistic permutations!).

As with most things in life, formal rules and reality are somewhat different. An array of working practices involving less than the full complement of languages are used for many preparatory meetings below the level of the Council which are attended by member states' civil servants. When ministers and delegates meet informally in the margins of Council or preparatory meetings, they communicate in whatever language happens to be common to them. Most ministers can hold their own in either English or French. Linguistically challenged ministers may make discreet use of an available interpreter in one-to-one conversations in the margins of meetings. As in the other EU institutions, staff working in the Council secretariat will normally communicate with colleagues and delegates in English and/or French, the two *lingua franca* in common currency. Proficiency in both is therefore a prerequisite for operating effectively in the Brussels system, and most delegations' staff based in the permanent representations and Council officials are able to work in both. Other languages tend to be used on an *ad hoc* basis. The multilingual delegate or official has a distinct advantage in being able to interact more effectively with their peers and is able to judge the quality or political interest of suggested amendments in different languages, making it easier to find formulations which suit their particular ends. Many Council officials are fluent in three or four languages; the authors know of at least one Council official proficient in all official languages before May 2004 (eleven at that time), but are not aware of any with mastery of all twenty official languages (yet)!

The basic principles and rules governing the use of languages in the Council are found in the treaties, secondary legislation and the Council's rules of procedure. The treaties exist in twenty-one equally authentic linguistic versions, since primary law (i.e., the treaties themselves) also exists in Irish, although it does not enjoy the status of an official and working language. Article 290 TEC on the use of languages in the Union's institutions stipulates that: 'The rules governing the languages of the institutions of the Community shall, without prejudice to the provisions contained in the rules of procedure of the Court of Justice, be determined by the Council, acting unanimously.'

On this basis, the Council adopted regulation No. 1 of 15 April 1958 (the very first regulation adopted by the EEC Council) which, as amended following successive accessions, stipulates that the Union has twenty official and working languages. Under article 6 of this regulation, the institutions may stipulate in their rules of procedure which of the languages are to be used in specific cases. Article 14 of the Council's rules of procedure accordingly contains provisions regarding the translation of documents (but not interpreting), providing that all texts before the Council must exist in all official languages. Moreover, *de facto* equality of languages is acknowledged in institutions' dealings with the general public. The treaty confers on all citizens the right to write to the Union's institutions in any of the languages in which the treaties exist and receive an answer in the same language (article 21 TEC).[4]

Operating with twenty official languages understandably raises numerous practical, logistical and administrative problems. Each of the Union's institutions has had to face up to the implications of this. The Commission has, not without some controversy, adopted the informal practice of operating in three working languages (English, French and German), though all formal proposals must be presented in twenty languages. The European Parliament, as a legislative institution representing the people, has much less scope for operating with limited language arrangements, given the legitimate requirement for committee and plenary documentation to exist in all languages, and discussions to receive full interpreting. The issue of languages is not an arcane question confined to the internal workings of the institutions. For example, work on establishing a Community patent was delayed for years in part because of objections to the language arrangements governing the submission and translation of patents.

While a disinterested observer of the Union might feel that common sense should dictate using a limited number of working languages (as is the case in the UN or other international organisations), efforts in this direction have come to little. A suggestion to this effect made by France in 1994 before it assumed the Council presidency was quietly shelved (see Forrest, 1998, p. 305). The idea of a limited standard interpreting regime was also mooted in the report by the presidency to the December 2002 Copenhagen European Council on the use of languages in the Council (Council, 2002a), more as an academic idea than with a serious expectation of being followed up. As outlined in chapter 1, the Union is much more than an international, intergovernmental organisation. Formally establishing any limited language regime would run counter to the principle of the formal equality of languages, and hence is a political non-starter.

There are entirely valid reasons for the Council continuing to operate in twenty languages. First, it cannot be taken for granted that ministers, who in most cases are members of their national parliaments, will be completely at ease in a foreign language (although in practice many are – even members of the UK government!). When discussing a complex piece of legislation which may have significant political ramifications in their country, it is perfectly legitimate for ministers to expect to be able to put their point in the language with which they are most comfortable. Second, since the Union enacts laws which are directly applicable to citizens and residents in member states, these laws have to exist in a language comprehensible for the people who have to apply them – a directive on water quality which only existed in Greek would have little impact in Scotland! All legislative acts adopted by the Council or by the Parliament and the Council must be published in all official languages in the Union's Official Journal.

On the other hand, efficient use of resources, value for money for the European taxpayer and common sense dictate that interpreting and translating resources should be concentrated where genuinely needed. However, this illustrates a not uncommon situation in the Union where what might at first appear to be a rational and practical solution to a problem is, for reasons of political acceptability and presentation, simply not a viable proposition. Many member states view language arrangements inside the Union as a vehicle for furthering national language policy and a matter of national prestige and 'presence'. Governments would be quickly taken to task by national media if they were perceived to be 'going soft' on the use of their national language in the European Union. As a consequence, this was a taboo subject for many years, off limits for any rational and dispassionate discussion. On the rare occasions when Coreper reluctantly had to broach language issues (usually in an informal setting over lunch), the outcome, after heated and often bad-tempered exchanges, was invariably inconclusive. As a result, arrangements for translating and interpreting in the Council developed over the years in an *ad hoc* and haphazard manner, without any underlying rationale. The prospect of finding any rational solution to the problem as far as the Council was concerned was, at least until recently, a pipedream.

It was only as enlargement became a looming prospect that a change occurred. In the light of a study conducted by the secretariat on the administrative consequences of enlargement (Council, 2002b) and following pressure from certain member states, particularly Sweden, there was a growing realisation in 2002 that the difficulties in managing the language requirements of the Council would be significantly compounded after enlargement. Limited physical, human and financial resources mean that flexibility has to be applied out of necessity in managing available resources to ensure that the Council can work efficiently, without undermining the basic principles underlying the Union's language arrangements. The Seville European Council in June 2002 accordingly asked the Council to 'study the question of the use of languages in the context of an enlarged Union and practical means of improving the present situation without endangering basic principles' (Council, 2002c). While the subject remains politically difficult, given the limited room for manoeuvre for governments in such a visible area impinging upon national pride, it has at least become possible to discuss it in a rational and less emotionally charged manner – an achievement in itself.

Translation of documents

Translation (as opposed to interpreting) refers to the process of rendering a written text in different languages. Article 14 of the Council's rules of procedure states that: 'Except as otherwise decided unanimously by the Council on grounds of urgency, the Council shall deliberate and take decisions on the basis of documents and drafts drawn up in the languages specified in the rules in force governing languages.' The second paragraph reads: 'Any member of the Council may oppose discussion if the texts of any proposed amendment are not drawn up in such of the languages referred to in paragraph 1 as he may specify.' The Council's rules of procedure only mention 'documents' and 'drafts' and therefore only cover rules relating to document translation; they make no reference to arrangements for inter-preting. Strict application of article 14 led to curious results. For example, annual reports relating to the work of the European Police College and Europol, both of which use English as their sole working language, pre-viously had to be translated despite the fact that the translations are not used by the agencies in question, simply because the Council was required to endorse or approve these reports.

All documents which are a basis for Council deliberations are translated into all twenty official languages, whether they are submitted under part A or part B of the agenda (see chapter 3). The only exception is for items added to the agenda under 'other business', where no substantive decision can be taken, and, on rare occasions, for certain acts on foreign policy matters, which in cases of particular urgency are adopted in a single language, and are only translated after formal adoption. Moreover, all legal acts are reviewed by specialised legal-linguistic experts (currently there are around

Box 2.1: *Translation in the Council*

The translation and document production directorate is the largest in the Council secre-tariat with around 1,200 staff, around 700 of whom are translators (this represents nearly two-thirds of the Council's administrative grade staff, including all policy depart-ments). Currently there are twenty linguistic divisions. The linguistic divisions for the new languages consist of twenty-five translators and revisers, plus around fifteen secre-tarial support positions. The staff of the linguistic divisions of the existing languages are gradually being reduced in size, in line with the new approach for document translation, with the result that the incorporation of ten new languages will be achieved over time with only a slight increase in the overall size of the Council's translating staff.

In 2003, a total of 28,417 documents were processed by the Council's central coordi-nation, representing 245,896 pages. Of these only around 30% were translated into at least one other language by the Council secretariat. A total of 732,077 translated pages were produced.

Fifteen years ago most documents in the Council were drafted in French, but the situation has altered substantially in recent years. While in 1998 roughly the same per-centage of documents were drafted in French and English (41% and 44% respectively), by 2003 64% of documents (accounting for 72% of total pages) were drafted in English, while 26% were drafted originally in French (representing 18% of pages). This is of course not the result of any conscious policy decision, but simply a consequence of the accession of Austria, Sweden and Finland in 1995, resulting in a greater number of 'anglophone' presidencies. This trend is likely to continue with the accession of new member states primarily using English as their first foreign language, and with greater numbers of Council staff who have English as their first foreign language.

sixty in the Council secretariat) to ensure the exact correspondence of the different linguistic versions, each of which is equally authentic and may be produced before the Court in legal proceedings.

The Council has taken practical steps to ensure that it will be able to cope with the impact of enlargement on translation. This approach involves reducing the overall demand for translating by identifying more rigorously what are termed 'core' documents, namely legislative texts and papers for Councils and the European Council, making greater use of the 'relay' and 'two-way' methods[5] of translation and, in so far as possible, using a reduced number of languages for internal administrative purposes. Following this approach will over time result in a reduction in the size of most of the Council's linguistic divisions.

Interpreting in the Council

Interpreting (as opposed to translating) involves rendering orally a statement from one language into another. Practically all interpreting provided in the Council is simultaneous, requiring glass-fronted booths for interpreters to sit in and provide a real-time rendition of a speaker's words. The thing that strikes visitors to the Council meeting rooms for the first time is the sheer number of interpreting booths built in and around the walls. Of the two existing meeting rooms equipped to accommodate the Council, one has twenty-five booths, and the other twenty-two. Each booth can accommodate up to five interpreters. The presence of so many booths restricts natural light in the meeting rooms, which have to be artificially lit, and creates a slightly claustrophobic atmosphere. Delegates around the main table have a microphone, into which they have to speak, and a single earpiece in order to hear the interpretation they require. Each delegate can choose the language he or she wishes to hear by selecting the appropriate channel. Interpreting is provided simultaneously as the speaker talks, albeit with a slight time lag. Because of the number of possible linguistic permutations not all languages can be interpreted directly into all others – it is not exactly easy to find interpreters who can operate directly from Finnish into Maltese! Consequently, a number of languages have to operate through a 'relay' system, usually via the English, French or German booths. While effective, it inevitably increases the time lag between the original speaker and the listener hearing what has actually been said, and also allows greater opportunity for slippage in meaning to occur.

This inevitably has a detrimental impact on the quality of debates. Having to use microphones makes it difficult for speakers to interject quips or heckle (heckling is practically unheard of and, if it occurs, it is usually off microphone, so cannot be interpreted!). It adds to the formality of meetings and tends to dampen spontaneity. Working through the medium of an interpreter, no matter how good they are – and many of them are first class – inevitably reduces the directness of communication and understanding, since many of the subtle nuances, irony and dramatic effects available to the speaker when able to address the listener in a language he or she understands are inevitably lost. It is also difficult, unless interpreters are particularly sure-footed, to render humour well. The last resort either involves them telling an entirely different joke with the punch line coming at the right moment for collective laughter, or if all else fails, the rather lame *'the speaker is telling an untranslatable joke – just laugh … now!'* Indeed, in the cut and thrust of intense political argument on particularly important or sensitive points, it is not uncommon for ministers (including heads of government in the European Council) to revert to English or French to hammer their point home more forcefully. The invigorating effect on the discussion is immediately perceptible.

However, for the reasons outlined earlier, all sessions of the Council (around 75 per year) in its usual places of work (Brussels and Luxembourg) and the European Council operate using a full, twenty-language regime. The Council does not have its own interpreting service, but leases interpreting services from the Commission's interpreting directorate-general (DG SCIC), which also provides interpreting for other institutions and consultative bodies, apart from the European Parliament and the Court of Justice. For discussions by ministers over lunch, which are not formally part of the Council, more limited interpreting facilities are used in practice, since dining rooms are not equipped with large numbers of booths and ministers like to use the lunch environment in any case for discussing sensitive items on a more intimate basis than in the Council meeting room. In this setting the actual languages used vary from meeting to meeting.

The problem for managing interpreting is not ministerial meetings, but the arrangements to be used for the some 160 preparatory committees and working parties that meet within the Council (see chapter 12). Over the years, a wide variety of language combinations of less than the full complement of languages evolved as a result of long-standing understandings or established practices which in many cases did not always reflect real or objective needs. These ranged from meetings without any interpreting, when delegates used English and French as the two most common *lingua franca*, through a variety of interpreting arrangements, from three languages up to full interpreting. In some cases interpreting is available on a so-called 'passive' basis. This means that a delegate may speak in their language and be interpreted into other languages, but no booth exists for that language, so the speaker cannot hear interpretation into their language.

In reality, it would be impractical to provide full interpreting arrangements for all meetings attended by diplomats at working and preparatory level. First, there are not enough meeting rooms which could accommodate twenty-language interpreting. Only two such rooms exist at present, and other rooms will not be available before 2007. Second, the availability of suitably qualified interpreters is limited. On any single day, up to eleven teams of interpreters can be made available to the Council, only a few of which could theoretically cater for all twenty languages; the other teams are made up of various configurations depending on requirements for that particular day. Third, full language interpreting would in any case be unaffordable. With twenty official languages, offering full interpreting arrangements for a single Council meeting requires the presence of a minimum of sixty interpreters and costs upwards of €40,000 during normal working hours (if only one shift of interpreters is required). Providing this level of service in all meetings of civil servants would require a more than threefold increase in the Council's annual interpreting budget from its current level of around €70 million to cover the cost (even discounting the prohibitive cost of converting meeting rooms for this purpose) – an unrealistic prospect.

In the period immediately preceding enlargement, an heroic attempt to put in place arrangements for interpreting at the working level ensured at least a manageable if not a perfect system. Following detailed work by the Danish, Greek and Italian presidencies at the level of the Antici Group (see chapter 11), a system has been put in place which allows a practical approach to be taken to the problem while respecting the basic principles underlying the Union's language arrangements. There are three components to this approach: an increased number of working parties and committees in which no interpreting is requested, a limited number of such bodies which may meet with full languages interpreting (twenty), and interpreting available 'on request' in all other preparatory bodies, with each language receiving an allocation of around €2 million under the Union budget to cover requests. Should requests exceed the budgeted amount, member states which use the official language in question must top up the funds required. While this system is still under trial, it has allowed the problem of languages after enlargement to be managed; it ensures that over time there will be no explosion in the Council's interpreting budget and it should encourage greater planning and discipline in convening working party and preparatory committee meetings.

Managing the linguistic needs of a Union in which the number of official languages will continue to grow with successive enlargements will remain a daunting challenge for the foreseeable future. While the Union will continue to be the only entity in the world to operate with so many official languages, it is not impossible for the institutions, despite the obvious practical and logistic difficulties this entails, to find ways of coping. In this case, necessity is indeed the mother of invention.

Chapter 3: The ground rules

Like any institution, the Council organises and structures its work according to a variety of rules, practices, traditions and conventions. The treaties lay down who makes up the Council, and the Council's rules of procedure establish the framework within which negotiators in the Council conduct business and engage in the process of bargaining and consensus building described in part 4. An institution's ability to set its own internal rules is an important power in a system like that of the Community, where the treaties set out a basic framework and leave much else to custom, precedent and jurisprudential case law (see, for example, Bieber, 1992a). The Council's internal autonomy is established under article 207(3) TEC, which states simply that: 'The Council shall adopt its rules of procedure.' The Council, like its predecessor, the Special Council of the European Coal and Steel Community, has always had this power. Following the creation of the EEC, the rules of procedure adopted in 1958 endured without change until 1979. Since then they have been revised or amended on no fewer than ten occasions (six times in the past five years – one measure of the pace of change in the Council in recent years!).[1]

In a system founded on the rule of law, the power to establish rules and take decisions brings with it responsibility. Article 230 TEC provides that 'the European Court of Justice shall review the legality of acts... (*inter alia*) of the Council...'and that 'It shall for this purpose have jurisdiction in actions brought...on grounds of lack of competence, infringement of an essential procedural requirement, infringement of this Treaty or of any rule of law relating to its application, or misuse of powers.' In the eyes of the Court, the provisions of an institution's rules of procedure represent essential procedural requirements, and failure to respect them can result in the annulment of decisions. For example, in the hormones case (Case 68/86, *United Kingdom v. Council*), the Court treated as grounds for annulment the Council's failure to comply with the provisions of the then article 6(1) of its rules of procedure on the adoption of acts by written procedure (see below), which required the agreement of all members. It is for this reason that the Council and Coreper regard the rules, and any amendments to them, with great seriousness. The Court factor also explains why the Council's rules do not cover every eventuality. Practices constantly evolve in the Council, as they do in the Commission and the Parliament. To adopt a rule is to introduce an element of rigidity where flexibility might be preferred. Unlike the European Parliament, the Council does not have a standing committee with responsibility for considering and drafting amendments to the rules of procedure and to decide in cases of disputed interpretation. That role falls on the heavily over-worked Coreper structure.

What follows is not a detailed exegesis of these rules (for that, see Council, 2004) since, to echo Voltaire's aphorism, the best way to be boring would be to leave nothing out! It is, rather, a working description of who makes up the Council, how its work is programmed and its agenda set and the nature of the decisions it takes and the acts it adopts. It is the body of basic rules and practices that newcomers to the institution must rapidly understand as the framework within which the art of negotiating, bargaining and consensus building takes place.

Who is 'the Council'?

Composition

The composition of the Council – that is, who exactly can sit as a Council member – is laid down in the treaties. Until the entry into force of the Maastricht Treaty in 1993, EEC article 146 ordained that: 'The Council shall consist of representatives of the Member States. Each Government shall delegate to it one of its members.' Two principles sprang from this wording. The first was that the Council was to consist of representatives of *states*. The language was deliberately designed to distinguish between the Council and the European Parliament, EEC article 138 describing members of the European Parliament as 'the representatives in the European Parliament of the *peoples* of the States.' Thus, in this sense at least, the 'founding fathers' saw a classic bicameral division between a 'lower house', composed of representatives of the peoples, and an 'upper house' consisting of representatives of the states (although it is the latter which would wield real powers).

The second clear principle was that member state representatives had to be members of their national government. The Maastricht Treaty changed this. Article 203 now reads: 'The Council shall consist of a representative of each Member State at ministerial level, authorised to commit the government of that Member State.' The first principle, of state representation, remains. But the new wording, introduced at the request of the German government, henceforth enabled ministers from the German Länder (and from other self-governing regional entities in other member states) to participate in Council meetings as fully-fledged Council members.

From the Council's earliest days, ensuring full representation at ministerial level proved difficult. Ministers are never entirely masters of their domestic diaries. In the very early days, Brussels was a long way from Rome, whether by plane or, even longer, train. Moreover, the opportunity cost of travelling to and from Brussels has always seemed very high when a Council agenda is, from the point of view of a particular minister, relatively anodyne or consensual – particularly if, for example, an urgent parliamentary debate is scheduled back home.

As a pragmatic response to this, the Council's rules of procedure (article 4) provide that 'a member of the Council who is prevented from attending a meeting may arrange to be represented.' The most common form of such substitution is for a (Brussels-based) permanent representative ('perm. rep.' in the jargon) or deputy permanent representative to take a minister's place.

This is not simply a matter of filling the minister's chair. Permanent representatives may, and sometimes do, take the floor and intervene on behalf of their governments in the Council itself. They may therefore wield considerable derived influence and power. As chapters 11 and 17 describe, permanent representatives are intimately involved in producing their country's positions on policy issues. They can therefore be (and frequently are) better briefed than ministers, more familiar with the arguments on all sides of an issue, and better able to expound a winning case. Ministerial substitutes in the Council can also wield the positive power of signalling tacit or explicit agreement (or, in more nuanced fashion, failing to signal disagreement) or the negative power of signalling disagreement upstream of any formal vote.

Such fine distinctions may be of academic interest, and are, in the end, of little real political importance, since the substitutes will always follow the same 'line to take' that the minister would have taken, albeit with less flexibility to manoeuvre on politically difficult items. Indeed, it is not unheard of for ministers to be conveniently absent when a difficult item is being taken in the Council either to avoid conceding a point or simply being outvoted on a particularly sensitive issue.

A variation on the substitution theme concerns formal voting. Another article (11(3)) in the Council's rules of procedure provides that: 'Where a vote is taken, any member of the Council may also act on behalf of not more than one other member.' This language is taken directly from article 206 TEC. It enables the minister of one country to enable the minister of another to wield that country's vote. Again, since the Council rarely votes, this potential empowerment is of limited formal significance.

Seating arrangements

Ministers rarely find themselves on their own in a Council session. The Council's rules of procedure provide that members of the Council 'may be accompanied by officials who assist them.' The most important of these is the member state's permanent representative or the deputy permanent representative, and a senior advisor in the policy area in question. A minister's entourage will also typically include the expert on any particular subject on the agenda, either from the permanent representation or from the national capital.

Before enlargement, the normal configuration for a Council session was that each delegation had three seats at the main table and three seats behind. The presidency, the Commission and the Council secretariat generally had more seats. In recent years, sheer pressure of space in the Council's meeting rooms has led to this number being reduced to five (two at the main table and three behind) from 16 April 2003 (the date on which acceding states were accorded active observer status and from which they were admitted to all meetings of the Council and its preparatory bodies). The Council makes 'overflow' rooms available to those unable to squeeze into the chamber itself. The reservation of places for member states and the Commission mimics that to be found in the Council chamber itself. A large screen broadcasts images of the current speaker and simultaneous interpreting is relayed to the 'overflow room'. Thus, though reliable statistics are unavailable, the new edict limiting the number of officials allowed to sit with their minister or commissioner in the Council chamber seems to have done little to reduce the overall number of officials in attendance.

However, with the inevitable increase in numbers with enlargement, the recent Italian (2003) and Irish (2004) presidencies have made a concerted effort to hold Council meetings in a more restricted and intimate format. If deliberations are to be effective and allow ministers to engage in detailed argument or substantive discussion, this cannot be done with nearly 150 persons in the room. Recent sessions of the Ecofin (Economic and Financial) and General Affairs and External Relations Councils have therefore organised part of their proceedings in a format with ministers alone at the main table, and two seats for advisers placed immediately behind them (UN Security Council-style). For certain Council formations, however, particularly where more than one minister is frequently in attendance for certain members, or where more technical sectoral matters are being discussed and ministers wish to avail themselves of the expertise of their deputy permanent representative at their side, delegations prefer to retain the format of two per delegation at the main table. From 1 May 2004, Council meeting

Box 3.1: *Seating order in the Council and Council preparatory bodies July-December 2004*

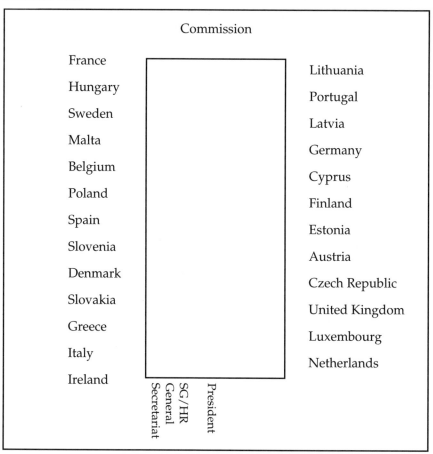

rooms have allowed a configuration with one, two or three persons at the main table, and up to three persons behind. However, at any Council session, when dealing with particularly sensitive issues, or where it is felt that a compromise might be easier to obtain under less 'public' circumstances, the presidency may propose that the item be handled in a 'restricted format', i.e., 'ministers plus two', or 'ministers plus one', or occasionally just 'ministers alone' ('super-restricted sessions), with transmission to the overflow room switched off.

Delegations are seated in the order of succession of presidencies, which was fixed in a decision adopted by the Council in 1995. Previously presidencies rotated in alphabetical order. However, with the accession of Austria, Sweden and Finland in 1995, the order was changed so that the troika of the previous, current and incoming presidencies would always include a 'larger' member state. Immediately to the right of the presidency is the national seat of the delegation holding the presidency (presidencies cannot overtly defend national positions from the chair). The incoming presidency is next to the right. As each new presidency moves into the chair, all delegations rotate one place around the table. To the left of the presidency is the Council secretariat (typically the secretary-general, deputy-secretary general and/or the relevant director-general, as well as the director-general or a director from the legal service). The ten new members are interspersed, in alphabetical order, between the current members, starting after the next presidency but one (see box 3.1). For the time being, they do not move round the table every six months. Under the arrangements foreseen in the Treaty of Accession, a decision on the order of succession of presidencies should be taken at the latest one year after the entry into force of the treaty – i.e., by spring 2005.

The Commission in the Council

Article 5(1) of the Council's rules of procedure provides that: 'The Commission shall be invited to take part in meetings of the Council... The Council may, however, decide to deliberate without the presence of the Commission...' (Since Maastricht, the Council's rules make exactly the same provision for the European Central Bank 'in cases where it exercises its right of initiative'.) The Commission is almost always represented in Council meetings and, indeed, is not infrequently described as an additional member state. It sits opposite the Council president. On very rare occasions, when sensitive internal matters are under discussion, the Commission may not be invited to attend. However, such rare occasions are the exceptions that prove the rule. Indeed, depending on the nature of the Council and the subjects under discussion, it is not unusual for several members of the Commission to be present for part or all of a Council meeting. Like ministers, members of the Commission are generally accompanied by a delegation of officials and experts.

Rooms for manoeuvre

Within the Council's Justus Lipsius building an entire floor is given over to suites of rooms for the delegations of the member states and the

Commission. It is in these rooms that ministers and permanent representatives 'camp out' when not in Council or Coreper meetings. When a minister or a permanent representative says that they must consult with their national capital or 'political authorities', it is from the delegation's rooms that the call will be made. From here constant contact can also be kept with the permanent representation. The presidency also has at its disposal a suite of rooms on the main meeting level that can be used for receiving dignitaries, for briefings or bilateral 'confessionals'.

Programming, timetabling and agenda setting

Article 204 TEC provides that 'The Council shall meet when convened by its President on his own initiative or at the request of one of its members or of the Commission.' This wording, which is faithfully reproduced by article 1(1) of the Council's rules of procedure, might give the impression of considerable flexibility. In reality, the dates and the rhythm of the Council's meetings are established up to a year in advance of any particular presidency. Indeed, to a considerable extent incoming presidencies are locked into pre-established rhythms and all they can do is choose the precise dates of particular meetings.

The Council is a heavily over-charged institution where carefully calculated organisation is at a premium. National ministers, who themselves belong to heavily over-charged governments, need to know a long time in advance which dates they should block in their diaries. The Council's general secretariat has to plan well in advance for the organisation of Council meetings in budgetary and human resource terms. Moreover, all of the Council's preparatory bodies (see chapters 11 and 12) must know the dates of the Council's meetings in order to schedule their own. Since the Council has only a limited number of meeting rooms and is able to provide only a limited number of interpreters, a presidency, advised by the general secretariat, must frequently arbitrate between the competing requirements of different preparatory bodies (the most thankless job in the permanent representation is that of presidency meeting coordinator!).

Programming and agenda setting

The formal draft agenda established for any Council meeting effectively preordains what the Council can and cannot do on a particular occasion. However, over the years a series of mechanisms have been introduced which greatly diminish the possibility of the Council behaving spontaneously. Presidencies are now locked into these mechanisms, which are designed to ensure greater continuity in the Council's work. Part of the pressure for introducing them was the feeling that the Council often had sharply changing priorities every six months without any consistent follow-up on certain new policy initiatives.

In political terms, the Council's agenda is determined by a number of factors. In the first instance, the treaties themselves are an important agenda-setter for the Council. In many areas the treaties set out framework goals and overall deadlines, leaving the Council to work out the legislative detail. The creation of the common agriculture policy (CAP) was an early example, the realisation of the single market a more recent one. The annual budgetary cycle, as set out in the treaties, largely governs the Council's work in the budgetary sphere (see chapter 5.2).

Second, the European Council has increasingly assumed the role of political agenda setter for the Council's work, by endorsing or adopting legislative programmes or action plans in specific sectors, or by specifying target dates for the Council to conclude its deliberations on a particular dossier. It is often the forum where commitments are given by the Commission to legislate (the Commission president is a member of the European Council). While a catch-all article in the treaties (article 208 TEC) provides that 'The Council may request the Commission to undertake any studies the Council considers desirable for the attainment of the common objectives, and to submit to it any appropriate proposals', the increasing importance of the European Council in this role, coupled with the creation of overall programmatic objectives such as the creation of the single market or the establishment of the single currency, have much reduced the need for the Council to bring such pressure to bear. Consequently, use of this article has been much diminished. In the European Council institutional form is preserved by the European Council or the Council noting the Commission's intention to come forward with an appropriate proposal on a given item.

In 2002 and 2003, two further mechanisms to improve continuity in the Council's work were introduced – an annual operational programme and a three-year strategic programme of work (for the background to these instruments see chapter 21). The first annual programme was drawn up jointly by the Greek and Italian presidencies for 2003, and the European Council in December 2003 adopted the first multiannual strategic programme for 2004-2006 (Council, 2003). It is not only the Council and government ministers who wait on such longer-term planning. The Commission makes its own calculations about the best time to table proposals so as to ensure a smooth or rapid passage of particular legislative proposals, and the European Parliament also looks to the Council's planning and schedules its legislative work and many of its debates accordingly.

The European Commission is among the most important of the Council's agenda-setters, particularly under the so-called 'first pillar'. Because it holds virtually the sole right of legislative initiative, it is the Commission which primarily determines the Council's legislative activity. But the Commission's legislative proposals do not come from a vacuum. At the outset, its underlying objectives were set out in the treaties (common agricultural and transport policies, for example), but since the 1987 Single European Act the Commission has increasingly made its proposals on the basis of pre-established legislative or work programmes endorsed by the European Council (the single market, the single currency, the Tampere agenda, the Lisbon strategy, etc.). The Commission's other tasks and functions also affect the Council's agenda. The Commission frequently issues communications and consultative documents (such as green and white papers), all of which require a Council response or position. The Commission also often comes before the Council simply in order to keep it abreast of developments in areas where the Commission is primarily responsible, such as trade negotiations. Even in those policy areas where the Commission's formal role is much reduced – from the second and third pillars through to the so-called 'open method of coordination' – it retains a central coordinating role which effectively enables it to influence the Council's draft agenda.

Finally, unfinished business from the previous presidency and external events also play an important part in determining the Council's agenda. If the preceding presidency has failed to clear the decks as anticipated, the incoming presidency will have to take up any outstanding business. External events also dictate the pace of business. These can range from the everyday (for example, shifts in world prices for agricultural products), to the routine (for example, preparations for IMF meetings), to the unexpected (for example the events of 11 September 2001).

Fixing Council agendas

Even though presidencies have to slot into multi-annual and annual programmes, ongoing legislative processes, rolling programmes, action plans and strategies and the like, they can brake or accelerate negotiations, concentrate the Council's firepower, and take initiatives.

The Council's rules of procedure set out the mechanics of drawing up the agenda for any particular Council meeting. Article 3(1) states that: 'Taking into account the Council annual programme, the President shall draw up the provisional agenda for each meeting. The agenda shall be sent to the other members of the Council and to the Commission at least 14 days before the beginning of the meeting.' The rules go on to stipulate that:

> 'The provisional agenda shall contain the items in respect of which a request for inclusion on the agenda, together with any documents relating thereto, has been received by the General Secretariat from a member of the Council or from the Commission at least 16 days before the beginning of that meeting.'

This means that any delegation and the Commission may as of right have an item included on the agenda provided this deadline is respected (i.e., the agreement of the presidency or other delegations is not required). These basic provisions are hedged with a series of qualifying provisions. Thus, the provisional agenda has to indicate (by an asterisk) those items on which the presidency, a Council member or the Commission may request a vote. Asterisks are automatically included on the agenda once all the procedural requirements under the treaty are fulfilled for the Council to act (i.e., EP opinions and opinions of other bodies required are available). Items relating to the adoption of a legislative act under the third pillar (justice and home affairs) cannot be put on the provisional agenda for a decision until the six-week period provided for in the protocol on the role of national parliaments has elapsed. Only items in respect of which the documents have been sent to the members of the Council and to the Commission at the latest by the date on which the provisional agenda is sent may be placed on that agenda. The Council's rules allow for requests for the inclusion of items on the agenda which have not respected all of the above constraints, provided unanimity exists among the Council members for their inclusion. The same rules provide that, where legislative dossiers are concerned, if Coreper has not completed its examination then the items must be removed from the provisional agenda. Clearly, all of these provisions are designed to channel the Council's work through the appropriate preparatory and control bodies and to reduce the possibility for surprises to a minimum.

Coreper and the Council's other preparatory bodies can also be important agenda-setters. The permanent representatives cannot themselves take policy initiatives, but to a considerable extent their work rate – which is very high – determines the work rate of the Council. It is Coreper's astute and experienced political judgement, together with that of the presidency (and the general secretariat) which mainly decides when and how items will rise to ministerial level. Similar observations can be made about the Council's other preparatory committees.

Since the entry into force of the Single European Act, with its derived raft of legislative proposals designed to create the single market, it has become increasingly necessary for the Council to schedule its meetings according to the rhythm of legislative work. This led to the practice of 'rolling programmes', whereby incoming presidencies would take over work in progress. A combination of the growing quantities of draft legislation to be dealt with and the greater complexity and duration of the co-decision procedure (which can take up to eighteen months) has placed an even greater premium on long-term planning. This requirement is reflected in article 1(2) of the Council's rules of procedure, which states that: 'Seven months before the beginning of its term of office, after consulting the Presidencies preceding and following its term of office where appropriate, the Presidency shall make known the dates which it envisages for meetings that the Council will have to hold in order to complete its legislative work or take operational decisions.'

Article 2(6) of the Council's rules of procedure provides that: 'The incoming Presidency shall establish indicative provisional agendas for Council meetings scheduled for the next six-month period, showing the legislative work and operational decisions envisaged. These indicative provisional agendas shall be established at the latest one week before the beginning of its term of office, on the basis of the annual operational programme and after consulting the Commission. Where necessary, extra Council meetings may be provided for, in addition to those previously planned. Similar indicative provisional agendas for Council meetings scheduled for the six-month period following that referred to in the first subparagraph shall be established by the Presidency concerned, after consulting the Commission and the next Presidency, at the latest one week before the beginning of its term of office.'

These provisions are generally respected, although in Council configurations dealing mainly with non-legislative matters, such as the General Affairs and External Relations Council and the Ecofin Council, the actual agendas of the Council meetings in question turn out to be significantly different, particularly in the light of fast-moving international events. Nevertheless, they do confirm the trend towards more planning and coordination, thus tying individual presidencies in to an overall process and reducing their autonomy.

One provision of article 2 would appear to be more like wishful thinking than the others. A closing paragraph states that 'If during a six-month period any of the meetings planned during that period proves to be no longer warranted, the Presidency shall not convene it.' In reality, it is extremely difficult to cancel an already-scheduled Council meeting. The presidency, disaggregated to the level of the individual sectoral Councils, feels honour-bound to produce meetings, even if agendas occasionally need to be padded out with inessential items. The Commission is always happy to oblige by fast-tracking proposals in the pipeline. In short, the very fixing of a date in the diary effectively sets off a series of mechanisms designed to ensure that the agenda of the meeting concerned is as full and substantive as possible.

The Council's attempts to render its activities more open and accessible, particularly when acting in a legislative capacity, have added yet further imperatives for forward planning (see chapter 20). The Council's rules of procedure set out how the Council's deliberations on acts adopted in accordance with the co-decision procedure should be open to the public. These include the presentation by the Commission of its most important legislative proposals and the ensuing Council debate and votes on legislative acts, together with the final Council deliberations leading to the votes and any subsequent explanations of vote. The rules require the secretariat to inform the public as far as possible in advance of the dates and approximate time on which such transmissions will take place.

It is thus increasingly rare for the Council to meet outside the preordained schedule, although such meetings can and do occur. Convening a Council meeting at much shorter notice (for example, to deal with an unforeseen crisis) creates huge logistical problems, but it can be done. In this context, the General Affairs and External Relations Council is a special case. On the one hand, it has an overall coordination role; on the other, it is at the apex of the Union's emerging foreign and security policy and must therefore have the capability to react at short notice to urgent events. Nevertheless, even this particular Council formation is increasingly bound by planning mechanisms.

There is one other reason why exceptional meetings of sectoral Councils (apart from the General Affairs and External Relations Council) are rare. The Council is, in the eyes of the treaties, one and indivisible. Consequently, any and every sectoral Council may deal with any matter. This orthodoxy is most apparent in the case of 'A items' (see below), i.e., items where no discussion is required. A glance at the press release of any Council meeting will show that many of the 'A items' adopted do not fall within the normal scope of work of the sectoral Council concerned (since there is no discussion, this does not matter). However, on occasion, a sectoral Council may be called upon to deal with the substance of a matter that does not fall within its generally acknowledged competences. This can occur, for example, where a legal void might otherwise result if the Council does not act. On such occasions, ministers and the presidency will be appropriately briefed by their permanent representatives and the competent experts and officials. Clearly, the possibility of dealing with urgent matters in this way greatly reduces the need to hold exceptional meetings of a sectoral Council outside the presidency's pre-established timetable.

'A items', 'B items', and 'false B items'

Under article 207 TEC, Coreper is described as a Council preparatory committee, but in its rules of procedure the Council has given a broad interpretation of Coreper's preparatory duties. In particular, article 19(2) declares that 'Coreper shall endeavour to reach agreement at its level to be submitted to the Council for adoption.' This deck-clearing operation is, in practice, one of Coreper's primary roles (see chapter 11). Where the representatives of the member states have been able to reach complete agreement at Coreper level, the matter is submitted to the Council as an 'A item' – derived from the tradition whereby matters requiring no further discussions are always placed on part A – the first part – of the Council's agenda. Matters requiring discussion by the Council itself are placed on the second part of the Council's agenda and have therefore come to be known as 'B items'. No formal distinction is made between a decision taken as an 'A item' and a Council decision taken following debate by the institution. By the Council's reckoning, about two-thirds of Council decisions are dealt with as 'A' items.

In recent years, there have been claims that the 'A item' procedure is somehow less 'legitimate' than having items adopted following proper debate by the Council. However, such criticisms fail to take account of two factors. First, before agreement is reached on an item, it will have been debated intensively by civil servants who, in each national context, will have referred any matter of political consequence up to the national minister for a view before a final decision is taken. It may well already have been the subject of a number of deliberations at ministerial level on one or more occasions. Second, all 'A items' must be notified ahead of the Council in a published list, which is scrutinised thoroughly by national administrations, and which ministers themselves must approve in the Council session. In the event of objections being raised in the Council to a particular item, it is withdrawn from the agenda without discussion and referred back to Coreper.

There remains one other form of 'B item'. This has been described thus: 'It can occur that items of considerable importance to delegations have actually been settled at a lower level. Since the agendas for Council meetings circulate openly, it is considered undiplomatic for such issues to 'go through on the nod'. Hence the invention of the 'false B point' – in effect, an A item in disguise for reasons of public relations.' (Spence, 1995, p. 15)

Legislative and decision-making procedures

Article 249 sets out the ways in which the Council may act, either alone or together with the European Parliament, in the Community context. The Maastricht Treaty added two further contexts for formal acts under the second and third pillars. The various formal acts which the Council may adopt are set out in box 3.2. In some areas within the Community pillar where Community powers are exercised with powers reserved for the member states, use is made of so-called 'mixed' acts, done jointly by the Council and the representatives of the governments of the member states 'meeting within the Council'.

The Council, as underscored by article 202 TEC, is first and foremost a decision-taking body. The way in which those decisions have to be taken, together with the role or involvement of other institutions, is laid down in specific articles in the treaty. These procedures range from the simplest legislative procedure involving a Commission proposal and a Council decision, with no consultation of the European Parliament or any consultative body, to the fully-fledged co-decision procedure under which the Council and the European Parliament act as co-legislators on an equal footing. One of the main objectives of the draft constitution is to simplify the number of such procedures, and as the draft currently stands their number would be reduced substantially. Some of the variants of these procedures

Box 3.2: *The various types of formal Council acts*

Regulations (alone or together with the European Parliament)

Directives (alone or together with the European Parliament)

Decisions (alone or together with the European Parliament)

Recommendations

Common strategies (second pillar)

Joint actions (second pillar)

Common positions (second and third pillars)

Framework decisions (third pillar)

which are particular to different policy sectors are described in the subsequent chapters.

The written procedure

Although the Council meets frequently, occasions occur where acts must be adopted urgently and where otherwise a legal void would ensue. Article 12 of the Council's rules of procedure allows the Council to decide on urgent matters using a so-called written procedure (either at its own behest or at the proposal of the president). The Council or Coreper must unanimously agree that the written procedure be used. The Council secretariat, which has general responsibility for managing written procedures, typically sends an e-mail to member states' capitals setting out the text of the proposed decision and the agreed deadline, which is usually in about two or three days but can be shorter for very urgent matters. Member states can reply yes or no, and they may submit statements for the Council's minutes, but they must all reply. The general secretariat establishes whether the required majority has been attained. A summary of the acts adopted by the written procedure is drawn up every month. Though the written procedure was designed to deal with urgent matters, the procedure has increasingly been used to dispatch relatively minor business, such as formal decisions to consult the other institutions on Commission proposals, the approval of draft answers to written parliamentary questions, or the accreditation of third country ambassadors.

In cases of extreme urgency on foreign policy matters, the Council's rules provide for a simplified written procedure, known as the 'silent procedure',

PART 2: THE COUNCIL IN ITS DIFFERENT GUISES

The Council is a single entity, institutionally and legally; there is only one Council. However, this single entity is multi-cephalous. Originally the Council was composed of ministers of foreign affairs (the Foreign Affairs Council, then General Affairs Council, or as it is now dubbed, the General Affairs and External Relations Council). However, from its earliest days, foreign affairs ministers found it increasingly difficult to cope themselves with ever more specialised agendas. The practice emerged of different sectoral 'configurations' or 'formations' of the Council meeting alongside the Foreign Affairs Council, which remained primus inter pares with a general coordinating role (see chapter 4). The first truly sectoral Council – that is, specialised ministers meeting on their own to discuss matters falling within their competence – was that of transport ministers (25 February 1960), and the second that of the social affairs ministers (10-11 May 1960). The development of the common agricultural policy is frequently thought to have given rise to the first sectoral Council but, although agriculture ministers had previously accompanied foreign ministers in the Foreign Affairs Council, the Agriculture Council did not make its first appearance until 14-15 November 1960 (see chapter 7).

Over the years, more and more sectoral Councils were established. The first edition of this book listed some twenty Council configurations. The Council seemed to have embarked on an inexorable process whereby, with each extension of the Union's competences, a fresh configuration sprang into being, with the attendant tendency to increasing policy compartmentalisation. The Council's machinery had long been protesting and its resources – particularly meeting rooms and interpreters – were becoming increasingly stretched. At the 1999 Helsinki European Council meeting, faced with the prospect of enlargement, heads of state and government decided not only to put a stop to the process but to cut back the number of Council configurations to just sixteen (the European Council actually suggested fifteen as a target, but at the time agreement could only be reached in the Council to reduce to sixteen). This number was subsequently radically pruned back further to nine at the Seville European Council in 2002. This list, reproduced in box 4.1, is now incorporated into the Council's rules of procedure. New Council configurations may only be created by the General Affairs and External Relations Council.

The practice of holding joint meetings of two or more sectoral Councils at the same time – known in the jargon as 'jumbo' Council meetings – was effectively outlawed by the 1999 Helsinki package of Council reforms. These

Box 4.1: *List of Council configurations*

- General Affairs and External Relations
- Economic and Financial Affairs
- Justice and Home Affairs
- Employment, Social Policy, Health and Consumer Affairs
- Competitiveness (Internal Market, Industry and Research)
- Transport, Telecommunications and Energy
- Agriculture and Fisheries
- Environment
- Education, Youth and Culture

state that 'Joint sessions of different Council formations shall no longer be convened, save in exceptional circumstances.' The original logic behind 'jumbo' sessions was to facilitate agreement where issues straddled the competences of different sectoral Councils. The method was not a success and had already been largely abandoned. The prospect of impending enlargement made the ban imperative – it is practically impossible to hold two Council sessions side-by-side in a Union of twenty-five members. On the other hand, annex I to the Council's rules of procedure provides that 'Several Ministers may participate as full members of the same Council configuration...', thus enabling issues that do straddle ministerial competences to be dealt with by a single Council configuration.

In addition to formally convened Councils, the practice has evolved of holding informal meetings of sectoral ministers at a venue in the country holding the presidency. Although sometimes referred to as 'informal Councils', this is strictly speaking incorrect, since they are not formally convened meetings of the Council in its recognised seat. According to the rules laid down by the Helsinki European Council, such informal meetings are designed to permit 'as free as possible an exchange of views on topics of general scope. They are not Council sessions and cannot replace the Council's normal activities.' The Helsinki package goes on to impose a series of restrictions and conditions: no official agenda, ministerial assistants limited to two, no Council documents to be prepared, and, above all, no formal conclusions or decisions to be taken. In reality, informal Council meetings are an integral part of what might be termed the 'presidency culture', a chance for the president to play host. They are therefore part of the scenery, and the Commission in particular tries to turn these sessions to good advantage by encouraging informal discussions about proposals in the legislative pipeline. In principle, presidencies should limit themselves to six such meetings during each presidency (which always include foreign ministers - the so-called 'Gymnich meeting', Ecofin ministers, justice and home affairs ministers, agriculture ministers and defence ministers).

The following chapters in this part set out the history, specific features, working practices and idiosyncrasies of four Council configurations – the General Affairs and External Relations Council (chapter 4), the Ecofin Council (chapter 5), the Justice and Home Affairs Council (chapter 6) and the Agriculture Council (chapter 7). While much could also have been written about the other five configurations, these four have been selected in order to provide a cross section of all three 'pillars' and because of their particular role in the Union's development in the past or at present. They also show that even if in name certain Council formations have been merged, much of the culture and atmosphere of the previous formations still exists. Thus, chapter 5.1 describes the workings of the Economic and Financial Affairs Council, while chapter 5.2 provides a description of the same Council when it is wearing its hat as successor to the now extinct Budget Council. After an initial period of disorientation, the Council has settled down reasonably well with its new configurations, although the feeling persists that certain configurations are somewhat artificial creations (e.g. the Employment, Social Policy, Health and Consumer Affairs Council). In such cases, a series of pragmatic arrangements have been devised which effectively enable the same Council to meet in different formats under the same formation (e.g. spreading a meeting over two days, so that ministers with one portfolio can attend on one day, and be replaced by ministers responsible for the other portfolio on the other). What emerges clearly from the following chapters is that markedly different histories, working cultures, atmospherics and methods of the various formations belie the legal orthodoxy and convenient fiction of a single Council!

Chapter 4: The General Affairs and External Relations Council

The General Affairs and External Relations Council has been known variously as the General Affairs Council, the Foreign Affairs Council (because of its composition), and, since June 2002, under its present longwinded title (usually abbreviated, somewhat indigestibly, to GAERC). In analyses of the Council, it is invariably described as being *primus inter pares*. There was at the outset no legal basis for this pre-eminence. It is only since 2002 that its pre-eminent role has been formally and explicitly acknowledged in the Council's rules of procedure (article 2). Its particular status stems from the fact that it is the embodiment of the dominant role played by member states' foreign ministries in building Europe.

The General Affairs and External Relations Council is a curious hybrid. It is formally a single Council formation, although it meets in two distinct sessions, each with its own agenda. This represents the compromise reached in 2002 between proponents of a complete split into two separate Council formations dealing respectively with horizontal internal and external aspects of EU policy, and those who wished to retain both aspects in a single Council formation attended by foreign ministers. Once the new constitutional treaty enters into force, this split will have been accomplished.

The following section recounts the history and development of the General Affairs Council and describes the working methods of today's General Affairs Council sessions, while section 4.2 analyses the Council's external relations functions. Section 4.3 relates in greater detail the history and debate about the emerging defence structures in the Council. Most of the changes in the structure and working methods of the General Affairs and External Relations Council were introduced ahead of enlargement as part of the reform process to ensure an effective Council with twenty-five members. Chapter 21 sets out in more detail the background to these changes and gives an assessment of various reforms, explaining why to date they appear to have had only a limited impact.

4.1 The General Affairs Council

History and development

The General Affairs Council's pre-eminence was evident from the inception of the European Coal and Steel Community in 1952. As described in chapter 1, coal and steel and the industrial sovereignty that went with them were vital national interests yet, with one exception (a young Italian Christian Democrat politician, Emilio Taviani), it was diplomats from the foreign ministries rather than technocrats from the ministries directly concerned that represented their countries in Jean Monnet's restricted negotiating group (Hallstein, Suetens, Spierenburg, Wehner). The reason for this was simple; the only mechanisms that countries had with which to deal with each other at that time were the classic intergovernmental mechanisms of foreign ministries and diplomatic services. Rare were the occasions when, say, economics ministers might venture abroad to meet, let alone negotiate with, their counterparts in other countries.

It was entirely logical, therefore, that foreign ministries should play leading roles in the diplomatic negotiations which led to the creation of the ECSC. It was also logical that the foreign ministries retained their predominance thereafter in the ECSC's 'statist' Special Council. Throughout the 1950s, the practice developed whereby routine and technical matters were dealt with by the ministers of economics, trade or industry (if they were not themselves replaced by high-ranking diplomats), but all sensitive and 'political' matters were reserved for ministers of foreign affairs. Thus, it could be argued, the division into 'sectoral' Councils and the pre-eminence of the General Affairs Council were effectively established during the early years of the ECSC.

A similar process took place in relation to the EEC and Euratom. Messina was a conference of ministers of foreign affairs. The principle author of the report they commissioned, Paul-Henri Spaak, was himself a foreign minister. In Germany, it was the ministry of foreign affairs (together with the chancellor) that defended Spaak's ideas against his critics in the federal ministries of economic affairs, atomic energy and agriculture. It was again Spaak who chaired the subsequent July 1956-March 1957 intergovernmental negotiations. At sub-foreign ministers' level, the heads of delegation committee made up of senior foreign ministry officials played an influential preparatory and coordinating role and, as chapter 11 describes, was ultimately to transform itself into a vital integrationist organ, Coreper. Indeed, Coreper, composed of ambassadors appointed by foreign ministers, consolidated the Foreign Affairs Council's pre-eminence.

Again, it was entirely logical that the EEC Council of Ministers should be predominantly composed of foreign affairs ministers. However, a countervailing sectoral logic began to assert itself. In the first place, the Euratom Council of Ministers could in itself be characterised as a sectoral Council (even more so after the 1967 merger of the Councils). The first six EEC and Euratom Council meetings were held concurrently. Although some foreign ministers were accompanied by energy ministers, the majority of foreign ministers simply switched 'hats' from the EEC to Euratom matters. However, the eighth Euratom Council meeting was held separately (31 July

1958). Only the Dutch foreign minister attended; the other five member states were represented by their economics or trade ministers.

A second factor was the sheer frequency of Council meetings. In its first year of existence, the EEC Council met seventeen times (Euratom thirteen times); eleven in Brussels, four times in Paris, once in Strasbourg and once in Venice. This was an entirely new, always considerable and at times onerous demand on limited ministerial time, particularly if the greater time and less comfort involved in travel of that era is taken into account.

A third related factor was the technical nature of much of the EEC Council's work. The EEC Treaty was a framework treaty; it described policy goals and sometimes set out timetables, but it was largely mute on policy development and implementation. It made little sense for foreign ministers to discuss the minutiae of, for example, a common customs tariff, and the Foreign Affairs Council was soon happy to leave such spadework to Coreper or trade ministers (or the Special Committee on Agriculture and agriculture ministers), whilst reserving for itself sensitive or political problems as well as the role of overall coordination and impetus.

Paradoxically, although the logic of sectoralism was countervailing, it nevertheless consolidated the pre-eminence of the Foreign Affairs Council, for how could a particular Council be *primus inter pares* if there were no others? The Foreign Affairs Council owed some of its pre-eminence to the sum of its parts. In most of the member states the foreign ministry was the first of the great ministries of state (though this honour went to the economics ministry in Germany). It also owed some of its pre-eminence to its subject matter, the 'high politics' of foreign affairs, and hence to the implicit principle that specialised work was 'delegated' to the sectoral Councils. Some of its pre-eminence was due to its diplomatic expertise and the diplomatic network, with Coreper at its apex, at its command.

Convinced federalists had always seen the Council as an alien, intergovernmental body in the Community's supranational institutional structure. They took solace from the conviction that the foreign ministers and their traditional diplomatic methods would, sooner or later, be ousted by sectoral ministers and technical specialists. Vertical division would weaken the Council's grip and strengthen the Commission's hand; international diplomacy (as the federalists perceived it) would give way to specialised negotiations. That the Council retained its grip, and the Foreign Affairs Council its pre-eminence, can be attributed to a number of factors.

The first, and perhaps the most important, was President de Gaulle's prejudice against the avowedly supranational EEC, which he had grudgingly inherited from the collapsed French Fourth Republic, and his preference for the intergovernmental – a preference which culminated in the ill-fated Fouchet Plan. Already, during an official visit to Italy in June 1958, de Gaulle had proposed the organisation of periodic meetings between foreign ministers (under the nascent Fifth Republic's constitution, foreign policy was primarily a presidential competence), and the 1960-1962 Fouchet negotiations were undertaken by foreign ministers entirely outside the Community framework. The Intergovernmental Committee on Political Union was chaired by diplomats, first Christian Fouchet himself and then an Italian, Attilio Cattani, and classic diplomatic procedures were used – summits between heads of state and government, and meetings of foreign ministers, prepared by national foreign ministries. Although the Fouchet talks themselves broke down, they underlined the pre-eminence of the foreign ministers in two ways. First, the nature of the talks meant that the foreign ministers were discussing the fate of the EEC whilst simultaneously being outside and above it. On several occasions foreign ministers broke off their Fouchet talks to don their Community 'hats'. Second, the majority of foreign ministers ultimately defended the Community method against Fouchet's de Gaulle-inspired proposals. This irony has continued to the present day. The foreign ministries are traditionally suspected of being too pro-integrationist at home, whilst in Brussels the Council, including the General Affairs Council, is traditionally suspected of being too pro-nation state.

A second factor in the Foreign Affairs Council's continued pre-eminence was the central preparatory role played by Coreper; only the Special Committee on Agriculture and the Monetary Committee escaped its grip. As was described above, Coreper's role and powers were tantamount to a composite consolidation of the role of the ministries of foreign affairs. At the same time, Coreper developed a - European - mind of its own. Once again, there was a certain irony in this situation. Federalists had vilified Coreper as an unwelcome statist/intergovernmental rival to the supranational Commission, yet Coreper played (and still plays) a vital role in making the Community method work and in developing a collective consciousness within the Council.

A third important factor was the Community's continued need for the traditional diplomatic tools of negotiation and coordination. The two went hand in hand, with the permanent representatives and Coreper much to the fore. In this context, the Commission subtly encouraged the Foreign Affairs Council's pre-eminence, preferring a body with an overall, and not unsympathetic, view to a collection of sectoral interests (a point of view ironically opposite to that of federalists in the late 1950s).

A fourth, and related, factor was the growing perception of the Foreign Affairs Council as a sort of Council of last resort. This owed something to its inherent superiority, something to its command of diplomatic and negotiating mechanisms, something to its implicit practice of 'delegating' work to sectoral Councils, something to its overall coordinating role, and something to its implicit brief for tackling politically sensitive matters. In addition, success begat success, and the habit grew of referring thorny problems to it. However, as the 1960s progressed, this role was undermined. Foreign ministers could not always act any more decisively than their sectoral Council colleagues, and this was especially true after the 1966 'empty chair' crisis and the advent of the 'Luxembourg compromise' (see chapter 14) with the concomitant need for unanimity. Nor did the foreign affairs ministers necessarily have greater seniority in terms of rank than their sectoral colleagues. An early example was the German Federal Republic, whose economics minister traditionally carried at least as much weight as the minister for foreign affairs. The relative weight of a member state's representatives could also depend on the political clout of the personalities involved or of their comparative hierarchical level (for example, ministers vs. secretaries of state).

Perhaps most significantly, sectoral Councils proved increasingly unwilling to refer disputes 'upwards' or 'sideways' to the Foreign Affairs Council.

As sectoral Councils consolidated their roles, so their reluctance to hand over difficult problems was reinforced. This reluctance was bound up in the socialisation of specialised ministers, and their increasing identification of a common sovereignty. If a sectoral Council passed on its problems to another Council, the twin implications were that it could not resolve its own policy issues and that ultimate policy-making power lay elsewhere. The Agriculture Council's grim determination to resolve all agricultural matters, even when these involve painful reforms – still a feature of the Union today – is a good example of this socialisation at work (see chapter 7). With unanimity the norm, thorny problems were as likely to remain blocked in a sectoral Council as they were to be passed on to the Foreign Affairs Council.

Whilst these developments undermined the 'troubleshooter' or 'star chamber' role of the Foreign Affairs Council, the 1969 outbreak of European summitry, following de Gaulle's abrupt departure and the election of the more emollient Pompidou, were shortly to have three important consequences, simultaneously boosting and consolidating the Foreign Affairs Council's pre-eminence within the Council structure.

The first was the Pompidou-initiated negotiations which led, via the 1969 Hague Summit and the 1970 Luxembourg report it commissioned, to the emergence of European Political Cooperation (EPC). Following the Gaullist model, EPC was initially purely intergovernmental in nature; the European Commission had to fight hard to achieve even minimal input. However, the foreign ministers who met in the EPC context were the same foreign ministers who met in the Foreign Affairs Council. EPC matters inevitably overlapped with Community affairs, especially where trade was concerned, and the frontier between the two contexts gradually became blurred. Throughout the 1970s, the Commission made slow but steady progress in inserting itself into EPC mechanisms, including participation in the work of the Coordinating Group which had been set up to report to the Political Committee (EPC) and Coreper (EEC).

The 1981 London report consolidated an apparently inexorable trend towards closer foreign policy cooperation, ultimately leading to the 1986 Single European Act, which placed EPC on a legal footing within the treaty structure, and to the 1992 Maastricht Treaty, which established the Common Foreign and Security Policy. With the entry into force of the Maastricht Treaty, the need for the foreign ministers of the General Affairs Council to swap 'hats' before discussing EPC matters finally disappeared. The high politics of foreign policy – the stuff of foreign ministers' professional lives – had finally been admitted into the European Union (though not the European Community) fold. This admission broadened the General Affairs Council's formal competences and consolidated its pre-eminence.

A second important consequence of the new summitry was the December 1974 Paris summit's decision to create the European Council. The communiqué issued by the heads of state and government also gave birth to the General Affairs Council by declaring that: 'In order to ensure consistency in Community activities and continuity of work, the ministers of foreign affairs, meeting in the Council of the Community, will act as initiators and co-ordinators. They may hold political cooperation meetings at the same time' (EC Bulletin 1974/12). By any standards, this represented a substantial boost in the role and powers of the General Affairs Council; not only would it alone be present alongside the government heads in the inner sanctum of the European Council, but it was expressly asked to act as initiator and coordinator (coincidentally extending the role and powers of Coreper). It would thus enjoy considerable agenda-setting powers. As importantly, its new duties formally established its pre-eminence over the sectoral Councils, whose work it was expected to coordinate. The close relationship between the Foreign Affairs Council and the European Council was subsequently confirmed by the 1977 London declaration on the European Council, the 1983 Stuttgart Solemn Declaration on European Union and, ultimately, the Single European Act.

The third consequence of summitry was the altered dynamics of European integration. Such factors as growing international monetary instability, Europe's increasing weakness *vis-à-vis* the United States, and the growing economic strength of West Germany convinced President Pompidou of the need for fresh progress. The Gaullist veto on British accession was lifted (the UK was seen as a potential counterweight to German strength); the Common Agricultural Policy was completed, common financial resources elaborated and concomitant budgetary powers for the European Parliament accepted; the EPC and economic and monetary union processes were launched. This new dynamic bestrode any number of sensitive issues which the Foreign Affairs Council would have been expected to discuss even if it had not, in the European Council context, had new coordination and preparation duties. Since the 1970s, the number of sensitive issues under discussion at any moment has constantly increased, and hence so has the scope and competences of the Foreign Affairs Council.

The recommendations of the 1979 Report of the 'Three Wise Men' are analysed in more detail in chapter 19. One of their deepest concerns was the fragmentation of the Council's authority through the development of increasing numbers of sectoral Councils. The Wise Men's apprehensions ultimately bore fruit in the 1983 Stuttgart Solemn Declaration on European Union, which declared that:

> 'The consistency and continuity of the work needed for the further construction of European Union as well as the preparation of meetings of the European Council are the responsibility of the Council (General Affairs) and its members.' (EC Bulletin, 1983, N° 6, p 26)

Functions of the General Affairs Council

The work of the General Affairs Council can be divided into three distinct functions. The first involves handling dossiers which are multidisciplinary or horizontal in character and which cannot be slotted easily into the remit of any other sectoral Council formation. Subjects such as the Union's multi-annual financial framework, structural funding for Europe's less developed or disadvantaged regions, institutional issues and enlargement (which covers the entire sweep of EU policy) need to be treated in a ministerial forum with a correspondingly broad remit and where sufficient time can be set aside for them. Part of the problem, however, in handling these types of dossier is that foreign ministers in many cases do not necessarily have the time nor the inclination to immerse themselves in what can be complicated issues which by their nature are not at the forefront of their domestic concerns. In certain cases these issues are handled by junior ministers for European affairs. While this has the advantage of ensuring the presence of ministers with some degree of expertise, in many cases their junior status means that they lack the authority and clout of their superiors when important policy matters need to be decided.

The second main function, as described above, is to ensure coordination and consistency in the Council's work, given the *primus inter pares* status of the GAC. However, while various mechanisms have been devised to try and strengthen its hand in this function, it is in practice difficult for the General Affairs Council to assert itself in this in more than a cursory way. If governments are sufficiently joined-up with properly working internal coordination mechanisms, there is no reason to suppose that different positions will be taken by different cabinet ministers within the same government in different Council formations (see chapter 17). Nevertheless, this is not always the case, and differences of nuance (rather than major substantive differences) can and do emerge between different Council formations. Moreover, foreign ministers in many cases are no longer necessarily the most senior members in the national cabinet, which renders any exercise involving the General Affairs Council exerting authority over another Council formation somewhat futile.

Its third role, which is performed more effectively, is preparing discussions in the European Council, including on matters where the latter is being called on to arbitrate between positions being taken by different Council formations. It is in effect the gatekeeper for the European Council (see chapters 9 and 21) by both helping to set the agenda and defining in advance the nature of and general content of the European Council's conclusions. In the past, preparation of European Councils was mainly handled by the presidency, Council secretariat and the Commission in a relatively closed circuit, with little substantive detail of the draft conclusions emerging until the European Council itself. However, since the introduction of an annotated draft agenda for European Councils following Seville in 2002, the General Affairs Council and Coreper have had a greater hold over the substance and presentation of the European Council conclusions than in the past.

These three types of tasks are now explicitly reflected in article 2 of the Council's rules of procedure which formally lists the responsibilities of the General Affairs Council as being: 'preparation for and follow-up to European Council meetings, including the necessary coordination of all preparatory work, overall coordination of policies, institutional and administrative questions, horizontal dossiers which affect several of the Union's policies and any horizontal dossier entrusted to it by the European Council, having regard to operating rules for economic and monetary union'. The General Affairs Council's competences are thus, at least in theory, extremely wide-ranging.

One of the main purposes of these reforms was to transform the General Affairs Council into a more effective negotiating forum in the wake of a certain drift which had occurred in the late 1990s, coupled with apprehensions about the operational consequences of the looming prospect of enlargement. This drift in general affairs matters was at least in part due to the tendency towards greater declaratory output on foreign policy matters rather than action- and outcome-oriented discussions in which something was genuinely at stake. This stands in stark contrast to the Ecofin Council which, like the General Affairs Council, has agendas the bulk of which are non legislative in character. In the Ecofin Council formation, debates are conducted in a busi-ness-like manner and focus exclusively on essential points, since in many cases, these items are real policy problems on which the outcome actually matters and ministers are focused on the issue at hand (see chapter 5).

A further problem is getting foreign ministers to give the necessary atten-tion to some of the subjects being handled in the General Affairs Council, such as technical aspects of enlargement or discussions on institutional topics. This is partly understandable, since in national terms they are not the main focus of the work of the foreign ministry. General affairs issues were often shunted off to the beginning of the meeting, and many foreign minis-ters would refrain from turning up until near the lunch. Often discussions on such matters were conducted by junior ministers or permanent repre-sentatives. Part of the problem undoubtedly lies in the fact that attendance at General Affairs Councils is so great (there may be up to 150 people pres-ent in the meeting room!) that ministers find it difficult to enter into sub-stantive discussion on more sensitive matters with such a large audience. As a result, ministerial lunches frequently became extremely lengthy affairs, lasting up to four hours on occasion, since they offered a forum in which ministers could discuss matters among themselves without their negotiating tactics and concessions being faithfully reported home by national civil ser-vants. Recently, to counter this effect, the Council has adopted the practice of having short lunches and meeting in a restricted format with ministers only at the main table and two civil servants in the back row.

Anatomy and working methods of the General Affairs Council

A General Affairs Council session is held practically every month, with the exception of August – usually immediately before or after an External Relations session. It is rare that matters of general affairs lead to unexpected meetings being called at short notice, although this has occurred in the past (for example, after the first 2 June 1992 Danish referendum vote against the ratification of the Maastricht Treaty, the General Affairs Council met in Oslo on 4 June, in the margins of a NATO meeting). However, because of the logistics involved, such emergency meetings are very rare. Twice a year, under the 'Gymnich' formula, the foreign ministers meet informally at a location – typically a castle or a stately home – in the member state holding the presidency. The original logic of these meetings was informal prepara-tion for European Council meetings by giving ministers a chance to hold exchanges of views away from the usual swarms of accompanying officials and without any obligation to reach decisions. Pressure on ministerial time and burgeoning agendas have undermined the original logic, and 'informal' ministerial meetings are increasingly likely to take important decisions, at least in principle if not formally. While informal meetings of foreign minis-ters generally focus on foreign policy issues, recent meetings have spent some time on enlargement and treaty reform. Foreign ministers (as foreseen in article 4 of the TEU) also attend the European Council and, as has been described, the General Affairs Council holds important gate-keeping, agenda-setting and preparatory functions in relation to the European Council's meetings.

Foreign ministers see much of each other. The European Union and its General Affairs Council is just one of a number of overlapping forums – the United Nations, NATO, the Council of Europe, G8 – where they may rub shoulders. Indeed, an old adage has it that the foreign ministers see more of one another than they do of their fellow ministers in government. Frequently appointed because they are regarded as safe hands and judicious wordsmiths, foreign ministers tend to enjoy long periods of service and hence come to know one another very well. Friendships develop, mutual respect grows. All of these factors encourage a particularly intense *esprit de corps* which is further enhanced whenever member states are able to present a united front on an issue.

As a general rule, the General Affairs and External Relations Council tends not to vote. Like the Council in most of its compositions, it is not, in the sense of decisions being taken by raised hands, a voting Council. This has much to do with the General Affairs Council's composition and its subject matter. Perhaps more than any other group of ministers, with the exception of Ecofin, foreign ministers straddle the fault line between national and European politics and between executive and legislative work in the Council. The high politics of constitutional affairs and foreign policy constantly touch on issues dear to the member states' cultural and political sovereignty but so, frequently, do trade and commercial issues (given the colonial past of certain member states and special trading relationships). Because of this, Coreper and the General Affairs Council go to great efforts to accommodate even the most awkward of positions. The search for consensus is a constant background theme to the General Affairs Council's work. Because it is not usually involved in nitty-gritty legislative work – such as the internal market or environmental law – in recent years much less emphasis has been placed on the speed and efficiency of the decision-making mechanism and much more on accommodation of interests. There is another important reason for this emphasis on consensus; the reverse of the consensuality coin is solidarity. Emphasis on voting procedures is in any case slightly misleading, since taking formal decisions is only a part of the General Affairs Council's work, given that it is more an executive policy-making body than a legislative one. Other important functions include – not necessarily conclusive – discussions, listening to and perhaps discussing communications from the Commission and other institutional actors, consideration of progress reports on important negotiations, consideration of opinions from the Political Committee and of reports from Coreper, taking stock or note of political situations, and the formulation of political gestures.

The General Affairs Council is thus a body with wide-ranging and disparate competences. Box 4.2 (over) illustrates the range of General Affairs Council business through a typical agenda from a recent Council session.

Box 4.2: *The agenda of a typical General Affairs Council session*

2,562nd session of the Council (General Affairs) held in Brussels on 23 February 2004

1. Approval of Agenda
A standard formality at the start of each meeting, which also allows delegations to add any additional 'other business' items not previously announced (although this is rare).

2. Adoption of the list of 'A' items
Nineteen items were approved under part 'A' of the agenda without discussion, ranging from restrictive measures to be taken against the leaders of Transnistria in Moldova to the preliminary rectifying budget for the European Data Protection supervisor. For a detailed list see document 6449/04 and the Council press release. A description of the 'A' item procedure can be found in chapter 3.

3. Resolutions, decisions and opinions adopted by the European Parliament
This is a routine item placed on the agenda which allows the presidency to draw members' attention to specific points contained in resolutions adopted by the European Parliament at its most recent part sessions. This item rarely detains the Council more than five minutes.

4. Progress of work in other Council configurations
This is also a standard feature and affords the Council an opportunity to take stock and comment on the most important files dealt with in other configurations of the Council, in order to enable it to ensure overall coordination of the Council's activities and their consistency with the general objectives of the Union. The main dossiers highlighted in the presidency's note (doc. 6348/04) were preparation of the Spring European Council and the state of play on negotiations for a savings tax agreement with certain third countries discussed in the previous Ecofin Council. This item is generally a formality (chapter 21 explains the background to this procedure).

5. Preparation of the European Council (Brussels, 25/26 March) – draft annotated agenda
Under the new method for preparing the European Council, the Council is required to draw up an annotated draft agenda on a proposal by the presidency at least four weeks before the European Council (article 2(3) of the Council's rules of procedure). The initial draft, which on this occasion already contained detailed conclusions language on most of the agenda, was presented to Coreper the previous week and is being presented to the Council for the first time (see doc. 6351/04). Over the coming weeks the presidency will refine the language in the light of comments made in the Council/Coreper and received bilaterally so that a near final draft can be presented to the General Affairs Council on 22 March immediately prior to the European Council.

6. Future Financial perspective
This was the first meeting in the Council on one of the most difficult package negotiations to be undertaken by the Union, with the initial presentation by Commission President Prodi of its communication on the new financial framework beyond 2006. After his presentation, ministers gave preliminary comments, staking out the ground with their starting bids in negotiations which would last at least until the summer of 2005.

7. Other business
No items were raised under other business.

4.2 External relations, foreign policy, security and defence, by Paul Reiderman

From ambition to reality

All policy areas are unique, but some are more unique than others. In the context of the European Union, the area of external relations is the most unique of them all. This distinction is due not only to the recent development of external relations as a sphere of EU activity, but also to its significance in terms of the overall process of integration, the singularity of the institutional architecture chosen, the working methods used, and the visibility of this policy area to the wider public.

The arrival of a genuine EU external relations policy is a recent event in EU history. Chastened by the early failure of the ambitious leap forward represented by the European Defence Community in 1954, the architects of European integration chose instead to build incrementally on solid economic foundations. Thus the 'Monnet method' eschewed the high politics of foreign or defence policy, preferring to make steady and less controversial progress by elaborating common policies in the various economic, technical and social fields. In method and activity the emerging entity was, as its name implied, a European *Economic* Community. However, from its earliest days a clear political ambition underpinned this project: the strategic goal of replacing national rivalries with a European identity. Moreover, important external aspects were never completely absent: trade and aid became important policy areas, and the proliferation of the European Commission's overseas 'delegations' looked and behaved like ersatz embassies.[1]

By the 1970s a limited form of foreign policy coordination began to be formalised. A loose framework known as European Political Co-operation (EPC) was established outside and alongside the EC Treaty structures and enabled member states to work together to find common approaches on foreign policy issues. Although it remained limited, EPC did at least begin to encourage a culture of consultation and cooperation between foreign ministries. In 1986, the Single European Act formalised this intergovernmental cooperation without changing its nature or methods of operation.

Decisive progress to realise the ambition of a meaningful common foreign policy began in earnest in the 1990s. The end of the Cold War ushered in a period of adjustment and evolution that fostered the development of a more ambitious and meaningful European foreign policy. The disappearance of an external threat, the reduced strategic importance of the European theatre and the increasing US focus on other priorities removed some of the glue from EU-US relations. The reunification of Germany, completion of the fourth wave of EU enlargement, and preparation for the fifth, strengthened the case of those arguing for greater 'deepening' to accompany the 'widening'. Perhaps most decisively, Europe – public and politicians alike – was stung by its inability to respond decisively to diplomatic and humanitarian challenges in the Balkans without American assistance. Together, these factors helped create a consensus that 'Europe's hour'[2] would never come without a significant step beyond the limited and rather *ad hoc* foreign policy co-ordination that had been achieved until then.

Negotiations towards the Maastricht Treaty confirmed that as the EU approached the completion of the economic phase of integration, the time had come to begin a more explicitly political phase. The treaty's entry into force on 1 November 1993 allowed, for the first time, the European Union as such to make its voice heard on the international stage. The goals of the new 'common foreign policy' were set out in general and wide-ranging terms. Title V of the treaty, as amended by the Amsterdam Treaty, states that the Union:

> 'shall define and implement a common foreign and security policy covering all areas of foreign and security policy, the objectives of which shall be: to safeguard the common values, fundamental interests, independence and integrity of the Union...; to strengthen the security of the Union in all ways, to preserve peace and strengthen international security...; to promote international co-operation to develop and consolidate democracy and the rule of law, and the respect for human rights and fundamental freedoms.'

The Treaty of Amsterdam gave further impetus to the Common Foreign and Security Policy (CFSP) with the agreement to create the post of high representative for the CFSP.[3] In doing so, the member states were responding to the widespread perception that the next phase of development of the Union's external policy required a more visible and permanent face than the six-monthly rotating presidency alone could provide. That the treaty put this face firmly in the Council (making the post-holder simultaneously secretary-general of the Council) rather than in the Commission was recognition that, while the member states were prepared to advance to a new phase of integration in this policy, they were not yet (and for some, not at all) ready to do so according to the traditional 'Community method', which would have implied a greater centrality for the Commission. Nor were the member states ready yet to make the logical and practical leap that the creation of the high representative offered: the ending of the increasingly anachronistic rotating presidency.

The Cologne European Council in 1999 appointed Javier Solana as the first high representative for the CFSP.[4] The appointment of a high profile political figure to the post and the subsequent construction of some of the requisite diplomatic and institutional machinery gave decisive momentum to the new position.

Though the construction was far from complete, by the end of the decade the EU was acquiring a policy with genuine operational capacity. This marked an important new phase in the overall process of European integration. The Union itself was now becoming an active player in a policy area traditionally reserved for sovereign states. Though the route chosen certainly did not represent the triumph of the 'Community method', neither was it a purely intergovernmental one. Indeed, it is somewhat misleading to describe foreign policy formulation in the Council as an intergovernmental activity. The developing CFSP is part of a treaty whose preamble proclaims that it marks a new stage in the process of European integration and continues the process of creating an ever closer union among the peoples of

Europe. The Commission is an important actor in this process, and the European Parliament can and does flex its budgetary muscle, although it cannot exercise any direct legislative control. Qualified majority voting on specific aspects of policy implementation is foreseen. More generally, working inside the single institutional framework places policy formulation within a framework where consensus building and collective problem solving on the basis of broadly defined common interests is a reflex.

In truth, the development of the CFSP was a pragmatic compromise between the competing federal and intergovernmental theologies. This compromise was made possible for two fundamental reasons: firstly the growing realisation by the member states that their influence on the international scene would continue to wane unless they could agree new patterns of cooperation at EU level, and secondly, the tectonic changes underway at the geopolitical level. Of all the Union's policies, the CFSP is probably the one that is grounded most firmly in executive rather than legislative functions. Until recently, the Council has fulfilled a role in many respects more akin to legislature than executive. Anchoring CFSP within the Council has obliged the Council to develop further its mechanisms of executive action. Finally, the CFSP is the policy with the highest profile of any. Although all other Council formations have their moments of drama, only the External Relations Council so regularly captures and holds the attention of press and public.

Tasks and scope

'External relations' is a phrase that covers all aspects of the Union's complex relationships with the wider world. As explained in chapter 1, since Maastricht the treaties have made an important distinction between various 'pillars' (though without ever using this convenient terminology). Broadly speaking, the economic aspects of external relations fall under the 'first pillar' (and are thus subject to the 'Community method'), whereas the more recent political aspects, including the CFSP, fall under the 'second pillar' (where methods have a stronger intergovernmental flavour). The different pillars allow for a specific allocation of powers among and within the EU institutions, depending on the policy area. By placing the external economic powers (trade and development aid) in the first or Community pillar, the Commission's central role is confirmed. Conferring powers on the Community in these areas is largely an extension of the internal logic of creating a single market in Europe, in which identical rights and obligations are imposed on member states, economic actors and citizens. The second pillar involves the member states exercising in common through the Union's single institutional framework the powers reserved to them in the area of foreign, security and defence policy. Since these are powers reserved to the member states, the Commission's role is more limited than in the first pillar.

The conceptual and legal space between the pillars allowed for a differentiation in terms of institutional powers and mechanisms. However, in policy terms, it is totally misleading to portray the distinction between the pillars as a distinction between the economic and the political. The first pillar contains elements essential for the definition and execution of a common foreign policy. The extension (or withdrawal) of commercial preferences, macro-financial assistance or development aid by the EU may have far-reaching political consequences. Similarly, agreeing a customs union with Turkey in 1995 was as significant for political as it was for economic reasons. Indeed, one of the Union's main and most effective instruments of foreign policy over the past decade falls firmly under the first pillar – its own enlargement. Moreover, ministers discussing relations with any third country do not make any distinction in their minds between 'economic' and 'political'. This is a purely artificial distinction, simply reflecting the fact that different procedures and work methods apply inside the Union. Recognising the indivisibility of external relations, the EU as a matter of routine now inserts human rights, counter-terrorist and non-proliferation goals into trade and cooperation agreements that it negotiates with partners.

The European Union and the member states can no longer ignore their combined weight in the world. They have a population 60% greater than that of the United States and four times that of Japan. They are the world's largest provider of development assistance and the biggest trading partner. They have an unparalleled web of relations and contacts with others in the world. Javier Solana, the EU's first high representative for CFSP put the point thus:

> 'It is my belief that because of our size and interests, because of our history and values, we have an obligation to take our share of responsibilities in this global age. We could, in theory, walk away from these responsibilities – but we could not escape the consequences of doing so.' (Javier Solana, Europe's place in the world, The Hague, February 2001)

European Security and Defence Policy

The assertion, first made in the Treaty of Maastricht, that the EU 'shall define and implement a common foreign and security policy covering all areas of foreign and security policy' left the door open for the subsequent development of a military component. Heads of state and government retained control as to the shape of any such subsequent development by adding: 'The European Council shall define the principles of and general guidelines for the common foreign and security policy, including for matters with defence implications.'

Five years later, the European Council did proceed to such a definition, but only after the two key players on the European defence scene, the United Kingdom and France, struck a bilateral bargain, at the December 1998 Franco-British St Malo summit, as to the strategic route to follow. Selling this bargain to other members of the European Council, including traditionally neutral countries such as Ireland, Sweden and Austria, was facilitated by the background of events in the Balkans: a US-led NATO intervention to reverse a humanitarian disaster in Kosovo. Accordingly, the European Councils at Cologne (June 1999) and Helsinki (December 1999) placed crisis management at the core of the ESDP and set the EU on course to develop the military (and civil) means required to fulfil this role. An off-the-peg mission statement was found by borrowing from the Western European Union (WEU) its 'Petersberg tasks' defined in 1992 as 'humanitarian and rescue tasks, peacekeeping tasks and tasks of combat forces in crisis management, including peacemaking.' To these ends, EU leaders committed themselves at Helsinki to the European headline goal of being capable, by 2003, of deploying 60,000 troops within 60 days and of sustaining these forces for at least one year.

An important part of the original Franco-British bargain on ESDP was that, although its development would be incremental and dependent at each stage on agreement within the European Council, the ambition would be open-ended. As described above, to date the European Council has allowed ESDP to develop with the focus clearly on crisis management. Moreover, the treaty does not exclude further developments, 'including the progressive framing of a common defence policy, which might lead to a common defence, should the European Council so decide.'[5] The ambiguity as to the ultimate shape of ESDP, although a deliberate and necessary part of the political bargain that allowed ESDP to be launched in the first place, has guaranteed an on-going tension between those member states which emphasise the importance of the EU's decision-making and operational autonomy in the military domain, and those which stress the centrality of the North Atlantic Treaty Organisation (NATO) and the complementarity of ESDP with NATO. The treaty makes clear that ESDP does not affect the specific nature of the security and defence policies of certain member states, and is also compatible with NATO. Elsewhere, the European Council has decided that, 'the Union must have the capacity for autonomous action, backed up by credible military forces, the means to decide to use them, and a readiness to do so, in order to respond to international crises without prejudice to actions by NATO.' Each successive European Council has gradually given substance to this desire to give the Union a capacity for autonomous action in international crisis management, where NATO as such is not engaged, in compliance with the principles of the UN Charter and acknowledging the prerogatives of the UN Security Council.

The development of ESDP does not mean that the EU is in the business of establishing a European army. The commitment and deployment of troops continues to be based on sovereign decisions taken by member states. However, a central objective behind ESDP is to enhance the military capacities of the member states. Hence, a process was launched to collect member states' voluntary commitments and to analyse the progress towards the achievement of capability objectives. Based on the outcome of that process, the European Council at Laeken stated that the Union was operationally able to conduct some crisis management operations. It also recognised that, in order to be in a position to take on more demanding operations, the assets and capabilities at its disposal would have to be developed. To that effect, a European Capability Action Plan (ECAP) was launched to boost the development of European crisis management capability and achieve the goals set by the European Council. ECAP aims to rationalise member states' respective defence efforts and increase the synergy between their national and multinational projects, thus enhancing military capability.

Keen to fulfil its potential as a 'one-stop shop' for crisis management, the Union decided to develop the civilian as well as the military aspects of crisis management. In June 2000 the Feira European Council defined four priority areas: police, strengthening of the rule of law, strengthening civilian administration and civil protection. Concrete targets were defined in those areas (and have since been met): member states should be able to provide, in the

common positions and joint actions. The Council secretariat, the Commission and the member states' capitals are permanently linked by a protected communications system that enables them to exchange messages and hold consultations.[12]

The centrality that the Commission enjoys in traditional community policies is diluted in the case of the CFSP. According to the treaty it is 'fully associated' with the CFSP. Such association is needed to ensure the consistency of the CFSP with those Community policies in which the Commission plays a leading role: external economic relations, development cooperation and humanitarian aid. The Commission's representatives are usually active participants in foreign policy discussions at all levels; the president of the Commission joins the heads of state or government within the European Council and the Commission participates in meetings of the Council and its preparatory bodies and in the political dialogue with third countries. Crucially, in the field of the CFSP the Commission does not have the exclusive right to submit initiatives. These come mainly from the presidency, a member state or the high representative. Nevertheless, the Commission remains a highly significant actor for a number of reasons. First, it has the political and administrative resources to make a telling contribution in the formulation of policy. Second, it has the financial and administrative resources to make it an indispensable actor as far as the implementation of certain CFSP policies are concerned. Third, it controls a number of important levers in community policies that, although formally outside the scope of the CFSP, are of critical importance in ensuring its success.

On paper, the European Parliament appears to be the poor relation in the institutional triangle that it forms together with the Council and Commission on CFSP. The treaty gives it a consultative role, while carefully avoiding that this gives rise to precise constraints or obligations. Thus, the Parliament is consulted by the presidency on the fundamental choices of the CFSP (notably via an annual debate) and is regularly briefed on developments (at both the plenary and committee levels) by the presidency, high representative and Commission. However, the real influence of the Parliament goes beyond the limited role that the treaty suggests. The Parliament performs a quasi-watchdog role through the many questions it asks of the Council, presidency, high representative and Commission. Though it may lack the formal power to censure, it is adept at exploiting the power to embarrass. In addition the Parliament is skilful at using its budgetary powers to give expression to its political priorities, including in the external relations field. Though the influence of the Parliament exceeds its formal powers, there are limits. The intergovernmental nature of ESDP is reflected in the fact that critical decisions on the deployment of forces and on defence budgets continue to be reserved for national parliaments.

Every six months a member state assumes the presidency of the European Union and in that capacity chairs the European Council, the Council and the subordinate bodies responsible for preparing proceedings (Coreper, Political and Security Committee, committees and working parties) (see chapter 18). A well-functioning presidency provides the impetus, ensures coherence, articulates Union positions and ensures their follow-up. It represents the Union in CFSP matters, notably by conducting political dialogue with third countries on behalf of the Union. It has responsibility to express the position of the Union in international organisations and at international conferences. It is responsible for implementing CFSP decisions. The presidency is assisted in these tasks by the secretary-general of the Council/high representative for the Common Foreign and Security Policy, in association with the European Commission. The presidency may also be assisted by the member state that will hold the following presidency.[13]

Over time, the drawbacks of the six-monthly rotation have become more apparent. In the area of external relations, continuity among interlocutors plays an important role. The current system of rotation denies the EU this continuity. It is not only names and faces that change: each incoming presidency has its own set of priorities that it will wish to see pursued during its term in office. This is not to say that presidencies pursue narrow national agendas at the expense of the wider EU interest, simply that the EU interest suffers with a constant re-ordering of priorities (the 'northern dimension' may be top of the list from January to June, only to be replaced by relations with the southern Mediterranean from July to December). Inevitably, also, there are temptations to ensure success during a six-month period that lead to a negotiating line that is weaker than would otherwise be the case. The success of any individual presidency is much dependent on the political personalities involved. Assumption of the presidency places a very big administrative burden on the member state concerned.

In appointing Javier Solana, the European Council responded to its own guidance set out at the Vienna European Council in December 1998 that the high representative should be 'a personality with a strong political profile'. According to the treaty, the role of the high representative is to assist the Council by helping to make and implement political decisions. When mandated to, he acts on behalf of the Council or the presidency in contacts with third parties. As the first incumbent of the post, Solana has made the most of the political aspects of the post. Within the External Relations Council and wider afield, he has succeeded in giving a face to the CFSP. 'He has', according to one observer, 'put the EU on the map, in the Balkans, in the Middle East and elsewhere.' (Everts, 2002)

Wearing his administrative hat, Javier Solana is also secretary-general of the Council. Together with the deputy secretary-general, Pierre de Boissieu, he is in charge of the general secretariat of the Council which assists the Council at all levels, in particular by counselling the presidency, and ensures that work proceeds smoothly (see chapter 19). The directorate-general for external relations (DG E) covers three major areas: *external economic relations; CFSP geographical and thematic affairs;* and the *politico-military structure for the security and defence policy.* In addition to DG E, three entities are currently under the direct authority of the high representative: the Policy Planning and Early Warning Unit (Policy Unit), the Joint Situation Centre (SITCEN) and the EU Military Staff (see Box 4.3).

Box 4.3: *Machinery of the CFSP*

General Secretariat of the Council - DG E
- is staffed by EU civil servants and officials on secondment from member states
- provides practical and intellectual support to the Council and its subsidiary bodies
- is responsible for preparing, participating in and following up political dialogue
- manages the working relationship between the European Union and international organisations in the areas falling within its sphere of competence

The Policy Unit
- set up by a declaration annexed to the Amsterdam Treaty
- staffed by diplomats and officials put at the disposal of the secretariat by member states, the Commission and the Western European Union (WEU) and by officials from the Council secretariat
- tasked to monitor and analyse developments and provide timely assessments and early warning of events or situations which may have significant repercussions, including potential political crises; to provide assessments of the Union's interests and identify areas where the CFSP could focus in future, and to produce argued policy-option papers as a contribution to policy formulation in the Council
- provides direct policy suport to the high representative and its staff act as contact points between their seconding member states or institutions

The Situation Centre (SITCEN)
- staffed with civil and military officials
- provides timely assessments and early warning of events or situations which may have significant repercussions for the EU's CFSP
- reports to the high representative and the competent bodies for crisis management; acts as a round-the-clock operational contact point for the high representative and close collaborators as well as for similar situation centres/crisis cells inside and outside the EU

The European Union Military Staff (EUMS)
- consists of military experts seconded from the member states
- reports directly to the high representative
- is headed by a senior military official on secondment from a member state tasked to provide early warning, situation assessment and strategic planning for crisis management operations, including the identification of national and multinational European forces, and to implement policies and decisions as directed by the Military Committee it is to assist

EU Special Representatives
- appointed by the Council by qualified majority
- operate with a mandate in relation to particular policy issues (currently: Middle East; Great Lakes; Stability Pact; Macedonia; Bosnia; Afghanistan; Southern Caucasus)
- act under the authority and operational direction of the high representative

Meetings of the External Relations Council

Once a month the foreign affairs ministers of each member state meet in the External Relations session of the General Affairs and External Relations Council. It is here that the Council takes the decisions concerning the formulation and implementation of the CFSP on the basis of the general guidelines or common strategies laid down by the European Council. As described above, since the Seville European Council decided on the new constellation of Council formations in June 2002, the External Relations Council and the General Affairs Council form a single Council formation, albeit with separate sessions. Consequently, the distinction between the two is less well defined than might be imagined. Although each has its separate agenda, there is often a seamless transition from one of the sessions to the other. Many of the participants are the same, and it is not always clear on which session's agenda a particular item should feature. A more meaningful distinction would arise if the External Relations Council were to be chaired by the European Foreign Minister, as proposed in the European Constitution. At present, each of the two Councils typically lasts a half or whole day, depending on the length of the agenda and the complexity of the issues to be discussed. In recent years the agendas of the External Relations Council have been formulated so as to guarantee the participation of defence ministers for part of one session during each presidency. A consensus on creating a specific 'Defence Council' has not so far emerged, though this seems a distinct possibility for the future.

The role of the External Relations Council is to ensure that the Union's actions in the field of CFSP are unified, consistent and effective. To that end, the Council goes about its business through a combination of discussion and legislation. Compared to Council formations in the first pillar sectors the emphasis is on the former rather than the latter. Discussions usually focus on the pressing international issues of the day, as identified by the presidency (with input from the high representative, the Commission and the member states). It falls most often to the presidency to launch discussion on a particular issue, either through a presentation of its own analysis, or by inviting the high representative or Commission to make their own presentation, before giving the chance to member states to outline their positions. Depending on the number of speakers and their brevity, the debate may last minutes or several hours. The outcome of the discussion may be either a simple oral summary by the presidency or general agreement on written conclusions to be released to the press. Discussions on the most delicate or most confidential issues are usually reserved for the working lunch or dinner, at which the absence of all but a handful of senior officials encourages an atmosphere of greater frankness and compromise. The enhanced quality of debate at these informal mealtime sessions is confirmed by the growing tendency for an ever greater number of agenda items to be discussed there rather than at the formal sessions and by the habit of some ministers to attend these informal sessions only, leaving their deputy to attend the formal sessions. Recently attempts have been made to stem this tendency by organising more discussions in the formal session in 'restricted' format (typically minister plus two for each delegation).

The Council frequently invites guests to attend part of the meeting, allowing them to make their case and to exchange views with the members of the Council. For legal reasons, the participation of guests takes place outside the formal sessions of the Council. Guests may include the foreign ministers of third countries, the heads of other regional organisations, or the EU's own special representatives. In addition to its meetings with guests, each session of the Council usually enjoys one or more 'political dialogue' events in its margins (see below).

The proceedings of the Council are prepared by the permanent representatives committee (Coreper) and by the political and security committee. The permanent representatives act in this area in the same way as for other Union policies. The political and security committee (PSC) brings together senior Brussels-based officials (usually at ambassadorial rank) from the foreign ministries of the member states. Meeting at least twice each week, its task is to monitor the international situation, contribute to the formulation of policies by giving the Council opinions, either at the latter's request or on their own initiative, and to the implementation of the policies that are agreed. In the event of a crisis, the political and security committee plays a central role in defining the Union's response; it is responsible for the political control and strategic direction of all operations, with the support of the opinions and recommendations of the military committee assisted by the military staff for military operations. The military committee is responsible for the military direction of all military activities within the EU framework. It is composed of member states' chiefs of defence (CHOD), represented by their military delegates in Brussels. The chairman of the military committee is a four-star general, elected by his fellow chiefs of defence and appointed by the Council for a period of three years. The Treaty of Nice has enabled the political and security committee, under certain conditions, to take certain implementing decisions with regard to crisis management, making the Committee's political control and strategic direction of operations easier.

Instruments of the CFSP

The working methods and instruments of the External Relations Council differ substantially from those of the other Council formations. Of all the Union's policies, the CFSP is the one that is most grounded in executive rather than legislative functions. In most other, more established, formations, the Council's role has principally been one of legislature rather than executive. Anchoring the CFSP within the Council has obliged the External Relations Council to develop mechanisms of executive action alongside its more limited legislative role.

Much of the External Relations Council's activity is of a declaratory nature. In part this is an inevitable consequence of the nature of external relations: the oldest and still most central feature of diplomacy is the passing of messages, many of which have a public character. The values, interests, views and concerns of the European Union find their expression in the many public messages that the Council agrees and publishes at its monthly meetings. For the most part these messages are agreed and published in one of several possible written forms. At their most formal, they are 'statements' or 'conclusions' of the Council. Occasionally, if time or the divergent positions around the table do not permit complete agreement on the wording of the message but the broad political content is undisputed, the presidency, high representative, or commissioner could be mandated to convey the Council's views orally.

At a typical meeting of the External Relations Council, declarations will be issued on a large number of geographical issues and several thematic or horizontal issues. Although without immediate legal impact, they can represent a strong political message in being an official statement of the Union's policy, unanimously agreed by the member states and Commission. As such they can be an indication of possible future action by the EU. They have an internal function too – defining a policy line that member states and the Commission henceforward have an obligation to defend and further in the interests of solidarity. Some may do so with more or less enthusiasm, some may emphasise one aspect or other of the declaration, but all will feel guided by the content of the declaration. The impact of such declarations is cumulative. Over time they come to represent a framework within which the EU speaks or acts. Rare are the instances when a member state can depart with impunity from the policy line established by successive declarations.[14]

Contacts with third countries take place mainly through 'political dialogue' meetings and 'démarches'. The European Union holds a political dialogue with a very large number of countries or groups of countries on questions of international policy. Such meetings, over 200 every year, take place at all levels: heads of state, ministers, political directors, senior officials and experts. The European Union can be represented at them by the presidency (assisted by the high representative for the CFSP), or by the high representative alone at the request of the presidency, or by the troika (presidency assisted by the high representative for the CFSP and the Commission and, where appropriate, the next presidency), or (in a limited number of cases) by member states' delegates and the Commission representative. 'Démarches', which are usually confidential, are undertaken vis-à-vis third countries by the presidency or the troika, on behalf of the European Union. It is generally their purpose to resolve with the state in question matters relating to human rights, democracy or humanitarian action.

The treaty gives the CFSP several instruments: common positions, joint actions, decisions and the conclusion of international agreements. In addition, common strategies involve and facilitate recourse to CFSP instruments. Declarations and contacts with third countries also continue to be important diplomatic tools for the CFSP. The CFSP does not have legal instruments such as the 'directives' or 'regulations' used for Community policies: instead it uses certain specific instruments (see box 4.4).

Box 4.4: *Formal instruments of the CFSP*

Common strategies
- are decided, unanimously, by the European Council, in areas where the member states have important interests
- each strategy specifies its objectives, its duration and the resources that will have to be provided by the Union and the member states
- are implemented by the Council through joint actions and common positions (in theory by qualified majority, except in relation to questions with military or defence imnplications)
- three common strategies adopted to date on Russia, Ukraine and the Mediterranean region

Common positions
- are adopted by unanimity in the Council
- their purpose is to formally define the Union's approach to a particular geographical or thematic issue (vis-à-vis a third country or at an international conference for example)
- member states are obliged to ensure national policies are in line with the common position

Joint actions
- are adopted by unanimity in the Council
- are used in situations requiring operational action committing the member states of the European Union
- each action specifies its objectives, scope, the means to be made available to the Union, the conditions for its implementation and (if necessary) its duration

Decisions
- in theory, are adopted by qualified majority in the Council
- as with common positions and joint actions, CFSP decisions are binding on the member states

International agreements
- the Council may authorise the presidency to enter into negotiations with one or more states or with international organisations
- during such negotiations, the presidency is assisted by the general secretariat and, where necessary, by the Commission
- agreements are then concluded by the Council, acting unanimously, on a recommendation from the presidency
- an agreement is not binding on a member state whose representative in the Council states that it has to comply with the requirements of its own constitutional procedure
- other members of the Council may agree that the agreement shall apply to them provisionally
- agreements may not imply any transfer of competence from the member states to the European Union
- such agreements are binding on the Union's institutions

Persistent singularity

The external relations policy of the European Union, and the Council that remains its focus, are likely to undergo further change in the years to come. The singular nature of the sector is, however, set to persist. That outcome is guaranteed by a political consensus that is broadly shared by all EU member states, whether old or new and regardless of whether their government is of left or right. This consensus is built around two convictions. The first is that the European Union can and must do more to strengthen its voice in the world and its capacities to tackle problems that transcend national borders. The short history of the CFSP has been enough to demonstrate that acting together is more effective than acting alone. The second conviction is that the foreign policy of the Union will remain, for the foreseeable future, a common policy rather than becoming a single policy. Member states want to pool their sovereignty on foreign policy in order to generate efficient outcomes, but they are not prepared to relinquish that sovereignty.

The constitutional convention and the subsequent intergovernmental conference agreed a number of innovations that mark significant departures from orthodox thinking about European integration. The Constitution for Europe creates a European 'foreign minister' who will combine the jobs of high representative and commissioner for external relations. The minister will chair meetings of the External Relations Council and will be vice-president of the European Commission. These innovations offer the potential of a significantly more coherent EU foreign policy. They will reduce the current multiplicity of foreign policy actors and allow for greater coordination of the disparate policy instruments available to the Union. It will take some time yet before these changes will be implemented, and longer still before their impact can be gauged. One thing is sure however. The unique character of external relations as an area of the European Union's activities is set to continue.

4.3 The nascent defence structures,
by Toon Digneffe

In November 1998, European defence ministers gathered for the first time in the history of European integration. The ministerial meeting was initiated by the Austrian presidency and was informal in nature. One month later France and Britain adopted a joint declaration in St Malo, France, in which they asked the Union to have a 'capacity for autonomous action' in the field of defence. These events represented an unprecedented step towards a more unified European defence policy. Since then meetings of EU defence ministers have been held on a regular basis. At least one informal meeting takes place during each presidency and defence ministers are invited to one session of the External Relations Council devoted to politico-military questions. While a Defence Council as such does not exist formally, defence ministers have now become an embedded part of the Council's ESDP architecture. This section retraces briefly the history of this particularly fast moving policy area.

For several years the debate on defence fell silent after the discussion on Combined Joint Task Forces (CJTF) – to allow Europe-led operations with the use of NATO assets – and the rapprochement of France and NATO. Since 1998, qualitative steps have been taken towards strengthening European defence policy. The fact that European defence ministers come together – albeit informally – to discuss defence issues can be seen as symbolic in this respect. Understanding why it took until 1998 before a gathering of defence ministers took place requires a more probing examination of the complex issue of European defence as it has developed in recent years both inside and outside the EU institutional framework. In essence, it is another illustration of the fact that the Union works best where clear political objectives are agreed and political will exists to implement them.

The institutional landscape

The first thing that strikes any newcomer to European defence is the complex institutional overlapping and interplay that exists in this field. Apart from the UN and the OSCE, which also have a role to play in European security, there are three institutions – NATO, WEU and EU – that can be viewed as the 'triangle of European defence'. Without going into detail about their functioning and background, a brief review of the main developments within each organisation and its membership will help to explain how developments within the organisations are closely interlinked through overlapping membership. Thereafter, the developments of the relations between the three organisations are described in more detail.

NATO

The North Atlantic Treaty was signed in Washington on 4 April 1949, creating an alliance of twelve independent nations. For most of its fifty year existence the central focus of NATO was providing for the immediate security and defence of its members within a mutual defence alliance. However, with the end of the Cold War the organisation's immediate focus had to be fundamentally rethought. This change began to take shape in 1991 with the adoption of the Strategic Concept in Rome. The Concept provided for major changes in NATO's integrated military structure, including substantial reductions in its size and improvements in its flexibility. Against the background of the crises in Yugoslavia, NATO increasingly directed its attention to crisis management and peacekeeping.

At a 1996 Berlin summit the NATO members came to an agreement on the CJTF concept. This decision was part of the process of NATO's internal restructuring, but also contributed to the development of the European Security and Defence Identity (ESDI) within the Alliance. At the Washington summit in April 1999 to celebrate the alliance's fiftieth anniversary, three new members joined: Hungary, Poland and the Czech Republic. On 29 March 2004 another seven countries joined the Alliance (Estonia, Lithuania, Latvia, Slovakia, Slovenia, Bulgaria and Romania) increasing NATO membership to 26 countries. Other members include Belgium, Canada, Denmark, France, Germany, Greece, Iceland, Italy, Luxembourg, the Netherlands, Norway, Portugal, Spain, Turkey, the United Kingdom and the United States.

Western European Union

On 17 March 1948, the Brussels Treaty was signed by Belgium, France, Luxembourg, the Netherlands and the United Kingdom as a response to Soviet moves to impose control over the countries of Central Europe. This was followed on 23 October 1954 by the signing of the modified Brussels Treaty, the act that gave birth to the Western European Union and incorporated Germany and Italy as members. The main feature of the founding act was the commitment to mutual defence should any of the signatories be the victim of an armed attack in Europe.

Although the WEU played an important role in some dossiers in the early years of its existence, it got off to a rather inauspicious start. Its main achievements were as a stepping stone for the integration of the Federal Republic of Germany into the Atlantic Alliance and as a forum for consultation between the European Community founding member states and the United Kingdom, as the WEU was the only framework in which the Six and the United Kingdom met regularly. However, the early 1980s witnessed something of a revival of the WEU. The practical consequences of this revival came a few years later, with the involvement of the WEU in the Yugoslav conflict. The WEU contributed to the efforts of the international community to contain the Yugoslav crisis by mounting three operations: a naval operation in the Adriatic conducted jointly with NATO, a police operation in the city of Mostar carried out on behalf of the European Union and a customs operation on the Danube, in cooperation with Bulgaria, Hungary and Romania. In this respect the foreign ministers widened the remit of the WEU to include peace-making, peace-keeping, humanitarian and rescue tasks in their 'Petersberg Declaration' of June 1992. One year later the Treaty of Maastricht entered into force, which declared the WEU to be 'an integral part of the development of the Union' and invited the WEU to 'elaborate and implement decisions and actions of the Union'. The institutional innovations of Petersberg and Maastricht were further complemented with an operational reactivation of the WEU. The headquarters moved from London

to Brussels and the organisation started to elaborate new operational capabilities, including early warning and intelligence facilities, an effective
telecommunications system and armed forces available for WEU missions.
Several WEU member states took initiatives to make forces available to the
WEU (FAWEU). The best known of these was the Franco-German initiative
to establish the 'Eurocorps'.

The membership of the WEU involves a myriad of different types of
status: full members, observers, associate partners and associate members.
The difference in membership clearly shows the complexity of the European
security system. The seven original members (Belgium, France, Germany,
Italy, Luxembourg, the Netherlands and the United Kingdom) have since
been joined by Portugal, Spain and Greece. Denmark, Ireland, Austria,
Finland and Sweden have observer status (the so-called 'neutrals'). The
Czech Republic, Hungary, Iceland, Norway, Poland and Turkey are associate members (members of NATO). Following the Kirchberg Declaration of
1994 seven countries have the status of 'associate partners': Bulgaria,
Estonia, Latvia, Lithuania, Romania, Slovakia and Slovenia. Only the ten
member states are signatories to the modified Brussels Treaty and have full
decision-making rights in WEU. The other eighteen countries have been
increasingly associated with WEU's activities.

European Union

Even before the European Community came into existence France,
Germany, Italy and the Benelux signed the 1952 Treaty for a European
Defence Community. In a declaration that René Pleven read before the
French Assembly in 1950 he mentioned for the first time the appointment of
a European minister for defence accountable to the Council of Ministers.
The Pleven plan later led to the Treaty for a European Defence Community
and was signed in 1952. However, because there was no majority in the
French parliament, it was never ratified and the initiative collapsed in
August 1954. The same six countries subsequently signed the Rome Treaty
establishing the European Economic Community. As its name implies, the
main focus of the EEC was economic, and it was to remain so for many years
to come.

The preceding sections of this chapter have traced the development of
foreign policy coordination from the late 1960s, through to its gradual incorporation into the treaties by means of the successive changes embodied in
the Single European Act and the Maastricht, Amsterdam and Nice Treaties.
The Maastricht Treaty explicitly covered all foreign policy and
security/defence issues, with article J.4 stating: 'The Common Foreign and
Security Policy shall include all questions related to security of the Union,
including the eventual framing of a common defence policy, which might in
time lead to a common defence.' The treaty made explicit reference to
NATO and the WEU and conceived the latter as an 'integral part of the
development of the Union'. Furthermore, the Union could request the WEU
to elaborate and implement decisions and actions which had defence implications. Regarding NATO the member states agreed that the policy of the
Union 'shall respect the obligations of certain Member States under the
North Atlantic Treaty'.

After having recounted briefly developments within each organisation

individually, it is important to see how relations between these three organisations developed after the end of the Cold War. A brief overview of these
interorganisational developments is given below and is illustrated by Figure
4.1

Figure 4.1: *The development of the 'European triangle of Defence' in the 1990s*

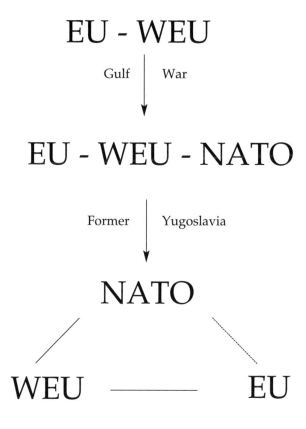

European Security and Defence Identity (ESDI)

The ESDI concept can be traced back to the Maastricht Treaty, where it was
codified for the first time. A declaration on the WEU, attached to the treaties,
stressed the 'need to develop a genuine European security and defence
identity'. The declaration refrained, however, from giving a clear definition
of what this entailed. The only indications given were that an ESDI had to
be established 'through a gradual process involving successive phases' and
'in the longer perspective of a common defence policy within the European
Union, which might in time lead to a common defence'. This common

defence, however, would need to be 'compatible with that of the Atlantic Alliance'.

The end of the Cold War presented Europe with an unprecedented opportunity for the development of ESDI. With a transformed external environment, the US preoccupied with reassessing its post-Cold War role and pressure in Europe for deeper integration, the moment appeared propitious for ESDI to come of age. The WEU appeared the most likely vehicle to advance this identity but the enhancement could only be achieved at the cost of encroaching upon NATO's position of primacy (Rees, 1998, p. 38). In this respect the Treaty of Maastricht saw the WEU as 'an integral part of the development of the Union'. But in the annexed WEU declaration it was also seen 'as a means to strengthen the European pillar of the Atlantic Alliance'. This meant that the WEU fell between two stools, since there was no consensus to give priority to developing the EU-WEU partnership as the main instrument of ESDI. The first military crisis to follow the end of the Cold War, in the Gulf, further showed the limitations of developing the EU-WEU tandem. The Gulf War highlighted the Europeans' lack of capabilities to project military power over long distances and their inability to present a unified front in the crisis. This tempered the high ambitions for the WEU to be the premier defence organisation on the European continent. The WEU was in fact squeezed between the EU and NATO. NATO adapted itself in the meantime extensively in response to the challenges it faced after the end of the Cold War. This was shown in the first real test case in the aftermath of the Cold War, namely the wars in former Yugoslavia, when NATO proved to be an indispensable part of the European defence structure. As Cornish puts it: 'Europe's defence and security requirements are still not entirely clear…Nevertheless, it is now clear that NATO has more credibility in matters of security and defence than any conceivable rival' (Cornish, 1996, p. 768). The confrontation with reality – the Gulf War and the wars in former Yugoslavia – had radically tempered the theoretical ambition of the EU and the WEU to become Europe's primary crisis managers. NATO, by contrast, had shown the capacity to change and modify its structures. The absence of political will in Europe made it clear that the WEU would remain an actor of subordinate importance to the Alliance. As the then Belgian minister of foreign affairs Erik Derycke concluded: 'Some predicted that NATO, as an organisation, would die a slow death. Some also saw in this the opportunity to abolish armed forces while others – on both sides of the Atlantic, moreover – were of the opinion that Europe would henceforth be capable of solving its own defence problems unaided and that a commitment on the part of the US was no longer desirable. The Gulf War was the first challenge to such views and the calamitous war in the former Yugoslavia further increased the disillusionment' (Derycke, 1996, p. 6).

The individual relations of the 'triangle of European defence' are described in the following sections. The relationships between the various entities developed in a certain chronological order, with the foundation for the NATO-WEU relationship being laid before the WEU-EU relationship took a more or less definitive shape. The development of a relationship between the EU and NATO is relatively recent, but has evolved rapidly into today's primary relationship.

Combined Joint Task Forces (CJTF)

The failure of the WEU and EU to become the premier defence organisation for the emerging ESDI made it possible for the US to adopt a more benign attitude towards the WEU's role as a European pillar of the Alliance. The formal acknowledgement of this development occurred in the 1994 NATO Brussels summit. In the summit's final communiqué the US gave its 'full support to the development of a European Security and Defence Identity'. The US was now willing to embrace a division of labour with its allies and searched for ways to improve WEU-NATO cooperation. This raised the potential for consultations to take place during a crisis and for the US to consider providing support to Europe-led operations, where American interests were not engaged. The general framework under which such operations could be managed was called 'Combined Joint Task Forces' (CJTF). The concept can be placed under the NATO-WEU side of the European defence triangle.

What exactly is a CJTF? US joint-forces doctrine describes a 'task force' as a temporary force for carrying out a specific mission. 'Joint' task forces involve components from two or more services, while 'combined' task forces include forces from two or more countries. (Barry, 1996, p. 83.) This provided Europeans with the means to undertake missions on their own, using NATO equipment, via the WEU which lacked the resources to do so. However, the concept clearly stated that this could only be done in a way which was 'separable but non separate' from NATO. The implementation of the CJTF concept, moreover, raised several fundamental questions with regard to the genuine development of a European Security and Defence Identity. Firstly, the release of NATO resources to a WEU-led operation would necessitate North Atlantic Council approval, giving NATO a *'droit de regard'* over all operations set up under CJTF. Secondly, the CJTF concept remained mainly a NATO instrument to adapt the organisation to the post-Cold War challenges. It assisted NATO to give its integrated military structure sufficient flexibility to respond to new missions beyond the traditional article 5 collective defence tasks. Maybe initially CJTF was focused both on flexibility within NATO and operations led by the WEU. Today however, as van Eekelen points out, it centres much more on internal reform. (Barry, 1996, p. 210.) Finally, tensions between France and the US prevented further implementation of the concept. The Americans wanted to tie CJTF closely to the existing NATO structure, while France argued that CJTF command should lie outside the NATO structures. While the prospects remained unclear for the future of CJTF, the member states of the European Union got together again in the scheduled follow-up to Maastricht. The resulting treaty reform took new initiatives in the second pillar and revived the debate about the relationship between the EU and WEU.

The Treaty of Amsterdam and the St Malo declaration

After the Treaty of Maastricht had enabled the Union to have recourse to the WEU to implement any Union decisions with defence implications, the Treaty of Amsterdam made new attempts to bring EU and WEU closer together. First of all, the treaty empowered the EU to order CJTF operations led by WEU with the support of NATO. The inclusion of the WEU Petersberg tasks – humanitarian, peacekeeping and rescue tasks – into the EU treaties was important in this respect. Furthermore, the treaty foresaw closer institutional relations between the EU and the WEU, but full integration was made dependent on a decision by the European Council.

All this provided the EU with the framework for further developing its defence policy, but the political will to do so was still lacking. The event that helped to bring about the momentum for change was the Kosovo war. Once again the Europeans had to call upon the US to resolve a war in Europe's backyard. The support of British Prime Minister Tony Blair in October 1998 for independent European defence capabilities changed the tone of the debate on ESDI. For the first time there seemed to be something of a European consensus to develop an EU defence policy. The first sign of this was the Franco-British declaration of St Malo of 4 December 1998, which called upon the EU to have a 'capacity for autonomous action, backed up by credible military forces, the means to decide to use them, and the deadlines to do so...(which requires) strengthened armed forces that can react rapidly to new risks'. This development was welcomed by all member states a week later in Vienna. The recognition by the US came in March of the following year at the NATO summit in Washington, but at the same time it was stressed that 'non-necessary duplication' should be avoided.

The growing political momentum reopened the discussion about a possible merger of the WEU and EU. That discussion had already taken place during the Maastricht IGC, but had not led to a definitive conclusion. But at a ministerial meeting of the WEU in May 1999, a qualitative step was made towards integrating the WEU into the EU. The ministers formally backed the idea of gradually merging the WEU into the EU. At the European Council of Cologne in June 1999, all these developments were formally adopted in a 'declaration on strengthening the common European policy on security and defence'. Another historic decision at the summit was the appointment of Javier Solana, NATO secretary-general at that time, as the first high representative to coordinate the Union's common foreign and security policy. This was a clear sign that the member states were serious about their commitment to boost Europe's political role in the world. In November 1999 this commitment was reinforced by the decision of the General Affairs Council to authorise its secretary-general and high representative also to serve as secretary-general of the WEU. So, when Solana formally took up his new position at the end of 1999 he combined his functions both in the EU and WEU. As Solana put it: 'I can at least say that co-operation between the current secretaries-general of the EU and WEU is beyond reproach!' (*Bulletin Quotidien Europe*, 1999, p. 4). Since then, the WEU has retained some residual functions, while de facto most of its structures have been dismantled and subsumed into the Council (see below).

Helsinki and the Treaty of Nice

The Helsinki European Council in December 1999 took further steps towards a 'Common European Security and Defence Policy' (CESDP or ESDP). In the conclusions the member states underlined their 'determination to develop an autonomous capacity to take decisions and, where NATO as a whole is not engaged, to launch and conduct EU-led military operations in response to international crises'. However, they added that this process will 'avoid unnecessary duplication' and 'does not imply the creation of a European army'. Nevertheless, the text gave a clear commitment to develop the necessary capabilities and institutional mechanisms to conduct EU-led military operations. Where Cologne had set out the general principles of the ESDP, Helsinki elaborated those principles with regard to its concrete organisation and military equipment. Hence the European Council concluded that by 2003 member states must be able to deploy within 60 days, and sustain for at least one year, military forces of up to 50,000-60,000 persons capable of the full range of Petersberg tasks. As described in the previous section, new political and military bodies and structures have been established within the Council to enable the Union to ensure the necessary political guidance and strategic direction to such operations, including a standing political and security committee (PSC) based in Brussels and composed of national representatives of ambassadorial level, two politico-military directorates in DG E in the Council secretariat, an EU military committee (EUMC) composed of chiefs of defence or their representatives, a military staff (EUMS) and an EU situation centre within the Council structures. Another decision with major consequences for the institutional structure of the Council is that 'defence ministers will be involved in the CESDP; when the GAERC discusses matters related to CESDP, defence ministers as appropriate will participate to provide guidance on defence matters.'

Less eye-catching, but nonetheless very important, was the provision calling for 'modalities for full consultation, cooperation and transparency between the EU and NATO' (see the presidency progress report on strengthening the Common European Policy on Security and Defence annexed to the presidency conclusions of the Helsinki summit). This opened for the first time the possibility of establishing institutional links between the EU and NATO. Until then no formal relationship existed between the two organisations. The NATO-EU side of our 'triangle of European defence' was in fact the only side that still lacked formalised modes of interaction. The Nice European Council in December 2000 agreed that the development of the ESDP will lead to 'a genuine strategic partnership between the EU and NATO'. Annex 7 of the report points out the 'standing arrangements for consultation and co-operation between the EU and NATO'. The text specifies that regular dialogue will be established by holding meetings between the Ministers of both EU and NATO 'at least once during each Presidency'. There will be routine contacts between the EU and NATO military staff by means of meetings of the military committees or subsidiary groups of both organisations. This dialogue can be supplemented by inviting, for example, the NATO secretary-general to EU ministerial meetings, 'in particular those attended by Defence Ministers'. Other means of communication include exchanges of information and contacts between the secretaries-general of the two organisations.

The final shape of the triangle

The 1990s saw the development of a fully-fledged 'triangle of European Defence' with close interinstitutional links between all three organisations.

The institutional basis for each of the interinstitutional relations has been described in the previous sections. Each of them describes a critical milestone in the individual relationships: the CJTF concept created a standardised platform for cooperation between the WEU and NATO; the provisions of the Treaty of Amsterdam made the opening for the integration of the WEU and the EU; and the Treaty of Nice formalised the arrangements for consultation and co-operation between the EU and NATO.

However, with the de facto integration of the WEU into the EU, the evolving relationship between NATO and EU and the strengthened commitment of the EU in the field of defence, the definitive shape of the triangle is far from decided. Rather than giving a chronological overview of the most recent developments and their influence on the interinstitutional relations of the triangle of defence, the remainder of this chapter highlights three interrelated priorities for the future which are currently at the forefront of discussions. Each of the points starts with a quote from the draft Constitution for Europe and relates it to a key challenge the EU will face in the further development of its ESDP.

> 'The common security and defence policy shall include the progressive framing of a common Union defence policy. This will lead to a common defence, when the European Council, acting unanimously, so decides... The policy of the Union in accordance with this Article shall not prejudice the specific character of the security and defence policy of certain member states and shall respect the obligations of certain member states, which see their common defence realised in the North Atlantic Treaty Organisation, under the North Atlantic Treaty, and be compatible with the common security and defence policy established within that framework.'[15]

First of all, this text shows that tensions between 'Europeanist' and 'Atlanticist' visions of European defence are still present. Since the ESDP has been conceived up to now as distinct from 'collective defence' and from 'alliance' policies and since it is oriented towards the WEU 'Petersberg missions', in order not to duplicate existing NATO structures, the question about a suitable division of labour between EU/WEU and NATO remains to be answered. A major step forward in this respect has been the conclusion of the so-called 'Berlin Plus' package. While the Treaty of Nice provided the institutional framework for the EU-NATO relationship, the Berlin Plus agreement put more flesh on the bone including more practical arrangements for the assured access to NATO planning capabilities and availability of NATO assets and capabilities for EU-led crisis management operations as well as arrangements for consultation and capability requirements. On 16 December 2002, the EU and NATO signed a joint statement bringing together this comprehensive package of agreements.

While this opened the way for a strategic partnership between the EU and NATO in the field of crisis management, implementation of the permanent agreements between the two organisations based on the exchange of letters between the Council secretary-general/high representative and the secretary-general of NATO finalised in March 2003, allowed the Union to take over the operation Allied Harmony in Macedonia on 31 March 2003.

Nevertheless, the discussions within the 2003 IGC on a mutual defence clause and the establishment of an EU military planning unit showed that the final word has not yet been said on the EU-NATO division of labour.

Some considered that the inclusion of a mutual defence clause within the draft Constitution seemed to imply that the EU could become a collective-defence organisation to rival NATO. In this respect, the presidency proposal for the Naples conclave of 28-29 November 2003 clearly stipulated that commitments and cooperation in the area of mutual defence 'shall be consistent with commitments under NATO, which for those States which are members of it, remains the foundation of their collective defence.'[16] Another contentious issue between NATO and the EU was the move by Germany, France, Belgium and Luxembourg to launch a separate military planning cell. A compromise was reached between the UK, France and Germany ahead of the Naples conclave in November 2003 on establishing an EU planning cell within NATO (SHAPE, Mons), while at the same time strengthening the capacity of the EUMS in Brussels to conduct early warning, situation assessment and strategic planning through the establishment within EUMS of a military planning cell. The Brussels European Council of 12 December 2003, on the basis of a document submitted by the presidency, formalised this agreement by requesting the secretary-general/high representative to propose the necessary measures for establishing within the EUMS a 'cell with civil/military components.'[17]

'Those member states whose military capabilities fulfil higher criteria and which have more binding commitments to one another in this area with a view to the most demanding missions shall establish structured cooperation within the Union framework.'[18]

The general challenge of diversity within the Union also applies to the area of defence. The draft Constitution incorporates the possibility for some member states to move ahead in the field of defence within the EU institutional framework. The diversity of the EU member states in the field of defence is also reflected in the variation in membership of the institutions. While most member states are members of both NATO and the WEU, some are still 'neutral and non-aligned' (Austria, Ireland, Sweden and, to a certain extent, Finland). Therefore the ESDP is partly inside NATO and the WEU, partly only within NATO (Denmark) and partly outside NATO and the WEU (the above-mentioned partners). The whole geopolitical configuration is narrower than NATO with Norway and Turkey inside NATO but outside both WEU and EU. It is less coherent in geopolitical-strategic terms with Sweden, Finland, Austria and Ireland outside the core territory of the 'Euro-Atlantic' alliance and the combined collective defence treaty areas. (Ruhl, 1999.) The draft Constitution further states:

'Member States shall undertake progressively to improve their military capabilities. A European Armaments, Research and Military Capabilities Agency shall be established to identify operational requirements, to promote measures to satisfy those requirements, to contribute to identifying, and where appropriate, implementing any measure needed to strengthen the industrial and technological base of the defence sector, to participate in defining a European capabilities and armaments policy, and to assist the Council of Ministers in evaluating the improvement of military capabilities.' [19]

A third challenge is related to European military capabilities. Although the total amount European governments spend on defence is considerable (around €200 million per annum), the Kosovo war clearly showed the technological advantage of the Americans. An audit of assets and capabilities performed by the WEU in November 1999 indicated Europe's military weaknesses. The WEU ministers agreed unanimously that 'considerable efforts are still needed to strengthen European capabilities' and this in the areas of strategic intelligence and planning and capabilities for projecting forces to theatres of operation. In Kosovo, for example, only 2% of European forces were able to be moved to the theatres of operation as Europe has nothing comparable to the 80 jet transports that the US has available for military airlift needs. On 20 November 2000 the member states took part in a Capabilities Commitment Conference in Brussels. At the conference each member state committed itself to making national contributions corresponding to the rapid reaction capabilities identified to attain the headline goal set at the Helsinki European Council.

However, the conference also made clear once again that much effort needed to be made in the field of military capabilities and especially in the fields of transport, control, command and communication and intelligence capacity. Following the launch of the European capability action plan in November 2001, a new capabilities conference was held in May 2003, making further progress on capabilities and infrastructure. An important step forward in this respect was the decision to create an agency in the field of defence capabilities development, research, acquisition and armaments at the Thessaloniki European Council in June 2003, implemented by the GAERC of 17-18 November 2003.[20] The basic functions and tasks of the agency will include: developing defence capabilities in the field of crisis management, promoting European armaments cooperation and contributing to policies and measures aimed at strengthening the European defence industrial and technological base. Work is progressing in 2004 so that the agency can be formally established by the end of the year.

What the foregoing shows is that this is one of the fastest-moving policy areas inside the Union at present, and is likely to remain so for the coming years. With an increased focus on operational capabilities, the Union engaged in 2003 in three historic missions: the EU Police Mission in Bosnia-Herzegovina, the Union's first-ever civilian crisis management operation; the Concordia mission in the former Yugoslav Republic of Macedonia, the Union's first ever military operation; and the Artemis mission in the Democratic Republic of Congo, the Union's first-ever autonomous peacekeeping intervention outside Europe. Five years previously, the developments described above would have been unthinkable. This again bears out the point that the Union always works best when it sets itself clear political objectives, and discussion focuses not on the objectives themselves, but rather on how to go about implementing them.

Chapter 5: The Economic and Financial Affairs Council (Ecofin)

5.1. The Ecofin Council and the Eurogroup,
by Sixten Korkman

The EU is a veritable laboratory for common policies and policy coordination, and it has a system of economic governance and an economic policy regime with a number of particular characteristics. One of these is variable geometry; roughly half of the member states participate in the euro area, while the others have either an opt-out (the UK and Denmark) or a derogation. Another is the great diversity of the methods of involving the Community level in the process through which economic policies are formed. While the treaties refer to the Council in the singular, this is clearly a legal fiction. In practice, the Council meets in different formations with different agendas according to the subject matter under consideration, and each Council formation has its idiosyncrasies with regard to the organisation and character of work.

The aim of this chapter is to shed light on this rather complex policy regime by answering the question 'who does what and how?' in the area of economic policy. It first describes the main institutions and bodies involved in economic policy-making in the monetary union. It then sets out the allocation of competencies and the assignment of tasks more generally, and distinguishes between different methods of Community involvement in economic policy-making. The chapter describes the instruments and procedures of economic policy coordination and sets out the main features of the preparatory machinery. The final comments aim at conveying some impressions of the deliberations of the Ecofin Council and the Eurogroup with a view to illuminating how economic governance operates in practice.

Decision-making bodies in monetary union

The Community level actors in economic policy are, with the exceptions explained below, basically the same as in other policy areas: the Commission, the European Parliament, the Council and the European Council. However, the roles of the actors differ between policy areas, and there are certain characteristics in the area of economic policy which deserve attention. The area of economic policy also includes actors beyond the familiar 'institutional triangle' (the Commission, the Council and the European

Parliament). In particular, any account of the institutional set-up of the monetary union must necessarily refer to the European Central Bank (ECB) and the Eurogroup.

The central role of the Ecofin Council

The key institution at the Community level in the economic policy area is the Council meeting in the composition of ministers of economy and/or finance, universally known by the acronym 'Ecofin'. Together with the General Affairs and External Relations Council, it is one of the two most important Council formations. The first identifiable meetings with the presence of finance ministers took place at the beginning of 1960, but these meetings did not evolve into a regular sectoral Council until 1974. Throughout the 1960s, finance ministers met informally every three months to discuss common issues such as budget orientations, economic policy coordination and positions to be taken in international monetary affairs. However, this was a loose and informal framework which evolved more as a discussion than a decision-taking forum. Although article 103 of the EEC Treaty foresaw economic policy coordination, there was no ultimate objective, nothing to work towards. However, the first moves towards economic and monetary union in the 1970s firmed up Ecofin's role, which was formalised in a Council decision on convergence in 1974 which declared that 'the Council shall set aside each month a specific day, chosen in advance, for meetings on economic and monetary matters'. Thus the Ecofin Council was born.

The Ecofin Council plays a key role in the area of economic policy coordination, though in this respect its work should be seen in conjunction with the deliberations in the Eurogroup; much of the debate takes place in the Eurogroup, but only the Ecofin Council can take formal decisions (occasionally with only member states participating in the euro area having the right to vote). It is the Ecofin Council which decides on legislation in the area of financial services (in co-decision with the European Parliament) and taxation. The importance of the Ecofin Council is enhanced by (or reflected in) the tradition of inviting finance ministers to participate in the meetings of the European Council when issues of economic policy are the subject of discussion.

The institutional role of the Commission is weak since many Council decisions are based on Commission recommendations rather than proposals, and the Council can therefore decide on amendments by QMV. (For proposals, by contrast, the Council may amend texts by QMV rather than unanimity only if the Commission does not object.) Similarly, the role of the European Parliament is weak as most of economic policy is outside the co-decision procedure, and as the treaty does not even foresee consultation of the Parliament in matters of economic policy coordination.

Monetary authorities

The *European Central Bank* (ECB) and the national central banks (NCBs) of the euro-area countries together constitute the *Eurosystem*, while the *European System of Central Banks* (ESCB) consists of the ECB and the NCBs of all EU member states. The ESCB is only of some limited administrative significance; it is the Eurosystem and notably the ECB which are the key actors in the monetary area. The main task of the ECB and the Eurosystem is to formulate and implement the monetary policy of the euro area. Other tasks include the conduct of foreign exchange operations, the holding and management of official foreign exchange reserves, and the promotion of the smooth operation of payment systems. Also, the ECB has an obligation to contribute to the smooth conduct of policies pursued by the authorities in charge of the prudential supervision of credit institutions and the stability of the financial system, though the ECB is not accorded any power to regulate or supervise financial institutions (unless the Council were unanimously so to decide).

The main decision-making body of the ECB is the *Governing Council*, which consists of the six members of the *Executive Board* and the governors of the central banks of the participating countries. The Governing Council takes all key decisions on monetary policy, while the Executive Board prepares the decisions by the Governing Council and oversees their implementation. The articles of the treaty and the statute of the bank (attached to the treaty as a protocol) stipulate that the ECB and the NCBs, as well as members of their decision-making bodies, are forbidden to seek or take instructions, be it from Community institutions or national governments. The independence of the ECB is further bolstered by the fact that the members of the decision-making bodies of the bank have long and non-renewable terms of office, and by the financial independence of the ECB. Also, the treaty forbids any provision of central bank credit to the public sector. As the safeguards of its independence are in the treaty, and can therefore be changed only in an intergovernmental conference with the consensus of the member states, one may conclude that the ECB is institutionally highly independent, probably the most independent central bank in the world. The ECB is accountable, in the sense of having reporting obligations, notably to the European Parliament.

The most important task of the ECB is to decide on the objectives, strategy and implementation of its monetary policy. As set out in the treaty, the key objective of the ECB is price stability, and this objective has been defined by the Governing Council as an annual rate of increase of the harmonised consumer price index below (but close to) 2% in the medium term. The monetary policy strategy is based on a two-pillar approach, the first pillar consisting of a reference rate for the growth of money (broadly defined), and the second pillar amounting to a comprehensive and forward-looking analysis of price developments in the light of various economic and financial indicators. Within this framework the practical decision-making of the Governing Council focuses on key short-term interest rates and associated operations in the interbank market. In special circumstances the ECB may also intervene in the foreign exchange markets with a view to reducing misalignments in the external value of the euro.

The Eurogroup

The European Council in Luxembourg in 1997 decided to set up the Eurogroup as an informal grouping of the finance ministers of the euro-area countries, who meet regularly (mostly on the evening before the meeting of the Ecofin Council) to discuss matters of common interest and related to the single currency. The Commission and the ECB are invariably invited to participate in these meetings, which have become the most important forum in the EU for dialogue on economic policies. Discussions cover a number of issues such as the economic situation and outlook, including identifiable risks, budget developments within the euro area, the implementation of the fiscal policy rules, the macroeconomic policy mix and exchange rate developments.

The Eurogroup, being an informal body, has no decision-making powers, these being reserved for the Ecofin Council. However, there are a number of issues on which only the countries participating in the euro area have a vote when decisions are taken in the Council, and discussions within the Eurogroup often serve to define the position that euro-area countries will take, notably in decisions on the implementation of the fiscal rules. A main purpose of the Eurogroup is to arrive at a common understanding of the economic situation, the risks and the challenges for policy action. Such a common understanding is an important precondition for peer pressure with a view to better coordination of the policies of member states. The Eurogroup occasionally issues communiqués on the economic situation or on policy issues, including on the external value of the euro.

Competence and assignment

Stipulations on competence and assignment are of fundamental importance and go a long way towards defining the 'hard core' of the EU policy framework. Competence refers to an actor being empowered, by a national constitution or by a treaty, to take decisions on the use of some instrument or set of instruments. Competence may be general or specific as well as exclusive or shared.[1] However, the allocation of competence over policies is not enough to define a policy regime; it is, as a minimum, also necessary to specify the objectives or assign the tasks that decision makers should pursue. Also, it is helpful to identify systems of monitoring or surveillance giving rise to feedback from developments to policy planning.

General economic policy

The essential structure of the EU economic policy regime is as follows: *Monetary policy is the competence of independent central banks and notably of the ECB in the euro area, while other economic policies remain the responsibility of governments of member states.* Also, the treaty makes it clear that the primary objective of the ECB shall be to maintain price stability, and similarly for the independent NCBs in the case of the countries not participating in the euro area because of a derogation or an opt-out. Other economic policies, by contrast, can be used by member states to pursue objectives that they deem important.

There are, however, a number of qualifications to the above:
– the ECB shall not focus exclusively on price stability but 'shall support the general economic policies in the Community with a view to contributing to the achievement of the objectives of the Community'. However, the ECB shall support the general economic policies only to the extent that it

can do so 'without prejudice to the objective of price stability' (with similar stipulations holding for the NCBs of countries outside the euro area);
– member states are treaty bound to maintain sound public finances. The Excessive Deficit Procedure (EDP) and the Stability and Growth Pact (SGP) forbid 'excessive' government financial deficits and foresee early warnings, recommendations for action and the possibility of sanctions if this fiscal rule is not adhered to properly. Member states remain competent and responsible for their fiscal policies but have to acknowledge a legal obligation to comply with a specific constraint in the form of the fiscal rule agreed at the Community level;
– there are a number of other 'quasi-constitutional' constraints in the treaty, notably concerning the ways in which national budget deficits may or may not be financed. These provisions support the independence of the central banks and the fiscal discipline of governments;
– there is Community competence in the area of the internal market (exclusive for much of competition policy and shared in other domains), and the economic policies of member states must comply with internal market legislation as well as competition and state aid rules;
– member states shall take account of their interdependence and 'shall consider their economic policies as a matter of common concern and shall coordinate them within the Council'. In practice, this is predominantly done in the framework of the broad guidelines of economic policies (see next section). Such coordination shall be done 'with a view to contributing to the achievement of the objectives of the Community', 'in accordance with the principles of an open market economy with free competition' and 'in compliance with the principles of stable prices, sound public finances and monetary conditions and a sustainable balance of payments'. This guidance is not very precise but it underlines attachment to a free market economy and to financial discipline;
– there is a close link between monetary and exchange rate policies. It is therefore of some importance for monetary policy that the responsibility for exchange rate policy is shared between the ECB and the Council. However, the treaty (article 111) is somewhat ambiguous with regard to their respective roles. It is for the Council to conclude formal agreements on an exchange rate system for the euro in relation to non-Community currencies, but this provision is in present and foreseeable circumstances of limited or no practical relevance. More relevant is that the Council is empowered to formulate 'general orientations for exchange-rate policy' in relation to third currencies. However, such orientations 'shall be without prejudice to the primary objective of the ESCB to maintain price stability'. Presumably it is for the ECB to decide whether this condition is met (otherwise its independence would be more apparent than real). Also, foreign exchange intervention, the instrument for giving effect to exchange rate orientations, is in the hands of the ECB (article 105). This suggests that exchange rate orientations need the backing of both the Council and the ECB[2]

The qualifications are of some importance but do not change the overall picture: monetary policy is run by the ECB (or independent NCBs) and geared to price stability, while member states are free to use other economic policies to enhance their own policy objectives, though subject to certain rules. This assignment of responsibilities is simple and clear. It is also mark-edly asymmetric, as the single monetary policy in the euro area is combined with nationally decentralised policies in other respects. EMU entails 'a cur-rency without a state', and this feature is at the heart of much of the debate about economic policy coordination in EMU.

Legislative action: financial services and taxation

It has so far been (implicitly) assumed that economic policy amounts to gov-ernance by the ECB and by national governments within a given legal framework. However, in a broader sense economic policy also encompasses legislative action; in some areas this is a main instrument of policy. Two areas of special importance to economic policy are taxation and financial services. Decisions in these areas, at the Council level, are the responsibility of the Ecofin Council.

Financial services share many of the characteristics of other parts of the internal market. Legislation is thus by co-decision with the European Parliament and decisions in the Council are taken by QMV. Work in this area has for a long time been lagging behind as compared to work on mar-kets for goods, mainly because integration of financial services is made dif-ficult by a number of country-specific institutional considerations and concerns. Recently, however, work on the Financial Services Action Plan (FSAP) has been very intensive and successful, though a lot of work is still needed to achieve a well-functioning internal market for financial services by 2005 (the deadline set in the FSAP).

Tax policy is a sensitive area, close to the heart of national sovereignty. The treaty defines the objective for Community action in the area of indirect taxation as 'harmonisation of legislation covering turnover taxes, excise duties and other forms of indirect taxation to the extent that such harmoni-sation is necessary to ensure the establishment and functioning of the internal market'. The treaty does not make any explicit reference to direct taxation. Also, unanimity is required in all Council decisions on tax matters, while the European Parliament has only a consultative role. Given the una-nimity requirement and pronounced differences in view as between member states, progress in the tax area has been and is bound to remain slow. Nevertheless, the Council has in recent years (against the odds) man-aged to agree on a number of directives in the area of both indirect and direct taxation.[3]

Methods of Community involvement in economic policy

As seen above, the Ecofin Council's activities are quite heterogenous in char-acter. It is, in fact, useful to make a distinction between four different methods of Community involvment in economic policy decision making in the EU. These are as follows (for a summary comparison see table 5.1).

Delegation of power to a supranational institution

This is the method used for monetary policy. The treaty empowers the ECB to plan and implement monetary policy for the euro area (and, in conjunction with national legislation, the NCBs to do so in the other countries). This delegation is accompanied by instructions, which assign the central bank the primary objective of maintaining price stability. However, the mandate is not overly precise as it is for the ECB itself to define its strategy and give operational reality to the meaning of price stability. Other examples of delegation of power to a supranational body are competition policy and state aid policies, where the Commission is empowered by the treaty to take the relevant decisions.

The legitimacy of delegation of power is based on three considerations. First, delegation is specific and related to the implementation of (relatively) well-defined tasks. Second, the decision on delegation has been taken in a manner (in an intergovernmental conference) which in itself has democratic anchoring. Third, there is accountability in the form of reporting so as to allow evaluation of how the task is accomplished. Needless to say, legitimacy is enhanced if the delegated power is used with competence and good judgement.

The Community method or legislation

The Community may enact legislation if there is a legal base in the treaty. This is the traditional and most important method for Community involvement in decision-making, and this is what is usually referred to as the 'Community method' (see chapter 14). It involves a mutual interaction and a particular balance of power between the main Community institutions. The role of the Commission is to take the initiative and make a proposal (based on its analysis, consultations and planning). The Council and the European Parliament then deliberate and decide. The decision may be taken by the Council alone if the parliament only has a consultative role, while the two institutions decide together in the case of co-decision. As noted above, amendments to a proposal normally require unanimity in the Council if objected to by the Commission (which may also withdraw its proposal at any time if it considers that modifications introduced in the Council are unacceptable). Member states are responsible for the national implementation of EU legislation, and the Commission may initiate legal (infringement) procedures against a member state failing to implement or enforce EU legislation properly.

The Community method has a double legitimacy. First, Council decision-making amounts to a 'pooling of sovereignty', in which ministers and governments of member states jointly take decisions, and all governments are accountable domestically (though not separately for decisions taken in the Council). Second, decisions bind the European Parliament (notably in the case of co-decision), which is accountable to the European electorate.

Policy coordination

This method is increasingly used to give the EU a role in areas in which the Community is not empowered to take decisions. Lack of competence does not exclude a role for the Community level in the policy process, understood as a sequence of planning, decision-taking, implementation and evaluation. In particular, the Community may in various ways be involved in coordination of the planning and evaluation of policies even if competence (power to take decisions) rests with member states. Such coordination may be 'strong' or 'weak'. The former refers to coordination based on legally binding rules, and is exemplified above all by the Excessive Deficit Procedure. Weak coordination activities (which have increased, or escalated, in recent years) are quite diverse in terms of both subject matters and modalities. They include, inter alia, exchange of information, policy dialogue, benchmarking and identification of 'good' or 'best' practices, the setting of common or national targets, monitoring and surveillance, and peer review within the framework of certain instruments and procedures (see below).

Table 5.1. *Economic policy in the EU: Who does what?*

Function	Monetary policy (in the euro area)	(Other) economic policies	Legislative action	Community budget
1. Decisions (competence)	ECB	member states	Council+EP or member states	Council+EP
Qualifications	Objectives in treaty	Principles and rules in treaty	Depending on the treaty	Special rules in treaty + IIA
2. Implementation	ECB+NCB	member states	member states	Commission + member states
3. Monitoring + surveillance, dialogue + peer review	ECB, EP, Eurogroup	member states, Commission, Council and Eurogroup	Commission and/or member states	Commission, Council+EP, Court of Auditors
4. Planning	ECB	As above	Commission or member states	Commission
Overall	ECB	member states	Commission+ Council+EP or member states	Commission+ Council+EP
Method of Community involvement	Delegation	Coordination	'Community method' (legislation)	'Community method' (special rules)

Coordination, in its weak form, does not pose a real issue of legitimacy as power over decisions rests with member states. However, there is a risk that policy coordination at the Community level, particularly when it involves setting objectives, may create confusion as to the allocation of responsibilities for policy decisions. Also, the proliferation of coordination activities has been such in recent years as to call for streamlining to reduce the bureaucratic workload involved. Strong coordination, by contrast, may lead to situations in which individual member states come into difficult conflicts with the rules and procedures agreed at the Community level.

The Community budget

Finally, policy actions may be undertaken by programmes in the Community budget (provided there is an appropriate legal base). Again, decision-making is by the Community method, though through a special version set out in the treaty and in an Inter-Institutional Agreement (IIA) between the institutions, with considerable power for the European Parliament. However, the scope for policy action via the Community budget is limited as it amounts to no more than roughly one per cent of GDP in the EU. The agricultural and regional programmes of the Community are of considerable financial interest to certain member states, and the financial burden of the Community budget occasionally raises tensions between 'net payers' and 'net recipients', but basically the EU is a rule-making machine rather than an instrument for raising revenue for spending purposes. Chapter 5.2 below sets out in detail the stakes in the annual budget procedure.

The picture which emerges of EU decision making is one of heterogeneity in the area of economic policy with regard to competence and diversity with regard to the method employed. Many actors are involved in the policy process, and there is a notable asymmetry in competence as between monetary policy and other economic policies. The methods of Community involvement differ with regard to their degree of supranationality and the way in which they derive their legitimacy. All this gives rise to a certain complexity, which often has its legitimate and understandable reasons, but which is not helpful from the point of view of easy understanding of who does what in the policy process.

Instruments and procedures of economic policy coordination

The economic policy regime in the treaty amounts to a rules-based framework with a specific allocation of competences and assignment of tasks. This is complemented by the principle of coordination, according to which 'member states shall regard their economic policies as a matter of common concern and shall coordinate them within the Council'. Coordination aims at ensuring that appropriate policies are effectively implemented, and that national policies take account of their implications for the Community. Monitoring and surveillance of economic developments and policies, and the associated policy dialogue at the EU level, aim at giving national decision makers appropriate feed back with a view to guiding them in their evaluation and planning of policies. This section briefly sets out the most important instruments and processes that form part of economic policy coordination in the EU.

One may, in this context, make a distinction between three cases. First, deviation of policies of member states from agreed rules may lead to warnings and even sanctions. This is the case for *legally binding rules*, which clearly belong to the 'hard core' of the policy regime or the domain of 'strong' coordination (as is the case for the obligation to avoid excessive budget deficits). Second, the specification of objectives and their surveillance may aim at *peer pressure* in the form of advice and non-binding recommendations (as is the case for the economic policy guidelines). This is what differentiates a normative process of policy coordination from the third case, which involves only exchange of information and dialogue with a view to *mutual learning*.

It may be recalled that the institutional position of the Commission is rather weak in the area of economic policy coordination. It still has the sole right of initiative for legal acts, but Council decisions are based on Commission recommendations rather than proposals. This means that the Council is free to modify the text by qualified majority and does not need unanimity to introduce amendments going against the view of the Commission (as is the case for legal acts based on Commission proposals). This needs to be seen in the light of the fact that general economic policy basically remains within national competence.

Fiscal policy rules

The background to the fiscal rules is twofold. On the one hand, it has been widely felt that there is an inherent political bias towards excessive budget deficits. There is broad agreement that persistently large budget deficits and a rapid build-up of public debt cause harm by adding to risk premiums in interest rates, complicating the task of monetary policy, reducing the room for manoeuvre of future fiscal policies, weakening capital formation and tilt-ing income distribution in favour of present as opposed to future gener-ations. On the other hand, EMU may aggravate the fiscal deficit bias; borrowing might be encouraged by the fact that even large national budget deficits would be unlikely to trigger sizeable increases in the (area-wide) interest rates. Such behaviour, if widespread, could have systemic conse-quences and would risk undermining the good functioning of EMU. There is, in other words, concern about 'free-riding' behaviour in the EMU, as the financial repercussions of national budget deficits may indirectly become a shared burden of all member states.

While leaving competence for fiscal policy with national governments, the treaty therefore also imposes obligations and constraints on what fiscal authorities can and should do. In particular, it obliges governments to finance budget deficits at market terms, allows no 'bail-out' of defaulting governments by the Community or other member states, and imposes ceil-ings on the size of acceptable government financial deficits and debts. The *Excessive Deficit Procedure* (EDP) forbids, as a rule, general government deficits in excess of 3 % of GDP. The treaty-based EDP was in 1997 comple-mented by the *Stability and Growth Pact* (SGP), which requires member states to produce stability or convergence programmes (of euro-area member states and of other member states respectively), and to aim at budgetary positions of close to balance or surplus in the medium term.

The SGP consists of two Council regulations and a European Council res-olution, and it should be seen in conjunction with the treaty-based EDP. The fiscal rules operate along two main lines. First, member states are commit-ted to aim at balance or surplus in government finances in the medium term, and this should create a safety margin against the risk that the 3% of GDP ceiling on budget deficits is violated. As part of the surveillance of budget-ary policies, member states notify the Commission about their budget devel-opments and submit annual updates of their stability and convergence programmes. The Council, assisted by the Commission, assesses the programmes and gives opinions on them, monitors their implementation, may give 'early warnings' to countries which seem not be on track for their medium term target, and may issue (non-binding) recommendations to member states concerned to take corrective action if slippage from targets is detected.

Second, the EDP becomes operative if a country runs an excessive deficit or comes close to doing so. If so, the Council will give recommendations to the member state concerned with a view to redressing the situation and may, if the member state fails to take sufficient action, decide on sanctions. These may take the form of an obligation for the member state concerned to make non-interest bearing deposits or even to pay fines of up to ½% of GDP. Also, the EDP should induce member states to take corrective action rapidly to rectify a situation with an excessive deficit. However, the provisions on sanctions apply only for member states participating in the euro area. Discussions on the implementation of the EDP and the SGP take place primarily in the Eurogroup for member states participating in the euro area, though formal decisions are taken in the Ecofin Council. The EDP and the SGP complement each other in the sense that the latter is designed to help ensure that the former is applied strictly. However, both procedures are highly discretionary and they always require an overall assessment and a political decision by the Council on a case-by-case basis.

The fiscal rules, in the case of member states participating in the euro area and if the rules are strictly applied, impose limits on and thereby restrain national discretion or sovereignty in budgetary matters. However, they have the great attraction of simplicity in that the target of budget balance and the avoidance of excessive deficits can be well understood by decision makers, financial markets and the general public. If duly followed, the rules should safeguard debt sustainability while leaving sufficient room for 'automatic stabilisers' to operate.[4] Also, compliance with the rules can be monitored with readily available statistics. The restriction on national sovereignty need not be perceived as severe, as it does allow member states to opt for a big or a small public sector and high or low tax burdens. The rules only aim at ruling out persistently large budget deficits of a sort which should normally be contrary to the interests of both the Community and each of the member states. However, the fiscal rules have always been controversial and they have recently given rise to a lot of critical debate.

An incident which has attracted particular attention in the media is instructive in this context. France and Germany were running excessive deficits in 2002, and were therefore given recommendations under article 104(7) to bring the situation to an end in 2004 at the latest. In October 2003 it was clear that this would not happen; France and Germany were foreseen to have excessive deficits in 2004 for the third year in a row. There was broad agreement that both countries would need more time (until 2005) to correct their deficits, but also that they should undertake more fiscal adjustment in 2004 than foreseen in their budgets. While the size and timing of the needed fiscal consolidation was a subject of some debate, it was really the procedure that became the sticking point.

The Commission recommended to the Council to 'give notice' under article 104(9) to France and Germany to take the measures judged necessary by the Council to remedy the situation. France and Germany considered that this would bring them dangerously close to possible decisions on sanctions, and mustered a blocking minority to prevent the decision. They wanted the Commission instead to give a new recommendation under article 104(7), which the Commission refused. Given the deadlock, the Council agreed on political conclusions as a substitute for a formal decision effectively putting the normal procedure on hold.

The failure of the Council to apply the 'proper' procedure was heavily criticised and seen as a blow to the credibility of the SGP by the member states being outvoted, the ECB, and many commentators in the media. Also, some of the small member states complained that the rules are not implemented equally for large and small member states. The Commission subsequently decided to bring the matter to the Court of Justice to clarify the legal status of the Council conclusions. The incident illustrates both the economic and the political difficulties of the SGP. Given three years of stagnation and a weak economy, it arguably did not make sense to ask France and Germany to make big cuts in expenditure or embark on tax increases. Politically it is very tough for the Council to impose fines on sovereign nations. Rules are useful, even essential, but there must inevitably also be discretion, and rules need to be backed up by political will and skilful implementation. As for the governance in EMU, the Council is still in a process of learning by doing.

Economic policy guidelines

The most important 'overarching' instrument of economic policy coordination is set out in article 99 of the treaty, which requires the Council to develop *Broad Economic Policy Guidelines* (BEPGs) of the member states and the Community. These contain assessments and recommendations both for the EU as a whole, for the euro area, and for the individual member states. The treaty also foresees that the implementation of these guidelines should be monitored and assessed, and allows the Council to make recommendations if the economic policies of member states deviate from the BEPGs or risk jeopardising the proper functioning of the EMU.

The process of producing the BEPGs starts with national reporting by member states (using the annual updates of stability and convergence programmes as well as special reports on structural issues). A 'Key Issues Paper' (KIP) on the BEPGs is presented by the Ecofin Council and is the subject of debate in the spring meeting of the European Council (see below). On the basis of further work (by the Commission and committees), the Council presents the BEPGs to the European Council in June and then adopts them. It has been agreed that the BEPGs should be subject to a full review with three-year intervals, the focus during the other years being mainly on implementation.

The coordination process involves information sharing and peer pressure through multilateral surveillance of policies in the light of agreed guidelines, and it allows the EU level to have a helpful role in areas of national competence. The BEPGs have been the inspiration for many other coordination processes (see below).

The BEPGs are expected to influence policy planning and action in member states but are not binding; there are no sanctions for failure to abide by the guidelines or associated recommendations. Instead, the main significance of the BEPGs is that they give expression to the agreed common view of member states on the economic policy strategy that the Community and its member states should follow. Needless to say, the views of member states often differ depending on national traditions and experiences, specific events and the political composition of governments. Drafting of the BEPGs is mostly done by consensus (though formally only qualified majority is needed), and the text unavoidably tends to reflect the 'lowest common denominator', therefore often lacking in boldness and clarity. Nevertheless, there is normally rather wide agreement on the main lines of the policies to be pursued. This concerns both the assessment of the economic outlook and the macroeconomic policy mix as well as the long-term challenges and priorities for structural policies.

Figure 5.1: *The Broad Economic Policy Guidelines*

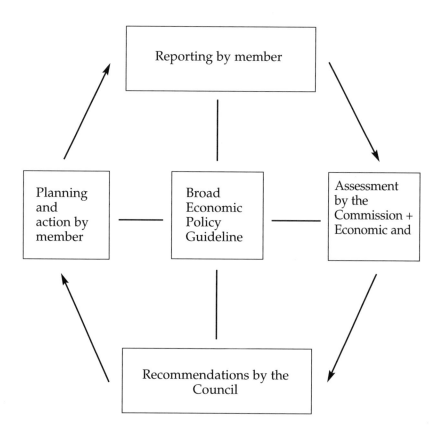

The emphasis in the BEPGs is on the medium term strategy and on structural or microeconomic policies. These policies, which may cover a very broad area, aim at improving the market mechanism and at strengthening the supply side and the growth potential of the economy. Action may be called for in the form of Community legislation, but often the structural reforms relate rather to actions which are the competence of member states. Indeed, structural policies tend to be associated with country-specific institutions and traditions, and their cross-border linkages are less obvious than the macroeconomic interdependence. The subsidiarity principle thus implies a presumption that such policies should be and remain a matter for national decision-making. On the other hand, there are also considerations pleading for coordination or action at the Community level, the most important being that structural policies may have a bearing on the functioning of the internal market.

The Lisbon process

The European Council, meeting in Lisbon in March 2000, agreed that it should devote annually a spring (March) meeting to discussion of economic and social issues. The March meeting is unique in that all the broad economic and social issues are on the table for consideration by the heads of state or government. The stated purpose of the Lisbon process was to relaunch a process of dynamism and structural reform, the strategic goal being that of making the Union by 2010 'the most competitive and dynamic knowledge-based economy in the world capable of sustainable economic growth with more and better jobs and greater social cohesion'.

The basic documentation for the spring meeting includes notably a 'synthesis report' by the Commission and the 'Key Issues Paper' on the BEPGs by the Ecofin Council. However, recent years have witnessed an escalation of policy coordination procedures, not only in the area of economic policies but also for, inter alia, employment and social policies. Some of these are treaty-based, such as the 'European Employment Strategy', which consists of employment guidelines, recommendations on employment policies to member states and surveillance in the form of examinations of annual national action plans for employment. Other processes have been set up on the basis of the conclusions of the European Council in Lisbon. In particular, it suggested an 'Open Method of Coordination' (OMC), to be applied in areas where no treaty-based instruments exist (such as pension systems, health expenditure or social inclusion). It takes the form of exchanges of information, benchmarking on the basis of structural indicators and the definition of best practices, and it aims at policy dialogue with a view to mutual learning as well as healthy competition and concerted action.

The goal of the Lisbon process (quoted above) is sometimes deemed to reflect political rhetoric rather than realism. Yet, the annual spring meeting of the European Council is important in that it allows the heads of state or government to get an overview of and assess progress achieved in the economic and social area, to reconcile differences between sectoral Council formations, to set priorities and to give impetus for further work through initiatives with specific remits and deadlines. The Lisbon process and the annual spring meeting have thus become the focal point for many of the Community's procedures in the economic and social area.

The preparatory machinery

The following will not attempt any detailed exposition of the Union's preparatory machinery but will mainly draw attention to the dichotomy in the Ecofin area between preparation of legislation as compared to economic policy coordination. Also, it will refer to some of the important committees involved.

Special committees

Work on policy coordination is mostly prepared for the Council by special committees, which combine technical expertise with some degree of political authority based on close relations to the relevant minister. The most important of these committees are the *Economic and Financial Committee* (EFC) and the *Economic Policy Committee* (EPC), both of which are bodies of high-level officials from ministries of finance or economy and central banks.

The EFC is the more senior committee, and most of its members work closely with their respective ministers. This allows the committee to play a key role in the preparation of Ecofin Council meetings. The EFC focuses on macroeconomic and financial issues, including international financial issues, and assumes the main responsibility for the preparation of both the BEPGs and the implementation of the EDP and the SGP as well as the work of the Eurogroup. The EFC meets in different compositions; in its broad composition it includes the representatives of central banks (the vice governors), while in its narrow composition only treasury officials participate (and representatives of the ECB and the Commission). Also, work of the EFC is prepared by the alternates of its members and occasionally by specific ad hoc groups. The work of the Eurogroup is prepared in the context of EFC meetings by the 'Eurogroup working party', which includes only the treasury officials of the member states participating in the euro area (in addition to the representatives of the Commission and the ECB).

The EFC has a chairman elected for a period of two years by the committee members rather than following the rotating presidency, which helps give the chairman an authoritative position, and a secretariat located in the Commission (DG/ECFIN) but acting under the instruction of the chairman of the committee. This secretariat arrangement has advantages of specialisation and synergy. The EPC deals more with structural and long-term issues and contributes notably to work on the BEPGs. It also has an elected chairman and shares a secretariat with the EFC. Work prepared by these committees often goes directly to the Council without passing through Coreper, though the latter is in all cases be informed of the preparatory work for the Council.

Other high-level committees in the Ecofin area include the Financial Services Committee (FSC), which advises the Commission and the Council on policy matters in the area of financial services and markets,

level of the working party or Coreper. The Ecofin Council (which in this context does not include the Budget formation) discussed the Community budget mainly at the stage preceding agreement on the last Financial Perspective. 'Other' is a heterogeneous category (including discussions of matters relating to the EIB, macrofinancial assistance, other external aid, and so on).

Table 5.2 *The Ecofin agenda: frequency of items*

	Taxation	Financial services	Policy coordination	Community budget	Other
1995	8	6	18	8	26
1996	6	0	13	10	19
1997	10	2	31	6	13
1998	11	6	40	17	16
1999	19	3	20	13	21
2000	11	9	32	5	16
2001	21	16	33	9	18
2002	24	23	31	9	22
2003	20	12	31	3	18

Such a table is potentially misleading because it covers only the agenda of formal meetings. In reality, it should be noted, the Ecofin Council meets in different formations and the informal discussions are often as relevant (if not more so) as what happens in formal session. In particular, the informal meetings of Ecofin ministers are important. These take place once during each presidency and ministers are on that occasion joined by the central bank governors. The agenda of the informal meetings is heavily tilted in favour of issues related to policy coordination, financial markets and services, the IMF and international developments, but these meetings occasionally also discuss strategic matters of tax policy. The lunch discussions, in the context of regular Council meetings, are often used with a view to seeking agreement on particularly controversial points in politically important dossiers. More recently, finance ministers have developed the habit of meeting over breakfast (before the normal Council meeting) for free-floating discussions of issues of common interest (ranging from structural policies to the IGC). It should also be noted that the Eurogroup (the ministers of the euro area, together with the President of the ECB and the relevant Commissioner) meets for a dinner discussion during the evening preceding Ecofin Council meetings.

While the character of the deliberations differs depending on the issues at stake, the personalities involved and a number of circumstances specific to each situation, three characteristics of the deliberations may nevertheless be seen as being representative or important. First, the ministers meet each other frequently (also in other international meetings such as in the OECD and the IMF) and they therefore often get to know each other well. Also, they are all in similar situations domestically; they typically have the ungrateful task of saying no or of setting strict conditions in their discussions with the 15-20 spending ministers of their governments. Even more than some other Council formations, the Ecofin Council thus develops a 'club-like' atmosphere. Ministers and their officials tend to see themselves not as representing a sectoral interest but as lobbyists for the general interest. They are the advocates of stability, financial prudence and structural reform with a view to sustained and healthy economic activity as a basis for a balanced development of society. Given the role that finance ministers play domestically, with the national budget being a key instrument of policy coordination, they expect by analogy the Ecofin Council to have an important role in the Community.

Second, the Ecofin Council works relatively effectively compared to most other Council formations. Ministers are mostly well briefed and focus their discussion on the key outstanding issues in a business-like manner. They tend to avoid long discussions (*tour de tables*) and rarely spend time on general resolutions of declaratory rather than operational significance. The close links between ministers and their representatives in the EFC facilitate efficient preparation of key issues in dossiers on economic policy coordination. The various configurations of meetings all have their particular role, formal sessions of the Council being used mainly for taking decisions and for deliberations on legal acts, while much of the discussion of policy coordination takes place in restricted composition over breakfast, lunch, or dinner (in the Eurogroup).

Third, while politicians inevitably have to focus on (perceived) national interests, finance ministers are very much aware also of their common interests in enhancing favourable economic developments and of their shared responsibilities. This is the case particularly for the members of the euro area and the Eurogroup. Lack of credibility of economic policies and of policy coordination risks undermining market confidence and sentiment with negative consequences for interest rates and exchange rates as well as for investment and growth. The strength of the common interest makes each participant aware of the need to act together with a view to bolstering confidence and to support sound and sustainable policies. Also, ministers mostly accept the key role that dialogue and peer review has to play in this process, though there are also cases where policy coordination requirements have led to dispute and conflict.

The EU has no government to decide on the economic policies pursued in the Union. Instead, the economic policy regime of the EU and the EMU is essentially based on a clear separation of the roles of monetary and other economic policies, in combination with respect for subsidiarity within a rules-based framework. The framework can function satisfactorily only if supported by economic policy coordination backed up by commitments to agreed norms of behaviour as well as multilateral surveillance of commitments. Given occasional tensions between what is perceived as the national interest and the broader Community or euro area interests, policy coordination faces political difficulties and serious risks of failure. Success of the economic policy regime is ensured only if and to the extent that the Ecofin Council and the Eurogroup are capable of facing up to these challenges.

5.2 The budget procedure, by Sir William Nicoll and Merrick Bryan-Kinns

Eloge du budgétaire

'L'appellation n'est pas contrôlée. Existe cependant dans la Communauté une race d'hommes et de femmes seuls à posséder le secret et qui se reconnaissent, comme dans Les Pléiades de Gobineau, sans avoir à s'annoncer: du côté de la Commission, le Commissaire compétent, quelques membres de son cabinet et de la Direction générale, une ou deux personnes de chez Delors; du côté du Conseil, quelques hauts fonctionnaires nationaux, un ou deux ministres en place depuis suffisamment longtemps (ce qui est rare), quelques bureaucrates accusés de tous les maux, mais qui ont au moins une mémoire; du côté du Parlement, quelques coordinateurs, officiels ou non, certains fonctionnaires des groupes, le secrétariat de la Commission des budgets....' (*Jean-Pierre Cot, a former president of the European Parliament's committee on budgets, in L'événement européen, 1988 N°1 (317, p. 207))*[5]

The Budget Council: past and present labels

Until the July 2002 changes in the structure of the Council, the Budget Council met in a distinct and separate configuration. Under the new arrangements, the Economic and Financial Affairs Council is also responsible for budgetary matters, but when it meets to consider such matters, the Ecofin Council mutates into more than a passing imitation of the former Budget Council, with the budgetary specialists eloquently described by Jean-Pierre Cot above slipping into the places of their senior ministers. Notwithstanding the disappearance of the Budget Council as a distinct configuration, the specificity of the budgetary procedure nevertheless obliges the Council to act in different and particular ways, hence a specific section devoted to the topic in this book.

The distinction between 'senior' and 'junior' Ecofin configurations can perhaps best be illustrated in the budgetary field through their agendas: the 'senior' Ecofin debates at its March meeting each year the annual EU budgetary guidelines, an elaborate policy statement designed to emulate the annual policy statements drawn up by the European Parliament and Commission respectively,[6] and it also deliberates in March on the discharge recommendation to be forwarded to the European Parliament under article 276 of the treaty,[7] a very solemn and important part of the financial process. It is also the 'senior' Ecofin that in May (chaired by the incoming presidency - see below) listens to a presentation by the Commission of its preliminary draft budget, before handing the baton to the 'junior' configuration whose job it is to conduct the July and November readings under the budgetary procedure!

The specificities of the budgetary procedure

Uniquely, the Council's budgetary work cycle is subject to a treaty timetable – reflected in the financial regulation – onto which has been grafted a 'pragmatic timetable' designed to achieve a rational rhythm of work by advancing the enshrined deadlines. Moreover, unlike the Council in the formations described in other chapters, the Council in the budgetary sphere has always voted its decisions. It is one of the two exceptions to the general rule[8] which prescribes that, if the Council wishes to change a proposal which it has received from the Commission, it needs unanimity within its ranks. The Budget Council was also the first to negotiate directly with the European Parliament to reach an overall agreement on a given matter (the budget). This so-called 'conciliation procedure' was in large part the model on which the similarly-named stage in the legislative co-decision procedure introduced by the Treaty of Maastricht was based.[9]

The nuts and bolts of the Community's budgetary procedure are set out in article 272 TEC, but have been much qualified and clarified by interinstitutional agreements and evolving custom (see below). Nevertheless, the basic rounds in the procedural cycle remain. The Commission draws up a preliminary draft budget and forwards it to the Council. Using this as its basis, the Council adopts the draft budget by qualified majority and forwards it to the European Parliament. The treaty stipulates a deadline of 5 October, but pragmatically this is done in July. The Parliament returns the draft budget, together with its proposed amendments, to the Council. The strength of the Parliament's power to amend the different parts of the budget depends on the classification of the expenditure involved. The treaty article distinguishes between compulsory and non-compulsory expenditure. Basically, the Parliament has the final say in the latter, the Council in the former.[10] Article 272(5) provides that the Council may modify any of the European Parliament's amendments by qualified majority, and it goes on to stipulate (referring to compulsory expenditure) that:

– where a modification proposed by the European Parliament would not increase the total amount of expenditure, the Council may, acting by a qualified majority, reject the proposed modification. However, in the absence of a decision to reject it, the proposed modification is deemed accepted;
– where a modification proposed by the European Parliament would increase the total amount of expenditure, the Council may, acting by a qualified majority, accept the proposed modification. However, in the absence of a decision to accept it, the proposed amendment is deemed rejected;
– where, acting in accordance with one of the two preceding sub-paragraphs, the Council has rejected a proposed modification, it may, acting by a qualified majority, either retain the amount shown in the draft budget or fix another.

This whole process is known as the Council's 'second reading' and takes place in November. The Council forwards its modified draft budget to the European Parliament which may, acting by a majority of its members and three-fifths of the votes cast, amend or reject the modifications made to its amendments by the Council. Once the Parliament has voted on all of its amendments again, it may then adopt the budget, and it is the president of the Parliament alone who declares that the budget has been adopted. However, where it feels there are important reasons, the Parliament may, acting by a majority of its members and two thirds of the votes cast, reject the draft budget and ask for a new draft to be submitted to it.

From this brief description, it will be gathered that the budgetary procedure is a complex and arcane business. The Parliament has enjoyed its budgetary powers since the early 1970s, and it is hence the area where the Council is most used to working with the Parliament. The annual budget cycle has traditionally involved lengthy voting sessions and many long nights, and a mutual camaraderie has grown up between the two institutions (albeit clothed in the terminology of warfare). Under the rules discussed later, both phases (July and November) are preceded by lengthy 'conciliation' meetings, themselves prepared in 'trialogues' so that the bare treaty procedure which deals with the transmission of drafts between the two institutions is in fact to be seen as a face-to-face quasi-permanent negotiation process.

The Economic and Financial Affairs Council in its budgets guise and the Council's budget committee are unique in that they always vote formally and, with the occasional exception of particularly sensitive matters, they always vote just as soon as the required majority has been attained. The reason for this is simple; the Community budget is a highly complex document to which annual, treaty-based deadlines apply, but yet has to be adopted in detail. Formal voting is the only practical solution.

The EU budget is an expenditure budget; so when it meets on budgetary matters, the Ecofin Council has only one responsibility - to influence (where it can) the overall level of expenditure, the level of each given category of expenditure, and the priorities to be chosen within each such category. So far as it is concerned, the quantum of revenue of each type ('own resource') is a given, calculated by the Commission on the basis of the reports which it receives from the member states, giving estimates of how much Community revenue they expect to be responsible for. The Commission's calculation is discussed with the member states in an advisory committee under the Commission structures. Once confirmed or revised, the revenue is incorporated into the budget drafts. It would be indeed strange for the Ecofin Council or its specialised preparatory committees to discuss the revenue estimates afresh, except as a technicality. This is mainly because, although there is a clear treaty obligation for the budget to be in balance (article 268), in practice the Ecofin (Budget) Council and its preparatory bodies only discuss the expenditure side, which in present circumstances (the existence of a 'financial perspective', see below) is considerably below the level of theoretically available revenue.[11] The only occasion on which the budget *filière* becomes considerably excited about the revenue side is when the annual amending budget arrives, spelling out the amount of budget surplus due to be reimbursed to member states.[12]

Just as it does not discuss revenue except as an adjunct, the Council does not discuss spending on agricultural guarantee either in any detail. The Commission calculates, from the price-fixing and other decisions of the Agriculture and Fisheries Council, the cost of EAGGF guarantee in the coming financial year. The calculation is discussed with the member states in an advisory Commission committee (the EAGGF Committee), and the agreed figure-work is incorporated into the budgetary drafts. The Ecofin Council and its budgetary preparatory bodies do not re-examine the figures except at the margin. The European Parliament can, and does, seek to modify them, but the Council has the 'last word', at present[13] and moves only as part of an overall deal (see below). Thus for all practical purposes some 45% of the budget is processed without detailed discussion.[14]

The Ecofin (Budget) Council has, in other words, several specific characteristics that set it aside from other Council formations: the habit of voting[15] as a matter of course (and therefore without any 'high drama'); negotiations with the European Parliament – either as a body or by delegation – on what could be described without much exaggeration as a continuous basis, and therefore also as a matter of course; the fact that it acts not as legislator but as a partner in a compulsory annual process, which in turn means that the Commission's role changes subtly from that of initiator to that of conciliator; the fact that whenever it convenes it has an *obligation de résultat*. There is one other specific worth recording: special arrangements agreed at the Seville European Council on 22 June 2002 and then incorporated into the Council's rules of procedure[16] mean that, once the Commission's preliminary draft budget is tabled, preparatory work relating to the Council's first reading (July) carried out in the first half of the year is chaired by the member state holding the presidency of the second half of the year. Meetings of the subordinate budget committee have therefore to be divided between two chairpersons, and human nature being what it is, this arrangement is only as efficient as the participants wish it to be.

Broad budgetary and tax policy

When the Ecofin (Budget) Council meets on budgetary matters, 'budgetary policy' is also a given. The budget *filière* is not involved in decisions about 'own resources' or in the periodic internal and institutional discussions and decisions about budgetary discipline in the legislative sense. It does not discuss the relief of national budgetary imbalances either. Increases in own resources (and changes to their mode of collection) are proper to the General Affairs and External Relations Council (GAERC), acting as the antechamber to the European Council. For its part, the senior Ecofin Council does indeed, very frequently, discuss VAT, but then under the aspect of general tax policy harmonisation issues, never under the aspect of revenue-raising for the EU! The Ecofin (Budget) Council is likewise not the major participant in the periodic interinstitutional negotiations which establish the medium-term financial planning (the 'financial perspective', of which more below) which are indeed the province of the European Council with preparation by the GAERC (see chapter 16).

To sum up, then, it can be said that the body that used to be known, with the merits of clarity, as the 'Budget Council', in fact has a very narrow remit: to allocate, in a specialised type of 'co-decision', expenditure within a framework that it has not itself decided and using revenue on which it has not itself decided either. Lastly, it should be remembered that – unlike the European Parliament – the Council's constant position is that the budget should finance existing policies and not be used as a vehicle to create new ones.

Macroeconomic effects

The Community budget is far too small, currently at a maximum of 1.24% of EU GNI (a limit which will remain valid until 2006), to have a significant effect on macroeconomic conditions across the Union, which is not the same as saying that its out-turn, up or down, is not of vital importance to many, if not all, member states - for example, the United Kingdom as a well-known net contributor. The Ecofin Council (Budget) is not in the business of determining the resource flows which are the expression of 'economic and social cohesion' (the title, XVII, which was first introduced into the Community lexicon by the 1987 Single European Act).[17] Redistribution of resources is mediated by the budget, but is not a subject for discussion as such within the junior Council. For it, Union expenditure 'lies where it falls'. Any correctives to secure 'cohesion', otherwise termed as 'reducing the disparities between the various regions and the backwardness of the least-favoured regions'[18] are the concern of other instances in the Union.

Composition and support

When it meets to discuss budgetary matters, the Ecofin Council is composed of junior ministers mostly from national finance departments (including, in those member states which adopt the practice, senior officials holding ministerial rank). Their bosses are the senior members of the Ecofin Council. The president of the Ecofin (Budget) Council has had a higher profile, though in a publicly less conspicuous way, than most of his colleagues in other Councils, to the extent that he or she represents the Council in most of its exchanges with the European Parliament and speaks in Parliamentary plenary sessions when presenting the Council's handiwork for it to debate.[19]

The work of the Ecofin (Budget) Council is prepared by the permanent representatives committee, as the treaty requires (article 207). Until the 1995 budgetary cycle, it was 'Coreper I', the deputy permanent representatives, who thus acquired budgetary expertise. In practice, however, the Coreper I legislative workload became so onerous that by default it largely entrusted preparation of the Council to the lower-powered budget committee. With effect from the 1996 budgetary exercise, Council preparation was assumed by Coreper II, the permanent representatives themselves. They were already charged with preparing meetings of the more senior version of the Ecofin Council and it was thought that they would therefore have a greater awareness of the financial implications of the widening scope of Union policy.

The budget committee is one of the hundred and sixty or so Council preparatory bodies (see chapter 12) whose work is funnelled through the permanent representatives committee (Coreper) to the Council. These bodies are composed of officials from member state administrations. Those serving on the budget committee are drawn from finance or revenue departments (or central banks) and are usually attached to permanent representations and resident in Brussels.[20] They are all on first-name terms. When the work intensifies, they may be joined by colleagues from capitals, bearing fresh instructions to supplement those coming by telex from HQ. Like its peers, the budget committee has no powers of decision. Its recommendations need the fiat of the Council. But it sifts out of the 1,800 pages and

3,000 lines of a budget document the essential and disputed matters which ministers have to decide if there is to be a budget. These are presented to the Ecofin (Budget) Council in a series of reports, showing what could be agreed and what, taking account of such agreement, remains for decision. Although qualified majority voting is now widespread, there is still a difference between the Ecofin (Budget) Council and others. The latter go to great lengths to reach a consensus, voting only when the room for compromise is exhausted. The Budget Council stops negotiating when a qualified majority is reached. The arithmetic is simpler if the calculation is of a blocking minority. As soon as it shrinks, the Council has decided.

The presidency's very skilful task (usually performed in practice at the lowest level, and sometimes at Coreper) is to 'buy off' a sufficient number of opponents to its compromise package so that it can conjure up a qualified majority by the skin of its teeth. Since delegations have different voting weights and very specific individual priorities (cynics christen this the 'shopping list' approach) a juggling act of the utmost precariousness is called for, and always succeeds.

When the Council's preparatory bodies work on the preliminary draft budget, they tend to do so in the guise of a 'hearing' rather than a traditional working party; much in the same way as the European Parliament works, each body requesting a block of appropriations, including of course each institution, must make a presentation and undergo a robust and probing interrogation by the budget committee. Perhaps it should also be recalled that the Council not only acts on figures (in the specific decision-making process vis-à-vis the European Parliament) but also on the minutiae of the staff establishment plans of each institution, and indeed quite often on the 'remarks' to the individual budget lines.

By way of completeness, it should be recalled that the budget *filière* (nominally the Council but of course in practice Coreper, fed by the budget committee) also processes on a day-by-day basis a myriad of proposals for transfers internal to the budgets of the various institutions, and, in addition, does have a role outside the strictly budgetary field: its role in the discharge has already been mentioned, where conclusions are drafted on the basis of a 'hearing'-type procedure; its own annual policy statement (like the discharge, reserved ultimately to the 'senior' Ecofin); its legislative work on, inter alia, successive financial regulations.[21]

The financial perspectives and the working methods they have engendered

At the time of writing, the two arms of the budget authority (Parliament and Council) will have been working together for some fifteen years (i.e., since 1988) within the constraints of a 'financial perspective' and an 'Interinstitutional Agreement on budgetary discipline and improvement of the budgetary procedure'; we are now in our third such perspective and our third Interinstitutional Agreement, and both are due for no doubt arduous re-negotiation.[22] It is not the purpose of this chapter to rehearse the detailed history of this financial framework on the last fifteen years,[23] but rather to point out those salient features that have come to influence the budgetary climate, and thus the Council's own work. The specific hermetic ceilings within the successive financial frameworks, together with the accompanying codification of negotiation procedures, undeniably constitute a form of voluntary self-restraint (particularly by the European Parliament, whose prerogatives on expenditure under the treaty are defined mathematically) and a judicious set of concessions by both parties; in other words, we now have a very specific – and indeed very complicated – type of co-decision which to all practical purposes obliges both partners to come to agreement. Like all intelligently constructed structures, the framework has some built-in safety valves (which probably explain why the system still works): the 'emergency aid reserve' (as its name suggests, it is a budgetised reserve, but it can be mobilised – and has been – and thus relieves pressure on the allocation for external action); the 'flexibility instrument' which, like any true safety valve, has been used with the Council's obviously reluctant concurrence in every recent budget year so far, as part of an overall 'deal';[24] finally, and most recently, the European Union Solidarity Fund created on 11 November 2002[25] with its accompanying interinstitutional agreement, in the wake of the disastrous flooding earlier that year, which allows for the mobilisation – in co-decision – of up to €1 billion above the existing ceilings, clearly a major safety valve.

Perhaps because of the careful construction of the successive interinstitutional agreements (including such safety valves),[26] perhaps because of public opinion's attitude to public expenditure in general, perhaps because the agreed procedures oblige both partners to meet at least seven times a year, and in practice far more frequently,[27] perhaps also simply because of the conciliatory character of some of the individuals prominently involved in the negotiation process (explanations can sometimes be that simple!), outsiders generally agree that the annual negotiating climate has improved radically over the last decade: the stalemate, the legal action before the Court of Justice, the December 'crisis' Council meetings in Strasbourg, the 'provisional twelfths' provoked by Parliament's rejection of the draft budget, all these seem mercifully to be becoming a distant memory. The attitude is businesslike, the negotiation is real but loyal (the rhetoric of battle is naturally still there...), meetings are appearing to become shorter.

Isolated incidents arguably became a pattern: *4 June 2002* saw an important financial conciliation meeting (on the new financial regulation) end successfully in the space of just a few minutes by spontaneous applause; *22 October 2002* saw the first budgetary conciliation conducted by video conference; *25 November 2002* saw the first conciliation meeting and Council 'second reading' to be held the same day (as opposed to the traditional arduous night session involving two notional 'days');[28] *16 July 2003* saw the first Council 'first reading' and prior conciliation to be conducted – by agreement – without the traditional tripartite lunch (indeed without anything to eat at all) while *24 November 2003* saw a Council 'second reading' and prior conciliation lasting just one day with, again, no formal lunch.[29] It is no secret that informal moves behind the scenes were recently afoot, unfortunately to no avail as yet, to explore even the possibility of conducting business with reduced delegations on both sides (considerably less than the twenty-five each that represents current practice) but it may well be that this idea will need a long germination period.

These outwards signs are admittedly trivial if taken individually; taken together, they hopefully form a pattern – the outward signs of a gradually less confrontational approach – and it can only be hoped that this situation will last. It is probably no use to gaze into a crystal ball to wonder how the atmosphere might change when the new treaty is applied: that possibility is still too far down the road, but it is arguably obvious that if a future financial perspective – unlike the present one – were to be set at a level extremely close to current real budget (as recently advocated by six member states),[30] so that all safety valves and growth prospects are removed, then this would not be conducive to the controlled and constructive annual negotiating climate to which we have recently become accustomed.

This improved state of affairs could, however, at any moment prove fragile, and indeed came perilously close to tumbling down completely when, in March 2003, the member states fixed in the draft Accession Treaty the revised financial perspective for enlargement. This gesture, which in hindsight can most charitably be classed as insouciance, provoked a fierce counter-reaction, immediately escalated to the highest level,[31] by the European Parliament (which felt its prerogatives had been ignored) and among the threats issued was that of simply denouncing the interinstitutional agreement and its attached financial perspective. Peace was bought inevitably, but at a heavy price (a further 480 million euros added to the ceiling foreseen for internal policies) and it is probably fair to say that the lesson has not been lost on the Council.

It is extremely dangerous to over-simplify, but schematically one can summarise the annual negotiating round – at least over the last few years – by saying that the Council's main strategic priority is to obtain as low a level as possible of payment appropriations ('real money'), to ensure a satisfactory allocation for the CFSP, and to resist until the eleventh hour any question of using the 'flexibility instrument' to breach a given ceiling; concomitantly, it tries to ensure that sufficient margins are left under each category of the financial perspective.[32] Parliament's priority – at least as perceived by the Council – is to demonstrate that the various ceilings are woefully inadequate, that Parliament is able to exert a certain influence on agriculture spending and to obtain from the Council suitably guaranteed information flows regarding CFSP expenditure so that the CFSP does not remain a sort of *'chasse gardée'* for the member states alone.[33] Clearly, this sort of menu offers all the ingredients for a deal, and once the rhetoric and the cliff-hanging has been gone through, the deal has always been done in recent times.

What strikes the observer of any of the recent budget conciliation meetings is that the figures ostensibly on the table for negotiation are simply the vehicle for a traditional struggle for influence; aside from the issue of payment appropriations, the total of the figures up for discussion as such (the margins under each ceiling, the flexibility instrument, the CFSP...) never amount to much more than 0.5% of the budget at most!

The Council's own budget

No account of the Council as an institution would be complete without a brief comment on the Council's own administrative budget (known to the initiated as 'section II') and how it affects preparatory work within the Council. The Council, and indeed the European Parliament, have a curious dual role; they act as arms of the budget authority in the decision-making process governing the whole of the European Union's general budget, but at the same time they are individually the arbiters of their 'own' small administrative budgets. Indeed, with this duality in mind, a 'gentlemen's agreement' was born thirty-four years ago – and is still thankfully going strong – under which neither institution interferes (by amendment or hearing) with the administrative budget of the other.[34]

This factor only adds to the intensity with which the Council's preparatory bodies, particularly Coreper, focus on their own institution's budget. In terms of sheer person-hours, it can be said without any exaggeration that the preparatory bodies on average spend more time and effort on the Council's own budget than on all other elements of the Union's general budget put together (even though the Council's budget represents a mere 0.5% of the sums involved!). There are two reasons for this: firstly, Coreper is acting as a quasi-board for its 'own' staff and buildings, for example going into great detail on building plans/staff levels/interpreting problems etc. This is normal. Secondly, the Council's budget – precisely because of the interinstitutional agreement – has to be fixed at the July first reading – and the European Parliament will not reopen it by amendment – whereas all other headings, and particularly the administrative budgets of all institutions, are fixed at the Parliament's second reading. So the Council only has 'one shot',[35] and this can occasionally give rise to unfortunate presentational problems at the first reading (July) where the Council is seen, for example, as awarding itself a treatment more favourable than that it gives to other institutions. The unbalance is *trompe l'oeil*, of course, because the other institutions will, as a general rule, be able to improve their situation thanks to the second reading of the European Parliament, while the Council's situation will remain static.

The European security and defence policy (ESDP)

The recent development of the ESDP, principally in the wake of the European Council's conclusions handed down in Helsinki (December 1999) and then in Feira (June 2000) and Nice (December 2000) have had a very specific impact on the Council's own section of the budget, and therefore by definition on the work of the Council and its preparatory bodies, as well as its general secretariat; these developments are therefore worth recalling in the context of this chapter. For the sake of clarity, we have to emphasise that we are not in any way dealing here with financial arrangements that fall outside the general budget.[36]

The Council general secretariat was faced with the task of acquiring, housing and equipping an advisory military staff in a very short time-frame: more precisely, this entailed the acquisition of a dedicated building and communication system to an obviously high security specification and the concomitant build-up of a large team of military 'seconded national experts'[37] to be remunerated by their national authorities backed up by a daily allowance[38] scheme.

This type of expenditure which was, at the time, both exceptional and unforeseeable qualified *par excellence* for the technique of a supplementary and amending budget (SAB); initial building acquisition costs, along with a bid from the European Parliament, were thus entered into a draft SAB by the Council on 29 June 2000 and approved by Parliament on 6 July 2000. So far so good; but for 2001 when the build-up would gather speed, it was far too late – in mid 2000 – for the Council to incorporate any estimates in its first reading of the draft budget for 2001. The approach had to be step-by-step. So it was only in March 2001 that the Commission tabled a preliminary draft SAB for 2001 (on the Council's request and specific to the Council); the Council proceeded to its first reading on 9 April 2001 and the Parliament, which did not seek to amend it, approved it on 17 May 2001.

To permit this swift adoption, there had however been a fairly arduous trialogue at which the European Parliament insisted that as from 2002 all administrative expenditure relating to the ESDP should be identified clearly by means of a separate title III in the Council's budget, in the name of transparency, and this has been carried out ever since.[39]

But the issue goes far deeper than mere presentation techniques; we can detect an underlying malaise within the European Parliament on this issue[40] and, at the time of writing, it is uncertain how this will develop in a new legislature. Because of the 'gentlemen's agreement' (see below), Parliament would not normally seek a *droit de régard* on the Council's budget, but there is a feeling there that this particular expenditure in the ESDP field, despite assurances that such expenditure is in no way 'operational', should in fact not be shielded from scrutiny by being incorporated in the Council's budget in this way, albeit transparently. Watch this space! This issue between Parliament and Council, which has so far mercifully not even developed into a major skirmish, is the perfect example perhaps of what this chapter has tried to demonstrate: that on-going budget negotiations are not really about figures (the ESDP budget within the Council budget is microscopic) but about institutional prerogatives.

Concluding remarks

The Budget Council, now no longer even called the Budget Council, is unique in the Community system; it only actually meets as such twice a year, it does not legislate, it approves drafts for ultimate approval by Parliament; it negotiates collectively or by delegation on an almost continuous basis; it works within a financial framework that other ministers will have decided; its 'votes' are in almost all cases pre-arranged at the level of national officials; it appears to the outsider to devote enormous energy to discussing a few sums of money which are microscopic on the scale of the general budget as such. Last but absolutely not least, it is the 'bursar' for its own house, so to speak (the one area where it can work conscientiously without being challenged by Parliament).

Take a few steps back, and the bigger picture becomes clear: the history of the budget procedure, which in a few years will undergo yet another upheaval, is one of a perpetual struggle-for-influence ('power struggle' is too journalistic an expression), between Parliament and national governments, and arguably – at a perhaps less spectacular level – via the Council's own budget section, between national governments and the concept of an independent European civil service.

It is impossible to tell at this point if the relatively constructive 'peace' of the last fifteen years will survive the new treaty; there will certainly be a rough passage ahead; the key to the relative peace of recent times is that all parties have accepted with reasonably good grace the financial framework; if a new financial framework (either by its absolute figures or by its pro- cedure) were to change this fundamental, then life in the former Budget Council might revert to the ancient pattern of night-sessions, emergencies and conflict. It is to be hoped not.

Chapter 6: The Justice and Home Affairs Council,

by Hans G. Nilsson

The introduction of cooperation in the fields of justice and home affairs ('JHA' – though even in English the French acronym, 'JAI', is frequently used) into the framework of the Union Treaty (in a new title VI, commonly referred to as the 'third pillar') during the Maastricht Treaty negotiations attracted limited attention. Many still consider this area to be more the natural preserve of national administrations or legislatures rather than EU institutions. The special provisions in the treaty governing this area reflect the fact that justice and home affairs matters are among some of the most sensitive areas of public policy, close to the heart of member states' national sovereignty. There are a number of reasons why they have nevertheless emerged as major and high profile areas of Union policy.

First, the policy areas covered by justice and home affairs touch upon some of European citizens' most acute political concerns: internal security, combating drug addiction, terrorism, organised crime and the problems of immigration. These issues are much closer to the immediate interests of citizens than, for example, the technical harmonisation of lifts or even a more efficient and visible common foreign and security policy. The major role played by immigration and internal security in recent elections in some EU member states is one indication of the importance citizens attach to these issues and the political relevance they have already acquired at national level.

Second, the scale of the revision of the JHA provisions undertaken in the Amsterdam Treaty (not to mention those envisaged in the new constitutional treaty) inevitably generated public attention. The scope of the Amsterdam changes was spectacular, both in terms of sheer volume – over one hundred new or amended treaty provisions, six protocols and twenty declarations – and in substance: not only were the basic provisions of the existing title VI TEU extensively amended, but major sectors of justice and home affairs were transferred to the EC Treaty in an entirely revamped title IV covering visa, asylum and immigration policy and cooperation in civil law matters. A broad range of new objectives were established, and improved legal instruments were designed to help the Union meet them. In addition, both the 'old' intergovernmental and the 'new' Community part of justice and home affairs were opened to a wide range of actual or potential differentiated integration within the framework of the treaties, the most substantial being the incorporation of Schengen (see below) into the EC/EU framework. All these reforms were placed under the overall objective of making the Union an 'area of freedom, security and justice' (referred to in shorthand as AFSJ), adding a new programmatic element to the overall integration process.

Third, it is within the 'area of freedom, security and justice' that the Union faces some of its most important challenges. Among those challenges are the many problems linked to increasing migration and asylum claims. Although the figures have diminished lately, the pressure of international migration combined with the systematic abuse of asylum systems has already transformed some of the member states into de facto net importers of migration, a development which could easily give rise to significant political, social and economic problems. Indeed, it is an important factor in domestic political debate in some member states. The increasing flows of international migration in some member states and the abolition of internal borders inside the Union make it impossible for member states to find adequate responses to this major challenge on an individual basis. The growing internationalisation of crime represents a further challenge. Out of necessity, the member states are developing common approaches and actions in order to be able to respond effectively to the increasing sophistication of international crime. The Union's annual organised crime reports provide ample proof of the growth of international drug trafficking, terrorism and fraud. A common response at the Union level to all of these questions has been deemed both logical and urgent.

Cooperation in justice and home affairs is therefore at the centre of the Union's development. In October 1999 a special session of the European Council in Tampere was dedicated to justice and home affairs (only the second time that a European Council meeting had been devoted to a single subject). The European Council's conclusions set down major political guidelines for the further construction of the EU as an 'area of freedom, security and justice'. New objectives have since been added, such as those for the fight against illegal immigration adopted by the Seville European Council in June 2002. In its draft Constitution of July 2003, the Convention on the Future of Europe proposed further major reforms in this area. Failure by the Union to fulfil its objectives would mean not only increased risks for the internal security and stability of the member states but also a severe blow to the Union's political credibility. The Tampere and Seville European Council conclusions; the adoption of the European Commission's 'scoreboard' system to speed up implementation of justice and home affairs decisions; the increased number of legally binding texts adopted and the series of action plans in key areas such as organised crime; the fight against drugs and external border controls – all these indicate that member states and EU institutions have increasingly regarded the development of the 'area of freedom, security and justice' as a central political priority for the EU. The question arises as to how it is that, in such a short period of time since the Maastricht Treaty's entry into force (November 1993), the trend described above could so accelerate.

The origins of EU action on justice and home affairs

Most writers on EU cooperation trace the origins of JHA cooperation back to the mid-1970s and the violent terrorist attacks perpetrated in a number of member states (*Rote Armee Fraktion* in Germany, *Brigate Rosso* in Italy and *Action Directe* in France, among others). In fact, member states' police forces had been working within Interpol (which was set up in 1914) for decades and European justice ministries had cooperated within the framework of the Council of Europe since 1958 (when the European Committee on Crime Problems was established).

With its formal structures (expert groups, steering committees and committee of ministers), intergovernmental cooperation taking place in the Council of Europe context since the early 1950s had already socialised justice and, to some extent, interior ministries into a certain style and form of cooperation. Within that framework, more than 30 conventions were developed and over 100 recommendations made on issues as varied as access to justice, family law, asylum and immigration, terrorism, money laundering, extradition and mutual legal assistance in criminal matters. A solid base for intergovernmental cooperation was therefore present already by the 1970s. However, interior ministries (police departments in particular) did not have an appropriate forum in which to express themselves. This was one of the reasons why the TREVI structure was set up on 1 July 1975. (Some believe that the 'TREVI' acronym stands for Terrorism, Radicalism, Extortion, Violence and Intimidation – or International Violence in some French textbooks, although the explanation is somewhat simpler. The first TREVI meeting at the level of senior officials was held in Rome and was chaired by a Dutchman by the name of Fonteijn (who asked to be remembered by the name of the famous fountain!).

TREVI initially met once a year at ministerial level, but the frequency of ministerial meetings declined. TREVI had a number of working groups (TREVI I-VI) which, following Maastricht, were incorporated into the Council – incidentally one of the reasons why the Council found itself with five layers of decision-making instead of the ordinary three-tier structure of working parties, Coreper and Council. (It should also be noted that countries such as Switzerland, the USA, Canada, Norway and Morocco often participated in TREVI meetings.) The TREVI working groups examined questions relating to terrorism, public order and training, organised crime and drugs, nuclear safety, compensatory measures for the free movement of persons, and Europol. Other TREVI structures also existed during different periods of its existence; for instance, CELAD (drugs), immigration, MAG (mutual assistance between customs' administrations) and MAG 92 (training and exchange of information between customs).

The most important part of the process was the coordinators' group, which prefigured the senior 'K4' committee created in the Maastricht Treaty. This group of coordinators (senior level officials at the ministries of justice and interior) was created at the 1988 Rhodes summit, with the task of coordinating and driving all of the Union's work relating to the free movement of persons and compensatory measures for the abolition of border controls.

Schengen (1985 onwards)

In 1985, in the small Luxembourg town of Schengen, France, Germany and the Benelux countries signed an agreement on the gradual removal of border controls. Five years later, on 19 June 1990, a convention was signed concerning the application of the agreement, the so-called Schengen Implementation Convention. In effect, Schengen cooperation was born out of the failure of the European Community to make progress on free movement of persons. France and Germany had decided at the 1984 Rambouillet summit to reinforce their cooperation by abolishing all formalities hindering free movement of persons between the two countries. Later the same year, at the Fontainebleau summit, the Benelux countries joined this Franco-German initiative.

The 1985 agreement was more a letter of intent than an instrument with operational content. Its objective was to ensure greater freedom while at the same time increasing internal security through concrete measures. Italy joined Schengen cooperation shortly after the convention had been signed, followed by Spain and Portugal in June 1991. The other EU member states gradually followed suit. All of the fifteen 'old' member states have since joined Schengen cooperation inside the EU (but for the UK and Ireland with the exception of the parts that relate to the control of frontiers, and for Denmark in accordance with their 'opt out' – see chapter 8). The ten new member states are able to join Schengen cooperation gradually, with some measures being immediately applicable and others applicable only later.

Schengen was incorporated into the Union framework with the Amsterdam Treaty, which also, uniquely, allowed for Norway and Iceland to join in the Union's decision-shaping (though not its decision-taking) procedures. These two non-member states had joined the Schengen cooperation through their links with the Nordic Council cooperation and under the freedom of movement among Nordic countries. The unique mixed committee procedure (COMIX) in the Council adopted as a result of this latter feature of the Schengen cooperation is described below.

One of the trickiest practical difficulties which existed when Schengen was incorporated into the Amsterdam Treaty in 1997 was how to divide up and slot the existing Schengen *acquis* into the new treaty structures, under which part belonged to Title IV under the EC Treaty (visas, asylum, immigration and free movement of people) and part was to be subject to Title VI TEU (police and judicial cooperation in criminal matters). This breakdown took nearly a year to conclude (and was not without importance since the procedures in the two titles, including, in certain cases, voting rules, are different).

Maastricht (1993)

The Maastricht Treaty was a compromise; the member states' justice and home affairs departments were used to intergovernmental cooperation and it was felt necessary to begin any shift of method cautiously. Hence, in the Maastricht Treaty, JHA affairs were considered to be matters of 'common interest', and competence was given to the Union in nine different fields of cooperation. Some member states reportedly accepted this compromise on the understanding that the third pillar would be purely intergovernmental and that no power to act would be given to the Union. This interpretation was always debatable, since a number of the legal instruments created, particularly joint positions and joint actions, were considered to be binding once adopted, and its proponents laboured under the misapprehension that the third pillar was somehow entirely dissociated from the existing Community institutional framework. However, TEU Article C declared that the Union was served by a single institutional framework and, therefore, all of the Union's institutions had roles to play in the third pillar as well. Thus, the first steps towards the full incorporation of the JHA matters into the Community/Union were taken in Maastricht.

The new third pillar introduced a number of features that were unfamiliar to proponents of the Community method. The right of initiative was excluded for the Commission in three areas (cooperation in criminal law matters, customs cooperation and police cooperation) and in others was shared with the member states. All decisions were in principle taken by unanimity and the European Parliament was only consulted. Conventions had to be ratified by all member states before they entered into force, although there was a (frequently used) possibility for the member states to apply the conventions in relation to member states that had made the same provision for early application. Joint actions were at least binding on member state governments but their legal value was contested and, in any case, the real value of the instrument was limited since there were no follow-up mechanisms to ensure proper implementation. A bridging clause provision, enabling the transfer of Union competences in the third pillar to the Community was provided for but was in fact never used – though it clearly had symbolic value for the third pillar's future development.

The Maastricht working structures, largely a duplication of the old TREVI structures and thus a heritage of the past, were decided by the European Council two days before the treaty entered into force on 29 October 1993. The so-called 'K4' (after the TEU article) committee of senior officials was in effect the group of coordinators decided upon by the Rhodes European Council and the three steering groups were direct descendants of the TREVI working groups on asylum/immigration, police cooperation and judicial cooperation.

At the beginning tensions existed between the various working levels: customs officials felt that their interests had not been taken care of sufficiently and that their work was split up between several working parties; there was open competition between the steering groups and the K4 committee; and the K4 committee was alleged to be seeking to impose itself as a 'Coreper III' but was unable to wield the political power of the permanent representatives, nor able to take decisions at the same level as Coreper. The incorporation of these structures into the formal Council structures resulted in the setting up of a complex decision-making process in which nobody initially took responsibility for decision-making and where difficult decisions were always pushed up to the next level. This confusing situation has been described as a clash between two different cultures; that of the traditional Council/Coreper method and that of the traditional intergovernmental method.

The first JHA Council met on 30 November 1993 and drew up an action programme. Decision-making was slow and frequently blocked because of the unanimity rule. Use was often made of non-binding political instruments (resolutions, recommendations and conclusions) rather than legally binding acts. Conventions were negotiated, but took a long time to agree and even longer to ratify. Of the first 100 decisions taken by the JHA

Council, only one (no. 99!) was a binding instrument. Frequent problems occurred in relation to procedures and legal issues and concerning demarcation lines between the first and third pillars.

Moreover, the officials working in this area (in the Commission, the Council secretariat, successive presidencies and national delegations) were understaffed and inexperienced in Council procedures. The Council secretariat was set up with just a few officials who had to service a number of working parties that had simply been incorporated from the old TREVI structures; the Commission set up a small 'task force' that bore no resemblance to a normal Commission DG; and successive presidencies had to receive training on how to deal with Council structures and working methods. Moreover, member states assuming the presidency frequently availed themselves of the opportunity to table legislative initiatives in order to demonstrate political 'action', but in doing so failed to take due account of the general interest (as the Commission does when it takes initiatives in the first pillar) and often simply replicated internal legislation.

By the mid-1990s, the third pillar was being severely criticised by commentators, the European Parliament and some politicians for not having met with the expectations that the draftsmen of Maastricht had placed upon it. Around 1995/1996, the third pillar slowly began to yield some results. The Europol Convention had finally been adopted, as had several conventions on judicial cooperation in criminal matters (protection of the financial interests of the Community, simplified extradition and extradition). Moreover, the legal position of joint actions was becoming clearer and that instrument was even used to approximate criminal law (racism and xenophobia, corruption). By then, however, the decision to launch a new intergovernmental conference had already been taken and it was clear that a revision of the third pillar would be one of the major topics.

The criticisms levelled at the decision-making structures had to some extent been answered. The five-level decision-making structure had been reduced to four levels when, at the beginning of the 1997 Luxembourg presidency, it was decided no longer to convene the steering groups. During the two previous presidencies (Italy and Ireland), the steering groups had been infrequently convened and had gradually lost their role in the decision-making process, thus strengthening the role of the K4 committee. Moreover, the member states had posted JHA counsellors to Brussels, and this began, slowly but surely, to have an impact on decision-making by smoothing out queries from capitals and through the advice they gave to Coreper and the K4 committee.

At the same time, a process was initiated that would have a thorough impact on decision-making and on the substance of the work, in particular as regards organised crime, but which would also spill over into other fields of the third pillar. This was the process that led to the setting up of the high level group on organised crime and the adoption, by the Amsterdam European Council in June 1997, of the action plan on organised crime.

The high level group on organised crime (1996/1997)

In the summer of 1996 two events shaped the future of the third pillar more than any others: the killing of an Irish journalist, Veronica Guerin, who had specialised in reporting on drugs-related crime; and the kidnapping, abuse and murder of several children and young girls in Belgium, allegedly by a paedophile gang (the so-called 'Dutroux affair'), as a result of which more than 300,000 Belgian demonstrators took to the streets of Brussels in August 1996, coinciding with the start of the Irish presidency. The Belgian government deposited a draft joint action on child pornography and sexual exploitation of children at the meeting of the K4 committee on 9 September in Dublin. In parallel, the Irish presidency pledged that it would make organised crime a priority of its presidency.

Negotiations progressed extremely rapidly on the joint action and were mostly carried out by JHA counsellors, by the K4 committee and in Coreper. Political agreement was reached at the December JHA Council, which effectively meant that negotiations on such a complex instrument had taken just two and a half months. At the same time, the Irish presidency prepared an extra meeting of the K4 committee devoted to the development of the action against organised crime. This document contained several proposals that would be implemented over the following years. It was submitted to the European Council on 16 December 1996 in Dublin. The presidency conclusions called on the IGC to work to reach agreement on a strengthened capacity for action in relation to visas, asylum, immigration, the crossing of external borders, the fight against drugs and international crime including terrorism, offences against children and trafficking in persons; 'Europol should have operative powers working in conjunction with the national authorities to this end. These issues are of the most serious concern to citizens in all member states and the Union must be given the means to act effectively in these areas.' On organised crime, the Dublin European Council decided to create a high level group to draw up a comprehensive action plan containing specific recommendations, including realistic timetables for carrying out the work.

Contrary to what had happened in Maastricht, it was clear that the ministries of foreign affairs had realised the need for involving more closely ministries of justice and home affairs in matters falling within their competence (while of course the ministries of foreign affairs jealously guarded their prerogatives in the IGC), since otherwise implementation problems would result. For the first time, a group outside the IGC would de facto have close formal links with the IGC and, as it in practice turned out, it was the high level group that negotiated the JHA treaty provisions, in particular in relation to the sensitive issue of Europol and its role. It was also clear that the JHA area would become one of the most challenging issues for the ongoing IGC, and one where clear results would have to be produced.

The high level group began its work during the early stages of the Dutch presidency and met surprisingly little (only six formal meetings were held, of which the first three were devoted to discussions of a general nature and on issues of structure). Several member states sent high level representatives, such as senior police commissioners, who did not normally participate in Council meetings. The group would report directly to the Amsterdam European Council, but was also tasked with drafting a letter on its results by April 1997 so that these could be taken into account by the IGC. The group had to work under considerable time pressure. In making its proposals it was somewhat detached from the ministries of justice and home affairs.

Much of its time was devoted to the drafting of 15 'political guidelines' that
would be adopted as the European Council's own political orientations, and
less time was devoted to the 30 detailed recommendations that, at the end
of the day, had most importance in the implementation of the action plan.
The practical drafting of the action plan was carried out by the Council secretariat, in liaison with the presidency, on the basis of the discussions in the
high level group and preparatory documents. The action plan was submitted to a special meeting of the JHA Council on 28 April, and then adopted
by consensus by the Amsterdam European Council.

The action plan, which was the end result of the high level group, was not
so visible at the time, since the focus of attention was the Amsterdam Treaty,
but it is fair to say that the action plan was an instrument as important as the
Tampere or Seville European Council conclusions for developing the third
pillar action on organised crime and beyond. It is clear that a number of the
30 recommendations of the group go far beyond the remit of organised
crime and that the plan is in fact a complete work programme on judicial
and police cooperation in criminal matters (see box 6.1 below).

By the time the high level group had been set up, the IGC had already

Box 6.1: *The action plan on organised crime*

---

1.   An approach to the phenomenon of organised crime
This section contained recommendations on coordinating the fight against organised
crime at national level and collecting and analysing data. A pre-accession pact on
organised crime was drafted for the candidate states. Cooperation was to be developed
with the USA, Russia and Ukraine.

2.   Prevention of organised crime
This set out a comprehensive policy against corruption, public tender procedures were
examined, the issue of legal persons and their involvement was examined, the use of
structural funds was contemplated and fraud was analysed. The Falcone financing
programme on organised crime was set up.

3.   Legal instruments, scope, implementation
Ratification of specific conventions was targeted, a mutual evaluation mechanism was
set up (this was a considerable novelty in the third pillar where no mechanism for
evaluation of implementation existed), a joint action on defining the offence of participation in criminal organisation was adopted, the issue of the liability of legal persons
and fraud and counterfeiting of payment instruments was addressed.

**4.   Practical cooperation between police, judicial authorities and customs in the
fight against organised crime**
Central contact points were established for certain issues, multidisciplinary teams were
set up, the European judicial network was established and a specific Council working
party (the multidisciplinary group on organised crime – the MDG) was set up.

**5.   Development of a fully-fledged Europol and extension of Europol's mandate
and tasks**
This mainly set out provisions on Europol which were to become part of the
Amsterdam Treaty.

6.   Organised crime and money
This section addressed issues relating in particular to money laundering and confisca-
tion of proceeds from crime.

come a long way in its deliberations on JHA, and a major reform which some considered unnecessary was underway. By 31 April 1999, the day before the entry into force of the Treaty of Amsterdam, the JHA Council had adopted 335 measures (conclusions, decisions, recommendations, resolutions, joint actions, common positions and conventions) of which 125 could be considered to be of a substantive nature (de Lobkowicz, 2002), 86 of an original character and 39 to be implementing measures for existing decisions. For an organisation that had begun work on 1 November 1993, this was not a bad quantitative result. In terms of quality, however, the result was more nuanced as, mainly due to the unanimity rule, there was always a tendency to strive for the lowest common denominator. However, a number of achievements were made already under the Maastricht regime, primarily in police and judicial cooperation and combat against organised crime, and should not be underestimated. Progress on asylum and migration was slower.

Amsterdam (1997)

Much of the Amsterdam IGC debate was about whether or to what extent JHA matters should be incorporated into the EC Treaty or remain as a separate 'pillar' of the TEU. The report of the Westendorp reflection group set up to prepare the IGC showed clearly that the opinion of member states was still divided, in particular on how to deal with abolition of internal border controls, decision-making procedures, involvement of the European Parliament, the role of the Court of Justice and on the extent to which parts of the third pillar should be incorporated into the EC Treaty. Two main tendencies emerged during the negotiations: those who preferred the continuation of negotiations and decision-making strongly 'intergovernmental' in formal character, and those who wanted a further extension of the Community method and an enlarged role for the EU's institutions. The Amsterdam compromise led to an extremely complicated legal and institutional arrangement. For an explanation of the decision-making structures in Title IV, see below. Box 6.2 summarises the main features of the changes agreed in the Treaty of Amsterdam.

The integration of Schengen and the creation of the mixed committee (COMIX) procedure involving Norway and Iceland changed considerably the legal framework and how the Council had to operate in all Schengen related questions. Owing to the opposition of the UK and Ireland to the abolition of internal border controls, these two member states obtained an opt-out of all measures concerning free movement of persons. Under the protocol integrating the Schengen *acquis* into the framework of the European Union, the Council decided by unanimity on the legal basis for the *acquis,* and it did so for everything except the Schengen Information System (SIS) which remained therefore in the third pillar. The Court of Justice became competent for the entire Schengen *acquis* in accordance with the rules relevant to Titles IV and VI, something which was not the case hitherto. This aspect of the integration of the Schengen *acquis* is often forgotten but must be said to represent considerable progress by the Amsterdam negotiations . The Court of Justice has also had occasion to adjudicate a case relating to the Schengen *acquis* where the Court took a very

Box 6.2: *Main features of the changes agreed in the Treaty of Amsterdam*

- The objective of the creation of an Area of Freedom, Security and Justice (AFSJ) was laid down in the treaty.

- Asylum, immigration and judicial cooperation in civil matters were brought to the first pillar in Title IV whereas police and judicial cooperation in criminal matters remained in Title VI.

- The Commission's right of initiative was generalised to include also police and judicial cooperation in criminal matters.

- The entire Schengen *acquis* was incorporated into the Union which had as a consequence that Norway and Iceland participate in meetings of the Council and its subordinate bodies when it acts as a mixed committee, although Norway and Iceland do not take part in the decision-making, only in the discussions and decision-shaping. (It also meant that the Council's secretariat was reinforced through the integration of the Schengen secretariat.)

- Consultation of the European Parliament became mandatory.

- New legally binding instruments, similar to directives and regulations, but called 'framework decisions' and 'decisions', were instituted in what remained in the third pillar; so-called 'joint action' in the third pillar was abolished.

- The Court of Justice was given the power in general to hear cases concerning requests for preliminary rulings in relation to most member states and the member states were entitled to bring proceedings before the Court of Justice in relation to incorrect implementation of framework decisions and decisions. (This power has never been used, but it is possible that the application of the European arrest warrant may change the situation. Several requests for preliminary rulings concerning third pillar subjects, *ne bis in idem*, have however been made to the Court.)

- The arrangements relating to financing by the Community of actions in the third pillar changed so that Community financing became the rule.

- Conventions would enter into force after half the member states had ratified them, and the Council, when adopting a convention, would set a date for the beginning of internal ratification procedures.

---

progressive stance in relation to the issue of *ne bis in idem* (joined cases C 187/01 and C 385/01; two other cases, C-469/03 and C-493, are currently pending) and noted that: 'In those circumstances, whether the *ne bis in idem* principle enshrined in article 54 of the CISA (i.e., the Schengen Convention) is applied to procedures whereby further prosecution is barred (regardless of whether a court is involved) or to judicial decisions, there is a necessary implication that the Member States have mutual trust in their criminal justice systems and that each of them recognises the criminal law in force in the other Member States even when the outcome would be different if its own national law were applied.'

The handling of Schengen matters is a good example of 'variable geometry' in the Council, with thirteen member states participating fully, the United Kingdom and Ireland enjoying an opt-out (but having opted in to a large extent into those measures not linked with border controls), Norway and Iceland participating in the discussions, and Denmark having a special position whereby the measures adopted under title IV TEC are not considered to be Community law in respect of Denmark but, rather, public international law in the classical sense. This means that the measures adopted in so far as Denmark is concerned do not have the same legal standing as ordinary Community law. As regards the Danish situation in respect of police and judicial cooperation in criminal matters, Denmark de facto participates fully in all decisions after the agreement of the Danish Parliament, which has to approve every measure decided by the Council.

As far as Norway and Iceland are concerned, there are two agreements defining arrangements for the COMIX procedure at the level of ministers, senior officials and at expert level. Through this procedure (which is chaired both at the level of ambassadors and ministers alternately by the Union – i.e., by the presidency – for six months and by Norway or Iceland for six months). Norway and Iceland participate and freely express their opinion in all discussions concerning questions which are considered to be a development of Schengen.

However, determining what is and is not Schengen development is not always easy and may imply a good deal of discussion both at the level of working groups and in Coreper. For instance, when the Commission proposed the European arrest warrant, it considered that the proposal was a development of Schengen. (The same is true for the proposal on a European evidence warrant adopted by the Commission on 14 November 2003.) However, the presidency and the Council secretariat did not consider this to be the case, and the document was sent out without the COMIX code that normally indicates that an issue should be discussed under the mixed committee procedures foreseen in the agreements with Norway and Iceland. The issue was finally settled by Coreper, but in a way that proposed a negotiation on the inclusion of Norway and Iceland into the 'mechanism' of the European arrest warrant without, however, necessarily including all of its elements. It should also be noted that the ultimate recourse if Norway or Iceland cannot accept a decision by the Council is that the Schengen agreements are considered to have been denounced and that Norway and Iceland no longer participate in the Schengen cooperation (the so-called 'guillotine' clause).

The Schengen *acquis* has been applied in its entirety by the new member states since 1 May 2004. Under the Schengen acquis, the abolition of border controls at the internal borders may occur only after a satisfactory evaluation has been carried out by the member states belonging to the Schengen area. This evaluation consists in sending teams of experts to the borders of the new member states and checking how border controls are actually carried out.

From the point of view of the working of the Council, the integration of the Schengen *acquis* and its secretariat was an enormous task but also served as a welcome pretext for further rationalisation in the AFSJ. In fact, many of the working parties in the Council duplicated Schengen working groups, to the point that two groups (one in the Council and one in the Schengen structures) often existed on the same subject or at least dealt partially with exactly the same topics. The integration of Schengen enabled Coreper to halve the number of working parties to 27 and, at a later stage, to further rationalise work so that the number of preparatory bodies working in the JHA sector is currently 21 (see below).

Amsterdam served as a catalyst for further development of the AFSJ, and the drive that had begun with the high level group on organised crime continued. Although the member states retained the right to make proposals for five years in the areas of asylum and immigration and judicial cooperation in civil matters, de facto the Commission increasingly exercised that right. During the Maastricht era, the policy of the Swedish Commissioner Anita Gradin was not to take initiatives in the area but gradually to gain the confidence of the member states. The next Commissioner, Antonio Vitorino, sought to exercise due Commission influence. This meant that Commission proposals were appropriately prepared and reflected perceived common interests. However, in the area of asylum and immigration, blockages remained in the senior Strategic Committee on Immigration, Frontiers and Asylum (SCIFA) due to the differences in policies between member states and the sensitive nature of the discussions.

During the Amsterdam 'regime' – that is, from 1 May 1999 until the 1 February 2003 entry into force of the Treaty of Nice – the JHA Council passed 500 measures, including 26 regulations (asylum immigration and civil law), nine directives (mostly in the field of asylum/immigration), 29 decisions under article 34 (setting up Eurojust, CEPOL, various networks, etc), 15 framework decisions (harmonisation of criminal law), three common positions and 94 other decisions (negotiating mandates, decisions on signature, etc); 22 resolutions, 15 recommendations and 42 conclusions. It further approved 240 reports, action plans, and took other types of more administrative decisions in 240 cases. The activity of the Council in this field nearly doubled in 2002 and 2003 compared with 1999 and 2000. In 1999, the Council took some 70 decisions and the figure was roughly the same the following year. In 2001, the figure had increased to nearly 100 and in the following two years to about 140 – a clear indication of increased use of the new instruments asked for at Tampere.

A few figures demonstrate the impact the inclusion of civil law and asylum/immigration in the EC treaty had on the Council's activities. Whereas very few – just 23 – decisions were taken in the 1999-2000 period, over the next two years, once the role of the Commission had been enhanced, the figure rose to 67. The figure for 2003 was 51, thus illustrating the increased political pressure on the asylum/immigration sector in particular, with ten regulations and four directives adopted in 2002-2003. The extent of the vast programme of approximation of criminal law is illustrated by the fact that, of the 15 framework decisions adopted in the entire period, 12 were adopted between 2001 and 2003. Regarding police cooperation, the high figures for non-binding decisions are noteworthy; most of the binding decisions, meanwhile, concerned the setting up of networks. A high number of reports and budgetary decisions concerning Europol have also been adopted. These are reflected in the substantive number of decisions that have been taken in the police sector. Whether they actually improve police cooperation in the EU is another matter. Unsurprisingly, customs cooperation, with its focus on practical results rather than papers, has made less statistical impact.

Tampere (1999)

The implementation of the Amsterdam Treaty was managed mainly during the 1998 Austrian and UK presidencies. The working group structure of the Council needed to be reformed, the successor of the K4 committee – the article 36 committee (commonly referred to as 'CATS' – Comité de l'article trente-six) – could no longer work both in the first and the third pillar, the Schengen structures needed to be integrated, the follow-up of the high level group on organised crime had to be taken forward and preparations had to be undertaken for ensuring a smooth transition from the old Maastricht regime to the considerably different Amsterdam regime and the beginning of the creation of the AFSJ.

One of the consequences of this work was the drafting during the Austrian presidency of a new action plan – the so-called 'Vienna Action Plan', since it was to be adopted by the Vienna European Council. This action plan, which was drafted mainly in CATS and SCIFA, had a relatively low level of ambition – a mixture of ongoing work, long-term aims and short term goals, ad hoc actions and general statements, possible action ('the Council shall study, examine, take into account, give attention to, discuss, consider, begin consideration of, etc') – in short, an instrument typical of intergovernmental negotiation. Nobody was happy with it. It was therefore decided at the Vienna European Council that a special European Council should be held devoted entirely to the AFSJ. This was only the second time that such a special European Council had been held on a single subject, bearing witness to the growing importance of the JHA Council. Again, the European Council showed that it had to step in to break the deadlocks that were habitual already in the area.

The presidency conclusions were agreed on 16 October 1999 and contained the so-called 'ten Tampere milestones' (see box 6.3), where a full programme was laid down for the implementation of the AFSJ until 1 May 2004. Often forgotten, but equally important, was the Tampere European Council's decision laying down the procedures for adopting the EU's Charter of fundamental rights. The importance of the Tampere conclusions cannot be overestimated. They were often referred to as 'the bible' by insiders. Every word, every comma, had been scrutinised and agreed at the highest level. A number of important actions had been decided and simply had to be undertaken – the European arrest warrant was decided (at least as a principle – it is another matter that its application was considerably extended as a result of the events of '9/11'), the principle of mutual recognition was enshrined as a 'cornerstone' of judicial cooperation in both civil and criminal matters, a 'common' asylum and migration policy should be forged, a plan for harmonisation of criminal law was adopted, the setting up of Eurojust was decided and it was agreed that stronger external action in the area should be taken. Tampere was a success; a balanced, measured but ambitious response was given to the expectations of heads of state and government and citizens alike.

The European Council's conclusions stated that it was: 'determined to develop the Union as an area of freedom, security and justice by making full use of the possibilities offered by the Treaty of Amsterdam. The European Council sends a strong political message to reaffirm the importance of this objective and has agreed on a number of policy orientations and priorities which will speedily make this area a reality.' It went on to state that: 'The European Council will place and maintain this objective at the very top of the political agenda. It will keep under constant review progress made towards implementing the necessary measures and meeting the deadlines set by the Treaty of Amsterdam, the Vienna Action Plan and the present conclusions. The Commission is invited to make a proposal for an appropriate scoreboard to that end. The European Council underlines the importance of ensuring the necessary transparency and of keeping the European Parliament regularly informed. It will hold a full debate assessing progress at its December meeting in 2001.'

Box 6.3: *The Tampere milestones*

A. A COMMON EU ASYLUM AND MIGRATION POLICY

I. Partnership with countries of origin
A comprehensive approach to migration was agreed, to the effect that political, human rights and development issues in countries and regions of origin and transit should be developed with greater coherence of internal and external policies of the Union, and with partnerships being established with third countries.

II. A Common European Asylum System
The Union and member states undertook to work towards establishing or finalising, inter alia:
  – a common European asylum system and common standards for a fair and efficient asylum procedure;
  – common minimum conditions of reception of asylum seekers, and
  – the approximation of rules on the recognition and content of the refugee status;
  – uniform status throughout the Union for those who are granted asylum;
  – temporary protection for displaced persons;
  – Eurodac (the system for the identification of asylum seekers).

III. Fair treatment of third country nationals
Third country nationals should be given rights and obligations comparable to those of EU citizens, by enhancing non-discrimination in economic, social and cultural life and developing measures against racism and xenophobia. Under this heading the following is foreseen:
  – approximation of national legislation on the conditions for admission and residence of third country nationals;
  – a person, who has resided legally in a member state for a period of time and who holds a long-term residence permit, should be granted in that member state a set of uniform rights;
  – long-term legally resident third country nationals should be offered the opportunity to obtain the nationality of the Member State in which they are resident.

IV. Management of migration flows

In order to achieve more efficient management of migration flows at all their stages:

– information campaigns should be developed, on the actual possibilities for legal immigration, and for the prevention of all forms of trafficking in human beings; and,

– a common active policy on visas and false documents;

– illegal immigration should be tackled and severe sanctions against trafficking in human beings should be laid down and rights of victims catered for;

– the Council was invited to conclude readmission agreements or to include standard clauses in other agreements between the European Community and relevant third countries or groups of countries.

B. A GENUINE EUROPEAN AREA OF JUSTICE

V. Better access to justice in Europe

This would be ensured by:

– An information campaign and publication of appropriate 'user guides';

– The establishment of an easily accessible information system should be maintained and up-dated;

– Minimum standards ensuring an adequate level of legal aid throughout the Union as well as special common procedural rules for simplified and accelerated cross-border litigation on small consumer and commercial claims, as well as maintenance claims, and on uncontested claims should be set up;

– Common minimum standards should be set for multilingual forms or documents;

– Minimum standards should be drawn up on the protection of the victims of crime.

VI. Mutual recognition of judicial decisions

The principle of mutual recognition should become the cornerstone of judicial cooperation in both civil and criminal matters within the Union. In particular:

– measures should be taken to enable the recognition and enforcement of a decision or judgement in the requested State;

– intermediate procedures should be abolished;

– this could be accompanied by the setting of minimum standards on specific aspects of civil procedural law. Formal extradition procedure should be abolished among the member states as far as persons are concerned who are fleeing from justice after having been finally sentenced, and replaced by a simple transfer of such persons. Consideration should also be given to fast track extradition procedures;

– the principle of mutual recognition should also apply to pre-trial orders, evidence lawfully gathered by one member state's authorities should be admissible before the courts of other member states.

VII. Greater convergence in civil law

New procedural legislation in cross-border cases (e.g. provisional measures, taking of evidence, orders for money payment and time limits) should be prepared.

C. A UNIONWIDE FIGHT AGAINST CRIME

VIII. Preventing crime at the level of the Union
Integration of crime prevention aspects into actions against crime as well as further development of national crime prevention programmes should be made. The exchange of best practices should be developed, a Community funded programme should be decided. The first priorities for this cooperation could be juvenile, urban and drug-related crime.

IX. Stepping up cooperation against crime
The European Council called for:
– joint investigative teams to be set up without delay. The rules to be set up should allow representatives of Europol to participate in such teams in a support capacity;
– a European Police Chiefs operational Task Force to be established;
– Europol to be provided with the necessary support and resources. It should be authorised to ask Member States to initiate, conduct or coordinate investigations or to create joint investigative teams in certain areas of crime;
– Eurojust to be set up to reinforce the fight against organised crime;
– a European Police College for the training of senior law enforcement officials to be established;
– efforts to agree on common definitions, incriminations and sanctions to be focused in the first instance on a limited number of sectors of particular relevance.

X. Special action against money laundering
The measures decided include:
– implementation by member states of the money laundering directive, the 1990 Strasbourg Convention and the financial action task force recommendations in all their dependent territories;
– improved transparency of financial transactions and ownership of corporate entities and expedited exchange of information between the existing financial intelligence units (FIU) regarding suspicious transactions;
– approximation of criminal law and procedures on money laundering;
– extending the competence of Europol to money laundering in general, regardless of the type of offence from which the laundered proceeds originate;
– Developing common standards to prevent the use of corporations and entities registered outside the jurisdiction of the Union for hiding of criminal proceeds and money laundering.

Finally, the Tampere conclusions also contained recommendations for stronger external action of the Union in the JHA area.

The events of 11 September 2001

Immediately after October 1999 the institutions began their implementation of the Tampere milestones: the Commission began work on the proposals for a European arrest warrant and a framework decision with the aim of defining terrorist offences; the Council secretariat convened the future Portuguese, French, Swedish and Belgian presidencies to begin drafting the discussion papers and (later) the initiative of the 'group of four presidencies' on Eurojust. Attempts were made during the Portuguese presidency to lift out article 13 of the Convention on Mutual Assistance in Criminal Matters so as to speed up the implementation of the Tampere decisions to set up joint investigative teams on terrorism, drugs and trafficking in human beings; a new protocol on provision of banking information was approved during the French Presidency; a crime prevention network was set up under the Swedish presidency, and so on. However, the negotiations were slow and tedious and the results were relatively unambitious, particularly in the criminal law area and as regards police cooperation.

The European institutions reacted quickly to the events of 11 September 2001. The Commission advanced by one week its proposals on the European arrest warrant and the framework decision on terrorism and submitted them to Coreper on 19 September. The Belgian presidency and the Council secretariat drafted an extensive action plan, which was to become the EU's 'roadmap' on antiterrorism measures. This action plan was submitted to a special meeting of CATS on 18 September, to Coreper the following day and to the extra JHA Council on 20 September. On 21 September, the European Council adopted elements of that comprehensive action plan as its own, and inter alia decided that the JHA Council should 'define the modalities' of the European arrest warrant at its meeting of 6-7 December. There was no longer any question of agreeing only the main principles of the arrest warrant.

The roadmap illustrates the depth and breadth of the Union action against terrorism. In principle, all of this action was discussed and decided within the space of ten days in September 2001. It illustrates how the JHA Council can act when there is political pressure and willingness. Agreeing the European arrest warrant (in the space of only two-and-a-half months) represents one of the most significant and radical pieces of legislation ever adopted by the European Community or Union in terms of driving forward the process of European integration. The warrant epitomises the aspirations of the Union to create a genuine judicial area, where judicial decisions circulate freely and where full faith and trust (as under the United States' constitution) is placed in judicial decisions of another member state. The previous extradition system was based on a concept of cooperation and a request from a requesting state – the new system of mutual recognition is based on trust and on the proposition that a decision that has already been taken in a member state, will be immediately recognised and executed in another state. The warrant also got rid of political interference in essentially judicial decisions and of obstacles to surrendering own nationals. The very essence of the warrant is the abolition of double criminality for some 32 categories of offences, which implies a high level of trust in other member states' legal systems, coupled with a high degree of harmonisation.

The events of 11 September provided yet another fillip to Union action in the third pillar, in the same way as the 'Dutroux affair' had done in the field of sexual exploitation of children or the death of fifty-eight Chinese in a sealed container lorry in the UK had done in the field of trafficking in human beings. Its impact was of course greater and more sustained, due to the magnitude and character of the attacks. The fact that a very important policy element – the EU's relations with the USA – was involved also contributed to the fact that the '9/11' effect lasted longer and had a greater impact on policy and decision-making in the JHA area.

The changes in Council decision-making were little short of amazing. As noted above, there had been a failed attempt during the 2000 Portuguese presidency to 'lift out', in the form of a framework decision, article 13 of the Mutual Assistance Convention, with a view to facilitating the implementation of the Tampere conclusions on the setting up of joint investigative teams. In Coreper on 3 October 2001 the same file was discussed, the scope of action was enlarged and the draft was agreed in the space of three minutes! The Eurojust draft, which had been discussed during 32 meeting days at the level of the working group, had 14 contentious points, each of which would have taken lengthy discussions by ministers under normal circumstances. Coreper and Council solved them on 5 and 6 December 2001 after rapid negotiation. Doubts had been expressed previously about the use of articles 24 and 38 of the treaty in relation to negotiation of agreements on extradition and mutual assistance in criminal matters, although the treaty expressly foresaw this possibility. It suddenly became easy for the Council to discuss and adopt a negotiating mandate during the 2002 Spanish presidency (and the treaties between the EU and the USA were signed later on 25 June 2003, thus reaffirming that the Union on its own had become a player also in this field and confirming that the Union has legal personality with treaty-making powers).

Ahead of the March 2004 European Council, the secretary-general/high representative appointed Gijs de Vries, a former Dutch junior home office minister, as EU coordinator on counter-terrorism. Working inside the Council secretariat, and responsible to the secretary-general/high representative, his brief is to coordinate action in terrorism matters inside the secretariat and between different Council bodies, as well as liaising with member states. This appointment was made in the context of work on preparing further proposals under the European Security Strategy agreed at the December European Council. Because of the complex nature and the wide array of instruments involved in combatting terrorism (which cut across many areas of policy competence), coordination of work is a major issue. Moreover, since responsibility for combatting terrorism lies primarily with the member states, the Union as such can and should intervene only where it can offer demonstrated added value or effectiveness.

At the time of writing, the Council is experiencing yet another flurry of activity in the wake of the tragic events in Madrid on 11 March 2004. A special JHA Council met on 19 March to discuss implementation of existing measures against terrorism, accelerate implementation of decisions already taken and consider new action. The European Council adopted a declaration and action plan on 25 March. This is yet another example of how the Union can act swiftly when the political will exists.

Nice (2001)

The Treaty of Nice did not change much in the JHA area. An extension of recourse to QMV was foreseen in some areas under title IV TEC and some adjustments were made in relation to article 24 TEU to clarify the status of international agreements negotiated by the Union. The biggest novelty was that Eurojust was introduced into the treaty together with the European Judicial Network. An attempt by the Commission to include a provision on a European public prosecutor was however rejected by the European Council.

The Seville European Council (2002)

As noted above, the negotiations under Maastricht and Amsterdam had been difficult in the fields of asylum, immigration and border controls, although the Commission had rapidly confirmed itself as the driving force in these areas by the use of the Community method. The Commission had taken a number of initiatives but the Council was slow to follow suit. The work had been concentrated on visas, free movement of Union citizens (Schengen) and on protection against disruptive migratory flows. Less discussed were issues relating to legal immigration, integration and the status of long-term residents. The member states acted as if their frontiers still existed physically, and as if they could decide autonomously on their immigration policies, whereas there were of course no longer physical frontiers for most of them. The European Councils in Seville in 2002 and Thessaloniki in 2003 decided on measures to combat illegal immigration, on the gradual introduction of the coordinated, integrated management of external borders, on integrating immigration policy into the Union's relations with third countries and on speeding up legislative work on the framing of a common policy on asylum and immigration, and set very specific deadlines for the Council's work. While the heat had largely been taken off the third pillar, issues relating to title IV were now at the political forefront.

Structures of the JHA Council and how it works in practice

It is broadly true that 80% of the Council's 'decisions' are settled at working party level. This is not as surprising as it seems, because many of the measures adopted by the Council fall within the scope of decisions which in the national context would be taken by executive act or statutory instrument rather than as a legislative measure. The subjects treated and the high level of technical complexity would require an enormous amount of personal investment by ministers if they were in practice to decide collectively on all these matters. At national level the situation is in practice not so different in most member states. Although ministers or governments are, under national constitutions, those that formally take decisions, in practice it is often an individual minister or senior civil servant who takes certain decisions. There is therefore nothing illegitimate in translating this system to European level (although at European level, scrutiny is often much greater than at national level).

The Union's decision-making structures on JHA matters are complex, and complicated further because of the role and influence of national parliaments, the national sensitivities involved and the vigilance of civil society in general and civil liberties groups in particular. This complexity means that the sensitivities at national level have to a great extent been translated into an enormously complex decision-making structure of the Council, with a very top heavy reporting line where working parties are supposed to keep to largely technical matters. The reality is different, however, and a number of ostensibly highly political matters are finalised at working party level, although all decisions must formally be endorsed by the Council under part A of its agenda (see chapter 3).

As has been noted above, the integration of Schengen led to a large-scale rationalisation of the Council's structures. More than 54 working parties were rapidly reduced to 27. Successive adjustments have been carried out and the official number of working parties is now 21. The structure in 2004 is set out in figure 6.1.

In the field of justice, a great number of adjustments have been carried out, and the policy of setting up new working parties in response to every major new piece of draft legislation has been abandoned. Instead, it is the subject matter of discussion which is important and not the specific text. For instance, civil law cooperation has only one working party but works in reality in five or six different formations depending on the drafts under discussion. When it deals with general questions, usually at the level of senior officials, it meets as the 'civil law committee (general questions)' but when it discusses a specific project it meets, usually with a different chairperson, as the 'civil law committee (European enforcement order)', to take an example. This has meant that it has been possible in the justice field to focus more on the substance of the work rather than on the group itself. This in turn has had good effects on the management of the presidencies and the focus on the adopted action plans. It has also meant that, in the civil law field, there is no longer any fourth layer of decision-making, as the working parties now report direct to Coreper.

The rationalisation has been more difficult as regards the working parties attended by representatives from interior ministries, although there has been some adjustment. SCIFA has in practice worked as the equivalent of the CATS, although it has no treaty basis; SCIFA meets in the form of SCIFA (ordinary composition) and 'SCIFA+' with the composition of heads of frontier guards for discussing matters relating to the Union's frontiers. The reason for this arrangement is that Coreper has not wanted to set up a specific committee for that question, knowing well that it is easy to set up a new committee, but more difficult to abolish it.

Three groups have a horizontal remit – i.e., they do not report through either CATS or SCIFA. These are the collective evaluation working group (COLLEVAL), the horizontal working party on drugs (GHD) and the Schengen evaluation group (SCH-EVAL). (There are an unusual number of animals in the JHA area; to cite but two, *cheval* in French means 'horse', and CATS are also well known creatures. Senior policy makers are apparently not totally devoid of a sense of humour!) The multidisciplinary group on organised crime (MDG), which works horizontally with customs, police and judicial cooperation but may also according to its mandate specifically deal with first pillar matters, is one of the few Council working parties which has

Figure 6.1: *Council Preparatory structures in the JHA sector*

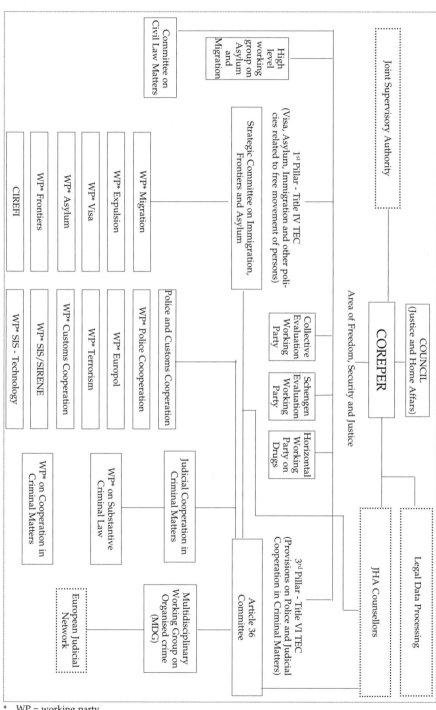

* WP = working party

been given real decision-making power by delegation from the Council. A joint action from 1997 designates it to be the holder of the power to adopt reports on evaluations in the field of organised crime following the mechanism of so-called 'peer-evaluation', whereby expert teams are sent out by the presidency to evaluate on the ground how member states are carrying out the fight against organised crime in practice. Three evaluation rounds have been carried out – mutual assistance in criminal matters, the fight against drugs, and information sharing among law enforcement agencies inside and among the member states and with Europol. The peer evaluation has become such an effective mechanism that it has been taken up in the draft constitutional treaty.

The European judicial network (EJN) in criminal matters (there is another EJN in civil matters, working under the auspices of the Commission) also has a special position. It is considered to be a Council working group for its internal working (it is run by the six-month presidency, meets under the Council's rules of procedure and is subject to the rules of convocation of Council working party meetings). The reality of the EJN is more complex, as it consists to a large extent of independent judicial authorities, designated by the member states as contact points under the Joint Action setting up the EJN. A practice has been developed by which the EJN meets regularly in the country holding the presidency and once a year on the Council premises in Brussels.

CIREFI is a centre for information of the member states and sometimes also third countries dealing with migratory flows in the field of immigration.

The legal data processing group deals with information exchange on development of new information technologies and legal data bases within the Union. It is one of the seven Council preparatory bodies chaired by the Council secretariat.

The JHA counsellors working party has no formal status. Its functions are purely preparatory but its real importance is hard to measure. It depends largely on the personal investment of the JHA counsellors in the applicable sector (title IV TEC, civil or asylum/immigration, title VI TEU, police, criminal or police) and may take on an important role, particularly if the counsellor of the presidency is a strong personality. The group reports both to CATS and to Coreper and has the double benefit (and sometimes the curse) of serving two masters: the ministry that sent the counsellor (and pays his/her salary) and the permanent representation/ministry of foreign affairs that gives it the diplomatic status and rank in the national administration. On certain occasions, the JHA counsellors have been known to solve questions where CATS, Coreper or the Council could not achieve a result because of the high level of technical complexity coupled with the political sensitivity of the file.

The advantage of the JHA counsellors is that they, like Coreper, are permanently based in Brussels, and that they know each other through numerous personal contacts which create, over time, trust. They also know the technical details of the subject as they follow the meetings of working parties. They are very closely linked with the national administrations through the SCIFA or CATS representative while at the same time having a very close link with the permanent representative through whom all preparations of the Council are made. It is often said that they negotiate more with their capitals than with Brussels. The quality and personal approach of the JHA counsellor is very important but that is not different in comparison to a normal working group. An additional advantage of the working of the JHA counsellors is that they do not require interpretation, with English and French normally used.

Most member states, realising the value of the JHA counsellors, have sent several counsellors specialising in the work of the different working groups and representing ministerial departments. For instance, Germany has about ten counsellors and France close to that number. Smaller member states have fewer, but it is usual to have at least four or five: one for civil law, one for criminal law, one for police cooperation and one or two for asylum/immigration.

The respective roles of CATS and SCIFA are similar, although they have a different legal basis. CATS is enshrined in the treaty whereas SCIFA was set up by Coreper decision under the Council's rules of procedure. This is slightly more comforting for CATS but, as the natural heir of K4 and the TREVI group of coordinators, it has never been able to assert itself against Coreper. At one point, there was some discussion about whether a 'Coreper III' dealing exclusively with justice and home affairs should be set up with Brussels-based representatives, but this idea failed to gain support, both because of resistance from Coreper II (permanent representatives, who feared the impact of further sectoral compartmentalisation in the Council) and the K4 coordinators themselves, since they for personal or other reasons did not see the advantage of having a permanent residence in Brussels. Instead, the K4 committee, and later CATS and SCIFA, became a senior committee subordinated to Coreper II, thus confirming the now classic four-tier JHA decision-making procedure.

Decision-making structures have always been a problem in the JHA area. Inevitably, where there are five levels of decision-making (as there were in the Maastricht structure), there will always be a tendency to push the decision to the next level. With four levels it is relatively difficult to take decisions at the lower level. In addition, the stultifying effect of unanimity on the negotiating dynamics means that working parties tend to refer diffi-cult problems up to SCIFA or CATS in the hope that they will agree, but those senior groups sometimes do not have the expertise to find the appro-priate solutions. This means that there is a tendency to arrive at the lowest common denominator or to push decision-making up to Coreper or Council also in questions that are not truly political. The result is that the Coreper agenda has become overburdened with a large number of unresolved items, many of which are not points which should normally be dealt with at that level.

Apart from the attempts to improve the working methods of the Council in general described elsewhere in this book, special attempts have also been made to improve decision-making within the JHA area. In particular the 2001 Swedish presidency sought to render more efficient the decision-making in the JHA area. The so-called 'Haga process' was launched after the name of the Swedish castle where the first meeting of the article 36 com-mittee was held to discuss reforms in this area. The process had some effect in terms of better coordination between the presidencies, better initiatives

taken by the member states and better use of working groups, but never led
to any real changes in the working of the JHA Council. However, ideas are
still circulating about radical changes in the number and structures of the
working groups with a view to focusing work better on the priorities of the
Council, in particular by reducing the number of preparatory bodies to ten.

How then does the Council work in practice when a proposal has been
made, either by the Commission or by a member state? The JHA Council is
not unlike most Council formations. Negotiations begin most often directly
in a working group, sometimes after having been presented at a higher
level. The presidency is the master of the agenda. The subject matter to be
discussed is put to the working group and the negotiations begin. Since
most of the questions are decided by unanimity, the negotiations are long
and complex; a 'normal' legislative proposal is often discussed over two or
three presidencies or more. Delegations hide their cards and tend not to
rush to compromise. Frequently, the delegation's negotiating aim is to
avoid changing its national law by ensuring that the proposed instrument is
compatible with that goal. But where, on occasion, a matter may be decided
by QMV, the negotiations become more rapid, the delegations seek quickly
to achieve a majority view and are in general more willing to disclose their
hand for that reason.

Where the issues have been considered sufficiently at a technical level, the
file, or at least some key aspects of it, is pushed to a higher level, CATS and
SCIFA, often with a view to deciding whether a specific issue should be
taken to the Council. If the file is very political, such as in the area of asylum
and immigration, the matter is taken quickly to Coreper/Council. Since the
JHA Council meets roughly once every two months and occasionally more
frequently, there are numerous occasions to deal with such questions rapidly.

Depending on the file, the European Parliament is consulted or sometimes involved in co-decision according to the treaty-ordained procedure.
Where consultation is mandatory, the European Parliament often has to be
reconsulted since many instruments are substantially changed in comparison with the original proposal. The European Parliament has in most cases
at least three months to give its opinion. When the Council has agreed politically (most often the terms 'agreed on a general approach' is used to indicate that the issue may still be under consideration in national parliaments)
there are often parliamentary scrutiny reservations pending. Such reservations may sometimes not be lifted for up to eighteen months or two years.
This is because the constitutional practice of some member states is such
that the legislation must be enacted in conformity with the Council act
before the parliamentary scrutiny reservation may be lifted. This sometimes
causes frustration in some member states since they may not be able to
submit the proposal to parliament before the Council act has been formally
adopted.

When the last parliamentary scrutiny reservation has been lifted, the
working party of legal linguists ensures that all translations are legally identical to the 'model version', which in nearly all cases will be the French or
the English text. This is a very delicate matter in some cases as the choice of
words is often crucial and it is very difficult to render the exact meaning of
complex legal texts in twenty languages. But the text is a text of the Council

and not of the member state concerned, so the Council must take the ultimate responsibility. It should also not be forgotten that, for instance,
'Swedish Swedish' may not always be 'Finnish Swedish' and that thus several member states are interested in a particular language version.

The Council secretariat

In the JHA sector, the Council secretariat has played a role which is mark-
edly different from that of other areas of the secretariat. Apart from the
normal role of note-taking and reporting, advising on procedures and being
the 'honest broker' and 'institutional memory', the Council secretariat has in
this particular field played the role of a motor, legal drafter and initiative-
taker. There are many reasons for this.

First, when member states began to cooperate within the framework of
the Council, they did as they always had done within the framework of
'normal' intergovernmental cooperation within the Council of Europe, the
OECD and the UN; i.e., they expected the secretariat to play a driving role
in producing and drafting texts. Ministries of justice and, in particular, of
interior had little or no experience of the working of the Council and the
experts that went to Brussels often had experience in meetings in other
international fora. In such fora, and in particular in the Council of Europe,
it is often the secretariat that draws up the first text of a draft convention and
it is often on that basis that discussions take place. It was therefore easy for
the experts from the outset to accept that the secretariat took on greater
responsibility than would be the case in the first pillar, where the
Commission has the sole right of initiative. (It is often, incidentally, the same
persons that attend meetings in the Council of Europe and the EU.)

Secondly, as with most international relations, the role of individuals is
important. The Council secretariat (at the time only three persons) in the
JHA area was initially attached to the secretary-general, but it was then
established as a separate directorate general, under its first director-general,
Charles Elsen. Elsen already had substantial experience as a Rhodes
Coordinator within the TREVI structures and he was a former chairman of
the European committee on crime problems (CDPC) of the Council of
Europe. At the time of writing, it should be noted that Elsen, a Luxembourg
national having been the closest counsellor to the minister of justice, has
thirty-seven years of experience of cooperation within the JHA area. In
addition, another former chair of the CDPC was chosen as the director of the
legal service responsible for the JHA area; a former head of cabinet of the
previous Belgian minister of justice was chosen as the director of DG H; and
a former judge and administrator for ten years from the Council of Europe
was chosen as head of division. All this, coupled with the personal qualifications of staff already in place, meant that the member states' administrations could count on the Council secretariat to give sound advice legally and
politically and that personal engagement and quality in the drafting would
be guaranteed.

Thirdly, given that the Commission's right of initiative was curtailed
during the Maastricht regime, and the fact also that the Commission began
with a very limited staff as a 'task force' attached to the Commission's general secretariat, the member states did not look to the Commission as a

motor, but rather with suspicion. Instead, the member states looked in the direction of the presidency and noted that the Council secretariat was working closely with the presidency. In that sense, the Council secretariat became a permanent institutional memory being able to ensure a driving force and coordination over time between various initiatives.

Fourthly, the right of initiative at the beginning, although theoretically lying with the Commission in some areas, was mostly exercised in practice by the presidency (or, in more exceptional cases, by a member state), in many cases assisted by the Council secretariat (sometimes described as 'the Brussels branch of the presidency').

An example may illustrate the role of the Council secretariat. The idea of setting up Eurojust was born within the Council secretariat and was floated in a paper that was proposed by the Irish presidency in 1996. However, the idea was premature, even in its modest form, and could not be realised until the preparations for Tampere began, in particular before and at the meeting of the ministers of justice in September 1999. At that meeting, Eurojust was officially proposed after intensive contacts between the Council secretariat and the German and French ministers, and found its way into the conclusions of the Tampere European Council. After Tampere, the Council secretariat worked together with the Portuguese presidency and the three incoming presidencies to draft all discussion papers on the detailed shaping of Eurojust and on the draft 'instrument' that would be proposed by the group of four presidencies. At a final meeting between the four CATS coordinators at the French permanent representation the text for a Council decision was presented and discussed. That text had been drawn up entirely by the Council secretariat on the basis of the discussions in CATS and among the four delegations. The text was amended to take account of the views expressed and was officially submitted by the four governments taking the initiative. At the same time, an initiative was prepared for the setting up of the provisional Eurojust unit and discussed and agreed at the informal meeting of the ministers of justice held in France. The Council secretariat also drafted that initiative and was actively involved in the negotiations between the delegations concerned.

The role of the Council secretariat has changed since the first days of Maastricht. It is clear that its role was greater in the beginning, while the Commission was building up its resources and expertise. Moreover, as the questions concerning asylum, immigration and civil law cooperation moved over to the first pillar in the Amsterdam Treaty, the institutional role of the Commission changed, it began to affirm its right of initiative more, although formally shared with the member states, and the member states have become used to working with the European Commission. In what remained in the third pillar, the member states continued to keep the Commission at arm's length for a few more years (and consequently turned to the Council secretariat) but gradually became used to working with the Commission in a more 'peaceful' climate built on trust and comprehension for each others' roles and constraints. The Commission also began to use its right of initiative more frequently and has become an important player in negotiations, in particular in the person of Commissioner Antonio Vitorino, whose personality set an imprint on the JHA Council.

Justice and home affairs is now one of the largest directorates-general in the Council, with some sixty persons working within it. This is partly explained by the fact that its role is different than in those sectors where the Commission is the driving force, and partly by the fact that the Council secretariat is carrying out certain tasks which are atypical for the Council, such as the missions concerning evaluation to the member states which are normally carried out by national experts seconded to the secretariat for periods of 2-4 years by the member states. These national experts may be senior policemen, frontier experts, judges or prosecutors. They work in the field of Schengen evaluations, terrorism, organised crime and evaluation of candidate countries, fields where specific expertise is required.

Coreper

As noted above, in the early stages of setting up the K4 committee there was some discussion as to whether it would take on the role of a 'Coreper III' and effectively prepare the JHA Council. Coreper II, however, affirmed itself as the preparatory organ for the Council and has since played its role to the full in preparations for the JHA Council. This role has however depended very much on the personal interest of permanent representatives and on the willingness of the relevant ministry of interior and/or justice to let Coreper become involved. The role that Coreper has played in practice has therefore varied very much from presidency to presidency.

For instance, it has been said that, during the Danish presidency in 2002, 78% of all items on the agenda of Coreper II related to JHA. During other presidencies, the figure has certainly been lower. What is sure, however, is that each presidency since 1993 has had to face an increasing number of JHA items. It is not unusual for reference to be made to the 'marshes of JHA', with Coreper frequently getting bogged down in a level of detail which normally should have been addressed more fully by working parties before filtering its way up the system. In fact, the setting up of the AFSJ can rightly be compared to the setting up of an internal market for freedom, security and justice. When one adds all the proposals in the Vienna Action Plan, Tampere and other programmes adopted by the Council, at least 300 measures should have been adopted by 1 May 2004. The magnitude of the work is compounded by the fact that many of the topics have political implications, are headline news, and that ministers are closely involved in the discussions. It is clear that the JHA Council, after a modest start, has become one of the three most important Council formations.

Coreper has also showed a remarkable tenacity and inventiveness in negotiations in JHA. It has often been faced with seemingly irresolvable problems but has always managed to find formulae acceptable to all. As a rough estimate, Coreper will solve about ten per cent of problems in a file, whereas CATS and SCIFA may contribute about five per cent. The Council itself would then solve the remaining problems of a difficult political nature.

The JHA Council

The Justice and Home Affairs Council (which also includes issues relating to civil protection) is itself often de facto divided into two meetings, i.e., two sets of ministers are often involved (even three in some member states), depending on the subjects to be discussed. Justice issues are in most member states dealt with by the justice minister. In Ireland it is the minister of justice, equality and law reform who is responsible for all matters relating to the JHA Council, something which is a considerable advantage when Ireland holds the presidency due to the ease of organising internal coordination. In the UK the home secretary is responsible for all matters relating to criminal justice and interior matters, whereas the lord chancellor deals with civil justice. Most member states have specific interior or public order ministers but police questions are dealt with by some justice ministers (Sweden, Netherlands, Denmark, Ireland, Luxembourg). Asylum and immigration questions are often dealt with by the ministers of interior but there are in some countries specific ministers dealing with such matters and they are sometimes placed in the ministries of foreign affairs.

These differences in the internal organisation of the member states occasionally render the organisation of Council meetings a difficult exercise. Ministers have a busy schedule and do not want to wait while others are doing business. Presidencies therefore, assisted by the Council secretariat, often have to arrange the agenda so as to cause as little waiting time as possible. The Council also often spans two days and there have in recent years been several events that have taken time from the 'real' business of the Council. These special events have included a number of public debates (where ministers usually read pre-prepared statements; all involved agree that they are of little value), meetings with the candidate countries/new member states, meetings with ministers from western Balkan countries or other countries.

A Council meeting is always prepared in detail. The presidency and the secretariat are in constant contact in the context of the meetings leading up to the Council, and the closer the Council comes, the more detailed the negotiations become. In this context, the JHA counsellors play an important role. They act both as advisors to their ambassador to prepare Coreper and as advisors to their respective ministerial departments. Since they have most often followed the work of the working group and have special knowledge of the file, they can also participate in smaller bilateral negotiations where compromises of Coreper/Council can be prepared. In fact, the JHA counsellors group has been likened to a 'mini-Coreper'.

When Coreper has prepared the Council there may still be some questions outstanding. The Council secretariat, together with the presidency, prepares the papers for the Council and drafts speaking notes for the Council president which are translated into his or her language. On a number of issues fall-back positions and alternative drafts are prepared, room documents are drafted and the contacts between delegations, the presidency, the Council secretariat, and, increasingly, the Commission are multiplying. The presidency seeks to establish what can be achieved at the Council and where there are possibilities to find compromises. Sometimes, the Council president will have direct bilateral contact with a minister from a country that 'has a problem' or even travel to that country in advance of the Council if the issue requires personal discussions. The Council secretariat is sometimes associated with such bilateral meetings, which may often also be held in the margins of the Council.

Immediately before the Council, the presidency and, increasingly often, the incoming presidency meets with the Council secretariat (director-general and his close collaborators and the Council legal service) and the commissioner, and his collaborators from DG JAI in the Commission to discuss the latest developments and to fine-tune the Council. At this meeting an assessment is made on what may be achieved and final drafts for possible compromises are agreed. Some of the discussion is also devoted to negotiating tactics and how to present compromises.

At the Council, the Council secretariat sits next to the president and is able to give immediate advice as questions may arise. Often, however, the Council is so well prepared that the president is able to follow the 'script' (which will contain options and fall-back positions) practically in its entirety, which of course does not rule out the occasional surprise. Most ministers are experienced politicians used to negotiations. Therefore, the Council can often achieve results which may not be achievable at any other level. Increasingly, the ministers know each other personally and this also contributes to the good functioning of the Council itself. However, in recent years, some parts of the Council have been devoted to negotiations in detail (footnotes in documents). This has led to an unfortunate tendency in some member states not to send the minister in person but a junior minister or the ambassador instead.

The draft constitutional treaty

The long and winding road towards the incorporation of the JHA into EU policies has been complex, and riddled with compromises which are difficult to understand, even for those working within the system. This chapter has attempted to show the main tendencies and main decisions in order to help the reader understand the system. A constant tension exists between those advocating a greater role for the Community/Union, and those wishing to preserve national systems and seeking to hold back developments. When the first JHA commissioner, Anita Gradin, made a tour of all member states she came back and reported that the Union had fifteen perfect systems! Things changed however, and it was inevitable that these tendencies also would come up in the heated debate within the European Convention drafting the draft constitutional treaty. At the time of writing, not all issues pertaining to the most sensitive areas in JHA have been completely resolved.

The critics of the system argued that there was a lack of effectiveness in the Union's law and of efficiency of its decision-making process, something which emerges clearly from the description in this chapter. Moreover, they considered that the JHA area was unduly complex and lacked democratic and judicial accountability. These issues were all raised in the context of the Convention itself and in its working group 'X' chaired by the former Irish prime minister, John Bruton.

The draft Constitution will, if adopted, lead to a number of important changes for the JHA Council. The following are among the most significant:

- There will in principle only be one single legal framework for negotiation and adoption of texts in the JHA area;

- European framework laws and European laws will in principle, in specified fields, be adopted by QMV and co-decision with the European Parliament; for further measures unanimity will be required;

– The European framework laws and European laws will have direct effect;

– The Commission will in police and judicial cooperation have the sole right of initiative, unless one-quarter of the member states agree on an initiative;

– It will be clearly provided that JHA area matters are shared competencies. The legal basis for some questions such as criminal law will become more restrictive but also more precisely drafted;

– The principle of mutual recognition will be laid down in the Constitution;

– A safeguard clause for criminal law and police cooperation will be introduced;

– The control of the Court of Justice will be generalised with a few exceptions;

– National parliaments will be more involved in the legislative process;

– Competencies in civil law will be extended and clarified;

– Reinforced cooperation will be possible between eight member states (this follows already from the Nice Treaty, but the procedure is made simpler).

As discussions within the intergovernmental conference have only just conlcuded at the time of writing, it is difficult to conduct further analysis at this stage. It is however clear that the changes that are proposed will affect the entire JHA area and the way the JHA Council works, and will in all likelihood be no less far-reaching than the previous reforms described in this chapter. Such is the incremental nature of European integration!

Chapter 7: The Agriculture and Fisheries Council

by Paul Culley

There is a general perception that the EU, its policies, procedures and institutions are remote and unrecognised by the great majority of the Union's citizens in their daily lives. This generalisation is not true of those of the Union's citizens who are farmers or who trade directly with those who work the land. Although not always popular, the Agriculture Council's debates and decisions, as well as the Commission's management of agriculture policy, and even the pages of the *Official Journal*, have long been familiar to farmers and to managers and workers in the agrifood business, very many of whom can quote the articles and subparagraphs of Council regulations because they have a direct bearing on their lives by laying down milk quotas, compulsory wine distillation measures, rules for organic agriculture and so on.

Although its visibility has been eclipsed in recent years because of the higher profile of other expanding policy areas and their respective ministers, as well as the European Parliament, the Agriculture Council has traditionally been responsible for the largest share of the budget, and so remains. Some of the more theatrical antics of the Agriculture Council – marathon negotiations ending at daybreak, walkouts by angry ministers (just before the main evening television news), 'stopping the clock', street demonstrations by irate farmers (who on one occasion herded a cow into the Council building where the ministers were in session) – remain engraved in the public's mind decades later as emblems of the Council or 'Brussels', long after they have been overtaken by more sober and disciplined practices.

Total spending on agriculture in 2003 was some €44.3 billion, representing about 45% of the total budget (down from about 66% fifteen years ago). Most of this (roughly €39 billion) is spent on market measures for the various agricultural products. This merits two comments. First, unlike many other Council formations, the Agriculture Council adopts both regulatory legislation (with little or no impact on the Community budget) and 'spending legislation'. Second, since much EU activity is regulatory (dealing with the environment, industrial policy, transport, etc) or creating common policies (immigration and asylum, foreign policy and defence questions) without large expenditure programmes, it can appear that agriculture consumes a disproportionate amount of the EU's budget. It is therefore instructive to situate agriculture spending in another context – that of EU GDP, of which it represents roughly 0.5%. According to current estimates, this will be reduced to about 0.33% by 2013.

Inevitably, any sketch of the Agriculture Council will reflect two trends: the development of the Common Agriculture Policy (CAP) and general on-going institutional reorganisation. In this latter respect, the Agriculture and the Fisheries Councils were merged following the decision by the European Council in June 2002 to reduce the number of Council formations.

The first session of the merged Council took place in September 2002. Council sessions, regardless of their formation, are numbered sequentially. Chance determined that many of the milestone sessions of the Council of the European Union (1,000th, 1,500th, 2,000th, 2,500th) were held in the agricultural formation (remarkably, all in Luxembourg) – likewise, in 2004, the first ministerial meeting following enlargement to an EU of 25 members was of agriculture and fisheries ministers (albeit an informal meeting in Ireland on 9 May). However, chance was considerably assisted by the relative frequency of the agriculture sessions, especially in the early decades. Today, the Agriculture and Fisheries Council normally meets every month except August. While in the past there were frequent additions of end-of-presidency sessions in order to conclude, for example, price negotiations, the trend has reversed in recent years and some meetings have been cancelled, especially in January or July after the out-going presidency has 'cleared the table'.

Historical origins

At the very origins of the European Economic Community, special arrangements were put in place for developing agriculture policy. These entailed the participation of agriculture ministers alongside foreign ministers in Council sessions and the creation of a 'special committee' at the level of officials in order to prepare the agriculture dossiers.

Article 39 of the Treaty of Rome (1957) (now article 33) gave a prominent position to agriculture in the overall objectives that were set for the new economic community. Subsequently, the Stresa Conference of Governments (3-11 July 1958) discussed what steps should be taken in pursuit of those objectives and the Commission was invited to present proposals based on the conclusions of the conference. At that time, Council meetings consisted of the foreign ministers of the six, whose deliberations were prepared by Coreper, which had been established in January 1958.

In May 1960, the governments of the member states took a general decision to speed up the achievement of the treaty objectives.[1] In that context, they took specific decisions concerning agriculture and laid down a timetable for the presentation of proposals by the Commission and for debates in the Council on the construction of a common agriculture policy (CAP) (article 5 of the decision).

In particular, a 'special committee' was established in May 1960 to prepare decisions related to the creation of the CAP. The establishment of the special committee for agriculture (SCA) was confirmed by a decision (curiously, an intergovernmental decision!) taken at the session of the Council on 19-20 July 1960 when agriculture ministers participated for the first time. It was also envisaged that agriculture ministers would participate in subsequent meetings of the Council when matters concerning them were discussed.

The role and functions of the Agriculture Council

As a result of recent developments, the scope of the Agriculture and Fisheries Council is divided into three distinct categories. This subdivision resulted both from the reallocation of responsibilities in the 1999-2004 Prodi Commission and from reorganisation of the Council itself. The 'three category' structure determines the arrangement of the Council's agenda and the practical organisation of meetings, in particular concerning the attendance of the commissioners responsible. However, even before this distinction was created at the level of ministers, the Council dossiers in each of the three categories had always been prepared, at official level, via different channels. Depending on the legal basis and the category into which the Commission's proposals fall, the Agriculture and Fisheries Council legislates either with relative autonomy from the European Parliament (simple consultation procedure) or as a joint legislator (co-decision procedure).

The Common Agricultural Policy

The first category of issues is development of the CAP. This means the market organisation measures for all agricultural products produced in the EU together with rural development measures (that is, measures not related to production but geared to strengthen the competitiveness and economic structures of rural communities). These are the issues that account for the lion's share of the agriculture budget. This category also includes many cross-sectoral questions such as organic agriculture, quality policy (including some food labelling questions) and measures to promote agriculture products, as well as forestry. Until relatively recently, most journalists, academics and commentators referred to the Agriculture Council as the 'Farm Council' because this was a perfect reflection of its orientation towards on-farm producers.

The CAP has always been under the responsibility of a single commissioner (traditionally chosen from a 'small' member state) and is almost entirely handled in the Commission by DG Agriculture. All CAP issues are prepared for the Council by the SCA.

Almost all of the legislation adopted by the Council in this category is subject to simple consultation of the European Parliament. This means that, while the Council cannot normally adopt a proposal until the Parliament has adopted an opinion, it is not in any way constrained by the substance of the Parliament's opinion. However, the Parliament levers as much influence as possible with this procedure, often through the Commission. There have been cases, on important dossiers, where the Parliament has refused to adopt an opinion until it got a political commitment from the Commission (in the absence of a legal obligation) to amend its proposal in a certain way and not to make concessions to the Council regarding such amendments. Even without resorting to such bold tactics, it is usually through persuasion of the Commission that the Parliament makes its voice heard in the Council. As a result, the Commission will often urge the Council (sometimes at the level of SCA or working party) to accept a textual amendment from the Parliament. At the level of ministers, the political thrust of the Parliament's opinion is often cited by individual delegations when it suits them, but rarely specific textual amendments.

While it is not in the scope of this chapter to analyse the development of the CAP, it is important to highlight how the Council in recent years has broadened its vision of the role of agriculture in society, culminating in the radical reforms of 2003. Whether this is the result of enlightenment, pragmatism or bowing to external pressures is a matter for debate.

Firstly, the Council recognised and defined the multifunctional character of agriculture – this is a basic principle of the European model of agriculture adopted by the Luxembourg European Council (1999). This establishes that agriculture must not just be economically sound and competitive, but that it should also be spread throughout the whole European territory, including regions that have specific problems. Furthermore, policy should be socially acceptable and make it possible to ensure a fair income, striking a fair balance between sectors, producers and regions.

Secondly, arising from this, Agenda 2000 created the rural development programme as the 'second pillar' of the CAP. After the initial programme from 2000-2006, this is likely to be expanded in the next financial perspectives (2006 onwards). Thirdly, the Council developed a food safety dimension (see below) and took decisions that imposed controls, new practices and costs on its traditional constituency – the agrifood sector. It was by no means inevitable that the Agriculture Council would retain responsibility for this dossier – had it failed to meet its responsibilities, the dossier would have been dealt with elsewhere. Finally, the political message of the 2003 reform is that the CAP, in line with society's demands, imposes food safety, environmental and animal welfare requirements as conditions for the payment of public funds to farmers. In line with the 'multifunctional' doctrine, it widens the political definition of farmers not just as food producers but as providers of these 'public goods'. In a substantial stepping-up of the 1992 MacSharry and Agenda 2000 reforms, most subsidies are disconnected from production, making farming more market-oriented. In taking these decisions for internal reasons, the Council also expected the Community to be in a stronger position in the WTO Doha Development Agenda negotiations.

Food Safety and Animal Welfare

The second category is food safety and animal welfare. It is difficult today to imagine that prior to the BSE crisis ('mad cow' disease) in the mid-1990s, food safety was almost unknown as a policy issue either in the Union's institutions or in member states; it did not appear in job titles or in organisation charts, it did not have a separate heading in annual programmes, reports or manifestos. Issues that had an impact on food safety (for example, regulations on pesticides or animal feeding stuffs) were discussed in different contexts and with different aims, but without political priority or profile. It took the BSE crisis and cases of food contamination for certain issues to be brought together and given a food safety, public health and consumer protection perspective.

The issues in question were not traditionally distinguished from 'mainstream agriculture'. As far as the Commission was concerned, they were handled by the same commissioner and the same department until 1999. As far as the great majority of member states were concerned, they were handled by the same minister in the same ministry. As far as the Council was concerned, there was no rationale for making any distinction between agricultural production and consumer or other interests. The Council, like everybody else, dealt with the issues concerned under the heading of 'harmonisation of technical legislation'.

This title, taken from the treaty, described a programme of work designed to underpin the common market for agricultural products by harmonising technical standards relating to production inputs or practices. These included national rules and regulations on veterinary and hygiene issues; animal feeding stuffs; pesticides; plant health; food additives; and food labelling. The objective was progressively to replace the various national rules by common Community rules usually adopted in the form of directives.

Harmonisation of food additives and food labelling was taken out of the scope of the Agriculture Council after the adoption of the Single European Act (1986), not for reasons of food safety, but because they were identified as a priority for the completion of the single market for which a new legal basis was created (article 100a), enabling decisions to be taken by qualified majority rather than unanimity under the previous arrangement (article 100). As part of the same exercise, the Council developed a new formation ('internal market') that became responsible for food additives, among other things. These dossiers were transferred therefore from Commission DG Agriculture to DG Internal Market and from the Agriculture Council to the Internal Market Council.

The other 'harmonisation' dossiers remained in the domain of agriculture, both in member states and in Community institutions, until the food crises of the 1990s. In response to public and parliamentary concerns, both member states and the Commission reallocated responsibilities in order to separate producers' interests from consumers' and public health interests. The 1999-2004 Prodi Commission created a new portfolio covering health and consumer protection (known by its French acronym, SANCO). A commissioner was entrusted specifically with giving a public health and consumer focus to a broad range of former 'harmonisation' dossiers transferred mainly from the agriculture services, including, in particular, animal health, plant health, food hygiene, animal feeding stuffs, pesticides, and food labelling as well as the food safety aspects of genetically modified organisms. Most important of all, the Commission's legislative programme planned a framework food law establishing basic objectives and principles of food safety in accordance with which the various technical standards would be reviewed and updated. In the same exercise, SANCO was also given responsibility for animal welfare.

It was therefore an historic occasion when David Byrne, commissioner responsible for SANCO, took a seat alongside Franz Fischler, commissioner responsible for agriculture, at the September 1999 session of the Agriculture Council in order to deal with an agenda item on animal feeding stuffs. A policy separation had been created and institutionalised where none had existed before.

During the Italian presidency in 2003, ministers had informal discussions about whether the title of the Council should not be changed to 'Agriculture, Food and Fisheries' in order to reflect the fact that much of its work concerns food safety. The idea did not get very far because there are other food issues besides food safety that are dealt with in other formations of the Council, such as the Competitiveness Council, which incorporates the former Internal Market Council.

Pressure for a reorientation of the Agriculture Council did not come only from external events such as Commission reorganisation and pressure from the European Parliament, but also from within its own ranks. As described later, agriculture ministers traditionally represented farmers' interests and were sometimes farmers themselves or had emerged from farming politics. Substantial changes took place in the 1990s after the food crises. There was a trend in many member states for the agriculture ministries to be broken up, given a new orientation and counterbalanced by other ministries or agencies representing public health and consumer interests – just as was happening in the Commission. As part of this process, certain member states (such as Italy and Germany) governed by multi-party coalitions nominated members of 'Green' parties as ministers for agriculture. These parties were elected on manifestos promising that food safety, animal welfare and environmental protection would change established, farmer-oriented agriculture policy. The Agriculture Council saw the arrival of ministers who were not ministers for agriculture but, for example, minister for consumer affairs, food and agriculture (Germany) or minister for environment, food and rural affairs (UK). This was a rejection of any notion that the Agriculture Council could continue to be a farm council focused exclusively on the needs of farmers. It should also be remarked that the accession of Sweden to the EU in 1995 helped to tip the balance in favour of member states such as Denmark, the Netherlands and the United Kingdom, where consumer, environmental or animal welfare issues already played a more prominent role in the formulation of agriculture policy.

The Council's deliberations on these questions were always prepared by Coreper. The legal basis for 'harmonisation' was article 100 or 100a of the treaty. This was replaced in the Treaty of Amsterdam by a specific legal basis for food safety (article 152). Animal health and animal welfare remain based on article 37. The Maastricht Treaty included a protocol on animal welfare, giving an impetus to this aspect of food production. In the area of animal health and animal welfare, the working party of Chief Veterinary Officers is very influential and plays an important role in preparing, or finalising, dossiers for Coreper and the Council. In particular, it has the power to prepare 'I' items for Coreper that become 'A' items for the Council.

The Council's legislation in this second category is subject to the co-decision procedure with the European Parliament for article 152, and simple consultation for article 37.

Fisheries

This is the third category of issues dealt with by the Agriculture and Fisheries Council. The first elements of a Common Fisheries Policy (CFP) were put in place in 1970. The fisheries resources policy based on total allowable catches (TACs) and fish quotas allocated to member states was introduced in 1983. The Council's ongoing role is to adjust the CFP in line with requirements – the policy was subject to a major reform in the second half of 2002. The main features of this reform were a multi-annual management of fisheries resources based on sustainability and an adaptation of fishing effort and capacity to bring it into line with available resources. Council legislation deals typically with technical conservation measures for fish stocks (such as specifications for nets), monitoring and inspection rules (for checks on catches, landings and transhipments) and multi-annual stock management (including recovery plans for endangered stocks).

When the Fisheries Council was 'independent', it usually met four times annually (April, June, October and December). Now, unless there is a good reason to do otherwise, these are the months when fisheries items normally feature on the agenda of the Agriculture and Fisheries Council.

The main annual task for the Council is to fix the TACs and quotas for the Union's fishermen. This exercise involves striking a balance between economic and environmental considerations – the latter having become more compelling in recent years, both because of the objective state of fish stocks as well as increased societal demands for sustainable fishing.

Fisheries legislation, therefore, is highly technical but has major political consequences. It has a direct impact on the livelihood of fishermen and the economy of their local communities. Because fishing is a 'primary' economic activity, entailing considerable physical risks and concentrated in traditional communities, fishermen have a strong political voice. However, the Council is not a 'fishermen's Council' either, because of the ever-increasing political weight of environmental concerns.

Whereas food safety and agriculture are major concerns for all member states, the importance of fisheries is more variable, ranging from Spain (a major fish-catching and fish-consuming country) to landlocked Austria and Luxembourg, where it is of minor importance. Enlargement has added both to the fishing countries (Poland, the Baltic States, Cyprus and Malta) and to the landlocked group. Most likely, the issue of aquaculture (that falls in the scope of the Council) will increase in prominence in future.

Fisheries legislation is based on article 37 of the treaty, requiring simple consultation of the European Parliament. It is worth noting that the annual, high-profile TACs and quotas exercise is based on a derived legal basis – that is, an existing Council regulation – with the result that a consultation of the Parliament is not required.

Fisheries dossiers are prepared for the Council by Coreper which is, in turn, prepared by two working parties that meet weekly.

Coordination with other formations of the Council

The Agriculture and Fisheries Council is the main protagonist in the Union's legislative process concerning agriculture, food safety and fisheries. Like most other sectoral councils, it has 'corporatist' tendencies, meaning that it acts as a forum to express the interests of a specific group, possibly with cross-institutional support. This is a natural organisational tendency that should be counteracted by the coordinating role of the General Affairs Council in its function of ensuring the coherence and consistency of all EU policies. However, this role is not fully exploited (see chapter 4).

Nonetheless, the Agriculture Council is much less corporatist than in the past because it has redefined itself in the light of the changed context in which it operates, as described above.

Different formations of the Council (including Agriculture and Fisheries) often hold parallel discussions on the same issue, usually at the request of certain delegations and often to the annoyance of others. Delegations making such a request hope that the views they express in the debate (often not agreed as official conclusions of the Council formation concerned) will influence the outcome of the Council formation responsible for taking the decision. As an example, the Agriculture and Fisheries Council has in the past debated the agriculture aspects of the WTO negotiations that are the responsibility of the External Relations Council. This is partly due to the fact that the agriculture commissioner holds specific responsibility for these aspects alongside the trade commissioner who holds general responsibility for WTO issues.

The Agriculture and Fisheries Council is also a 'reporting point' or forum for discussion on important agricultural or fisheries questions. Both ministers and the Commission use the Council to make statements or present information about important political questions in the agriculture or fisheries domains. Under 'other business', delegations often draw colleagues' and the Commission's attention to specific problems in their country which require Community attention; for example, drought, flooding, collapse of market prices or outbreaks of disease.

The organisation of the Council - Membership of the Council

In a European Community that grew from six to twelve members between the 1950s and the 1980s, agriculture ministers were usually senior members of their national governments, reflecting the importance of the agriculture constituency in most cases. However, the agriculture sector's declining share of both national output and employment caused the agriculture portfolio to slip down the hierarchy, at least in some member states, over the decades. Today, most ministers for agriculture are also responsible for fisheries and for forestry and many are responsible for 'rural development'. As described above, some ministers hold the agriculture portfolio as a subsidiary responsibility to environment or consumer affairs.

In the past, the Agriculture Council was characterised by stability and continuity (which some observers termed 'clubbish') in the sense that several held the portfolio for a long time (some held it for ten years) or came from an agricultural background or occupied international posts in agriculture. For example, several members of the Agriculture Council later became commissioners responsible for agriculture – Sicco Mansholt (Netherlands), Poul Dalsager (Denmark), Ray MacSharry (Ireland), René Steichen (Luxembourg) and Franz Fischler (who had been an observer prior to Austrian accession). Indeed, on occasions, certain member states have nominated an experienced agriculture minister to the Commission in order to enhance their chance of being awarded the agriculture portfolio. It is noteworthy that Franz Fischler, in addition to being one of only four members of the Santer Commission to survive into the Prodi Commission, was the only commissioner to retain his former (agriculture) portfolio. Having held the Commission portfolio for ten years, having previously been Austrian minister for agriculture during the accession negotiations, and coming from a previous background in farming politics, Fischler is a good example of a 'veteran' of the sector.

Politically, the agriculture ministry and associated participation in the Agriculture Council can be a step either towards obscurity or higher office. Some ministers have had their domestic political reputations irreparably damaged by appearing to fail to defend national interests in Brussels or by being held scapegoats for food scandals. Others emerge with enhanced reputations from their service in the Council. For example, Loyola de Palacio, after high-profile negotiations in the Council on Agenda 2000 and the olive oil sector, was nominated by Spain to the Prodi Commission where she additionally secured one of the two vice-presidencies. Further in the past, Edith Cresson and Michel Rocard spent periods in the Agriculture Council prior to becoming prime minister of France, as did Jacques Chirac prior to becoming President of the Republic. In the case of Chirac, it was observed that his background in agriculture was a distinct asset, at least as far as achieving certain agricultural objectives were concerned, when the European Council in Berlin (1999) concluded the Agenda 2000 negotiations, including important adaptations of the agriculture component (see chapter 15).

The special committee for agriculture (SCA)

The SCA is one of the main focal points of agricultural interests in the EU policy-making process. It provides a guaranteed weekly forum for senior agriculture officials from the member states and the Commission to come together to discuss agriculture questions in preparation for the monthly Council meeting. Whereas other sectors, such as transport or internal market, must compete, in effect, for scarce discussion time in a busy Coreper programme, the agriculture sector has a standing arrangement which enables it to discuss questions to the extent it considers necessary. In addition, the member states have the opportunity to hold these discussions directly with the most senior representatives of the Commission's directorate general for agriculture (rather than its general secretariat, as is the case in Coreper) which represents the Commission at the SCA.

Origins and legal basis

In creating the SCA in May 1960, it was not the Council's intention to delegate technical matters from Coreper to a subordinate committee of experts, but to speed up agreement on the CAP through the involvement of high-level officials having specialist knowledge of agriculture. The SCA had a similar mandate to that of Coreper – 'to prepare the work of the Council'.

In this first stage, the SCA worked alongside Coreper. While the SCA worked on the construction of the CAP, Coreper had responsibility for preparing other questions for the Agriculture Council which had significant non-agricultural policy implications. The distinction was a matter of judgement rather than legal definition but, in practice, Coreper was responsible for questions which had, and now has, implications for commercial trade policy, public health (such as foodstuffs, veterinary and plant health matters) and financial implications of impending decisions.

After the first stage of the creation of the CAP, some adjustment was necessary and the Council confirmed, on 1-2 April 1963, that the SCA was responsible for agriculture questions while Coreper had overall responsibility for all questions going before the Council. This horizontal authority gave Coreper an element of rank in relation to the SCA, giving it the right to consider the non-agricultural aspects of any question prepared for the Council by the SCA. The current rules of procedure (adopted in February 2004) confirm the overall authority of Coreper in preparing the work of the Council, although this has not been exercised in practice in relation to dossiers prepared for the Agriculture Council by the SCA.

Unlike members of Coreper, the capital-based members of the SCA are involved to varying degrees in implementing Council and Commission legislation in their member states, whereas members of Coreper are never involved in the practical implementation of Community legislation.

The closeness of the relationship between ministers for agriculture and the members of the SCA is noteworthy and differs from members of Coreper, who are responsible to their foreign ministers but also deal with many other ministers (transport, environment, health, industry, etc) at the sessions of the different Councils (which in many cases are only three or four times a year).

The SCA's debates are prepared by about twenty-two working parties that report directly to it, not to counsellors/attachés as in some other sectors. As a result, the SCA does not have an 'I' point procedure to approve dossiers without debate.

Membership

The composition and chairmanship of the SCA were much debated before it was established, as was the role of the Commission representative. Today, all its members are senior officials from agriculture ministries with extensive experience of the CAP. Many occupy a senior post in their ministries in their national capitals, such as director for European or international affairs. Some are posted to the permanent representation in Brussels. The SCA had a woman chairman (Kate Timms (UK) in 1992) before Coreper and has had several women members.

In EU-15, about half of the SCA members were Brussels-based; however only two of the new members from the ten new member states are Brussels-based. Under the new language interpretation arrangements introduced after 1 May 2004, the SCA is one of the limited number of preparatory committees to have full interpretation in all 20 official languages.

The stability and continuity which used to characterise the Council also characterises the SCA. Some of its members served an 'apprenticeship' in subsidiary working parties, some served for ten years in the committee, some chaired the committee two or three times, some went on to be directors-general of their ministries and some even went on to be ministers for agriculture. Three UK spokesmen in the committee went on to represent the Commission in the committee. Two of the four secretaries-general of the Commission (probably the most senior EU civil servant post) since 1958

(David Williamson and Carlo Trojan) served in the SCA in national delegations at earlier stages of their careers.

The Commission is represented at the SCA by one of the deputy directors-general from DG Agriculture, almost always a veteran of the sector. Although the director-general for agriculture rarely attends the SCA, it is worth noting that only four people have occupied this post since 1958, further confirming the pattern of continuity in decision-makers in this sector.

Right to agree 'A' items

One of the most important powers of the SCA is the right to agree 'A' items for the Council to adopt without discussion – a right otherwise exclusive to Coreper. This greatly facilitates decision-making both from the practical and political viewpoints.

A clear example is the CAP reform of 2003. After several months of negotiations, and at the end of a marathon negotiating session (such sessions having become rare in recent years), the Council reached political agreement on a compromise at its session in Luxembourg at the end of June. The 31-page political agreement substantially altered the Commission proposals. When the political agreement was examined in the cold light of day in order to prepare a legal text for adoption, it was discovered that there were ambiguities, loopholes and even contradictions in the text that could obviously not be transposed into a legal act. Since it would have been ill-advised to ask the Council to re-open the discussion, and hence risk unravelling the fragile agreement, it fell to the SCA, over the course of many meetings from July to September under the Italian presidency, to clarify and resolve the problems so that a legal text – running to 136 pages in the Official Journal and representing one of the biggest reforms of the CAP in 40 years – could be adopted by the Agriculture and Fisheries Council as an 'A' item on 29 September 2003. As it is hard to imagine how Coreper could have spent so many days in negotiation on such a text, the value of a 'special committee', on this occasion, was demonstrated.

In the past, there may have been occasions when the existence of a 'special committee' resulted in dossiers being 'over-discussed', especially in the absence of an 'I' point procedure. However, in May 2003 the committee adopted guidelines for its working methods, based on the code of conduct adopted by the Council, in order to streamline its proceedings, especially with enlargement in mind (see chapter 21).

Concluding reflections

It is worth dwelling upon why the Agriculture Council is subject to criticism from many quarters, including from committed Europeans.

In the first instance, the Agriculture Council and the CAP have provided abundant material to sustain eurosceptics in their convictions – allegations of fraud (for example, smuggling to attract subsidies or avoid taxes), allegations of waste (unsaleable beef or wine surpluses stored as symbolic mountains or lakes), allegations of absurdity (milk processed into butter, stored at great cost and finally subsidised to feed calves). These illustrate that Community policies are no more immune to management or policy errors than national policies in agriculture, health, education or defence. However, to focus exclusively or obsessively on these aspects – deplorable as they are – is to lose from sight the fact that the CAP was the flagship of European integration in political, economic, financial and legal terms during the first three decades of the Community. No other policy area saw such a transfer of national sovereignty to the Community, combined with financial solidarity where the Community budget largely replaced national budgets, and a common market for agricultural products that went further and more rapidly than for non-agricultural products or for services. Indeed, no other Community policy reached so many Community citizens in so many regions, bringing economic and social modernisation. To characterise the current work of the Agriculture Council exclusively in terms of certain eye-catching, past mistakes is to deny recognition of a major, pioneering European achievement.

However, many euro-idealists also feel uncomfortable with the CAP and the Agriculture Council. There are several possible reasons for this. Any sector or body that appears to benefit from special treatment or that appears to escape the common rules is likely to attract scepticism. It is easy to see how the working method of the Agriculture Council, with its special preparatory committee, falls into this category.

Furthermore, it is not just a perception but a reality that the decisions of the Agriculture Council often derogate from common rules. For example, while the treaty prohibits state aids in general, it also provides a procedure in article 88 whereby the Council, acting unanimously, can approve state aids on request from a member state – a procedure used almost exclusively by the Agriculture Council. Similarly, Community legislation on the labelling of foodstuffs requires that ingredients and additives be indicated on the label for all products, but makes an exception for wine and spirit drinks; this dates back to the period when the Agriculture Council was responsible for foodstuffs legislation. Although not a decision of the Agriculture Council, it remains a fact that CAP subsidies were outside the scope of GATT trade liberalisation agreements until the Marrakesh Agreement (1994). Agriculture's 45% share of the Union's budget, viewed in isolation from its 0.5% share of the Union's GDP, is also a source of criticism but it does not take account of the fact that the EU has no jurisdiction, and no intention to propose, to spend money in most of the areas that make up a large proportion of national budgets – health, education, social security, defence.

The cumulative effect of these apparent privileges in procedure, policy and budget that are exclusive to the Agriculture Council is to create a degree of frustration in many other policy-makers. However, when viewed objectively, a trend can be observed, going back to the late 1980s, whereby the Agriculture Council has been progressively subjected to budgetary, policy and procedural disciplines.

The 1980s were perhaps a watershed because the Single European Act was the first in a series of treaty amendments leading to cooperation and co-decision with the European Parliament as well as an expansion of Community policies on environment, consumer protection, food safety and animal welfare that had to be integrated into the farmer-oriented CAP. Many questions previously discussed in the Agriculture Council were transferred logically to newly-created policy instruments – e.g. agricultural research was integrated in the Framework Research Programme and many forestry questions are now part of environment policy. In 1988, the European Council imposed the first budgetary discipline that was later confirmed and remained in place until replaced by Agenda 2000. The discipline was reinforced by the European Council (October 2003) when it froze CAP marketing spending until 2013 with a fixed indexation for future inflation that almost certainly means a reduction in real terms for the first time in history.

On the international scene, the Agriculture Council had to factor trade liberalisation and concerns for developing countries into its decisions. Within its own institutional framework, the Agriculture Council has been subjected to general rules on transparency, disclosure of documents and public debates as well as a more rigorous management of resources by the Council secretariat resulting in efficient programming of its work. Many of these changes were alien to a Council that established its personality during decades when there was no budgetary discipline on its spending decisions, when there was minor input from policy areas that had little or no legal basis in the treaty and when all documents and deliberations were shrouded in professional secrecy.

This is the Council that faces the future in a Union of 25 or more. It is neither a farmers' nor a fishermen's Council. Some EU-15 ministers are guardians of consumers' interests rather than farmers' interests. Many of the agriculture ministers from the new member states are market-oriented with expanding, competitive national food industries. Some of the ten new member states, as well as the two pre-accession countries, have large proportions of their population living in poverty on subsistence agriculture; they also have food industries that are uncompetitive or that do not yet meet EU food safety standards. Market expenditure in the next financial perspectives may be reduced well below the level of financial discipline, counterbalanced by a strengthened rural development instrument both in budgetary and in organisational terms. Internationally, the WTO Doha Development Agenda, the UN Millennium Declaration and FAO World Food Summit Declaration exert increasing pressure on domestic as well as trade policy.

Other formations of the Council take an increasing number of decisions that are certainly more significant in terms of political integration, such as foreign policy and defence. However, the Agriculture and Fisheries formation of the Council will continue to be the forum whose decisions most directly affect the daily business of many millions of citizens in the enlarged Union – over 11 million farmers and fishermen, together with their families and neighbours living in rural communities centred on food production. As a result, agriculture and fisheries is a barometer to measure the strength of citizens' Europe as well as the health of integration achieved under the 'first pillar'.

Chapter 8: 'Variable geometry' in the Council

'Variable geometry' is one of the buzz phrases which has emerged in the vocabulary of European integration in recent years to describe flexible arrangements in the Union involving fewer than the full complement of member states. The concept (also referred to as 'flexible' or 'differentiated' integration or 'enhanced' or 'structured' cooperation) is not a new one; it has been an integral part of the longstanding deepening versus widening debate on the development of the Union. There are, however, a multitude of terms used to describe variations on this concept, each meaning slightly different things (as explained below). One of the difficulties in any debate on this subject, including among treaty draftsmen in the IGC, is to define exactly what is being talked about in a way that ensures that all participants in a discussion on the topic are talking about the same thing at the same time.

For the purposes of this chapter, the term 'variable geometry' is used in the very specific sense of compositions of the Council where fewer than the full complement of members either are involved in decision-making or take part in deliberations. This has been a feature of the Council in a number of policy sectors for many years, as a result of structured cooperation (or what are more commonly referred to as 'opt-outs' or 'opt-ins') foreseen in the treaties. This chapter describes the various circumstances in which the Council can and does meet in such compositions. Before doing so, the background of the history of the debate on 'differentiated' or 'flexible' integration is briefly recounted and the typology of forms of structured cooperation which exist among member states is explained.

The debate on 'differentiated' integration

In the years preceding the Single European Act and the enlargement to include Spain and Portugal, politicians and academics began to reflect on ways of dealing with the Union's increasing diversity. Willy Brandt triggered the debate in a speech to the European Movement in 1974, setting out his 'Emergency Programme' that called for *'Eine Politik der Abstufung der Integration'* (Brandt, 1974, p. 36). This idea was taken up by Leo Tindemans in his report to the European Council in 1975 in which he suggested a *'multi speed'* concept to overcome financial and economic differences in Europe (Tindemans, 1975). The approach put forward by Ralf Dahrendorf, in a speech to the European University Institute in Florence (Dahrendorf, 1979), injected a dose of both realism and radicalism into the debate. Dahrendorf's concept, which later became known as *'à la carte'*, offered the member states the possibility of 'picking and choosing' the policy fields in which they would like to participate. A set of core policies, however, would remain untouched. A third concept, *'variable geometry'*, originated from the then MEP, Jacques Delors. It was situated in the evolution of the late 1970s when, mainly at French instigation, international industrial, technological and energy cooperation was established through projects such as Eureka, Airbus and JET (joint European torus). Those initiatives were a pragmatic response to the need for flexibility in setting up cooperation between a limited number of operators in certain sectors outside the *acquis communautaire* (see box 8).

Similar concepts were again put forward in the run up to, and following, the 1996 IGC that led to the Treaty of Amsterdam. This time the 1994 Schäuble-Lammers paper kicked off the debate (Schäuble, Lammers, 1994). The controversy surrounding the paper stemmed from the idea that a hard core of able and willing member states should have the possibility to integrate further. This core was not, however, meant to be exclusive. On the contrary, its force of attraction would draw other member states to participate in due course *(multi-speed)*. Furthermore, the document explicitly renounced the notion of a Europe *'à la carte'*. The reaction to this document followed rapidly. In a speech delivered to the University of Leiden, UK Prime Minister John Major called for more flexibility for the member states to choose whether or not to participate in a certain policy field. According to Major, the single market was the only field in which member states had to act together, in other fields groups of countries could cooperate together if they wanted to *('à la carte')*. He also opposed the notion of a 'hard core' Europe or a Europe with inner and outer circles. A concept close to Delors' variable geometry was proposed by French Prime Minister Edouard Balladur, who argued for a Europe of 'concentric circles'. These circles would be based on the degree of integration and membership. The three circles, as proposed by Balladur, would consist of a circle of Community legislation, a monetary and military circle and a large circle consisting of all countries staying outside the EU for the moment (Balladur, 1995).

During negotiations leading up to the Nice Treaty, European leaders vied with one another in offering a flurry of new constitutional blueprints for the Union. In the context of that debate, French President Jacques Chirac and others argued for a 'pioneer group' of member states to pull out of the 'convoy' into the 'fast lane' and step on 'the accelerator' of European integration. The loosening up of the treaty provisions on so-called enhanced cooperation (see below) was viewed by some as a potential first step in this direction.

The definitional quagmire

This brief history shows that, like much euro-jargon, 'flexible' or 'differentiated' integration can mean different things. The term is often used as a generic label describing all types of flexible arrangements found in the treaties that differentiate among member states in the scope and pace of integration. Flexible arrangements in one form or another have always been a feature of the Union. Examples include transitional periods in treaties of accession, flexibility in the scope of application of certain directives, member states with opt-outs or moving at different speeds towards full economic and monetary union, the opt-outs (or potential opt-ins) for Denmark, the UK and Ireland on visas, asylum, immigration and other Schengen matters, 'enhanced cooperation' enabling clauses and so-called constructive abstention on CFSP decisions (see below). As explained, an array of concepts have been devised to describe these arrangements, including 'structured cooperation', 'enhanced cooperation', 'flexibility', 'closer cooperation', 'differentiated integration', 'variable geometry', 'multi-speed Europe' and 'Europe à la carte', to cite but a few. These terms are sometimes used interchangeably, though subtle distinctions exist between them, relating either to time ('multi-speed'), space ('variable geometry') or substance 'à la carte'.

One of the main problems is the difficulty in conceptualising different forms of cooperation between member states in and around the Union. Much confusion prevails, even among EU policy specialists. This is because no agreement exists about the precise political purpose of developing opportunities for enhanced co-operation in the treaties, although it is generally perceived as a vehicle for fostering further integration. The fact that prior to the Nice Treaty negotiations Jacques Delors and William Hague found themselves unlikely bedfellows in embracing the idea of more flexibility in the Union, albeit for diametrically opposed reasons, amply demonstrates that the concept can be viewed potentially as an accelerator for, or a brake on, further integration, depending on where the emphasis is put. An extensive body of academic literature has helped clarify the concepts (e.g., Stubb, 1998) and analyse the impact of such arrangements on the Union's past and future development (Philippart, 2000). Box 8 outlines the various concepts of cooperation among member states inside and outside the treaties, and how they relate to the debate on structured or enhanced cooperation in recent IGCs.

Box 8.1: *Forms of cooperation between EU member states*

In addition to normal action under the treaties, member states may cooperate in any one of a variety of ways. The term 'structured' or 'enhanced' cooperation in a generic sense is usually only applied to cooperation of the second type described below (i.e., inside the Union's institutional framework):

1.   COOPERATION *OUTSIDE* THE UNION'S INSTITUTIONAL FRAMEWORK

(i)   Cooperation 'overlooked' by the treaty

It is sometimes forgotten that the treaties do not prevent any two or more member states from cooperating among themselves. As sovereign entities they are free to organise relations between themselves as they deem fit, provided, of course, they do not undermine the Union's objectives and that obligations entered into as Union members are fully respected. This ranges from bilateral diplomatic and political agreements (such as the Franco-German Cooperation Treaty) to more organised forms of cooperation involving a number of member states, sometimes with third states (e.g. Airbus, Eurocorps, European Space Agency, Eurocontrol, etc).

(ii)   Cooperation mentioned in the treaty

Article 17(4) TEU does not preclude closer cooperation among member states within NATO and article 306 TEC allows for regional unions such as the Benelux to the extent that the objectives of these regional unions are not attained by the treaty. Explicitly mentioning such cooperation in the treaties highlights the fact that they are compatible with treaty obligations. During the Nice IGC, the conference considered briefly whether cooperation between two or more member states which contributes to the Union's general objectives, even if it takes place outside the institutional framework, should be given some more loose but systematic recognition under the umbrella of the treaty. This idea met with widespread scepticism, mainly because of fears of creeping Union competence.

(iii) Special case of the Eurogroup

The Eurogroup of finance ministers which meets in the margins of the Ecofin Council is an example of cooperation outside the Union's institutional framework which is nevertheless closely linked to the Union's single currency, in which not all member states are yet members. This group was established entirely outside the institutional framework on the basis of the 1997 Luxembourg European Council conclusions. It has been suggested that one of the reasons this arrangement did not anticipate seeking a basis under the enabling clauses in the Treaty of Amsterdam was precisely because they were deemed too constraining and unworkable even before the treaty entered into force.

2. 'STRUCTURED' COOPERATION *INSIDE* THE UNION'S INSTITUTIONAL FRAMEWORK

(i) 'Pre-determined' or 'pre-defined' structured cooperation

To date, structured cooperation in any meaningful form has only actually been realised in areas singled out in the treaty or in treaty protocols for which all the relevant principles, rules and procedures governing that cooperation are spelled out. These types of arrangements, best exemplified by EMU and 'Schengen' matters, are often referred to as 'pre-determined' or 'predefined' structured cooperation, because the precise area covered is clearly pre-defined in the treaty itself.

(ii) 'Enabling clause' structured cooperation

Enabling clauses specify general principles, conditions and procedures for allowing a number of member states to cooperate more closely on a case-by-case basis. Unlike pre-determined structured cooperation, detailed arrangements would have to be set out in the act establishing the cooperation in question, in particular to define precisely the area in which it would apply. Enabling clauses were introduced into the Treaty of Amsterdam under the EC Treaty and the third pillar (cooperation in police and criminal justice matters).

(iii) Structured cooperation by default

In this case structured cooperation is not the result of the desire by a number of member states to move forward, but rather the possibility for member states to 'opt out' on individual decisions. Examples include constructive abstention under the CFSP and the possibility under article 34(2)(d) TEU for certain conventions on cooperation in police and criminal justice matters to enter into force for a limited number of member states.

Structured cooperation under the treaties

'Structured' or 'enhanced' cooperation is a term of art that refers to allowing a number of member states less than the full membership to use the Union's institutions and procedures to act collectively on matters covered by the treaties. This concept exists in three forms: areas singled out in the treaty or in treaty protocols for which all the relevant principles, rules, criteria and procedures governing such cooperation are spelled out ('pre-defined' structured cooperation); co-operation by groups of member states on the basis of 'enabling clauses' originally introduced in the Treaty of Amsterdam; and structured cooperation 'by default' (e.g. constructive abstention in CFSP, or the non-participation of Cyprus and Malta in discussions in the Council involving NATO classified information).

Pre-defined structured cooperation

To date structured cooperation under the treaty in any meaningful form has only actually been realised in clearly defined areas where all the relevant principles, rules and procedures governing that cooperation have been pre-determined in the treaty or in treaty protocols. These types of arrangements, best exemplified by EMU and Schengen matters, have worked because underlying them was a clear political objective in a particular policy area backed up with the necessary ways and means to achieve it. IGCs offer an ideal opportunity to emulate this approach in other areas. However, this is only possible if an IGC is able to identify suitable areas at a sufficiently early stage in its work to be in a position to specify the relevant ground rules in the new treaty. During the Nice IGC, no tangible proposals were forthcoming for new areas where 'pre-determined' structured cooperation might be envisaged. In the 2003-2004 IGC, however, in the light of the experience acquired by the Union in conducting crisis management operations and of the decision to work towards establishing a European armaments and capabilities agency, it was felt that security and defence lent itself to such treatment. At the IGC conclave of foreign ministers in Naples in November 2003, a text was tabled by the presidency, building on work undertaken by France, UK and Germany, which would allow member states whose military capabilities fulfil higher criteria, and which have made more binding commitments in this area with a view to the most demanding missions, to establish permanent structured cooperation within the Union (IGC, 2003). This is now enshrined in the draft constitutional treaty.

Structured cooperation 'enabling clauses'

The term 'enhanced' or 'structured' cooperation in recent IGCs has often been understood as referring specifically to one brand of flexible arrangement; namely cooperation by groups of member states on the basis of 'enabling clauses' originally introduced in the Treaty of Amsterdam. The problem for negotiators in the Nice IGC was that these clauses had never been used, arguably because the conditions had been so tightly drawn as to make their use all but impossible (Weatherill, 1999). The Nice IGC accordingly found itself in the somewhat surreal position of considering amendments to treaty provisions which had never been used, to deal with situations which could not be clearly identified and for no clearly defined objective. If ever there were a subject in the realms of virtual reality this was it!

Some argued that, since the enabling clause provisions were as yet untried, it would be premature in the absence of practical experience to contemplate amending treaty text which had barely been in force for a year. Advocates of change on the other hand argued strongly that it was precisely because they had been too rigidly framed that the existing enabling clauses had not been used. The increasing heterogeneity of the Union as a result of enlargement was likely to make unanimity to launch enhanced cooperation impossible to obtain. Rendering the provisions more flexible might also, paradoxically, encourage the conference's efforts to extend QMV in order to reduce the likelihood of them being used. Easier access to enhanced cooperation was also seen as the best way of reducing the temptation for member states to develop forms of closer cooperation, including potential 'pioneer' or 'vanguard' groups outside the EU treaty framework as mooted at the time in speeches by President Jacques Chirac and German Foreign Minister Joschka Fischer.

During the Nice IGC negotiations, defining the coverage of the enabling clauses was an issue in the EC Treaty and for the second pillar. As far as the third pillar was concerned (cooperation in police and criminal justice matters), the existing broad potential coverage was retained. Under the EC Treaty, while enhanced cooperation is necessarily ruled out in areas such as the CAP or the Common Commercial Policy (CCP) – since member states cannot cooperate in areas where practically no national room for manoeuvre exists – there was justified concern that relaxing the requirements for launching enhanced cooperation risked fragmenting some of the Union's hard-won achievements, particularly the internal market. Allowing enhanced cooperation on regulatory or normative matters associated with establishing or preserving the internal market or the Union's financial solidarity would unquestionably be harmful to the interests of the Union as a whole and of those member states not involved from the outset.

The debate in the latter stages of the Nice IGC focused inevitably on how to safeguard these core areas of Community business. Provided the internal market and economic and social cohesion policies (i.e., structural and cohesion funds) were explicitly ring-fenced, there would be no objective reason not to ease the conditions for enhanced cooperation in areas where member states in any case already had a significant measure of autonomy to act, without damaging the Union's coherence or the interests of other member states. Suggestions were put forward for using enabling clauses for policy coordination within the limits of the margins for action left to member states in areas such as certain specifically targeted environmental protection measures and measures for securing the Union's external borders. The treaty accordingly permits enhanced cooperation provided it 'does not concern areas which fall within the exclusive competence of the Community' and 'does not undermine the internal market as defined in article 14(2) of the TEC, or the economic and social cohesion established in accordance with Title XVII of that Treaty' (article 43 (d) and (e) TEU). Apart from in CFSP (see below), no significant changes were introduced into the enabling clause provisions, other than fixing the minimum number of member states as one third and allowing the possibility for member states engaged in enhanced cooperation to decide that QMV could apply where the treaty provided for unanimous decision-making.

Structured cooperation under the second pillar (CFSP) was in the past viewed with scepticism. Attempts to introduce such enabling clauses at Amsterdam failed. The value and strength of a common foreign policy is its unity and, on the face of it, the use of enabling clauses allowing separate initiatives would seem incompatible with the desired objective. Moreover, the treaty already contains provisions allowing a measure of flexibility. Article 23(1) TEU allows an 'opt out' for any member states which do not wish to apply a particular policy decision. It has been argued that constructive abstention in this way, which allows a number of member states not to apply a measure while accepting that it commits the Union, already provides sufficient flexibility without undermining the unity of the CFSP. While ways have been sought in the past to bind in all member states to the CFSP, particularly in the light of previous experience with contact groups, enhanced cooperation enabling clauses could never become a means of constraining member states' autonomy on the international scene.

While the Nice conference originally considered texts which were broad in scope, including security and defence matters, the final outcome was much more restricted, in particular by excluding matters having military or defence implications. This is evidently very different in nature from structured cooperation under the first and third pillars. In reality, it is akin to a form of implementing measure for an already agreed policy, accepted in principle by all member states, but under which specific tasks are delegated to the member states involved in enhanced cooperation. The term 'enhanced cooperation' is therefore something of a misnomer. Under the draft constitutional treaty, substantial changes have been introduced which will allow structured cooperation under the CFSP with no exclusion for ESDP and no limitation simply to policy implementation.

'Variable geometry' in the Council under 'pre-defined' structured cooperation

There are currently three areas where 'pre-defined' structured cooperation results in altered geometry in terms of Council deliberations and decision-making: economic and monetary union; justice, home affairs and movement of persons; and security and defence. The impact of arrangements in these sectors on the composition of the Council are summarised below.

In the past, variable geometry also applied in the case of the social policy, where the UK's non-participation in the social protocol appended to the Maastricht Treaty meant that the UK could not participate in votes on matters decided under the protocol. For decisions to be taken by qualified majority, the UK's votes (10) were simply subtracted from the threshold for a qualified majority of the Twelve (54), as a result of which the threshold dropped from 71% to 66% of weighted votes. During negotiations on the Treaty of Amsterdam, following a shift in the position of the UK government, the provisions in the protocol were integrated into the treaty proper. The Council of the social protocol is therefore defunct.

Economic and monetary union

Thirteen member states have not adopted the single currency. All thirteen may decide to join the single currency provided the convergence criteria are met and the Council takes a decision to that effect. As far as the UK, Denmark and Sweden are concerned, any such decision, for internal or constitutional reasons, would require a favourable vote in a referendum.

Two practical consequences flow from this as far as the Council is concerned. In the first place, ministers from member states which have adopted the single currency meet once a month in the 'Eurogroup', usually on the eve of Ecofin Council meetings. While the Eurogroup is an informal forum and cannot take binding decisions (only the Ecofin Council can do that), most of the serious policy discussion on matters which concern euro members takes place in that forum, with the Ecofin Council simply formally rubber-stamping any decisions to be taken (see chapter 5.1). Second, under the treaty, a number of decisions relating to economic and monetary policy (as set out in article 122(3) TEC) are only taken by member states which have adopted the euro. Those not inside the euro-area, although present in the Council deliberations, cannot take part in votes or decisions. Where such decisions are taken by qualified majority, the qualified majority requires a two thirds majority of weighted votes of Council members entitled to vote. If decisions are to be taken involving measures against one of the euro members under the excessive deficit procedure, the votes of the members concerned are excluded from the calculation of the qualified majority.

Justice, home affairs and free movement of persons

Under various treaty provisions relating to justice, home affairs and free movement of persons, three member states have various opt-ins/opt-outs under the treaty. As regards border controls for persons moving *inside* the EU, under article 1 of the protocol to article 14 TEC, the UK has the right to retain internal border controls in order to check persons coming from other member states. Ireland also has the right to retain border controls in order to maintain the common travel area with the UK. However, if Ireland were to renounce the common travel area, it would no longer apply border controls for persons coming from member states other than the UK. As a result of the position of the UK and Ireland, the other member states have the right to maintain their border controls towards the UK and Ireland. However, both the UK and Ireland take part in discussions and vote on measures based on article 14 TEC. Under the treaty of accession, border controls will be maintained between the Fifteen and the ten new member states until such time as it has been established, following verification, that they fulfil the necessary criteria to become part of the Schengen area and a decision to that effect has been taken by the Council.

The situation is somewhat different in relation to title IV TEC (visas, asylum, immigration and judicial cooperation in civil law matters). Three member states (UK, Ireland and Denmark) have various types of opt-out/opt-in. Under a protocol annexed to the treaty, Ireland and the UK do not take part in the adoption of any measures based on title IV TEC nor in the substantive costs arising from them unless they decide to opt in by either

(i) participating in specific measures on an ad hoc basis if they indicate within three months after a proposal or initiative is made that they wish to participate in its adoption or (ii), after obtaining the Commission's approval, they accept that a title IV TEC measure becomes binding on them after its adoption. In practice, both Ireland and the UK in most cases opt in to title IV measures before they are adopted, particularly those related to asylum and judicial cooperation in civil law matters. Ireland may, under the protocol, give up its special position by means of a simple declaration. In cases where the UK and Ireland choose not to opt in, they are present at all deliberations but may not vote. The qualified majority is calculated as the same proportion of the weighted votes of the members of the Council concerned as laid down in article 205(2) TEC; unanimity of the same members is required for decisions requiring unanimity in the Council.

Again via a treaty protocol, Denmark has completely opted out of all measures adopted on the basis of title IV TEC (except in relation to the adoption of certain visa measures in which it *does* participate). There is no possibility for Denmark to opt in on an ad hoc basis. Apart from the limited exceptions in the case of visas, Denmark does not therefore participate in the adoption of any measures based on this title, nor in the substantive costs arising from such measures (although it is present during Council deliberations and in all preparatory bodies). It can only participate in title IV TEC by renouncing completely or partially its opt-out, in which case all relevant title IV TEC measures would become applicable to Denmark without the need for a change to the TEC. For measures under title IV TEC which involve developing the Schengen *acquis* (see chapter 6), Denmark must, within six months after the adoption of the measure, decide whether it will implement the measure in its national law! If it does not, the other member states concerned will consider appropriate measures to be taken. In practice, Denmark always aligns its national law with all measures decided.

With regard to title VI TEU, although, as far as the UK and Ireland are concerned, the Schengen protocol applies in relation to title VI TEU measures building on the Schengen *acquis* (i.e., opt-out with a potential opt-in), in practice both member states are deemed to have opted in to practically everything (with the exception of hot pursuit for both UK and Ireland, and discreet surveillance in the case of Ireland). Denmark has no special provisions in relation to title VI TEU, and so is 'in' on everything.

Security and defence

There are currently two cases in the context of the EU's security and defence policy where variable geometry configurations occur in the Council. In the first case, Denmark, under its treaty protocol, is not involved in any matters with defence implications, and has no possibility of opting in. This means that Denmark does not participate in decision-shaping or decision-making in the Council on any matters with defence implications (i.e., no speaking or voting in the Council), and does not contribute to the financing or operational expenditure of such measures. While Denmark is present in the Council and its preparatory bodies when defence questions and military operations are discussed (including in the military committee), Danish

Council members cannot intervene in the discussion nor participate in decisions.

The other case where fewer than the full complement of Council members can take part is deliberations on defence matters, where NATO classified information is being discussed or referred to in the Council or any preparatory bodies. Under the EU-NATO agreement on security of information, NATO classified information may only be exchanged with states which have concluded a security agreement with NATO. This means that in any Council preparatory body where NATO classified information is discussed, Cyprus and Malta may not be present or take part in the deliberations. As a result, Cyprus and Malta at present do not take part in EU military operations conducted using NATO assets, although this does not affect their right to participate in decisions launching such operations. However, they are not involved in any decisions which concern the implementation of such operations (Council, 2002).

As mentioned above, security and defence is one area where concrete proposals have been made in the 2003-2004 IGC for establishing structured cooperation based on pre-defined criteria. Under the new treaty, structured cooperation in this area would be open to any member state which undertakes (i) to proceed more intensively to develop its defence capacities through the development of its national contributions and participation, where appropriate, in multinational forces, in the main European equipment programmes and in the activity of the European armaments agency; and (ii) to have the capacity to supply by 2007, either at national level or as a component of multinational force groups, targeted combat units able to respond within five to 30 days, and which can be sustained for an initial period of 30 days and be extended up to at least 120 days. The decision to put this cooperation in place would be taken by qualified majority, as would any decision taken by the participating members allowing other member states which fulfil the basic criteria to join. Operational decisions by members participating in the structured cooperation would be taken by unanimity.

Variable geometry under the structured cooperation enabling clauses

One of the principles underlying enhanced cooperation put in place through the treaty enabling clauses is that it should be open to all member states (article 43 TEU). While the decision to initiate enhanced cooperation under the first and third pillars is taken by all members of the Council by qualified majority (unanimity in the case of enhanced cooperation under the second pillar), for acts and decisions taken under the enhanced cooperation once it has been launched, all members of the Council may take part in the deliberations, but only those representing member states participating in enhanced cooperation will take part in the adoption of decisions. A member of the Council may delay a decision by requesting that the matter be referred to the European Council. Since the European Council meets every three months, this does not represent a significant delay. This referral does not constitute a veto, since the matter will revert to the Council after it has been discussed by the European Council.

In such cases, the relevant institutional provisions of the treaties shall apply (as appropriate, unanimity or qualified majority, the latter being the same proportion of weighted votes and Council members concerned – but not the population clause foreseen in article 205 of the treaty). Expenditure, other than administrative expenditure entailed by the institutions, is borne by the participating member states, unless all Council members unanimously decide otherwise.

Easing some of the procedural requirements to make enhanced cooperation easier to initiate depended on striking a balance between member states participating in enhanced cooperation and those electing not to participate at the outset. At Nice, adjustments were made in order to define more clearly the respective rights and obligations of 'ins' and 'outs' in any enhanced cooperation, thereby finding a balance between making enhanced cooperation easier to launch in a particular area for those who wished to pursue it, and securing the interests of non-participating member states, both in terms of safeguarding the Union *acquis* and of ensuring that they would not be arbitrarily excluded from taking part if they elected to do so and fulfilled the relevant criteria laid down in the treaties. As far as the procedures for launching enhanced cooperation are concerned, the minimum number of member states required to launch any initiative was altered from a majority of member states to eight, a figure which will remain unchanged after the enlargement.

'Variable geometry' by default

There is currently one case where a 'variable geometry' configuration can result by default under the second pillar on foreign and security policy matters. Under article 23(1) TEU, a member of the Council may qualify any abstention with a formal declaration stating that it shall not be obliged to apply the decision (so-called 'constructive abstention'). While any such states might participate in the deliberations leading up to such a decision, once they had constructively abstained, they would not be involved in decision-making in any subsequent implementing decisions (although they would be present in discussions). To date, this provision has never been invoked.

Structured cooperation – a necessity for the Union?

The variety of flexible arrangements which already exist or which would come into effect after the entry into force of the constitutional treaty is a direct reflection of both the depth of integration in certain policy sectors and of an increasingly diverse and heterogeneous Union. This has also had an impact on the working of the Council in the various ways described above. The real question for the coming years is whether the elements of flexibility which are currently built into the EU's structures provide sufficient 'give' while maintaining a broadly cohesive whole, or whether the strains of an increasingly diverse Union generate pressures for more concrete shape to be given to ideas for deepening integration via a more limited 'inner core' group inside the Union. While such ideas have not yet emerged in any seriously developed form to date, that does not preclude such steps being taken in future.

Structured cooperation, like most projects in the Union, has worked most successfully where clear objectives and criteria have been defined in the treaty. On this basis, the provisions on pre-defining cooperation on security and defence matters in the new constitutional treaty have at least a credible chance of working. However, structured cooperation of this type has frequently been overshadowed by the attention given both in policy discussions and in the academic literature to the so-called 'enabling clauses' in the treaty. There are several reasons for this.

First, with enlargement involving states with levels of prosperity well below that of existing member states looming, the view was that in a larger and more heterogeneous Union it might be wise to take out an insurance policy for the future in the shape of workable enhanced cooperation enabling clauses. Even if no clearly perceived purpose exists for these clauses at present (to date they have never been used), the more instruments at the disposal of the Union the better equipped it will be to deal with unforeseen eventualities. Even if ideas on precisely how these clauses might be used in the context of enlargement were sketchy, recourse to enhanced cooperation enabling clauses is not generally considered to be a vehicle which would result in a de facto 'core' Europe. Interestingly, there did not appear to be any real concern during the Nice IGC that easing the conditions might lead to them being turned into a means for across the board, systematic cooperation by a group of member states seeking to establish an integrationist 'vanguard' within the Union. The general view was that the enabling clauses should be an instrument of last resort to be used on a case-by-case basis by discrete groups of member states on specific issues when circumstances genuinely warranted their use.

Much of the ideological rhetoric which was a feature of discussions at Amsterdam has given way to a more pragmatic view. The Union will in all likelihood proceed cautiously in considering recourse to these new instruments; clearly, the first occasion they are used will constitute an important precedent. Irrespective of the way in which they might be used in future, these re-worked provisions, coupled with possibilities for structured cooperation in security and defence matters, may have weakened the case for structured vanguard groups of member states organising themselves outside the treaties. It is one thing for a number of member states to agree among themselves to act as a unit and coordinate their positions as far as possible inside the EU institutions using all the means available under the treaties to promote the interests of the group. At the end of the day, if certain member states wish to take a political initiative to work within the system according to their own code of behaviour as a sort of internal pressure group, they cannot be prevented from doing so. It would however be quite another to conclude a treaty in parallel to the existing Union. However, with further enlargements of the Union becoming a real prospect on the horizon, this debate is one which is likely to remain open for the foreseeable future.

PART 3: THE EUROPEAN COUNCIL AND INTERGOVERNMENTAL CONFERENCES

Although it may at first sight appear somewhat odd, not everything which happens in the Council building is 'of the Council'. There are a number of occasions where decisions are taken inside the Council buildings by representatives of twenty-five governments, yet which are not Council meetings. First, there are the regularly quarterly meetings of the heads of state or government of the European Union and the president of the Commission, collectively known as the European Council, which, since the latter part of 2003, have all taken place in the Justus Lipsius building in Brussels. Chapter 9 describes the history, functions and working methods of the Union's supreme political body and its intimate relationship with the Council.

Chapter 10 considers the second case, i.e., where ministers act collectively on matters for which the member states themselves (rather than the Union or Community as such) are competent. Decisions taken in this way are 'intergovernmental' in the conventional sense, unlike decisions taken by the Council itself, which, even in the areas of foreign policy and cooperation in police and criminal justice matters, are *not* intergovernmental. This may seem a legalistic distinction, but at a time when the question of the extent of the Union's powers relative to those of member states is a political bone of contention, such distinctions are significant. These meetings are referred to as 'conferences of the representatives of the governments of the member states', or 'intergovernmental conferences' for short.

Chapter 9: The European Council

A student coming afresh to today's European Union would look instinctively to a body such as the European Council, composed as it is of member states' heads of government, as the logical apex of the decision-making structure. Yet, for most of its existence, the European Council has acted outside the Union framework with ambiguous legal status and a somewhat vaguely defined role. It was only when the Maastricht Treaty entered into force in November 1993 that this fundamentally ambiguous situation changed.

The European Council is not, at present, an institution of the Union, but features in the general preambular articles of the Treaty on European Union, where it is described as providing 'the necessary impetus' and defining the 'general political guidelines' of the Union. This is distinct from the specific tasks in the emerging 'economic government' of the Union which are conferred on the Council meeting in the composition of heads of state or government (e.g. article 122(2) TEC). The Council is an institution with legal powers, whose decisions are subject to the jurisdiction of the European Court of Justice and which operates according to rules of procedure. The European Council is the Union's supreme political authority, its decisions are not subject to the Court's jurisdiction and it has twenty-six members (unlike the Council, the president of the Commission is also a member of the European Council). Its composition, *modus operandi* and 'feel' are very different from the Council (see below).

With Maastricht, the European Council started to come of age, after a meandering existence that traces its roots back to February 1962, in the earliest days of the European Community's existence. This chapter recounts the chronological development of the European Council, highlighting some of the most significant meetings in recent years. As the closing section of this chapter will show, the draft constitution, when it enters into force will take the European Council to a new plane, as a formal and integral part of the Union's institutional framework. But in many respects this is what it already is …

De Gaulle-inspired summitry

When General Charles de Gaulle came to power in 1958, he inherited a Rome Treaty on which the ink of the signatures had barely dried. Much of it was anathema to him. Having fought to re-establish a free and powerful France during the 1940s, he was particularly distrustful of the treaties' federalist slant. Initially distracted by the Algerian crisis, by the early 1960s de Gaulle had turned his thoughts to an alternative structure for cooperation

between European states which would, simultaneously, assert European
(and hence French) independence vis-à-vis the United States, and avoid the,
as he saw it, dangerously federalist leanings of the European Economic
Community. On 10 and 11 February 1962, he convened a summit of the
heads of government of the other five member states of the European
Economic Community in Paris. This was the first time that the heads of the
Six had met, but de Gaulle expressly convened the meeting outside, and
without any linkage to, the Community framework – it was to be a meeting
between the leaders of sovereign states. De Gaulle launched the idea of a
European political union based primarily on intergovernmental cooperation
and, though wary, the other member states agreed that the idea should be
studied. The smaller member states were apprehensive on two counts. First,
they did not want Europe to be detached from the United States. Second,
there was a resurgence of the old fear, prevalent at the very beginning of
negotiations for the European Coal and Steel Community in 1951-52, that a
new framework would lead to Franco-German dominance (the fear was
exacerbated by the fact that the Paris summit was an entirely Franco-
German bilateral initiative). A second summit was held in Bonn on 19 and
20 July 1961 to study the Fouchet Plan, but the member states' misgivings
could not be overcome, and de Gaulle's initiative collapsed.

De Gaulle's summitry was based on his own particular, patrician logic
about sovereign states and their leaders. Only leaders, he felt, had the legitimacy to commit states, and then on the basis of intergovernmental cooperation. The Paris and Bonn summits were the means to a precise end - an
intergovernmental platform and forum for the Fouchet Plan, but summitry
was also to have been an integral part of the Fouchet Plan, just as bilateral
summitry was to form an integral part of the vestigial 1963 Franco-German
Treaty. The result of de Gaulle's ill-fated initiative was to create a deep dis-
trust of summitry among European Community circles which was not completely overcome until the 1980s.

Pompidou-inspired summitry

The heads of government of the Six met again in Rome on 29 and 30 May
1967, but this was a purely ceremonial occasion to mark the tenth anniversary of the signing of the Treaties of Rome. By the end of the 1960s a number
of worrying trends were becoming apparent to French policy-makers. The
economic boom Western Europe had enjoyed earlier in the decade was
fading, and the Western European economy was becoming markedly
weaker than that of the United States. At the same time, the Western
German economy was growing in strength. De Gaulle's departure and the
election of Georges Pompidou as the new French president created the
opportunity for reassessment and fresh initiatives. British accession to the
EEC, which had twice been refused by de Gaulle on the grounds that Britain
was too close to the United States, was now seen as a possible counterweight
to Germany's growing strength.

These broader, traditional diplomatic and geopolitical considerations
combined with narrower concerns about the stagnation of the European
Economic Community. Once the few specific policy objectives in the Rome

Treaty had been achieved, it had become more difficult to reach agreement. The Luxembourg compromise (see chapter 14) had exacerbated this problem, undermining the European Commission's 'visionary' role and pushing it towards more pragmatic, lower-common-denominator solutions. Positive initiatives foundered. The over-worked Foreign Affairs Council was unable to arbitrate among the disputes of the growing number of technical and sectoral Councils (see the introduction to part 2). There was little apparent overall policy evaluation or direction. The continued absence of direct elections to the European Parliament deprived the Community of legitimacy, at least in the eyes of some. Economic problems were becoming increasingly important, and economics was becoming increasingly internationalised.

All of these considerations combined in Pompidou's proposal for a new summit meeting of the heads of government. Since the meeting occurred during the 1969 Dutch presidency, it was held at The Hague, on 1 and 2 December. Though it is now fading into history, the Hague summit was one of the great watersheds in the Community's development. The summit was devoted to three interlinked themes; completing, widening and deepening the Community. On the evening of the first day, President Pompidou and the German Chancellor, Willy Brandt, were able to reach agreement on enlargement. This served as the key to progress elsewhere. There was an agreement in principle on the Community's 'own resources' (see chapter 16) with, as a quid pro quo, an agreement that the European Parliament should be awarded budgetary powers. The Council was requested to draw up a plan for the phased introduction of economic and monetary union. The foreign affairs ministers were instructed to study ways of making progress in foreign policy cooperation. Integration was unblocked. Pompidou proposed that summits should be institutionalised, but the idea was not taken up, in part because of residual prejudices against the old, Gaullist method.

Despite a backdrop of continued monetary upheaval, the next summit was not convened until the subsequent French presidency. The 19 and 20 October 1972 Paris summit was judged a failure. The chief themes discussed were the already faltering process of Economic and Monetary Union (linked to social and regional policy), strengthening the institutions towards political union, and the European Community's international role. Preparations by the foreign affairs ministers and their officials were fraught. The communiqué issued after the summit was pre-cooked and avoided many of the real political issues. Once again, President Pompidou unsuccessfully proposed that summitry should be institutionalised.

By the time of the next summit, international economic conditions had deteriorated still further. Western European relations with the United States had soured. The October War in the Middle East had led to the oil crisis. This in turn had exaggerated the effects of impending recession, exacerbating divergent economic tendencies in the member states and blowing the Werner Plan for Economic and Monetary Union off course. Like Paris, the 14 and 15 December 1973 Copenhagen summit was regarded as a failure; ill-prepared, chaotically run, with limited decisions, mostly not implemented. Earlier in the year, in October, President Pompidou had once more proposed that summits should be institutionalised in order to deal with European political cooperation matters. At Copenhagen, the heads of government went halfway towards this proposal, deciding that summits would be 'held whenever justified by circumstances and when it appears necessary to provide a stimulus or lay down further guidelines for the construction of a united Europe'.

The ad hoc summits had not been a complete failure; the Hague summit in particular had been a success. Though the meetings had been ill-prepared and badly managed, though there had been discontinuity between the objectives they set and the follow-up given to them, the member states had identified common problems and agreed on the need for common solutions. Pompidou's repeated calls for institutionalised summitry had sparked off a debate, albeit within limited circles, about the desirability of such a move. Some pro-integrationists warned against summitry. Building on latent hostility from the Fouchet Plan days, they saw summits as intergovernmental structures designed primarily to counter integration and ensure French influence. The imposition of an intergovernmental structure at heads of state level would sap the Commission of its role as the Community's driving force and create a new dynamic of rivalry between the supranational and the intergovernmental. More pragmatically, Georges Vedel, who had chaired a working party on the problems associated with the enlargement of the Community (European Commission, 1972), argued that frequent use of summits would reduce their impact and authority. But some pro-integrationists saw summits as an obvious response to the Community's post-Luxembourg compromise lack of direction. Altiero Spinelli, ever the imaginative constitutionalist, suggested they be institutionalised as a 'supreme council' (Spinelli, 1972, pp 176-178). Jean Monnet was a warm supporter of the French initiative, telling Giscard that 'what is lacking more than anything else in European affairs is authority. Discussion is organized: decision is not.' (see Monnet, 1978, pp 751-765; see also, Fontaine, 1979).

The constitutional status of institutionalised summits was debated at length; would they be in, beside, or above the European Communities' framework? Would summits be subject to the jurisprudence of the European Court of Justice, or accountable to the European Parliament? How would summits interact with the European Commission's treaty-based right of initiative? Would summits legitimise the Communities, or would this be better done through direct elections to the European Parliament?

Broader elements began to inform the debate. For example, the growth of summitry was not a phenomenon restricted to Western Europe. Monetary and economic problems caused by the collapse of the Bretton Woods system and events such as the oil crisis, together with the growth in economic power of countries like Japan and Germany, led to institutionalised 'Western' economic summitry. As the Western world grew more interdependent, government leaders were expected to play a more prominent international role.

Giscard and Schmidt-inspired summitry – the birth of the European Council

As young finance ministers in the early 1970s, Valéry Giscard d'Estaing and Helmut Schmidt had met together with their British and American counterparts (Anthony Barber and George Schulz) in a series of informal secret sessions to discuss economic and monetary problems. The first of these took place in the White House library, and hence the meetings became known as the 'library group'. Both Giscard and Schmidt had been impressed by the library group format; no officials were in attendance and ministers could speak freely and completely off the record (the fact that both Giscard and Schmidt spoke good English helped). By 1974, Giscard and Schmidt had become president and chancellor, respectively, of their two countries. When Giscard, acting in the tradition of his predecessor, urged the holding of a summit in 1974 under the French presidency, both men had their library group experience in mind.

In fact, Giscard's initiative led to two summits. The first, known as the 'picnic summit' took place in Paris on 14 September 1974. Its primary purpose was to prepare the main themes for a major summit later in the year. The 'picnic summit' was adjudged to have been a success:

'All participants, including the Benelux states, seemed to be satisfied by this meeting. The participants had been able to reflect on the most appropriate way of maintaining the EC as a "going concern", capable of tackling the main problems concerning the Member States. The success lay in the opportunity for a frank exchange of views without pressure for a firm set of decisions.' (Bulmer and Wessels, 1987, p 43)

Despite apprehensions about the attitude of the British Labour government, which had been returned to office in October 1974 with a working majority, the second Paris summit, held on 9 and 10 December 1974, was also a great success. Just as the key at The Hague had been enlargement, so the key at Paris was the creation of a regional fund. Germany, already the Community's 'paymaster', made concessions over the size of the fund, and other elements of the jigsaw then fell into place. Indeed, the Paris summit was a complicated example of the package deal at work (see chapter 16). The opposition to summitry of the pro-integrationist Benelux countries was bought off by the promise of direct elections to the European Parliament and the commissioning of a report on European union. UK prime minister Harold Wilson's position over re-negotiation was facilitated by a Schmidt-led compromise to create a 'corrective mechanism' which could be presented as a negotiating success by the British government, but which allayed French fears of any reform of the common agricultural policy.

Progress was made in a great number of areas but, for the purposes of this chapter, the most important development was agreement to the creation of institutionalised summitry. (Several governments, particularly the Danish, objected to the term 'European Council' which was therefore not formally used, but Giscard repeatedly used the term in his pronouncements until the Danish government gave in.) The communiqué issued after the meeting of the heads of state or government declared that they had 'decided to meet, accompanied by the ministers of foreign affairs, three times a year and, wherever necessary, in the Council of the Communities and in the context of political cooperation.' The European Council had been born.

A number of characteristics of the early European Council deserve comment. A first is the importance of Giscard's and Schmidt's shared vision. The importance of personalities and the chemistry between them is a recurring theme in the evolution of the European Council. If the Paris summit succeeded it was not only because of the friendship between the French president and the German chancellor and their shared experience in the library group, but because they shared a common political vision. Giscard was not a Gaullist but a pragmatic Europeanist. Both he and Schmidt were sceptical about the Commission's role and had no compunction, if it suited their interests, in encroaching on the Commission's prerogatives. The Paris communiqué ambiguously stated that 'the Commission will exercise the powers vested in it and play the part assigned to it', but what powers, and what part? In truth, both Giscard and Schmidt believed that, if only for purely pragmatic reasons about where the balance of power now lay, political leadership in the Community had to be exercised by the heads of state or government.

The composition of the European Council was the result of a series of compromises. It should first be noted that, because of the particular constitutional status of the French president, the practice has grown of referring to the European Council as 'the heads of state or government' although, in fact, there are normally only two heads of state who attend – the French and Finnish presidents. Second, account had to be taken of the differing status of heads of government in the various member states. In Belgium, Italy and the Netherlands the prime minister is traditionally regarded as *primus inter pares*, whereas in the French fifth republic the French president normally holds uncontested primary responsibility for foreign policy. Further, coalition governments were standard practice in a number of member states, and thought had to be given to equitable and balanced political representation. The resulting compromise was that the leaders were to be accompanied by their ministers of foreign affairs.

This provision coincided with other considerations. One was the need for an overall view and 'steer' for the evolving European political cooperation. The 1970 Luxembourg report on political cooperation had already booked the heads of state or government a seat at the European political cooperation table by stating that if the foreign ministers felt 'that the gravity of the circumstances or the importance of the subjects in question so justify, their meeting may be replaced by a Conference of Heads of State or Government.' Another consideration was the need for coordination. Thus, the Paris communiqué stated that:

'In order to ensure consistency in Community activities and continuity of work, the Ministers of Foreign Affairs, meeting in the Council of the Community, will act as initiators and co-ordinators. They may hold political co-operation meetings at the same time.'

The position of the European Commission, and whether it would be represented in the European Council was another consideration. However, the Commission president was invited to the first true European Council meeting at Dublin in March 1975, and the practice of the Commission's full participation was later confirmed (see below).

A third consideration was the organisational basis of future summits. The communiqué stated simply that: 'The administrative secretariat will be provided for in an appropriate manner with due regard for existing practices and procedures.' The opaque phraseology circumvented a major potential stumbling block, for a fear expressed in more pro-*communautaire* circles had been that the creation of a permanent secretariat would lead to a direct rival to the European Commission. It was therefore decided that, notwithstanding the chronic organisational problems the ad hoc summits had encountered, there would be no permanent secretariat, and the organisers would just have to 'muddle through'. Gradually, the organisational role devolved upon the Council, Coreper, the presidency and the Council's general secretariat. If the Paris summit's decision condemned the European Council to ad hoc organisation, the lack of a permanent structure also reinforced its position as an occasional forum – the European Council was to meet three times a year, a provision faithfully respected until 1985 – and final arbiter.

Though there was no formal provision in the Paris communiqué, it was clear that there were to be very few civil servants in the meeting. This was a legacy of Giscard's and Schmidt's library group days and was intended to free up discussion, but the absence of clear provisions on minute-taking and conclusion drafting was to cause severe headaches in the early years of the European Council's development.

A fourth consideration concerned the European Council's status and role – what was it to do? The Paris communiqué spoke about 'the need for an overall approach' to the Community's internal problems and the external problems facing Europe, and the need 'to ensure progress and overall consistency', but said nothing about how these objectives were to be achieved. What is clear is that, once established, the European Council quickly grew into 'the most politically authoritative institution of the EC' (Bulmer and Wessels, 1987, p 2), and it is no exaggeration to say that, since 1975, most of the major political decisions of the European Community have been taken in the European Council; the European monetary system, the decisions that led to the Single European Act and the Maastricht Treaty, German unification, further enlargements, the *ouverture* to the East, to name just a few. In effect, the absence of a clearly-defined role enabled the European Council to evolve organically, based on the natural authority of its membership.

A fifth consideration concerned the effects of the very existence of the European Council:

'The Three Wise Men ... specifically accepted that the European Council had imposed a hierarchy on the Community institutions whereas the Treaty of Rome had rather suggested a balance between them.' (Duff, 1981, p 244)

The 1977 London declaration

As the European Council's role grew in importance, so its organizational shortcomings became more apparent. At the initiative of Valéry Giscard d'Estaing, the 1977 London European Council discussed and adopted a declaration setting out in some detail the role of, and practical arrangements for, the European Council. The declaration foresaw three sorts of discussion: confidential and informal discussions in library group style; discussions leading to specific actions; and an occasional role as star chamber and court of last resort in disputes referred up to it from the Council. Substantive discussions intended to lead to conclusions or action and any statements to be issued were to be prepared in advance. There was to be no record of the participants' exchanges, but a written record of conclusions, issued on the authority of the presidency. There were, at Giscard's continued insistence, to be as few officials as possible.

The 1983 Stuttgart solemn declaration

In November 1981, the German and Italian governments submitted to their partners a 'draft European Act' designed to further European integration (the so-called 'Genscher-Colombo Act'). The November 1981 London European Council charged the foreign ministers with the task of studying the draft Act with a view to further action. The foreign ministers reported back to the 19 June 1983 Stuttgart European Council, which subsequently adopted a 'Solemn Declaration on European Union'. The solemn declaration devoted several paragraphs to the European Council.

The composition of the European Council was defined as before, but now expressly included the president of the Commission assisted by one other member of the Commission (six months later, at the Athens European Council, the Commission's secretary-general was allowed, for the first time, to attend the European Council, and has attended ever since).

The European Council was now allotted five specific tasks: providing general impetus; defining approaches and issuing general political guidelines; deliberating, with a view to consistency; initiating cooperation in new areas of activity; and expressing common positions on external relations questions. These definitions were far more specific than the Paris communiqué or the London declaration.

There were three significant innovations. The first was the statement that 'When the European Council acts in matters within the scope of the European Communities, it does so in its capacity as the Council.' This gave the European Council a curiously bi-cephalic status. When it acted within the Community framework, it acted as an extension of the Council, but it otherwise functioned on an ad hoc basis. The provision gave substance to the category of discussion, as foreseen by the London declaration, which was 'designed to produce decisions'. In effect, the European Council could, if it so wished, act as the Council.

The second innovation concerned the European Council's relations with the European Parliament. *Communautaire* observers felt that the European Parliament's role had suffered, perhaps more than the European Commission's, from the creation of the European Council. The creation of a body made up of heads of state or government was thought to have detracted from the legitimation function the European Parliament might have been expected to have played, had it been directly elected. Nor was the European Council accountable to the Parliament. However, under the terms of the Stuttgart solemn declaration, the European Council was now obliged to report to the European Parliament after each of its meetings. In the same context, the third innovation concerned the role of the presidency, which was now expected to present a report to the Parliament after each European Council meeting.

The Single European Act

After the extensive provisions of the Stuttgart solemn declaration, the Single European Act proved to be surprisingly terse. A single article confirmed the composition of the European Council as consisting of the heads of state or government and the president of the Commission, assisted by the ministers of foreign affairs and one other member of the Commission. The minimum frequency of meetings was reduced from thrice to twice a year. The most significant innovation was however that, for the first time, the European Council had a basis in the treaties.

The Maastricht Treaty

As William Nicoll has pointed out, 'the easily forgotten Solemn Declaration of Stuttgart was to become the quarry for what the Treaty of Maastricht was to say about the European Council' (1994, p 203). Much, though not all, of the solemn declaration's provisions were taken over and embodied in the Treaty. However, if the Maastricht Treaty did not go quite as far as the solemn declaration, this does not mean that the solemn declaration's other provisions no longer apply (these being, debating questions relating to the Union and ensuring coherence, opening the way to cooperation in new sectors, and solemnly expressing common positions on external relations questions).

The most significant development in the Maastricht Treaty was that the European Council would henceforth play a treaty-based role in providing the European Union with the 'necessary impetus for its development', defining the Union's general political guidelines and, in the context of economic government, defining the Union's broad economic guidelines. As late as the 1983 Stuttgart solemn declaration, heads of state or government were prepared to 'underline the particular importance of the Commission as guardian of the Treaties of Paris and Rome and as a driving force in the process of European integration,' thus reaffirming the traditional role of the European Commission as the 'motor of integration'. A decade later, the same heads of state and government seemed to have reserved this role to themselves. Was this, as some commentators believe, a decisive shift towards intergovernmentalism?

The truth is more complex. In one sense, article 4 TEU was merely a confirmation of current practice. The old integrationist model of the early 1960s, which saw a supranational Commission championing federalism as the nation states withered on the vine of national sovereignty, was effectively shattered by the Luxembourg compromise. When European integration once more got under way at the 1969 Hague summit, it was on a far more pragmatic basis, necessarily involving the nation states as an integral part of the process. This was the *raison d'être* of the European Council. But this did not lead to a displacement of the Commission. Within the Community framework, the Commission retained its right of legislative initiative; the member states were powerless to act in the absence of a Commission proposal. The Commission also retained its role as *penseur*, as the only institution able and willing to reflect upon the development of the Community and the European integration process from a central position (though the European Parliament was to develop a similar role after the 1979 direct elections had finally rescued it from obscurity and powerlessness).

In retrospect, it is clear that, far from discouraging the European Commission from embarking on major integrationist projects, the existence of the European Council encouraged it in this role. The Luxembourg compromise had taught the Commission that it could only embark on major projects if it brought the member states – or at the least an influential majority of them – on board. In effect, the European Council provided the Commission with a recruiting ground for its ideas. Closer examination of the major initiatives emanating from the European Council reveals that many were the result of Commission initiatives; for example, the European monetary system was the fruit of an initiative launched by the then Commission president, Roy Jenkins (Ludlow, 1982); the internal market programme embodied in the 1985 Single European Act was drawn from a Commission initiative and white paper. Two academics have calculated that, between the first European Council meeting in 1975 and the Fontainbleau European Council meeting in 1984, the Commission submitted over 60 proposals to the European Council (Jacqué and Simon, 1984, pp 24-25). As the 'Three Wise Men' put it, the Commission was 'finding new ways to play its traditional role' (The 'Three Wise Men', 1979, p 21). The phenomenon was particularly true of the three Commissions presided over by Jacques Delors – for example, the December 1994 Essen European Council's initiatives to combat unemployment were directly derived from a Commission white paper on growth, competitiveness and employment; Jacques Delors' parting gift, as it were. Delors' preference for the European Council over the Council was well known. He became adept at recruiting the member states to his causes, which were then referred down to the Council for action. He also developed a finely-honed instinct for producing compromise proposals at the eleventh hour (which were invariably greeted with relief) and was able to use skillfully the presidency's desire for a successful European Council. Delors himself responded to critics in the European Parliament, who had criticised the Commission for its 'lack of leadership', by noting:

'The Commission has a right of initiative. But a distinction needs to be made according to whether we exercise it within a specific institutional framework or in a more political context. Within a specific institutional context, our duty is to give effect to what has been formally decided by the European Council or by an amendment to the Treaty ... We might well dream of a Commission that had more powers. But we have to operate within our actual terms of reference.' (*Debates of the European Parliament*, 16.12.89)

Amsterdam

The Amsterdam Treaty made few fresh provisions regarding the European Council, but those it made were important. The most significant were in the context of the nascent common foreign and security policy. The European Council's role was strengthened by conferring upon it the competence to define the principles and general guidelines of the CFSP and to decide on common strategies (which were to be fleshed out by the Council, acting by qualified majority). Where a member state opposed such a decision for stated reasons of national policy, no vote would be taken but the Council could, by a qualified majority, refer the matter up to the European Council for decision by unanimity – a provision commonly described as the effective incorporation of the much-vilified Luxembourg compromise.

Both a common defence policy and the possible integration of the Western

European Union into the EU were to be subject to decisions by the European Council. The European Council could establish guidelines for the WEU where the EU had 'availed itself of the WEU'. A further consolidation of the European Council's role was the apparently minor, but nevertheless significant, express provision for decision-making. This, in combination with the lack of an explicit dividing line between strategy and implementation measures, gave rise to fears in the European Parliament that the new provisions might be sapped if a tendency developed to push decisions up from the Council (QMV) to the European Council (consensus). As the Parliament saw it, 'For the first time the voting procedure is determined not by the substance of the decision but by the level at which it is taken.' (European Parliament, 1997, p. 41)

Helsinki

To borrow from American parlance, by the 1990s the European Council's hull was covered in 'barnacles' – that is, a series of practices which had grown up organically but, by creating 'drag', threatened the European Council's efficiency. The most notorious of these was the way in which the European Council had become increasingly prolific, as one statistic demonstrates: the conclusions of the first European Council meeting in 1975 took up seven columns of the *EC Bulletin*; despite smaller print, the conclusions of the December 1994 Essen European Council took up 48 columns of the same *EC Bulletin*! Long-serving German Chancellor Helmut Kohl was among a number of European Council members to complain about the General Affairs Council's practice of tacking all manner of pronouncements and declarations onto the back of the European Council's conclusions proper.

In 1999 the then Council secretary-general, Jürgen Trumpf, drafted a paper setting out a series of proposals designed to steam off at least some of the barnacles from the hull not only of the Council, but also of the European Council. The December 1999 Helsinki European Council largely took over the Trumpf recommendations. 'The European Council,' it declared, 'must remain an effective forum for policy leadership in providing necessary impetus for the Union's development and defining general political guidelines.' It went on: 'One means of helping it better fulfil these tasks is to make the Presidency conclusions more concise (maximum 15 pages), thereby focusing them on the political decisions taken on the items actually discussed at the meeting.' This recommendation, immediately implemented, has been largely respected, but on occasion the conclusions have burgeoned beyond this under pressure from bureaucracies which view the conclusions as a vehicle for underwriting the importance of their particular sectoral interest. This is bad, because the public message being delivered by the European Council can often be lost in descriptive or over-detailed verbiage. What matters to the outside world is not what the European Council thinks, but what it has decided.

Lisbon

The Lisbon European Council in March 2000 provided a graphic example of the way in which the European Council could provide the 'necessary impetus' and, in so doing, proposed a new working method for the Council and the European Council. At Lisbon heads of state or government set the Union an ambitious new strategic goal of becoming 'the most competitive and dynamic knowledge-based economy in the world'. The European Council proposed to achieve this goal inter alia through the introduction of a 'new open method of coordination at all levels, coupled with a stronger guiding and coordinating role for the European Council to ensure more coherent strategic direction and effective monitoring of progress. A meeting of the European Council to be held every Spring will define the relevant mandates and ensure that they are followed up.' The Lisbon European Council set down detailed operational recommendations on how the new method was to be implemented, in the process introducing new terms to the EU's jargon, such as 'best practice', 'indicators', 'benchmarking' and 'peer review'. These recommendations were designed 'to help member states to progressively develop their own policies' by:

> 'fixing guidelines for the Union combined with specific timeta-bles for achieving the goals which they set in the short, medium and long terms;
>
> establishing, where appropriate, quantitative and qualitative indicators and benchmarks against the best in the world and tailored to the needs of different Member States and sectors as a means of comparing best practice;
>
> translating these European guidelines into national and regional policies by setting specific targets and adopting measures, taking into account national and regional differences;
>
> periodic monitoring, evaluation and peer review organised as mutual learning processes.'

The 'relevant mandates' concerned the various sectoral Council configur-ations on whose shoulders the bulk of the work was going to fall.

While the 'open method' itself has proved controversial, the Spring Lisbon strategy review European Council meetings are now an accepted fix-ture in the Union's calendar and, perhaps of deeper and more lasting sig-nificance, nobody and nothing contested the European Council's prerogative in establishing such an ambitious strategy (contrast this with the provenance of the internal market and single currency – both Commission-led initiatives).

Indeed, one of the more controversial aspects of the Lisbon strategy was the way in which it effectively circumnavigated such traditional 'Community method' characteristics as Commission initiatives and European Parliament legislative and control mechanisms. The Commission subsequently (and very quickly) scrabbled back a central role of sorts by offering itself as secretariat and coordinator of the strategy (a role the Council needed and the European Council had not really foreseen), but the Parliament was largely reduced to a consultative role at best. At the same time, both Commission and Parliament were broadly supportive of the strategy itself, and both have performed their 'ad hoc' roles with gusto. Rocket science is not required to predict that, should the strategy fall significantly short of reaching its avowed objective (as would currently seem a strong probability), both institutions will point to more traditional mechanisms as providing a more reliable means of doing business. In the meantime, however, 'best practice', 'indicators', 'benchmarking' and 'peer review' will long since have become accepted parts of the Council's methodology and the Union's lexicon.

Nice

As part of the process of reaching an overall agreement, the Nice Intergovernmental Conference agreed to include the following declaration in the final act: 'As from 2002, one European Council meeting per presidency will be held in Brussels. When the Union comprises eighteen members, all European Council meetings will be held in Brussels.' Feelings about this declaration were mixed. Some emphasised that, in addition to cost savings, basing European Council meetings in Brussels undoubtedly represented a further step towards institutionalising the Union's supreme political authority. With the trend towards holding at least four meetings a year, including an annual meeting on economic and social matters in the Spring, the establishment of a fixed venue consolidated the European Council's position as the body driving the Union's political agenda. It also emphasised the fact that the European Council should also be viewed as a 'normal fixture' in the Union's political life, rather than a special 'cup final' media event.

Others, in contrast, regretted what they saw as a risk – by basing the European Council in Brussels the Union might render itself even more remote from citizens, since this removed a regular opportunity to somehow bring 'the Union' to the member states in a very visible way. However, as chapter 18 demonstrates in regard to the presidency, such arguments lost their force in the light of violent demonstrations which marred European Council meetings in Göteborg and Nice, and the closer the prospect of a Union of between 25 and 30 member states became; in particular, it could just as easily be argued that the right of each member state to host a European Council meeting once every twelve to fifteen years would merely serve to reinforce the distance of 'Brussels' from the people it purports to serve. All European Council meetings since the second half of 2003 have taken place in Brussels (see appendix 1).

Seville

As the 2004 enlargement grew ever closer, as the central role of the European Council was increasingly consolidated, and as the need for reform of the European Council's organisation and working methods became more apparent, the June 2002 European Council returned to the reform theme in a more determined fashion, codifying some existing practices and laying down new rules for the preparation, conduct and conclusions of its proceedings. The European Council itself characterised this package as 'a substantial change to present practices in the direction of enhancing the efficiency of the institution on the eve of an unprecedented increase in the

number of member states of the Union.' In summary form, the new rules
were as follows:

- The European Council to meet four times a year, with allowance
  for additional meetings under exceptional circumstances;

- Meetings to be prepared by the GAERC;

- GAERC to have an enhanced gatekeeping function by preparing
  draft annotated agendas four weeks before European Council
  meetings setting out items for debate, approval, etc;

- GAERC to meet on the eve of European Council meetings and
  adopt the definitive agenda (to which no item may subsequently
  be added);

- Meetings in the margin of European Council meetings to be held
  in exceptional circumstances only and have prior approval of the
  GAERC;

- The presidency to ensure smooth conduct of business, including
  by restricting speaking time;

- Each delegation to have two seats in the meeting room, and the –
  total size of delegations limited to 20 for each delegation and for
  the Commission;

- The conclusions should be 'as concise as possible' and set out
  policy guidelines and decisions reached, indicating the stages of
  procedure to follow on from them;

- An outline of the conclusions to be distributed on the day of the
  European Council meeting, with a distinction between parts of
  the text 'which have been previously approved' and those parts
  which the European Council must discuss.

Today's European Council

As currently constituted, the European Council consists of the heads of state
or government of the member states and the president of the Commission,
assisted by the ministers for foreign affairs and by another member of the
Commission. The European Council meets twice under each presidency,
i.e., at least four times a year. (The draft Constitution further consolidates
this by forthrightly declaring that the European Council 'shall meet quarterly'.) Its treaty-based role is still defined as providing 'the necessary impetus', but in reality the European Council plays a vital role in all of the
European Union's fields of activity, whether by giving impetus to the
Union, defining general political guidelines, or by coordinating, arbitrating
or disentangling difficult questions. As the Council's website puts it:

'Currently, only the European Council can really give the European
Union a shot in the arm...This is explained mainly by the legitimacy which
the heads of state or government enjoy, but also by the fact that the
European Council can stand back to some extent and, unlike the Council,

the Commission and the European Parliament, is not involved in day-to-day decision-making.'

Participants sit in the sequence used for the rotation of the presidency, moving clockwise every six months (see chapter 3), and the meeting is chaired by the prime minister or president of the member state holding the presidency. In addition to the interpreters (the 'formal' sessions have interpretation to and from twenty languages), attendance is restricted to a handful of officials: the Council secretary-general and deputy secretary-general (seated at the main table), and, seated well back from the main table, the Commission secretary-general and the head of the private office of the Commission president, four officials from the presidency (one normally being the chair of Coreper II), and four from the Council secretariat.

The Council general secretariat also maintains a rota of note-takers, who take it in turns to sit in on the European Council meeting for fifteen to twenty minute periods. Emerging note-takers brief the members of the Antici group seated in a nearby antechamber (see chapter 11) on the European Council's proceedings. There is no verbatim report or record of proceedings. The lack of an official record may at times be an irritation and a frustration, and it can give rise to ambiguity about what was decided (although the secretary-general is able if necessary to give an authoritative account of what actually transpired), but it is also an important guarantee for frank discussions. Each head of government has a red button in front of him or her, and pressing it immediately summons their 'Antici' into the room. They may bring in or take out messages, or summon a senior official to come to offer some advice to the head of government. However, officials cannot remain in the room. As seen above, Seville restricted official delegations to twenty in number, but member states are able to supplement their official delegations with other officials, described as 'non-official' or 'technical' delegations.

European Council meetings are typically spread over two days, from late afternoon on day one to lunchtime on day two. They invariably begin with a brief formal session which is followed by two separate dinners, one of the heads of state or government plus the president of the Commission, and the other of the foreign affairs ministers and another member of the Commission. The president of the European Parliament addresses the plenary session before the formal start of the European Council, a practice instigated in 1988, setting out the European Parliament's views on the main issues to be addressed. The dinners are an occasion for informal and more open exchanges, but may also used by heads for bilateral discussions.

The second day's formal proceedings begin with another formal plenary session, possibly followed by another lunch. Several hours are typically set aside for the purpose of agreeing the text of the conclusions, most of which will have been elaborated by the senior presidency and secretariat officials in attendance at the meeting and have been reviewed by Coreper. The meeting is followed by a press conference, given jointly by the president of the European Council, the president of the Commission and the Council secretary-general/high representative, where the president gives a summary of the conclusions reached by the European Council. Each member state representative gives separate press conferences for the benefit of the national press corps, and these are noted for the different glosses that can be put on what occurred in the meeting room. In one sense European Councils are highly transparent affairs – by piecing together what is said in various press conferences (and what all the 'spin' machinery is putting out), a very accurate picture can be constructed of what has transpired inside the European Council.

The European Council's basic methods are discussion and the adoption of conclusions. Discussion need not necessarily be conclusive. European Council meetings are an obvious way, for example, for the heads of state or government to keep in touch with one another collectively about developments of common interest. Because there is no written record or verbatim report, these discussions and their subject matter may remain unreported, though there is a fair possibility that most matters covered will leak to the attendant press. Dinner discussions (so-called 'fireside chats' of heads of state or government – see below) are the nearest the European Council comes to the library group method.

Most of the conclusions adopted at European Council meetings are the result of a large-scale preparatory process which increasingly takes place within the Council structures (see chapter 21), on the basis of input provided by the presidency, with the assistance of the Council secretariat. For its part, the European Commission is frequently called upon to draft reports and table documents for the European Council. Increasingly intensive preparations in Brussels are matched by increasingly extensive preparations in the member states, which liaise through their permanent representations and bilaterally. The presidency may well engage in 'shuttle diplomacy', making a round of capitals to clarify the member states' positions in advance (although routinely carrying out a 'tour of capitals' before each session is logistically difficult in a European Council with twenty-five members).

It is rare for the European Council to find itself bogged down in major contention, although it can happen that if 'something is at stake' discussions become more animated. On such occasions most heads will intervene in English and French. Indeed, it is not unheard of for a UK prime minister to intervene in French and a French prime minister to intervene in English. The European Council's basic ethos is consensuality, and great efforts are made to ensure that all of the member states can agree to the proposed conclusions. Members of Coreper II will be present in national delegations, and it is part of Coreper's camaraderie that they should be involved in finding acceptable solutions. Usually the presidency will table a full set of draft conclusions early on the second day reflecting previous preparatory work in Coreper and the discussions the previous evening.

Another important participant in drafting sessions is the Council's deputy secretary-general, who, along with the chief legal adviser, can help find imaginative solutions to apparently intractable problems. The legal adviser's role was publicised during the December 1992 Edinburgh European Council, when his advice enabled the European Council to find a solution to the 'Danish problem' caused by the 'no' vote in the June 1992 Danish referendum on the Maastricht Treaty. The work can be highly technical, particularly where budgetary and finance questions are involved, and this explains the numbers of technical experts present in the national delegations, since they will be called upon to verify the fine print to the political agreements reached by their political masters. The European Council cannot, strictly speaking, take decisions in the formal, 'Community method' sense. However, article 13(2) TEU provides that the European Council shall decide on CFSP common strategies. The European Monetary System, for example, was brought into existence through a European Council resolution, and the Council was charged with the task of taking the necessary decisions.

The basic ethos of consensuality has broken down on only a few occasions in the life of the European Council to date. For example, at the December 1983 Athens European Council, the member states were unable to reach agreement over the thorny problems of CAP reform and finance, and no conclusions were issued. At the June 1985 Milan European Council, the Danish, Greek and United Kingdom governments were outvoted in a decision to establish an intergovernmental conference. A similar disagreement occurred with the United Kingdom at the December 1989 Strasbourg European Council on convening an intergovernmental conference on economic and monetary union, although there was also a difference over the social charter. Lastly, at the October 1990 Rome European Council the United Kingdom found itself in a dissenting minority over the setting of the date for the second stage of the economic and monetary union process.

The European Council is not entirely master of its own agenda. It has tended increasingly to create its own sort of 'rolling programme' of commitments and measures decided at previous meetings (demonstrated *par excellence* by the Lisbon strategy). It is inevitably drawn to discussion and possible action in response to important current issues and, as was explained above, the Commission has, at least in the past, been adept at harnessing the European Council to its own agenda. The fourth source of points for the agenda is the presidency's own priorities. The Council secretary-general and deputy secretary-general traditionally play a valued role in advising the presidency (including briefing notes) about narrowing down the agenda of a meeting or the ordering of points. Other points may fall or be introduced following discussions in the preparatory Coreper and Council meetings. In exceptional cases, the agenda may be dominated by a single issue. This was the case, for example, in the Brussels February 1988 European Council (budgetary problems), the April 1990 Dublin European Council (German unification), the October 1990 Rome European Council (economic and monetary union) and the Brussels 1994 European Council (nomination of the Commission president). More recently, the European Council has convened special sessions devoted to a single policy area, as was the case in Luxembourg in October 1997 (employment) and Tampere in October 1999 (justice and home affairs – see chapter 6).

Notwithstanding the Seville European Council's good intentions, European Council meetings typically harbour an alternative agenda or, rather, a series of alternative agendas. Bulmer and Wessels have described this as 'multiple bilateralism' (1987, p 54). Member states see European Council meetings as important occasions to engage in bilateral diplomacy. Dinner on the first evening and breakfast on the second day are the usual times for this sort of activity, and some lobbying goes on to ensure that the guests are seated at the dinner table in a way which enables bilateral talks to be held. Bulmer and Wessels cite the case of French president François Mitterrand, who held thirty bilateral meetings with other government heads in 1984. Former Irish prime minister Garrett Fitzgerald has attributed some of the success of the 1985 Anglo-Irish peace initiative to the fact that he and Margaret Thatcher were able to conduct bilateral business in the margins of the European Council meeting. Bilateral contacts may or may not result in announcements to the press, but they are an important, though mostly hidden, aspect of the European Council's overall success.

The European Council is at one and the same time a forum, a policy initiator, and a decision-maker. Basing themselves on the Stuttgart solemn declaration's list of functions, Bulmer and Wessels (1987) and Nugent (1993) ascribed a series of ad hoc functions to the European Council: informal exchanges of view; defining the guidelines for integration; policy orientation; enlarging the scope of European cooperation; policy coordination; issuing declarations on foreign relations; de facto decision making; policy monitoring; court of appeal and *deus ex machina*. To these should be added the European Council's new, treaty-based tasks in providing necessary impetus through the European Union's general political and economic guidelines (and in relation to the passage to the third stage of economic and monetary union), but also less tangible qualities such as the overall enhancement of mutual understanding and the introduction of more predictability into relations between governments, as well as the provision of a valuable showcase for the presidency and for its head of government, both on the international and the domestic stage.

In the twenty years of its existence, the European Council has concentrated the bulk of its activities in a number of discernible policy areas: the economic and social situation of the Union; international economic and monetary issues; international political questions; institutional and constitutional matters; and problems specific to the European Community, such as finance. There have been periods when the European Council seemed to concentrate on some issues to the neglect of others. This was particularly the case during the early 1980s, when all minds were concentrated, willingly or not, on the problem of the British budgetary rebate. However, there is another way of looking at things, bound up in dominant personalities and dominant alliances as much as dominant policy issues. Early summitry and the European Council have mostly been characterised by alliances of French and German leaders: de Gaulle and Adenauer, Pompidou and Brandt, Schmidt and Giscard, and Mitterrand and Kohl. From this perspective the early 1980s, when Margaret Thatcher was able, through the force of her personality and of her arguments, to wrest the agenda away, seem almost an aberration.

Looking to the future

This chapter began by pointing out how the European Council now seems a logical necessity rather than an awkward historical afterthought. The Commission has long since learnt to work with and through the European Council. For a long time, the European Council's existence offended the European Parliament's purist constitutional vision of the way the European Union should develop, but the Parliament now not only accepts the need for the European Council but criticizes it when it fails to fulfil its tasks. When the Maastricht Treaty was adopted, few criticized it for giving the European

Council specific tasks in the context of economic and monetary union. Amsterdam and Nice have since built on those foundations. However, discussions in the convention and the intergovernmental conference about creating a permanent president of the European Council rekindled the debate about the role and place of the European Council in the Union's institutional set-up. Once the Constitution has been ratified, the European Council will consolidate its current roles and powers and become a formal institution of the Union. It will elect its own president, by qualified majority, for a term of two and a half years, renewable once. The president will chair and drive the European Council's work, ensure its proper preparation and continuity in cooperation with the Commission president and endeavour to facilitate cohesion and consensus.

What is at stake is where executive power (i.e., political leadership) should lie in the Union. While it is generally recognised that executive power needs to be strengthened against the background of a more heterogeneous union resulting from enlargement, the debate about the European Council revived the ideological argument between supranationalists and intergovernmentalists regarding the Union's future evolution. Inevitably, executive power in the Union will remain shared between the European Council/Council and the Commission. The outcome of the IGC represents a compromise which recognises the need for greater consistency and direction in the European Council's work. In fact, in the light of the shortcomings at political level lower down the system (see chapter 4), the European Council remains the one supreme political authority in the Union capable of deciding on issues ranging from defence, milk quotas, immigration policy and satellite navigation systems to constitutional reform.

One of the most critical factors for the Union's success in the future will be the extent to which this forum's decision-making capacity can be preserved. This is one of the real challenges facing the Union. If the European Council were to become 'councilised' and its ability to act effectively were to be diminished, the Union's system of 'government' would be seriously weakened. There is no further supreme authority beyond it. The buck stops there!

Chapter 10: Intergovernmental Conferences

There are two distinct types of intergovernmental conference: conferences to implement certain provisions of the existing treaties which foresee decisions of this type ('simple' intergovernmental conferences); and conferences convened 'outside' the treaties to agree amendments to EU primary law. The latter take two forms: 'constitutional' IGCs foreseen in article 48 TEU, and 'enlargement' IGCs provided for in article 49 TEU. Slightly different procedures apply in each case. A common feature of all such conferences is that decisions are taken by 'common accord'. This means that the positive assent of all contracting parties is required. Unlike unanimity in the Council (see chapter 14), it is not possible to 'abstain'; indeed this would be completely illogical, since it would be tantamount to a member state declining to exercise its competence, thereby rendering a decision by all member states impossible.

'Simple' intergovernmental conferences

Various articles in the treaties themselves foresee decisions by the governments of the member states. For example, article 289 TEC states that: 'The seat of the institutions of the Community shall be determined by common accord of the Governments of the Member States'. A number of such provisions in the treaties relate to appointment of members of certain institutions (e.g. judges and advocates general of the Court of Justice – article 223 TEC) While in the past most appointments to the institutions were decided by common accord, important inroads into this principle were made in the Treaty of Nice, where for a number of provisions (most significantly the nomination of the president of the Commission), the decision in future will be taken by the Council by qualified majority (see chapter 14).

There are no rules and few conventions for such conferences, which can take place at any level, from heads of state or government down to permanent representatives. In the majority of cases, it is the latter who switch over to intergovernmental mode. In practice, this is usually done by the simple expedient of 'swapping hats'. For example, when a decision is to be formally approved, this usually occurs in the margins of a Coreper meeting, and permanent representatives swap hats either before commencing or at the end of their agenda (since the item cannot be part of the Coreper agenda as such) to become the 'representatives of the governments of the member states' to adopt a decision requiring common accord. While the conference is not formally a body of the Council, usually a decision will have been prepared in a Council working party in the course of normal business, and if discussion is required at a higher level, that debate would be undertaken in Coreper. It is only at the stage of a formal decision that 'hats are swapped'. A further example of how closely the Council and the conference may work is provided by so-called 'mixed acts' (that is, acts combining matters which are of Community and member state competence). The best example of this is when deciding to conclude agreements negotiated with third parties. Where such agreements extend to areas where the Community has not been given powers to act (e.g. trade agreements which also cover trade in services), then such agreements have to be concluded both by a Council decision and by a decision of the representatives of the governments of the member states.

Intergovernmental conferences to revise the treaties (IGCs)

'Constitutional' IGCs are the mechanism for undertaking revisions of the treaties to reform the powers, structures and workings of the Union and its institutions. They are convened in accordance with article 48 of the TEU. Since the mid-1980s, the Union has been involved in a rapid succession of major negotiations on both treaty revision and enlargements. Like history, this cycle is repeating itself. Following the Nice IGC in 2000 and the treaty which entered into force in February 2002, the Union entered the final stages of the enlargement of the ten which culminated in the signature of the Treaty of Accession in Athens on 16 April 2003. As it was doing so, the Union was already embarking on yet another major treaty reform which reached its conclusion in June 2004.

As far as constitutional IGCs are concerned, they are formally a diplomatic negotiation among member governments, the outcome of which is enshrined in a treaty amending the existing treaties. These amendments enter into force once all member states have ratified them in accordance with their respective internal procedures, which either involve a parliamentary procedure or, in certain circumstances in some member states, a referendum. Typically, ratification procedures take from eighteen months to two years to complete following signature of the treaty. Under this process, which is very much in the realms of international treaty law, the member states remain the 'masters of the treaties'. Once the conference has been launched, the institutions themselves no longer have any formal role to play in negotiating and adopting the outcome. Although the Commission and the European Parliament are politically involved in this process to varying degrees, the Council's role ceases completely once it has given a positive opinion on launching a conference. This is entirely understandable; there would be no point in the Council trying to reconcile its members' views since the substance is negotiated among member governments during the conference.

The Commission, given its particular role as independent guardian of the treaties and by virtue of the fact that article 48 TEU gives it the right to table proposals, participates at all levels of the conference. Through its detailed opinion, formal and informal contributions and interventions in meetings, the Commission is an active participant in the conference. However, its impact is more limited and it is involved to a much lesser extent in the process of elaborating compromise proposals than in normal Community business. There are two main reasons for this. The first is that while the president of the Commission is a fully-fledged sixteenth member of the European Council, when heads of government are meeting in IGC configuration the Commission is in a much weaker institutional and political position by virtue of the fact that it is not a government and therefore not part of the conference. The second is that in a number of politically high profile areas where it had taken a strong public stance, such as seeking a significant extension of QMV on taxation, social policy and foreign policy and on certain institutional issues, the Commission has traditionally defended politically difficult positions.

The European Parliament's role in successive IGCs has been a matter of some controversy. Under article 48 TEU, the European Parliament has no role in the IGC itself, either to submit proposals or attend sessions of the conference, nor does it have any formal role at the end of the process. However, over the years it has gradually acquired the right to have two observers attend preparatory and ministerial meetings, and during the 2003-2004 IGC, the president of the Parliament attended all sessions of the conference at the level of heads of government.

Given the fact that the logistics, negotiating style and compromise-building process replicate established patterns of negotiation within the Council, including similar vertical negotiating structures involving largely the same players, both the presidency and the Council secretariat (traditionally designated the conference secretariat by the European Council – see chapter 19), play a role similar to that in normal Council business. The presidency acts as the engine, driving the conference by setting the overall pace of work, planning and organizing the agenda, producing discussion papers and brokering compromises. While other member states, the Commission and the European Parliament produce papers setting out their positions in general terms or on specific points, it is the presidency working papers which constitute the negotiating basis for the conference. The presidency's role is neatly encapsulated in this description from the Amsterdam IGC:

'A Presidency cannot invent a way forward out of thin air. It must, at the same time, guide and shape the direction of the Conference. It is not a scissors and paste job. Defining the real underlying agenda – identifying the European interest, recognising what will run and what will not, developing language that will be both effective and acceptable – is a complex and subtle challenge. It is an art form rather than a science.' (McDonagh, 1998).

Over the years, criticism has been levelled at the treaty revision process on the grounds that it should be both more efficient and more legitimate. The methods used for negotiating treaty change had been criticised for being ill suited to the negotiation of texts of legal and constitutional importance. Critics claimed that the negotiating method, often based on multitiered vertical negotiating structures, suffered from structural weaknesses similar to those found in the Council. In particular, failure to resolve items at a lower level led to heads of government being faced with a problem of overload with a large number of complex technical and legal points being left open for resolution in the space of three days. This suggested that an effective political filter below the level of heads of government was lacking.

Second, achieving an acceptable outcome on difficult issues inevitably involves striking a political balance in the drafting of treaty language.

Hence, the outcome occasionally suffers in terms of legal clarity and quality of drafting. More significantly, because texts are approved by heads of government, it is in practice impossible after the event to alter language which has received their blessing unless the changes are deemed unanimously to be of a purely legal and linguistic nature. Even apparently neutral changes suggested as part of this exercise, which every treaty undergoes before it is signed, do not always command universal approval and cannot therefore be taken on board. Various suggestions have been made for improving the process on both counts (McDonagh, 1998), and these shortcomings were one of the major factors in the birth of the European Convention as a new preparatory exercise compared to that used on previous occasions.

The legitimacy of the process has also been challenged on two counts. First, given that the Union is much more than a conventional international organisation and that the treaties already have a constitutional dimension, many, including the European Parliament, consider that a broader based participation than national governments is required for negotiating treaty change. The Parliament, supported by a number of heads of government, had advocated that a body similar to the convention used to negotiate the charter of EU fundamental rights alongside the Nice IGC, and which was composed of representatives of national governments, national parliaments, the European Parliament and the Commission, should be used for preparatory work for the 2003-2004 IGC.

Second, some have argued that successive transfers of powers to the Union effected by previous treaty changes have resulted in a de facto extension in the discretion of national executives in the domestic arena at the expense of political control through national parliaments, without any corresponding increase in parliamentary control at EU level (Lord, 1998). They have consistently contended that, in addition to broader participation in the preparatory process, this warrants a greater degree of legitimation than that afforded by a simple 'take-it-or-leave-it' basis on which either national parliaments or electorates give their backing to their government's position. While the legitimacy of gatherings of heads of government, as the supreme political authority in the Union, is unquestioned, heads of government themselves accepted the need for a broader based political preparatory process leading up to the 2003-2004 IGC than had been the case in the past.

The purpose of holding a European Convention prior to convening the 2003-2004 IGC was therefore designed as a response to both types of criticism. While the Convention produced a single agreed text, the difficulties encountered during the subsequent IGC again demonstrated that no matter how effective or broad-based the preparatory process is, it cannot guarantee an easy result in an IGC. Since the IGC had been preceded by the Convention, which had conducted a detailed examination of all the treaty provisions, there was considerable pressure to convene the IGC formally at political level only (i.e., without a preparatory body of senior officials to prepare the deliberations). It was felt that the work undertaken had examined all available options sufficiently in depth and that the basic choices on the relatively limited points of contention on the Convention's draft were essentially political rather than technical in nature.

Recent IGCs such as Amsterdam, Nice and the most recent in 2003-2004 are somewhat different in character from the two which preceded them (leading to the Single Act in 1986 and to the Maastricht Treaty in 1992). In the latter cases, the IGC was a negotiation on the means to achieve clear and unambiguous political objectives which had been largely pre-determined from the outset. This is what the Union does best. The three most recent IGCs lacked a similar underlying pre-ordained political objective; aims such as streamlining structures and improving the efficiency or the democratic legitimacy and transparency of the institutions for enlargement, while worthwhile in themselves, are diffuse and open ended, and since no common view exists they are essentially divisive inside the Union. This partly explains some of the difficulties encountered in recent IGCs. While they were ostensibly about improving institutional efficiency, efficiency in the minds of most was about preserving power and influence in an enlarged Union. Redistributing power inside the Union is always a fraught exercise particularly when the scope for final trade-offs is limited by a narrow agenda, such as was the case in Nice.

One way of approaching the power politics behind recent IGCs is to consider the different ways in which the concept of balance is used in the Union. Balance is a recurring theme in literature describing the workings of the Union – e.g. 'balanced blend' of supranationalism and intergovernmentalism, the Union's 'institutional balance', an 'overall balanced outcome' to negotiations. It is hardly surprising therefore that architecture, with its concerns for engineering stability and aesthetic equilibrium, provides one of the most common metaphorical crutches for describing the Union's structures and processes. Understanding three layers of balance in the Union highlights the fact that any constitutional debate ultimately involves a dynamic shift in existing power balances, albeit between different players.

First, there is the *balance between the member states and the European Union*, which can be more accurately described as the constitutional share-out of powers between the Union/Community and the member states – i.e., what the Union and the member states respectively can and cannot do. The treaties circumscribe the limits of Union action, so the notion of equilibrium between the Community and the member states in a static sense is relatively unproblematic. The Community has a clear legal existence separate from the member states and can only act 'within the limits of the powers conferred' by the treaty (article 5 TEC), thus debunking the myth that the Union can somehow acquire unlimited powers by its own institutions' actions. If need be, any grey areas can be clarified by the Court of Justice. More interestingly, however, is the dynamic shift of this 'equilibrium' over time as successive treaty revisions have extended the Union's powers. Indeed, evolving towards *'ever closer Union'* created a natural presumption in IGCs prior to Nice that powers should be extended and, between IGCs, at least in the Community's early days, that as broad an interpretation as possible should be followed in implementing the treaty. However, the logic of the 'Monnet method' (i.e., fostering political integration beginning by pooling sovereignty in a limited number of specific economic sectors and relying on gradual 'spillover' effects into new policy areas) has probably reached its limits with the transfer to the Union of certain core powers relating to monetary union, foreign policy and internal security. Handling these core powers at Union level has required the devising of new procedural approaches for handling economic and monetary union (EMU), foreign policy (CFSP) and justice and home affairs (JHA). Questions such as the extent to which these core powers in the latter two cases should be exercised by the Union, and, conversely, whether the Union has not gone too far in detailed regulation of certain economic and social areas, was at the forefront of the debate in the European Convention.

Second, there is the system of *checks and balances* that operate between the Union's policy-making and legislative institutions (the Commission, the Council and the European Parliament) – the so-called 'institutional triangle'. This 'institutional balance' – a term which is not without its critics (Wallace, 2000) – is in reality a shifting, dynamic equilibrium which has evolved over time as the powers of certain institutions – most notably those of the European Parliament – have increased with successive treaties and as a result of subtle shifts in the ways the institutions interact and exploit their powers within the framework laid down in the treaties. This was also one of the main topics on which the European Convention focused in its work, in particular in defining the concept of legislative act in the Union and thereby taking to its logical conclusion the approach of co-deciding legislative acts by the Council and the Parliament.

Third, there is the *equilibrium within the Union among the member states themselves*; in other words how the Union reflects in its institutional structure the power balance between equally sovereign member states of very different sizes and levels of prosperity. The treaty explicitly mentions that the Union is an 'ever closer union among the peoples of Europe', although no similar mention is found of the member states. Article 1 of the TEU states, however, that the Union's tasks shall be 'to organise, in a manner demonstrating consistency and solidarity, relations between the Member States and between their peoples'. Nevertheless, the Union, although it has a constitutional dimension, is a creation of treaties under international law, the contracting parties to which are the member states, hence the frequent allusions in the IGC debates to its dual nature as a '*Union of states and of peoples*'. By focusing the Nice IGC agenda on the institutional changes necessary to accommodate new member states within the Union's existing institutional structure, issues of 'balance' among member states (i.e., their relative power and influence in the Union's institutions) inevitably featured prominently. It was power issues of this type that drove the Nice IGC and that also resurfaced during the 2003-2004 IGC.

'Enlargement' intergovernmental conferences

'Enlargement' IGCs differ from 'constitutional' IGCs in a number of respects. The purpose of an 'enlargement' IGC is to agree '*the conditions of admission and the adjustments to the Treaties on which the Union is founded which such admission entails*'. Enlargement always has been and still is one of the Union's main instruments of foreign policy towards its immediate European neighbours in bringing peace and stabilising democracy in central and eastern Europe. The Copenhagen European Council in June 1993 set out the three conditions (usually referred to as the 'Copenhagen criteria') for becoming a member of the Union: the political criteria (stability of institutions guaranteeing democracy, the rule of law, human rights and respect for and protection of minorities); the economic criteria (a functioning market economy and ability to cope with the competitive pressure and market forces of the Union); and the ability to take on the obligations of membership (i.e., accepting and actually implementing around 80,000 pages of EU *acquis*). While there is only a single treaty of accession for all states joining the Union at the same time, each IGC is conducted separately with each acceding state. This reflects the underlying principle that negotiations are conducted with each applicant on their own merits, with each progressing at its own rate depending on its degree of preparedness.

Enlargement negotiations involve a two-stage process: first an internal negotiation inside the Union to determine its common negotiating position on each of the various various *acquis* chapters, then an actual accession conference involving the member states and the applicant country concerned. The objective of these conferences is to discuss whether an agreement can be reached on the Union's common position, drawn up in response to each candidate's negotiating position on a particular chapter. The outcome of discussions is then recorded in summary conclusions agreed by both sides which, along with the agreed common positions, are the basis on which the relevant provisions of the accession treaty are drafted.

The internal preparation of common positions for the accession conferences is carried out inside the structures of the Council. Member states have conferred on the Council preparatory bodies (the enlargement working party and Coreper) the task of preparing the position to be presented by the presidency to the candidate state. In line with previous accession negotiations, in recent negotiations member states also conferred on the Commission the right of initiative and requested it to prepare draft common positions, initially on matters under the EC Treaty although as the negotiations progressed, it was also requested to prepare common positions on the common foreign and security policy (CFSP) and justice and home affairs (JHA). Common positions are approved by Coreper as a 'roman I item' and then presented to the candidate state.

Accession conferences are then usually held at deputy level (i.e., ambassadors), and chaired by the permanent representative of the member state holding the presidency. Accession conferences themselves are usually rather formal, stage-managed affairs, with, in addition to the presidency and the Commission, all member states present, and an equivalent number on the other side. However, as with most negotiations in the Union, conferences are preceded and followed up by intense informal contacts between the candidate state and the Commission, the presidency and the Council secretariat. Before the end of each presidency, all of the common positions agreed internally by the Union are submitted to the General Affairs and External Relations Council for approval as an 'A' item before the accession conference is convened at ministerial level in order to approve the work undertaken by deputies over the previous six months.

These are important political events in the calendar of each presidency and of the candidate state since they provide a regular 'photograph' of the state of progress in the negotiations which can be used as a yardstick to measure both the success or otherwise of the EU presidency and progress by the candidate state. For the recent enlargement of the ten, a total of 260 meetings of the accession conferences were held. Readers interested in a detailed account and assessment of the Council process in the Union's recent enlargement should consult Willocks, 2004.

Concluding remarks

With the preservation of peace as one of its primary founding aims, the Union's ultimate vocation to incorporate all European states is now heralded as an ever more distinct possibility. The combined impact of the Union's expansion in the medium term virtually to the geographical limits of Europe, coupled with a widely-held desire to avoid watering down the integration process, have prompted the wider rethink of the Union's institutional structure and its relationship with the member states which has taken place in the European Convention and the recent IGC. At stake is how to tailor the Union to the future needs of extended membership while retaining broad public support and ensuring that the Union remains a dynamic and cohesive unit. Whether or not these aims can be successfully reconciled will only become clear in time.

PART 4: PREPARING THE COUNCIL

The Council itself meets around eighty times a year. A sizeable vertical structure of preparatory bodies exists to prepare the ministerial meetings. It would be unrealistic to put a complex piece of legislation directly before ministers and expect them to have a meaningful discussion on it! Discussions on sensitive political matters require careful preparation in order to identify precisely the political difficulties that ministers themselves need to resolve, and to separate them from second order issues that can normally be resolved at the level of diplomats or officials.

Below the Council itself is the main interface in the Council between the political and the technical – the permanent representatives committee (Coreper), a body formally responsible for preparing the work of the Council and for carrying out the tasks assigned to it by the Council (s ee chapter 11). Coreper is the Council's backbone and the engine room of Council business; it is here that the work of the various sectoral working parties converges, before being channelled up to the separate Council formations. It is in effect the only point in the Council system where a complete overview exists of the entire range of EU business.

Alongside Coreper a number of specialised senior committees are involved in coordinating work in particular policy areas. A number of these committees also have a basis in the treaties. Some of them wield considerable power and influence in the preparation of matters in certain policy areas, as previous chapters have shown. At the base of the pyramid are the Council working parties. These are attended by member state experts in the particular policy area which falls within each working party's remit (see chapter 12). It is in these rather technical and unglamorous fora that the bulk of the formal process of negotiation is conducted. Of all the Council's component parts, the working parties (or working groups as they are also commonly referred to as a translation of the French 'groupes de travail') are perhaps the least well-known yet among the most vital. There is no mention of working parties in the treaties (the Council's rules of procedure provide that committees or working parties may by set up by or with the approval of Coreper with a view to carrying out certain preparatory work or studies defined in advance); they are nevertheless the Council's lifeblood.

Chapter 13 looks at how a national negotiator operates within this vertically structured framework as the focal point of overlapping and intersecting circles of interest involved in a particular negotiation. The policy process is not confined to what happens between delegates in Council meeting rooms – this is merely the tip of the iceberg. It extends across informal networks between delegations in Brussels, between the Council and other EU institutions, between Brussels delegates and their respective national administrations, and between different government departments within national administrations as well as between national administrations in different EU capitals.

Chapter 11: The Permanent Representatives Committee (Coreper)

Coreper as prism and fulcrum

A treaty article (article 207 TEC) provides for the Council to be assisted by 'a committee consisting of the permanent representatives of the member states.' This committee, universally known by its French acronym Coreper (*Comité des représentants permanents*), is one of the most powerful organs within the European Union's institutional structure. It is also one of the most obscure. A prime reason for this obscurity is that Coreper is composed of career diplomats whose theoretical task is to prepare the work of their political masters. In reality, those diplomats collectively wield considerable executive and legislative influence. Until recently, these powers were mostly de facto, but the Amsterdam Treaty has given Coreper de jure (albeit mainly procedural) decision-making powers. In its quiet and low-profile way – indeed, perhaps *because* of its quiet and low-profile way – Coreper has made a continuous and lasting contribution to the construction of the European Union.[1]

Coreper's status rests on its role as the Council's prime preparatory body. Everything destined for consideration by the Council has to come via Coreper. This primacy is anchored in a number of articles in the treaties and in the Council's rules of procedure, and is linked to the status of the Council's *primus inter pares* formation, the General Affairs and External Relations Council (GAERC). Since Coreper prepares the GAERC's work, and since the GAERC prepares the European Council's work, it is also intimately involved in preparing the deliberations of the European Union's supreme political authority. It is therefore part and parcel of the Council's 'backbone' (Coreper – GAERC – European Council).

Coreper remains a powerful organ but over the past decade its role has, paradoxically, been both consolidated and undermined. The root cause for this dual tendency was the Maastricht Treaty and, in particular, the pillar structure it introduced to the Union's constitutional topography. As the breadth of the Union's policy competences was extended, so the need for preparation and coordination increased. Coreper's primacy had always been contested by the Council's need for specialised preparatory work in areas such as agriculture (see chapter 7) and economic and financial affairs (see chapter 5.1). But the Maastricht Treaty introduced two new policy areas – economic and monetary union and justice and home affairs – and extended external relations to include foreign, security and defence policy (see chapters 5.1, 6 and 4.2 respectively), all of which applied different procedures than the traditional Community method.

Ironically, Coreper has also been a victim of the collective success of that self-same Community method. The work rate of the permanent representatives and their deputies has never been less than superhuman, but even superhumans cannot continue to extend their competences indefinitely; decisions must inevitably be delegated downwards or handed out sideways (after all, Coreper already exists in two configurations). Already, as chapter 6 recounts, an attempt to 'steal' Coreper's competence sideways through the creation of a specialised justice and home affairs Coreper has been seen off. Indeed, the existence of such a specialised body would have spelt the death of Coreper's overall coordinating role. But the delegation downwards has continued apace and hence promoted the role and de facto powers of other, lower preparatory bodies. Until the Maastricht Treaty, Coreper could validly be described as the Council's prism but, even where its prismatic role has been undermined, it remains the Council's fulcrum: the universal point of leverage.

Origin

In one respect the early evolution of the Council followed closely the model established by an earlier European organisation, the Council of Europe. When the Council of Europe was first established in 1948, it was intended that it should be led by its Committee of Ministers, made up of the foreign ministers of the member states. Indeed, in the early days of that organisation the foreign ministers flew out to Strasbourg on several occasions. Such meetings had to be prepared. Article 14 of the Council of Europe's statutes allowed for alternates to be appointed and, as the Council evolved into a form of standing diplomatic conference, so the member states appointed high-ranking diplomats, most permanently based in Strasbourg, whose primary job was to prepare the work of the ministers. This was an entirely logical development. Ministers' time was, as it continues to be, precious. An increasing proportion of the Committee of Ministers' work was uncontroversial and everyday and could safely be delegated to officials. However, over time, these ambassadors steadily accrued real policy-making functions, since their principal task became to boil off all but the most intractable of problems for their political masters.

The Special Council of Ministers of the ECSC and, later, the Council of Ministers of the EEC, followed a similar course. There was no provision for any preparatory body in the Treaty of Paris (ECSC), but the need for one soon became apparent, and in February 1953 the Special Council of Ministers created a Comité de Co-ordination (COCOR) to prepare its meetings and undertake any studies it considered necessary. COCOR, which was composed of high-level national civil servants, first met on 5 March 1953 and thereafter met monthly. Before very long, it had created a number of specialised technical working groups – precursors of the modern day Council's working parties – to assist it in its preparatory work. COCOR members were based in their national capitals rather than Brussels – an important consideration for Jean Monnet, who had been determined to avoid the creation of any permanent Luxembourg-based body.

In Messina, on 1 and 2 June 1955, the foreign ministers of the ECSC member states decided to establish an intergovernmental committee to study ways of furthering European integration. The committee, headed by the then Belgian foreign minister, Paul-Henri Spaak, reported back to the Venice conference of foreign ministers on 28 May 1956. Following the Spaak committee's recommendations, the foreign ministers decided to convene an intergovernmental conference.

There was general recognition within the IGC that the envisaged Council of Ministers should be assisted by a preparatory body of some sort, but there was some discussion as to whether such a body should itself be at ministerial level. In the end, the negotiators compromised and left the question open. Thus, article 151 EEC and article 121 Euratom laid down that the internal rules of procedure of the Council 'may provide for the creation of a committee composed of representatives of the member states'. It was therefore left to the future Council to decide whether or not such a body was necessary and what form it should take.

In the event, on signature of the EEC and Euratom treaties in Rome (25 March 1957), the foreign ministers immediately decided to create such a body. The initial task of this 'interim committee', composed as it was of the heads of the national delegations who had attended the IGC (they were unofficially known as 'qualified representatives') was to prepare the entry into force of the treaties. The interim committee's role was consolidated by a 6-7 January 1958 meeting of the ministers of foreign affairs, which created the function of 'permanent representative' and officially instituted a committee of permanent representatives, thereafter universally known as Coreper. The foreign ministers decided that the permanent representatives should be high-ranking diplomats with ambassadorial status. Since the diplomats were primarily answerable to their foreign ministers, the creation of Coreper consolidated the pre-eminent role of the member states' foreign ministries in the early development of the European Communities.

Evolution

Unlike its ECSC precursor, COCOR, Coreper was a permanent, Brussels-based organ. It was seen by many enthusiasts of a purer, more supranational model of European integration as a direct, state-led rival to the new Commission, which had already been rendered far less pre-eminently powerful than the ECSC's High Authority. At the Council's very first meeting, the president of the new Commission, Walter Hallstein, sought direct assurances that political authority would remain at ministerial level. The then Belgian foreign minister, Victor Larock, assured him, with the unanimous backing of the Council's other members, that responsibility for taking decisions would remain entirely in the hands of the ministers themselves (Noël, 1966, p 18). This decision was fundamental to the Community's subsequent institutional development, establishing beyond doubt the political nature of both the Council and the Commission.

Italy and Luxembourg appointed their permanent representatives in February 1958. The last, that of Germany, was appointed in June of the same year. As senior diplomats enjoying ambassadorial status, the permanent representatives were entitled to their own diplomatic staff and premises, and thus were born the permanent representations. Staffing levels at the permanent representations has steadily grown over the years, primarily as a consequence of the Union's growing policy scope and competences.

In the early 1960s, the permanent representatives took to appointing specialists from other national ministries to help with the preparation of technical dossiers. Nowadays, specialists outnumber career diplomats in most permanent representations, thus to some extent reversing the earlier trend towards concentration of European policy in foreign ministries. As Hayes-Renshaw *et al* put it, this 'hints clearly at an infringement of the diplomats' traditional monopoly in dealing with international affairs'. But this could be put another way: 'European' policy is becoming increasingly domesticated, and can no longer be reduced simply to an aspect of foreign policy.

The trend towards the delegation of technical work to specialists was reinforced in 1960, when the Council decided to speed up its efforts to negotiate the common agricultural policy foreseen in article 38 EEC. The 12 March 1960 decision was accompanied by the decision to create a special agriculture committee. As chapter 7 describes, the SCA effectively acts as a specialised Coreper and its members, high-ranking delegates from member states' ministries of agriculture, deal directly with the Council.

The trend was further consolidated in 1962, with the decision to divide Coreper up into what have effectively become two different bodies. Coreper I (part one), composed of deputy permanent representatives, deals with most sectoral legislative activity, while Coreper II (part two), composed of the permanent representatives themselves, prepares the General Affairs and External Relations Council, the Ecofin Council and the Justice and Home Affairs Council, as well as overall preparation of the European Council.

Until 1967, the ECSC, EEC and Euratom Councils were serviced by three theoretically distinct preparatory committees. Article 4 of the 1965 Merger Treaty, which came into force in 1967, provided for a single preparatory committee, Coreper. The Merger Treaty represented another important consolidation of the permanent representatives' role and status. Under the Treaty of Rome, Coreper was a *'comité formé des Représentants des Etats membres'*, but the member states were under no obligation necessarily to send their permanent representatives to Coreper. This important nuance was resolved by article 4 of the 1965 Merger Treaty, which provided for *'un comité composé des Représentants permanents des Etats membres'*; henceforth, the permanent representatives *were* Coreper, and Coreper was fully integrated into the Community system.

Two other developments in the early 1960s were of particular importance to the evolution of Coreper. A first was the development of the written procedure, which was created primarily because of the relative infrequency of Council meetings, but which had as an important consequence the effect of focusing power and responsibility upon the permanent representations. The second was a revision of the Council's working practices in 1960 and 1962 and, in particular, the creation of 'A' and 'B' items (see chapter 3) which has been elegantly described thus: 'Un certain assouplissement ultérieur a conduit maintenant à interpréter cette procédure plutôt comme une renonciation unanime à une discussion dans le Conseil' (Noël, 1966). Many years later, in the 1979 report of the Three Wise Men, this 'desk-clearing' function of Coreper was again to be stressed as vital[2].

The permanent representations

In formal legal terms, the permanent representatives are 'diplomatic missions created by a unilateral act of the relevant government, and there is no accrediting procedure' (Hayes-Renshaw et al). However, although there was no specific treaty provision on the privileges and immunities to be accorded to the permanent representatives, Belgium (as the host nation) early decided that article 10 of the Rome Treaty's Protocol on Privileges and Immunities (which covered members of the Common Assembly and the Commission and EEC officials) should apply. Permanent representations (with the exception of the Belgian permanent representation) therefore enjoy the same rights and privileges as traditional embassies.

Most non-member Western European countries established some sort of diplomatic representation to the European Communities in Brussels, frequently linked to a country's bilateral Belgian embassy. Those countries with longer-term ambitions of membership developed the practice of 'shadowing' the Communities and, as countries applied for membership, so the practice grew of establishing a negotiating team in Brussels which, after accession, could be transformed into the country's permanent representation. Sometimes, the diplomatic teams negotiating membership were already separated off from the parent embassy before accession. This was the case, for example, with Ireland. This practice of establishing Brussels-based 'shadow embassies' has enabled the permanent representations of the newly-acceding member states to 'hit the ground running'.

The numbers of officials in the twenty-five member states' permanent representations vary considerably. There is some relationship between a member state's size, its geographical proximity to Brussels and the number of officials based in the permanent representations. Each has an idiosyncratic mix of diplomats, officials from other ministries, and in some cases regional representatives. For example, the Belgian permanent representation includes officials representing the Belgian French-speaking community, the Flemish community, the Walloon region, and the Brussels region. The Danish permanent representation has a representative from Greenland. The Austrian permanent representation has a representative of the National Bank, and so on. On the other hand, the German permanent representation has no representatives of its powerful Länder, all of which have their own Brussels-based representations. Relative size depends also on the division of labour between home- and Brussels-based officials. Thus, Ireland has just two officials from its department of agriculture, food and forestry, and Italy two from its ministry of agriculture, whereas Greece has seven, and Spain and the Netherlands five.

'Socialisation'

As noted above, officials from national ministries generally outnumber career diplomats within permanent representations. This gives rise to an interesting phenomenon. Diplomats, particularly junior diplomats, will see a posting to Brussels as one of a number of postings during their careers. Technical specialists, on the other hand, see 'Brussels' as a more permanent fixture. Although detailed statistics are not available, it is generally accepted that technical specialists' postings are of longer duration than their colleagues from the diplomatic services. Even when returning to the national capitals after their postings, national civil servants are likely to continue with 'Brussels'-related work, whereas junior diplomats may well end up doing something completely different and unrelated (though they may return to EU affairs later on in their careers). The technical specialists are, therefore, an important source of stability and continuity in policy formation and implementation, both within the permanent representations and within the national ministries.

This phenomenon is absent at the most senior level. Appendix II gives a complete list of all permanent representatives and their deputies for each of the member states from the inception of the EEC until the present day. An interesting feature of this list is the average length of service of permanent representatives. This contrasts strikingly with the three years average length of time in office of Western European ministers (Blondel, 1991), and indeed of commissioners (until 1994, a commissioner's term of office was four years; the Maastricht Treaty extended this to five years). Clearly, the individual members of Coreper therefore represent an important element of stability, not only in the context of the Community's inter-institutional relationships, but also in the context of individual member states' European policies. Permanent representatives frequently outlast their political bosses. Indeed, criticism is sometimes heard in the national capitals that the career diplomats have 'gone native', becoming too understanding of their counterparts' problems and insufficiently 'hardline' in defending their own country's position.

Permanent representatives are typically high-flying diplomats, who may be at the end of an illustrious career (as was the case with Sir Michael Butler, UK permanent representative from 1979 to 1985), or who will probably go on to other senior postings, perhaps in other international organisations. For example, Sir David Hannay, UK permanent representative from 1985 to 1990, was next posted to the British permanent representation to the United Nations in New York. Sir John Kerr, the UK's permanent representative from 1990 to 1995 was next posted to Washington, before becoming permanent under-secretary at the foreign office, then secretary-general of the European Convention. (Indeed, for the British foreign office, the EU permanent representation in Brussels is seen as one of a handful of top postings, together with Paris, Berlin, Washington and New York.) In the case of most member states, appointment of their permanent representative will involve consultation with the minister of foreign affairs, and perhaps with the head of government. The reason for this is clear; a confident and trustful relationship with a permanent representative is a vital aide for a government, particularly during crises and at sensitive times, such as during the run-up to an IGC and during a member state's turn at the presidency.

Whether rumours of 'going native' are well founded or not, such criticism reveals another important phenomenon related to all levels within the permanent representations; what, in social sciences parlance, is referred to as 'socialisation'. The two Corepers meet every week and so, clearly, the permanent representatives and their deputies see a lot of one another. Inevitably, such close and regular contact leads to familiarity, if not friendship, and mutual trust and respect. (In addition permanent representatives have in common their calling as professional diplomats.) In time – permanent representatives have far more time to develop relationships than their political masters – a sense of institutional solidarity develops, so that they find themselves defending not only the interests of their respective member states but also the more general institutional prerogatives of the Council (a tendency encouraged by the Council's general secretariat). There is a definite sense of teamwork among Coreper members. The permanent representatives may frequently find themselves on different sides of a discussion, but they are all engaged in the same basic activity. Even when a permanent representative is totally isolated and under great pressure, there is mutual understanding and a tendency to criticize, implicitly or explicitly, the national capital and its instructions rather than the individual concerned. This solidarity extends to the presidency, since everybody at the Coreper table knows that they will, sooner or later, find themselves in the same position and role. (In passing it should be noted that in 2001 Coreper welcomed to its ranks its first, and to date sole, female member, the Irish permanent representative, Anne Anderson – in 2004 she became the first female president of Coreper.)

A traditional part of any diplomat's work is the entertainment of their counterparts on what is informally known as the 'cocktail circuit' (most diplomats receive an entertainment allowance). In Brussels, lunch and dinner are more likely than cocktails, and the guest list will extend beyond diplomats to officials working in the institutions, but the principle is the same. Such informal contacts are explicitly designed to facilitate the familiarisation and socialisation processes. However, lunches and dinners, whether formal or informal, have long since become an integral part of the Council's working method, at both ministerial and Coreper level. This development in part arose out of ministers' and Coreper's increasingly large work loads and subsequent time pressure, but also out of a pragmatic recognition that sensitive matters and potentially thorny problems could sometimes be usefully addressed outside the more formal circumstances of a full Council or Coreper meeting, with their banks of interpreters and attendant officials and the need for official, on-the-record pronouncements. Such a development is a further example of the way power and influence is diffused throughout the Council's structure.

The process of socialisation also takes place among the specialised staff within permanent representations. Diplomats are linked by their common calling, and so are many specialised staff. Some of the legislation dealt with at the Community level is highly technical and esoteric. Specialists from the national ministries will be very few in number and may have met in other international organisations or industrial or academic fora. Inevitably, friendships will be struck up and people who meet at work will also meet outside it. The result is a network of alliances and relationships which further enhances the Council's overall stability and its amorphous sense of identity.

Coreper's working methods and functions

According to article 207 TEC, Coreper is responsible 'for preparing the work of the Council and for carrying out the tasks assigned to it by the Council'. In practice, underneath its preparatory umbrella, Coreper, and its component permanent representatives, fulfil a number of complementary functions which could be summarised as information, coordination, interpretation, negotiation and defence. Chapters 15 and 17 consider negotiation and coordination in the overall context of the Council. Here Coreper's working methods are first examined, before considering its various functions.

Working methods

Coreper is serviced by a large number of standing and ad hoc working groups. When a Commission proposal is forwarded to the Council, the matter is habitually referred down to the appropriate working party for technical, specialised consideration (see chapter 12). At a time of the presidency's choosing, but generally when the working party has worked its way completely through the proposal, the party will report back to Coreper.

Coreper uses an agenda system similar to the Council's distinction between 'A points' and 'B points'. Where a working party has reached complete agreement on a proposal, it is placed on Coreper's agenda as a 'roman I item'. Roman I items are grouped together at the beginning of Coreper's agenda in much the same way as A items are grouped together at the beginning of Council agendas. Roman I items are not normally the subject of discussion, but are noted and sent on up to the Council as A items.

Proposals where working parties have been unable to reach complete agreement are placed on Coreper's agenda as 'Roman II items' ('*Points II*') and are the subject of discussion. Coreper may itself boil off all outstanding problems, and the problem will then be sent up to the Council as an A item. More commonly, Coreper will boil off some problems, clarify others, and identify potential solutions. The proposal is then typically referred back to the responsible working group for further consideration. Like a 'convection current', proposals may be referred back to working groups and back up to Coreper several times before ultimate referral up to the Council.

Coreper's working method is informed by two fundamental considerations. The first, generalised at all levels within the Council, is the search for maximal consensus on each issue. In the final analysis, it falls to the presidency to decide when maximal consensus has been reached. The second consideration is more practical. Council time is a precious asset, and Coreper takes pride in using it as sparingly as possible. Even where sensitive or intractable problems are reluctantly handed up to the ministers, they are frequently accompanied by the tentative foundations of a solution.

The principal record of Coreper's work is the reports it sends up to the Council on each particular dossier. The summary record (minutes) of Coreper's meetings are prepared by the Council secretariat. They are very succinct documents, and are normally made up of references to the reports to Council. On rare occasions, a permanent representative may choose to make a statement for entry in Coreper's minutes. The aim of and the technique for such statements is exactly the same as statements in the Council's minutes. Again, as is sometimes the case in the Council, an 'extract' from Coreper's minutes may sometimes be drafted to facilitate agreement. Such extracts will ultimately be incorporated in the body of the minutes of a particular Coreper meeting.

Information

Coreper and the permanent representations are at the interstice of a two-way information flow between the state apparatus of the individual member states and the formal institution of the Council. When formal proposals are made to the Council or formal communications addressed to it, these are fed back to the national capitals, and hence the national ministries and parliaments, via the permanent representations. The permanent representations also feed back to the national capitals a great deal of unofficial information, ranging from the minutes of the Commission's weekly meetings to the preparatory meetings of commissioners' *chefs de cabinet*. The permanent representations relay on to the national capitals all formal documentation received from the Community institutions, ranging from the Council secretariat's minutes of meetings to Commission research documents. In addition, permanent representations engage in constant reporting back on meetings, from forthcoming agendas of meetings through to outcomes and decisions. Such meetings can be formal (e.g. Council working groups, coordination meetings, advisory committee meetings, European Parliament committee meetings) or informal (e.g. bilateral meetings with other delegations, presidency briefings, visits of VIPs).

The speed of the information process varies. In the case of the United Kingdom permanent representation, for example, the standard foreign office practice of a 'telegram' to London on the same night is broadly respected. Formal written information can be generously supplemented by telephone conversations. When relaying on information and, above all, when reporting back on meetings, permanent representations engage in a considerable amount of selection and preliminary analysis. This may range from, for example, general estimations of how much room for manoeuvre exists on a particular matter through to, say, a detailed analysis of the negotiating position of each member state. Such analyses will build upon and supplement the Council secretariat's traditionally succinct reports and minutes of meetings. Thus, although a great deal of information is relayed back to the national capitals, the relaying is methodical, selective and analytical.

A similar process is taking place in the opposite direction at both formal and informal levels. At the formal level, member state representatives in working groups and Coreper meetings are constantly informing their counterparts within the Council (as well as Commission representatives) about their positions on legislative proposals or political issues. At the informal level (see 'socialisation' above), member state representatives are engaged in constant exchanges of information, whether specific or more general and background.

Coordination

The coordination of national and European policy is considered in chapter 17 and will be dealt with only briefly here. Coreper is not the only preparatory committee beneath the ministerial level and is itself divided into two separate levels. Nevertheless, Coreper, and its component permanent representatives, play an important role in coordinating, first, the policies of the member states and, second, the work of the Council itself, for it is axiomatic that virtually all items on the Council's and the European Council's agenda will first have passed through Coreper (or another of the Council's preparatory committees). Thus in one sense Coreper plays an important gate-keeping function for the Council and the European Council but in another each permanent representative and deputy representative acts as a point of policy focus for his or her member state. This policy focus also enables permanent representatives to assess the overall balance of their member states' interests which, in turn, enables deals and concessions to be made (see 'interpretation' below).

The Antici and Mertens groups

The Antici group plays a vital part in coordinating the work of Coreper II. Although suggestions for such a body had been in the air for some time, the Antici group was the result of a joint Belgian and Luxembourg initiative and was established under the Italian presidency in the first half of 1975. It is named after a then official in the Italian permanent representation, Paolo Antici, who was the first to chair the group.

The establishment of the Antici group was a functional response to Coreper II's and the Council's increasingly heavy workloads. The aim was to clear Coreper's and the Council's agendas of as much organisational detail as possible, leaving ambassadors and ministers to discuss substantive issues only. It is not generally a negotiating body in itself but, rather, prepares the timetables and agendas for Coreper II and Council meetings so as to allow the member states and the Commission to coordinate and finalise their negotiating positions before the formal meetings take place. It may, however, act more like a traditional Council working party in examining particular sensitive or horizontal dossiers conferred on it by Coreper (for example, buildings or interpreting and translating – see chapter 2). The Antici group meets on the eve (Tuesdays or Wednesdays) of each weekly Coreper II meeting. When its meetings are over its members hurry to inform their ambassadors and permanent representations of the procedural decisions taken and the state of play on more sensitive dossiers on the Coreper agenda. Antici group members are also responsible for agreement on draft Council minutes.

The group is composed of representatives from the member states' permanent representations and the Commission and chaired by a representative of the presidency. The 'Anticis' are in effect the close advisers and coordinators for their permanent representatives. They also have a particular role in the margins of European Council meetings, where they are the relay to delegations for debriefings given by the secretariat on proceedings in the European Council itself. Members of the Antici group are among the few national civil servants with direct access to the European Council meeting room to give information to, or receive instructions from, their respective heads of state or government. This right suggests a more privileged and influential role than straightforward coordination might imply. Antici group members, who usually sit in an ante-room to the European Council meeting room, also act as messengers to foreign ministers and heads of government from their permanent representatives. Thus, Antici group members display an idiosyncratic combination of privileged access and relatively junior status. They are, in effect, confidential advisers to their permanent representatives.

Once the Antici group was up and running, it was not long before suggestions were made for a similar body to be established to prepare and coordinate the work of the ever more over-burdened Coreper I and sectoral Councils. However, it was only under the Belgian presidency in the second half of 1993 that these suggestions ultimately bore fruit. The Mertens group, named after Vincent Mertens de Wilmars, the Belgian permanent representation official who was first to chair it, is similarly composed of representatives from the permanent representations and the Commission and exercises parallel coordination functions to those of the Antici group.

Above all, both the Antici and Mertens groups are important coordinating tools for the presidency. On the one hand, they enable the presidency to find out where problems lie and judge what the best possible approach to a problem might be. For example, it is at Antici or Mertens group meetings that the presidency will discover whether delegations intend to insist on maintaining reservations or might be inclined to lift them (perhaps after behind-the-scenes bilateral or presidency negotiations). Where delegations seem intent on maintaining reservations and where unanimity is required the presidency might well consider it inappropriate or untimely to bring certain points before the Council. On the other hand, these groups are also the forum in which the presidency will inform the other Council members how it intends to handle particular problems. For example, it might announce its intention to propose new compromise ideas, limit discussion to certain specific items of the dossier under discussion or seek further clarifications from the Commission or certain delegations. Permanent representatives or their deputies need to be prepared accordingly. Moreover, in recent years the Mertens group has undertaken most of the work in preparing items which should appear in the agendas of the sectoral Councils, thereby saving much Coreper I time. It also clears the deck on the 'I' (i.e., non-discussion) items on the Coreper I agenda.

The Antici and Mertens groups' status and their idiosyncratic mix of functions and privileges is a further example of the diffuse nature of policy-making functions within the Council. Precisely the same points about 'socialisation' apply to the members of the Antici and Mertens groups as they do to members of other preparatory bodies. Through their informal system of confidence and mutual understanding, they share sensitive advance negotiating information with the common aim of making the decision-making machinery work. They take pride in their work, share common status and, naturally, an *esprit de corps*, and such sentiments of attachment can continue long after the civil servants concerned have moved on to other more senior tasks.

Interpretation

The Council's working parties necessarily have a narrow, purist approach to their work. Each member state's representative deals only with the proposal on the table. In time, the working party will report to Coreper (through the general secretariat), the presidency representative will report back to the presidency, and the individual representatives will report back to their ministries. By the time a matter reaches Coreper, all problems will normally have been identified and member states' positions flagged. Similar reports are constantly reaching Coreper and the presidency from a large number of working parties covering very different subject areas. Thus, as was explained above, the Coreper level is a level of focus, and hence of coordination. But it is also a level of *interpretation*, since it is at the Coreper level that a member state can first weigh up the relative importance of dossiers and of its objections on particular issues.

It is also mainly at the Coreper level that the possibility of deal-making first emerges, with member states able to make comparative calculations as to whether and where concessions on relatively unimportant dossiers and issues might result in worthwhile gains on other, more important, dossiers and issues. The presidency will also be making similar calculations from a more objective point of view. The way in which such interpretation and deal-making will take place depends to a considerable extent on a member state's mechanisms for coordinating its European policy-making. In the case of some member states, the permanent representative will receive detailed instructions, but in probability all permanent representatives receive detailed instructions where particularly sensitive issues are concerned. Whatever the degree of detail, there will always be scope for permanent representatives to interpret their instructions in the light of ongoing negotiations in Coreper. For example, a permanent representative might be instructed that their member state is prepared to drop its objections to a particular clause if it receives sufficient satisfaction on another matter. But it will be left to the permanent representative to decide whether sufficient satisfaction has been given and whether the initial objection should in fact be dropped.

Thus Coreper embodies two levels of interpretation. The first is an overall interpretation of a member state's (or the presidency's) interests and the *relative* value of issues. This is a highly dynamic process, with permanent representations and the national coordination mechanisms behind them engaged in constant evaluation. Moreover, the relative value of issues can change. For instance, a previously obscure matter can become politicised in one or more member states, and issues can take on, or lose, importance as the Council's agenda shifts. The second level is the interpretation of instructions, which can involve a considerable amount of political judgement on the part of the permanent representatives, particularly as negotiations progress.

Negotiation

The negotiation process is considered in detail in chapter 15. By the time a matter reaches a formal Coreper meeting it should, if the preparatory mechanisms have worked well, be stripped to its barest essentials. The appropriate working party will have settled most minor technical issues and flagged up major differences. The Antici group (or the Mertens group) will have decided its position on the agenda, made a shrewd guess as to how much time will be required to deal with it, clarified the initial negotiating positions of the member states and the Commission, and outlined the way in which the presidency intends to proceed. The member states' permanent representations, competent ministries and coordination mechanisms will meanwhile have established their positions and set out negotiating guidelines or instructions for their permanent representatives. The stage is set.

There are four sorts of negotiator in Coreper. The first is the member state, whose interests are defended by its permanent representative. Coreper is little different to any other body in the types of negotiating techniques that are used. Although Coreper can vote on procedural decisions, there are rarely 'votes' on legislative proposals. Permanent representatives may, however, indicate the position their minister is likely to take in Council. At the same time, all seated around the table know that Coreper is not the forum of last resort, and that a member state's position can still change. In short, Coreper is the first level at which political, as opposed to purely technical, battle lines are drawn up, but those lines are not necessarily set in stone.

The second negotiator is the presidency. As chapter 18 describes, the presidency has its own agenda which could be roughly summarised as having two aims; to reach agreement on as many dossiers as possible, and to reach as broad an agreement on each dossier as possible, insofar as this is compatible with the first aim. The presidency's tools are the typical tools of a non-executive chairmanship: to cajole, persuade and convince through argument, and to use privileged information to facilitate compromise. However, although the presidency has its own agenda, it would be wrong to assume that it is entirely independent in its pursuit. The presidency is drawn from the member states and is always of them. The presidency's ingrained bias is further enhanced by its reliance on the Council secretariat and on the advice of the Council's legal service.

The third negotiator is the Commission, which has often been characterised as an additional member state at the Council table. Where 'first pillar' (Community) legislation is concerned, the Commission has a proprietorial right over its legislative proposals and is free to withdraw them or modify them until (if under co-decision) the second reading stage. This right gives both the Commission and Coreper important bargaining tools. In the first place, the Commission can threaten to withdraw a proposal if it considers that the Council negotiations risk distorting it out of all recognition, but there is a concomitant risk that the Commission's bluff will be called. In the second place, judicious use of the Commission's right to modify its proposal can greatly facilitate agreement but, in the third place, a coalition of member states can subject the Commission to great pressure to modify a proposal in a way it would otherwise not have done. Outside the legislative process, the Commission remains a significant and influential political force whose views can be consequential.

Over the past decade a fourth negotiator has asserted its interests in the Council's meeting rooms, though it is never physically present in either

Coreper or the Council: the European Parliament. Since the implementation of the Single European Act in July 1987, the European Parliament has had an increasingly important legislative role in an increasing number of EU policy areas. The co-decision procedure, introduced by the Maastricht Treaty and refined by the Amsterdam Treaty, has left the Council and the European Parliament as twin arms of the legislative authority for many categories of legislation. The underlying point is that the Council and hence Coreper are now obliged to take account of the European Parliament's position. Its formal legislative position is made known through amendments. Since it is physically absent from the meeting room, its informal position can only be made known via a proxy. In the past, this tended principally to be the Commission, with an occasional sympathetic intervention from a friendly member state. But since the advent of the conciliation committee procedure foreseen under the co-decision procedure, the presidency has increasingly found itself in the role of go-between, reporting back from formal or informal encounters with the parliamentary delegation. The dynamics of the co-decision procedure are mostly dealt with at the Coreper level (most codecision procedures are handled by Coreper I, which means that deputy permanent representatives are the Council's co-decision experts).

The defensive role

'Defending the national position' has been identified as one of Coreper's three basic functions. (Hayes-Renshaw *et al*, 1989). There are four identifiable levels of defence involving Coreper. The first is the defence of individual member states' interests. The spirit of maximum consensus is as strongly present in Coreper as it is in the Council and the European Council; member states' problems are mutually respected and great efforts are made to find a solution satisfactory for all. Inevitably, there is strength in numbers (formalised where majority voting and qualified majority voting is the norm), and this factor, which applies just as much to the larger states as it does to the smaller ones, leads to a second level of defence, that of the interests of groups of member states. Alliances can be shifting or static, single issue or general, but the foundations of most are constructed in Coreper. (The phrase 'in Coreper' is here intended in its broadest sense, since by the time the ambassadors or their deputies sit down formally to discuss an issue such alliances will already have been forged in bilateral contacts between similarly interested permanent representations.)

The third level of defence is that of the institution, particularly vis-à-vis other EU actors and institutions. Coreper's Brussels-based permanence and the lengthy periods of office of its component permanent representatives encourage a strong sense of identification with the overall interests of the Council. In practice, this means that Coreper is a jealous and doughty defender of the rights and prerogatives of the Council – far more so, indeed, than the Council, at the formal ministerial level, itself. This combination of defensive spirit and institutional solidarity manifests itself in many different ways; decisions about Court cases, mandates to the presidency during the negotiation of inter-institutional agreements, monitoring intergovernmental conferences, positioning vis-à-vis the Commission and the Parliament, and vis-à-vis parliamentary amendments.

The fourth level of defence could be considered to be a variation on the third; it is the defence of the institution, of its actions and decisions, back to the national capitals. As Brussels-based residents, constantly monitoring the EU policy-making process, permanent representatives are frequently better placed to see the full implications and ramifications of particular policy issues or stances and they are often intimately involved in the brokering of deals. It falls to them, subsequently, to explain their views, based on their insiders' vantage point, to their national capitals.

Permanent representatives in the Council

Permanent representatives or their deputies accompany 'their' ministers whenever the Council formally meets. Coreper will already have expedited the ministers' work by boiling the Council's agenda down to its political essentials. For the most part, it is Coreper that effectively decides what the ministers will discuss. Since virtually all items on the Council's agenda have passed through the Coreper filter, the permanent representatives are ideally placed to advise their ministers on how best to proceed, not only because of their familiarity with the national capital's instructions and the detail of the dossier, but also because of their shrewd insider's view as to what will 'play' and how best it should be played. Should a compromise be suggested, by the presidency or the Commission or another member state, they will know how to react to it, and they will have briefed their minister beforehand as to how far he or she may realistically go in the search for compromise. Thus, permanent representatives play a vital role in the Council itself. Moreover, they frequently replace ministers in Council.

It is rare for the Council to vote, and though the presidency is perfectly entitled to proceed to a vote, it is loath to force issues where any potential for compromise might still exist. However, following the entry into force of the Single European Act, the Council's rules of procedure were amended so as to allow the Commission or a member state to request a vote, and the presidency is thereafter required to open voting proceedings if a majority of the member states so decides. The result of these provisions has been a certain increase in voting in Council (see chapter 13, box 13.1). Under article 206 TEC, 'Where a vote is taken, any member of the Council may also act on behalf of not more than one other member.' However, in practice a minister is invariably replaced by their permanent representative or the deputy permanent representative. In such circumstances, the permanent representative can do pretty much everything except vote. The member state's position can be explained and defended, and the permanent representative can indicate how the delegation would vote.

Coreper today and tomorrow

The Maastricht and Amsterdam Treaties and the conclusions of the Helsinki European Council meeting have consolidated and extended Coreper's role considerably. Article 207 TEC states that Coreper 'shall be responsible for preparing the work of the Council', and article 3 TEU states that the Union 'shall be served by a single institutional framework'. The preparatory work of Coreper therefore covers all EU policy areas. The Amsterdam Treaty additionally provided that Coreper 'may adopt procedural decisions in cases provided for in the Council's rules of procedure,' thus extending and reinforcing its horizontal, coordinating competence. The Council's rules of procedure set out those areas where Coreper may adopt procedural decisions. These include: holding a Council session elsewhere than in Brussels or Luxembourg; allowing Council debates to be broadcast or to publish the results of votes; using the written procedure; consulting an institution or body; and deciding to set or extend a time-limit for the consultation of an institution or body.

Despite the increasingly heavy load on Coreper's shoulders, the December 1999 Helsinki European Council meeting further consolidated Coreper's role and its competences. 'Given that Coreper has responsibility for the final preparation and presentation of all agenda items to the Council,' argued the document, 'it shall be responsible for assembling all preparatory work undertaken by different vertical bodies for both multidisciplinary and interpillar dossiers.' Even with the proliferation of specialised senior committees pre-empting much of the substance of Coreper's preparatory work in certain (generally non-legislative) policy areas (see chapter 12), Coreper nevertheless retains a general overall competence for horizontal legal, institutional and financial issues.

The twin keys to understanding the true extent of Coreper's apparently far-reaching political and legislative powers are, on the one hand, the preparatory processes into which they are bedded and, on the other, the formal nature of much of what occurs at the Council level. If permanent representatives acted as free agents, they would not remain in Brussels for long! As this study shows, Council meetings are but one level in a mechanism made up of a multitude of formal and informal processes which have evolved to ensure maximal representation of member states' interests. Moreover, although it is true that ministers are the repositories of political power, whereas diplomats are servants to their national capitals' instructions, the vast bulk of the Council's work is of a highly technical nature. As Noël remarked in 1966, 'the creation of such an organ as Coreper was not only necessary but inevitable' (1966, p 52). As the work of the Convention has demonstrated, such an organ remains indispensable; article III 247 of the draft constitution takes over the wording of article 207 TEC concerning Coreper in its entirety! It is therefore a certain prediction that Coreper will continue to remain the Council's prism and its fulcrum; just as certainly, pressure to delegate downwards will grow.

Chapter 12: Other Council preparatory bodies

Aside from Coreper, a large number of senior policy committees and working parties make up the base of the Council's internal structures. Until 1999 no official list of Council preparatory bodies existed. Numbering about 400, they had grown up over the years in an organic and rather haphazard manner as the Council's responsibilities expanded. Given the increasing cost of holding working party meetings and the more limited usefulness of such bodies as a negotiating forum with twenty-five members, an official list was first agreed by Coreper in 1999 as part of the Council's internal reforms to prepare for enlargement (see chapter 21). Further rationalisation of working parties was agreed following the reduction in the number of Council formations decided at the Seville European Council in June 2002. The list of preparatory bodies is updated approximately every six months by the secretariat and can be consulted on the Council's website. At present there are around 160 preparatory bodies covering the full range of EU business. They can be divided into two basic categories: committees of senior officials with overall responsibility in a particular policy area, and working parties composed of relatively junior experts with narrower technical competence.

Senior policy committees

As outlined in the previous chapter, Coreper has overall responsibility under the treaty for preparing Council meetings. Over the years a number of complementary, specialised senior committees have been established with overall policy responsibilities in certain sectors. These fall into two broad groups: committees established by the treaties or by intergovernmental act (box 12.1), and committees established by Council decision (box 12.2). The role and functions of some of these committees have been described in part two of this book dealing with the Council in its various guises, and the detail is therefore not repeated here.

A major consequence of this increasing policy compartmentalisation inside the Council has been a perceptible weakening of Coreper's overall position inside the Council's structures. Given the volume of work now being processed through the Council, it would be unrealistic to expect Coreper to deal with all policy details in every sector of work. In some cases, a certain rivalry has developed between Coreper and the policy committee in question, with some committees viewing their role as one of 'gatekeeper' for the Council in a given policy sector. Steps were taken as part of the Council's preparations for enlargement to strengthen Coreper's hand in

Box 12.1: *Senior Council preparatory bodies established by the treaties or intergovernmental act*

The economic and financial committee (EFC) (the successor of the former monetary committee) has its basis in article 114 TEC and is something of a hybrid animal in that it delivers opinions and reports on the economic and financial situation of the member states and the Community to both the Council and the Commission. It is the body which prepares the substance of all the Ecofin Council's non legislative discussions (i.e., most of its work), yet it meets in the Commission and its secretariat is provided by the Commission. The member states and the Commission each appoint two members, who are senior officials from finance ministries and central banks. The EFC's chair is elected from among his or her peers for a duration of two years. Details of its role and functions are given in chapter 5.

The employment committee was established in the follow-up to the Treaty of Amsterdam under article 130 TEC to promote coordination between member states on employment and labour market policies. It also formulates opinions at the request of either the Council or the Commission, and like the EFC, each member state and the Commission appoints two members and the Commission acts as secretariat for the committee.

The article 133 committee follows and guides Community action and policy formulation in external trade. Under the EC treaty, the common commercial policy as defined in article 133 is a matter of exclusive competence, on which the Commission negotiates agreements (on the basis of a mandate given by the Council) and submits the agreed outcome to the Council for conclusion. The article 133 committee, which meets at the level of full members (directors-general of external trade), deputies and technical expert formations, has three main tasks. First and foremost, it advises the Commission in its role as negotiator where the latter is negotiating trade agreements on behalf of the Community. Second, it advises the Commission on routine matters on which the Commission makes 'démarches' to third countries in the management of the Community's common commercial policy. Third, it acts as a typical Council preparatory body when preparing certain legislation for adoption by the Council.

The social protection committee was also placed in the treaty following the Treaty of Amsterdam, where article 144 sets out its terms of reference. Like the employment committee and the EFC, it is an advisory body composed of two members from each member state and the Commission and its secretariat is provided by the Commision.

The special committee on agriculture (SCA) was established by a decision of the representatives of the governments of the member states on 12 May 1960 to prepare decisions of the Agriculture Council. Its functions and interaction with Coreper are explained in chapter 7.

The political and security committee (PSC), first established in the Maastricht Treaty, has responsibility for monitoring the international situation in the areas covered by the common foreign and security policy and issuing opinions to the Council. It also exercises, under the responsibility of the Council, political control and strategic direction of crisis management operations (see chapter 4).

Box 12.2: *Council committees established by Council act*

The EU military committee (EUMC) consists of the chiefs of defence of the member states, represented by their military representatives (milreps) and was established by Council decision 2001/79/CFSP of 22 January 2001 (see chapter 4). The chairman is appointed by the Council on the recommendation of the committee for a term of three years.

The committee for civilian aspects of crisis management (Civcom) was established by Council decision 2000/354/CFSP of 22 May 2000 and its function is to provide information, formulate recommendations and give advice on the civilian aspects of crisis management to the PSC (see Box 12.1).

The economic policy committee (EPC), although formally established by an act of the Council (decision 2000/604/EC of 29 September 2000), is actually mentioned briefly in the treaty (in article 272(9)). Its job is to contribute to the preparation of the work of the Council of coordinating the economic policies of the member states and of the Community and provide advice to the Commission and the Council. This includes economic analyses, opinions on methodologies and draft formulations for policy recommendations, particularly on structural policies for improving growth potential and employment. Along with the EFC, it plays an important role in preparing the deliberations of the Ecofin Council on these issues. Its chairman (elected by the Committee for a term of two years) always attends meetings of the Ecofin Council (see Chapter 5).

The financial services committee (FSC) was established by Council decision 2003/165/EC of 18 February 2003 to help define the medium- and long-term strategy for financial services issues and provide political advice and oversight on internal issues such as the single market and the financial services action plan, and external issues such as the WTO. The Commission and each member state appoints a high-level member and the chair is elected from among the committee's members for a two year term.

The security committee, established by Council decision 2001/264/EC, is responsible for issuing recommendations to the Council and to the secretary-general/high representative on all matters relating to the Council's security regulations, such as on handling classified information and implementing agreements on the security of information with third countries. It normally meets twice a year and, unusually for a Council preparatory body, its composition is laid down in the Council decision (members are each member state's national security authority (NSA)). It is chaired by a representative of the Council secretariat.

---

matters where it alone should logically play a strong and effective role. Many of the specialist committees represent the interests of particular government departments in the Council system. Coreper, on the other hand, is supposed to maintain a horizontal overview of issues going before the Council, particularly where they involve principles of legality, subsidiarity, proportionality, or institutional issues, matters with financial implications and/or matters of procedure or transparency. Since most permanent representatives come from foreign ministries, they are all too often perceived by the specialists as the voice of their foreign ministry, rather than that of the 'general interest' inside the Council. A member of the economic and financial committee would not consider him or herself in any way subordinate to a permanent representative, for example.

While these other committees have no formal decision-making powers, their influence and reach can be considerable. As has been described in previous chapters, in some cases they are the natural forum for coordinating work in certain sectors and, if they are effective (and effectiveness and efficiency vary widely), most or all substantive points will have been resolved before the dossier comes to Coreper, before being in turn submitted to the Council, with little or no need for Coreper subsequently to reopen discussion.

Working parties

While around 160 preparatory bodies exist on paper (including the committees mentioned above), their practical existence – that is, whether they actually meet at all – depends on the flow of work within each particular area of responsibility. In many cases, this depends on the previously established legislative priorities of the Commission and the presidency. Some working parties may meet infrequently or not at all during a presidency. Others, particularly in a sector where a presidency is determined to make progress, may meet as often as once a week, though the need to produce, translate and circulate documents places a practical limit on the frequency of meetings. Over the years, there has been a steady increase in the number of meetings of preparatory bodies. In 1997, there were 2,705 meetings in the Council (excluding Coreper and Council meetings). By 2003, this number had increased to 4,333 per year, slightly down on the peak of 4,420 meetings reached in 2002.

There are no fixed formal rules about the composition of working parties. They are attended by experts from member states together with a representative or representatives of the Commission, which attends all working party meetings (including certain items discussed in the EU military committee and the military committee working party). With a few exceptions, it is up to each member state to determine who to send to working party meetings, which all take place in Brussels in the Justus Lipsius building. 'Expert' is an amorphous term. An expert will generally be an official from a ministry on secondment to the permanent representation in Brussels, or somebody flown in to Brussels from the national capital for the duration of the meeting. In highly technical fields, an expert may be a non-governmental co-opted scientist or technician. At the other extreme, where a working party is dealing with more general or political issues, the expert may be a career diplomat. In most meeting rooms, only one delegate can actually sit at the main table for each delegation, although up to two further members of each delegation can be seated behind.

Most preparatory bodies are chaired by a representative of the rotating presidency. Four senior policy committees and one working party have a permanent elected chairman for a fixed duration (the economic and financial committee, the economic policy committee, the financial services committee and the military committee, as well as the military committee working party). Seven bodies are permanently chaired by a member of the Council secretariat (see chapter 19).

Delegates are seated around the table in the same order as in the Council itself (i.e., in the order of succession of presidencies, with the ten new member states interspersed, in alphabetical order starting after the next presidency but one (see box 3.1)). The presidency, flanked by the general secretariat, including, in most instances, a member of the legal service, sits at the head of the table. The Commission representatives sit directly opposite the presidency.

The degree of independence, and hence of flexibility and deal-making capacity, of experts can vary considerably. Some are kept on a tight leash by their national ministries. They are frequently obliged to issue waiting reservations so that they can consult with their authorities. In pressure situations, they may have to leave the meeting room to telephone their capitals. Others have far more independence. This may be because a delegate occupies a relatively senior position within their ministry (or in the broader scientific community), but on occasion it may be simply because a member state is relatively indifferent to the outcome on a particular piece of legislation or policy (see following section).

The effectiveness of a working party depends to a considerable degree on the skills of its chair. Aware of this, member states prepare carefully for the presidency. The chair of each working party will be selected some time before the presidency begins and in the case of many member states will be given some tutoring on how to conduct meetings. The best chairs combine expertise in the subject area with authority and diplomacy. A chair must be aware of the sensitivities of the different member states and, at the more human level, of their representatives and will carefully avoid being seen as overtly favouring the position of their own delegation.

Working party meetings are convened by the presidency, assisted by the Council general secretariat. Once the date has been fixed, the interpreting booked, and the secretariat has received a green light from the presidency, the members of the group will be informed of the date of the meeting and of the agenda by e-mail. If a presidency feels that it can reach a successful conclusion on a particular dossier during its term of office, it may plan a succession of meetings at increasing frequency, using as a deadline the date of the next appropriate sectoral Council (and a preceding Coreper meeting). This is why Council meetings tend to be bunched towards the end of the six-month presidential term.

The rhythm of working parties has been affected by three developments. The first is the increasing use of programming in the Council's work (see chapter 21) which came about at least partly in response to the tendency for the Council to have rapidly shifting priorities from one six-month period to the next as each new presidency took over the helm. In December 2003, the Council adopted the first multiannual strategic work programme covering the three-year period 2004-2006. In addition, since 2003, the two member states which hold the presidency over the calendar year are obliged to draw up an annual operating programme for the Council's work. This both forces member states to work together in preparing the programme and to produce a jointly agreed document which is presented to the Council. No presidency can therefore adopt an entirely *à la carte* approach to adopting its priorities. (The transition from one presidency to the next is facilitated by the fact that the incoming presidency may already begin chairing items in a working group after the last relevant sectoral Council has taken place during the presidency and where discussion on these items will continue during the next presidency.)

A second constraint has been the imposition of legislative deadlines under the co-decision procedure with the European Parliament. As a result, working parties need to meet to consider parliamentary amendments and the attitude which the Council should adopt towards them. This has in turn instilled the need for further discipline in working parties' proceedings. The third more practical constraint is that, as a result of the increased numbers of meetings in the Justus Lipsius building, meeting rooms and interpreters generally need to be reserved more than two months in advance if the presidency wants to secure facilities for a meeting. This, combined with a need to programme requirements for document translation to ensure proper preparation of a dossier for examination by Coreper or the Council, means that the chair of each working party needs to have a fairly well-developed work programme at the micro-level.

Most working parties operate in a fairly informal manner; in many cases the delegates are on first name terms (long gone are the days in Coreper where permanent representatives used to be addressed in the meeting as 'Ambassador Smith/Dupont/Schmidt', etc.). In many cases the discussions can be very straight talking, with no holds barred. Indeed, the first thing that struck some of the new member states' representatives, perhaps expecting a more 'diplomatic' type forum, was how animated the cut and thrust of debate could be at times and how directly delegations could express their views and comment on the arguments of others. The budget committee (which is in the habit of 'voting' regularly – see chapter 5.2) is perhaps one of the finest examples.

Chapter 13: The national negotiator in Council preparatory bodies

What follows is a stylised account of the working methods in the Council's preparatory bodies, describing how a national negotiator operates in working parties. While the formal rules and voting procedures in the Council are outlined in chapter 14, voting rules are only one – albeit an important one – of the factors affecting the behaviour of individual negotiators in this process. It is the national negotiator in the Council who represents the focus of overlapping interests in shaping the negotiation and pulling the end point of equilibrium in a particular direction.

The Council rarely takes the initiative itself to begin work on a given topic. In many areas it has no power to do so. For most matters falling under the EC Treaty, the right of initiative lies exclusively with the Commission. Negotiation in the Council on EC matters can therefore only begin once the Commission has formally approved a proposal in the twenty working languages and forwarded it to the Council. The Commission does not, of course, propose in a vacuum; before collectively approving a proposal, the Commission will have engaged in an extensive consultation process among its own services, with member states, economic and social interests and other representative associations and with other institutions – by means of green and white papers where major initiatives are concerned. The Commission tries to gauge as closely as possible the general interest, given that it wants to table viable proposals which will have a reasonable chance of coming through the legislative mill more or less intact (see chapter 15). Increasingly, the Commission's legislative intentions are flagged up through multi-annual legislative and work programming exercises.

For subjects falling under the second and third pillars, initiatives may originate from any member state, but in most cases the lead is taken by the presidency, or the secretary-general/high representative on certain matters on foreign and security policy. The secretariat and legal service will assist the presidency or member states in ensuring that any initiative tabled is prepared in the correct legal form.

Once a proposal or initiative has been tabled, the presidency will schedule discussion in a particular working party. Usually it is obvious which working party is competent to deal with a particular proposal. In cases of doubt Coreper will adjudicate, or may decide to set up a new permanent or ad hoc working party. It is at this point that negotiation formally begins in the Council.

The formal framework

A national delegate negotiates on the basis of instructions provided by his or her administration. These may leave a greater or lesser margin of discretion for the negotiator to shape a deal at working level (see following section). The main factor in determining negotiating tactics is whether unanimity or QMV applies for the final adoption of the decision. Under unanimity, a national negotiator is in a fairly comfortable position if the Commission has proposed a politically unpopular measure for his or her government. Unless and until the government is willing to acquiesce and let the measure go through, pressure can be exerted in order to wrest concessions until such time as a politically acceptable outcome is found. Under qualified majority voting, no such comfort zone exists. Delegations are obliged to determine what their realistic bottom negotiating line is, and need to seek alliances with other like-minded delegations in order to construct what is usually referred to as a blocking minority – sufficient votes to prevent the measure being adopted (see chapter 14).

Once such a blocking minority exists, it is easier to extract concessions from the Commission. An important element in the overall balance of influence between the institutions is the fact that the Commission cannot be forced to amend its proposal against its will – even where qualified majority voting applies. This gives the Commission considerable influence in determining what concessions to make on its initial proposal in order to buy off a qualified majority. Delegations must therefore make a tactical assessment of the cohesiveness of any blocking minority, in which delegations may have similar or entirely different reasons for opposing a proposal by the Commission. The skill of the national negotiator lies in making realistic assessments not only of their own negotiating position, but also the bottom line positions of all the main players in a particular negotiation and what they will be prepared to accept politically at the end of the process. Deal making therefore requires much more than attending a once-fortnightly meeting of a working party. In any case, in meetings with more than twenty-five participants the scope for meaningful negotiation is limited.

Some academics, based on a detailed statistical analysis, have argued that recourse to qualified majority voting has had little measurable impact on the Council's decision-making output (Golub, 1999, 2000). Actual recourse to a vote in the Council tends to be infrequent. In adopting the 280 or so directives necessary for the creation of the single market, consensus was achieved on 260 of them (Barnier, 2000). Box 13.1 indicates voting outcomes in the Council from 1999 to 2002. What it shows above all is the extent to which QMV is now the rule in EU decision-making, and how relatively infrequently the Council actually votes.

However, the present cannot be extrapolated into the future. What worked with fifteen member states will not necessarily continue to do so in a Union of twenty-five or more where consensus will necessarily be more difficult to achieve. Recourse to voting is undoubtedly going to become more commonplace since, in a system where debating time is severely constrained, the existence of a qualified majority will in most cases determine the cut-off point in negotiations.

Furthermore, decision-making effectiveness and, arguably, the quality of

Box 13.1: *Voting outcomes in the Council on definitive legislative acts*

	1999	2000	2001	2002
Total definitive legislative acts adopted	199	191	187	195
Acts with a legal basis allowing adoption by qualified majority	132 (66.3%)	135 (70.7%)	130 (69.6%)	139 (71.3%)
Number of acts adopted: –without votes against or abstentions	104	115	100	106
–with abstentions	4	4	10	17
–with votes against/ abstentions	24	16	20	16
Acts with a legal basis requiring unanimity	67	55	57	56
Number of acts adopted with abstentions	1	1	1	4

Source: Council Secretariat

legislation are both enhanced through the negotiating dynamic generated by virtue of the very existence of QMV in a particular area as a result of what Weiler terms 'the shadow of the vote' (Weiler, 1999). It provides a strong incentive for delegations to break deadlock in the Council by making concessions without actually resorting to a vote. It encourages the Commission to contemplate amendments to its proposals as part of the process of compromise building. Finally, in certain sectors, such as agriculture or the budget, votes tend to be threatened or used as a matter of course, since any further concessions are likely to be financially costly. Cost containment in any sector involving significant financial outlays is best served by QMV; unanimity inevitably increases the cost of side-payments to secure adoption of a particular measure (see, for example, Council, 1999b, paragraph 44).

In the formal context of the working party, delegations will set out their positions on the text under consideration (either orally or in writing). To begin with, delegations may be asked to outline their overall position on a proposal as a whole, or on compromise ideas put on the table to take a particular issue forward. Traditionally this was done by means of a 'table round', i.e., going round the table allowing each delegation to speak. However, with twenty-five delegations around the table, the round is now a dying breed.

At the Council level, the rules of procedure now state that 'full table rounds shall be proscribed in principle; they may only be used in exceptional circumstances on specific questions, with a time limit on interventions set by the Presidency.' It would clearly make no sense for each member of a Council of twenty-five to take the floor on each agenda point. Even allowing three minutes per delegation, a table round would take nearly an hour and a half! An exception comes with the Council's scheduled debates (see chapter 20), where each member state would normally have its say on an issue which, after all, had been chosen by the Council for open debate precisely because of its importance to the European citizens.

When a member state representative, at whatever level (Council, Coreper or working party) cannot agree to something in a text proposed by the Commission or the presidency, they place what is known as a reservation on it (often referred to in Franglais as a 'reserve'). Often, alternative wording will be proposed, or an explanation will be given as to why the proposed wording is unacceptable.

There are different sorts of reserves, and gradations among them. The most simple is the waiting or scrutiny reservation. A scrutiny reservation means that the member state representative is unable to take a position on a matter and cannot therefore agree to any decision involving that matter. The representative may not be briefed on an issue, or have received instructions on it, or they may not yet have read or analysed a provision; they may be unsure about the full implications of a compromise solution and wish to check with more senior members of the delegation or with authorities back in the capital. On occasion, a representative may simply want to wait until a translation in his/her language is available (this is usually referred to as a 'linguistic reservation'). Often delegations will continue working on a text they do not have in their own language, in the knowledge that once their language version is produced, their linguistic reservation will be lifted immediately. Waiting reservations are not considered important, since most will evaporate in due course. Delegates in working parties sometimes put scrutiny reservations on articles to create bargaining chips in negotiations on other articles, but this is a fairly transparent tactic.

A number of national parliaments have obtained undertakings from their governments that formal decisions should not be adopted in the Council before the proposed decisions have been communicated to the parliament and a nominal amount of time has passed to enable the parliament to scrutinise the proposal. The House of Commons has a particularly well-developed scrutiny system, and it is common to hear British (and other) delegates placing 'parliamentary scrutiny reservations' on decisions which may otherwise be ripe for adoption. Again, parliamentary scrutiny reservations are not considered to be of particular importance, since they too can be expected to evaporate in due course, albeit at a slower rate than simple scrutiny reservations.

A formal reservation is the sternest and most inflexible variety. It means that a member state cannot accept a provision on substantial rather than procedural grounds, and that a political solution must be found. Formal reservations issued in working parties generally boil up to Coreper and from there, if not settled by permanent representatives, to the Council.

Informal networks

An important part of any negotiating process is the understanding of opponents' positions. While the formal setting of a working party allows delegates to explain their position or to question other delegations on their positions, delegates also need to establish good working contacts with their counterparts outside the meeting room in order to understand what their real concerns are. Many working parties meet at least once every few weeks, and typically those dealing with politically difficult or high priority dossiers will be meeting practically on a weekly basis. In the case of many working parties, delegates tend to change relatively infrequently (usually every three years or so) and so usually get to know each other reasonably well both professionally, as well as socially. More than a few marriages have been made in Council working parties! Delegations will communicate by telephone and meet their opposite numbers (who, in a particular negotiation, may share their basic viewpoint, or whose government takes a radically different view) in order to assess the scope for compromise and prepare the way for political deal brokering at a later stage in the process. Such informal contacts also extend to representatives of the presidency, the Commission and the Council secretariat, who are all expected to help broker the compromises necessary at the end of any negotiation to secure agreement. Informal contacts and relationships play an important role at all levels of the process, including in the Council and the European Council.

Informal networks may also involve two or more member states meeting on a particular issue in order to defend a particular tactical negotiating line in any negotiation. The effectiveness of such alliances depends on the cohesiveness of the group and the solidity of the position being defended. The presidency may also convene groups of member states which have something at stake on a given item of negotiation in order to see whether an acceptable way forward can be forged. Provided such small groups of delegates are selected to represent both extremes of an argument involving the major parties with a direct interest in a particular negotiation, such meetings can be productive in the sense that any solution that can be bought by the extreme views in the negotiation will most likely be accepted by the other member states which have perhaps less at stake. Following enlargement, greater recourse will probably be had to such methods.

National position formation

Delegates in working party meetings (and in Coreper and Council) do not negotiate on their own whims, but in the knowledge of the overall policy stance of their government and based on specific instructions which are issued before each meeting suggesting the line to take in a discussion in order to defend 'the national interest'. However, determining what constitutes 'the national interest' is not as self-evident as it may at first sound. Governments are not monolithic organisations, and the interests of different government departments in a national administration may well be at odds in determining ideal, realistic and fallback negotiating positions in relation to a Commission proposal. For example, if the Commission proposes to fix limits on motor vehicle emissions, the UK department of trade and industry, the department of employment, the department of the environment, the foreign office and possibly the Scottish and Welsh offices may all have specific and diverging interests on how this proposal should be handled and what the optimum outcome should be. A national negotiator who receives two or three conflicting instructions will be, to say the least, in a somewhat weak negotiating position! This is why all member states have in place more or less sophisticated internal coordination procedures to reconcile differing positions into a single national negotiating position (see chapter 17).

The national position, however, must not simply reconcile the interests of different domestic ministries, but must also take account of the realities of what may be a fast moving negotiation in Brussels. The national delegate on the front line will have a better feel for where the endpoint of equilibrium is likely to fall in a particular negotiation, and what scope realistically exists for building an acceptable compromise. The input from a delegate in Brussels can be vital in ensuring that he or she receives viable negotiating instructions on a given dossier. Indeed, many national delegates will readily admit that they spend more time negotiating with their national capital to ensure they get the 'right' instructions, than with colleagues from other member states (who may well be encountering similar problems in their national administrations).

Interinsitutional dynamics

The national negotiator must also factor in to his or her tactical considerations the likely behaviour of other key institutions, in particular the Commission and the Parliament.

The role and impact of the Commission has already been described in some detail above (see also the chapter by Wessels and Diedrichs in Spence (ed.) *The European Commission*). In the past, it was commonplace to hear the Commission described as 'an additional member state at the Council table', and there is some truth in this description from one particular angle, for the Commission is a sophisticated negotiator which, particularly in the Community pillar, has some strong cards in its hand. Its officials, like those of the Council general secretariat, tend to be more permanent fixtures than the national delegates, and a complex symbiosis has grown up between them. Council and Commission officials acknowledge their respective wisdom. The Commission, through its own dealings with member states' delegations, may have a pretty shrewd idea about negotiating positions, but does not enjoy the same intimate relationship of trust that the Council general secretariat has won for itself over many years of studiedly objective work. On the other hand, in the Community pillar, where the Commission enjoys proprietorial rights over its proposals, a shrewdly placed and timed modification to the initial proposal – or even a concession about implementation downstream from the legislative process itself – can win consensus. The Council and Commission general secretariats therefore generally work closely together; both want a positive result, and both have privileged roles that can help bring this about.

The positions taken by the European Parliament, particularly on acts adopted by the co-decision procedure, also need to be factored into national negotiating positions. Support by the Parliament for a delegation's basic position can be helpful in ensuring an acceptable outcome in the Council, in the same way that positions taken by the Parliament which are at odds with a delegation's national negotiating position may make an ideal outcome difficult or impossible to achieve. This explains why certain delegations, particularly on matters subject to co-decision, spend considerable time lobbying members of parliamentary committees where legislative discussions are often conducted in parallel with discussion in the Council. Indeed, the larger and more resourceful permanent representations now see the permanent cultivation of good relations with 'their' MEPs as an integral part of their overall role.

Until Maastricht, there was relatively little cooperation between the Council and the Parliament outside the budgetary sphere. The co-decision procedure made it increasingly important for the two to work closely together, at both political and administrative level. The cumulative effect of this cooperation has been to normalise relations and to socialise both administrations. Scorn and suspicion have been replaced by interest, respect and mutual understanding. As with the Commission, the reason for this is that both 'sides' would prefer to achieve a positive result, and both can help to bring it about.

As part of its shrewd tactics, the Commission is also not averse to seeking alliances in the Parliament which can help win concessions in the Council and, almost invariably, the Commission looks to the Parliament to re-establish the budgetary amounts in its legislative proposals which, just as invariably, the Council will have cut. Thus, in an apparent paradox, the negotiating arena has become more complex since Maastricht but also, it has to be observed, more consensual.

The big picture

National negotiators find themselves not only at the centre of the Council's formal pyramid structure but also at the point of overlap of the various negotiating levels and factors described above. Grafted on top of these elements, which are common to most negotiations in the Council, is the tendency for participants in many policy sectors to operate in a vertical 'closed circuit' where national administrations, the Commission officials working in that sector, the parliamentary committee and professional associations often share a common interest in collaborating to secure outcomes which collectively serve the sector as a whole, but which might be less than optimum in terms of overall consistency of EU policy. While policy compartmentalisation is inevitable to some extent given the complexity of the Union as a political system, it is less than optimal for one sectoral formation of the Council to take a position which is out of kilter with the Union's overall policy line. As part of the reforms agreed by the Seville European Council in 2002, the number of Council formations was reduced from sixteen to nine, partly to help counter this tendency to policy compartmentalisation in the Council (see part two). The following part considers the behaviour of negotiators in the process of coalition and consensus building working within the structures described above.

PART 5: NEGOTIATING AND BARGAINING IN THE COUNCIL

Negotiating and bargaining is the very essence of what the Council is about. As the previous chapter has shown, the main players, representatives of member state governments, engage in a multi-tiered and vertically compartmentalised process in which they are motivated to varying degrees by a will to defend national interest and a desire to cooperate in joint problem-solving within a framework of formal rules, informal arrangements and accepted conventions. The system's formal decision-making rules are laid down in the treaties and in the Council's rules of procedure. However, as described in the previous chapter, the role and influence of governments in the Union's system are dependent on many institutional and informal factors other than voting rules and procedures and formal manifestations of each member state's size. While important, these are not the sole determinants of government behaviour. An overall commitment to the system, creative institutional interplay, informal personal networks, the extent to which national administrations are joined up and coordinated, the ability of non-institutional actors to articulate influence in different policy areas, personalities, events and circumstances may all play a significant part in determining policy outcomes.

This part examines the formal rules and procedures governing Council decision-making and how these have evolved with successive enlargements (chapter 14), analyses the behaviour of national negotiators in the process of coalition building and conflict resolution (chapter 15), describes the nuts and bolts of the consensus-building process in a major package negotiation (chapter 16) and considers how member states go about coordinating their EU policy (chapter 17).

Chapter 14: The formal framework – voting and decision-making

The legal bases in the treaties determine the voting rule which applies for decisions on any particular matter, while the Council's rules of procedure determine when and how formal votes on a given dossier may be requested. The rules of procedure require that for a meeting to be quorate and a vote to be taken, a majority of Council members must be present (currently, at least thirteen out of twenty-five). If a vote is requested, the decision to proceed to a vote is taken by simple majority (article 11(1) of the rules of procedure). While it is rare for there to be fewer than thirteen ministers present, a quorum will only be verified if so requested by a Council member. Items on the Council agenda on which a vote may be requested (i.e., once all the procedural requirements laid down in the treaty, such as consultation of other institutions or bodies, have been fulfilled) are marked by an asterisk.

This might suggest that the Council votes as a matter of routine. In fact it is relatively rare for the Council to vote formally. This, however, does not mean that the calculation of majorities is unimportant. The presidency and the Commission both spend time calculating how a necessary majority could be constructed. The member states' representatives know when they are in a minority position and could be outvoted. Any further negotiations once a required majority has been established will be the result of a magnanimous presidency's determination to go 'that extra mile' and bring on board as many member states as possible, or they may flow from the realisation that further compromise or concession is possible. In both cases, the presidency's action is based on the Council's fundamental consensual urge, as considered below. Nevertheless, the existence, or potential existence, of an appropriate majority is always at the back of the president's mind.

While it is relatively rare for votes actually to be called in the Council, it is not unheard of. The Ecofin Council on 5 December 2003 provides an interesting example of a meeting where a series of formal votes were called in the course of debate on the implementation of the excessive deficit procedure for Germany and France. Votes were taken on whether to adopt Council decisions under articles 104(8) and 104(9) TEC in respect of both France and Germany. In all four cases, no qualified majority was achieved. The Council then adopted by qualified majority two sets of conclusions assessing action taken by France and Germany. In total, including votes by simple majority on whether the Council should proceed to a vote, a total of ten votes were called in rapid succession! The Council press release for that meeting details the voting record of individual Council members (Council, 2003b).

Simple majority

There are three main ways in which the Council can take decisions. The first is by simple majority; that is, a straightforward majority headcount of members of the Council. Under article 205(1) TEC, this is at present the default rule unless the treaty provides otherwise – which it usually does. The simple majority voting rule applies mainly for procedural matters and in a very limited number of policy areas (e.g. adoption of the Council's rules of procedure (article 207(3)) or decisions to impose anti-dumping duties on third countries, where simple majority voting is provided for in the basic anti-dumping regulation). Under the new constitutional treaty qualified majority voting (see below) will become the default procedure.

Unanimity

The second way is by unanimity, which requires the approval or at least the acquiescence of all members of the Council for a measure to be adopted (abstention does not prevent unanimity from being achieved (article 205(2) TEC)). Hence, it is theoretically possible (if somewhat improbable) for an act to be adopted unanimously with one vote in favour and twenty-four abstentions! Indeed, it is possible for decisions to be adopted unanimously for which a qualified majority could not be attained as a result of abstention by members of the Council who do not wish to vote in favour but who do not want to prevent the act in question from going through. Under QMV such abstentions do not count towards attaining the majority.

The obverse of the unanimity requirement is the veto. When in ancient Rome the tribunes of the people opposed measures proposed by the senate, they would reject them by saying *'veto'* – 'I forbid'. The word 'veto' has made frequent appearances over the years in debates about the union and the extent of majority voting, despite the fact that it appears nowhere in the treaties. It is typically brandished by member state politicians in the same breath as 'national sovereignty', perhaps because it places emphasis on the rights and powers of individual states. Clearly, where unanimity applies for the Council to act in a particular area, member states which have political difficulties in accepting the proposal on the table are in a relatively comfortable negotiating position (see chapter 13). Ultimately, any such measure cannot be adopted for as long as it is opposed by at least one Council member.

There is another sense in which the term 'veto' is applied in the Community context. This is under what is commonly referred to as the 1966 'Luxembourg compromise'. This was a political agreement that no decisions would be taken by a majority vote if a member state felt that very important national interests were at stake. While arguably no longer actually applicable, it dogged decision-making processes in the Community for more than twenty years (see Teasdale, 1999, for a detailed account of the origin and impact of the Luxembourg compromise). Its effect was to create a national veto over all key EC decisions where qualified majority voting was foreseen under the treaty (see box 14.1.).

One other variant of unanimous decision-making exists under the treaties – decisions by common accord of the representatives of the governments of

Box 14.1: *The Luxembourg compromise*

The 'Luxembourg compromise' resolved an acute crisis in the Community's development which had two linked but distinct components. The first was the rejection by France in June 1965 of a series of key European Commission proposals – on the financing of the common agricultural policy (CAP), the introduction of EC own resources and the widening of budgetary powers for the European Parliament. The second was the refusal by France to accept that when the so-called third stage of the transitional phase of the Community's development came into effect in January 1966, majority voting should automatically be introduced for the first time in a significant range of issues in the Council.

After a six-month 'empty chair' policy by France, the Council on 28-29 January 1966 reached conclusions which in effect constituted an agreement to disagree. The Council conclusions stated that if one member state considered that 'a very important national interest' was at stake (often incorrectly referred to as 'vital' national interest), the Council would endeavour to reach, within a reasonable period, solutions that could be adopted unanimously. The French delegation considered that when very important interests were at issue, discussion 'must be continued' until unanimous agreement was reached. However, this more maximalist formula, which is the one most widely associated with the compromise, was not accepted by the other member states. It was simply noted that there was a difference of opinion on what precisely would happen when a complete resolution of a dispute within the Council could not be achieved.

Although still theoretically on the books as part of the Union *acquis*, under current practice, majority voting now applies in all areas in which it is provided for under the treaties. A member state can no longer veto a proposal unless unanimity is explicitly specified as the decision-making method.

the member states. These are legally intergovernmental decisions (see chapter 10). Decisions by common accord require a positive vote in favour by all member governments (i.e., governments cannot abstain). Until the entry into force of the Treaty of Nice in February 2003, this was the procedure followed for most important political appointments in the Union, such as the president and members of the Commission. Under this procedure, an objection by a single member state was enough to block a nomination. This sort of veto was wielded in a blaze of publicity by British prime minister John Major in 1994 when he refused to accept the proposed nomination of the then Belgian prime minister, Jean-Luc Dehaene, as president designate of the European Commission.

Under the Nice Treaty at least seven provisions relating to appointments to the institutions moved from Council decision by unanimity or intergovernmental decision to Council decision by qualified majority. While the introduction of QMV for appointments to EU institutions or bodies with members from each member state (e.g. the Court of Auditors, the European Economic and Social Committee and the Committee of the Regions) is arguably somewhat artificial, the important point is that significant inroads were made into what was previously a no-go area for QMV. In the case of the appointment of the president of the Commission and the secretary-general of the Council/high representative for the CFSP the breakthrough is almost revolutionary. The nomination of the president designate of the Commission in June 2004 under article 214(2) TEC was the first time that the Council at the level of heads of state or government acted under this provision.

A final point in relation to unanimous decision-making is that it is not always a 'bad thing' – not even from the point of view of the most ardent European integrationist. In certain cases where action by the Union would constitute either a retrograde step or derogate from normal treaty rules, unanimity is stipulated in the treaty. Examples include measures constituting a step back as regards the liberalisation of the movement of capital to or from third countries (article 57(2) TEC); measures constituting a step back as regards transport (article 72 TEC); and decisions not to charge CFSP and third pillar operational expenditure to the EC budget (articles 28(3) and 41(3) TEU).

Qualified majority voting (QMV)

The third method of voting is by so-called qualified majority. Under this method, the vote of each Council member is given a weighting, and decisions are carried once a given threshold of total weighted votes has been achieved (traditionally around 70% – see below). There can be few more recondite areas of debate than the matter of majority voting in the Council. However, since qualified majority voting is now the rule for most Council decision-making, voting weight (i.e., the relative voting strength given to each Council member) matters. At Nice in December 2000, this was the issue that detained heads of government the longest and was the last to be settled, at around 4.20 am in the morning at the end of the longest EU summit in its history. It is also one of the issues on which negotiations on the new constitutional treaty faltered in December 2003. Before considering in more detail how votes are weighted in the Council, it is worth considering some of the claims about the desirability or otherwise of QMV as a method for taking decisions.

Over the years, QMV has been something of a bogey word. The first transition to QMV in the mid-1960s prompted the French empty chair policy which resulted in the Luxembourg compromise (see box 14.1 above). It is also a concept with which successive UK Conservative governments have felt uncomfortable, although that did not stop them agreeing to significant extensions of QMV in 1986 and 1992 to secure and consolidate the internal market. Three main arguments are often put forward for opposing extending QMV: it extends the Community's powers; it is tantamount to a loss of sovereignty; and it weakens the legitimacy of decisions by the Union. However, in some respects, the arguments are misleading or misplaced and, on closer examination, are somewhat less convincing than they appear at face value.

The first is that extending QMV amounts to an *extension of the Union's powers*. This misconceived view arises from confusion about the nature of the Community. The Community operates on the principle of conferred powers as stipulated in article 5 of the EC Treaty (Dashwood, 1996). The powers conferred under the treaty establish the limits for action by the Community; the institutions can therefore only act insofar as they have the power to do so under the treaty. The decision-making procedure used to exercise the powers given to the Community cannot alter their scope. Therefore, agreeing in an IGC to switch from unanimity to qualified majority voting does not imply any extension of Community powers. Discussion in previous IGCs on some issues has highlighted difficulties in distinguishing clearly between an extension of the Community's powers, exercising potential powers which already exist under a particular treaty provision, and an extension of QMV. It is perfectly possible to agree to extend the Community's powers as part of the treaty revision process, but this is an entirely separate operation. What is true is that shifting a particular provision to QMV makes it easier for the EU to *exercise* powers which already exist under the treaties and which previously may not have been used.

The second argument is that recourse to QMV is tantamount to a *loss of sovereignty*, with sovereignty meaning the ability of an individual member state to defend and articulate its interests in the Union. This argument is typically deployed to resist removal of a member state's ability to veto measures that its government deems to be contrary to its national interest for political or constitutional reasons (see above). On this latter aspect, the need to retain unanimity on matters of a constitutional or quasi-constitutional nature linked to the *sui generis* nature of the European Union is unquestioned by any member state or the Commission, even those advocating wholesale extension of QMV. The real issue therefore is whether removal of a member government's veto for politically sensitive measures undermines a member state's sovereignty, either because it would run counter to particular national interests or because it involves issues that are deemed crucial in determining voters' domestic political choices. While it is undeniably true that QMV no longer allows an individual government to block any measure it disagrees with, it is far from self-evident that this equates to a loss of sovereignty. Even where the Community is given new powers to act in a particular area, it is misleading to portray that as a 'loss of powers' for member states, since this suggests that they no longer have any say in exercising them. The powers pooled in the Community are, however, exercised collectively through the Union's institutions (by national government ministers in the Council and directly-elected members of the European Parliament) in which all member states and their electorates have a stake. It is perfectly legitimate to argue that relinquishing de jure sovereignty can paradoxically enhance a state's de facto sovereignty, by making politically desirable outcomes possible (Patten, 2000). In an IGC package-type negotiation, an assessment has to be made about whether the economic and political cost of losing the ability to block in one sensitive policy area is compensated by gaining easier decision-making in other areas, where failure by the Union to decide may be equally or even more damaging to a particular state's national interest than the risk of facing unpalatable decisions in the specific area in question. In weighing up these factors, governments must have a degree of confidence in the system's ability to deliver.

The dynamics of Council negotiation is as much about cooperation as conflict (see chapter 15). Even where QMV is the voting rule, there is a natural tendency for Council members to seek consensus if at all possible when confronted with intractable political problems. All member state governments know full well that they may find themselves in a minority on specific issues and would expect some understanding when confronted with difficult political choices. While a case can be made that QMV on all non-constitutional policy matters is always desirable, since the overall balance of gain for the Union will be greater than that from member state governments retaining the power to block, member states, even within a 'club' such as the Union, can and do make assessments which lead them to identify certain policy matters for which their interests are best served by retaining unanimity. While the number of such areas are relatively few, they tend to be those which feature prominently in domestic political agendas (such as taxation and social security), in which many governments wish to retain maximum room for manoeuvre in making domestic political choices, not least because of the constraints imposed on them through the Union's economic policy coordination process (see chapter 5). By the same token, they are also deemed to be areas where action by the Union is both logical and necessary, particularly in the context of securing and maintaining an effective internal market.

The third argument is that QMV results in a *loss of legitimacy* of Council decisions and contributes to the so-called 'democratic deficit' in the Union. Legitimacy in the Union derives mainly from two sources: directly elected governments taking executive and legislative decisions in the Council (or the European Council), and a directly elected European Parliament co-deciding legislation with the Council and scrutinising the Commission, backed up by the power of censure. Scrutiny over the performance of national governments in the Council can only be exercised via national parliaments on an individual basis, since the collectivity of the member states – that is, the Council – cannot (logically) be accountable to the European Parliament. As long as unanimity is applied for Council decisions, national parliamentary scrutiny can (in theory at least) be exercised over each individual government's decisions in a particular area. Once QMV is introduced, the fact that individual governments may be outvoted on specific issues is seen by some as undermining the legitimacy of such decisions, because national parliaments can no longer exercise the same degree of scrutiny.

However, as a point of general principle, and leaving aside theoretical questions about the boundaries of polities in which majority voting can legitimately be applied, the concept of majority voting, which is central to any democratic system, does not necessarily render decisions any less legitimate provided the system is accepted as fair and no member government finds itself in a permanent minority. In practice, this never happens. Moreover, a partial response has been found by giving greater powers to the European Parliament, which, since the entry into force of the Amsterdam Treaty, has a genuine co-legislative role alongside the Council in most legislative matters.

This only accounts, of course, for part of the Council's work, the rest of which resembles that of a national executive or government. A legitimacy gap arguably does exist regarding the collective accountability and scrutiny of the Council and the European Council, which cannot simply be addressed by giving the European Parliament more powers. This is not to say that there is no case to answer, only that the case should not be overstated. Moravcsik has developed a powerful counter-argument to claim that most of the EU's work not covered by co-decision (and even a great deal which is), if transposed into a national context, would be handled by statutory instruments which are the prerogative of the executive rather than by legislative procedures, the EU's so-called 'democratic deficit' does not exist:

'...any useful and realistic assessment of the EU's democratic performance must be based on a comparison with the actual functioning of national democracies. The assessment must take into account the tight constitutional constraints imposed on the EU by its lack of fiscal, administrative, procedural and coercive resources. It must compare EU policies to the management of similar issues nationally... And it must take full account of the primary position of national governments in most EU decision-making. When this is done, we find that EU decisions closely approximate the general practice of most modern democracies. The EU's democratic deficit is a myth.' (Moravcsik, 2003).

The system of Council vote weighting

Voting weight and voting power

Vote weighting refers to the voting strength given to each Council member when, and only when, decisions are taken by qualified majority (otherwise, each member state has one vote of equal weight). Under the current system, agreed under the Treaty of Nice and which has been applicable since 1 November 2004, the largest members have a weighting of 29 votes, while the smallest, Malta, has three votes. Two further criteria must also be fulfilled for a qualified majority to exist: a threshold in terms of the number of Council members in support of the act, and (if verification requested) a minimum population threshold. If the Council is deciding on the basis of Commission proposal, the qualified majority must include a majority of members; in all other cases a majority of two thirds of Council members is required. The minimum population threshold is 62 per cent.

In the Nice IGC and the subsequent IGC on the constitutional treaty, this issue more than any other was portrayed by the media as a 'big' versus 'small' power struggle. It is easy to understand why; after all, the Council of the European Union is designed for the articulation of the interests of member states' governments in the Union's legislative and executive decision-making processes. A shift in the relative voting strength of any individual member is easy to portray as a measurable change in the relative power and influence of that member state in determining negotiating outcomes. Hence, it appeared easier on this issue to single out 'winners' and 'losers' than on some of the other more arcane institutional reform questions.

Appearances, however, can be deceptive. As far as member states' voting strength is concerned, a distinction has to be drawn between voting *weight* and voting *power*, both being important. Voting *weight* refers to the relative voting strength accorded to any individual member state under a system of weighted votes: i.e., the percentage of the total vote held by a member of the Council. Voting *power* refers to the ability of any individual member of the Council to cast a decisive vote for adopting or blocking a decision: i.e., the likelihood of a member of the Council being instrumental in constructing a winning or blocking coalition. This depends not only on the actual number of votes held, but also on the threshold for achieving a qualified majority or, if seeking to prevent a piece of legislation from being adopted, the number of votes required to construct a 'blocking minority', as well as on the likelihood of other like-minded members of the Council joining a coalition.

The difference between voting strength and voting power can be graphically illustrated by considering the original system of weighting in the Union of six. France, Germany and Italy each had four votes, the Netherlands and Belgium each had two and Luxembourg had one. A qualified majority required 12 votes out of 17 in favour. While Luxembourg's voting *weight* was one out of 17 (or 5.9 per cent of total votes), its voting *power* was zero, since its single vote could never be decisive in forming any qualified majority of 12 votes, nor any blocking minority of six votes! The design of this system is explained in box 14.2 below.

An extensive body of academic literature exists attempting to measure voting power of members of the Council on the basis of various power-value indices, such as the Shapley-Shubik or the Banzhaf indices (Hosli, 1996; Winkler, 1998). An interesting and perceptive independent quantitative analysis of the various voting systems on the table for Nice was carried out comparing their relative merits in terms of efficiency, legitimacy and acceptability (Baldwin *et al.*, 2000). While such indices and quantitative analyses may provide revealing insights into the power of an individual member of the Council to shape decisions or into the statistical likelihood of successful decision-making outcomes, they do not in themselves provide a fail-safe guide for designing a new system of vote weighting – any such system being largely determined by political factors difficult to quantify. Altering the system required calculations by individual governments of more than the way in which the overall legitimacy and efficiency of the system would be affected, important though this was. The primary concern was the way in which national voting strength and power would be affected. However, other factors included broader political linkages to other issues, in particular the distribution of seats in the European Parliament and the need to 'compensate' member states for foregoing the right to nominate a second commissioner. Probably the most important factor was the perceived political 'saleability' of any outcome to national parliaments and the general public. This issue, perhaps more than any other, was as much about public presentation of the outcome as about the substance and impact of the changes agreed.

Portraying the issue as a confrontation pitting large against small ignores three facts about Union decision-making. The first is the extent to which the current institutional arrangements have been devised and have evolved since their inception precisely in order to ease large versus small state concerns. The second is that within the Council, a regular large/small split practically never occurs in reality. Alliances form and disband on the basis of shared or discrete negotiating objectives that are determined by national interests and priorities rather than size. The third is the way in which qualified majority voting lends a dynamic to negotiating in the Council in which member states are forced to seek compromises, to consider what their key bottom-line objectives are and to focus their negotiating effort accordingly (see chapter 13). This dynamic goes some way towards explaining why the Council is often more than simply the sum of its twenty-five component members seeking least-common-denominator solutions, and possesses its own collective institutional 'culture'. The Council, supported by its preparatory bodies, has developed into a well-oiled machine in which the interests of governments with very different national priorities and political complexions can be reconciled in outcomes (often with the help of the Commission) in the interest of the Union as a whole – outcomes which, more often than not, represent much more than a minimalist solution.

The principle of weighted votes in the existing system

That Council members of different sizes should be given different voting weights is not as self-evident as might be assumed. The basic principle underlying all organisations or groupings of states in international law is the sovereign equality of states; in other words *'one state – one vote'*. As we have seen above, this is the case when the Council is deciding by unanimity (for quasi-constitutional or politically sensitive matters) or by simple majority (in a limited number of mainly procedural matters). Outside the European Union, examples of formally unequal representation of states at international level tends to be the exception rather than the rule; e.g. international financial institutions in which voting power is directly linked to capital share. Unequal weighting can also be found in systems of representation within states. The German Confederation between 1815 and 1866, where, in the Plenary Assembly, votes were distributed among the 41 states and a threshold of two-thirds was set, provides an example. This ensured that Austria and Prussia, the largest states representing some 58 per cent of the population, even if they acted together with the four kingdoms of Bavaria, Saxony, Hannover and Württemberg, could not outvote the rest (Best, 2000). Modern day examples also exist in federal or confederal states such as Germany and Switzerland, where the upper parliamentary chamber provides for differentiated voting strength of the component entities on the basis of size (even if the Council cannot be compared to an upper parliamentary chamber).

The main purpose of a system of weighted votes in the Council today, as in the German Confederation in the early nineteenth century, is to ensure a reasonable balance of influence between member states of different sizes when majority decisions are being taken. The present system was constructed during the negotiations that gave birth to the Treaty of Rome in 1957. The principle of applying a weighting to the votes of the member states was itself fairly readily accepted: a system of weighting had applied in the ECSC Treaty. However, it was felt that a new system was required to reflect the new reality of a common market, and the question was how to determine the relative size of the votes to be attributed to each member state (see De l'Ecotais, 1996a, 1996b, 1997). The solution was to distinguish between three groups of states – large member states (Germany, France and Italy) which would each have four votes, medium-sized member states (the

Netherlands and Belgium), which would each have two votes, and a small member state (Luxembourg), which would have one vote. This gave a total of 17 votes. The critical political question, and one that has remained a real political bone of contention ever since in determining voting power (includ-

Box 14.2: *Description of the system of Council vote weighting pre-Nice (up to EU-15)*

The weighting system for EU-15 ranged from 10 votes each to the four largest member states to 2 votes for Luxembourg. Relative population size is not reflected in an absolute, linear way, but is based on a political agreement reflecting the principle of 'degressive proportionality'. In other words, the less populous member states are over-represented in terms of voting strength (i.e., their percentage of total votes is greater than their percentage of the EU population), while larger member states are under-represented (i.e., their percentage of total votes is lower than their percentage of the EU population). This represents a compromise between the principle of 'one state/one vote' and 'one citizen/one vote', reflecting the dual nature of the EU as a Union of both peoples and of states.

The system was constructed so as to ensure a certain relationship between member states based on a system of 'groups' or 'clusters' of large, medium and small member states, with states in each cluster having an identical number of votes. In 1957, the threshold for determining a qualified majority was fixed to ensure that the three large states (France, Germany and Italy) voting together could achieve a majority and could not be prevented form moving forward against the combined opposition of the Benelux countries. However, the opposition of any one of the large member states, even if combined with Luxembourg's vote, would not be sufficient to block a decision. Prior to the Treaty of Nice, the system had the following characteristics:

Apart from an adjustment in voting weights to accommodate new categories of member states at the first enlargement in 1973, the system underwent straightforward extrapolation at each successive enlargement;

The system of 'clusters' was maintained. With each successive enlargement, new member states were categorised in accordance with the same principle, although new categories had to be inserted into the system as required on the basis of member states' size (e.g. Denmark and Ireland were allocated 3 votes each, Spain 8 votes and Austria and Sweden 4 votes each);

The threshold for achieving a qualified majority in terms of weighted votes remained practically unchanged for each successive configuration of the EU at around 71% of total votes (currently 62 out of 87 votes, or 71.26%);

The minimum population of the Union represented by qualified majority (forming a qualified majority with members with the highest voting strength compared to their population – that is starting with the least populous member state and counting up until a qualified majority is achieved) was 67.81% in 1957 (EU-6), but, following an initial blip after the first enlargement to 70.49% (EU-9), steadily declined following successive enlargements to 70.13% (EU-10), 63.21% (EU-12) and to 58.16% (EU-15) in 2000;

A qualified majority always represented at least half of the member states as an automatic, in-built feature (i.e., not as a separate necessary criterion). The treaty has, however, always provided for a specific threshold in terms of numbers of member states when the Council is deciding on a basis other than a Commission proposal (two thirds of the member states).

ing at Nice), was where to fix the threshold in terms of votes for a qualified majority. This was fixed at 12 votes out of 17 for EU-6 (see box 14.2).

It should be remembered that, at the outset of the Community, unanimity was the general rule for voting in the Council, and qualified majority voting very much the exception. It was only after the entry into force of the Single European Act in 1987 that the issue of Council vote weighting again came to the fore with the significant extension of qualified majority voting associated with the creation of the single market. Vote weighting has become such a key political issue because qualified majority voting now applies for most decisions taken in the Council.

Following successive enlargements (to nine in 1973 with the accession of Denmark, Ireland and the UK, ten in 1981 with the accession of Greece, twelve in 1986 with the accession of Spain and Portugal, and fifteen in 1995 with the entry of Austria, Finland and Sweden), the system was adjusted and extrapolated without changing its fundamental character. Table 14.1 shows that the threshold for the qualified majority in terms of votes remained more or less constant at around 71% following successive enlargements up to EU-15, but has subsequently begun to creep upwards.

Table 14.1: *Evolution of the QMV threshold in terms of weighted votes up to EU-25*

EU-6	EU-9	EU-10	EU-12	EU-15	EU-25
70.59%	70.69%	71.43%	71.05%	71.26%	72.27%

Nice – the problem of redesigning the system for enlargement

The system constructed back in the 1950s was based on a political balance which did not reflect size in an absolute, linear way in direct proportion to some objective factor such as population. Less populous states have always been 'over represented' in terms of voting strength relative to population, while the largest member states are 'under represented'. However, the system could not simply be extrapolated for subsequent enlargements, as had been done in the past, for three reasons.

The first was the formal requirement enshrined in the treaty to 'compensate' the larger member states for relinquishing the right to nominate a second commissioner through the system of Council vote weighting. While this linkage always tacitly existed during the Amsterdam IGC, the protocol on the institutions with the prospect of enlargement annexed to the treaties following Amsterdam explicitly mentioned this requirement as one of the relevant factors to be taken into account in the new system of weighting.

The second was the impact on the voting strength of the most populous states of admitting a large number of small and medium-sized candidate states. Some argued that the impact of successive enlargements had been borne equally by all member states, large and small. This is certainly true if one considers the relative reduction in each individual member state's percentage share of the total vote. In other words, following the accession of Sweden, Austria and Finland, Germany's share of the total votes fell from

10/76 to 10/87. Luxembourg's share fell from 2/76 to 2/87. In both cases this represents a loss of just over 12.5% in voting strength (i.e., the percentage of total votes added through the new accessions). However, the view that all members of the Council were equally affected by enlargements was challenged by the more populous member states, which argued that a relative loss of voting power penalised to a greater extent states whose population sizes under the system were already 'under-represented' in terms of voting strength than smaller member states who were already 'over-represented' in terms of their population size. This warranted, in their eyes, an increase in the number of votes for the largest member states.

Third, a potential political legitimacy problem was in the making. Over successive enlargements the minimum percentage of the Union's population represented by a qualified majority had steadily declined from 67% to 58% in 2000. If the current system were simply extrapolated to EU-27[1], the minimum population threshold for a qualified majority would decline to 50.2%. The explanation for this decline lies in the degressive proportionality of the system. Since successive accessions in future will involve a high proportion of small and medium-sized states, a larger share of the total votes will be held by countries that have a proportionately higher share of votes compared to their population size. Given the substantial increase in qualified majority voting that has occurred since the Single Act in 1987, the legitimacy argument has come increasingly to the forefront of debate, even if some saw no problem in coming down to a minimum of just over 50%. The only way to halt or reverse this trend under the system of weighted votes would be by giving the larger member states more votes, thereby ensuring a greater correlation between voting strength and population, without necessarily calling into question the principle of degressive proportionality.

At the Nice IGC, the negotiators were not starting with a blank sheet of paper. As a so-called Amsterdam 'leftover', the treaty itself, in the protocol on the institutions, called for the system of vote weighting to be altered either by 'reweighting of the votes or by dual majority, in a manner acceptable to all Member states, taking into account all relevant elements, notably compensating those Member states which give up the possibility of nominating a second member of the Commission'. The Helsinki European Council conclusions also explicitly referred to both reweighting and dual majority systems, as well as the threshold for qualified majority decision-making as subjects to be examined by the Conference. On this latter point, declaration No. 50 attached to the Final Act of Amsterdam stated that the Ioannina compromise (see box 14.3) would be extended until the entry into force of the first enlargement and that by that date, a solution for the special case of Spain would be found.

Different systems of Council vote weighting

In the context of the Nice IGC, three methods of vote weighting were considered:

The first, referred to in EU jargon as the *'dual majority' system*, was expressed as a simple majority of members of the Council and a majority of the population of the Union. The adoption of any measure would be subject to simultaneous compliance with *both* conditions. The system had obvious

Box 14.3: *The 'Ioannina compromise'*

During negotiations leading up to the accession of Austria, Sweden and Finland, the level at which the QMV threshold should be set became a hotly disputed bone of contention. Until 1995, 23 votes (out of 76) were required in the Council for a blocking minority (i.e., two large member states, plus any other member state apart from Luxembourg). If the QMV threshold were to remain at around 71% of votes after enlargement, the number of votes in the blocking minority in absolute terms would increase from 23 to 26. The UK and Spain objected to increasing the blocking threshold in absolute terms, since this would reduce opportunities for constructing blocking alliances in the Council. The member states finally agreed to retain the QMV threshold in terms of votes at the same percentage level after enlargement, thereby increasing the blocking minority to 26 votes, while at the same time adopting the so-called 'Ioannina compromise' agreed by Council decision of 24 March 1994. This decision is framed as follows:

'If members of the Council representing a total of 23 to 25 votes indicate their intention to oppose the adoption by the Council of a decision by qualified majority, the Council will do all in its power to reach, within a reasonable time and without prejudicing the obligatory time limits laid down by the Treaties and by secondary law, such as in Articles 189b and 189c of the treaty establishing the European Community, a satisfactory solution that can be adopted by at least 65 votes. During this period, and always respecting the Rules of Procedure of the Council, the President undertakes, with the assistance of the Commission, any initiative necessary to facilitate a wider basis of agreement in the Council. The members of the Council lend him their assistance'.

The then UK prime minister, John Major, highlighted the legally binding character of the decision, while other member states considered it to be no more than a political agreement among the then twelve. The impact of this agreement depends on the interpretation given to the phrase 'within a reasonable time'. Article 7 of the Council's rules of procedure allows for any member of the Council or the Commission to call for a vote in the Council, and a simple majority could determine whether 'a reasonable time' had elapsed. Contrary to widespread fears at the time, the compromise had little practical effect on decision-making and has to date only been formally invoked (unsuccessfully) before a ministerial vote on rare occasions, such as by the United Kingdom on 24/25 October 1995 when the Agriculture Council was deciding on national compensation for loss of farm income through currency movements.

The Ioannina formula has been reborn in the new constitutional treaty (see below)

attractions; it was entirely objective, reflected clearly the dual nature of the Union, was easy to understand, had the potential to make decision-making easier if it involved lowering the threshold, and was supported for these reasons by the Commission and a number of delegations. While such a system was not deemed acceptable at Nice for reasons of political presentation, it was however proposed by the European Convention in the draft constitutional treaty, and has been incorporated into the new constitutional treaty, albeit with a higher population threshold (see below).

The second is the so-called *'weighted' dual majority*. This option, originally put forward during the Amsterdam IGC, involved retaining a system of weighted votes extrapolated to EU-27, and setting a dual threshold expressed as a majority in terms of weighted votes (either unchanged or with a slight reweighting); and a majority of the total population of the Union (which would logically be set at a figure higher than the percentage resulting from a majority of weighted votes). The adoption of a measure would require *both* conditions to be met. The attraction of this system lay in the fact that it need not necessarily involve the painful process of adjusting the existing weighting of votes, since any reweighting element could be 'concealed' in the population safety net. The proposal was also made to undertake a moderate reweighting as a means of helping to address the compensation question. (The outcome in Nice, although ostensibly a reweighting model, bore more than a passing resemblance to the system just described – see below).

The third is a straightforward *'reweighting' of votes*, i.e., retaining the system in its existing form and reweighting (i.e., increasing) the votes of the larger member states. As previously mentioned, the Council's present voting system does not reflect the relative size of each member state's population in absolute, linear terms (as it would under the dual majority approaches described above) but applies a degressively proportional formula resulting from a political approach described earlier in this chapter. Two strong arguments were marshalled in favour of reweighting: first, that it was the simplest and most effective means of compensating those member states relinquishing the right to nominate a second commissioner; and second, that it could halt the downward trend in the minimum threshold of the EU population represented by a qualified majority as an inbuilt feature, rather than as a supplementary condition to fulfil. It is axiomatic that the only way to achieve both requirements under the current system is to give more votes to the larger member states. For these reasons, it was favoured from the outset by most of the larger member states (except Germany which, for evident reasons, had a preference for dual majority options), although a number of medium-sized states also indicated early on that they were not opposed in principle to reweighting, provided that the operation was limited in scope and did not call into question the overall balance of the system.

The Nice solution on vote weighting

The Nice IGC considered solutions on vote reweighting which would apply in EU-27, taking account of all the states with which the Union was engaged in accession negotiations at that time. This would also cater for any intermediate configuration of the Union. The solution agreed was ostensibly a vote reweighting model under which the votes of the largest member states were increased in relative terms. However, in endeavouring to reflect fully the duality of the Union as a union of States and a union of peoples, heads of government resorted to a conservative, ad hoc approach by grafting a 'population' and a 'member state' element onto the existing system. Some have accordingly dubbed this a 'triple majority' system, in which three separate conditions need to be met in order to achieve a qualified majority:

i.   a majority of weighted votes (232 out of 321 in EU-25);
ii.   a majority of members of the Council (13 out of 25);
iii. a majority of members of the Council representing at least 62% of
      the Union's population (if verification requested).

A majority of weighted votes

A simple reweighting was the most straightforward means of compensating the larger member states for relinquishing the right to nominate a second national as a member of the Commission, and to achieve a minimum backing for a qualified majority in terms of population. This legitimacy issue was of direct concern to *all* member states. Even if the larger member states had not been giving up their second member of the Commission, the legitimacy problem would still have needed to be addressed as one of the 'relevant elements' mentioned in the treaty protocol.

As far as the demographic element was concerned, if a commonly agreed minimum 'legitimacy' level for popular backing of any QMV decision in the Council could be agreed, a quick arithmetical calculation would suffice in order to determine how many extra votes should be allocated to the larger member states to achieve that objective. However, no such agreed 'legitimacy' level existed, although the general view was that the figure should probably not be much lower than the current 58%. The second element (i.e., compensation for abandoning the right to nominate a second commissioner) belonged to the realm of pure politics. The adjustments agreed at Nice (combining the compensation and demographic elements) have managed to preserve the minimum population level in EU-27 at just above 58%, equivalent to the current level. However this is subject to application of an additional 62% minimum population threshold (see below).

In following this approach, one of the more delicate political issues was whether to tamper with the existing clusters of member states. Two very different types of issue arose in this context. The first, more 'technical' in nature, related to the need to create new groupings of member states, particularly at the lower end of the table, to take account of the relative size of new member states that did not fit readily into existing vote categories. Doubling of votes allowed new categories to be created.

The second issue was much more politically sensitive: whether the Netherlands (with a population some 50% greater than Belgium) and Germany (with 40% more inhabitants than France) should both be given additional votes in recognition of their size relative to other members in the same group. The greater size of the German population was already reflected in the European Parliament, where Germany's seats were increased from 87 to 99 following unification. While understandable in the context of the European Parliament (representation of the people), the issue of whether German representation should be 'decoupled' in the Council was not necessarily self-evident given the way in which the system of vote weighting had been constructed. A key question was whether France would accept a decoupling of Germany, thereby facilitating Belgian acceptance of an additional vote for the Netherlands.

While most of the larger member states appeared fairly relaxed about such decoupling, for historical reasons it was politically unacceptable to

France. Equality between the big four member states in terms of decision-making power was part of the fundamental design of the Community. Equality between France and Germany was based on the magnanimous attitude of Robert Schuman and Jean Monnet, and the principle was agreed at a meeting between Monnet and Adenauer in Bonn in April 1951. Monnet told Adenauer 'I have been authorised to propose to you that relations between Germany and France within the Community should be governed by the principle of equality, in the Council as in the Assembly and all the other Community institutions, whether France enters alone or with the French Union, whether Germany is the West alone or reunited' (Monnet, 1976, p. 516). Adenauer gave his full agreement reminding Monnet 'how much I am attached to equal rights for my country in the future'. The principle of equality was subsequently extended to the third large founding member state, Italy. The difficulty of whether or not to decouple Germany in the voting system was resolved by including a population criterion in determining the qualified majority (see below).

France's reluctance at that time to allow a clear-cut decoupling of Germany in the weighting figures in order to preserve the illusion of parity (although the result achieved is a real decoupling) made it politically more difficult for Belgium to accept decoupling the Netherlands (13 votes) from the other member states in the category with 12 votes. Decoupling the Netherlands could be justified on objective grounds, since this grouping had a greater 'stretch' in population percentage terms than even the grouping with the largest member states, and the ratio between the Netherlands' population and its voting strength constituted an acknowledged anomaly. Belgian misgivings could only be dispelled at the end of the negotiations once further concessions had been made on European Parliament seats, on its own vote weighting relative to the vote weightings of certain candidate states, and on arranging that the total Benelux votes (12 + 13 + 4 = 29) equalled that of the largest member states. The agreement on establishing Brussels as the venue for official European Council meetings (see chapter 8) also helped to secure Belgian agreement.

A majority of member states

The second element was the requirement to have a majority of member states in any qualified majority. The system of vote weighting as it existed up to EU-15 always involved at least half of the member states in any qualified majority as an in-built feature. This was an arithmetical consequence of the system, given the low spread of member states. The problem was that if more than a moderate reweighting was applied to the larger member states, this automatic, in-built condition would no longer be met, because of the larger spread of member states in the Union. A qualified majority could be achieved with fewer than half the members of the Council, albeit in the highly improbable event of all the most populous member states voting in favour of a measure, and all of the least populous member states voting against.

It became a matter of principle for the smaller member states to have such a requirement enshrined in the treaty as a legitimising factor for the system. Moreover, it constituted a political *quid pro quo* for reweighting the votes of the larger member states. While potentially representing a further compli-cating condition in taking decisions in the Council, it was deemed to repre-sent a fair point of equilibrium, since the member state criterion does not come into play in the reweighting for EU-15; and in EU-27 (as well as in intermediate configurations of the Union) its practical impact is likely to be negligible, as the scenario of the thirteen most populous member states voting in favour and the fourteen least populous voting against a particular measure is sufficiently improbable that it can be discounted for all practical purposes.

A majority representing 62% of the EU's population

To reconcile France's position with the German desire to see its greater rela-tive size reflected, the following provision was inserted in article 205 TEC alongside the Council vote weightings in order to include a population cri-terion as a potential condition for achieving a qualified majority:

'When a decision is to be adopted by the Council by a qualified majority, a member of the Council may request verification that the Member States constituting the qualified majority represent at least 62% of the total popu-lation of the Union. If that condition is shown not to have been met, the decision in question shall not be adopted'.

In practical terms, the effect of this clause in EU-25 will be to allow any three of the four largest member states to constitute a blocking minority, or for Spain or Poland together with Germany and another large member state also to constitute such a blocking minority. In EU-27, Germany, which will then account for around 17% of the EU population, will be able to constitute a blocking minority with any two of Britain, France and Italy. In other words, with a blocking minority fixed at ninety-one in EU-27 (see below), the population clause has the same effect as granting four additional block-ing votes to Germany! Since this is now expressly stipulated in the treaty as a verifiable and necessary condition for adopting legally binding acts, the Council has adopted a legal basis for applying this criteria.

The QMV threshold

Once the vote weightings had been fixed, the QMV threshold in terms of votes still had to be determined. This proved to be the most intractable bone of contention. It was impossible to determine at Nice an absolute figure in terms of votes for the QMV threshold for every intermediate configuration of the Union, since it would depend on which candidate states joined the Union in which order. Two issues had a particular bearing on the threshold. The first was the initial negotiating position of certain larger member states that were endeavouring to secure a blocking minority of three large member states. While this position was not pressed towards the end of the nego-tiation, it nevertheless played a role in dictating the final outcome in con-junction with the second issue, namely adjustments to accommodate the special case of Spain. Spain had been identified as a special case in declara-tion No. 50 attached to the Final Act of the Amsterdam treaty (see box 14.3 above). The Spanish government sought similar treatment to the large member states. The difficulty was that while Spain had the right to nomi-

nate two commissioners, it had two fewer votes in the Council than
Germany, the UK, France and Italy (eight as opposed to ten). Its population
size made it impossible for Spain to lay claim to the same number of votes
as the other large member states. So, a solution was found placing Spain on
an equal footing with the largest member states without awarding it the
same number of votes.

There were two possible ways of doing this. One was to set the threshold
for EU-27 at such a level that Spain could achieve a similar degree of blocking power as any three of the four largest member states, a position which
Spain had argued for throughout the negotiations. However, this would
have led to an unacceptably high QMV threshold. The other was to construct a minimum blocking minority of four members in EU-27, and then fix
the votes in such a way that *either* three large members, *or* two large plus
Spain would be able to form a blocking minority only with the support of
the same fourth member.

The constraints created by securing the position of Spain meant that
something had to give. That something was the QMV threshold, which for
the first time in the Union's history would be pushed above 71.5%. Any
decrease in the overall number of votes for the most populous member
states or, conversely, increase in voting strength for the less populous
member states would inevitably raise the QMV threshold. Both occurred.
The consequences of these movements provoked a reaction, particularly
from Belgium, Portugal, Finland and others, which feared that the rising
QMV threshold would result in more difficult decision-making after
enlargement because of the higher requirement facing other Council members in building coalitions. The compromise solution was the declaration
agreed at the end of the meeting regarding the level of the QMV threshold
and the number of votes for a blocking minority, which read:

'Insofar as all the candidate countries listed in the declaration to be
included in the Final Act of the Conference on the enlargement of the
European Union have not yet acceded to the Union when the new vote
weightings take effect (1 January 2005), the threshold for a qualified
majority will move, according to the pace of accessions, from a percentage
below the current one to a maximum of 73.4%. When all the candidate countries mentioned above have acceded, the blocking minority, in a Union of 27,
will be raised to 91 votes, and the qualified majority threshold resulting
from the table given in the declaration on enlargement will be automatically
adjusted accordingly'.

The new vote weighting system

Because of the linkage to the size and composition of the Commission, it was
agreed that the changeover to the new system would occur at the same time
as the shift to one commissioner per member state, as stated in article 3 of
the protocol on enlargement annexed to the treaties. Under the Treaty of
Accession, it was thus agreed that the changeover to the new vote weightings would occur on 1 November 2004, at the same time as the new
Commission takes up office.

Table 14.2 illustrates the Council vote weightings as from 1 November
2004 for EU-25, and table 14.3 indicates the additional weightings and the

threshold which will apply after the accession of Romania and Bulgaria anticipated in 2007.

Table 14.2: *Council vote weightings for EU-25*

MEMBERS OF COUNCIL	WEIGHTED VOTES	MEMBERS OF COUNCIL	WEIGHTED VOTES
Germany	29	Slovakia	7
United Kingdom	29	Denmark	7
France	29	Finland	7
Italy	29	Ireland	7
Spain	27	Lithuania	7
Poland	27	Latvia	4
Netherlands	13	Slovenia	4
Greece	12	Estonia	4
Czech Republic	12	Cyprus	4
Belgium	12	Luxembourg	4
Hungary	12	Malta	3
Portugal	12		
Sweden	10		
Austria	10	TOTAL EU 25	321

Council acts shall require for their adoption at least 232 votes in favour cast by a majority of members.

When a decision is to be adopted by the Council by a qualified majority, a member of the Council may request verification that the Member States constituting the qualified majority represent at least 62% of the total population of the Union. If that condition is shown not to have been met, the decision in question shall not be adopted.

Total votes =321	Votes	% votes	Minimum number of members	Minimum % of population
Qualified majority	232	72.27%	13 [1]	55.06% [2]
Blocking minority	90	28.04%	4 [3]	10.55%

[1] *Without the requirement for a majority of member states, it would be theoretically possible to constitute a qualified majority with 12 member states*

[2] *This figure indicates the minimum population represented by a qualified majority resulting from the application of the voting table. The actual minimum population figure under article 205(4) may be raised to 62% if invoked by any member of the Council.*

[3] *The minimum number is 3 members if the 62% population clause is invoked.*

Table 14.3: *Council vote weightings for EU-27 agreed at Nice*

MEMBERS OF COUNCIL	WEIGHTED VOTES	MEMBERS OF COUNCIL	WEIGHTED VOTES
Germany	29	Austria	10
United Kingdom	29	Slovakia	7
France	29	Denmark	7
Italy	29	Finland	7
Spain	27	Ireland	7
Poland	27	Lithuania	7
Romania	14	Latvia	4
Netherlands	13	Slovenia	4
Greece	12	Estonia	4
Czech Republic	12	Cyprus	4
Belgium	12	Luxembourg	4
Hungary	12	Malta	3
Portugal	12		
Sweden	10		
Bulgaria	10	TOTAL EU 27	345

Council acts shall require for their adoption at least 255 votes in favour cast by a majority of members.

When a decision is to be adopted by the Council by a qualified majority, a member of the Council may request verification that the Member States constituting the qualified majority represent at least 62% of the total population of the Union. If that condition is shown not to have been met, the decision in question shall not be adopted.

Total votes = 345	Votes	% votes	Minimum number of members	Minimum % of population
Qualified majority	255	73.91%	14 [1]	58.29% [2]
Blocking minority	91	26.38%	4 [3]	11.61%

[1]   *Without the requirement for a majority of member states, it would be theoretically possible to constitute a qualified majority with 13 member states.*

[2]   *This figure indicates the minimum population represented by a qualified majority resulting from the application of the voting table. The actual minimum population figure under article 205(4) may be raised to 62% if invoked by any member of the Council.*

[3]   *The minimum number is 3 members if the 62% population clause is invoked.*

It is difficult to escape the feeling that while the outcome at Nice on vote weighting represented a satisfactory outcome for all governments in terms of achieving their own political objectives, somehow the Union as a whole lost out. The larger member states achieved their goal of compensation for abandoning the right to nominate a second commissioner through a moderate reweighting. Germany's size was recognised by enabling it to form a blocking minority of three with any two other large member states (in a somewhat less than transparent manner). Spain found itself in many respects on a similar footing to the large member states, although not exactly the same footing. The Netherlands achieved its long-standing objective of increasing its voting weight. All of the current member states achieved some measure of upgrading, with the exception of Luxembourg, although the Benelux states collectively have as many votes as a large member state (29). The less populous member states achieved a political safeguard for their interests since no decision can be taken without their collective consent, as the treaty now stipulates expressly that a qualified majority requires the votes of a majority of Council members. In other words, everyone went home with a presentable result.

However, what will the impact be on Union decision-making? The two approaches (dual majority and reweighting), often opposed as different concepts in the negotiations on Council vote weighting, are in fact variants of one and the same system attempting to reconcile both a member state and a population element – i.e., a union of states and a union of peoples.

Given the need to fulfil three separate conditions as well as meeting a higher QMV threshold as the Union expands, the final outcome is complex, difficult to explain and undoubtedly runs counter to the general desire at the start of the negotiations *not* to make Council decision-making more difficult. The Commission, the European Parliament and many commentators have been critical of the outcome for these reasons.

Despite misgivings about the complexity of the voting system, when one moves from the abstract and hypothetical to the practical, the picture is much more positive than the above analysis might suggest. The requirement for any qualified majority to be composed of a majority of the members of the Council, although an essential point of principle which had to be written into the treaty to secure agreement, can for all practical purposes be disregarded. The extreme configuration required for this condition to come into play as the determining factor for or against a decision (all of the most populous member states in favour and all the least populous against) is theoretically possible but very unlikely in practice; the Council just does not work like that.

In October 2004, the Council decided how the 62% population threshold will be measured if it is invoked. The rules of procedure now contain a table setting out the official population figures for each Member State (i.e. legally resident inhabitants). This table will be subject to a technical update each year from 1 January on the basis of officially validated Eurostat figures. In reality, however, qualified majorities typically represent well over 62% of the Union's population. In EU-27 the population clause can only come into play when Germany is in a minority. But the actual impact is difficult to determine exactly. In EU-27, the clause could have an impact if three large member states including Germany sought to form a blocking minority. It is somewhat ironic that the de facto result of this clause, which is to accord four additional blocking votes to Germany in EU-27, probably goes well beyond what Germany itself would have regarded as a satisfactory outcome in terms of additional votes in the vote weighting table. However, if Germany had been given more votes in the vote weighting table this would have assisted the process of building qualified majorities in favour of any decision, whereas concealing the additional votes in the population clause means that they can only come into play in constructing blocking minorities. One interesting avenue for further research will be to assess the political impact of the new vote weighting table in various policy sectors and to attempt to measure the real power gain for Germany in the light of the enhanced relative position of both Spain and Poland in the vote weighting table.

Given the real advantages that many Council members (not least Spain and Poland) have acquired under the Nice system, it is understandable that agreeing a changeover to a fully-fledged dual majority system under the new constitution proved problematic. While this involves retaining two of the three elements agreed in Nice (i.e., the member state and a population criterion) while abandoning the existing vote weighting table, it is this latter element which favours Spain and Poland in particular.

It is an interesting academic exercise to compare whether the outcome of any decisions subject to QMV in previous years would have been different under the new voting system. None of the legislative decisions taken by qualified majority in 1999 would have had a different outcome under the new weighting system agreed in Nice. The Commission undertook a study during the Amsterdam IGC which purported to show that, had a dual majority system been applied, none of the negotiating outcomes in the Council over the previous three-year period would have been different (Petite, 2000).

It would, however, be wrong to deduce from such calculations and box 14.4 that the nature of the voting system used in the Council is totally irrelevant. The idea that 'nothing changes' is a static, one-dimensional view based on an *ex-post* analysis. As Chapter 13 has shown, negotiating in the Council is a dynamic process, in which negotiating behaviour is at least partly conditioned by the negotiators' knowledge of potential winning and blocking combinations and by a sense of what is 'achievable' in a given situation. The qualitative aspects determined by the voting system also need to be factored in. It is in these shifting power coalitions or potential coalitions that a particular negotiating outcome is achieved. Most importantly, the final voting outcome may have been the same, but there is no guarantee that with a system subject to different voting powers the *substance* of the outcome would have been identical. Macro-level quantitative analyses find it difficult to build in such qualitative factors.

Whatever the outcome, however, and despite the political posturing on the formal elements of the system, at the end of the day the precise numbers of any vote reweighting (aside from the political imperative of public presentation) probably do not actually matter that much. Much more important in determining negotiating outcomes, as chapter 13 has emphasised, is the very existence of qualified majority voting rather than precisely how that majority is arithmetically defined or constructed.

Qualified majority voting under the new constitutional treaty

The system described above will aply at least until October 2009. From 1 November 2009, provided the new constitutional treaty is ratified, the Council will move to a fully-fledged dual majority system. Under this system, the threshold for determining a qualified majority is expressed in terms of a minimum number of Council members representing a minimum percentage of the Union's population. Given the difficulties involved in arriving at the Nice system, it is hardly surprising that this was one of the final components of the compromise package to be agreed.

In the text proposed by the European Convention, the minimum thresholds were fixed at 50% of Council members, representing 60% of the Union's population. Under article 25(1) of the constitution, these percentages were increased respectively to 55% and 65%. However, this does not convey the full picture. Three further features of the system need to be borne in mind:

- First, and most importantly, the minimum population threshold in a Union of 27 member states will not be 65%, but 58%! This is because the treaty stipulates that a blocking minority must include at least four Council members, *failing which the qualified majority will be deemed attained*. This means that should a measure be opposed by, say, Germany, France and the UK, it will pass with the support of just over 58% of the Union population.

- Second, the constitution stipulates that the minimum number of Council members voting in favour of a measure must be fifteen. In the Union of twenty-seven, this number will in any case be attained under the 55% rule (which equates to a majority plus one). This clause will therefore have no practical effect, and was inserted for reasons of political presentation.

- Third, a decision will be adopted upon the entry into force of the constitution which effectively reintroduces a Ioannina-type procedure into the Council's deliberations (see box 14.3). The operative provisions of this decision mirror those contained in the Ioannina decision, including the essential reference to *"respecting the Rules of Procedure of the Council"*. This decision may be invoked if at least three quarters of the level of population or three quarters of the number of member states necessary to constitute a blocking minority (respectively 26.25% of the population or 10 member states (or 3 of them in the case of the first indent above)) indicate their opposition to the Council adopting an act by qualified majority. The practical impact of such a provision is difficult to gauge, but, based on the experience of the Ioannina decision, is likely to be minimal.

Leaving aside the latter two features, the practical impact of which is likely to be non-existent or minimal, the system agreed under the constitution is certainly more simple than Nice and should facilitate decision-making in the Council. Leaving aside the last two complications, it is also easier to explain to the public than the current system composed of three different elements (weighted votes, number of Council members and population threshold).

Chapter 15: Negotiations, coalitions and the resolution of inter-state conflicts, by David Spence

In 2004 the Union's membership grew from fifteen to twenty-five states, and it could grow to a possible thirty or more by 2010 and beyond. There are many implications of this growth in numbers. Working methods will need to adapt to meet the two, sometimes contradictory, challenges of greater diversity and greater efficiency of governance. Member states are therefore set to embark on a variety of new ways of interacting, and the way in which they negotiate with each other is not the least of the hurdles on the route to fundamental change.

This chapter will attempt to draw some conclusions about the future of Council negotiating style in this considerably enlarged EU. It analyses the evolution of the idiosyncratic framework in the Union for inter-state negotiation. It describes the negotiating process in terms of the procedures involved. It also describes negotiating practice at the various levels of the Council and attempts to categorise the types of coalition and alliance building typical of Council work.

The specific nature of EU Council negotiations

Sir Henry Wootton's view that 'an ambassador is an honest man sent to lie abroad for the good of the state' may have been an accurate account of diplomacy in the traditional 'billiard-ball' model of international relations, but it is not true of the interdependent world of European inter-state relations in the era of supranationality. The underlying premises of all negotiations are twofold. The process involves attempting to achieve something when others control – at least in part – the means for its achievement. But negotiation also implies a willingness to adapt aims in order to achieve what one wants. If the two, or more, sides in a negotiation are unwilling to give ground, there is no negotiation.

In the EU, as in other fora, negotiations may appear to be about issues where one state wins or loses, but there is a higher-order agenda. Negotiated agreements in specific areas limit the potential for conflict and dispute in other similar areas in the future, and this is the overall, yet unspoken, aim. Negotiation in the EU is as much about 'achieving a legally level playing field' in the long term as it is about achieving short-term national goals. As one British ambassador has put it:

'Negotiation is in essence an exercise in mutual confidence, in the recognition that "win one, lose one" is a sounder settlement than sweeping the board against a thoroughly trounced opponent'. (Jackson, 1981, p. 6)

This is but one of several features of EU negotiating, which distinguish the EU style from that of traditional negotiations. That EU style falls into two categories; contextual and legal/procedural. The overall political and economic framework, the actors involved and the premises of state interaction form the context. To begin with, increasing economic and political interdependence since the creation of the European Community has considerably changed the nature of interaction between states and their representatives. Of course, rivalry for influence between the member states persists, but what characterises the system is commitment to togetherness and the seeming unshakability of member states' resolve to strengthen the system of European governance. This may not be to the liking of euro-sceptics in one or other member state, for it gives perspective to the frequent crises in the EU and member states' recurrent carping about partners.

A second key feature of the EU's internal negotiation process is the multiple levels and origins of the national actors involved. International diplomacy is characterised by several levels of preparation of ministerial interaction. Most of what is discussed at summits has been pre-cooked by various hierarchical levels of interaction between civil servants. Yet, long the preserve of diplomats, international negotiations in the Union are now more the province of domestic than foreign ministries (see Hocking and Spence, 2002). Moreover, since home civil servants and diplomats often have rival interpretations of the national interest, a complex system of co-ordination has developed. Sophisticated coordination occurs both within the national context and with representatives of other states involved. Indeed, much negotiation, or pre-negotiation, occurs before the formal defence of national interests takes place in the Council.

What are the premises of interaction at all these levels? The underlying assumption about negotiation in the Council is that it is a quest for agreement on how vying national interests can be melded into a policy recognised by all as a superior European interest, with governments free to portray it as the *national* interest for domestic consumption. Negotiations in the Council are in one sense about joint problem-solving. They are generally 'positive-sum', rarely about distributive bargaining and almost always about integrative bargaining, where accommodation and rapprochement are the rule. This may not always seem the case during the periodic standoffs between recalcitrant governments, and obvious exceptions to this generalisation are high-profile negotiations involving the share-out of expenditure under the CAP or the structural and cohesion funds (see chapter 16) or the share-out of power and influence among the member states, a feature of recent IGCs on treaty reform. Yet even here, in the settlement of claims by one or other member state to an adjusted share, trade-offs are usually obtainable in terms of other benefits or commitments in major policy areas. So, despite the occasional rumpuses at ministerial level, the historical purpose of inter-state bargaining in the EU context can be seen as ending unilateral ability to hinder free economic and political relations between states and their component groups. The search for strength in numbers has been simultaneously a search for reduced complexity in international relations, a point often missed by those who claim that the EU has increased the degree of overall regulation.

These contextual features underline the specificity of EU negotiations. Several legal and procedural features complete the picture. They include:

- no binding mandate on negotiators from people or parliament;

- supranationality and binding results of international negotiation in domestic law;

- qualified majority voting;

- the European Commission;

- the club-like nature of the Community method.

Ministers and officials negotiate with no specific mandate from either the people or the parliament of the individual member states. With the exception of the Danish *Folketing*, and since January 1995 the Swedish parliament, no national parliament obliges ministers to operate within the framework of a restrictive mandate. Yet, supranationality has far-reaching implications for the process of domestic decision-making and legitimacy. Even if there were national mandates for negotiators, the process of qualified majority voting described in chapter 14 implies that regardless of national mandate or national interest, however defined, the national negotiator can simply be outvoted. So member states must be prepared to accept sub-optimal outcomes in one negotiation in return for enhanced gains across the range of EU policy areas. This is both the price and reward of EU membership. The role of the European Commission as a partner in the negotiations is also crucial. In the Community pillar (for a discussion of the pillar system, see chapter 1), the Commission has the virtual monopoly of legal initiative and can withdraw legislative proposals if member states try to introduce 'unacceptable' changes. It can also wield the threat of court action if member states subsequently fail to fulfil obligations arising from the negotiation process. One senior Delors cabinet member put it succinctly, arguing that the Commission 'set(s) the tone and limits of the debate...we've got to be quick and nimble, play as best we can...we've got the advantage of knowing more about other people's points of view than anyone else'. (Ross, 1995, p. 88)

The third original feature of EU negotiations is that the output of this inter/supranational negotiation process is binding on the participants in domestic law – it is *'law-making by diplomacy'*. ('Law-Making by Diplomacy' was the title of a 1975 Granada TV film in the 'The State of the Nation' series.) The outcome of diplomatic negotiations must either become national law (directives) or, more strikingly original in terms of traditional international relations, may already and without national implementation have primacy over any existing national legislation in case of a conflict of laws (regulations).

Finally, the club-like nature of the negotiating ambience implies that EU negotiators see themselves as both rivals and partners. Despite their defence of their own national brief, negotiators retain a commitment to understanding and even helping their fellow negotiators from other member states. Ministers and officials negotiating in Brussels operate with an agreed set of values and methods. Indeed, they are almost a circle of friends, often with loyalty to their opposite numbers in other member states, which crosses the boundary of national allegiance. National officials in Brussels are sometimes accused of 'going native' or even of treachery (see Barber, 1995). Part of the 'club' process is the fact that negotiators meet each other continually for new negotiations. The negotiation process is permanent. Unfair outcomes in one negotiation affect relationships and engender stakes and demands for others. Spain spent years attempting to put issues resolved against its interests in the accession negotiations back on the agenda[1] and much effort by UK officials in the 1980s went into reversing the financial conditions of UK membership. Sir Stephen Wall, a former UK permanent representative, summed up the underlying mentality succinctly:

'COREPER...is a place where deals get done. We are all there to promote our national interest and to reach agreement. We all wrestle with impossible instructions from our capitals. We like to think we are clever people, and tend to show off a bit'. (*European Voice*, 30 April-7 May 2003).

When Harold Nicolson said after the Versailles conference in 1919, 'nothing could be more fatal than the habit ... of personal contact between the statesmen of the world' (Dickie, 1992, p. 305) he clearly did not foresee the nature of European inter-state relations in the second half of the century. Nicolson believed that 'personal contact breeds, inevitably, personal acquaintance and that, in its turn, leads in many cases to friendliness: there is nothing more damaging to precision in international relations than friendliness between contracting parties'. In the EU the converse is true, and this not only at the level of working groups and permanent representatives, where negotiators are on first name terms both in private and in their formal, often weekly, meetings. It is also true, on their own admission, of ministers themselves: 'The Foreign Ministers know each other well, communicate with each other easily (almost all have a common language), and many of them like each other. There is a genuine feeling of a Foreign Ministers' club'. (Butler, 1986, p. 73) And as John Major, a former British prime minister, remarked, 'I've actually sat there negotiating with my fellow heads of government across Europe. I know the mind-set. I know how the deals are struck'. (5 January 1997 BBC TV interview with David Frost).

The essential point is that the club reaches compromise in the Council, because of overall commitment to the European Union. The premise of Council negotiation is that wise agreement will meet the legitimate interests of all sides as far as is possible. Conflicting interests, indeed conflicting reasoning, will be resolved fairly. The outcome of negotiations will be durable and take the interests of the EU itself into account. The public conception of EU negotiations may conform to the traditional model of negotiation – conflict of interests. While resolution is the desired outcome, the traditional tools of the diplomat (or the car salesman) – namely secrecy, concealment and the psychological skills of persuasion and rhetoric – seem par for the course. But, to conclude, in practice, while much of this tradition remains, a large element of partnership through collaboration in problem-solving has replaced traditionally conflictual relationships. Indeed, asked in a television interview whether MI6 deployed espionage resources across the Channel, former foreign secretary David Owen answered:

'A bit. I actually had a difference of opinion on this. These are our friends and allies. You have to make a distinction, they are no longer opponents and I think you have to be very careful about having intelligence within the framework of the European Union'. (*Guardian*, 2 January 1998)

Other foreign secretaries, interviewed in the same television programme were less forthcoming, though the inference has been that a degree of 'spying' is still prevalent. Yet, conflict resolution through negotiation clearly remains the key to understanding the settlement of sporadic acute conflicts between one member state and (some of) the others. So, while it is clearly still the case that there is a high degree of haggling, compromise, redrafting, re-apportioning of shares, etc., involved in the day-to-day operations of the Council, the majority of EU business is more fruitfully understood as a process of joint problem solving. The distributive consequences of individual negotiations may thus be seen, structurally, as cogs in the wheel of an integrative bargaining process, where the stakes in the creation of a manageable regulatory framework are much higher.

How does this impact upon domestic politics? One former UK permanent representative, Sir Michael Butler, has remarked: 'There will always be those who will applaud the 'sock it to 'em' defence of today's interests with yesterday's phrases. National leaders like to be seen to be battling for national interests, and public opinion likes to see them do it'. But, (this) 'enables progress to be made at the margin, unperceived and therefore with minimal controversy.' (Butler, 1986, p. 215)

Seemingly, therefore, there is one game being played for public opinion and another being played in the negotiating chamber. If the Council is club-like, what are the roles of individual negotiators and national styles in European affairs? While working styles may converge and while the structure of the negotiating process may define many of the parameters within which issues become 'yes-able' (see Fisher and Brown, 1989), negotiators recognise that national style and individual capability remain valid reference points in terms of successful outputs. The fact that much EU business is conducted in 'bilaterals', 'confessionals' and in informal, corridor discussion has been lamented from time to time. National style persists. One northern European diplomat is said to have described EU negotiations as 'the southern way of negotiating'. (Mann, 1996) Two British ambassadors have commented pertinently on French negotiating style. One describes the French negotiating style in the following terms:

> 'They take a very hard line for months. The time approaches when they judge that a decision is going to be taken soon. They soften on some minor points and indicate a readiness to negotiate. However, just before the crunch meeting, their line hardens and two or three points that have scarcely appeared in their speeches before suddenly assume great prominence. They announce that they cannot possibly move on them…(often) they are discards, points which have been blown up specially so that they can be elegantly abandoned at two in the morning on the last day, while preserving the things that really matter in France's original position'. (Butler, 1986, p. 75)

Another speaks of a French 'cartesian dedication to the national interest, which makes their formal internationalism and Europeanism in Community activity and representation largely a matter of convenience and tactics'. (Jackson, 1981, p. 39)

This view posits a high degree of rationality, an elaborate negotiating strategy and a series of sophisticated tactical moves. It may be. Yet consider this statement from a senior French negotiator, after the crucial negotiations on reform of the Common Agricultural Policy in 1992: 'Il ne faut pas croire que la délégation française est allée à la négotiation avec une position claire-ment définie. On a surtout découvert les problèmes au fur et à mesure qu'ils se présentaient.' (Le Theule and Litvan, 1993)

Clearly, attempts at generalisation risk falling foul of a somewhat more complex reality. Are there national styles, with negotiating teams in Brussels and national capitals working more or less to highly structured strategies where constraints, objectives and means are objectively assessed and the negotiating tactics planned in minute detail? Is it always necessary to dis-tinguish between the policy content of the overt negotiating strategy and the covert aims of member states in terms of how the balance between the national and the supranational is to be maintained or altered? It may, on occasion, be the case where major national stakes are involved, but the degree of sophistication in negotiation depends on the size of the state con-cerned and the efficiency of coordination procedures for European business (see chapter 17). In general, it is probably true to say that day to day nego-tiation is characterised more by absence of general principles and presence of short-term assessments of national interests in given sectors. National negotiators are fire-fighters, not architects. The 'line to take' in daily busi-ness is concerned with optimal outcomes in the policy area concerned. It is only when sensitive matters, such as budgetary affairs, CAP reform or insti-tutional issues, reach the Council or the European Council itself that long-term visions become perceptible.

As for individual negotiating styles, the former UK permanent representative, Sir John Kerr, was 'renowned for his sharpness in detecting political booby-traps in advance' and even held to be 'eminently capable of replacing a minister at Council level'. (Dickie, 1992, p. 316) At more senior levels, individual statespersons are known to block negotiations, rile their negotiating partners and drive what are to some unacceptable bargains. Margaret Thatcher, for example, was reputed to be a very tough negotiator, who did not accept the rule of compromise. Commenting on her recalcitrance, Jean Musitelli, Elysée spokesman, opined diplomatically that: 'Manifestement un état membre ne veut pas négocier, refuse des amendements et ne formule aucune proposition.' (*Le Monde*, 12 December 1991)

However such comments to the press are also part of the negotiation process itself (see below). To Thatcher, Sir Geoffrey Howe was often the carrot to her stick, working at foreign minister level with French foreign minister Roland Dumas to get the detailed budget deal, which Pesident Mitterrand, unwilling to have a summit failure, let through at Fontainebleau. '*Maggie is home with a bargain*' clearly belied the work of the foreign minister and the team of officials involved in the corridors and mul-tiple bilateral pre-negotiations. One former junior foreign minister sums this up well in commenting on a key foreign office official:

'I think the most difficult thing for the public to see is the sheer mental and physical skill of Foreign Office officials...the detail and complexity of (European) Community business these days is daunting...sometimes...when I am going along in a car with him, simply to tease him, I will say, "You know Michael, I'm still worried about article 122", and he just goes "Well, you're quite right, Minister, because if you look at the third tiret (indent), you'll find that the first five words..." and off he goes. I mean they just know this stuff backwards'. (Edwards, 1994)

EU negotiations are, then, a very specific form of international bargaining. In the next section some of the mechanisms involved are set out.

From bilateral pre-negotiation through alliances and coalitions to multilateral negotiation in Council

The preparatory phase

In the defence of the national interest negotiators are obliged to compromise. They thus settle for sub-optimal outcomes in strictly national terms. The assumption is that member states accept the premise of 'satisficing' rather than 'optimising'. (Wallace, H, 1990, p. 224) But what is the process by which these compromises are reached? In the preparation phase soundings are made in a series of contacts between officials in permanent representations, through direct contacts between lead ministries in the member states and a process of constant lobbying of the European institutions. Commission officials not only draft 'green' and 'white' papers setting out options in a formal manner and thereby enabling public debate. They also often visit national capitals for information gathering and lobbying purposes, before finalising their proposals. The nationality of commissioners and senior Commission officials is sometimes cited as a lever for the defence of specific national interests. (See, e.g., Le Theule and Litvan, 1993, p. 771)

Importantly, such preparatory talks establish the range of options available and the scope for 'yes-able' propositions. In thus reducing uncertainty, member states are able to manage complex, technical discussions at lower levels of risk than the immediate plunge into formal negotiations might imply. It is generally agreed that the well-prepared IGC on EMU was more successful than the precipitate parallel discussions on political union in the run up to the Maastricht Treaty. Allowing divergent views to be partially reconciled before the formal negotiations begin enables preliminary agreement on the limits of negotiability to be reached before public announcements of progress (or otherwise) in formal negotiations. Problem-solving discussions in advance of formal negotiations allow, at least in principle, an easy flow of incremental steps in formal negotiations. The work of the Reflection Group in preparation for the 1996 IGC and the Convention in preparation for the 2004 IGC are cases in point. These are pre-negotiations, admitted publicly, though with the caveat that the participants in the process are not formally negotiating and merely appear in their individual capacities. Participants can still withdraw from negotiations or resist inclusion of items on the agenda for negotiations. To sum up:

'pre-negotiation promises to lower the cost of critical information. In so doing it is attractive to leaders as a strategy of risk

> management in situations of uncertainty and complexity...the
> political costs of information are less at the outset of pre-
> negotiation than in negotiation...and (prenegotiation is) attractive
> to leaders whose interest is not exclusively in a negotiated
> agreement as the outcome'. (Gross Stein, 1989, p. 483)

Position-taking in initial Council working parties discussing technical
issues is exploratory and based on information gathering in the context of
an existing proposal and an agreement to negotiate on its contents. It is
exploratory, partly because the informal preparation of some delegations
has been imperfect and partly because agreements reached in pre-negotiations on technical questions need to be expressed as individual positions
to avoid impressions of clique building and ganging up – the downside of
the otherwise harmless expression 'coalition-building'. Thus, real negotiating positions begin to emerge only after formal positioning has begun. Some
delegates may be more concerned at this level with adumbration of their
own position (sticking to their brief) but, if they are clever, they are listening hard to the positioning of their rivals, preparing to report back to capitals and for the subsequent assessment of the margin for later manoeuvre,
the need for visits to national capitals, bilateral pre-negotiation and alliance
building.

What may be ultimately 'yes-able' emerges from the positions expressed.
After consultation in national capitals and the consequent revision of negotiating standpoints, proposals to shift from initial positions and to engage
the process of search for compromise can then occur at Council working
party level. There is usually no limit on the time Council working parties
can continue consideration of a proposal, though presidencies and the
Council secretariat are keen for business to be conducted efficiently – providing the proposal itself is a presidential priority. If it is not, a variety of
delaying tactics can be used to keep discussions going (see below).

After the first meeting of the working party a line-by-line analysis of the
Commission proposal takes place. Subsequent meetings produce revised
texts taking into account proposals for improvements or amendments
agreed around the table. Where disagreement persists on items in the text,
the revised version usually states that country X or Y maintains a reservation on the item and proposed changes to the text are underlined in successive textual updates (see chapter 13). There may also be reservations
expressed on the whole text, as opposed to the detail. The Agriculture
Council of June 1996 was said to have had no less than 160 reserves on a
paper concerning fruit and vegetables (Mann, 1996). Gradually, over a series
of meetings, such reserved positions are normally eliminated until the
working party feels (or, more precisely, the presidency believes) the proposal has been discussed sufficiently for Coreper to consider placing the
subject on a Council agenda. As chapter 7 makes clear, agricultural councils
are prepared not by Coreper but by the special committee on agriculture
(SCA). In the case of the Agriculture Council mentioned above, one official
is said to have claimed that the SCA could have reached compromises long
ago, had the tradition in agriculture not been to save up for the final Council
of each presidency issues for marathon sessions in which unrelated issues
form the basis of package deals (Mann, 1996).

By Council time, in principle, either all conflicts of view have to be settled or the remaining disagreements must be political rather than technical. Coreper (or the SCA) alone decides. If agreement in principle has been achieved it would then only remain for the Council to rubber-stamp the proposal. Any Council agenda may include the point as an 'A' item (see chapter 3). If Coreper is unable to agree, then ministers must engage in a final negotiation. This means the subject enters the appropriate specialist Council agenda as a 'B' item. Occasionally, Coreper considers an issue insufficiently well prepared for the Council and will send the issue back to the working party for further assessment and negotiation on the basis of guidelines from the permanent representatives. Presidencies 'putting issues up' to Coreper too hastily are unpopular with the Council secretariat and with well-coordinated member states, whose officials are known to criticise presidencies in private for their inefficiency.

Thus, with new information available from the first meetings of the working party, from bilateral pre-negotiation and alliance building, delegations can begin to shift ground and generate options. The key is the 'give and take' basis upon which moves must be based, if they are to be successful in the creation of agreed outcomes on a 'win-win' basis. If the negotiation turns into a 'win-lose' situation, negotiations may stall and previous negotiating steps may need to be retraced. The aim in both working parties and in Coreper is to close without damage to ongoing relationships. Not for ministers and officials the advantage of a one-off negotiation; in the EU the same negotiators reconvene in the same forum within days or weeks to consider new proposals.

There is an interesting point to be made concerning the relationship of Coreper to ministers in national capitals. Questioned on the relationship by a UK House of Lords select committee, Sir Michael Palliser talked of a sort of dialogue: ' "If it is impossible for us to do this we shall go back and see if we can negotiate more" or "Do you want me to leave it for further discussion and the ministerial council?" or "How do you want it played" and you get into a sort of dialogue. But when you are in the council, then there can be a certain element of the permanent representative trying to pull on the reins, partly because, simply by being there every day, he may have a better sense than the minister; he will know what the negotiating leverage may be. Ultimately, the minister is the one who knows what he can persuade the Cabinet or the Prime Minister to agree to, and he has to decide.' (1985, p. 215)

Some negotiations work to fixed deadlines, such as agricultural price-fixing, with its tradition of stopped clocks, etc., IGCs or the cooperation and co-decision procedures. Other negotiations are open-ended and may even remain stalled *sine die*. However, private interests need results and lobby for them energetically. Face can be lost if deadlines are not met and there is often a premium on efficient decision-making and the public presentation of the result.

Member states attempt to render individual details of new legislation less harmful by the addition of caveats and reserves, declarations for the record, etc., so as to leave margin for manoeuvre at a later date. The Danish insistence on Art 100A(4) in the Single European Act, allowing discrimination in the internal market if environmental considerations justify it, or the various declarations appended to the TEU explaining what member states feel they are signing up to are cases in point. No negotiator can return home without having attempted to counter measures likely to endanger national interests with the requisite caveats.

The process of bargaining and coalition building

When national officials negotiate in a Council working party, they work to a brief prepared in the national capital. If it is an effective negotiating brief, it will provide the negotiator with an ideal, a realistic and a fallback position enabling decision-making effectively to produce compromise. Nevertheless, national officials are constantly constrained by the limiting framework of the precise text, which is the subject of a negotiation and their detailed brief. Importantly, and contrary to widely held views amongst the uninitiated, 'package deals' are not entered into at this stage. There may well be cross fertilisation of points within the same area of business, but officials do not become involved in trade-offs across policy sectors. This is reserved to ministers in full Council meetings. Nevertheless, using the term 'negotiation' is not a misnomer, since a good deal of movement occurs within the working party framework. One British official has put it thus: 'when officials or ministers meet in capitals to decide on the brief for the Council at the beginning of a debate on a subject, they adopt a maximalist line. They know that they have to make concessions later, but equally, that they will not get a good deal if they do not ask for a lot at the beginning and stick to it for quite a long time' (Butler, 1986, p. 74). Although a UK Minister has wryly remarked that officials' aim is to: ' "expedite business" – i.e., not make a fuss about anything, however monstrous. Or at least, you could make a fuss, but only a "show" fuss in order to get kudos from, soon after, surrendering "in the interests of making progress" '. (Clark, 1994, p. 139)

The problem for officials in technical departments of domestic ministries is that ministers may well trade the hard-won gains at official level for other gains in totally different policy areas resulting from negotiated package deals. Only at a political level is there issue linkage in negotiations. This process of issue linkage brings with it a set of assumptions regarding log-rolling and side payments to other negotiating partners with differing stakes in the game. 'Log-rolling' is the process by which within a given issue-area bargains are struck along the lines of the basic negotiation principle 'if you...then we...'. 'Side-payments' is the term used when bargaining stretches across functional areas, thus interlinking issues, which, to all intents and purposes, have nothing to do with each other, but which may prove the coinage which permits transaction. 'If you accept our view on agricultural reform, we will expand the criteria for aid under the structural funds' or 'if you agree to an intergovernmental conference on political union, which we want, we will agree to an intergovernmental conference on economic and monetary union, which we would otherwise rather not have at this time'. The result is an intricate system of alliance building and shifting sets of bilateral and multilateral coalitions based on issue linkage not only of a functional kind, i.e., linking disparate European policies, but also involving procedural issues, i.e., changes to decision-making structures.

The originality of the EU negotiating process is not the package deals which form part of the *Community method* – these can be observed in many multilateral negotiating frameworks - but two further features of the process. First, since the seemingly last word at one negotiation stage can be reformulated as part of a package deal or a series of bargains, one must conclude that in the EU more than elsewhere what seem at times to be irreducible minimum negotiating objectives actually turn out to be quintessentially negotiable when side-payments are on offer. The seemingly absolute can thus be adapted and amended if the negotiating environment is changed. EU negotiation is hence, *par excellence*, an example of a 'nested game', where focusing on one negotiation and its outcomes may mislead the observer in his attempt to identify the overall stakes in the game and where a compromise in one area may seem to contradict much-published views on minimum requirements. The point is that any one negotiation is part of a whole series of other negotiations, each in some way incorporating spin-offs for the others. An outcome in one area may only be explicable if set against the background of other elements in the package. (See Tsebelis, 1990).

Secondly, and in extension of the nested game theme, what characterises EU originality is the way in which relations between member states form a complex web of long-term interests. Alliances of member states turn around several key long-term interest groupings. They are geographical (Southerners, Northerners, wine or beer drinkers), interest based (farmers, industrialists, etc), simply based on the fact of being large (France and Germany) or small (Benelux) states, liberal or protectionist, left or right-wing, etc. The net contributors, for example, all have the problem of persuading finance ministers to finance new policies, however worthy, when additional expenditure is involved.

On the other hand, however, these long-term 'objective' alliances are of a different order from tactical coalitions, which have little profound impact on ongoing bilateral relations between the member states concerned, such as agreement on restricting tobacco advertising, milk quota adjustment or the technicalities of domestic gas boilers. Thus, one-off coalitions make alliances shift from issue to issue since there is always a readiness at two levels to put one or other policy or alliance on hold – either for a short-term gain in a key policy area or as part of a higher-order set of trade-offs including transient coalitions of interest engaged in log-rolling and side-payments. Indeed, while negotiating one set of issues, new subjects for discussion may arise and the negotiating agenda be changed. Member states often begin negotiations, find obstacles in the path of compromise, suspend negotiations and return to pre-negotiations. The fraught discussions over the EU's position in negotiations with the US on farm policy reform in the GATT context in 1993 was a case in point, as was the similar situation prior to the September 2003 WTO discussions in Cancun.

Coalitions that block or promote policies are not the only structured rigidities in the negotiating framework. Individual member states also have their negotiating taboos. As Butler has commented,

'The Greeks, for example, for home political reasons, would much rather not take a common position with the major West European countries on East-West or Arab-Israeli questions and no one feels the way they do about the Turks. For Ireland, it would be politically damaging to do anything which could be taken to mean they were moving nearer to NATO. For the

Danes, there are questions on which it is painful for them politically to separate themselves from the other Scandinavians. Denmark and Greece are
unable, for quite different reasons, to take a relaxed view about human
rights in Turkey. For France, it seemed good politics to get ahead of others
in being tough with South Africa. And so on.' (1986, p. 73)

Wallace (1986) and Moravcsik (1991) have argued that European negotiations have retained the large-power dominant nature of the early
Community days. The shift from two-power domination of policy-making
in the Europe of the Six to the three-power dominance in the European
Union of fifteen has not changed the basic rule that when the large countries
need a decision, they are prepared to buy off the opposition of the small
countries. The Southern countries and Ireland, for example, have silence
encouraged by increased structural funds and cohesion funds and are rarely
the source of major EU initiatives. This might be expected on a neo-realist
view of international relations. It is surprising if the analyst starts from the
assumption of belief in the European common good adumbrated in the first
section of this chapter.

The domestic link

Structuring negotiations at all levels is the need for politicians to explain
negotiating outcomes to domestic constituencies, whether public opinion at
large or the elites representing the various sectoral interests that are the subject of the negotiation. As Putnam has suggested, there are two levels in successful international negotiation; the first to reach tentative agreement and
the second to ensure that the constituent groups at home can ratify the
agreement (1988, p. 436). This can be hard when there is a divergence
between predicted outcome or publicly announced bottom lines for the
negotiation, which turn out not, after all, to be the irreducible minimum.
Bottom lines and fallback positions may move as the pressure to compromise produces negotiating alternatives. There is thus often a practice of
maintaining one discourse for negotiations and another for public consumption. If the two can coincide, politicians' jobs are easy. If, however, sensitive negotiations lead to renunciation of one or other national policy line
as a contribution to the negotiation or as part of a higher order package deal,
there is a delicate job of public relations to be done. Not only this, but timing
is of the essence in the negotiation itself and a premature freeing of the
proverbial cat from the bag may alter the terms of the negotiation itself. The
corollary, of course, is that the statements of politicians for their home
market may require some interpretation in terms of what they may portend
for negotiations. Negotiators must 'deconstruct' the texts of their partners.
Former foreign secretary Douglas Hurd has complained that foreign secretaries are regarded as weak and compromising figures, eager to sell out
British interests, when at home. But as soon as they arrive in Brussels they
are seen as 'better briefed, devious and ruthless in the pursuit of British
interests.' (*Guardian*, 2 January 1998)

Ministers often appear 'holier than thou' for domestic consumption, pre-
tending they support or oppose a policy, when they know and agree that the
final decision may well be different. (EU watchers studied closely, for
example, the evolution in the statements of health, and trade and industry

ministers on tobacco advertising in the UK, Germany and Holland, the three states forming the blocking minority preventing its total ban in the EU for years.) The protagonists in the opposing case can, on occasion, be later blamed. Thus, as former permanent representative Sir Michael Butler has commented, if one minister judges another will refuse to agree a given policy, 'he may be tempted to propose or support it (even if he does not want it much to happen), so that the foreign government concerned and/or his national parliament (if it is a popular cause) can be told he has proposed it but that it could not be agreed...Of course it is not possible to prove that a minister is playing games of this kind...all the same, a lot of games do get played!' (Butler, 1986, p. 74) A good example of this is the continued official French reticence to reform the CAP long after it had been decided by the French government in October 1991 that reform was on the cards and therefore to be supported, albeit with an attempt at damage limitation. (Le Theule and Litvan, p. 769)

Problems are posed for the negotiator by a lack of domestic consensus, not only in terms of interest groups bringing pressure to bear on government and the consequent difficulty in establishing an agreed line in the 'national interest', but also in terms of the bureaucratic disagreements and ministerial demarcation disputes to which such social and economic divergences give rise. In some member states, this problem is compounded by the addition not only of the various private sector interests in play, but a further set of sub-national governmental pressures of constitutional significance. The more open the political system, the more subject is government to the pressures of pluralist interests. The more federal the national political system, the more diverse the pressures of a formal, constitutional nature. Indeed, just as in one member state, Denmark, parliament has carved out a specific, constitutionally anchored role in shaping the government line, so in another, Germany, the Länder have achieved the right to sit alongside the governmental representative in Council negotiations where the competence of the Länder is at issue (e.g. culture) (see Leonardy, 1993).

Sometimes there is even a process by which compromises resulting from the confrontation of member states' views in Brussels put the national official into the position of defending a view contrary to an original departmental line or to a position advocated by a key 'national' interest group. National officials often have to persuade their own colleagues in capitals that the limits of negotiability have been reached, a task often more difficult than persuading other delegations to accept one's own national viewpoint. Readers of the literature on international negotiations will not be surprised by this. Gilbert Winham, for example, has pointed out that international negotiations are often characterised by the preponderance of negotiating *within* the team in order to reach an agreed line, rather than with the other side. (Winham, 1977) It also occurs that representatives of interests who have not managed to have their view accepted as 'the national interest' may seek an alternative route to policy acceptance by bringing pressure to bear on the Brussels machinery. Majone quotes the case of 'a British safety expert who originally had sought to reform the British approach to safety at the workplace. Having failed to persuade the policy-makers of his own country, he brought his innovative ideas to Brussels, where they were

welcomed by Commission officials and eventually became European law.'
(Majone, 1996, p. 74 and Eichener, 1992)

Finally, the press is also part of the negotiating process. Everything
becomes known to the press, though meetings are generally not open to
journalists. Member states use the press to win public and elite support and
to isolate opponents. *Agence Europe*, for example, gives a near-inside view of
Coreper and Council meetings. The problem for officials and ministers is
that if a hard-line position becomes known, questions in the media and in
parliament can arise. The hard line may be a tactic, but the raising of
national voices in sympathy with or against the line may affect the progress
of the negotiation itself. It is difficult for negotiators to 'open the oven
during the baking process', and thus difficult to portray a starting position
in a negotiation as precisely the objective one hopes to achieve. The pressure of opposition parties in parliaments, bent on embarrassing ministers,
has clear reverberations for a country's negotiating stance.

Reaching compromise

Seeing other viewpoints, whether of other member states, the Community
as a whole or of 'the lobby' has become the *sine qua non* of the effective
national negotiator in the EC context. In practice, 'seeing other viewpoints',
may have unsavoury consequences for an individual government department or for a private sector interest. Officials negotiating in Council may
have been provided with a brief containing ideal, realistic and fallback positions. But, the ideal position is not always, or even perceived by the negotiators themselves as being the rational line to take in terms of persuasion of
the negotiating partners. (Wallace, 1989) Since the Single European Act
expanded the scope of decisions taken by qualified majority, national governments are frequently outvoted on issues where their 'ideal position' as
set out in the 'line to take' agreed in national capitals is simply a non-starter.
Indeed, sometimes the more nuanced 'realistic position' is not acceptable
either. And in the worst-case scenario, even the 'fallback position' may still
leave a negotiator isolated and outvoted. (For a discussion of negotiating
strategies in Council, see Wallace, 1985)

Compromises, clearly an integral part of bargaining in the EU, take many
forms. One frequent form results from key member states reaching agreement on a package of issues where all participants can find a measure of
advantage greater than the disadvantage of no policy at all. Here, the role of
the Commission is extremely important. While the Commission is a non-
voting member of the discussion, it has often been described as an extra
member state, since the Commission's right to amend its proposal or withdraw it if Council compromises are unacceptable neatly counterbalances the
absence of the right to a vote. It did this in November 1986 in the case of the
Erasmus programme of student exchanges, when Commissioner Marin
argued that the Council was depriving the scheme of all significant content
(Usher, 1994, p. 147). However, the Commission does not always have to
wield the stick for the underlying point to be made.

The Commission or the presidency often formally proposes compromises
hammered out bilaterally, so the message to the outside world tends to
downplay the 'win-lose' theme in relations between member states. While

the Commission cannot be instructed to adapt its positions to help reach a compromise, it can play an important brokerage role akin to that of the presidency. The Commission's relationship to the Council and to the Council secretariat is thus a vital element in negotiating between member states. The Commission, the presidency and the Council secretariat live in a symbiotic relationship in this search for compromise, where the roles of initiator, broker, helper of the process itself and shaper of the outcome are constantly shared and where the lead is mutually agreed. The role of the Council secretariat in aiding the presidency is not to be underestimated. Officials sit beside the chairman in negotiations at all levels. The secretary-general himself, currently Javier Solana, who is also the high representative for foreign policy, briefs the president of the External Relations Council and sits beside him in the meeting itself as a permanent advisor on strategy and tactics. Deputy secretary-general Pierre de Boissieu perfoms a similar function for the General Affairs Council sessions and for Coreper. The secretary-general or deputy secretary-general often accompanies the president of the European Council on the tour of capitals prior to European Council meetings.

The presidency is, of course, the prime 'shaper' of the meeting. Its role is effectively to broker compromise, sometimes after a series of 'confessionals' where delegates negotiate bilaterally with the presidency after admitting what they feel is their 'bottom line' or fall-back position. During this process, other delegations might well be using the adjournment time for bilateral negotiation and coalition-building. By mediating between rival positions, the presidency gains status, but it must be sure that its proposed compromise is likely to achieve acceptance. Failure to gain a qualified majority reflects on the efficiency of the presidency itself. Indeed, forcing an issue to a vote is sometimes more a way of creating a long-term grudge than an instrument for conflict settlement. The obligation to resort to the veto in 1985 (see below) still rankles in the minds of German policymakers, highlighting, as it did, Germany's lack of authoritative inter-ministerial coordination. The lessons drawn by the British after their failed attempt to invoke the Luxembourg compromise in 1982 led to similar rancour, as did their failure at the Milan summit in 1985 to prevent the establishment of an inter-governmental conference.

Presidencies disrupted by domestic factors face problems in negotiations. The Irish in the second half of 1996 were the first for some time not to have domestic events crowd in on them. Previously, the Germans, French, Spanish and Italians had had elections, which had prevented them fulfilling the customary aim of effective chairmanship of EU business. In addition, the Italians, in the first half of 1996, had been plagued by almost permanent governmental change, the British BSE crisis and the consequent UK blockage of EU business. At the outset of the Florence summit, the presidency and the Commission were able to persuade UK Prime Minister John Major to give up both the blockage and the resistance to Europol; the day before energy ministers had reached agreement after six years of negotiation on the mutual opening of electricity and other energy markets. Add to this agreement on a new TV without frontiers directive and a common extradition agreement and the Italian presidency could claim a balancing success to offset the problems with which it had been beset – the failure of the first three months of its presidency, when Prime Minister Dini had resigned (by the Florence Council he had become foreign minister in a new government); new elections on 21 April and the new Prodi government in power on 17 May. Importantly, despite such high political level problems, the Italian administration was able to cope – largely due to the efficiency of Luigi Cavalcini, the Italian permanent representative, the diligence of the Council secretariat and the excellent working relations it maintained with the Commission.

Frequently, when issues become sensitive, Council meetings go into 'restricted session', where only those at the main table remain, or 'super-restricted session', where all except the ministers themselves and the permanent representatives withdraw. Similar to the restricted session are the frequent informal lunches, commented on by former UK foreign secretary Lord Howe as evidence that 'diplomacy is inseparable from gastronomy', since some European statesmen seem to hold that 'if you are not eating at the same time you are not sincere.' (*Guardian*, 2 January 1998.) Informal lunches and the holding of several informal ministerial meetings in the country of the presidency are the bane of national officials. Giving ministers a free rein to come to agreements beyond carefully structured official briefs may facilitate compromise, but officials are wont to suggest that ministers are sometimes guilty of short-sightedness, in effect unable to see all the technical and political implications of a seemingly simple compromise. Procedurally, therefore, a presidential summary once the formal session has resumed is a vital part of anchoring what is otherwise informal agreement. Even then it is not unknown for delegations to renege on the agreements they have sometimes hastily or tardily reached.

Delaying, persuading and other tactics

There are many ways in which member states can disguise their true aims. One aim may be to delay or to keep an issue off the agenda. The formal system of *reservations* in the negotiating chamber itself is a procedural means of introducing delay, while negotiating positions are reviewed, parliaments consulted, etc. But this is an overt tool that the presidency, Commission or impatient member states can bring into question. There are also covert means to keep issues off the agenda. If a negotiated settlement is on the cards, or if an outcome looks likely and a member state risks isolation, various tactics may be used. They include use of a principle to avoid a practical policy discussion, such as an attempt to argue that the Commission's proposal is based on the wrong treaty article or that the proposal assumes Community rather than national competence. In the negotiation itself, Parliament's view may be cited as a reason for further reflection.

It is necessary, therefore, in reading between the lines of a negotiator's standpoint, to distinguish the overt strategy from the covert aims. The principle of 'subsidiarity', for example, has often been used as a means of preventing an issue reaching the Council agenda. Douglas Hurd, then British foreign secretary, when introducing the UK presidency's agenda in 1992 to the European Parliament was accused, for example, of using the subsidiarity issue to move social issues off the agenda of the Twelve. 'Listening to you', said the Socialist spokesman, Jean-Pierre Cot, 'the subsidiarity principle seems like a magic vanishing powder.' (*The Times*, 9 July 1992) Commenting on a leaked UK presidency strategy paper on social policy, the *Guardian* commented at the time on the 'approach required' from British ministers... '*the word "delay" is marked after each issue.*' (10 July 1992)

Another way to deal with unpalatable issues is simply to attempt to change the tacit rules of negotiation behaviour and 'refuse to budge'. But the argument that compromise is a key structuring feature of governmental interaction in the EU means that negotiators unready to shift from their 'ideal' to a 'realistic' position in a negotiation are not 'playing the game'. They become caught in a contradiction between the positive sum environment and their own zero-sum negotiating approach. Lady Thatcher remarked in her maiden speech in the House of Lords that she 'always found that the most effective weapon was "no". Or sometimes "*no, no, no*"', adding that she was 'glad this continues to be the policy, even if it is more sweetly expressed' (*Guardian*, 3 July 1992). A former UK permanent representative, Sir David Hannay, has recounted how she corrected him when he said negotiating in Brussels was like a game of snakes and ladders, stating that 'that is where you are quite wrong. In Europe they are all snakes.' (*Independent*, 28 July 1995) Arguably, this kind of attitude to the negotiating environment has put the UK at a distinct disadvantage over time. Rather than seeing success for UK positions as others rally round, the agenda has constantly been set by others – usually the Franco-German tandem, but quite frequently Italy and the Benelux countries. As a senior Commission official has commented 'the British under Major could be a lot more mischievous than under Thatcher. She usually manoeuvred them into a corner. Everyone could then take for granted that they wouldn't deal and ignore them.' (Ross, 1995, p. 88)

A minister unwilling to compromise is not playing the Community game and, because the game is not one of traditional diplomacy, tact and discretion, interest groups and the press may be used to foster the arguments of one or the other side. As one British Conservative minister has put it, 'Despite the rhetoric with which politicians seek to allay domestic anxieties about the growing influence of Europe, the governments of the Twelve are moving more decisively towards fulfilment of the European Community's purpose than at any time since its foundation. Behind the headlines, beneath the flamboyant national gestures, there is a relentless momentum.' (Heseltine, 1989, p. 23)

Importantly, however, achieving the desirable does not necessarily mean advocating one's desirable position. Others may be used as a shield to defend a view that might provide a source of embarrassment to a particular member state. The Germans were doubtless grateful to the British in the past for making the running on budget discipline. Because of the differences of view in the government coalitions mentioned above, strong advocacy of budget discipline might kindle resentment in those sectors liable to profit from increased spending. German original initiatives are generally thin on the ground. They are usually co-presented either in tandem with the French or with an alternative partner, such as the Italians in the case of the Genscher-Colombo plan. British negotiators often smart at the memory of too much isolation in the 1980s when dogmatism and ideology was overt and negotiating style arguably unsubtle. On many issues the British have stood alone in the defence of views many would accept, though they might be reluctant to make an admission of the fact.

Issue linkage and package deals

As described above, officials at junior levels must negotiate on the basis of their briefs, but as issues move up the negotiating hierarchy to Coreper and into Council, issue linkage begins to emerge. In a technical Council formation, bargaining clearly involves a good measure of log-rolling; bargains within the same issue area providing a give-and-take basis for the trade of concessions. It is in the General Affairs Council, in preparation for the final European Council, that the negotiation process is the most fascinating. The GAC, as chapter 4.1 points out, is overburdened and still burgeoning, but it is still here that the side-payments may be discussed, political trade-offs are made, deals are done and the policy packages constructed in times for the quarterly jamborees of the European Council.

Yet, not all European Councils produce the complex packages which have come to characterise the Community method. The 1965 negotiation linking budget reform to CAP consolidation and institutional reform was an example of a package that came apart because the Commission's efforts to amalgamate disparate issues in order to produce an integrative momentum was ill-judged. Later examples, once the European Council was introduced in 1974, are the Fontainebleau summit of 1984, which resolved the British budget problem, or the Luxembourg Council of 1985, which led to the 1986 Single European Act (see de Ruyt, 1987). The latter set ambitious deadlines for key policy areas such as the internal market and introduced, simultaneously, new policy areas, such as the environment, institutional reforms designed to facilitate success (extension of qualified majority voting), provide democratic legitimacy (a new procedure for relations with the Parliament) and square the recalcitrant poorer member states (a boost to the structural funds principle called 'cohesion'). Other headline-grabbing packages were the Treaty of European Union, signed at Maastricht, the final agreements of the EFTA enlargement and the enlargement to Central and Eastern European countries, both jeopardised by Mediterranean resistance in the closing stages and a consequent need for appeasement. (The following chapter describes in greater detail the negotiations which led up to the agreement at the Berlin European Council in March 1999 on the Agenda 2000 financial framework for the Union from 2000 to 2006.)

The future of EU negotiating style in an enlarged Union

The environment in which member states conduct negotiations with each other has grown enormously in complexity and in the degree of bureaucratisation and subtlety that characterises it. Package deals between member states can range right across the gamut of all ministerial activity. No home ministry remains untouched by European Union policies or policy constraints, as a simple glance at the number of areas requiring negotiation for the entry of new member states shows (Granell, 1995). As this complexity has grown, so too has the complexity of the European institutional framework.

One of the structuring features of Community business set out in the introduction to this section was the way in which foreign policy and domestic policy have reached a new stage of symbiosis in the European Union. Decision-making in the specific context of the Council has bureaucratised the process of inter-state bargaining, leaving the large majority of decisions through negotiation to officials at various levels with only the 'package deals' and the high politics left for ministers. Thus, the simplistic notion of 'negotiated settlement' in EU affairs hides a degree of complexity which defies the understanding of the non-specialist. As positions are tabled, decomposed into their separate elements, divided between levels of Commission, then Council meetings from working parties through Coreper to the Council meeting itself, progress is incremental and often hidden in complex detail an understanding of which is only available to one key level, Coreper, which sits at the interface of the political and the technical.

The Council's bottom-up negotiating approach leads to the package-building with which the press regales the public at times of European Councils. But it is a bureaucratic approach to which only initiated outsiders are privy and it sets as a premise for its success the willingness to be 'satisficers rather than optimizers'. All this raises serious questions about the democratic accountability of the process, only partially answered by the Council's willingness to accept, under the constraint of increasingly hostile public opinion, openness in its dealings through, for example, the televising of some of its sessions (see chapter 20). This question has become a marker in the ongoing debate about the nature of EU business, in particular since the arrival of further Nordic member states in 1995. Yet, it is not entirely cynical to observe that cakes only continue to rise if the oven door is kept closed. If it is opened on demand, the nature of the baking process may have, inevitably, to change.

EU negotiations progressing through the institutional hierarchy from consultative meetings chaired by the Commission, through Council working parties, Coreper and on to ministerial level only partly conform to a model based on the rapprochement of opposites by a series of small-step compromises. Much of the time, national bureaucrats are searching for ways of extricating ministers from the detail in which much of Community negotiation becomes 'bogged down'. Procedural devices such as presidency confessionals, pre-negotiation at bilateral level, the Antici group and coalition-building are vital stages in the negotiations, but they are also bureaucratic steps towards political settlement.

Attempts to make parallels with international negotiations of the classic, intergovernmental type are misleading, since there is in the EU a genuinely different conceptual framework within which the actors must operate. There are, naturally, features common to all negotiations present in EU negotiating, as this section has shown. Underlying EU negotiations lies the omnipresent notion that negotiation is possible, because the players are not in a zero-sum game, despite ministerial attempts to portray negotiations as precisely that. It is rare for an individual negotiation to be perceived in simplistic, zero-sum terms by the negotiators themselves. If one issue area seems to present the features of a win-lose negotiation, the intricate system of linkages between issue areas quickly turns an apparently (and often professedly) zero-sum game into a positive-sum *set* of games. In EU business, despite occasional triumphalism of the ministers involved, there can be no 'game, set and match' (former UK Prime Minister John Major's view of the negotiating outcome at Maastricht). EU business is far too complex for there to be only one clear winner, though national political rhetoric seems bent in all cases on proving the opposite.

Some positions, such as the UK view on EMU, tax or social policy, are seemingly non-negotiable, but even here there is a sense in which the EU emerges strengthened despite appearances, since member states recognise the difficulties of other member states and adapt. Rather than put the Maastricht Treaty at risk, for example, the Eleven accepted the opt-out principle for EMU at Maastricht, though it has subsequently become clear that this was precisely what Commission president Jacques Delors had predicted, and the strategy upon which the Commission had based its negotiating positions a year before. Thus, while holding together and accepting a 'multi-speed Europe' may have seemed to some to be a damage limitation strategy destined to ensure increased integration with all member states on board, there is also an argument for viewing the compromise involved as a skilful method by which the prime agenda-setters in the Community (France, Germany and the Commission) were able to sideline the UK, while apparently bowing to UK domestic political pressure. George Ross, who spent six months in Delors' cabinet in 1991 has commented that as early as February/March 1991 he knew 'Delors was already cooking up a scheme for a British 'opt-out' of stage 3.' (1995, p. 88)

Indeed, the TEU, like all subsequent treaty negotiations, was a series of compromises. All countries achieved what was essential to them at the expense of the less essential. Interestingly, the underlying aims of the protagonists are not the actual subject of the negotiations in many cases. The TEU was about further economic and political integration, but France's aim was to curb German hegemony through EMU, while Germany wanted the political union it made a condition for agreement to EMU. The UK wanted a flexible Europe allowing for enlargement. Unfortunately, it seems that one significant result of the constant resort to complex compromises which please everyone is that the public remains bewildered – at best ill-informed and at worst disabused by European Union politics.

At times it appears that the traditional view expounded in this chapter of the EU negotiating process as a joint attempt to find policy solutions that enhance the 'European interest' may not explain the full story. The UK has largely remained a Euro-recalcitrant since it joined the Union, but it has clearly, on a number of occasions, weighed the cost of withdrawal or isolation from the European mainstream against the short-term definition of the national interest. British decision-makers have not always found their way easily through the negotiating jungle. An element of coercion has often occurred, as the decision to hold an intergovernmental conference (which led to the Single European Act) despite British reticence at the Milan summit in 1985 demonstrated. Indeed, as Moravcsik has argued, 'if two major states can isolate the third and credibly threaten it with exclusion and if such exclusion undermines the substantive interests of the excluded state, the coercive threat may bring about an agreement at a level of integration above the lowest common denominator' (1991, p. 47). Perhaps traditional power

political analyses still have much to teach the student of Council negotiations.

Whether the current model of Council negotiation can survive the challenges of the current enlargement is a moot point. The obvious changes
enlargement will bring about may change the assumptions upon which the
EU bargaining style has developed. Like most popular clubs the EU has to
think hard about the costs of moving from an elite membership with established traditions and working methods to an arguably unwieldy and untidy
new membership structure, where the aims of the new members diverge
from the aspirations of the founders. At the same time, the new members
have inevitably brought with them new demands in terms of membership
fees and the benefits to be drawn from membership. Their demands may not
be the basis of negotiations that are 'yes-able', and they may also unleash
centrifugal forces in the existing member states. Helen Wallace has
observed, for example, that there will be more financial constraints and
reduced opportunities for financial side payments, yet there will be 'more
claimants for side-payments, the currencies of their claims (will be) diverse,
and there (will be) less margin for the free rider' (Wallace, H, 1989, p. 198).
Indeed, it is not unlikely that the notion of side-payments may prove a misnomer. Major policy alterations may be the cost of enlargement, not least the
likely requests for 'opting out' of policy areas where the national costs may
not be worth the price of the benefits obtainable.

Such fundamental changes, occurring after a decade of navel-gazing, constitutional debate and pronounced weakening of public support for the EU
may so fundamentally alter the premises and the logic on which the
Community was based, that the Community method may be sacrificed in
the endeavour to construct some kind of architecture to meet the challenges.
From the negotiating point of view, as the game conceivably changes, win-
win negotiations may end up as merely negotiators' memories and be found
only in their memoirs. The costs in terms of Council decision-making ability
may be high.

Chapter 16: Negotiating a package deal – the example of Agenda 2000*

The political backdrop to Agenda 2000, the shorthand label describing reform of the EU's major spending policies and of the financial means to fund them over the period 2000-2006, did not augur well for a smooth or straightforward negotiation. Member states were struggling to meet the Maastricht convergence criteria ahead of the final decisions in May 1998 on the introduction of the euro, while confronting the implications of a number of external factors in drawing up a new seven-year financial framework for the Union. Reform of the common agricultural policy would be undertaken on the threshold of a new millennium round of WTO multilateral trade negotiations in which agriculture would feature prominently. With the EU embarking on its biggest ever enlargement, the financial implications of admitting a large number of less wealthy members were likely to be hotly disputed among existing member states. Amid the general squeeze on public finances across Europe, the issue of payments to the EU budget by the largest net contributors (Germany, the Netherlands, the UK, Sweden and Austria) was being propelled to the forefront of domestic political agendas[1]; in Germany in particular, the perceived 'excessive' net contribution to the EU budget was developing into a major electoral issue in the run-up to the September 1998 general elections. The UK government, faced with calls from other member states either to abolish the 1984 budget abatement mechanism or to make significant inroads into it in relation to the cost of enlargement, argued that the UK's continued status as a major net contributor meant that the abatement was non-negotiable.

Given that reframing spending policies is essentially a zero-sum exercise in dividing up a given budgetary cake, member states began their tactical positioning based on calculations of net gains and losses which might result from the Commission's Agenda 2000 proposals, the external pressures outlined above and demands likely to be pressed by other member states. The prospect of a rough ride ahead on one of the most complex packages ever processed by the Union loomed large at the outset of the negotiation.

1998 began with something of a phoney war following the initial frenetic activity on the Commission's Agenda 2000 communication in the run-up to the Luxembourg European Council in December 1997. The Commission had presented its communication in July 1997 in the wake of the Amsterdam Intergovernmental Conference in order to test the water before submitting its formal proposals. In political terms, the main question facing the December 1997 Luxembourg European Council was the extent to which markers on the future financial framework should be laid down at this early stage as a pre-requisite for the European Council to launch the enlargement process. While the Commission harboured ambitions that the European Council would provide substantive guidelines in support of the broad principles underlying its proposals, governments saw no need to hold any part of Agenda 2000 hostage as a condition for giving the green light to the start of the enlargement process. Hence the minimalist and general blessing of the Commission's ideas as '*an appropriate working basis for further negotiations for an agreement on the Union's policies and the financial framework*'. The major substantial element to emerge from the Luxembourg European Council conclusions was the requirement to ring fence expenditure for EU-15 in the next financial framework from that reserved for future acceding countries.

Nothing had therefore been pre-empted when the Commission duly presented its raft of proposals on 18 March 1998. The range and complexity of the Agenda 2000 reforms underlined the magnitude of what was at stake: a new financial framework fixing (in an Interinstitutional Agreement (IIA) between the European Parliament, the Council and the Commission) the medium-term financial ceilings within which the annual budgets for the Union should be drawn up over the period; six draft regulations reforming the Union's structural and cohesion funds; eight draft regulations reforming the arable crops, beef and veal and milk production sectors, including modifications to the CAP financing, direct support schemes and rural development regulations; amendments to the financing of Trans-European Networks (TENs) and Loan Guarantee Fund regulations; and three regulations on co-ordinating the pre-accession strategy and establishing two new pre-accession instruments respectively on agriculture and structural policies. The package lacked one vital element, which would only arrive in October (i.e., after the German general election): the Commission's report on the operation of the own resources system (the system for raising revenue for the EU budget).

Such a far-reaching and potentially explosive reform package, covering the two major spending items in the Union's budget (CAP and structural policies) would clearly put to the test the robustness of the Union's negotiating process. This chapter looks in turn at the method of managing the negotiating process in the Council and the European Parliament (EP), at some of the main substantive political issues which emerged during the negotiation as well as an assessment of the lessons learned for negotiations on the new financial perspective which began in January 2004.

Managing the negotiating process

Although precedents for this type of package negotiation existed in the shape of the Delors I and II financial packages following, respectively, the Single Act and the Treaty on European Union, the Agenda 2000 negotiations were compounded by two further complicating factors. First, because of the tight timetable if formal adoption was to be achieved before the June 1999 European Parliament elections, work would have to be pursued simultaneously on the overall political package to be agreed by the European Council, and on the actual texts translating the political deal into legislative form. Many of these texts required Parliament's approval in one form or other. In the case of Delors II, the legislative proposals were only presented after the

Edinburgh European Council had struck an overall political deal. Secondly, the Union would have to ensure that the content of its reforms and its financial framework would enable it to cope with the accession of new and less wealthy member states during the period of the new financial perspective. While the EU had not committed itself to any date for the completion of accession negotiations, the working assumption used by the Commission in its proposals and in drawing up the new financial perspective was the accession of six new member states in 2002.

Furthermore, the economic and financial context within which the negotiations took place was very different from the one that prevailed at the time of the Delors II reforms. At that time, the Community was undertaking a rapid expansion of its structural expenditure, to enable poorer regions and countries to derive maximum benefit from the internal market. The Cohesion Fund was created expressly in order to assist less wealthy countries in meeting the demands of preparing for the single currency. In 1998, however, the watchwords of budgetary rigour and efficient expenditure were writ larger than ever, with many member states, particularly the net contributors to the EU budget, seeking to impose on the Union's expenditure similar budgetary discipline to that being exercised at home in the context of preparing for the introduction of the euro. The big question mark was whether the European Parliament would be as willing to subscribe to a financial perspective which would probably give it substantially less leeway for increasing non compulsory expenditure in the annual budgets than the treaty provisions on the so-called maximum rate of increase (article 272(9) of the EC Treaty).

Work in the Council

Council presidencies were confronted with two main management problems. First, Agenda 2000 extended across the preserve of the General Affairs, Agriculture and Ecofin Councils. Processing such a complex and wide-ranging programme through the Council's vertical structures ran the real risk of fragmentation of the various components of the package, with civil servants in different national ministries naturally taking negotiating positions defending their own turf rather than the interests of the overall balance of the package. It was therefore vital for the presidency to obviate this risk by putting in place mechanisms to ensure consistency of approach on the dossier as a whole. Second, the UK and Austrian presidencies each had to consider carefully what their overall objective should be in terms of the outcome of their respective European Councils as important staging posts along the road to Berlin. This required striking the right balance between sustaining an adequate degree of momentum throughout the negotiations, while avoiding over-ambition at too early a stage, with the attendant risk of incurring a major setback in a Council or European Council meeting, which could reflect badly on the presidency, and more seriously, delay agreement on the package.

Careful planning was required in order to deal with both of these potential pitfalls, while following the twin-track of paving the way for an overall political agreement and undertaking a detailed examination of the legislative texts. The Council agreed early in 1998 during the UK presidency on a procedure for ensuring unity of work. The General Affairs Council, given its role in preparing the European Council, would have overall responsibility for Agenda 2000, and for preparing the reports to be submitted to the European Council. The Ecofin and Agriculture Councils would provide their input on the aspects of the package that concerned them. Coreper was to have its usual responsibility for preparing the General Affairs Council, assisted by a 'friends of the presidency' group[2]. In practice, however, while Coreper and the General Affairs Council had overall responsibility for the financial amounts to be fixed for agriculture, actual work on the detailed content of the CAP reform was carried out by the Agriculture Council and its preparatory bodies, given the highly specialised and technical nature of these negotiations. Provided agriculture ministers and their civil servants respected the financial parameters to be laid down as part of the overall negotiation, they would be largely left to their own devices on the content of the reform. The question was whether an acceptable reform package could be achieved in the context of a desire to impose strict curbs on agriculture spending.

Much of the initial work by the UK presidency on the Commission's proposals involved clarifying their content and what they actually meant, as well as assessing the assumptions underlying them. Discussions in the 'friends' group and Coreper were structured by presidency questionnaires in order to highlight relevant issues, and ensure that all delegations were talking about the same thing at the same time (something that is not always necessarily self-evident nor easy to achieve!). It became clear early on that three broad types of issue would have to be tackled.

- First of all certain issues which were *fundamentally political in character*, such as the overall financial amounts in each heading, the agricultural guideline, and eligibility criteria for the structural funds. It was generally recognised that on these matters, agreement could only be reached in an overall context in the endgame, and that the focus of work would be to clarify the Commission's underlying assumptions and calculations.

- *Substantive issues* on which the broad contours of agreement could be reached, such as the structure and breakdown of the financial perspective, the content of the IIA other than on the endgame issues, the financial management provisions of the structural funds, or the pre-accession instruments. On these issues progress, even on fairly political aspects, could be expected at the level of Coreper or the Council.

- Finally, there were *more technical issues*, such as the organisation and programming of structural funds and the pre-accession instruments, where experts could get into the nitty-gritty detail of the legislative texts from the outset.

The report drawn up for the Cardiff European Council in June 1998 provided a useful overview and description of the key issues which would have to be addressed in the subsequent negotiation. Cardiff was able to reach two tangible conclusions. First of all, it fixed a deadline of March 1999 for wrapping up the political package in the European Council, with the aim of completing the legislative work before the European Parliament elections in June 1999. Secondly it again underlined the ring fencing requirement by stating that 'a clear distinction must be made in the presentation and implementation in the financial framework between expenditure relating to the Union as currently constituted and that reserved for the future acceding countries, including after enlargement'.

Armed with an annotated 'bible' in the shape of the Cardiff report, and knowing that work on the package could not be completed by the Vienna European Council in December, the Austrian presidency was faced with a daunting challenge: how to keep work focused and achieve the 'substantial progress on the key elements of the package' in the knowledge that final agreement could only come later. Careful management was required to avoid investing too much political capital in trying to move substantially towards an agreement at Vienna, without the constraint of a hard deadline and an endgame scenario to concentrate ministerial minds. The presidency nevertheless had to ensure that real progress was achieved at Vienna, while dispelling early on any public misconceptions that Vienna would somehow have failed if no final agreement were struck.

Work was pursued actively at technical level and by the 'friends of the presidency' examining the detail of the Commission's proposals, particularly on middle-order issues relating to the structural funds, as well as on the pre-accession instruments where tangible progress was achieved. The first stage of the presidency's work involved looking at issues which had only been given a cursory examination to date, or those requiring a more detailed examination as a precondition for advancing on substance. From September, the presidency, by tabling questionnaires and options papers, sought to flush delegations out by asking them to take position on specific items. Work was brought forward rapidly on the pre-accession instruments and the TENs financing and the loan guarantee fund regulations, so that by the end of the presidency political agreement on those issues had largely been achieved, subject to a number of reservations linked to the overall outcome on Agenda 2000. The third stage of work involved preparing a comprehensive report for the Vienna European Council which highlighted the main outstanding issues which would have to be resolved as part of the political deal. As regards the new financial perspective, the report managed to establish the upper and lower parameters within which further negotiation would take place (see below).

It was crucial for the Austrian presidency to have an effective internal process for forging its Presidency (rather than national) position on both tactics and key issues of substance, particularly those to be addressed at each session of the General Affairs, Ecofin and Agriculture Councils[3]. Presidency positions were co-ordinated by a strategic co-ordinating committee in Vienna consisting of senior civil servants from the federal chancellery, the foreign, finance and agriculture ministries, as well as from the permanent representation in Brussels. In hammering out a strategic line, often operating to tight deadlines required by the pace of work in Brussels, this committee not only had to square the interests of different ministries within the social democrat and people's party ruling coalition, but also to avoid taking an overtly partisan stance in presidency papers on vital Austrian national issues (e.g. the negative budgetary position).

The German presidency from 1 January 1999 marked the beginning of a new negotiating phase in which the presidency would have to drive forward the process of narrowing the gap between delegations' positions on the key issues in order to meet the timeframe confirmed at the Vienna European Council. In early January, the presidency tabled what was dubbed its 'negotiating box'. This document was an issue-based paper which did not set out delegations' positions; it constituted, in effect, a skeletal pre-draft of what would eventually become the Berlin European Council conclusions[4]. Developed language already existed in certain parts; other parts consisted of options, square-bracketed language[5] or blanks! The content of the 'box' was fleshed out by means of a series of non-papers tabled in Coreper on the presidency's responsibility[6]. In the light of successive discussions in Coreper, Council and by heads of state or government, the text would be gradually firmed up by a process of successive approximations. The presidency had to firmly steer work forward, through successive revisions of the 'box' at the appropriate junctures, over the two-and-a-half months leading up to Berlin. Essentially, the presidency had to organise and facilitate four types of activity:

- Holding preparatory meetings with the Commission and the Council secretariat in order to prepare compromise ideas. Typically, an initial draft of conclusions language or options ideas would be drawn up by the Council secretariat and tested with the Commission before being sent to the presidency as a basis for internal interdepartmental coordination. The texts would then be finalised in one of the weekly or fortnightly coordination meetings between the presidency, Commission and secretariat, with the presidency, after hearing counsel from the Commission and the Council secretariat, having the ultimate responsibility for the content of its papers.

- Conducting bilateral contacts throughout this period both in national capitals and in Brussels in the margins of meetings in order to sound out informally some of the ideas being developed and to gauge what the market would bear in terms of possible compromises. The outcome of these discussions would assist the presidency in selecting options most likely to constitute a basis for achieving political agreement.

- Organising weekly discussions in Coreper on the 'negotiating box' or on supplementary non-papers fleshing out language and ideas for inclusion in the 'box'. At this stage in the proceedings, the friends of the presidency group was less actively involved, since the work of preparing the European Council had moved on to a more political plane.

- Making best use of ministerial meetings of the Council as a forum for negotiating on the key political issues. Through the work carried out in Coreper, political issues would be identified by the presidency for examination by the General Affairs and Ecofin Councils.

Deft handling was required to keep all the negotiating strands moving forward roughly in unison. The presidency, as is the case in most package negotiations of this nature, had to keep several moves ahead of the game in dealing with the rapid succession of Councils and an informal heads of government meeting in Petersberg one month before Berlin. While most experts intimately involved in the negotiation could roughly sketch out the contours of a final deal as early as January, the skill lay in charting a path to ensure that the negotiation remained on track over the various political hurdles before the finishing line is reached. Although the broad contours of a fair and balanced overall outcome may have been discernible ahead of a final deal, the specific details of the many aspects of a negotiation such as this could have a significant financial impact on any individual member state, which meant that the presidency had to remain vigilant right up until the last moment.

Legislative handling in the European Parliament

Agenda 2000 also provides a good illustration of the interaction between the Council and the Parliament on a major negotiation. At the same time as the Council was pursuing its Agenda 2000 work, the European Parliament had also begun putting in place its internal arrangements for examining the legislative texts. A steering committee was established within the Parliament under the chairmanship of its president, José Maria Gil-Robles, in order to coordinate work between the various parliamentary committees, and to prepare the overall position which the Parliament would take towards the Council and the Commission. The Agenda 2000 proposals covered practically the whole gamut of legislative procedures, including consultation, cooperation (which would become co-decision after the entry into force of the Treaty of Amsterdam) and assent. From the outset, the European Parliament's view was that the proposals should be considered as a single political package, that it would need to be fully associated with discussions in the Council and that it would be seeking arrangements for handling the proposals involving two readings by the Parliament on all of them. Initially, it sought to formalise these arrangements in an interinstitutional agreement (IIA) with the Council.

The Council recognised the need for, and the importance of, collaborating effectively with the Parliament, given that a constructive attitude would be required from both institutions if the legislative work was to be completed on time. It also acknowledged the need for regular contacts between the two institutions to ensure co-ordination and an exchange of information on discussions. However, the Council was more circumspect on the question of agreeing an IIA on how to handle the package. Its view was that the treaties provided for a specific legislative procedure for each proposal, and that while these legislative proposals had to be considered in an overall context, the pace of work on each should take account of objective timing constraints, which were not necessarily the same for each one. Moreover, the Parliament's goal of achieving a de facto co-decision procedure on the whole Agenda 2000 package went beyond the letter and the spirit of the treaties, and what the Council felt able to accept.

The European Parliament's tactical response was to follow a two-stage approach for all of the Agenda 2000 texts. It first of all delivered proposed amendments on the Commission's proposals by late 1998 or early 1999, but at the same time withheld its formal legislative opinion on the texts until after Berlin (except for those subject to the cooperation procedure, where formal opinions were produced before the end of 1998). This enabled it to assess the direction the Council was taking, and the extent to which its proposed amendments had been taken on board before delivering its definitive views.

However the Council, building on the precedent followed during the Delors II negotiations, agreed that over and above the formal procedures of assent and cooperation, an approach would be followed allowing the Parliament to undertake a second reading on all the structural and cohesion fund regulations. There was a certain logic to this approach. Given that co-decision would apply to both the regulations on the European regional development fund and the European social fund, it would be difficult not to give serious consideration to the Parliament's view on the general regulation containing the provisions on issues such as eligibility criteria for the various structural fund objectives, transitional support and financial management issues, for which the assent procedure would apply. Indeed, a number of amendments were negotiated on the general regulation before the final text was formalised by the Council with parliamentary assent. This serves to demonstrate the general unsuitability of the assent procedure for legislative texts, given that formally it only allows the Parliament to give a general thumbs up or thumbs down on a text finalised by the Council, without any scope for negotiation.

Throughout the Agenda 2000 negotiations, the presidency therefore had an important second front to deal with in keeping the European Parliament informed about work in the Council in order to pave the way for the intense period of negotiation with the Parliament which would follow any political agreement in Berlin. Individual delegations were of course involved in a process of lobbying key members of parliament on all aspects of the negotiation. The Parliament had set up three working groups dealing respectively with agriculture, structural funds and the pre-accession instruments designed to act as fora for dialogue and exchanging information among members of Parliament, as well as with the Council and the Commission. The presidency, over and above the regular series of trialogue meetings with the Parliament and the Commission, participated informally in each of these working groups on behalf of the Council in order to ensure coordination of work between the Council and the Parliament and to exchange information on the progress of work in the various policy areas. This allowed the Council, through the presidency, to be informed about the mood of the Parliament. The Parliament, particularly on pre-accession instruments and on structural funds, expected, even before Berlin, to enter into a detailed dialogue on its proposed amendments. However, it was difficult for the Council to respond to these in detail as long as no formal common positions existed. Some minor concessions were made to the Parliament on the pre-accession instruments in February in order to demonstrate the Council's goodwill, and it was only following the Berlin European Council that a meaningful dialogue could take place between the Parliament and the Council on the Parliament's specific amendments to the structural fund regulations.

Survey of the main political issues

While half a dozen or so points could be singled out as first-order political issues which could only be agreed as part of a final package, three in particular merit attention: the requirement to ring fence expenditure for EU-15 and that for countries joining the Union in the course of the new financial perspective; the approach for determining the overall expenditure ceilings in the new financial perspective in general, and the main spending categories in particular (agriculture and structural operations); and issues relating to the Union's own resources, in particular the efforts by the four largest net contributor member states to achieve a reduction in their negative budgetary imbalance.

Ring fencing of expenditure for EU-15 and new member states

It became apparent as early as the Luxembourg European Council that provision would have to be made in the financial perspective to ensure watertight separation between expenditure for EU-15, and that for the new member states, including pre-accession expenditure. This conveniently killed two birds with one stone: it provided reassurance for member states which were net recipients of EU funds that enlargement during the new financial perspective period would not place in jeopardy their portion of the cake, and it sent a clear political signal to applicant states that monies set aside for them, both immediately in the form of pre-accession assistance and later following their accession to the Union, would not be eroded due to any unforeseen spending contingencies confronting EU-15. The Commission's approach involved setting aside resources in the financial perspective from 2002 until 2006 as maximum amounts in payment appropriations to cover expenditure resulting from new accessions over the period[7]. These figures would represent the Union's common negotiating position for the accession negotiations. Under the Commission's original proposal, there was insufficient scope to cover the full cost of enlargement in terms of payment appropriations under the financial perspective EU-15; the remaining cost would be met by having recourse to part of the additional resources available as a result of the new accessions. It is indicative of the extent to which the overall financial perspective levels agreed at Berlin fell short of the Commission's original figures that the full cost of enlargement in terms of payment appropriations could be accommodated in the financial perspective for EU-15, as well as enormous margins for unforeseen expenditure (0.14% of EU GNP by the end of the period[8]; by way of comparison, the margin for unforeseen expenditure in the 1999 financial perspective was 0.01% of EU GNP).

The Spanish delegation considered at an early stage in the negotiation that this approach did not provide sufficient assurances that funds for EU-15 would be secure. Their preferred approach was to make the full cost of enlargement visible at this early stage by adopting a financial perspective for EU-21, including the full cost of enlargement in a separate financial perspective heading. The amounts in this enlargement heading would cover the requirements following enlargement for all expenditure categories, and would remain in this heading after enlargement without being reallocated to the other headings 1 to 6. This implied that no adjustment of the financial perspective would be made upon enlargement. This approach appeared, however, at the very least to be complex and impracticable to apply in drawing up the annual budget and was criticised by other member states for being contrary to budget orthodoxy as well as discriminatory against what were to become fully-fledged member states.

The underlying political problem in this case was a desire to highlight clearly the maximum cost of enlargement over the period in the various financial perspective headings, and ensure the safety of expenditure for EU-15, particularly for structural operations, a concern widely shared by all the cohesion countries. The solution was to draw up alongside the financial perspective an indicative financial framework for EU-21, including additional own resources resulting from the accession of six new member states, and set out in an additional heading 8 in that framework the cost of enlargement as maximum amounts in commitment appropriations. Since this table was purely indicative in character, upon enlargement, the financial perspective for EU-15 would still have to be amended, taking account of the actual number of acceding member states. In order to underline the fact that enlargement posed no risk for current spending in EU-15, the Berlin European Council conclusions expressly provided that in the event of any development of actual expenditure as a consequence of enlargement proving likely to exceed the ceiling on payment appropriations, the financial commitments for EU-15 agreed in the financial perspective would have to be respected.

It should be noted that even though the Cardiff European Council called for ring fencing of expenditure 'including after enlargement', in actual fact once a new member state is in the Union it is no longer possible to earmark money solely for that member state under the budget. Spending is effected via the relevant budget lines in accordance with the applicable Community legislation. Theoretically, at least, member states could potentially receive amounts in excess of the allocation indicatively provided for under a treaty of accession, for example on agriculture, if applying the relevant legislation, e.g. on price support, were to result in a higher figure.

Determining the overall levels of spending in the new financial perspective

A clear split emerged from the outset between those member states, particularly those with negative budgetary balances, which advocated a top down approach based on determining the means available for spending before agreeing the content of policy reforms, and those (mainly the net beneficiaries) preferring a bottom-up approach in defining the Community's policy development needs before tailoring a financial framework to fit. In reality, both approaches were applied in parallel, with neither prevailing. However, a new watchword emerged to describe efforts by those advocating a rigorous budget disciplinarian approach for the Union's spending – 'real stabilisation of expenditure'.

Stabilisation is of course an elastic concept with potentially ambivalent meanings. However, the clear aim of the member states which introduced the concept into the discussion was to maintain expenditure ceilings *in terms of payment appropriations* at an annual level of around 85 billion euros (i.e., close to the level of the 1999 budget rather than the 1999 financial perspective ceilings). The tactic behind this move was to pull the negotiating blanket downwards from the Commission's original proposals, which they deemed over-generous. Stabilisation appealed of course to those countries that are large net contributors to the Community budget, given that every euro not spent by the Union represents a greater saving in terms of their contributions to the EU budget from the national public purse. Other member states, particularly the net beneficiaries, felt that this approach did not take account of the objectives and scope of policy reforms, did not adequately meet the treaty-based requirement for sufficient resources for the Union's policies, nor take account of the distinction between a financial perspective and the annual budget.

A key feature of negotiation on the overall level of the financial perspective is that it cut across the work of both the General Affairs and Ecofin Councils. Both endeavoured to stamp their mark by laying down principles for fixing the overall financial ceilings. However, while attempts were made to use the Ecofin Council to promote the concept of real stabilisation of expenditure, no firm endorsement of this approach could be achieved by Ecofin. This clearly underlined the fact that a package negotiation like Agenda 2000 is indivisible, and that even if finance ministers share the same 'religion', it was impossible to push through Ecofin a rigorous approach on spending independently of other political considerations in the wider package which were of equal or greater importance for certain member states. Playing one Council off against another cannot work where member states have already carried out their internal arbitration (see chapter 17). The Ecofin Council conclusions and press releases on Agenda 2000 are striking in that they highlighted the disagreement at that stage in the process on many political issues, and therefore added little in terms of consensus building. Nevertheless, the Ecofin Council made a significant contribution as a forum where advocates of real stabilisation of expenditure could muster support for their idea and keep it alive on the political agenda. In doing so, they ensured that the Vienna report contained an alternative, 'stabilised' financial perspective table, thereby establishing the lower negotiating limit for further work. It was clear that the final compromise would have to be sought somewhere below the Commission's proposal, and above the figures in this alternative table. The implications of the stabilisation approach would be felt most in financial perspective headings 1 and 2 (agriculture and structural operations).

Agriculture expenditure

As far as agriculture was concerned, the Commission had proposed retaining the agricultural guideline as the ceiling for CAP expenditure. The agricultural guideline is a mechanism which has until now determined the level of heading 1 by providing for an automatic annual increase of 0.74% of the increase in EU GNP starting from a 1988 base. Its original purpose was to act as a brake on agricultural expenditure. However, in recent years, with CAP reform and implementation of strict budgetary discipline by the Agriculture Council, an increasingly large gap had opened up between the heading 1 ceiling and the level of the annual budgets, which were substantially lower.

The guideline therefore appeared somewhat anomalous since in practice it no longer served its original purpose as a means of containing CAP expenditure. While the Mediterranean member states were concerned about the potential impact of enlargement on agricultural expenditure, there was growing pressure from the disciplinarian camp to either rebase the guideline or review its method of calculation, or to retain the guideline, and introduce a ceiling for heading 1 at a lower level. The latter approach was preferred for optical and psychological reasons[9].

The difficulty lay in trying to establish what that ceiling should be, and whether it should be based on:

- maintaining a strict level of €40.5 billion (i.e., the 1999 level of spending) for each of the years of the new financial perspective;

- taking €40.5 billion as an annual average over the period, thereby allowing higher amounts at the start of the period, to be offset by lower amounts towards the end of the period;

- or taking €40.5 billion as the spending target for 2006, and allowing a 'hump' in the intervening years, provided it permitted a substantial and far-reaching CAP reform.

While largely unsuccessful attempts had been made at a number of meetings of Ecofin and the General Affairs Council to fix a ceiling more in keeping with actual levels of spending, a strong (albeit not unanimous) preference emerged at the informal meeting of heads of state or government at Petersberg on 26 February for taking the €40.5 billion figure as an average figure for the period (excluding rural development expenditure of around €2 billion per annum transferred from heading 2).

This was an important political signal to the farm ministers, engaged in the time-honoured ritual of a marathon Agriculture Council in order to hammer out an overall compromise on the agricultural reform package. The Council finally struck a deal on 11 March. The compromise reached, however, was open to criticism because it cost around €7 billion more over the period than the figure which emerged with broad support from the Petersberg meeting. Moreover, some felt that the scope of reform did not go far enough, particularly by watering down the Commission's original proposals and by not providing for any 'degressivity' of direct aids over time. The risk was that negotiations on the rest of the financial package might stall, making it practically impossible to reach agreement in Berlin. Politically, the Agriculture Council could not revisit the deal without the risk of it unravelling, given the finely balanced content of such compromise packages. Introducing some measure of degressivity in direct income support provided to compensate farmers for price reductions also appeared to be a politically untenable option, given the firm opposition expressed by a number of member states in the Council.

Even more politically unsellable for reasons of principle (creeping 're-nationalisation' of the CAP), particularly for France and others, was the idea, originally floated by the Commission, of part co-financing direct income support, in order to share the burden between the Community budget (75%) and national exchequers (25%), thereby reducing the overall level of agriculture spending financed through the Community budget. A further idea was to provide a mechanism for reducing each year a certain amount earmarked for direct income support under heading 1 and increasing the heading 1 sub-ceiling on rural development (where co-financing is usual practice) by some portion of that reduction. This would in effect maintain total agricultural financial flows unchanged, while reducing significantly the amount channelled through the Community budget. Although this idea offered a number of attractions, it also encountered resistance from certain member states, and it would have required the Commission to come forward with proposals to ensure that certain rural development measures were applied in such ways as to support farmers' incomes.

At the Berlin European Council, it was clear that bringing the CAP back into line would probably involve some substantive reopening of the compromise. This was indeed what happened, with President Chirac leading requests for a number of changes to be introduced in order to achieve the objective of stabilising agricultural expenditure in real terms at an annual average over the period of €40.5 billion (excluding rural development). The financial target for expenditure was achieved mainly by postponing implementation of the dairy reform until 2005/6, along with a less ambitious reduction in the intervention price for cereals. Attempts to pre-empt the Union's mandate for the forthcoming WTO negotiating round in the Berlin conclusions were, however, watered down in the face of objections from member states seeking to ensure that the Union's hands were not immutably tied at this stage. The decisions adopted regarding the reform of the CAP within the framework of Agenda 2000 constituted 'essential elements in defining the Commission's negotiating mandate for the future multilateral trade negotiations at the WTO'.

Structural funds

Heading 2, which contains the annual amounts for the structural and cohesion funds, proved to be another key battleground. The thrust of the structural fund reform proposals was to enhance the effectiveness of EU structural funding by concentrating assistance in areas of greatest need. This would be achieved by substantially reducing the number of structural fund objectives to three, and by strictly applying the 75% of Community average GDP threshold for objective 1 status, the most generous assistance level accounting for nearly 70 per cent of structural fund allocations. This would be coupled with reasonably generous transitional assistance arrangements for regions and areas no longer eligible for objective 1 or 2 funding in the next financial perspective.

Regarding the overall levels for heading 2, the initial negotiating position of the cohesion countries was that the Commission's proposal represented a step back compared to the Union's 1999 level of structural spending. For these delegations, if stabilisation of expenditure was to be used as a concept to guide further negotiations, the point of departure had to be the 1999 target level agreed at Edinburgh (0.46% of EU GNP for EU-15). Under this approach, any reduction in that figure had to correspond exactly to reductions in eligible regions in the fifteen member states during the period. The Commission's proposal, representing some €240 billion over the period, was based on maintaining the political commitment of 0.46% of EU GNP for structural operations, but applied to the enlarged Union.

The advocates of a rigorous approach, however, considered that stabilisation had to be based on the annual average of amounts over the period 1993-1999, rather than solely the 1999 level. This discussion was compounded by the fact that the advocates of the rigorous approach, who felt the Commission had been too generous in its proposals given the current economic and financial climate, questioned whether member states receiving assistance under the cohesion fund should continue to be eligible for such assistance if participating in the single currency. Despite the logical inconsistency of defending stabilisation in terms of an annual average over the period rather than the 1999 spending level, while for all other headings, the 1999 budget levels were the yardstick, these delegations advocated an overall figure for heading 2 in the vicinity of €190 million, or lower, for the new period. Clearly, a wide gulf would have to be bridged if positions were to be reconciled into an acceptable outcome.

Reconciling the seemingly irreconcilable is the essence of work of the Council and the European Council. The concept of stabilisation was one which advocates of both approaches could accept, albeit with different meanings. The key was to build on the concept in such a way as to find a politically acceptable outcome somewhere in the middle between the two extreme positions. The concept developed for determining the overall level of expenditure for the structural funds was that of maintaining average per capita aid intensity levels in the new period for objectives 1, 2 and 3 at the 1999 level[10]. This could be accomplished by fixing the overall level of allocations for the new period at around €195 billion. The cohesion fund was maintained for all of the current beneficiaries, although the final total of €18 billion over the period (62% of which would go to Spain) was down on the Commission's original proposal of €21 billion. Final agreement on heading 2 was therefore reached on an overall figure of €213 billion, which, as it happened, was neatly placed near the mid-point between the upper and lower limits set for the negotiation. While haggling over numbers could be (and sometimes is) done on a purely arbitrary basis, it is always preferable to seek an underlying rationale which can be used by politicians in order to sell a negotiating outcome after the event.

Own resources and budgetary imbalances

Nothing excited the media, the politicians and the civil servants more than the question of the Union's own resources and the issue of negative budgetary imbalances, which, in a number of member states, especially Germany, had become a highly politically charged topic.

As far as the own resources system itself was concerned, there was general acceptance that the Union's financial system should be equitable, cost-effective, transparent and simple, and that pursuit of other goals, such as financial autonomy, should not undermine these four generally accepted principles. It was politically impossible to contemplate the introduction of new autonomous own resources at this stage, because providing an autonomous source of funding (i.e., one that does not rely on 'contributions' from member states' exchequers, even if they are as of right due to the

Union) would probably not result in an acceptable distribution of payments 'from member states' into the Union's coffers.

The European Council agreed on a number of specific changes to the own resources system (see below). Given the room available beneath the own resources ceiling, there was no need to increase this ceiling above its current level of 1.24% of EU GNI, although net recipients were reluctant to endorse this figure until the end of the negotiation given concerns about the financial ramifications of enlargement. On this question, those who favoured maintaining the ceiling unchanged were in a comfortable position, since the present own resources decision, which entered into force in 1994, would remain in force indefinitely.

From the outset of the discussion, improving the net budgetary situation as soon as possible was a domestic political imperative for the major net contributors. Their solution was a straightforward one: introduce a correction mechanism to act as a safety net if any member state's budgetary imbalance exceeded a certain proportion of national GDP, drawing inspiration from the 1984 Fontainebleau European Council at which the UK's budget abatement mechanism was agreed, which stated that:

'Expenditure policy is ultimately the essential means of resolving the question of budgetary imbalances. However, it has been decided that any Member State sustaining a budgetary burden which is excessive in relation to its relative prosperity may benefit from a correction at the appropriate time'.

A measure of the sensitivity of this question can be gleaned from the Cardiff European Council conclusions, where paragraph 54 reads as follows:

'... In this context, the European Council notes that some Member States have expressed their view that burden sharing should be more equitable and have called for the creation of a mechanism for correcting budgetary imbalances, but that some other Member States have opposed this. In the same context, it also notes that some Member States have made proposals for changing the own resources, e.g., by creating a progressive own resource, but that others have opposed this'.

Divisive language such as this is highly unusual to find in European Council conclusions. Staking out the ground and putting down political markers in this way, highlighting the fact that no common view yet exists among member states purely as a hook for politicians to demonstrate their firmness of stance to domestic political and public opinion on matters of important national interest, serves no useful purpose in terms of building consensus within the Council. In the absence of the Commission's own resources report at this stage, more general or procedural language might have been more appropriate.

The request for a correction mechanism faced strong objections from other member states. They deemed such mechanisms to be contrary to the basic principles of the Community, and queried the validity of the Fontainebleau conclusions given the changes in the level and scope of Union finances since 1984. They also considered that the concept of net balances was a poor measure of the benefits of EU membership. While a number of member states voiced sympathy for the net contributors' plight, there was a feeling that a proper assessment of the magnitude of the problem could only be made after evaluating the impact of expenditure stabilisation efforts and of policy reforms, given the emphasis in the Fontainebleau conclusions that *'expenditure policy is ultimately the essential means of resolving the question of budgetary imbalances'*.

Once the Commission's report on the operation of the own resources system was submitted in the late autumn, notwithstanding the continued efforts of the net contributors in pressing for a generalised correction mechanism, it was clear that an approach had to be found combining various measures to meet the political objective sought by these member states. They recognised that, despite arguing a robust case, they would not be able to garner sufficient support in the Council to establish a safety-net correction mechanism to limit their net contributions to a certain proportion of their national GDP. Ways had therefore to be found of achieving a sellable political outcome for these countries by addressing their concerns through other means. Their concerns were largely met in the following general and specific ways:

- by following a restrictive approach in the growth of the Union's finances, endeavouring to stabilise or at least limit the overall increase in resources channelled through the Community budget;

- by continuing the shift from the VAT to the GNP resource by reducing the maximum rate of call of the VAT resource from 1% to 0.75% in 2002 and to 0.50 per cent in 2004, thereby continuing the process of making allowance for each member state's ability to pay and of correcting the regressive aspects of the current system for the least prosperous member states. Given its regressive effects, phasing out the VAT resource is likely to be a long-term objective; however, since doing so at this juncture would have placed a significant burden on Italy, it was not possible to complete the phase out during the period of the new financial perspective. It should be noted, however, that the actual impact on the net budgetary situation of the main contributing countries of this measure was marginal;

- by taking a number of specific measures on the resources and expenditure side targeted at individual net contributors. For example, the charges retained by member states for collecting so-called 'traditional own resources' (i.e., mainly customs duties on goods entering the Union) were to be increased from 10% to 25% from 2001, a measure principally designed to help the Netherlands. Moreover, a number of specific additional payments were made on the expenditure side for the Netherlands and Sweden under the structural funds (see footnote 11);

- finally, and perhaps most importantly, by altering the financing key for the UK budget abatement in order to reduce the cost of the abatement borne by Germany, Sweden, the Netherlands and Austria. The UK budget abatement is financed by all member states except the UK under the method set out in the current own resources decision. Under that decision, Germany already benefited from a reduction in its normal contribution to the abatement to 66% of what it would otherwise be. This idea was taken a step further by reducing the contribution of Germany, the Netherlands, Sweden and Austria to financing the UK abatement to 25% of their normal share!

The question of the UK budget abatement was a focus of discussion right down to the wire at the Berlin European Council. The UK's basic negotiating position was that the abatement was non-negotiable. However, it was apparent that any satisfactory outcome on Agenda 2000 would require some inroads being made on the abatement. The UK government made a robust case for retaining it unchanged since, according to the Commission's analysis, the UK remained a larger net contributor to the EU budget than member states with a higher capacity to pay, and that its ranking would not be likely to change following enlargement. Other member states, in particular France, while recognising that its abolition was not a realistic prospect, at least expected the UK to shoulder its full, unabated contribution to the cost of enlargement. It was politically inconceivable for the British prime minister to return to the House of Commons having made major concessions on this question, although it was recognised that some quarter would probably need to be given. However, the margin for negotiation was limited, given the media attention to this issue (although UK media reporting on the abatement at the Berlin European Council was largely crowded out by events in Kosovo).

The UK government accepted the principle (already accepted in 1988 and 1992) of continuing to neutralise 'windfall' gains resulting from the reduction in the VAT resource, as well as those resulting from increasing the percentage of traditional own resources retained by member states to cover their collection costs (this latter element being a new concession). The more substantial concession was accepting to remove part of the accession-related expenditure from the calculation of the abatement. Like so many successful outcomes, this concession had to follow a defensible rationale, for reasons of political presentation. The UK abatement is calculated on the basis of so-called allocated expenditure, which does not include expenditure made outside the Union. Pre-accession expenditure would not therefore be included, and would consequently remain unabated. Given the particular characteristics of pre-accession expenditure, which is similar to expenditure that would be received by the new member states when joining the Union[11], its nature would not in essence change after enlargement. The UK was therefore able to accept a reduction in total allocated expenditure by an amount equivalent to the amount being received by the new member states in the form of pre-accession expenditure, thereby ensuring that this expenditure would continue to be unabated after enlargement. The overall combined impact of the concessions accepted by the UK was estimated at €220 million by 2006.

Given the challenges mounted in the earlier stages of the negotiation, it was somewhat surprising that more pressure was not applied on the UK government for concessions at Berlin. There are two explanations for this. First, a great deal of the negotiating effort in the European Council was deployed on the content of the CAP reform, leaving little time or inclination for heads of government to cross swords in the early hours of the morning on what would in any case be the near impossible task of wresting further

concessions from the UK. Second, and perhaps more telling, in altering the
financing key for the UK abatement, the four member states which benefited
from this measure now had a clear vested interest in retaining the abatement
as it stood as a means of securing a significant reduction in their own net
contributions to the Union budget! This can only be described as a resound-
ing victory for the UK, which also managed to obtain in the Berlin conclusions the unequivocal statement that 'The UK abatement will remain.'

Berlin and beyond – preparing the new financial framework

March 1999 was the self-imposed deadline set by the Cardiff European
Council for wrapping up the political package. Timing was of the essence in
the end-game scenario. Completion by this date was desirable for a number
of reasons: it would be the only chance for the Council and the European
Parliament to complete the legislative work within the lifetime of the parliament before the June 1999 elections; it would ensure that the Commission
could begin structural fund programming and prepare the implementation
of the new pre-accession instruments; it would also clear the way for the
Union to take up work on its institutional reform agenda. Other than these
political imperatives, there were no absolute legal deadlines compelling
agreement by that date. The current own resources decision would remain
valid beyond 1999, and in the event of denunciation of the IIA and the
absence of agreement on a new financial perspective, the treaty provisions
on the maximum rate of growth of non-compulsory expenditure would
apply.

In general terms, it can be said that interinstitutional cooperation on
Agenda 2000 worked well. Following the political agreement reached at
Berlin, the process of finalising negotiations on the new interinstitutional
agreement was a relatively smooth one, and the Parliament and Council
managed to reach agreement on a number of modifications to the structural
fund regulations to enable formal approval to be achieved by June 1999.
Good cooperation also took place in the agriculture sector.

The interesting feature of the process of cooperation between the Council
and the Parliament on Agenda 2000 is that it threw up a twin paradox. First,
unlike previous negotiations on the IIA and the financial perspective, where
the Council had taken the view that the financial perspective amounts
agreed by the European Council were untouchable, the Council was willing
this time round to accept the Parliament's requests for an increase in the figures for heading 3 (internal policies), and a de facto increase in heading 5
expenditure (administration) by fixing the amounts net of staff contributions to pensions. This constituted an interesting precedent for a Parliament
ever on the lookout for extending its informal as well as formal powers. The
Council was willing to contemplate these concessions in circumstances
where, unlike at Edinburgh in 1992, the financial perspective represented an
overall volume of expenditure significantly well below what could be
achieved by the Parliament in the annual budgetary procedure by applying
the provisions of the treaty.

Second, the European Parliament, while receiving some minor concessions on its role in the conciliation procedure and on the establishment of a
new flexibility provision totalling €200 million per annum, was willing to

sign up to an IIA in which it in effect renounced some of its budgetary powers under article 272 of the treaty (amounting to tens of billions of euros over the period). Clearly, the Parliament was responding to the prevailing political climate by tacitly recognising that even if the treaty gave it extensive powers and the theoretical right to increase non-compulsory expenditure up to the 'maximum rate of increase', a mature and responsible Parliament could not in any case have wielded these treaty powers to their full extent in current economic circumstances.

In package negotiations of this type, success depends on certain important political objectives for key players being achieved in a presentable way. On the positive side, three broad political objectives evident from the start of the negotiations were largely achieved. For the cohesion countries, their prime concern was to ensure that future enlargement of the Union did not occur at the expense of the Union's structural and cohesion policies. The overall amounts agreed in the financial perspective for heading 2, which retain their status as spending targets rather than financial ceilings, have enabled the Union to consolidate its structural assistance at a level corresponding to 1999 average per capita aid intensity levels, thereby meeting their concern. The relatively small price to be paid in the form of a shopping list of side-payments to various member states was an acceptable part of the final political deal[12].

Secondly, an important political signal was sent to the applicant countries that in the context of a single currency, in which the applicants are all aspiring participants, enlargement of the Union will have to take place within tight budgetary constraints. The financial perspective was drawn up to accommodate the full cost of enlargement until 2006, along with a significant increase in the pre-accession strategy, while also substantially increasing the margins for unforeseen expenditure under the own resources ceiling fixed at 1.24% of EU gross national income (GNI). There will clearly be pressure to maintain that ceiling beyond 2006. Finally, politically unacceptable anomalies which had emerged in burden-sharing among the member states in the cost of financing the Union's budget were corrected to a sufficient extent to make the overall Agenda 2000 package politically acceptable without having recourse to new budgetary correction mechanisms.

There were, however, costs involved. One of the leitmotifs of the reform of the Union's structural operations was concentration of assistance. The question can be legitimately put as to whether the Union went sufficiently far down this road in preparing for enlargement. As far as heading 2 is concerned, to what extent can concentration of assistance be tightened further in the future? While both Ireland and Spain will probably have dropped out of the cohesion fund by 2006, and the 75% average EU GDP threshold for determining objective 1 eligibility has fallen as new and less wealthy member states joined the Union, it is easy to foresee the tough political bargaining ahead as the older member states seek to preserve as far as possible financial flows they had been receiving within the Union. Similar questions can also be raised about the scope of the CAP reform. Although reform has been achieved while maintaining an annual average ceiling on expenditure over the period of €40.5 billion (excluding rural development), the price for doing so was to undertake a less ambitious reform than that initially proposed. One of the peculiar features of agriculture spending is that reforms always cost more during the transitional stage to a new regime. Hence, the more ambitious the reform, the more expensive the cost. At the end of the day, cost-containment prevailed over reform ambition.

Over and above the political content of the reforms, there are fundamental lessons to be drawn about the conduct of future negotiations of this type within the Union. The fact that agreement was reached at all is in itself an achievement, given the prevailing political circumstances surrounding the negotiation. This was one of the most complex packages ever processed through the institutional system. It says much about the driving skills of the UK, Austrian and German presidencies that the vehicle was held firmly on the negotiating road without skidding off at the first bump. Agenda 2000 would still be under negotiation if a firm hand had not been used in managing the negotiating process by the presidency, the Commission and the Council secretariat. While there was never any guarantee that the method of the 'negotiating box' would work, what is certain is that it at least provided a reasonable opportunity for the Berlin European Council to reach agreement. As the Union enlarges to twenty-five and more member states, methods of work used by the Council need to ensure that in what is likely to be an even more difficult negotiating climate for the coming financial perspective, the Council is capable of reaching agreement at the right time. The upcoming negotiation on the new financial framework will constitute a litmus test for whether changes in Council working methods have been far-reaching enough for the Council to handle a serious package negotiation (see chapter 21).

While one element of that package – the overall ceilings for heading 1 under the new financial perspective (agriculture) – has already been agreed in the context of the accession negotiations and is included in a protocol annexed to the treaty of accession (although its precise coverage has not been established), the declared objective of certain net contributing member states to achieve ceilings totalling 1% of EU GNI (i.e., close to current levels of actual expenditure), means that a tense and hard-fought negotiation is definitely in prospect. Many of the issues described above will again emerge in the negotiation, albeit with different emphases, compounded by the changes brought about in the financial position of member states because of the effect of enlargement.

Chapter 17: The coordination of European policy by member states, by David Spence

This chapter focuses on national coordination of policy in the EU frame-work. It reviews EU policy-making through the lens of the governmental endeavour to defend 'national' interests. In this process of political persua-sion, national interests are treated as primordial for purely selfish national reasons (e.g. the UK is not yet ready to join the euro) or, because they are deemed to coincide with 'European' interests (e.g. too much regulation of labour market conditions is generally detrimental). In both cases, nego-tiation with other member states is required. So, willingness to bargain and to compromise underlies the process by which governments seek to maxi-mise their influence on the conduct and the outcome of EU business. The originality and the efficacy of the negotiation techniques involved are the subject of chapter 15. This chapter stresses how the relative efficiency of national policy coordination is a further important guide to effectiveness in achieving best possible outcomes (see Debbasch, 1987, and Wallace, 1973).

A report by the secretary-general of the Council in March 1999 (Council, 1999b) underlined the *raison d'être* of such an analysis of national and EU governance albeit in somewhat convoluted terms: 'The smooth functioning of the Council depends directly on that of national authorities, whether the political authority or the administration, involved in the Union's decision-making process'.

Analysing the smooth (or otherwise) functioning of national policy-making and coordination for European affairs requires a multi-level and multivariate analysis (see, e.g., Page and Wright, 1999. For foreign min-istries, see Hocking and Spence, 2002). Coordination is necessary at all the various levels of European affairs, from the initial influencing of the European Commission's legislative proposals through Council working parties to the meetings of the Council of Ministers and, ultimately, the European Council itself. But, whether national public administration has developed adequately to meet the coordination challenge of Europeanisation of domestic policy-making is not a moot point. National arrangements for policy-making in EU affairs are distinctly idiosyncratic. They diverge from typical domestic modes of administrative behaviour, where one might posit that rivalry between ministerial or sectoral interests is resolved through arbitration conducted for the most part by prime minis-terial offices. In EU affairs, such rivalry and arbitration exists, but it is made more complex by the existence of alliances and pressures from outside the

national polity. At the very least, this makes for a more complex and cir-
cuitous pattern of policy management.

   Stanley Hoffmann argues that the European Union is 'a collection of
bruised nations, whose states have traded visible and distinct power for diffuse collective interest.' (1995, p. 311) The governments of those nations
would probably argue that the collective interest is far from diffuse; it is
even measurable in terms of prosperity and world influence. But it does
imply that European integration requires more rather than less coordination
by national governments. This said, there is a clear discrepancy between the
influence on and involvement of all levels of national government in EU
affairs and the national arrangements for coordinating the resulting diverse
policy inputs and outputs. The European lobbying and negotiating system
is highly sophisticated. It is part of the originality of European governance
itself. But, it is not matched – at least, not in every member state – by governmental recognition of the challenge and operational consequences of
Europeanisation of the domestic policy agenda. Thus, as this chapter shows,
governments have diverse records in managing EU business to good effect.

National administration in the EU context

Since the Single European Act, and even more so since Maastricht,
Amsterdam and Nice, 'compromise' in European negotiations may often be
a euphemism for a policy reached after hard battle, with some member
states outvoted and others successful in setting the EU agenda along the
lines of their own national priorities. Indeed, European laws are frequently
even proposed by the Commission at the behest of one member state. As the
originator of all EC legislation, the Commission is 'lobbied' by governments
and the private sector, in the same way as the private sector has traditionally lobbied governments themselves. In the EU context, of course, lobbying
one government – even if it is 'one's own' – is less effective than lobbying a
sufficient number of national governments – and the Commission – to
ensure a qualified majority to pass the legislation or a blocking minority to
prevent it, when the Council comes to vote. The aim of lobbying in the early
stages of the legislative process might be to get the Commission to
strengthen a proposal or to abandon it. Constructing a coalition of interests
to encourage, dilute or delete a measure on the likely Council agenda is the
stuff of European politics. Some lobbying is part of pre-negotiation. It takes
place before and during the formal negotiations in Council and is an integral part of inter-action between member states and the European institutions until Council negotiations are completed and legislation is in force. For
this process to run smoothly, as the above mentioned report (Council, 1999b,
p. 75) stresses:

> 'Member States must have determined a starting position, having
> carried out the necessary internal arbitration;
>
> they must be in a position, in the course of the negotiations, to
> allow for the margins of manoeuvre essential for final agreement,
> which implies that the internal arbitration exercise should con-
> tinue throughout at the level of the national administrations;

the official position to emerge from such arbitration must be defended clearly and unequivocally in all Council formations and their subordinate bodies'

If, then, European negotiations are ultimately about how governments put their point across and defend their 'national' interests and about the search for acceptable compromise between those national interests, the way in which governments arrive at a definition of these national interests is an important part of the process. The ability of public administration to coordinate effectively between the potentially conflicting views of ministers and their officials and the various levels of government and the private sector likely to be affected by legislation is crucial. Governments must arrive at a 'line to take' in Brussels that will be consistently supported by all officials and ministers, and thus be an effective contribution to the EU policy process. A common feature of international negotiation, as one practitioner has observed, is that 'about nine tenths of my time of negotiation was done with my own side.' (Winham, 1977, p. 91) One former UK ambassador has echoed this, observing that:

'Behind this ambivalence of the "domestic" and the "foreign" lies a corresponding tug of professional interest and authority as between the diplomat and the technician. The chicken-and-egg question it poses is whether Community negotiation is best served by the traditional negotiating skills, reinforced by technical expertise from the home departments, or conversely by a staff of technical experts selected also for negotiating experience...(though) one and the same issue can be a "diplomatic" question in certain circumstances, and be – or become – a technical one in others or, just as often, vice-versa.' (Jackson, 1981, p. 42)

Certainly, the methods used by member states to prepare Council proceedings are the hinge upon which efficient problem-solving turns. National officials have two functions in the process. They are on the one hand subjected to influence from all levels of national government, and on the other from both the domestic and international private sector. They must adjudicate between the resultant pressures in determining just how the 'national' interest is to be defined. They are also required to exercise influence, not only on their counterparts in the Council, but also with their domestic constituency – both to gain support for bargains struck in Council and to ensure implementation of the subsequent legislation. Naturally, the national official is only one focus in the EU decision-making process. As Wessels has cogently put it, there is 'a golden triangle of Community civil servants, national civil servants and interest groups...based on elite interactions, trust and reputation...people whose loyalties remain primarily national but modify their expectations and behaviour to hold this highly valued system together.' (Wessels, 1990) So, while each national official's role remains vital in the overall EU perspective, it is not necessarily crucial; though individual governments continue to behave as if it were.

One consequence of this is a dilution and redefinition of the relationship between local/regional government, their local interest groups and their national governments (Jeffrey, 2000). 'Their' government may not end up defending 'their' line on a given issue, whereas the Commission or a majority of other governments may. Environmental pressure groups have had notable success in by-passing their own government or, after failing to persuade it of their convictions, achieving their aims by concertation with the Commission, or other national interest groups and governments – even the European Court. (Cichowski, 1999; Gehring, 1997) Indeed, it has been argued that the European institutions provide an authoritative alternative to purely national approaches in certain sectors (Kendall and Anheier, 1999). The exponential growth of European level competence has thus shifted the focus of interest groups from the purely national level, just as the working environment of many national officials has also shifted, as the control over policy shifts from the national to the European level (Mazey, 1993; Scharpf, 1997).

If the national stakes in European bargaining are confused and relativised in these ways, the job of coordinating a national position to be defended by national officials in the Council is crucial to effective overall management of member states' European policy. Government ministries influence Commission policy and other member states both directly and through the permanent representations in Brussels. And there are various points of access to decision-making both before the Commission reaches its final proposal and before the Council takes its final decision, months or even years later. Private sector lobbyists are active in promoting their interests throughout the process. So are national officials. Sometimes lobbyists and national officials work together. Sometimes, their views of the national interest conflict. Just as there are conflicts between private interest groups, there may also be conflicts between government departments, between a department and its 'clients' in the private sector and between the 'Brussels team' and the 'home team'. The need for national coordination is predicated on the existence of a functional division of responsibilities between ministries, but also on the realisation that each sectoral ministry might, without coordination and arbitration, view its sectoral interest as the national interest. Government in Western democracies relies on the ability of individual ministries with potentially divergent interests to work together as partners in the identification and defence of national interests. The understanding is that, in the last resort, a coordinated approach is required and that the resulting policy will be accepted as the national policy line once it is determined. Of course, states are more or less adept at achieving this. That is the point of this chapter. The difficulty for the analyst in this area is that politicians and officials can so define issues as to be either in the national interest or not, depending on the negotiating strategy they intend to employ. Here, for example, is a former British ambassador explaining this very point to a House of Lords select committee:

> 'very often you can achieve things more easily if you do it within a Community context. I think actually over the years this has been one of our weaknesses and perhaps one of the strengths of our partners, particularly the French, in that they have managed to identify – and I do not say this in a cynical sense, since this is what we need to be doing – their national interest with Community interest...and they can persuade people back home that to achieve a Community conclusion...is actually also in the national interest of that country. I think one is constantly striking

or trying to strike a balance between what you might call a narrow sectoral or sectionally narrow interest and a broader interest, which may be in the broader national interest as well as in the broader Community interest.' (Palliser, 1985, p. 216)

Since the potential rivalry of ministries in the national government setting explains the requirement for coordination, an analysis of the EU decision-making process and the points in the process where national coordination is necessary helps situate the crucial points in national policy formation. Box 17.1 illustrates these various points by juxtaposing progress in EU decision-making with an 'ideal-type' of national policy-making and coordination. The chart adapts somewhat the useful policy coordination scale developed by Metcalfe (1994).

If this is the model, then how should the national input into the EU policy process be conducted and how should conflicts of responsibility, power and policy within and between government ministries in member states be resolved? The issues arising are common to all governments, though each member state's arrangements to fulfil them differ in application and effectiveness. Indeed, since the first edition of this book, the realisation has grown that thought ought to be given by governments themselves on such issues as 'whether coordination and arbitration bodies or fora to prepare EU negotiations are in the right place in the government machine; whether they have adequate administrative and political weight; whether the relay procedures work well; and whether they are capable of making a sustained contribution throughout the decision-making process' (Council, 1999b, p. 77). This is the view expressed by senior officials of the Council secretariat. Future editions of this book will doubtless describe whether member states heeded the message.

The conduct of European Union affairs by governments

There are three integral parts of the machinery of policy-making and coordination in EU affairs common to all EU governments; individual ministries, i.e., the 'lead ministries'; ministries with a monitoring and coordination role, i.e., usually the ministries of foreign affairs (though in some member states this role is shared between foreign ministries and economics or finance ministries); and the permanent representations to the European Union. Permanent representations are often considered extensions of foreign ministries, since the permanent representative is customarily a senior diplomat and the permanent representation itself exercises many traditional diplomatic functions. Yet most permanent representations are at least equally staffed by officials from domestic ministries, who, while temporarily occupying the traditional foreign service grade of 'first secretary' or 'counsellor', will later rejoin their home department.

In some member states there are additional national coordination mechanisms. These may either stand outside the ministerial framework, as in the case of the European secretariat of the British cabinet office or the French secretariat général pour la coordination interministérielle des affaires économiques européennes (SGCI), or be found in other ministries, such as the German economics ministry.

Box 17.1: *A European decision-making and coordination chart*

Negotiation stage	National coordination
'Gleam in Commission's eye'	Independent decision-making by lead ministry to decide policy line
Commission announces likely policy initiative	Trigger mechanisms flag up potential inter-ministerial problems
Commission consultative meetings with member states and interested parties	Lead ministry reviews for potential implications for other ministries, informs concerned ministries and foreign ministry, decides lobbying strategy, takes soundings with other governments and decides potential approaches to commissioners in consultation with foreign ministry and /or central coordination mechanism
Commission meeting to formalise proposal	Inter-ministerial meeting of officials responsible for EU affairs reviews implications and decides line to take
Commission proposal to Council	Consultations between ministries to a) review points of divergence b) search for agreement c) arbitrate between differences d) settle government line
European Parliament begins review	Foreign ministries coordinate instruction to permanent representation to present national line to national MEPs
Council working group deliberates	Lead ministry official or permanent representation official presents national line and reports on progress As ground shifts, further inter-ministerial coordination meetings in national capital
Coreper	Meeting in national capitals between permanent representative and senior officials/ministers
Council	Agree limits on ministerial margin of manoeuvre - review central priorities and areas subject to negotiation, agree fall-back positions
European Council	Inter-ministerial coordination to agree possible elements in package deal

Lead departments

While the European Commission works closely with permanent representations, individual Commission directorates-general also maintain direct links with domestic ministries in the member states. In some sectors, where the Commission manages policy directly, such as the structural funds, this is essential. The Commission relies on ministries in member states to implement a good deal of policy, but retains close links with the ministries concerned in order to ensure policy is implemented effectively. This is particularly the case of agriculture, where, for example, ministries of agriculture and intervention boards are responsible for the day-to-day implementation of Commission decisions in the field of agricultural price fixing. Ministries responsible in member states for policy areas of exclusive Community competence live a symbiotic relationship with the Commission's DGs. They have also developed close links with their counterparts in other member states. Domestic ministries in member states have 'Europeanised' considerably in the years of the EU's existence (Mény *et al*, 1996).

The pattern for the evolution of European policy-making in domestic ministries has generally been based on an initial phase where the appropriate specialised unit or department of a ministry managed European aspects of individual policies. Overall coordination and monitoring of policy rested during this phase with 'international divisions'. These were responsible not only for Community affairs but all international aspects of the policies within the responsibility of the ministry concerned. Subsequently, as workloads increased, international divisions spawned 'European coordinating divisions'. European divisions of major ministries rarely become involved in day-to-day arrangements for specific technical negotiations or implementation of Community legislation. Policy management typically remains the task of functional departments involved. Coordinating divisions come into play when overlapping issues produce the need to coordinate the principles of policy as opposed to the detail.

The management of single market matters is a case in point. Here, hundreds of functional departments defend their own policy line, but coordinating units, when they work well, establish principles to which all adhere – a line on 'comitology', for example, or on the appropriate degree of national versus EU competence. It is the coordination units in lead ministries which are present at interministerial coordination meetings. Technical desk officers in charge of specific legislation are brought into the process when reaching an agreed interministerial line involves the technical detail as opposed to differences of principle. They also appear when the policy area has thrown up problems to be dealt with horizontally or when the coordination divisions of domestic ministries are working in close liaison with foreign ministries in preparing specialised meetings of the Council and ensuring that the national input into the negotiations is coherently prepared. Lead ministries typically function within highly decentralised decision-making systems. A system common to all member states has emerged where individual ministries enjoy a high margin of manoeuvre in their Community dealings without undue interference of a centralised kind.

What then of the need for coordination? Coordination in terms of information flows to other ministries should be routine. Guidance from foreign ministries should only be required in cases of disagreement or where policy implications are complex. Where national systems differ is in the strength or weakness of the reporting and coordination mechanisms, which ensure information flows and that agreed policy lines are respected by officials from all ministries. In such decentralised systems, if information flows according to agreed guidelines, the potential dangers of ministries 'going it alone' are tempered by a series of trigger mechanisms, which ensure other ministries are brought into the process and alarm bells are sounded at appropriate moments before damage is done.

The role of foreign ministries

Foreign ministries provide the institutional framework of day-to-day coordination through European Union departments and the permanent representations in Brussels. They monitor ministerial activity and coordinate between national capitals and Brussels through, usually, two European Union departments, one specialised in policies with domestic implications, such as internal market, environment, energy etc, and one specialised in external issues, such as trade, development and the common foreign and security policy. This mirrors the division of labour between Coreper I (domestic – deputy permanent representatives) and Coreper II (external affairs and general coordination – the permanent representatives themselves). Departments in foreign ministries dealing with bilateral relations between the states concerned are, to a certain limited extent, involved, but do not take the lead in European affairs.

Two other functional areas are covered by varying arrangements in member states; coordination of the presidency, sometimes an ad hoc unit usually set up some twelve months before a member state takes on the presidency of the Council, sometimes a strengthening of existing arrangements; and arrangements for the coordination of national input into the intergovernmental pillars of the TEU, common foreign and security policy and justice and home affairs (see chapters 4 and 6).

The EU departments

In principle, European Union departments in foreign ministries fulfil four functions. The first is the routine coordination function of daily business. This is partly a 'post-box' function of receiving and distributing all material from Brussels, including Commission reports and proposals, notes concerning the day's meetings, etc. Foreign ministries also transmit, in principle, material from domestic ministries in national capitals to permanent representations for further handling. But it is important to note the caveat 'in principle'. Since the widespread use of fax machines and e-mail, and the increased proficiency of domestic ministries to coordinate in their own policy areas, foreign ministries are increasingly bypassed. The volume of Community business probably justifies this, though it does represent a weakening of the chain of command. However, in principle, foreign ministries provide the key link in the coordination process by ensuring feedback and consultation between domestic ministries on policy issues.

This process of mutual influencing engenders increased cohesiveness between officials and departments in ministries responsible for European affairs. The role of the foreign ministries is to ensure information flows between the lead ministries with their administrative and policy-making autonomy. The system, if it functions well, is based on a high sense of collegiality. Where it functions badly, as in some member states without a tradition of domestic policy coordination between ministries, or where coalition governments give rise to interministerial rivalry of a political nature, the deleterious effects on policy-making are easily perceived by other member states.

The second major function of the EU departments in foreign ministries is the preparation of briefings for Council meetings. Here the essential coordination role of foreign ministries is clearly demonstrated. While individual ministries could arguably prepare alone meetings in which their own minister takes part, each Council must be seen as one part of a complex pattern of ministerial meetings where trade-offs in negotiations can draw extremely diverse policy areas into package deals. The mere fact, also, that much of Council decision-making is settled by means of the 'A item' procedure discussed in chapter 3 means ministers often have an agenda before them with subjects, albeit not for discussion, completely outside their purview. Given their overall responsibility for coordination of ministerial meetings, foreign ministries become a partner in domestic ministries' decision-making processes.

A third function is responsibility for the European common foreign and security policy. Here, the prime tool of an emerging European foreign policy remains the *acquis communautaire*. Thus, first pillar treaty articles are necessary to enforce concrete political measures taken in the second (CFSP) pillar, such as economic assistance, sanctions and changes in trade policy. Again the obvious need to coordinate the two areas of policy-making demonstrates the need for foreign ministries to play a coordinating role. In this particular case, there is an added complication arising from the nature of the three-pillar Maastricht structure. As chapter 4 makes clear, the decision to keep 'a single institutional structure' for the work of all three pillars created a series of problems with regard to the *'passerelles'* between the pillars. It also created a further layer of coordination mechanisms necessary to ensure that deliberations and decisions in the second and third pillar framework reach the General Affairs Council having transited through 'the single institutional structure', i.e., through Coreper and not merely through meetings of the PSC, and CATS. Coreper becomes involved since it is the coordinating body and negotiating instance of last resort before foreign ministers and heads of state or government meet. Yet the tradition built up through the years of European political cooperation was that political directors from foreign ministries performed these functions in the intergovernmental area of CFSP. There was considerable discussion about shifting the coordination responsibility from the PSC to Coreper, so that PSC ambassadors feed issues ripe for discussion in Council through the Coreper machinery. Coreper thus performs the coordination function, reconciling, where necessary, the aims of CFSP and the means of the first pillar.

Increasingly, however, the foreign ministries' role of objective arbitrator and coordinator of EU business may be compromised by the fact that CFSP introduces a distinct ministerial interest on the part of the coordinator. It will be instructive to observe whether national administrations find the need to create coordinating mechanisms outside the foreign ministries in order to avoid the challenge from domestic ministries that the coordinators (officials from the foreign ministry) are not masking their own foreign ministry interests in the rhetoric of the coordination of ministerial interests.

Finally, tasks of a horizontal coordination nature, such as the preparation and participation in intergovernmental conferences or the management of crises, such as the EU-Canada fishing dispute of spring 1995, usually lie with foreign ministries. But these are issues where the necessary coordination of domestic ministries raises the potential for substantial disagreement about the policy responsibilities involved. In such cases, where the susceptibilities and proprietary feelings of the coordinated are at stake, those member states with coordination mechanisms outside the foreign ministry benefit from an added focus of independent authoritative coordination and decision-making. The costs and benefits of such systems are reviewed below, but first a fundamental issue of foreign policy must be addressed, namely the role in EU affairs of bilateral embassies and the bilateral departments in foreign ministries.

Bilateral Relations in the EU

EU departments in foreign ministries run alongside other departments which retain responsibility for bilateral relations with European countries whether members or not of the European Community – Western, Eastern or Southern European departments. How far it is possible to dissociate specifically bilateral relations from the multilateral relations of the Community is a moot point. Depending on the nature and extent of the bilateral relations involved, the role of these bilateral departments is more or less great. The relations of the larger member states with major partners in other fora, such as the G8 or NATO, clearly encourage bilateral relations to retain a high political flavour in addition to the various low-political and trade related issues. But for smaller member states, there is a sense in which (apart from cultural relations or export promotion) most interest lies in concertation with others in the EU framework.

However, since domestic ministries now manage their own bilateral relations with their opposite numbers (and with pressure groups) in other member states, good coordination requires bilateral embassies and ministries of foreign affairs to be kept informed of direct approaches. Yet, it is clearly impossible, if only for reasons of staffing, for foreign ministries or bilateral embassies to conduct or even monitor closely such bilateral relations across the gamut of domestic policy areas now part of the EU purview.

The role of the bilateral European departments of foreign ministries is thus arguably in need of redefinition. It may decline as domestic ministries take on increasing responsibility for European affairs and European policy ceases to be regarded as 'foreign policy'. On the other hand, as the deepening and widening processes accelerate after the IGC and the enlargement of EU membership in 2004, new policy orientations may prove necessary. Indeed, from time to time special events already lead to increased activity by bilateral departments of foreign ministries in the EU context. For example, German unification saw a need for bilateral European departments to coordinate fact-finding operations in Bonn and other Community capitals in order to provide domestic ministries with the necessary data to assess the merits of Commission proposals for transitional measures applicable in the former German Democratic Republic. (Spence, 1991) Setting negotiating strategy across the gamut of Community policy required detailed briefing on the attitudes of individual German ministries and those of other member states. On this model bilateral departments could be drawn far more into the European decision-making process, thus ensuring more sophisticated preparation of European Community negotiations. Smaller countries, however, with far fewer functional issues to defend, clearly could not engage in the same degree of information gathering and possibly pre-negotiation as France and the UK in this specific case. Indeed, this emphasises the general point that the larger and older the national administration, the more the likelihood of an effective national style of European policy-making.

One radical option in terms of the future of relations between functional, domestic ministries, bilateral and EU departments in foreign ministries would be the creation of specifically European ministries. In the UK one of the recommendations of a review of foreign policy machinery was a 'merger of the home civil service and the diplomatic service and the creation within the combined service of a foreign service group which would staff most of the jobs in the UK and overseas.' (Central Policy Review Staff, 1997, p. xv) A combination of the external trade divisions of the department of trade and the ministry of overseas development into an integrated department of overseas affairs was proposed. The aim was to reduce the duplication of effort between parallel units and to improve coordination (Ibid., 20.43-47 and annex Q. See also Wallace, 1972, and Allen, 2002). Though nothing came of these proposals in the late 1970s, the qualitative leaps in Community affairs made in the 1980s and 1990s may well engender such reflections again – and in other EU member states. After all, most member states do not command the resources nor have the quantity of interests to defend of the larger member states. Resources and interests may reinforce competitive bureaucracies. Where both are limited there is a clear incentive to rationalise administration.

The permanent representations to the European Community

It is perhaps wrong to view the permanent representations as the extended arm of foreign ministries. More than half of the staff in permanent representations are drawn from domestic ministries. First secretaries with responsibility for technical affairs such as the internal market, transport or customs and excise are thus usually secondees from the domestic ministries concerned. Indeed, over time, the balance has switched from foreign ministry staffing of such posts to the representation of the interests concerned by the lead ministries. This is one of the concrete manifestations of the change in the nature of foreign policy-making stressed in the introduction to this chapter. Officials in national capitals responsible for policy-making in the areas concerned and requiring to visit Brussels for negotiations have a somewhat different relationship to the first secretary depending on whether he or she is a foreign ministry appointee or from the relevant domestic ministry.

As the permanent contact point between national capitals and the Community institutions, the permanent representations have a series of roles necessary for efficient government coordination of policy and for the defence of national interests in negotiations with other member states and the European Commission. The permanent representative himself (it was only recently that the first female permanent representative was appointed – see chapter 11 – although a number of deputies have been women) attends Coreper, itself the prime coordinator for the General Affairs Council and the European Council. As the *Financial Times* once remarked 'One of the best-kept secrets in Brussels is that 90% of EU decisions are resolved informally in Coreper before they even reach ministers.' (Barber, 1995) This may be an exaggeration. One academic estimates the total of final decisions taken by all the senior committees as more likely 70% (Wallace, 1990). Ministerial confirmation is provided, though with tongue in cheek, by the former UK trade minister, Alan Clark:

'Not, really, that it makes the slightest difference to the conclusions of a meeting what Ministers say at it. Everything is decided, horse-traded off, by officials at COREPER.... The Ministers arrive on the scene at the last minute, hot, tired, ill, or drunk... read out their piece, and depart.' (Clark, 1994, p. 139)

Permanent representations fulfil five key functions; they are a Brussels base for national negotiators, coordinate policy and procedures with the European institutions, interact directly with the representatives of other member states, maintain links with the press and provide the prime negotiators in most meetings at working party level in the Council. The permanent representations thereby mirror, on the spot, the coordinating role of the EU departments in national ministries of foreign affairs, while providing access to the main actors in the negotiating and lobbying framework, whether with the Commission, the Parliament or the other member states in the Council framework. However, where meetings are highly technical or scheduled to take place simultaneously with others falling under the portfolio of the permanent representation's officer concerned, they are attended by the appropriate desk officer from lead ministries in national capitals. Often, meetings are attended, at least part of the time, by officials both from the lead ministry and from the permanent representation.

The permanent representations provide a central point in Brussels for visits, whether at official or ministerial level. In the UK case the office of the permanent representation is a stone's throw from the Commission's headquarters and those of the Council. The European Parliament's offices and committee rooms are within walking distance. Other permanent representations are somewhat further away, but the institutions are accessible to even the most distant within a fifteen-minute drive. Permanent representations also keep a suite of rooms in the Council building where most Council working group meetings take place. From here domestic ministries can be telephoned or faxed in case of need and last minute briefing can take place in private. Negotiators from national capitals customarily arrive before

meetings to coordinate with the desk officers of the permanent representations, the presidency or the Council secretariat and engage in last-minute
pre-negotiations with other delegations.

Notice of meetings and their agendas are transmitted by the Council secretariat to permanent representations and the Commission. The permanent
representations send these to foreign ministries and/or the relevant ministry
concerned. Ministries often find it then necessary to get permanent representations to contact the Commission, the presidency and the Council secretariat to obtain a precise idea of the content of the meeting. Usually, of
course, individual working groups will continue with issues unsettled at the
previous meeting, but events and negotiating positions will have moved on
in the meantime. Discussing new initiatives may be the real purpose of the
meeting, so preparation by information gathering and bilateral lobbying by
the permanent representation is therefore essential.

Usually, regular visitors to Council working parties will know their
opposite numbers in ministries in other member states or in the
Commission and will take direct soundings by telephone. This may seem
an obvious route, but it was striking over the years how reticent traditionally domestic ministries were in cultivating the necessary contacts to
ensure tactical preparation of meetings. The absence of foreign languages
on the part of national officials in domestic ministries may have been part
of the problem. Today, mastering French or English has increasingly
become a prerequisite for work in the coordination departments of
national domestic ministries. The alternative is total reliance on the permanent representations, formerly a reason for domestic ministries to
attempt to ensure that one of their own staff covers the appropriate portfolio in the permanent representation.

Desk officers in permanent representations maintain daily links with their
opposite numbers in permanent representations from other member states.
They lunch together in the Council cafeteria or in the many restaurants
seemingly functioning precisely for the purpose of providing a social venue
for the furtherance of Community business. Yet, dependence on the permanent representations to provide all the background briefing, and ultimately
conduct the bilateral discussions which are an essential part of the pre-negotiation process, means lead ministries risk loss of control of the process. The
foreign ministries and permanent representations simply cannot be
expected to see all the implications of technical issues, as many lead ministry negotiators have learnt to their cost. Permanent representations, while
not reluctant to be involved in pre-negotiation, are overwhelmed by tight
agendas and heavy workloads. There is thus a conscious recognition of the
responsibility of functional ministries. If the monitoring and coordination
mechanisms function well, such decentralisation is highly effective. If it
fails, or has simply not been effectively provided for, decentralisation can
lead to uncoordinated and thus ineffective performance at Coreper and in
Council meetings.

For the permanent representations, heavy workload is compounded by a
major management problem arising from the short notice often given for
meetings. One of the administrative problems in running the presidency is
matching administrative requirements (rooms, timetables and availability
of staff to chair meetings) with political priorities. Complaints are common

that meetings are called at short notice, papers from the Commission or the general secretariat of the Council provided late or with some language versions not available even at the time of the meeting, or that the presidency has simply not had time to provide adequate distillations of previous meetings to facilitate effective preparation and coordination of a suddenly announced new meeting. Once again, those member states with centralised and efficient coordination mechanisms can usually rise to such challenges. The others are simply less effective in the negotiations.

Permanent representations also liaise closely with the national and foreign press in Brussels and control closely the information provided. Visiting delegates from national capitals customarily leave press briefings with the press officer and the desk officer responsible for the relevant subject area. Much journalistic reporting concerns technical progress on specific legislation, but even this can be part of the increasingly politicised agenda of EU business. Journalists constantly vie for information from all sources, not least from the permanent representations, and its provision can have effects on subsequent negotiations by alerting interest groups and thus encouraging the lobby to pressure governments to change their positions. In addition to skilful use of information and communication to the press, permanent representations need to keep a watching brief on the process, since leaking information or sounding off about another delegation's reticence to compromise can have an effect on the outcome of negotiations themselves. Managing press relations is therefore an important part of the negotiating process.

Permanent representations are the obvious focus for monitoring and influencing developments in the European institutions, whether as active negotiators in Council meetings or lobbyists. The Commission's role in the Community is as initiator of all Community legislation and executive for a large part of it. It also acts as mediator between the institutions and so-called 'guardian of the treaties', a role which often brings it into conflict with individual member states over questions of implementation of Community legislation. Permanent representations are involved in monitoring the Commission's activities in all these areas and in maintaining close links with Commission officials involved in them. They feed information to national capitals and represent national interests where the Commission's policies are thought to conflict with national priorities. Permanent representations thus become a prime focus for the private sector lobby as well as the lobbying arm of national government. Their job, in short, is to get early warning of Commission initiatives and to divert, correct or encourage them. This may be in the field of new legislation or in the field of implementation, where national governments may have failed to implement correctly and risk cases in the European Court of Justice. The permanent representations' role in bilateral negotiation with and lobbying of the Commission is thus clearly crucial.

In practice, all these tasks require officials in permanent representations to maintain close contacts with their opposite numbers in the Commission, forming a kind of permanent national lobby with the aim of influencing the Commission's forward thinking and obtaining early warning of proposals. To be effective permanent representations must act long before formal notice of new proposals, when proposals are mere gleams in the

Commission's eye. After consultation with national ministries, permanent representations encourage those proposals which suit national priorities and attempt to divert the Commission from those ideas which governments find inimical. They do this by making lead ministries' views known to the Commission or setting out implications Commission officials may not have thought through.

As to monitoring European Parliament affairs, usually two officials cover relevant committees and plenary sessions, reporting back to national capitals on the handling of legislation affecting individual ministerial responsibilities. They also construct close links with MEPs from other member states, so that in case of need they can help domestic ministries lobby parliamentarians on specific issues. The permanent representations maintain similar links to the European Economic and Social Committee, the Committee of the Regions and, of course to the Brussels representatives of private sector interests.

Overall coordination

The day-to-day coordination usually provided by foreign ministries is but one part of the coordination function. Ensuring information flows between colleagues with interests in other ministries is essential, but conceptually different from coordination as mediation and conciliation between rival ministerial interests. Member states coordinate between sectoral ministerial interests in a variety of different ways. The former secretary-general of the European Commission, Emile Noël, himself a Frenchman, told the *Financial Times* in October 1987 that the national administration for which he had the greatest respect was the British. (19 October 1987) Noël's view of the efficiency of UK coordination of EU policy-making has been confirmed by the research findings of the European Institute of Public Administration in Maastricht (see Metcalfe, 1987 and Metcalfe and Zapico Goni, 1991), which concluded that the UK and Denmark scored highest on an efficient coordination scale. Notwithstanding the apparent excellence of the machinery of these two countries, even the UK and Denmark have very different methods of coordination, though both seem to spend a good deal of energy in blocking others from progressing down the integration path – and not always successfully.

In the UK (Spence, 1993) and French (Lequesne, 1993) cases, the Cabinet Office and the SGCI are the central coordinators under the direct responsibility of the prime minister. Essentially, coordination is thus kept above the interests and objectives of individual ministers and their departments. As described above, the Foreign and Commonwealth Office (FCO) and the Quai d'Orsay run much of the practical day-to-day coordination. But the term 'coordination' means two different things. There is a clear difference between day to day monitoring and coordination and the arbitration role played by the central coordination mechanism in these two states. As Metcalfe has argued:

'attempts to rely on a central arbiter to "coordinate" are very likely to fail or prove cumbersome. Either the arbiter will be overloaded by coordination problems that could be more simply and effectively managed by the use of subordinate capacities, or the arbiter will spend a great deal of time recapitulating the lower order coordination functions; ascertaining the division of responsibilities among organisations, establishing a common understanding of the situation, promoting feedback and consultation and generally attempting to do for the organisations involved what, in a better developed network, they might do for themselves. Until all these things are done the arbitration function cannot be performed satisfactorily. And, when they are, it may prove unnecessary.' (Metcalfe, 1994, p. 10)

The question nevertheless arises of whether the Foreign Office or the Quai d'Orsay could take over the policy coordination role of the cabinet office and the SGCI as well. After all, other member states do not have an overarching coordination mechanism of this kind. The French and British position on this is similar. The problem is that foreign ministries are but one of many ministries with interests to defend in cases where an interministerial line is needed. The case of CFSP and inter-pillar coordination has already been mentioned. Indeed, domestic ministries often resent the views of ministries of foreign affairs, since their lead in specific policy areas is thereby undermined. One permanent representative has even informed journalists, perhaps with tongue in cheek, that he is known at home as the 'traitor' to, rather than the representative of, the national cause. (Barber, 1995: The German permanent representative was using a play on words in the German, describing himself as the 'Verräter' (traitor) rather than 'Vertreter' (representative).) Though Community membership has clearly blurred the distinction between domestic and foreign policy making, there is a clear sense in which bureaucratic rivalry exists and where the question of which ministry has competence arises.

The French and British agree that overall European strategy in the EU framework (in particular the arbiter role) should not be determined by a ministry with its own interests to defend; say, the economics ministry, as in the German case. (See Wessels and Rometsch, 1996.) In Belgium and Germany, responsibility for coordination and arbitration is shared between the foreign and economics ministries. Denmark leaves the foreign ministry responsible, while in Greece there is rivalry for power between the Ministry of the National Economy and the Ministry of Foreign Affairs. The UK's Cabinet Office and the French SGCI avoid the accusation of partisanship often levelled at these different arrangements in other member states. The following chart summarises (and clearly oversimplifies) responsibilities in member states (for more details, see Rometsch and Wessels, 1996).

The French and British systems can thus be seen as the centralised end of a continuum of European policy coordination, with the decentralised and, at times, uncoordinated German system at the other end. The French system does have one potentially destabilising feature in that the SGCI reports to the prime minister, though foreign affairs remains the reserved domain of the presidency. This may not matter in times of harmony between the two offices, but periods of 'cohabitation' between a president and a prime minister with different views, though rare in the system, bring about their own problems for policy-making (see Lequesne, 1987, 1988). Even apart from 'cohabitation' a senior official of the French permanent representation in Brussels once told the author that 'the SGCI is the principle – interministerial vying is the reality.' (Lequesne, 1996) This should not really be surprising. In 1992, for example, there were on average five conflict resolution meetings a day at the SGCI (Guyomarch *et al*, 1998, p. 59), and 'the key actors in Brussels have remained the foreign affairs minister, the permanent representative and his deputy, all diplomats, trained to find compromises, while most of those in Paris who coordinate negotiating positions for the Brussels team are from 'domestic ministries', whose goals are to find best practices and policies. The match between the two does not always work.' (Ibid., p. 72)

But the cabinet office and SGCI arrangements do carry authority with ministries. The cabinet office was described to the author by one senior cabinet office official as 'a bureaucrat's mechanism as opposed to a politician's'. Given the presidency/prime ministerial stakes in the French system, perhaps the SGCI is the reverse, but the overall effect of the coordination methods in the two countries is probably the same, since EU policy coordination is highly centralised and highly effective.

Understandably, though, individual ministries sometimes complain when their own policies are questioned by others. They also complain when their line in their own area of policy may have horizontal implications for others, which in turn lead to debate and questioning on the principle involved and where policy purity might be sacrificed. There can, for example, be cases where a particular policy line on an issue conflicts with a general political line. It may suit national government priorities to have a new Community policy in a particular area, but if the result is more government spending or political implications in other areas, the line taken in European negotiations may well be cautious. A good example was some member states' desire to keep the European Parliament out of deliberations on the common foreign and security policy. The European Parliament achieves involvement through its ability to control spending when the Community budget is involved. Officials used to admit privately that it would otherwise suit their government to keep spending on the CFSP within the European budgetary framework in order to avoid ad hoc increases in national expenditure. Meanwhile CFSP now formally falls to the Community budget.

It will be interesting to note whether spending on the new European security and defence policy follows the same trend. The European Councils of Cologne, Helsinki, Feira and Nice, while developing ESDP considerably, never questioned the national basis of military funding involved and the reliance on national 'pledging', the subject of a specific conference under the 2000 French presidency. Similarly, a committee procedure accepted in one policy area might prove inimical to other ministries if the Commission or other member states take it as a precedent. So a benefit of independent coordination rather than leaving a lead ministry to assume the coordination role as well is the centralised, impartial legal and administrative expertise which thus develops and which can be used to the advantage of all ministries in their negotiations. The next section analyses the precise purposes of EU coordination and draws some conclusions about the emergence of a European policy-making and coordination style, regardless of national differences in the approach.

Box 17.2: *Member States' coordination mechanisms in EU-15*

AUSTRIA

1. Routine coordination by foreign ministry.
2. The Federal Chancellery is responsible for preparing/coordinating the European Council and big issues like IGCs.

BELGIUM

1. Economic Affairs and Foreign Ministry share coordination responsibility, with two coordination committees; the interministerial economic committee and the Europe coordination weekly briefings committee respectively. Dual language use complicates.
2. The government has two ministerial committees – the foreign policy committee and the economic and social coordination committee.

DENMARK

1. The permanent secretary of the department of economic affairs in the foreign ministry chairs the EU coordinating committee, but lead ministries tend to chair coordinating sub-groups of officials from concerned ministries.
2. One European ministerial committee chaired by Foreign Minister.

FINLAND

1. Ministry of Foreign Affairs coordinates at all levels.

FRANCE

1. SGCI (Secretariat-General of the Inter-ministerial Committee for European Economic Cooperation), reporting to Prime Minister, provides centralised coordination, except for budget matters or CFSP, where Ministry of Finance and Foreign Ministry provide.
2. SGCI responsible, through PM, for coordination at ministerial level.

GERMANY

1. A committee of permanent state secretaries coordinates a highly decentralised system, where ministries enjoy considerable independence reinforced by the federal system and coalition politics.
2. Coordination made difficult by controversy between foreign, economics, finance and agricultural ministries.

GREECE

1. Ministry of National Economy and Ministry of Foreign Affairs vie for coordination power. High degree of lead ministry responsibility.
2. Prime Minister chairs an interministerial committee (KYSYM) for orientation and coordination.

IRELAND

1. High ministerial autonomy under Foreign Ministry supervision through European Communities Committee it chairs.
2. Minister of State for European Affairs reports directly to Taoiseach and provides high level coordination and arbitration.

ITALY	1. General coordination by Directorate-General for Economic Affairs in Foreign Ministry. 2. Minister of Coordination of European Affairs (reporting to PM) ensures higher level coordination and arbitration.
LUXEMBOURG	1. Foreign Ministry coordinates a highly decentralised structure, where lead ministries have high degree of autonomy. 2. Inter-ministerial ad hoc committees created to solve potential ministerial clashes.
NETHERLANDS	1. Interministerial Coordination Committee on European Integration (COCO) chaired by Foreign Ministry, but much informal coordination precedes. 2. Council of European Affairs (REZ) chaired by PM.
PORTUGAL	1. Ministerial autonomy is high. Two focuses of regular coordination – the European Union Interministerial Committee (CIUE), composed of officials from each ministry, chaired by the state secretary for EU affairs, himself head of the second committee, the State Secretariat for EU affairs (SEUE), which is an integral part of the foreign ministry. 2. The SEUE is the main focus of political leadership and coordination, since the CIUE provides only day-to-day coordination with no binding instructions at national level.
SPAIN	1. State Secretariat for the European Community (SECE) in Foreign Ministry chairs Interministerial Committee for Economic Affairs related to the EC (CIAERCE). 2. Governmental Delegated Committee for European Affairs (CDGAE) chaired by Ministry of Economy and Finance brings interested ministers together. Cabinet of the President of the Government further source of power.
SWEDEN	1. Ministries enjoy wide ranging autonomy under supervision of the European Secretariat of the Foreign Ministry, itself nominally independent, yet staffed by Foreign Ministry officials. 2. State Secretaries meet with European Secretariat in the chair on Tuesdays to coordinate for Coreper and Council meetings. Unresolved interministerial issues are arbitrated by the (Foreign Ministry) Minister for European Affairs and, ultimately, in cabinet.
UNITED KINGDOM	1. Lead ministries fairly autonomous under Foreign Ministry supervision. Cabinet Office, reporting to PM, provides coordination and arbitration function. 2. Cabinet Office coordinates at ministerial level.

The purpose of coordination and ministries' needs

As we have seen, there are three premises on which the need for policy coordination in the EU framework is based. Negotiation in the full Council forum is prefaced by lobbying and positioning by states and private interests. Bilateral pre-negotiation and coalition-building is the norm. Individual ministries take the lead in their policy areas, but the activities of ministries are not mutually exclusive and they cannot, in the 'national interest', be left to decide policy alone. Coordination ensures a common national line, a horizontal approach to the analysis of the implications and an increased ability to manage the environment. In practical terms, the objectives of coordination are:

- Foreseeing opportunities to promote national interests;
- Planning damage limitation;
- Elaborating negotiating strategy;
- Assessing trade-offs which may serve national interests in other areas;
- Centralising authoritative guidance on EU issues;
- Monitoring deadlines for implementation of legislation by lead ministries;
- Foreseeing legal implications of proceedings in the Court.

The need for coordination arises in practice as a response to various kinds of ministerial demand. The first is line-clearing. Individual ministries may know exactly what they require in terms of the negotiation of a specific piece of legislation, but may wish to ensure that other ministries are informed and have sorted out particular points of emphasis from their own point of view. They may also not have requisite expertise in a given area and wish to get 'cover' by ensuring there are no unforeseen implications. Ministries of health may, for example, have decided their own view on the Community's cancer action programme. But they need to ensure that potentially harmful spill-over into neighbouring areas has been foreseen and that lines have thus been cleared with the ministries concerned. Agreement by member states to a cancer action programme in the 1980s led subsequently to a Commission proposal (long resisted by key cigarette producing member states, but finally agreed) for a total ban on tobacco advertising with far-reaching implications for ministries of trade, industry, finance and taxation.

Effective coordination and the discussion and direct personal contact between officials that this entails can resolve such issues between officials and thus obviate the need for ministerial discussion. It also ensures that all ministries have a chance to analyse implications for their own policy areas. Without coordination, ministries could remain oblivious to such Community developments and to the principles involved. The risk, other-wise, is a public statement by one or other ministry that directly affects the negotiating stance of the lead ministry; opening the oven, as it were, before the cake has risen. The aim of coordination is to reach common objectives in the effort to ensure that all parts of national government do not so much 'toe the line', but accept that the 'line' is the expression of the 'national interest' as opposed to the specific functional interests of ministries involved.

Part of the line clearing function is the need for advice and guidance. Individual ministries may need guidance on procedural, tactical and strategic issues in negotiations. They may need procedural advice on the legal base of a Commission proposal, the scope of the Commission's powers or whether or not to contest an issue in the European Court. Individual ministries may also need guidance on 'comitology' – committee procedures. Advice on negotiating techniques and procedures is provided in general coordination meetings, where tactical measures required in negotiating are addressed and ministries confer with others about where compromises can be made without negative horizontal implications. Judging when to lobby a Commissioner's *cabinet*, how far to involve members of the European Parliament or when to get a minister to phone a Commissioner are often decisions taken during such consultation. Advice on the conduct of bilateral 'pre-negotiations' to ensure sympathetic coalition-building can also come about in this way.

Finally, coordination covers the arbitration function required between ministries, which simply cannot reach agreement on policy at lower levels of the coordination process. An umpire or even a central authority may be required in such cases – difficult in the case of coalition governments, like the German system, but manageable in a prime ministerial system with collective responsibility of the cabinet, like the British. Effective coordination requires the presence of all parts of the national administration described in this chapter.

For member states with capitals far from Brussels, distance and time involved in meetings complicates coordination. Some member states have obvious advantages resulting from their proximity to Brussels; London, Luxembourg, The Hague and Paris are within a few hours by car or train. In the British case, desk officers from the permanent representation in Brussels (UKREP) attend cabinet office coordination meetings within their sphere of responsibility. They do this to discuss precise details of 'the line to take' in meetings where they act as the negotiating representative, such as Commission and Council working parties. They also cover reporting to individual ministries on the evolution of bilateral and multilateral discussions in Brussels. In addition there is a regular Friday meeting in the cabinet office between the permanent representative and senior officials from ministries concerned by issues about to go forward to Coreper[1].

Similarly, the German arrangements involve a Friday meeting of the 'Europastaatssekretäre', i.e., the state secretaries in each ministry with European responsibilities. In the German case, the economics ministry is the convenor and provides the chair. The permanent representatives are the negotiators of last resort before matters proceed to Council. They report on the current week's Coreper meeting and on meetings of the Council, thus providing a crucial personal link between home officials and their colleagues in Brussels. Where necessary, they also visit ministers for further briefing. Such personalised high-level coordination guarantees the speed that coordination through officials might otherwise lack.

Coordination for Coreper and Council Meetings – the Antici group

National coordination for Council meetings reaches its high point after the procedural coordination between rival member states. The differences between international relations in the traditional context and the particular form of inter-state relationships found in the EU have already been alluded to. At the national level one can, in principle, assume common objectives, possibly an 'old-boy network' of civil servants and loyalty to the government (if not political loyalty at least loyalty to established policy as a function of political neutrality in government service). In the Council framework none of these assumptions holds. This chapter has argued that coordination is vital to the coherence and effectiveness of national policy-making, but it is precisely the above series of assumptions about national decision-making which do not yet go without saying in the EU framework. The Council and the Council secretariat do not, yet, enjoy the same authoritative role as their national government counterparts. Yet, to ensure efficiency of Council procedures and effective expression of rival national standpoints, coordination is essential in Council affairs. To a certain extent the Commission provides a focus of coordination of ideas and input to policy in its attempt to define the 'European interest' in order for member states to analyse whether their national interests are adequately protected by it. But the Commission is as much a rival policy-maker as an administration, even if its role in coordinating different national policy inputs and private sector interests in its initial proposals is crucial and its broker role between national viewpoints is marked in the daily workings of Council meetings (Rometsch and Wessels, 1995).

The presidency itself is the prime coordinator of Council meetings. Its role and that of the general secretariat of the Council are explained in chapters 18 and 19. Importantly, the emergence of the troika system and the tradition of rolling programmes for successive presidencies, form a structure of constraints from which individual presidencies escape with difficulty. Presidencies have to search hard for a really original role in policy-making. By default, most presidencies coordinate the initiatives of their predecessors. The six-month presidency cycle permits little more.

At Coreper II level, coordination is highly formalised between permanent representations, the Commission, the presidency and the Council secretariat by a regular weekly meeting of the so-called Antici group (for Coreper II) and the Mertens Group (for Coreper I) (see chapter 11). For the purposes of this chapter two points are relevant. First, a very high percentage of Council decisions are actually agreed by Coreper and merely rubber-stamped by ministers. Coreper's coordination role in preparing Council meetings is thus more aptly described as its decision-taking role. Second, as one journalist has observed, 'COREPER's role as a bridge to national capitals will grow in importance, so too its function as a clearing house for the Council of Ministers.' (Barber, 1995) The day before Coreper, the 'Anticis' meet to hear from the presidency how it intends to run the next meeting. The order of points on the agenda will be discussed, as will likely new Commission positions or those of individual member states. Typically, Anticis report to their colleagues that their permanent representative is likely to make certain points on known agenda items, the Commission gives the broad drift of its negotiating positions and officials announce any as yet unknown initiatives of their delegation. Originally, the Antici system developed in order to agree the minutes of Council meetings, so that they could be agreed as 'A' items and thus save time. Later, the preparation of Coreper was added to the functions of the Antici group. The advantage of the Antici system is that negotiators do not go naked into the negotiating chamber. It ensures that the permanent representatives are fully briefed and that new issues can be commented on after consultation with national capitals. Situations are thus avoided where delegations would be obliged to place a reservation on a particular issue and the presidency can be assured that Coreper will be efficiently prepared. It may contribute to the ritual and formality of Coreper meetings, but the overall standard of discussion and debate and efficient use of time is considerably raised.

From the national point of view, the Antici meeting in the Council secretariat provides last minute briefing allowing the coordination mechanisms to work efficiently. The Antici returns to the permanent representation and telephones major points to national contacts. In well-coordinated member states, a written minute follows a short time after and provides a basis for a national round-up in case of need.

Measuring Effectiveness in Policy Coordination

The discussion of the factors requiring national coordination in the EU framework leads naturally to an assessment of the relative effectiveness of member states' machinery for its fulfilment. Some governments, such as the French and British, are characterised by a combination of strong leadership, the absence of open coalitions and high quality civil servants. The principle of collective responsibility in the UK cabinet means the civil service can emulate the centralised and coordinated policy at the top. This is reflected in European policy-making in the successful coordination troika provided by the FCO European Union departments, the UK permanent representation to the EU (UKREP) and the European secretariat of the cabinet office. The system is as much a traditional British response to new administrative challenges as it is a reflection of the changed nature of government business since British membership of the Community. As for the French system, it too is a reflection of French administrative tradition with an administrative elite based on the system of ENA and the *grandes écoles* and the acceptance by those lower down the hierarchy of the need for a centralised, expert and decisive chain of command.

Effective coordination in both these cases rests on extremely tight and well-managed structures, but given the exponential growth of EU business in the 1980s and 1990s there is an emerging general tendency for national coordinating mechanisms to be streamlined. It is clear that effective coordination takes time and involves several levels of officialdom. In some member states, the absence of an overall coordinator outside the framework of functional ministries might lead to the assumption that these member states do not require an arbiter, because policy disagreement between ministries does not exist or is settled amicably at lower levels of coordination. The evidence is inconclusive, but at first sight it would seem that the opposite is the case. Germany's federal system and its lack of independent coordination, or Austria's or Greece's duopoly of leadership, are arguably causes of their frequent inability to produce a coherent policy line and, in extreme cases, to have ministers publicly contradicting each other over the line they have agreed to take. (For some historical examples of poor coordination see Bulmer and Paterson, 1988.) A telling example of this occurred when the German (CSU) agricultural minister I. Kiechle declared at the 'Green Week' in Berlin in January 1992 that the Commission's proposals for agricultural reform would have to be reconsidered and that price reductions would take place 'without me'. His subsequent resignation, when the liberal, free trade faction in German government had its way and obliged Kiechle to change his mind, may be the most extreme case of an apparently frequent phenomenon in the Federal Republic.[2]

There are increasing areas where the quantity and quality of European policy challenges the coordinating capacities of national governance (see Scharpf, 1994). This points to increasing complexity of national policy management. Coordination and arbitration, where they are effectively institutionalised, add further levels in the command structure. Yet, it is clear that lead ministries cannot settle differences with other ministries without some impartial arbitration mechanism. To be effective, the arbitrator may have to be proactive, must certainly be seen as the repository of skills and knowledge in European affairs of use to policy-makers and will certainly depend on effective prior coordination on a daily basis before issues reach the stage of outright bureaucratic rivalry. So coordination from the outset of the process is essential. This chapter has shown that it begins with the coordinating departments of individual ministries and climbs through the foreign ministry frameworks, sometimes through an independent mechanism or sometimes through interdepartmental bargaining without a recognised, impartial umpire, towards the ultimate level of European coordination, which is the Council itself. But it has also underlined the diversity of national practice.

In conclusion, while it may have been worth reiterating how much the development of an effective European policy-style depends on effective national coordination, one obvious question arises: is effective coordination both a necessary and a sufficient factor in the achievement of success in the EU process? The Council secretariat itself has pointed out in discussing the need for the General Affairs Council to take a more active role in the coordination of the work of other Council formations:

'the effectiveness of the Council decision-making process does not depend upon new initiatives to be taken at Union level, but upon a critical review to be undertaken by the Member States themselves of the methods used by them in preparing the Council's proceedings...given that all the Member States have different kinds of coordination and arbitration bodies or fora to prepare for Community negotiations, thought might be given to the following points: whether such bodies or fora are in the right place in the government machine; whether they have adequate administrative and political weight; whether the relay procedures work well; and whether they are capable of making a sustained contribution throughout the decision-making process.' (Council, 1999b, p. 77)

But, how much this contributes to success in achieving national goals is an altogether different issue. After all, one would need to demonstrate that well-coordinated governmental machines spell policy-making success for a causal relationship to be proven. National success in a given policy enterprise might be despite bad coordination and not because of it, and it need not necessarily tell us much about the efficacy of the coordination process. After all, what of states who also won, or lost, in the same policy area? Maybe a badly coordinated national administration might win in a given area, because there was anyway majority support for a directive or a regulation, or there may have been an effective blocking minority. Its own performance may not have been a decisive factor in winning desired policy outcomes. Nonetheless, this chapter has argued that there are costs of an unstreamlined system; costs both for the national administration involved and for the EU decision-making process itself. (See Neyer, 2004, for a discussion of the efficiency of Council decision-making.) Arguably, an uncoordinated system might involve more actors in the process. It may therefore be more democratic, a highly prized outcome in itself, even if the resource cost is correspondingly high. This chapter does not, therefore, claim that good coordination spells automatic success, only that it helps both the state concerned to master its dossiers and benefits the EU system itself, since business can be conducted more efficiently.

If there is no provable correlation between efficiency of policy making and outcomes, would the implication be that coordination is not necessary? Hardly. Efficient coordination is desirable, because it enables states to ensure that their 'line to take' is a tight one and that internal disagreements on the line to take are not aired in public. Success may not always be guaranteed, but good coordination surely implies that the decision-making process is managed without undue stress or cost in human resource terms and that all the chances are put on the side of the well coordinated. This, after all, is the message contained in the quotations cited above from official Council secretariat reflections. Importantly, also, the focus of this chapter has been on recognising the way in which doing business within the EU has placed constraints on governments, underlining that they must be well coordinated nationally if the system is to function well at EU level. In turn, the recognition by administrations of the relevance of this statement, by improving the rules of intergovernmental engagement, may contribute to improved outcomes.

PART 6: LEADERSHIP AND CONTINUITY IN THE COUNCIL

The European Union has evolved considerably over the past three decades. The number of member states has grown from six to twenty-five (and counting!). Cumulatively, the Single Act and the Maastricht, Amsterdam and Nice Treaties have considerably extended the policy scope and competences of the Union and its institutions. They have also resulted in a far more complex Union, with a welter of procedures and processes. Throughout all of these changes, the Council has continued to deliver; indeed, the fact that there has never been a major breakdown in the Council mechanism is one of the remarkable aspects of the Union's development. Two components of the system have made that possible.

The first, the Council presidency, has provided leadership – not only at political level but throughout the system in the Council's preparatory processes. As chapter 18 describes, the presidency is itself a complex form of power-sharing and 'joint investment' in the integration process. The administrative burden, political responsibility – and kudos – of this function have grown out of all recognition in the past fifteen years. As a vital part of the Union's executive leadership function in many areas, a properly functioning presidency is now an indispensable part of the system for the Union to work. This explains the attention which has been given to the Council and European Council presidency in recent discussions on the Union's new constitutional treaty.

The second, the Council's general secretariat, has provided continuity. It has been the rock on which all presidencies have been built. Latterly, the secretariat has found itself playing roles which, until recently, were more familiarly reserved to the Commission, but, as chapters 19.1 and 19.2 describe, in both negotiations and policy-shaping the secretariat has maintained its reputation as a totally reliable source of objective advice and information. In no small part, that reputation is built on the impartiality and high quality of its staff and the legal advice that the secretariat provides and on which member states know they can always rely. Chapter 19.3 describes the little known but important role played by the Council's legal service.

Chapter 18: The presidency

One and indivisible?

Litres of ink have been devoted in the recent past to the topic of the Council presidency. Seemingly, everybody has an opinion about its future shape and development. It was one of the 'hottest' issues during the work of the Convention and the IGC. What is it? Why does it excite such interest and passion? Should it?

The presidency is, at root, a simple concept. Collectivities of any sort need chairmanship. Thus the Council, like any collectivity, has always needed to be chaired. The founding fathers took the view that, in a Community where equality of treatment between member states was paramount, the duty of chairing the Council should be taken in turns. In a Community of six member states, six-month rotating stints seemed a reasonable arrangement. These simple and self-evident conclusions led to the provision for the Council presidency which has been in the treaties since the inception of the European Community in 1957. Since then, the European Community has evolved and transmogrified into today's European Union.

That transmogrification is the first key to understanding why the presidency has taken on such importance, for the presidency has long since ceased to be a simple matter of chairmanship; increasingly, the presidency has involved representation and leadership. Moreover, the European Union has long since extended beyond the simple 'Community method' structure of the Treaty of Rome. The Maastricht Treaty in particular created a new architecture which led to very different demands being put on the original concept.

Further demands resulted from enlargement, the second key to the increasing importance of the presidency. The dynamics of rotation among six (involving three 'large' and three 'small' member states) are clearly different to those among thirty (with six 'large' and twenty-four 'small' member states). Another important factor in the presidency's increasing importance has been the growing scope of the Union's competences. Cumulatively, collectively, the presidency has altered almost beyond recognition over the past five decades, not only in terms of competences and tasks but also in terms of demands on resources.

All of the preceding factors came into focus in the deliberations of the Convention and the recent IGC. In particular, there was a general recognition during those deliberations that the presidency need no longer necessarily be one, nor indivisible.

Early role and development

The presidency is neither an institution nor a body, but a function and an office which has become vital to the good working of the Council. The presidency's origins were modest. The second paragraph of article 203 TEC provides (as it and its predecessors have always done) that 'The office of President shall be held in turn by each Member State in the Council for a term of six months.' Thus, from the very outset of the European Communities two key principles were entrenched. The first was that representation of the Council, as it was to evolve, would be by the member states themselves, rather than through a collective representative, such as the secretary-general (as in the case of NATO, for example). The second was that each member state would occupy the office in turn, regardless of its size, economic power, or political weight (Wallace, 1985, p 2).

At the time, the treaty's draftsmen had in mind little more than an ordered sharing-out of the responsibility for chairing the Council's meetings, the modest responsibilities of which had been similarly carried out by the three-month rotating presidencies of the Special Council of the European Coal and Steel Community since 1952. There were, however, important differences of power and responsibility between the Special Council, where the High Authority held theoretical sway, and the Council of the Rome Treaties, which was a far more powerful beast. Nevertheless:

'During the first decade of the EEC, a combination of a clear and comprehensive mandate in the treaty itself, a forceful but nevertheless politically sensitive Commission, an effective and cohesive Committee of Permanent Representatives (COREPER) and the continued presence of some of the 'founding fathers' whose influence did not depend on whether or not their country held the Presidency masked the need for institutionalised political leadership within the Council and as a result delayed the emergence of the Presidency as a conspicuous player in its own right.' (Ludlow, 1995, p 145)

There were some early signs of potential. Already, the Italian presidencies of 1962, during the first, abortive, round of enlargement negotiations, and 1965, during the 'empty chair' crisis that led to the Luxembourg compromise, demonstrated how important a 'good' presidency could be.

An obvious reason for the emergence of the presidency was the fact that the Council, as a composite body, had no other evident means of representing itself vis-à-vis the other institutions, the press and media, or the wider world. For example, when budgetary dialogue was instituted between the Council and the Parliament in 1970, the role of representing the Council in the process naturally devolved upon the presidency (see also Ludlow, 1995, p 146). And it was the presidency which represented the Council in the negotiations leading to the 20 July 1963 Yaoundé Convention (forerunner of the 1975 Lomé Convention) and the 12 September 1963 Association Agreement with Turkey. Much later, the 1977 London Declaration decided that the European Council's conclusions would henceforth be issued on the responsibility of the presidency, and when the 1983 Stuttgart Solemn Declaration provided for regular reports on European Council meetings to the European Parliament, the task of representing the European Council logically fell to the presidency.

During the 1960s and 1970s a number of trends and developments combined to bring the presidency's organisational and managerial roles more to the fore. These included:

- the death or withdrawal from active politics of a number of important founding fathers, such as Spaak, Monnet, Schuman, and Adenauer, who had previously provided leadership and direction;

- the simultaneous rise of de Gaulle and the Gaullist patrician view of the role of the state and of its head;

- the shift in the institutional balance in favour of member state governments, caused and symbolised by the 1966 Luxembourg compromise;

- the more intergovernmental *'rélance'* of the 1969 Hague summit;

- the general growth in the Council's activity and in the number of sectoral Councils and preparatory working parties;

- the creation in 1970 of European political cooperation and the decision to devolve onto the presidency executive and representative functions;

- the rise of international monetary turbulence and the need for a concerted approach, and the 1971 decision to aim for economic and monetary union;

- the growth of summitry and the creation of the European Council in 1974 (see chapter 9);

- successive waves of enlargement, each wave making consensus in the Council more difficult to achieve.

Most of these developments were gradual, and the member states' responses to them were ad hoc. There was no manual of procedure for an incoming presidency; each presidency was free to acquit itself of the role and tasks as it saw fit. As a consequence, problems of coherence and continuity became increasingly apparent.

The Luxembourg (1970) and Copenhagen (1973) reports

When first established, European political cooperation (EPC) was firmly outside the European Community framework. Nevertheless, in the absence of agreement about whether the EPC should be furnished with its own independent secretariat, and with the Commission apparently excluded from any major role, EPC did borrow one feature from the Community method; that of the revolving presidency. The 27 October 1970 Luxembourg report adopted the rotating presidency (from the then EEC article 146) and charged it with the tasks of convening and hosting meetings and with providing the secretariat and material organisation (the rotating presidency thus ensured an equitable sharing of the costs involved). A report was to be made to the European Parliament once a year. The Copenhagen report of 23 July 1973 established a direct communications system (COREU) among foreign ministries which was to be coordinated by the presidency. It also foresaw enhanced links between the presidency and the embassies of the other member states. The presidency was further given the role of providing linkage between the EPC and the Community frameworks through Coreper and the Council. A June 1974 'Gymnich meeting' of foreign affairs ministers decided that the presidency should speak on behalf of the member states in EPC dialogue with friendly states.

The La Marlia procedure (1975)

The foreign ministers became increasingly concerned at the erosion of the Foreign Affairs Council's authority and overall managerial responsibility through the fragmentation of the Council into an increasing number of sectoral Councils. Discussions under the Italian presidency in the second half of 1975 resulted in an agreement at a meeting of the ministers at Lucca, on 18 and 19 October, later confirmed by the Council on 5 and 6 November, that in future the Foreign Affairs Council would be briefed at the beginning of each meeting on work in all of the sectoral Councils. The note was to be prepared by the Council's general secretariat. The foreign ministers' intention had in mind the possibility of constructive intervention where there was deadlock, but the 'La Marlia procedure' (named after the Italian president) became no more than a list of measures under discussion and lapsed into disuse.

The Tindemans report (1975)

In 1974, the Paris summit decided to entrust Leo Tindemans, then Belgian prime minister, with the task of drawing up a report on the concept and the scope of European union. The Tindemans report was presented to the European Council in December 1975. The fifth chapter concentrated on the institutions. In the case of the Council, Tindemans underlined the need for better coherence and coordination, particularly among the sectoral Councils, and the need to strengthen continuity (he proposed that this should be done by extending the presidential term from six months to one year). The Tindemans report's recommendations were noted, then largely forgotten. Nevertheless, they showed where informed insiders (Tindemans having interviewed a broad range of personalities within the institutions and the member states) thought the Council's growing responsibilities primarily resided.

The 1977 London declaration

In early 1977, French President Valéry Giscard d'Estaing proposed a revision of the European Council's procedures. It became clear, in correspondence between the member states' leaders, that Giscard's principal objective was to strengthen the powers of the presidency. In the event, the June 1977 London European Council gave the presidency the considerable responsibility of making public a summary of the conclusions of each European Council meeting. It was also given enhanced powers over the advanced preparation of the agenda (Duff, 1981, p 245).[1]

The report of the Three Wise Men (1979)

In December 1978, the Brussels European Council decided to set up a committee of 'Three Wise Men' to examine the functioning of the Community's institutions and ways in which their performances could be enhanced.[2] The Wise Men reported back in October 1989, a month before the November 1989 European Council meeting. Of thirty-one pages devoted to the Council, fully ten concentrated on the presidency. The opening paragraph was telling in its blunt appraisal:

> 'In improving the Council's performance, the first priority is to strengthen the Presidency in its dual role of organisational control and political impetus. It is no accident that the functions of the Presidency have been both expanded and more widely recognised in recent years. The strong central management which it can provide offers the most natural means of compensating for the centrifugal tendencies within the Council. It bears the prime responsibility for tackling the spread of specialized business, the ramifying inter-institutional relations, the differing interests and behaviour of the member states. The virtual breakdown in Council work under some 'bad' Presidencies (whether their faults lay in weakness, or an over-autocratic approach, or both) has shown that if the Presidency does not do this job, there is no longer anyone else who can fill the breach.' (The Three Wise Men, 1979, p 35)

The Wise Men argued that there had to be recognition that 'the State holding the Chair has certain *fixed responsibilities* for the management of Council business and the good working of the Community as a whole'. In the second place, the presidency had to have the *authority* 'to impose good order and discipline' in both the Council and its subordinate bodies. This authority, the Wise Men recognised, was conditional and based on advance and mutual acceptance of the ground rules. In the third place, a presidency had to have the organizational and personnel *resources* it needed to carry out its tasks.

Like the earlier, more radical, Tindemans report, the recommendations in the report of the Three Wise Men went largely unheeded.[3] Nevertheless, many of its recommendations about the main tasks of the presidency read uncannily like a description of the modern-day presidency's tasks and bear repeating here. For example, the Three Wise Men provided a 'practical, not legal' definition of the presidency's principal tasks:

> 'It convenes meetings of the *Council of Ministers*. It is responsible for advance preparation of the agenda; for the circulation of the necessary documents; for the allocation of time at the meeting and the conduct of debate; for the formulation and implementation of decisions. The Presidency's basic duty in this process is simply to get results. To do so it must work with technical efficiency, but also exercise a strong and politically sensitive control of the proceedings. It must select for the agenda the items which are most urgent, important and ripe for handling. It must prevent time-wasting and confusion at the meeting itself. It must

urge the debate towards conclusions by using the most appropriate combination of the weapons at its disposal (pressure, mediation, compromise proposals, time-limits, voting).' (The Three Wise Men, p 36)

Most of this is as valid as it was in 1979, and is the nearest there has been to an official description of the presidency's tasks. Much of the description seems self-evident, but it was a measure of just how bad matters had become that it had to be pointed out. Council agendas were over-crowded and badly organized; the Council was far too willing to undermine its own authority by passing problems up to the European Council; ministerial attendance, particularly of foreign ministers, was poor and erratic; and the Council's authority had become weakened by the growing autonomy of sectoral Councils and their preparatory bodies. The Three Wise Men saw the 'sins of omission' of various presidencies, their neglect of essential tasks, as the primary cause.

The Wise Men felt that the presidency should play a similar role at the level of the European Council, conducting proceedings with the 'right combination of flexibility and sense of responsibility', and ensuring that conclusions were recorded in 'proper terms'. They also identified a vital coordination role, both horizontally, as between the various specialised Councils and their preparatory bodies, and vertically, through the hierarchical process (working parties, Coreper, Council). In both cases, the presidency had to work through its chairmen at each level. The Wise Men stressed the self-evident role played by the presidency in relation to the other Community institutions. The presidency had to 'set the right tone', and maintain contact 'not only at Council level but through all the various stages of preparation'. Lastly, the presidency bore a heavy burden of responsibility for the management of the European political cooperation. Among the many options they explored as to how the presidency could be reinforced, the Three Wise Men paid particular attention to the role of the Council general secretariat and especially that of the secretary-general. Their recommendations in this field were reflected in the provisions made in the 1980 decision to appoint Niels Ersbøll as secretary-general (see chapter 19.1).

The London report (1981) and the formalisation of the 'troika'

The growing managerial, executive and representational tasks involved in the presidency of European political cooperation placed a heavy burden on the diplomatic services of smaller member states. At the same time, Council presidents were increasingly obliged to engage in 'shuttle' diplomacy, particularly in regard to EPC's efforts to broker peace in the Middle East in the late 1970s. Shuttle diplomacy required more flexibility than the traditional Council method of mandating its presidency would allow, since the president had frequently to react and to respond on the spot. There was also an unspoken feeling among the larger member states that the presidencies of smaller member states might sometimes need to be 'beefed up' when representing the EPC abroad.

On 5 and 6 September 1981, the foreign affairs ministers met informally under the British presidency at Brocket Hall. They agreed to a wider use of 'support teams' of three diplomats, drawn from the current, preceding, and succeeding presidencies. These 'support teams' could accompany the president when representing the EPC abroad, giving him access to a broader range of diplomatic expertise and simultaneously broadening the legitimacy of his mandate. The ministers also foresaw a similar, if more occasional, method at ministerial level. The foreign affairs ministers' report, which became known as the 'London report', was formally approved by the Council on 13 October 1981. The report stated that; 'If necessary, and if the Ten so agree, the presidency, accompanied by representatives of the preceding and succeeding presidencies, may meet with representatives of third countries.' (EC Bulletin, N° 11, 1981)

This decision formalised a method which has since generally been referred to as the 'troika' (after a Russian sled that seats three people). Since 1981, the troika has become a standard instrument in the presidency's *démarches* abroad. It has more than proved its worth as a way of spreading responsibility, strengthening and broadening the European Union's external representation, and broadening the presidency's base in the Council (see Nuttall, 1992, p 179). However, following the entry into force of the Treaty of Amsterdam in 1999, the troika has evolved into the presidency, the secretary-general/high representative and the Commission, and where appropriate the incoming presidency (see chapter 4.2).

The Stuttgart Solemn Declaration (1983)

At the June 1983 Stuttgart European Council, heads of state or government reaffirmed their desire to:

> 'strengthen and develop European Political Cooperation through the elaboration and adoption of joint positions and joint action, on the basis of intensified consultations, in the area of foreign policy, including the coordination of the positions of the member states on the political and economic aspects of security, so as to promote and facilitate the progressive development of such positions and actions in a growing number of foreign policy fields.' (EC Bulletin, 1983, N° 6, p 25)

Referring to the new arrangements in the 1981 London report, the European Council called upon the governments of the member states to make a 'constant effort' to increase the effectiveness of political cooperation. They made two proposals:

> 'Strengthening the Presidency's powers of initiative, of coordination and of representation in relations with third countries;

> 'Appropriately strengthening operational support for successive Presidencies, corresponding to the increasing tasks which they have to reform.' (Ibid, p 26)

A section of the conclusions devoted to foreign policy went on to list nine specific recommendations for the reinforcement of foreign policy, and each implicitly gave the presidency further managerial and representational tasks.

The Stuttgart Solemn Declaration charged the presidency with a large number of other representational tasks. The European Council was to address a report to the European Parliament after each of its meetings, and this report was to be presented 'at least once during each Presidency by the President of the European Council' – the first time that the head of state or government of a member state holding the presidency was given specific tasks. The European Council was also to address a written annual report to the European Parliament on progress towards European Union, and in the 'debates to which these reports give rise', the European Council would 'normally' be represented by its president.

The presidency was to address the European Parliament at the beginning of its term of office and present its programme, and to report to the Parliament at the end of its term of office on 'the progress achieved'. The presidency had long since already undertaken reporting tasks to the European Parliament, but these arrangements introduced, for the first time, an element of accountability. Presidencies would henceforth be judged by the Parliament, both on their initial programme and on how well they managed to achieve it. The presidency was charged with the task of keeping the Parliament regularly informed through its political affairs committee of the subjects of foreign policy examined in the context of European political cooperation.

Lastly, before the appointment of the president of the Commission, the 'President of the Representatives of the Governments of the Member States' had to seek the opinion of the enlarged bureau (the central political and managerial authority at the time) of the European Parliament.

Intergovernmental conferences (1985, 1991, 1996 and 2000)

The 1980s and 1990s saw further, major consolidation of the presidency's role through a number of developments. The major intergovernmental conferences held in the mid-1980s (resulting in the 1986 Single European Act) and the 1990s (resulting in the 1991 Maastricht Treaty and 1997 Amsterdam Treaty) created new roles for the presidency, and for the presidency-Council general secretariat tandem. On the one hand, the presidency had to organise and marshal the negotiations, on the other, it was expected both to bring vision and to seek consensus.[4] The presidency's IGC role was further consolidated at Amsterdam and Nice, where it was expected to act both as initiator and as engine, driving forward the work of the conferences.

The consequences of the return of majority voting

In the legislative sphere, the gradual breakdown of the Luxembourg compromise mentality at the beginning of the 1980s and the consolidation of the trend by the qualified majority voting provisions of the 1986 Single European Act placed more emphasis on the presidency's political and representational roles. On the one hand, there was a much greater need for political judgement on the part of the presidency, which shared the right to call votes (in practice it mostly exercises the right alone) and was best placed to know when matters were 'ripe' and maximum consensus had been achieved. On the other hand, the new procedures, particularly the aptly-named cooperation procedure, increased the need for Council represen-tation vis-à-vis the Commission and the Parliament. Lastly, the Single European Act contained the internal market programme and a deadline for its achievement. Successive presidencies played vital roles in ensuring, through rolling programmes and concerted prioritisation, that the bulk of the internal market programme was achieved on time.

On the legislative side, these trends were further accentuated by the Maastricht and Amsterdam Treaties. In particular, the Maastricht Treaty introduced a new legislative procedure involving co-decision with the European Parliament. The procedure was refined by the Amsterdam Treaty and its scope extended to cover a broader number of policy areas. Very early on in the life of the new procedure, both arms of the legislative authority realised that it was in their mutual interest to seek early agreement and not to let the procedure run its full course. The first (Maastricht) version of the procedure was particularly heavy in terms of procedural requirements. Increasing onus was therefore put on the presidency (and the general secre-tariat) to identify potential sticking points *and* potential solutions. Indeed, today's presidency habitually plays the role of inter-institutional honest broker, reporting to the Council working party on Parliament's position, and reporting to Parliament's rapporteur on the Council's position. The role is necessarily very informal, but it is increasingly indispensable, requiring a fresh set of skills from the presidency. Indeed, the judicious representations of a skilful president of a Council working party can avoid the need for a second reading.

The Helsinki European Council (1999)

The Helsinki European Council took further the Council's general prepara-tions for impending enlargement. With regard to the presidency, it concen-trated on enhancing cooperation between incumbent and incoming presidencies. In particular it provided that:

'The incoming Presidency shall assist the Presidency, while preserving fully the Presidency's powers and overall political responsibility for man-aging Council business in conformity with the Treaties and the Council's rules of procedure. The incoming Presidency, acting under the Presidency's instructions, shall replace the Presidency as and when required, relieve the Presidency, when needed, of some of its administrative burden and enhance continuity of work in the Council. The Presidency and the incoming Presidency will take all necessary steps to ensure a smooth transition from one Presidency to the next.'

At Helsinki the European Council also embarked upon a process of reform, with subsequent meetings in Göteborg (2001) and Barcelona (2002) hearing reports from the Council's secretary-general/high representative on ongoing reflections. Latterly, the European Council's deliberations took place against the backdrop of the Convention's work. Indeed, as will be seen below, much of the Council's preparatory work was fed into the Convention's deliberations.

Seville (2002)

The European Council's reflection process resulted in a set of conclusions, rules, recommendations and instructions, approved at the Seville European Council. With regard to the presidency, there were three sets of conclusions. The first again concerned coordination between incumbent and incoming presidencies. It was agreed that, with the agreement of an incumbent presidency, the future presidency could already begin to chair certain meetings during the current presidency. This was designed for those dossiers where it was clear that the matter would 'essentially be dealt with during the following six-month period' (the budget procedure being given as a specific example of where this rule should apply).

The second issue was an extension of the practice whereby certain working parties would be chaired by the general secretariat of the Council, rather than the presidency itself (see chapter 19).

The third issue concerned the conduct of meetings. The presidency was given the general duty of ensuring that meetings proceeded smoothly, but was empowered to limit speaking time and determine the order in which contributors spoke. The cumulative effect of these measures, which were later taken over in the Council's rules of procedure, was a radical departure from the previously genteel, but time-consuming, democratic process for Council debate, whereby everybody had their say in due course!

The modern presidency

The modern presidency performs a veritable galaxy of tasks, some set out in the treaty, some set out in the Council's rules of procedure, some set out in European Council conclusions and many others cumulatively resulting from the evolutionary steps reviewed in this chapter. The modern presidency is at one and the same time manager, promoter of political initiatives, package-broker, honest broker, representative to and from the other Community institutions, spokesman for the Council and for the Union, and an international actor. In organisational terms, a presidency must provide chairmen, at diplomatic and ministerial level, for literally hundreds of meetings, representing a huge strain on resources, particularly those of smaller member states. It must play a vital and delicate political role, diplomatically steering its way towards the broadest consensus whilst maintaining momentum and avoiding stagnation. It has the – increasingly important – support of the Council general secretariat , but it has few specialised tools to help it in its political tasks. In short, it has 'responsibility without power' (Dewost, 1984, p 31). Moreover, as Ludlow has forcefully argued; '...the Presidency will remain a crucial player for as long as the bases of the present political system are maintained and more particularly as long as the Council exercises executive as well as legislative functions.' (Ludlow, 1995, p 156)

The exercise of the presidency requires careful, long-term planning (see, for example, O'Nuallain, 1985). Presidencies must draw up programmes and present them to the Council and the European Parliament. Since 2003, they must help draw up three-year multi-annual strategic plans. They must defend their intentions and, when the presidency is over, their record. They must

intersperse themselves smoothly into rolling programmes, other ongoing legislative work, overall priorities or fresh initiatives established by the
European Council. In common foreign and security policy they must pick up
the baton and pass it on smoothly, and they must participate in the troika
before and sometimes still afterwards. They may have to react swiftly to
unforeseen circumstances. Presidencies cost member states a lot of money.
Given this onerous list of tasks and costs, the question arises; why do member
states do it?

The reason is at least partly bound up in the basic ethos of an equitable
Union of sovereign states. Fulfilment of presidential duty is a badge of
responsibility and honour (this has been perhaps particularly true of the
small member states and the more recent democracies). It redounds to the
good image of a member state (self image and external image), both as a
Union 'player' and as a mature European nation state, to acquit its presidential duties well.

The presidency also brings with it important considerations of privilege
and prestige. To take a popular example, over the fifty year existence of the
European Union the foreign minister of tiny Luxembourg has, for six
months roughly every three or four years, presided over Europe's richest
and most powerful states, including France and Germany. Latterly, he has
represented one of the world's largest trading blocs and markets, with a
combined population of over 420 million people, on the world stage.

Many member states also see the presidency as a welcome episodic discipline – recurring periods of intense preparation and activity that are not
without their pedagogic value in teaching the diplomatic and civil service
cadres about the mechanics of the European Union and the way in which
they are used. Clearly, the presidency also serves to educate member states
as to what the presidency involves – it creates fellow feeling and mutual
understanding – a sense of ownership in the European Union.

From a more self-interested perspective, occupation of the presidency
gives a member state the possibility of ensuring that its particular policy priorities are brought to the fore. For example, Spain, which held the presidency in the second half of 1995, established a list of six priorities. Top of its
list was the Euro-Mediterranean conference, held in Barcelona in November
1995, which was intended to introduce a new dynamic into the European
Union's relations with, in particular, the North African countries facing
Spain across the Mediterranean, and to balance the Union's eastward *ouverture*. The second priority was the reflection group preparing the work of the
1996 intergovernmental conference, which was chaired by a Spanish minister and reported to the December 1995 Madrid European Council. The third
was the liberalization of trade relations with Latin America. The fourth was
defence and security. The fifth was relations with the United States, and the
sixth was eastern Europe. The overall impression is of a balanced mix of
European Union and of more 'Iberian' concerns.

The advantages of the presidency from the European Union's point of
view are just as clear. It is an important part of what is known, in Brussels
jargon, as the *engrenage*, or gearing, of the European Union. Each member
state gets a regular chance to swap its role and position and to become a
larger and more important cog in the Union machine. These six-month
periods necessarily broaden a member state's perspectives and force them

to look beyond a narrower definition of self-interest to the European Union's interest. They also inculcate in member states the basic methodology of the Council: seeking the broadest consensus; relying on concession and compromise, and silent acquiescence rather than spoken opposition; empathy, if not sympathy, for member states out on a limb; diplomacy rather than confrontation.

For all of these reasons, the presidency has generally been regarded as a 'good thing'. But, while the presidency is considered to be a good thing, not all presidencies are considered good...

'Good' and 'bad' presidencies

Perhaps more in Brussels than in the member states, policy-makers like to talk about 'good' or 'bad' presidencies. Members of the Council general secretariat roll their eyes to heaven theatrically at the mention of certain notorious presidencies from the past. The combined weight of member states' diplomatic and political mechanisms is harnessed to the task of providing a 'good' presidency. The stigma of a 'bad' presidency rankles and may leave bad blood. But how can presidencies be judged?

There are a number of difficulties. The period of office is very short – just six months, and even less, given the holiday period, for presidencies in the second half of the year. Presidencies can be badly disrupted by unforeseen events; for example, wars, unexpected rows with major trading partners, or a sudden flare-up of an internal dispute. On the other hand, presidencies can benefit unexpectedly from, for example, peace, the settlement of trade rows or internal disputes. In other words, luck plays a part. Any judgement of a presidency should involve a composite picture, from chairmanship in working groups through to diplomatic representation abroad, and yet few observers are placed to make such informed judgements. Moreover, much can be good about a 'bad' presidency, and vice-versa.

Judgements of the presidency have also tended to be over clouded by the intense media focus on the European Council at the end of each presidency's term. Again, a good and productive European Council meeting may round off a bad presidency, and vice-versa. What is an ideal point of view to make such judgements? To take an obvious example, the European Parliament may have a very different set of criteria on which it judges the presidency than, say, the other member states, and judgements differ between 'Brussels' and the member state capitals.

An important explanatory factor for 'bad' presidencies is 'to be found in their inability – or unwillingness – to understand their role. The Presidency is first and foremost an office of the Union: it is not an instrument with which to pursue national objectives' (Ludlow, 1995, p 157). At a more practical and pragmatic level, most Brussels-based policy-makers would argue that one of the keys to the success of a presidency is its ability to capitalise on the support and advice of the Council general secretariat, rather than working against it. Stepping back from the debate, the point is that a member state's desire to be seen as a 'good' rather than 'bad' presidency is an important explanatory factor of the presidency's overall success as an increasingly important office.

Commentators have pointed to three shortcomings in the presidency system. A first is that there has been disappointingly little national parliamentary involvement in the presidential exercise. Some have argued that national parliaments should play a larger part in determining their government's presidential priorities and in judging its record. A second, linked, observation is that, with the exception of the European Council meetings, which tend to be high-profile media events, presidencies serve little pedagogic function outside diplomatic and political circles. Lastly, perhaps because of the growing complexity of the task, presidencies have been geared more towards coping, and overall initiatives have seemed difficult.

Future presidencies

The first and second editions of this book (chapter V) gave lengthy explanations of the way in which the order of rotation of presidencies has changed over time. Recurring enlargements led the member states to make adjustments to the order so as to take into account three increasingly important considerations. The first was the mixture of new and old member states, the desire being to avoid a succession of presidencies from new member states. The troika system would ensure that the new member states were preceded and succeeded by 'old hands' who could 'show them the ropes'. A second consideration was the mixture of small and large member states. A third consideration, was the need to ensure an appropriate mix in the troika for common foreign and security policy matters (especially given the fact that some member states were constitutionally neutral), although with the new-look troika and emerging role of the high representative, this is a less important factor than it once was. All three points were linked. The current order to succession of presidencies fixed by the Council in 1995 will continue to be followed at least until 2006. Appendix 3 sets out the rotation of Council presidencies from 1958 to 2006. In October 2002, the European Council decided that, 'In order to give new member states the time to prepare for their presidency the European Council confirms that the present rotation will continue until the end of 2006. The Council will decide on the question of the order of presidencies for 2007 and onwards as soon as possible and at the latest one year after accession of the first new member states.' This timing was essentially confirmed in a declaration to the final act of the constitutional IGC.

The future of the presidency

As the account in this chapter has demonstrated, the tendency has always been to adjust or modify the presidency system, rather than to reform it fundamentally. The 2000-2002 discussions in the Council had revealed a growing realisation that something more than tinkering might be required in a Union of twenty-five or more member states. A number of considerations had complicated the debate.

First, successive enlargements had undermined many of the arguments about the benefit of the six-month rotating presidency. In a Community of six, member states waited only a few years before their turn came around again. In a Union of twenty-five or more, the wait is much longer, and so all of the benefits of running a presidency – socialisation, familiarisation, and so on – are much diminished. Moreover, the decision to hold all European Council meetings in Brussels has removed a major perceived benefit of the presidency; even if it still possible to hold a limited number of informal ministerial meetings in the member state of the presidency, the old tradition of showcasing a European Council meeting in a major city is now over.

As this chapter has described, the presidency has been becoming increasingly complex and onerous. In this context, the Council secretariat's role in chairing certain working parties has been consolidated, as has the practice whereby succeeding presidencies take on chairing responsibilities during the preceding presidency. Such practices, it could be argued, have somehow diluted the 'purity' of the traditional method whereby, with only a few exceptions (Luxembourg traditionally relied on the help of its Benelux partners), member states did everything themselves.

An increasing number of policy processes (co-decision legislative procedures, etc) go beyond the six-month period and, in any case, the Council's new multi-annual planning mechanisms have reduced the scope for presidency initiatives.

Last but not least, with the consolidation of the common foreign and security policy, there has been an increasing recognition of the need for a more enduring presidency, at least in the CFSP sphere.

All of these considerations clearly came across in the reports put up to the European Council by the GAERC in 2002, culminating in the report put to the Seville European Council. Those reports recognised the vitally important contribution made to the development of the Union by the traditional presidency function, but argued that major change could no longer be avoided. There was broad agreement on a number of general objectives: better distribution of responsibility, consistency, maintenance of the institutional balance, and the need for national administrations to be involved. There was general acknowledgement of the special requirements of CFSP/ESDP. With these considerations came an increasing understanding that the presidency could no longer be considered as a one-and-indivisible institution, and with that, in turn, came an understanding that different solutions might be appropriate to the different component elements of the presidency.

A number of different models were put up to the European Council for consideration, but there was some reluctance to engage too deeply in this debate against the background of the European Convention's work, which involved looking at elements from all of the models which the GAERC and Coreper had been considering. The constitution foresees three distinct forms of presidency for the future, as set out in articles 22 and 24 of the constitutional treaty, and in a draft decision of the European Council.

The first, and over-arching, element is a new form of presidency of the European Council (article 22). The president would be elected by a qualified majority for a term of two-and-a-half years, renewable once. The president of the European Council would be responsible for:

–   chairing it and driving forward its work;
–   ensuring its proper preparation and continuity, in cooperation with the president of the Commission, and on the basis of the work of the General Affairs Council;
–   facilitating cohesion and consensus with the European Council.

The president of the European Council, who would report to the European Parliament after each meeting, would also ensure, at his or her level, the external representation of the Union on issues concerning its common foreign and security policy.

This would be done without prejudice to the responsibilities of the second element in the draft Constitution's presidency, the Union minister for foreign affairs, who will chair the External Relations Council. With the agreement of the president of the European Commission, and acting by qualified majority, the European Council would appoint the Union minister for foreign affairs, with responsibility for conducting the Union's common foreign and security policy, as mandated by the Council of Ministers (article 28). One of the most innovatory aspects of the Union minister for foreign affairs is that he/she would also be one of the vice-presidents of the European Commission, with responsibility for handling external relations. Moreover, in exercising these responsibilities the Union minister would be bound by Commission procedures.

The third element is that the system of six-monthly rotation of the presidency is effectively preserved for all other Council formations. While the Constitution stipulates in article 24 that the presidency of Council configurations other than that of Foreign Afairs shall be held by member state representatives in the Council on the basis of equal rotation, the decision to be adopted upon entry into force of the Constitution foresees a presidency consisting of pre-established groups of three member states for a period of eighteen months. However, that decision also states that each member of the group shall in turn chair for a six-month period all configurations of the Council (with the exception of Foreign Affairs). The IGC clearly took the view that the potential gain which might have resulted from having each Council formation chaired by one member state for eighteen months was likely to be offset by the effort that would have been needed to ensure effective coordination across the various players in the team. This confirms the tendency towards incremental adjustments rather than radical reforms. Preserving largely intact the six-monthly rotating presidency for most Council formations was more readily accepted given that the administrative and management burden on the presidency will be substantially reduced by removing the Foreign Affairs Council (and the associated meetings with third countries as well as the relevant preparatory bodies) from the rotation system. Moreover, building on the possibilities for the presidency to draw on assistance from other mmbers of the team should ensure that the system will work reasonably effectively in future. It is expected that the decision on the composition of the teams and the order of rotation from 2007 onwards will be taken in late 2004 or early 2005.

This chapter began by observing that many litres of ink had been devoted to the subject of the presidency. It seems clear that many more will be devoted to the same subject over the next few years, as the European Council, the Council and the Commission seek to implement the new forms of chairmanship of an increasingly complex and sophisticated Union.

Chapter 19: The general secretariat of the Council

19.1 Council secretaries-general

Christian Calmes (1952-1973)

At its very first meeting (8-10 September 1952), the Special Council of the European Coal and Steel Community set up a secretariat, headed by a secretary, to assist it. The choice for secretary fell to a 39 year-old Luxembourg diplomat, Christian Calmes. He was initially appointed for just six months, but his appointment was regularly renewed until July 1954, when his position was confirmed, and he was officially appointed as secretary-general.

The secretary-general's role was very much that of a secretariat. Under the Special Council's provisional rules of procedure, the secretary-general's two explicit tasks were to draft a verbatim report of proceedings which, once approved by the Council, was signed by him and the president-in-office, and to manage the funds at his disposal. Under the provisional rules of procedure of the Council of the European Economic Community, he helped prepare and distribute the Council's agenda, monitored officials in attendance, acted as repository for mandates for proxy votes, and signed Council acts, together with the president. One of his major tasks remained the drafting of verbatim reports of proceedings. This continued to be a major task until the 1970s, when the practice of drafting verbatim reports was abandoned in favour of more succinct minutes summarizing the main decisions taken at meetings.

When the foreign affairs ministers of the Six met in Messina in June 1955, they requested the secretary-general to provide, on an ad hoc basis, the secretariat for the interim committee and the subsidiary committees responsible for the negotiations leading to the new European treaties. Christian Calmes was deeply involved in the negotiations, recruiting a number of temporary agents to help him. His role was much appreciated by the national delegations and, when the Rome treaties were signed, the responsibilities of the old general secretariat of the European Coal and Steel Community were extended to the two new Councils of the European Economic Community and the European Atomic Energy Community. Thus, like Coreper, the general secretariat was born out of the Rome treaty negotiations. Altogether, Christian Calmes served for 21 years (1952-1973), his

presence as an *éminence grise* balancing that of the long-serving French secretary-general of the European Commission, Emile Noël (1958-1987).

Nicolas Hommel (1973-1980)

In July 1973, a 58 year-old senior Luxembourg diplomat, Nicolas Hommel,
was appointed to replace the retiring Calmes. Hommel, who had been his
country's permanent representative to the Organisation for European
Economic Cooperation (1949-1959) and NATO (1953-1959), and ambassador
to Belgium (1959-1963) and France (1963-1967), served as secretary-general
for seven years, until he reached retirement age in 1980. The appointments
of Calmes and Hommel established the tradition that the secretary-general
should be an experienced diplomat. The tradition was consolidated with the
appointment of the third secretary-general.

Niels Ersbøll (1980-1994)

A follow up to some of the recommendations of the 1979 report of the 'Three
Wise Men' became apparent in the Council decision appointing Hommel's
successor. The Council's choice was an experienced 54 year-old Danish
diplomat, Niels Ersbøll. In his early career, Ersbøll had served in his
country's representations to NATO, EFTA, and the GATT, and thus had
broad experience of European and international organisations. From 1973 to
1977 he served in Brussels as Danish permanent representative to the
European Communities, and thus also had first-hand knowledge and experience of the Council and the Community. (In 1995, following his retirement
as secretary-general, Ersbøll was appointed by the Danish government as its
representative in the reflection group preparing the work of the 1996 intergovernmental conference).

In appointing Ersbøll, the Council took the unprecedented step of pointing out the need for more continuity between successive presidencies, better
coordination of the work of the sectoral Councils, greater coherence in the
work of the Council's preparatory bodies and 'significant alleviation' of the
Council's workload through the reaching of preliminary agreement in
Coreper. While the Council recognised the need for 'determined contributions' by the member states and the 'special responsibility' of the presidency, it also pointed out that 'the task of the secretariat of the Council is to
assist the Council in general and the presidency in particular in the performance of their tasks' and that 'the office of secretary-general is of great
importance in bringing about the necessary improvements.' Ersbøll took
these pronouncements as a personal mandate and set about implementing
them faithfully:

> 'During the fourteen years that he has been in office, Niels
> Ersbøll has carried out the mandate that he was given to a
> remarkable degree and, in doing so, has consolidated the auth-
> ority of the presidency.' (Ludlow, 1995, p 150)

By the end of Ersbøll's stewardship, the role of the secretary-general as
the right-hand man of the presidency had been firmly established. As he
told the European Parliament in 1992, he had overseen: '...a gradual trans-

addition, the secretary-general has at his direct disposal a situation centre, responsible for monitoring and intelligence gathering, and the EU's military staff. A number of departments, while nominally responsible directly to both the secretary-general and the deputy secretary-general, are effectively run under the supervision of the deputy secretary-general and the director of his private office, given the deputy secretary-general's explicit policy responsibility under the treaty for 'the running of the general secretariat'. These include the security and infosec (i.e. security of electronic information) offices, health and safety at work, personal data protection and the internal audit service.

19.2 The general secretariat

Origin and development

The original secretariat of the Special Council of the European Coal and Steel Community was a small affair; just thirty officials, only five of them at AD (administrative) grade (this compares with a total today of more than 3,000 officials, nearly 500 of whom are AD grade or AD grade equivalent seconded national experts). This was in part due to Jean Monnet's fierce resistance to the creation of any potential rival to the revolutionary new High Authority which he headed and which was considered to be largely his brainchild.

The provisional rules of procedure of the ECSC Special Council stated simply that the general secretariat should 'assist' the Council, and this was largely interpreted as referring to secretarial duties, but the ministers of foreign affairs soon got into the habit of requesting the general secretariat to carry out 'intellectual' tasks (Ganshof van der Mersch, 1969, p. 251). The number of officials was doubled in 1954 and thereafter remained stable until the entry into force of the Rome treaties, when it jumped to 264, 58 of them AD grades. Some observers found this figure absurdly small given the extent of the new Council's activities, but federalist proponents of the Community method were deeply critical of what they saw as an attempt by member state governments to create an administration which would duplicate the work of the Commission and which went against the spirit, if not the letter, of the treaties.[1]

However, the general secretariat soon proved itself to be an indispensable part of the mechanism. Its nature changed rapidly, as it began to take on varied intellectual, technical and legal tasks. It was not an institution, but an important internal organ. By its very nature, it was *communautaire*, despite the fears of its critics. Since the general secretariat was the only Council organ with a permanent composition, it thus ensured continuity (Ganshof van der Meersch, 1969, p 252). This is important in an organisation which – unlike the European Commission and the European Parliament – has a non-permanent presidency in three respects. First, the duration of the traditional Council presidency (six months) was always much shorter than that of the Commission (five years) and the European Parliament (two and a half years). Second, the Council president does not work full time for the Union. He or she typically will only spend a few days each month dealing with EU business (although this may vary from sector to sector – foreign ministers generally have to devote considerably more time to EU business – see chapter 4). Third, the traditional Council presidency is fragmented, with each Council formation chaired by a different government minister. In addition, at the working level many national delegates generally only remain in post for around three or four years, and therefore there is a constant turnover in working parties. The only permanent feature in the Council structure is the secretariat as the repository of the 'institutional memory'.

Within the Council machinery, the Council secretariat has a very important coordinating role to play. The highly fragmented character of the

Council with its different formations and preparatory bodies and its growing problem of internal coordination make the secretariat an indispensable
part of the machinery. It is the only permanent element that can follow
dossiers throughout the whole Council hierarchy. To this end, officials
maintain a close relationship with delegations and the other institutions (see
chapter 13). The secretariat is de facto close to member state governments
and cultivates their confidence. Its members are in constant contact with the
permanent representations and with national experts. They act as confi-
dantes and as sympathetic advisers with inside information. When they are
not in meetings, they are on the telephone, receiving or imparting information, discussing, reassessing, absorbing, or simply providing a metaphorical
shoulder to cry on or an ear to bend. As working parties do not generally
review reports before they are sent to Coreper, there needs to be a large
degree of trust on the part of the national representatives that the secretariat
will represent the discussion in a balanced fashion.

The secretariat's 'traditional' functions

Today's Council secretariat provides the Council's administrative and practical infrastructure at all levels: working parties, Coreper, and the Council
itself. The secretariat's role has evolved considerably over the years and the
range of functions it performs has changed out of all recognition. At the
outset, the secretariat was established to fulfil three traditional functions:
logistics provider, amanuensis/record keeper and purveyor of legal advice.
The first of these has grown from the Council's modest beginnings and it
now requires an extensive logistic backup to enable it to function, ranging
from meetings rooms and facilities for delegations, to interpreting, production and circulation of vast quantities of documents and catering facilities
for staff, delegations, ministers and high level visitors (see chapter 2).
Increasingly the Council has to work in an environment where classified
information can be securely handled. The sophisticated physical and electronic security measures this requires are managed, with due discretion, by
the secretariat.

The second role of record keeper has also evolved over time. As noted
above, Council minutes used to be verbatim accounts of interventions, but
that practice was phased out in the 1970s. The Council rules of procedure
stipulate that the minutes should include, for each item on the agenda, the
documents submitted to the Council, the decisions taken or the conclusions
reached and the statements in the minutes made by the Council, a member
of the Council or the Commission (article 13(1)). Similarly, the record of
meetings at different levels generally takes the form of a summary of the
main conclusions reached as well as an indication of further procedure for
appropriate handling of a matter. The reason for this approach is that it is
not the detail of individual positions which is important in terms of bringing a negotiation forward, but what it is that the collective market will bear
and the paths which can be explored in subsequent discussions in order to
reconcile divergent positions and reach an acceptable conclusion. The role
of note taker extends to producing reports for Coreper or the Council (which
highlight the specific questions to be discussed, amending legislative texts
in the light of discussions, noting reservations and comments in footnotes in

the text), writing briefs for the presidency, providing draft answers to parliamentary questions put to the Council and providing draft speeches to the presidency. The secretariat ensures that deadlines and procedural obligations are respected. It also administers the Council archives.

The role of record keeper is in reality much more challenging than that of a glorified scribe. The most important tool of the trade of secretariat officials is their pens – or rather, nowadays, their keyboards. The papers produced for the Council are one of the instruments in helping the Council take decisions as expeditiously and efficiently as possible. Designing documents as effective negotiating instruments is an art form rather than a science, but it is a vital skill which must be acquired through practice by any official. The first thing that strikes the reader of reports produced by the secretariat for Council meetings is their succinctness and brevity. They generally only contain the minimum information necessary for comprehension of the matter under consideration and avoid needless deviation or repetition. The purpose of documents is to identify problems, possible solutions and the respective degrees of support which exist for various options for going forward. Purely descriptive documents setting out positions generally serve little useful purpose in that context (Council, 2003).

The third role is to provide legal advice to the Council and to represent the Council in cases brought by it or against it in the European Court of Justice. This role is performed by the Council legal service (see section 19.3 below).

The secretariat's 'new' roles

In addition to these 'traditional' roles, the secretariat has in recent years assumed a number of more 'political' roles with successive treaty changes and the increasing size of the Council. These range from being a more active negotiation 'manager', to acting as a political counselor to the presidency, a 'good offices' mediator, a political secretariat for the secretary-general/high representative, as well as assuming an executive role in planning and organising military and civilian crisis management operations.

Assisting with the management of Council business and the negotiating process is a logical extension of greater efforts undertaken in recent years to coordinate the Council's work more effectively. The Council's rules of procedure stipulate that the secretariat will 'be closely and continually involved in organizing, coordinating and ensuring the coherence of the Council's work and implementation of its annual programme' (article 23(3)). This begins with contacts with presidencies, up to a year in advance of them assuming stewardship of the Council, in order to plan the timing of Council meetings and overall programming of work. As the presidency nears, meetings at working party level need to be programmed (particularly where interpreting is required) at least two or three months in advance, taking account of the Council meeting to which a dossier is to be submitted, the need for intervening Coreper discussions, and the time required to consider a proposal in the working party.

In a negotiation on an individual dossier, the secretariat, through following discussions in the working party and through informal contacts with delegations, the Commission and the European Parliament secretariat, will

assist in the process of distinguishing real and false problems in a negotiation and predicting where the point of equilibrium is likely to be found.
An essential part of this process, as outlined above, is preparing papers for
the Council which help all delegations to approach discussion on a text on
the same basis, and which themselves are 'safe' (i.e., they do not elicit criticism from delegations because of biased presentation or misrepresentation
of their position or concerns). Poorly drafted papers can significantly
lengthen the duration of difficult negotiations if delegations do not accept
them as a valid basis for discussion. The primary objective of the secretariat
in accompanying this process with the presidency is to ensure that work
progresses as rapidly and as smoothly as possible.

It is in its capacity as a political counsellor to the presidency that the secretariat's role has changed most significantly, as the Council has grown in
sophistication and extended its reach of subject matters. While the secretariat is entirely at the service of the Council, supporting efforts to find compromise solutions and coordinate work, in practice this means operating in
close conjunction with the presidency. Although the secretariat is in practice
the right hand of the presidency, its fundamental loyalties lie elsewhere. As
Niels Ersbøll gnomically put it: 'our master is the Council – not the individual presidencies. We have ways of acting as a brake on national Presidency
initiatives if ever they should take on an excessive national colouring'
(Ersbøll, 1992). The potential role of the secretariat in conjunction with the
presidency was in fact already highlighted in the report of the 'Three Wise
Men' in 1979: 'It possesses a knowledge of procedures, an overall view of
the machinery, and an opportunity for neutral assessment of other States'
attitudes which even the largest national administration cannot match…The
definition of a more productive, and more consistently applied relationship
of support between the Council Secretariat and the Council Presidency
should be a natural accompaniment to the improved definition of the latter's
duties as a whole' (report of the Three Wise Men, 1979). The relationship
between the Council secretariat and the presidency has subsequently developed further along these lines, and the rules of procedure now expressly
stipulate that 'under the responsibility and guidance of the presidency, it
shall assist the latter in seeking solutions' (article 23(3)).

There are in fact no limits to the counsel that the secretariat may wish to
impart to the presidency. That advice can (and should) relate to the substance of the negotiation and the likely or possible outcomes, as well as the
strategy and tactics for handling specific meetings or dealing with the negotiation as a whole or the difficulties of individual delegations, as well as on
how matters should be presented to the Council. Advice is of course offered
at all levels, most visibly in draft documents to be circulated to the Council,
which are prepared by the secretariat, and in the briefs for Coreper and
Council meetings prepared for the presidency. These briefs include information about the state of play of the negotiations, member states' positions
and strategic and tactical advice on possible ways forward.

The secretariat can be seen as a promoter of the neutrality of the presidency. The involvement of the secretariat in drafting the presidency's compromise solutions is synonymous with neutrality and objectivity in the
quest for balance. This neutrality is important for the proper functioning of
the Council and the Union as a whole. As Ludlow argues: the explanation

of 'bad' presidencies 'is to be found in their inability – or unwillingness – to understand their role'. The presidency is not an instrument with which to pursue national objectives (Ludlow, 1995 p. 157). The secretariat prides itself on its independence from the presidency and its neutrality. This independence can be used as a way to control and to push for the neutrality. However, at the end of the day, it is the presidency which has to carry the can for papers presented in its own name, and, having heard the secretariat's advice, may on occasion prefer an alternative course of action.

The third of the secretariat's evolving functions is that of 'good offices' mediator. As one of the cogs in the Brussels machinery, the secretariat is constantly talking to the presidency, delegations and the other institutions involved in the legislative and policy process in Brussels. It is in this role that it can assist the process of compromise building. It has been extensively argued that this role of the secretariat varies from presidency to presidency. The most frequently voiced argument is that small presidencies tend to rely more heavily on the secretariat (Kirchner, 1992, p. 78). In practice, however, there is no big difference in the role played by the secretariat as between presidencies of big and presidencies of small member states, mainly because, as many practitioners have remarked, the larger resources that big presidencies can muster are often neutralised by difficulties in organising or coordinating internal positions. In the case of large presidencies, the secretariat can often provide an objective external input into the presidency's internal coordination system. In such instances, an external input from a 'neutral' source can greatly assist the internal coordination process on politically difficult issues, since such contributions are not immediately marked as 'questionable' by originating from one of the domestic actors in the internal coordination process.

Relations with the other major policy-shaping institutions are also an important part of the secretariat's mediating role. In addition to its intense contacts with delegations and the presidency, the secretariat has developed a network of relations with both the European Commission and the European Parliament. The relationship between the Council secretariat and the Commission's secretariat general is intense. First, the Commission attends practically all meetings in the Council at all levels. Second, the Commission's general secretariat has a horizontal directorate which deals specifically with relations with the Council. Third, the Commission's deputy secretary-general represents the Commission in Coreper and the secretary-general sometimes stands in for commissioners in Council meetings. Fourthly, frequent contacts occur between the secretaries-general of the Council and Commission (Egger, p. 306).

While there may on occasion be a measure of healthy mutual suspicion between the Council secretariat and the Commission when perceptions on a particular negotiation differ, part of the indispensability of the Council secretariat derives from a fundamental difference between it and the Commission. On any particular issue, especially where it has sole right of legislative initiative, the Commission will have a particular vision of how things should be; it has a prescriptive and normative role. The Council secretariat, on the other hand, has one primary aim: to broker the broadest possible agreement. Though it, too, has a normative role in ensuring respect for the institution's prerogatives and procedures, the Council secretariat is motivated primarily by a search for agreement. It is this constant dialectic between purity of vision and pragmatic agreement which characterises the relationship between the general secretariats of the two institutions. To the objective observer, however, the Council secretariat does not so much compete with the Commission (as federalists in the early 1960s feared), as complement it, for the Council secretariat's role is not one the Commission could easily, if at all, combine with its traditional tasks.

Relations with the European Parliament and the Council have developed extensively in recent years. Until the early 1990s, the 'institutional triangle' was very much isosceles shaped with the focus on the EP-Commission and the Commission-Council relationship. It was only in the budgetary procedure that the EP-Council relationship featured prominently. However, with the introduction of the cooperation and co-decision procedures this situation started to change. The introduction of co-decision in particular led to the creation inside the secretariat of a unit (located in the legal service, see section 19.3 below) acting as the interface with the corresponding horizontal unit in the European Parliament secretariat dealing with all co-decision matters. A consequence of this is that now people in the Council secretariat 'are obliged to follow the work of the EP much more closely and to take it more seriously than has been their practice in the past' (Wallace, 1997). Initial suspicion based on longstanding prejudices on both sides has now given way to a much more pragmatic relationship, involving also the Council presidency and the rapporteurs and committee chairs in the European Parliament in a concerted effort to ensure that procedures operate efficiently, with many less controversial matters already being agreed between the Council and the Parliament at the first reading stage.

The fourth of the Council secretariat's new roles is very different in nature from the three outlined above. The appointment in 1999 of Javier Solana as secretary-general/high representative saw the arrival of a political figure as head of the Council secretariat and has had fundamental consequences on the secretariat's working culture. Unlike other areas, the secretariat has a much more visible profile in foreign policy matters, resembling a political secretariat supporting the high representative in his institutional role under the treaty. Solana himself frequently speaks and contributes to discussions in the External Relations Council (see chapter 4.2), and in bodies lower down the structure members of the secretariat may intervene in meetings or present papers under the authority of the high representative, or chair committees on his behalf (such as the Council's security committee).

While Solana can draw on the resources of the policy unit for his own briefings, he also has at his disposal all the resources of the situation centre, the EU military staff (EUMS) and a directorate-general, as well as special representatives to assist him in his foreign policy tasks. The policy unit also assists in a policy-formulating role next to the policy-mediating role it has also acquired behind the scenes. Fears that assuming a more outspoken stance might impair the secretariat in its mediating role in first-pillar matters have proved largely unfounded, probably because member state governments have a high degree of confidence in Solana and any blurring of the two roles is confined to foreign policy and defence matters. However, there are signs that this more pro-active role in the field of the second pillar is spilling over to other fields (Digneffe, 1999), in particular in areas where working parties are chaired by the secretariat[2].

Finally, the secretariat's executive functions have been extended further in recent years in the context of planning and executing military and civilian crisis management operations (see chapter 4.2). This task, perhaps more than any other, has imposed great strains on the secretariat, by requiring functions for which the secretariat's original structures were not designed. Structures created to follow the regular pace of policy negotiations are ill adapted to the fast moving needs of crisis management operations. These often require the secretariat to acquire specific technical expertise at short notice, to plan certain operations and deal with issues, such as the procurement of sensitive communications material and technology, within tight timelines for which the Union's procurement rules were not designed. The secretariat has had to have recourse to the recruitment of significant numbers of seconded national experts on fixed-term contracts (currently there are around thirty). Moreover, much of this activity has elicited increased interest from the European Parliament, ever watchful of its budget prerogatives, since it views the significant growth in title III (administrative expenditure related to security and defence) of the Council's administrative budget in recent years as verging on the grey zone between administrative and operational expenditure (which would be contrary to the gentlemen's agreement between the Council and the Parliament regarding each institution's administrative budget – see chapter 5.2). This will remain one of the main areas where the secretariat will continue to develop, given the December 2003 European Council conclusions to put in place a civil-military planning cell which may conduct both strategic and operational planning with the potential to operate as an OHQ for certain types of operation.

With all of these roles, and the likelihood of having to assume an ever more proactive role in future, the Council secretariat has considerably grown in importance to become an indispensable part of the Council machinery. Its influence, although discreet and low-key, helps to shape the decision-making process. Its role in mediating outcomes derives from its expertise, the close institutional relations it has both with the Commission and the Parliament and within the Council system itself. In the logic that settling an issue at European level can be considered as promoting the European interest – getting twenty-five sovereign states to agree on something can be considered as an extraordinary feat – the Council secretariat, by boosting the Council's efficiency, can be seen as advancing the European interest. Moreover, through its objective, neutral and independent character, the Council secretariat strengthens the supranational character of the Council as a whole.

Not just the Council secretariat...

In addition to its role servicing the Council, the secretariat has over the years served as the secretariat for a number of other bodies closely associated with the Council either by their nature or because the structures and methods of negotiation equate closely to those of the Council, even if in legal terms they are different animals. The Council secretariat acts as the secretariat for the

European Council, which is a distinct entity from the Council (see chapter 9), a role carved out for the secretariat by Niels Ersbøll in the 1980s.

Similarly it acts as the secretariat for intergovernmental conferences to revise the treaties and for the accession of new member states. In their structure and negotiating methods, these two fora equate closely to the Council, and there is therefore a certain logic in having the Council secretariat providing the secretariat for such bodies (see chapter 10). The Council secretariat also acted as the secretariat for the convention which negotiated the EU's charter of fundamental rights in 2000. In the case of the European Convention, the secretariat was provided by an independent secretariat headed by a former UK permanent representative and head of the UK diplomatic service, Sir John Kerr, which contained representatives from the Council and European Parliament secretariats and the Commission. Finally the secretariat also acts for the secretariat of various joint bodies set up under international agreements concluded by the Union (e.g. the ACP-EU Council of Ministers and various association and cooperation councils with third countries).

The secretariat's administrative structure

In addition to the private office of the secretary-general and the deputy secretary-general, the modern day Council secretariat is divided into nine directorates-general (see figure 19.1). Traditionally, the various directorates-general in the Council secretariat were named by letters of the alphabet. Some of these, such as DG H (justice and home affairs), are a recent creation following the entry into force of the Maastricht Treaty. As Ersbøll has pointed out, although theoretically new ground, this was not exactly alien territory for the general secretariat: 'the Council Secretariat has for a long time been involved in activities of this kind, having served as Secretariat for intergovernmental cooperation on immigration...' (Ersbøll, 1992). Intergovernmental cooperation of this sort had previously been serviced by a small unit working within the private office (see chapter 6).

In recent years, the secretariat has consolidated and reduced the number of its directorates-general. With previous enlargements, there was a tendency to increase the number of directorates-general, with the result that at one time there was pressure to achieve a structure allowing the appointment of one director-general of each nationality of the member states of the Union. However, following this approach would ultimately be unsustainable, and in 2001 a substantial restructuring of the directorates-general took place to reduce them to nine in order to ensure that the secretariat's structures were more in line with the functional needs of the Council.

The Council recruits its own officials, as do all the institutions. They are EU civil servants, subject to the same staff regulations, which state that each official 'shall carry out his duties and conduct himself solely with the interest of the Communities in mind; he shall neither seek nor take instructions from any government, authority, organisation or person outside his institution'. Staff working in the secretariat are therefore independent not only from national governments, but also from the other Union institutions such as the Commission and the European Parliament. Their sole allegiance is to the Council.

Figure 19.1: *The secretariat's internal organisational structure*

Secretary-General
Private Office
Policy Unit
EU Military Staff
EU Situation Centre

Deputy Secretary-General
Private Office
General Policy Questions
General Administrative Questions
Security
Infosec
Health and Safety Internal Audit
Personal Data Protection

Legal Service

Directorate-General A
Personnel and Administration, Human Resources

Directorate-General B
Agriculture and Fisheries

Directorate-General C
Internal market, Customs Union, Industrial policy, Telecommunications,
Information society, Research, Energy, Transport

Directorate-General E
External and Politico-Military Affairs

Directorate-General F
Press, Communications, Protocol

Directorate-General G
Economic and Social Affairs

Directorate-General H
Justice and Home Affairs

Directorate-General I
Environment, Consumer Protection, Civil Protection, Health,
Foodstuffs Legislation, Education, Youth, Culture, Audiovisual

Source: Council Secretariat.

Note: Directorate-general D no longer exists.

The Council's 'AD' officials hail from a range of backgrounds. There is no privileged channel for recruitment, and all must pass a rigorous open competition or other selection procedure before they can be employed. One can find graduates from disciplines as diverse as the classics, theology and medicine. Some worked in their national civil service before joining the Council, while others were employed in professions as varied as teaching, banking, academia, economic analysis, lobbying, translating, town planning and IT programming! Given the multicultural mix of twenty-five nationalities found in the secretariat, and the particular challenges that poses in terms of coping with different work cultures, prejudices and stereotypes, there is no standard 'profile' of the typical Council official.

In the 2003-2004 period, the secretariat was involved in two reform processes which between them are resulting in significant changes for the working conditions of staff. On the one hand, the EU embarked on a substantial reform of the pay, pensions and career structure for permanent civil servants which was implemented on 1 May 2004, the date of enlargement. The second was an internal modernization of the Council's administrative structures and practices, implemented by the deputy secretary-general, and aimed at ensuring that the secretariat had at its disposal the structures, means and working methods to enable it to cope with some of the challenges outlined above.

19.3 The Council's Legal Service by Michael Bishop

The Council needs an independent legal service to help it respect the rule of law on which the EU is based, and to defend it in cases before the Court of Justice. These are no easy tasks: the former requires gaining the confidence of the national delegations, each of which has its own government lawyers to advise it separately; and the latter involves conducting litigation against some of the finest advocates to be found.

There is also a special group of 'lawyer-linguists' within the legal service, which is responsible for editing the final drafts of all legal texts to be adopted by the Council in each of the Union's official languages. Finally, the legal service is responsible for relations with the other EU institutions, in particular with the European Parliament, as well as for management within the secretariat of the co-decision procedure.

Organisation of the legal service

The legal service is under the responsibility of a director-general, who is the Council's legal advisor. There are nearly 50 lawyers and 65 lawyer-linguists, with one or more nationals from nearly every member state in both groups; this is necessary in order for the different legal systems to be properly understood. In addition, there are a dozen or so others (not necessarily lawyers by training) in the departments responsible for interinstitutional relations and for managing the co-decision procedure (these tasks, as well as those of the lawyer-linguists, are dealt with in separate sections below).

The legal service is organised into several teams, each headed up by one or two directors, and with the following areas of responsibility. Team I: internal market/competitiveness and other matters prepared by Coreper part I; the department responsible for managing the co-decision procedure is included within this team (see below). Team II: common agricultural policy, EMU/Ecofin and VAT/taxation. Team III: external relations (common foreign and security policy (CFSP)/ European security and defence policy (ESDP), trade policy, enlargement and questions of international law). Team IV: institutional, budgetary and staff matters. Team V: police and judicial cooperation, civil law, immigration and asylum. Team VI: interinstitutional relations, in particular with the European Parliament (see below).

The legal advisor attends at meetings of the European Council, the General Affairs and External Relations Council and Coreper part II. Directors from the legal service attend the meetings of other Council formations and Coreper part I, as well as the political and security committee, the 'Article 36' committee and the special committee on agriculture. The other lawyers are each responsible for following the various Council working parties. So there is always a member of the legal service on hand, to assist as necessary at meetings of the Council and its preparatory bodies.

Questions dealt with by the legal service

The legal service has a seat beside the presidency at meetings within the Council, and its representative will take the floor in response to any legal or institutional questions raised. The service is also responsible for drawing attention on its own initiative to problems which would not have been noticed otherwise.

Opinions may be given on many different questions. For example, a typical question will be to identify the correct legal basis for a proposal. The answer is important, because it determines whether the treaty provides the necessary power to adopt the proposal, according to what procedure (codecision or other) and by what voting rule (qualified majority, unanimity). These factors will obviously have an effect on the conduct of the negotiations and indeed on their outcome, in terms of substantive content. The same goes for the question of whether the Community has exclusive power to conclude an international agreement with a third country/countries, or whether that power belongs to the member states as well ('mixed agreement').

The legal service will also have to check whether the specific provisions of a proposal – or amendments which delegations may wish to introduce – comply with general principles of Community law, e.g. proportionality, non-discrimination, respect for legitimate expectations and the right to own property or carry on a business. Equally, it is necessary to ensure that a proper statement of reasons is given in the recitals to a measure, especially in problematic cases which could give rise to litigation. Another trap to avoid is that if the Council intends making amendments to a Commission proposal which are significant enough taken as a whole, then the European Parliament will have to be re-consulted, according to the case-law of the Court of Justice[3].

The preceding matters (legal basis, general principles of law, statement of reasons, etc.) all constitute grounds for the annulment of a Council act by the Court. So the advice of the legal service always has to be professional and independent, since the question could be taken to the Court subsequently.

The application of the Council's rules of procedure – some of which would also constitute grounds for annulment – also gives rise to many questions. For example: whether the necessary quorum of ministers is present; the adoption of the agenda (have the items been included in good time?); matters of confidentiality/openness (debates televised to the public); voting records; use of the written procedure for the adoption of Council acts; translation of documents; publications in the Official Journal, and so on.

Measures adopted by the Council in the foreign policy area (CFSP/ESDP) are not subject to review by the Court of Justice (although the Court does have jurisdiction to ensure that such measures do not encroach upon the powers of the Community). If anything, however, the absence of judicial review makes it even more important to ensure that the measures adopted in this area are lawful, i.e., that they respect human rights and fundamental freedoms, and comply with international law as well as with the provisions of the treaty itself.

The legal service has an important role to play in European security and defence policy, which has taken shape through the development of civilian and military crisis management operations. That presented a major institutional challenge: how to take account of NATO and those of its European members which are not EU member states whilst preserving the EU's decision-making autonomy. This matter has been successfully resolved, through the so-called 'Berlin plus' arrangements which were agreed with NATO in December 2002.

When the EU launches a crisis management operation, there is always a need for legal input. Firstly, it will be necessary to adopt a legal act (CFSP joint action), following a United Nations resolution or an invitation by the government of a third country for the EU to intervene. It would also be necessary to draw up rules of engagement and an agreement on the status of forces (SOFA), where an EU-led military force is deployed in order to enforce the peace (e.g. operation Artemis in the Congo in the summer of 2003). There could be legal questions about the use of airspace, freedom to navigate at sea, humanitarian law, etc. There are privileges and immunities to deal with, questions of contractual and extra-contractual liability, customs duties and other taxes, the recruitment of local staff, budgetary and financial matters, public procurement, etc. Similar questions arise in the case of EU police operations (e.g. the EU police mission in Bosnia and Herzegovina from March 2002). In order to prepare for these new challenges, the legal service has recruited several military lawyers with the necessary expertise.

In addition to advising the Council as such, the legal service gives advice to the presidency and the secretary-general/high representative, with regard to their responsibilities for implementing CFSP decisions and representing the EU externally.

Equally, the legal service gives advice to senior management within the secretariat, on administrative and budgetary questions such as delegations' travelling expenses, building projects, the administrative consequences of enlargement, the recruitment of officials and other staff, disciplinary proceedings, etc. Members of the legal service also agree to sit on various administrative committees, where their expertise is put to good use.

The legal advisor acted as advisor to the intergovernmental conferences in 1991 (Maastricht), 1995 (Amsterdam), 2000 (Nice) and 2003 (a Constitution for Europe). In the last case, this involved producing a re-drafted version – together with explanatory notes – of the text produced by the Convention, and chairing a working party of the delegations' legal experts, in order to complete the treaty/constitution.

Finally, the legal service sometimes combines its normal task of giving legal advice with a wider-ranging policy role. That was the case, for example, with the *Report on the Operation of the Council with an enlarged Union in prospect*, better known as the Trumpf/Piris report after its authors (respectively, the former secretary-general and the legal advisor) (Council, 1999b).

Production of legal opinions

The legal service produces more than a hundred written opinions or contributions every year, for the Council and its preparatory bodies. In addition, it produces a good many more internal notes for use within the secretariat, as well as briefing notes for the presidency when necessary. All written opinions and notes must be approved by the director responsible for the matter in question, as well as by the legal advisor who is in a position to take an overall view and thus ensure consistency in the legal service's positions.

Opinions and written contributions of the legal service are produced as separate documents, and may not be disclosed under the rules governing public access to Council documents[4]. For the same reason, oral advice given at a meeting by a representative of the legal service is not reproduced in the record/minutes of meetings.

Internal meetings within the service

If the legal service has to take a position on an important question, this will be discussed beforehand at a meeting between the legal advisor and the directors, as well as the lawyer responsible for the subject in question. There is also a regular 'information meeting' every week, for all the lawyers and a representative from the lawyer-linguists. It consists of going through the previous week's meetings of Council and Coreper, and pointing out any legal or institutional questions which had arisen. Each lawyer present may then report on any question of interest which they recently encountered in Council working parties or proceedings before the Courts. These information meetings give the members of the legal service a general overview of everything going on within the Council and its different formations, which helps them to contribute towards achieving consistency.

Research and know-how

The legal service has a special research and documentation unit, staffed by several assistants who undertake researches on request and help the lawyers with their own research. Each lawyer has a computer with access to the CELEX law system, the Official Journal on-line and the internet, together with an internal database of legal opinions and internal memos. The collection of paper files goes all the way back to the very beginnings of the Coal and Steel Community, over fifty years ago. The legal service also has its own law library separate from the secretariat's main reference library, and there is a wide range of law journals and periodicals which are circulated amongst the lawyers according to their specific interests.

Interinstitutional relations

As already mentioned above, the legal service (Team VI) also has the responsibility within the secretariat for handling relations with other EU institutions and bodies, in particular with the European Parliament. This includes preparing draft replies to parliamentary questions (written and oral questions by MEPs to the Council), in conjunction with the relevant directorate in the secretariat according to the subject. It is also necessary to attend the plenary sessions and committee meetings of the European Parliament, in order to give the necessary assistance there to the president of the Council and to the secretary-general/high representative during their regular appearances. Reports on the discussions are prepared and distributed to the delegations and to the relevant services of the general secretariat.

In addition, this team covers issues which have to be negotiated with the other institutions, in particular with the European Parliament, such as the question of a statute for MEPs (including their pay and expenses) and the regulations governing political parties at European level (adopted on 4

November 2003), as well the negotiations on interinstitutional agreements, e.g. the IIA on better law-making which was signed on 16 December 2003.

This team also covers day-to-day relations with the European Economic and Social Committee and the Committee of the Regions. This task includes reporting on the activities of plenary sessions and bureau meetings, as well as preparing the Council decisions to appoint the members of these bodies, and managing the consultation of them on legislative proposals where necessary.

Management of the co-decision procedure

As also mentioned above, the legal service includes a special department (the so-called 'backbone' in Team I) which is responsible for managing the co-decision procedure within the general secretariat. The backbone works in close cooperation with the other Council directorates responsible for the policy area in question (transport, environment, etc.).

The backbone follows the proceedings of the committee(s) within the European Parliament which examines a particular proposal, and it produces an information note on the outcome of both the first and second readings. If the conciliation committee has to be convened, the backbone is responsible for making the necessary preparations, including attendance at the trilogue meetings which take place beforehand between the Council presidency (the chair of Coreper), the European Parliament and the Commission. The backbone is also involved with the drafting of the joint text agreed in the conciliation committee, and it will ensure that the item is subsequently put onto the Council's agenda for formal adoption, signature etc. The backbone ensures consistency in the Council's handling of the co-decision procedure, by making good use of the expertise which it has built up in dealing with the European Parliament.

Quality of drafting

EU legislation often leaves much to be desired in terms of drafting quality, which is partly due to the fact that it is negotiated between a large number of parties ('committee document'): the Commission, the delegations within the Council and the European Parliament. The Council is aware of this problem, and has taken various steps to address it. Firstly, there is a provision in the Council's rules of procedure (article 22): 'the Legal Service shall be responsible for checking the drafting quality of proposals and draft acts at the appropriate stage, as well as for bringing suggestions to the attention of the Council and its bodies'. By a minutes statement on the same provision, the Council also instructed the legal service to give the necessary assistance to any member state wishing to put forward an initiative in the field of justice and home affairs, by tidying up the text before it is formally presented or at least before the initiative is published in the Official Journal.

The Council also concluded an interinstitutional agreement on 22 December 1998 with the European Parliament and the Commission on common guidelines for the quality of drafting of Community legislation, whereby the three institutions' legal services are invited to put forward appropriate drafting suggestions in order to make legislation clearer and more precise. The legal services subsequently drew up a joint practical guide for persons involved in the drafting of legislation, which was agreed on 16 March 2000.

The fact remains, however, that sometimes the only way to get a text agreed is by using a deliberately ambiguous form of words ('papering over the cracks'). In that situation, where delegations disagree over the substance, any attempt to improve the drafting quality of the text by making it clearer and more precise is likely to be in vain.

There is also an interinstitutional agreement of 20 December 1994 on an accelerated working method for the official codification of legislative texts, as well as an interinstitutional agreement of 28 November 2001 on a more structured use of the 're-casting' technique in order to achieve the same objective more effectively, i.e., by amending, codifying and replacing legislation all at once. Under these agreements, the legal services have been given a special role in identifying those parts of a Commission proposal which go beyond pure codification.

Finally, there is the interinstitutional agreement on better law-making signed on 16 December 2003, which contains further provisions for improving the quality of legislation, simplifying it and reducing the volume of legislation, as well as for better transposition and application by member states. The agreement also covers matters such as better coordination of the legislative process between the institutions, greater transparency and public accessibility, choice of legislative instrument and the possibility of using alternative methods of regulation where appropriate (for example, through the social partners).

The 'Lawyer-Linguists'

As already mentioned, there is a special group of 'lawyer-linguists' in the legal service, which is responsible for editing the final drafts of all acts to be adopted by the Council and published in the Official Journal. This task involves laying the text out properly, using the right terminology and ensuring that the act says exactly the same thing in all the official languages. This latter requirement is clearly vital for the uniform application of EU legislation, since each language version is equally authentic; and depending on the kind of act, it may be directly applicable without the need for transposing it into national legislation.

The lawyer-linguists work to the highest standards, but their scope for improving the drafting quality of the texts which they receive is limited, since these texts will have been already agreed within the working party and Coreper. The national delegations are invited to attend the meetings of the lawyer-linguists at which the drafts are finalised, and these delegations will naturally be reluctant to see any changes made to their painstakingly negotiated compromises, even when this appears necessary. Consideration is being given, however, to the possibility of involving the lawyer-linguists at an earlier stage in the process.

Cases before the Court of Justice

Litigation before the EU Court of Justice and Court of First Instance accounts for about one-third of the legal service's workload, although the proportion varies from one sector to another. This is a demanding and important task, which normally involves defending the Council against an action for the annulment or invalidation of one of its acts, or for damages.

Direct actions for annulment may be brought by the Commission, the European Parliament and any member state – e.g. after it has been out-voted in the Council. Actions for annulment may also be brought by private businesses or persons if they are directly and individually concerned by the contested measure. Even if that is not the case, the validity of the measure can still be challenged through the preliminary rulings procedure, whereby a national court may refer it to the Court of Justice.

The legal service defends the validity of Council acts (or possibly its failure to act) as a matter of course, whenever they are challenged in a direct action or by a reference for a preliminary ruling; in such cases, the legal service simply informs Coreper with a note about the proceedings. In other cases not involving the legality of a Council act, any decision to go to court would have to be taken by the Council itself, on a recommendation from the legal service. This would be the case if the Council decides to bring legal proceedings against another institution[5] to intervene in litigation between other institutions or between another institution and a member state[6], or to obtain the opinion of the Court on whether the treaty is compatible with the provisions of an international agreement which is envisaged.

The director-general normally appoints two members of the legal service to represent the Council as its agents in the case, under a standing delegation of authority which he has received from the Council. The agents will normally be the lawyer responsible for the subject-matter at issue, together with another lawyer who is fluent in the language of the case (the language is chosen by the applicant in direct actions, and it will be the language of the national court in the case of a reference for a preliminary ruling).

The Council's agents then prepare written pleadings which thoroughly address all the relevant facts and issues in the case. The draft pleadings are sent to the permanent representations one week before they have to be lodged at the Court, so the delegations have the opportunity to comment on them. However, there are no meetings held within the Council to discuss or approve the pleadings: the Council's agents are entrusted to defend the Council as they see fit. Each member state is entitled to intervene separately by making its own submissions to the Court.

Once the parties' pleadings have been lodged and exchanged, the written stage of the procedure is closed. The next stage is the public hearing, where the Council's agents have to present their case orally against the other parties' lawyers, and reply to any questions which the judges and the advocate-general may put to them. Most cases are heard by a chamber of five judges, but if the case is sufficiently important it will be heard by the full Court.

When the Court eventually gives its judgment, the legal service informs Coreper about it with a note. The Council hardly ever loses a case, but if that does happen then it may be necessary to take certain measures to comply with the Court's judgment. For example, the Council may have to re-adopt an annulled act on another legal basis or after re-consulting the European Parliament, or by amending provisions which have been found contrary to general principles of Community law.

Conclusion

The legal service plays a prominent role in all aspects of the Council's work, including questions dealt with at the highest level. For example, after the negative Danish referendum on the Maastricht Treaty, the legal advisor helped to devise an ingenious solution which was endorsed by the Edinburgh European Council, and the result was subsequently reversed in a second referendum.

Thanks to its proven independence and the quality of its work, the legal service is highly valued and the Council nearly always follows its advice. On the rare occasions when the Council fails to do so, then the Court of Justice will usually rectify the situation later – even though the members of the legal service appointed to defend the Council as its agents will then have had to plead in favour of what they had originally advised against!

PART 7: LOOKING TO THE FUTURE

an intergovernmental international organisation in which the member states' ministries of foreign affairs play a key role, both through the General Affairs and External Relations Council and through the permanent representatives committee. Thus, as some of the key actors in the Council's decision-making process are rooted in the tradition of confidentiality of diplomatic negotiations, it is not surprising that this culture also influenced the way in which the Council operates.

Second, the Council is often described as the institution in which the member states' national interests – as opposed to the Union's interests – are advanced and defended. However, as previous chapters in this book have shown, in general Council members do not pursue only their government's own interests, but also recognize that in the long run it is in their national interest to have a system that works, which requires give and take in order to strike a compromise. Regrettably, instead of explaining openly why they sometimes abandon initial positions for the sake of the common interest, ministers often chose to blame 'Brussels' for unpopular decisions. It is therefore hardly astonishing that the Council members were less than keen in making public their internal deliberations and preparatory documents.

The third element is closely linked to the preceding one. For some time, the Council did not put much effort into a serious information policy. The general secretariat understood its role as serving the Council, but not as playing an active role in public and press relations, and the Council lacked a 'corporate identity' of its own.

These factors led to almost total secrecy about the Council's deliberations. Citizens were unable to know how representatives of their governments had voted in the Council and why they took a particular position. Without exception, Council meetings took place behind closed doors. Legislative acts adopted by the Council were often accompanied by statements which gave an interpretation of certain provisions of those acts or explained why the Council or one of its members took a certain position. None of those statements were made public. Council members, their delegates and officials of the Council's general secretariat were bound by a strict obligation of professional secrecy, subject to practically no exception. There were no rules on access to Council documents. For all those reasons, it was very difficult, if not impossible, for citizens to follow directly the Council's debates and the arguments exchanged in the discussion between the Commission proposal and the final adoption of the act. One qualification, however, to this apparent veil of secrecy is the fact that Brussels journalists and lobbyists could always get a blow by blow account of what had gone on in Council meetings through press conferences and contacts with officials and civil servants. Indeed, there are few more leaky organisations than the European institutions.

The Maastricht Treaty: the emergence of transparency as a political concept

It is probably no coincidence that things started to change with the completion of the single market programme and the entry into force of the Treaty on European Union (the Maastricht Treaty) on 1 November 1993. Up to then, the European Communities were mainly occupied with creating a common agricultural policy, eliminating trade barriers and establishing the single market. With the Treaty on European Union, the integration process made a leap forward. A range of new policy areas emerged, notably in the field of economic and monetary union, justice and home affairs and foreign and security policy. The new co-decision procedure, by reinforcing the European Parliament's role, made it apparent that the Council and the European Parliament fulfil legislative functions in areas of direct concern to citizens.

In declaration No. 17 annexed to the final act of Maastricht, the Intergovernmental Conference underlined that 'transparency of the decision-making process strengthens the democratic nature of the institutions and the public's confidence in the administration' and invited the Commission to submit to the Council, no later than 1993, a report on measures to improve public access to the information available to the institutions. In the wake of the Danish 'no' and the French 'near no' in the referenda on the Maastricht Treaty in June and September 1992, respectively, a number of political initiatives followed, such as the so-called 'Birmingham Declaration' of 16 October 1992 entitled *A Community close to its citizens* and the conclusions of the Edinburgh European Council of 12 December 1992. The latter foresaw measures aimed at improving access to the Council's work (open debates, publication of votes) and information on its role, simplification of and easier access to Community legislation, and consolidation or codification of Community legislation. In the conclusions of its meeting in Copenhagen on 21 and 22 June 1993, the European Council re-affirmed its commitment 'to continue the process of creating a more open and transparent Community'.

The 1993 code of conduct: first legal rules on access to documents

In December 1993, the European Council's political orientations were translated into legal acts. On 6 December 1993, the Council adopted a new version of its rules of procedure (Council, 1993), which allowed public debates and publication of voting records and explanations of votes in certain cases. Although the Council could still decide not to publish the result of a vote, the Council never used this possibility when acting as legislator (Council, 1995). On the same day, the Council and the Commission agreed on a code of conduct (EC, 1993) 'the 1993 code of conduct', which laid down principles for the public's access to documents held by these institutions, with each institution implementing this code by legal decisions[1]. In the absence of another legal basis in the treaty, the Council's decision was based on article 151(3) TEC (now article 207) and article 22 of its rules of procedure, both of which concerned the Council's internal organization[2].

Both decisions were applicable to all documents held by the institutions, but because of the 'authorship rule' documents emanating from third parties were practically excluded from their scope. Access had to be granted unless the requested document was covered by a mandatory exception which protected certain public or private interests or by a discretionary exception, which protected the confidentiality of the Council's proceedings.

In the following years, the Council gradually acquired experience with the application of these legal instruments. On the basis of its rules of procedure and a code of conduct of 2 October 1995, the institution systematically published the results of votes on legislative acts and the statements to the minutes referring to these acts. In the area of access to documents, the Council, not least due to the case law of the Community courts and the recommendations of the European ombudsman, consolidated its implementation of the legal rules and its administrative practices to make the system more efficient and user-friendly. An important step in this direction was the creation of a public register containing titles, dates and reference numbers of Council documents, which was made available on the internet from 1 January 1999. In December 1999, the Council decided to extend the coverage of the register to classified documents, subject to certain restrictions necessary for the protection of public or private interests, and to make accessible to the public a list of the items on the provisional agendas of Council meetings and its preparatory bodies relating to the Council's legislative activities. Since 1 July 2000, the full content of documents released following requests under the 1993 access decision is made directly available to the public on the internet.

The Amsterdam Treaty and the 'Solana decision'

A landmark on the way to greater transparency was the Treaty of Amsterdam, which entered into force on 1 May 1999. It enshrined the 'principle of openness' in the Treaty on European Union, whose article 1(2) provides that decisions are taken as openly as possible. A new article 255 TEC explicitly anchored the right of access for any citizen of the Union and any natural or legal person residing or having its registered office in a member state to European Parliament, Council and Commission documents[3], subject to the principles and conditions to be defined in accordance with paragraphs 2 and 3. Under article 207(3) TEC, the Council is required to 'define the cases in which it is to be regarded as acting in its legislative capacity, with a view to allowing greater access to documents in those cases, while at the same time preserving the effectiveness of its decision-making process'. In line with the Council's constant practice, the results of votes and explanations of vote as well as statements in the minutes are to be made public when the Council acts in its legislative capacity.

However, the path to more openness was not without hurdles and temporary setbacks. The political impetus lent by the Helsinki European Council in December 1999 to the Union's emerging means for military and non-military crisis management and to the establishment of military structures within the Council, meant specific protection of sensitive documents relating to these matters was required. Therefore, on 14 August 2000, the Council amended its rules on public access to documents[4] in order to exclude documents classified 'confidential' and above on matters concerning security and defence or military or non-military crisis management from their scope of application. This decision, known as the 'Solana decision', gave rise to harsh criticism, in particular from the European Parliament which, alongside a number of member states, challenged its legality before the Court of Justice. The treatment of highly classified documents continued to be one of the most difficult issues during the subsequent negotiations on the new rules on access to documents foreseen in article 255(2) TEC. However, following agreement on these rules and the implementing provisions which repealed the 1993 access decision, as amended by the Solana decision, the actions before the Court of Justice were withdrawn.

The new legal framework

On 26 January 2000, the Commission presented a proposal for a regulation laying down the general principles and limits governing the right of access to European Parliament, Council and Commission documents. After intensive and difficult negotiations, the three institutions agreed a compromise text which was adopted, in first reading, as regulation (EC) 1049/2001 of the European Parliament and of the Council regarding public access to European Parliament, Council and Commission documents[5] ('the access regulation'). It has been applicable since 3 December 2001.

The specific provisions to be adopted by the European Parliament, the Council and the Commission regarding access to their documents pursant to article 255(3) TEC should ensure that documents are as far as possible made directly accessible to the public in electronic form or through a register. The Council had already adopted far-reaching provisions in this sense in a decision of 9 April 2001 which provided that certain categories of documents, in particular those relating to its legislative activities, are published on the internet through the public register, without any application being necessary. With effect from 3 December 2001, the content of this decision was taken over in a new annex III to the Council's rules of procedure (Council, 2001), which also laid down other specific provisions regarding public access to Council documents.

In the following years, further progress was made as regards the opening to the public of Council meetings when the Council is acting as legislator in accordance with the co-decision procedure: following the European Council meeting on 21 and 22 June 2002 in Seville, a new version of the Council's rules of procedure, adopted on 22 July 2002 (Council, 2002), provided for open debates during the initial stage and the final stage of the procedure (see below).

In parallel, the legal framework relating to access to documents was completed. The conclusion of the interinstitutional agreement of 20 November 2002 between the European Parliament and the Council concerning access by the European Parliament to sensitive information of the Council in the field of security and defence policy (EC, 2002), which is foreseen by article 9(7) of the access regulation, marked the end of the dispute between the two institutions over the issue of sensitive documents in the field of security and defence policy which began with the adoption of the 'Solana decision' and continued with the adoption of the Council's security regulations (Council, 2001a) on 19 March 2001, whose legality was also challenged by the European Parliament before the Court of Justice[6]. Furthermore, the rules on access to documents held by Community agencies and bodies and those institutions which are not covered by the access regulation as well as the rules concerning the historical archives were brought into line with the principles and limits laid down in the access regulation (see below).

At the same time, the institutions were gaining first experiences with the implementation of the new rules on access to documents. As for the Council, these are recorded in its annual reports for 2002 and 2003 (which are available on the public register). In January 2004, the Commission published a comprehensive report on the implementation of the access regulation (Commission, 2004), giving an overview of implementation of the access rules by all three institutions and problems encountered as well as proposing a number of measures to remedy those problems. It does not foresee any amendment of the access regulation in the near future, but suggests that it be revised in tandem with the process of ratification of the constitutional treaty on which the Intergovernmental Conference reached political agreement on June 2004 (see final section below), when more experience and case law are available and a broad public debate has taken place.

Openness of the Council's proceedings

Public debates

The general rule governing the Council's meetings and deliberations still reflects its diplomatic tradition. Under article 5(1) of the Council's rules of procedure, meetings of the Council are not public, except in the cases referred to in article 8. Nevertheless, as outlined above, exceptions to the principle of confidentiality of the Council's proceedings have become not only more numerous but, above all, more substantial over the past ten years. When open debates were first introduced in 1993, they were in fact not real debates, but rather monotonous monologues of ministers reading out speeches prepared before the meeting. They gave a false impression of openness, and their impact on transparency and public interest in them was minimal.

This changed with the conclusions of the Seville European Council in June 2002 and the subsequent amendments to the Council's rules of procedure. In addition to an annual public policy debate on the Council's operational programme and further public debates to be decided on a case-by-case basis on important issues affecting the interests of the Union, the rules of procedure foresee for the first time open debates at the end of the legislative procedure. As regards acts to be adopted under the co-decision procedure, not only the presentation by the Commission of its most important legislative proposals and the ensuing debate in the Council, but also 'the vote on legislative acts shall be open to the public, as well as the final Council deliberations leading to that vote and the explanations of voting accompanying it.'

Thus, within the co-decision procedure, the final debate on the Council's common position and the final act as a 'B' item which is meant to result in a political agreement is open to the public and transmitted by audiovisual means. Although this debate is usually not followed by a vote, it constitutes the last debate before the final adoption of the act in all language versions as an 'A' item in a later Council meeting, which is also public. The 'A' items relating to acts adopted under the co-decision procedure are grouped together and marked on the agenda, so that the president can publicly announce the adoption of each of those items and the vote. Delegations can intervene to give explanations of their vote. For practical reasons, public 'A' items are usually dealt with back-to-back with public debates on 'B' items during the same Council meeting.

Admittedly, application of these new rules is still not perfect. For instance, there were complaints that certain public debates were announced too late or that the initial timetable was changed during the meeting without advance notice. However, a start has been made. In 2003, there were public debates in 47 Council meetings, in which a total of 123 'A' items, 47 'B' items (all of them relating to legislative acts) and 11 other items, notably important legislative initiatives, like the CAP reform package, and policy-oriented issues, like the Council's operational programme for 2003 relating to the western Balkans or the presidency's work programme, were dealt with.

In practice, the adoption of acts as 'A' items and explanations of votes relating thereto in an open debate adds nothing to transparency, since this information is public anyway and, by definition, there is no debate on 'A' items. However, opening up final debates on acts in the context of the co-decision procedure as 'B' items amounts to a more radical change. For the first time in the Council's history, the public can follow a Council debate in which real negotiations take place. Of course, like all items on the agenda of Council meetings, the debate on acts in the context of the co-decision procedure is prepared beforehand by the presidency with the assistance of the general secretariat, sounding out possible compromises on open questions in bilateral contacts. Nevertheless, the majority of public debates on 'B' items which have taken place are not mere 'shows' of pre-cooked agreements for the public, but real discussions.

Making public votes, explanations of vote and minutes

Article 9 of the Council's rules of procedure sets out the cases in which the results of votes, the explanations of votes and the Council minutes are made public.

In many cases, publication is automatic. In addition to the cases where Council deliberations are open to the public, the results of votes and explanations of votes by Council members, as well as the statements in the Council minutes and the items in those minutes relating to the adoption of the act in question, are made public automatically where the Council adopts a legislative act (within the meaning of article 7 of the Council's rules of procedure) or a common position (under the co-decision or cooperation procedure), or where the Council establishes a title VI convention. The same rule applies to the results of votes and explanations of votes by Council members or their representatives in co-decision conciliation committees, as well as to the statements in the Council minutes and the items in those minutes relating to the conciliation committees.

When the Council acts on matters of foreign policy or in certain cases relating to cooperation in police and criminal justice matters, the publication of the results of votes requires a unanimous Council or Coreper decision, requested by one of their members. In all other cases, the Council or Coreper can decide by simple majority, when requested by one of their members, to publicise the result of the vote. When the result of a vote is made public, the explanations of votes are also made public by a decision taken by simple majority at the request of the Council members concerned, 'with due regard for the Council's Rules of Procedure, legal certainty and the interests of the Council' (article 9(2) of the Council's rules of procedure). Statements entered in the Council minutes and items in those minutes relating to the adoption of the acts referred to above are made public by Council or Coreper decision.

Votes and explanations of votes are published in Council press releases. Statements to the minutes are available the same day from the press office. In addition, monthly lists of acts adopted by the Council include the results of votes, the explanations of votes and the statements entered in the Council minutes which are public in application of the above-mentioned rules. These lists, as well as the items in the Council minutes which are made public in the form of addenda to the draft Council minutes, are directly accessible on the Council's internet site.

Access to Council documents

The applicable rules

Access to Council documents is governed by the access regulation and the Council's rules of procedure (Council, 2004). The general rule underlying the access regulation (see recital 11) is that in principle all documents of the institutions should be accessible to the public, whilst certain public and private interests should be protected by way of exceptions. Article 6(1) of the Council's rules of procedure provides that the obligation of professional secrecy covering the Council's deliberations applies without prejudice to its articles 8 and 9 and to provisions on public access to documents.

The access regulation and the Council's rules of procedure have been complemented by implementing rules which contain practical instructions on the production of various categories of documents and the types of documents that must be made directly accessible to the public. In addition, a comprehensive 'transparency guide' gives practical information on procedures for the implementation of the rules on access to documents and other aspects of transparency in the broad sense.

Who can get access to documents?

Under the treaty and the access regulation, the right of access is limited to citizens of the Union and natural and legal persons residing or having their registered office in a member state. However, in line with previous rules and practice, all three institutions grant access to their documents also to all other natural or legal persons[7]. In any event, as more and more applications are lodged by e-mail, it is impossible to verify an applicant's nationality or residence.

It follows from its purpose that the access regulation does not apply to requests for documents made by member states and the Community institutions and bodies. In their relations between themselves and with the member states, the institutions are bound by the principle of loyal cooperation and, on certain aspects, by specific provisions, like for instance the interinstitutional agreement of 20 November 2002 between the European

Parliament and the Council concerning access by the European Parliament to sensitive information of the Council in the field of security and defence policy (see above). However, individual members of the European Parliament can avail of the access regulation vis-à-vis the Council[8] and the Commission.

Which entities are bound by the rules on access to documents?

Like article 255 TEC, the access regulation applies only to the European Parliament, the Council and the Commission. However, in a joint declaration relating to this regulation, the European Parliament, the Council and the Commission agreed that the agencies and similar bodies created by the legislator should have rules on access to their documents which conform to those of the access regulation and undertook to adopt the necessary acts rapidly.[9] The other institutions and bodies were invited to adopt internal rules on public access to documents which take account of the principles and limits of the access regulation[10].

As regards the Council, the access regulation applies to documents submitted to or considered by the Council members at ministerial level and the Council's preparatory bodies, including Coreper and all other committees, groups and working parties. The presidency is part of the institution. As regards documents which have not been considered by the Council as such or one of its preparatory bodies, but only by officials in its general secretariat, the Council initially took the view that they were not held by the Council. However, following a recommendation by the ombudsman, the Council decided to release such documents since it had come to the conclusion that their content was not covered by any of the exceptions laid down in the 1993 access decision and thus implicitly accepted that documents in possession of its general secretariat are to be considered as Council documents.

As regards documents originating from member states, the situation is more difficult. On the one hand, it follows from the access regulation that member states are third parties vis-à-vis the Council. On the other hand, the Council consists of representatives of the member states (article 203 TEC). In order to give a useful meaning to each of these provisions, it is therefore necessary to distinguish between documents relating to the activities of members of the Council, which are to be considered as originating from the Council, and those relating to activities of the member states as such, which are third party documents. The former include documents summarising spoken interventions of Council members and their delegates and their written contributions to the Council's debate on a draft act, decision, letter or other, from the moment at which the activity of the institution has started, for instance by the transmission of a Commission proposal, a member state's initiative or a draft submitted by the presidency or the general secretariat. The latter include documents exchanged purely for information purposes between member states, documents relating to intergovernmental meetings or, generally speaking, each document emanating from a member state which, although it is circulated via the Council's general secretariat, is unrelated to a subject on which the Council is in the process of taking a decision.

Which documents are covered by the rules on access to documents?

The definition of 'document' in the access regulation is extremely broad. It covers 'any content, whatever its medium', i.e., texts written on paper or stored in electronic form, including e-mails, and sound, visual or audiovisual recordings. The only qualification is that the documents must concern 'a matter relating to the policies, activities and decisions falling within the institution's sphere of responsibility', as opposed to private documents which happen to be in the premises of the institution concerned. The legislator did not follow the Commission proposal which, in a bid to protect the 'space to think' of its officials, had foreseen to exclude 'texts for internal use, such as discussion documents, opinions of departments' and informal messages from the scope of application of the regulation.

Like the 1993 code of conduct, the access regulation applies to documents 'drawn up' by an institution. This wording could suggest that a document must present a certain degree of formalisation. However, the regulation does not contain any criterion relating to the official, final nature of a document. Even texts of an ephemeral, preliminary nature, like for instance drafting suggestions circulated during a meeting which have the function of replacing or supplementing oral intervention, are covered. However, they are not immediately recorded in the public register of Council documents.

The term 'content' in article 3(a) of the access regulation makes it clear that the object of access is not the document as such, but the information contained therein[11]. However, the right of access to documents does not entail a general right to information which does not exist in the form of a document[12]. Access is granted only to existing documents. Where an institution asserts that a particular document does not exist, there is a presumption that it does not, which may however be rebutted by the applicant by 'relevant and consistent evidence'[13]. Under the access regulation, the institution is neither bound to draw up a document which does not exist nor to reply to requests for information. However, under article 6 of the code of good administrative behaviour for the general secretariat of the Council and its staff in their professional relations with the public (Council, 2001d), members of staff of the general secretariat are obliged to provide the public with the information requested, falling within their area of responsibility, and to ensure that this information is as clear and comprehensible as possible.

The access regulation applies to documents covering all EU activities, including foreign policy and police and judicial cooperation in criminal matters. Since the treaty establishing the European Atomic Energy Community and the treaty establishing the former European Coal and Steel Community do not contain a provision similar to article 255 TEC, the access regulation does not apply to documents covered by those treaties, but pursuant to its recital No. 5 the European Parliament, the Council and the Commission should, in accordance with declaration No. 41 attached to the final act of Amsterdam, 'draw guidance' from this regulation. However, as article 305(2) TEC provides that the provisions of the EC Treaty shall not derogate from the Euratom Treaty, article 255 of the EC Treaty and the access regulation apply if there are no provisions to the contrary in the Euratom Treaty or in secondary legislation deriving from it. Therefore, as far as these two treaties are concerned, in practice only documents that have been classified in accordance with article 10 of Council regulation No. 3 of 31 July 1958 implementing article 24 of the Euratom Treaty and have not been declassified are outside the scope of the access regulation.

Third party documents

The access regulation abolished the 'authorship rule' contained in the 1993 code of conduct. The access regulation applies to 'all documents held by an institution, that is to say documents drawn up or received by it and in its possession'. Thus, the institution to which a request was addressed has to examine whether the requested document, even if it was drawn up by a third party, i.e., 'any natural or legal person, or any entity outside the institution concerned' (article 3(b)), is covered by one of the exceptions. In case of doubt, it must consult the author of the document (article 4(4)). This obligation also applies between the institutions[14] and between the institutions and the member states. Except where the request concerns a sensitive document or where the author is a member state, the originator's negative opinion is not binding on the institution. However, article 4(4) of annex II to the Council's rules of procedure provides for procedural safeguards. If the general secretariat disagrees with a third party's negative opinion, the Council is seized of the matter. If the Council envisages releasing the document, its author is to be given at least ten working days before the document is handed out in order to enable him to apply for interim measures before the Court of First Instance. In any event, a negative opinion of the originator may be an important factor in the institution's assessment of whether one of the exceptions applies.

The member states have a right to veto the disclosure of documents originating from them. The text of article 4(5) of the access regulation, which corresponds essentially to declaration No. 35 annexed to the final act of Amsterdam, is not without ambiguity (a member state 'may request' not to disclose a document 'without its prior agreement'). However, it is a *lex specialis* to article 4(4), according to which the opinion of a third party is purely consultative, and it explicitly mentions the 'prior agreement' of the member state concerned. The absence of such agreement is thus sufficient grounds to justify the refusal of access to the document in question, without it being necessary to rely on one of the exceptions laid down in article 4(1) to (3) of the access regulation[15]. However, since the majority of documents originating from member states and held by the Council relate to on-going Council proceedings and are thus not considered as third-party documents, the Council has only twice relied upon article 4(5) of the access regulation as grounds for refusal since the entry into force of that regulation.

Sensitive documents

The question of how to treat highly classified documents, in particular those relating to public security, defence and military matters, was among the most contentious issues between the Council and the European Parliament in negotiations on the access regulation. The aim was to set standards for the protection of sensitive information which conform to those by which NATO and its members are bound, without providing for block exemption for an entire category of documents.

'Sensitive documents' are defined in article 9(1) of the access regulation as documents originating from a Community institution or agency, a third country or an international organisation which are classified as 'TRES SECRET/TOP SECRET, 'SECRET' or 'CONFIDENTIEL' in accordance with the rules of the institution concerned in order to protect a public interest referred to in article 4(1)(a), notably public security, defence and military matters. Thus, this definition of sensitive documents does not cover all classified documents, but excludes documents classified 'RESTREINT UE'.

Although sensitive documents fall under the scope of the access regulation, they are subject to special treatment. Applications for access to sensitive documents can only be handled by persons entitled to acquaint themselves with them. It is for those persons to determine which references can be made in the public register to such documents, which can be recorded in the register or released only with the consent of the originator[16]. The reasons for refusing access to a sensitive document must be given in a way which does not harm the interests to be protected by this refusal[17]. The fact that a document is classified as 'TRES SECRET/TOP SECRET, 'SECRET' or 'CONFIDENTIEL' is not in itself a sufficient ground for refusing access to it. Disclosure can be denied only on the substantive grounds mentioned in article 4(1) of the access regulation. This is confirmed by recital 9 of the Council's security regulations, according to which these regulations are without prejudice to the rules on access to documents, and recital 9 of the access regulation, which justifies the concept of sensitive documents only by reference to their content. Once the Council has decided to release a sensitive document, it must be declassified before it can actually be handed out.

In practice, fears that classifying documents could be used to circumvent the access rules for large categories of documents have not been justified. In 2003, a total of 399 sensitive documents were produced (no 'TRES SECRET UE/UE TOP SECRET, 17 'SECRET UE' and 382 'CONFIDENTIEL UE'); 136 of these documents were referred to in the public register (Council, 2003).

Documents held by member states emanating from the institutions

Another hotly debated issue during the negotiations on the access regulation was the question of how to treat documents held by member states but originating from an institution, in particular from the Council. As seen above, the Council is composed of ministers representing national governments. They are not third parties in relation to the Council, but its members. It would thus have been logical to oblige the member states' authorities to apply the access regulation when they receive a request for a Council document. However, due to the firm opposition of a number of member states, in particular Sweden, article 5 of the access regulation stipulates merely that a member state receiving a request for a document originating from an institution must take a decision under its national law 'that does not jeopardise the attainment of the objectives of this Regulation'. In case of doubt, it must consult the institution concerned[18]. As a matter of fact, this provision constitutes nothing more than a concretisation of the principle of loyal cooperation laid down in article 10 TEC to which recital 15 of the access regulation refers. Information relating to member states' practice is rather fragmented and formal consultations in accordance with article 5 are rare. It is thus not possible to assess the extent of disclosure of documents emanating from the institutions by national authorities on the basis of their national law.

Exceptions to the right of access

General considerations

Article 4(1), (2) and (3) of the access regulation lays down the exceptions to the right of access. As these exceptions are quite similar to those in the 1993 code of conduct, much of the case law relating to them, in particular the general conditions for their application, is still pertinent. According to this case law, all exceptions are to be construed and applied strictly, in a manner not defeating the application of the general rule. The institutions are obliged to consider, in respect of each document requested, whether disclosure is in fact likely to undermine one of the protected interests (the 'harm test'). The risk of these interests being undermined must be reasonably foreseeable and not purely hypothetical. The reasons for refusal must be indicated at the very least by reference to categories of documents, without however jeopardizing the essential function of the exception in question. Where the applicant, in a confirmatory application, puts forward factors capable of casting doubts on whether the first refusal was well founded, the institution is obliged to state in its reply why those factors do not warrant a change in its position. Several exceptions can be invoked jointly.

The access regulation abandoned the distinction between 'mandatory' and 'discretionary' exceptions developed by the case law[19] relating to the previous rules. Article 4 of the access regulation establishes three categories of exceptions, which are all formulated in mandatory terms (access 'shall' be refused...), albeit with certain nuances as regards the requirements for the harm test and the balance with other interests (see below). In a further departure from the previous rules[20], this provision leaves no doubt that the list of exceptions is exhaustive.

Article 4(6) of the access regulation codifies the *Hautala* case law[21], which requires the institutions to grant access to those parts of a document which are not covered by any of the exceptions. The institutions must examine, in respect of each requested document, whether partial access can be given. The reasons for the refusal to grant access to certain parts of the document must be explained in the decision refusing access. In the Council's practice, whenever partial access is granted, those parts of the original document to which access is withheld are made illegible, without altering the structure of the document. In 2003, out of a total number of 12,552 documents requested, 8,824 were fully released, and 1,944 were partially released. In addition to documents which are automatically made available to the public, in many cases, only small parts of the documents concerned were concealed, in particular those permitting the identification of delegations whose positions were recorded in documents relating to ongoing discussions on legislative proposals (see below).

Public interest and privacy and integrity of the individual

The first category of exceptions protects certain facets of the public interest (public security, defence and military matters, international relations, and the financial, monetary or economic policy of the Community or a member state) and the privacy and integrity of the individual. No balance with other interests is required. Where disclosure would undermine the protection of these interests, access *must* be refused. In the Council's practice, the most important public interest exceptions are those relating to public security and international relations. Under applicable case law[22], the concept of public security covers the internal security of a member state and its external security, the interruption of supplies of essential commodities and attempts of authorities to prevent criminal activities. It can also be inferred from this case law that the exception covers operational matters, rather than policy matters.

As regards the international relations exception, the Court of First Instance has held that the Council's discretion as regards the release of documents relating to its activities under title V of the Treaty on European Union are connected with the political responsibilities conferred on it and that, in those circumstances, the Court's judicial review must be limited to verifying whether the procedural rules have been complied with, the contested decision is properly reasoned and the facts have been accurately stated, and whether there has been a manifest error of assessment or a misuse of powers[23]. The Court of First Instance examines, either on the basis of the litigious documents or similar documents which were produced in the proceedings, whether the reasons given for the refusal are plausible or whether there has been a manifest error of assessment. For instance, a document which 'contains formulations and expressions which might cause tensions with non-member countries' or which 'could compromise the European Union's position in current or future negotiations with third countries'[24] could be denied on 'international relations' grounds, unless the document consists of information which simply comprises descriptions and factual findings, in particular where those facts are already in the public domain or where there are other factors which remove any risks of negative repercussions on the relations with the countries concerned[25].

The exception relating to defence and military matters was newly introduced in the access regulation as part of the compromise package which consisted of including sensitive documents relating to defence and military matters in its scope whilst providing for specific protection of them where necessary. It has, however, scarcely been used: fewer than 1% of the refusals were based on it.

The privacy and integrity of the individual is protected 'in particular in accordance with Community legislation regarding the protection of personal data'. This seems to suggest that access must be refused where Community or third pillar data protection rules[26] forbid the disclosure of personal data. In practice, the interlinking of the rules on access to documents and those on the protection of personal data gives rise to subtle questions, in particular as regards the disclosure of names of persons – such as for instance officials and staff members, participants in a meeting or persons who have sent correspondence to an institution or are mentioned in a document. To date, these questions remain unresolved by case law. In any event, the practical importance of this exception for the Council is negligible: in 2003, only 0.3 % of refusals were based on this provision.

Commercial interests, court proceedings and legal advice, investigations and audits

The second category of exceptions protects commercial interests, court proceedings and legal advice and 'the purpose of inspections, investigations and audits', but only insofar as there is no 'overriding public interest in disclosure'. According to the ombudsman[27], the presence of an overriding public interest normally has to be established by the person seeking access, unless it is manifest. The institution must balance this interest against the interests protected by the exception in question. A private or personal interest is not sufficient to trigger this balance test, as any document made accessible following an application enters, as a result of this, the public domain and becomes accessible to all. Nor can the public interest be identical to the general interest of transparency, since this interest already underlies the access regulation. It could apply for example in a case where the interest in the protection of health of persons is to be balanced against the commercial interests of a company relating to information on the composition of certain of its products or the quantity of emissions of harmful substances. In their practice to date, the institutions have regularly concluded that the public interest in disclosure was not overriding[28].

For the Council, the most important exception within this category is the one relating to the protection of legal advice. It covers both external and internal legal advice, including opinions of the Council's legal service. On the basis of the case law[29], the Council consistently holds that any document or parts of it containing advice by its legal service, including opinions drawn up in the context of the Council's legislative activities, falls under this exception, unless there is an overriding public interest in disclosure. It argues that, even after the adoption of the act to which they refer, release of these opinions would undermine the public interest for the Council to be in a position to receive independent legal advice. On the contrary, the ombudsman holds the view that opinions relating to the Council's legislative activities do not fall under article 4(2), third indent of the access regulation, but are covered by article 4(3) of that regulation[30]. The question is currently the subject of court proceedings[31].

The protection of court proceedings applies not only to Community courts, but also to national courts[32]. This exception covers documents drawn up solely for the purposes of specific court proceedings, including pleadings or other documents lodged and internal documents and correspondence concerning the case[33]. However, apart from exceptional cases where disclosure of a document might adversely affect the proper administration of justice before the Community courts, parties are free to disclose their own written submissions[34], but not the pleadings of the other party[35].

The exceptions relating to commercial interests and intellectual property and to the purpose of inspections, investigations and audits are almost exclusively invoked by the Commission and have practically no importance for the Council. The latter exception succeeds the public interest exception relating to 'inspections and investigations' of the 1993 code of conduct, whose meaning has been clarified by the case law[36]. Although they are not explicitly mentioned[37], it mainly refers to infringement proceedings under Articles 226 to 228 TEC.

Protection of the institutions' decision-making process

The objective of the third category of exceptions is to protect the institutions' decision-making process. It replaces the previous discretionary exception which protected the confidentiality of the institutions' proceedings. Article 4(3) of the access regulation is formulated in mandatory terms (access 'shall be refused'), but the exception is subject to a more stringent harm test that its predecessor in the 1993 access decision. It has to be demonstrated, firstly, that disclosure would 'seriously' undermine the institution's decision-making process. The choice of the singular indicates that the potential harm for the decision-making process is to be assessed separately for each institution. Thus, documents relating to a decision already adopted by an institution disclosure of which would undermine an ongoing decision-making process of another institution are not covered. Secondly, even where the 'seriously undermine' criterion is fulfilled, the document must be released if there is an overriding public interest in disclosure.

Article 4(3) is divided into two subparagraphs. Both use the same criteria for assessing whether a document is covered by the exception (see above), but apply them to different categories of documents, depending on the stage of the decision-making procedure to which they relate. Where no decision has yet been taken on the matter to which the document relates (first subparagraph), the exception covers all documents 'drawn up by an institution for internal use or received by an institution'. Once the decision has been taken (second subparagraph), only documents 'containing opinions for internal use as part of preliminary consultations within the institution concerned' fall under it.

Since a large number of Council documents are internal documents drawn up in the context of ongoing deliberations of the Council and its preparatory bodies, it is not surprising that the exception laid down in article 4(3), first subparagraph is invoked in a considerable number of cases. However, as regards documents relating to ongoing discussions on draft legislative acts, it is frequently applied only to those parts which allow identifying the delegation which has taken a position recorded in the document concerned. In the Council's view, this method enables the applicant to take full cognisance of the arguments exchanged, while at the same time preserving the necessary flexibility for delegations to alter their positions in the course of the discussion, which constitutes a pre-condition for achieving progress on difficult questions[38]. Once an interim act in the co-decision procedure or the final legislative act has been adopted, all preparatory documents relating to this act and drawn up before its adoption, excluding legal service opinions and contributions and documents which are covered by another exception, are made public.

The main intention behind the exception laid down in article 4(3), second subparagraph, is to protect the 'space to think' within the institutions, which

was a matter of particular concern for the Commission during the negotiations on the access regulation (see above). It is scarcely used by Council,
as it would need to demonstrate that release of a document could seriously
undermine the Council's decision-making process in abstract terms.

Time limit for exceptions

Pursuant to article 4(7) of the access regulation, the exceptions laid down in
paragraphs 1 to 3 of this article apply for a maximum period of 30 years.
Only documents covered by the exceptions relating to privacy or commercial interests and sensitive documents may continue to be protected after
this period. This reflects the rule laid down in article 1(4) of regulation
354/83 concerning the opening to the public of the historical archives, which
provides that after thirty years the institutions' historical archives shall be
open to the public.

   Since regulation 354/83 excluded access to certain categories of documents even after thirty years from their creation, in particular all documents
relating to proceedings before the Court of Justice, it had to be brought into
line with the access regulation (Council, 2003d). Its Article 2 now provides
that access to documents covered by the exception relating to privacy and
the integrity of the individual can be refused after the thirty-year period.
This does not preclude the disclosure of files of staff of the institutions in
accordance with regulation (EC) 45/2001 on the protection of individuals
with regard to the processing of personal data by the Community institutions and bodies, 'and in particular Articles 4 and 5 thereof'. The latter provision could apply for instance to the use of data in an anonymous or
aggregated form for historical, statistical or scientific purposes. As regards
sensitive documents, article 2(4) of regulation 354/83 refers back to article 9
of the access regulation.

Procedure and remedies

Article 6 of the access regulation stipulates that the applicant is not obliged
to state reasons for the application. Applications must be made in writing,
including electronic form. Electronic mail is widely used since the public
register of Council documents provides a link to the general secretariat's e-
mail address. Applications must be sufficiently precise to enable the institution to identify the document. The applicant can be asked for clarifications.
If the application relates to 'a very long document or a very large number of
documents', the institution can confer with the applicant informally, with a
view to finding a 'fair solution' (article 6(3) of the access regulation). In
practice, this fair solution can consist, for example, in extending the time
frame for the reply beyond the legal limit, in particular where extensive
research is requested in order to identify the requested documents, or in an
invitation to consult documents on the spot. However, the access regulation
contains no safeguards against unfair, repetitive or clearly unreasonable
applications[39]. Invoicing of costs is optional and rarely used in practice, as it
is limited to the actual cost of producing and sending copies (article 10(1) of
the access regulation) and does not allow charging for identifying and com-
piling the documents, which is the biggest cost factor.

Articles 7, 8 and 10 of the access regulation and articles 6 to 9 of annex II to the Council's rules of procedure provide for a two-step procedure. The initial application is handled by the general secretariat, which has fifteen working days to decide on the request on behalf of the Council. This time limit can be extended by fifteen working days in exceptional cases. In 2003, the average time for answering initial requests was seven working days. The possibility of extending the time limit was used in only 4.7% of the cases. In the event of a total or partial refusal, the applicant can make a confirmatory application asking the Council to reconsider its position. The general secretariat then re-examines the documents and prepares a draft reply which, together with the documents concerned, is examined by the Council working party on information. The decision is adopted by the Council, acting by simple majority, within fifteen working days from the registration of the application, extendable by another fifteen working days. In practice, most requests are settled at the first stage of the procedure, in which a large part of the requested documents is already released, as is shown by table 20.1.

If access to the requested documents is totally or partially refused or if the institution fails to reply within the time limit, the applicant can bring proceedings to the Court of First Instance or complain to the European ombudsman under articles 230 and 195 , respectively. In this context, it is worth mentioning that with effect from 1 February 2001 a new article 67(3) was inserted in the rules of procedure of the Court of First Instance, providing that where a document to which access has been denied by an institution is produced in proceedings relating to the legality of that denial, that document must not be communicated to the other parties. While previously the Court of First Instance had to decide without seeing the documents at issue and was therefore reluctant to pronounce itself on the assessment of their content by the institutions, the Court now frequently requests the production of the litigious documents, which enables it to verify, whether the assessment made by the institution was flawed by a manifest error[40].

Register and access without request

In order to facilitate the exercise of the right of access, the institutions are obliged, under article 11 of the access regulation, to provide public access to a register of documents, which must contain references to documents (date, reference number, subject matter and, where possible, a short description of its content). Article 12 foresees that the institutions shall as far as possible make documents directly accessible, in particular legislative documents and documents relating to the development of policy or strategy.

The Council's public register is accessible via the internet. References to all non-sensitive documents submitted to the Council or to one of its preparatory bodies which serve as a basis for its deliberations, could influence its decision-making process, or reflect the progress made on a given subject, are entered via an automatic archiving system as soon as a document is produced. Documents of an ephemeral nature circulated during a meeting, such as room documents, non-papers, meeting documents and unnumbered ('SN') documents, are not immediately entered into the register, but must be transformed as soon as possible into official ('ST') docu-

Table 20.1: *Access regulation 2002-2003*

Number of applications pursuant to the access regulation

2002	2003
2,391	2,831

Number of documents concerned by initial applications

2002	2003
9,349	12,595

Number of documents provided by the General secretariat of the Council at the initial stage

2002	2003
8,157[1]	10,942[2][3]

Number of confirmatory applications (confirmatory aplications may be made if initial application is refused)

2002	2003
43	45

Number of documents released by the Council following confirmatory applications

2002	2003
89[4]	63[5][6]

Rate of documents released for the procedure as whole [7]

2002		2003	
76.4%	88.6%	71.7%	87.4%

(1)	7,089 documents released wholly, 1,068 documents released partially.
(2)	Based on 12,595 documents considered (including 1.9% public documents).
(3)	9,014 documents released wholly, 1,928 documents released partially.
(4)	24 documents released wholly, 65 released partially.
(5)	Based on 161 documents considered.
(6)	22 documents released wholly, 41 released partially.
(7)	Based on documents released wholly (left column) or wholly + partially (right column)

---

ments and recorded in the register. For sensitive documents, the author specifies the references which may be included in the register.

The system also allows the full text of documents to be made available in electronic form as soon as they are circulated and to be accessed directly via the register. This is the case in particular for provisional agendas of Council meetings and most of its preparatory bodies, a large number of legislative documents from the moment when the Council has reached agreement on the final act or an interim act in the co-decision procedure (common position or joint text approved by the conciliation committee), and, generally speaking, for all documents which are already in the public domain because they have been made public by their author or with his consent or were made available following a request under the access regulation.

As of 3 February 2004, the Council's public register comprised references to a total of 484,913 documents, including all languages. Out of these documents, 267,691 were fully available online. Another 10,394 documents were also public, but for technical reasons not accessible in electronic form. The introduction of the public register led to a significant increase in the number of applications for access – in 1999, when the register of Council documents was made available, the number of requests increased by 70% compared with the previous year – and to a diversification in terms of the source and subject matter of applications.

Not strictly indispensable in an act concerning public access to documents, but certainly useful in its context, is article 13 of the access regulation, which provides for minimum standards for the publication of documents in the Official Journal. The documents listed in paragraph 1 must be published in any case, whilst for those listed in paragraph 2 publication is optional. The institutions are entitled to provide for further categories of documents to be published. The Council made use of this possibility in article 17 of its rules of procedure.

The three institutions covered by the access regulation also made joint efforts to inform citizens of their right of access and on the Union's activities in general. They published a joint brochure with explanations on how to get access to documents and information and stepped up their internet presentation, in particular through a joint portal on the EUROPA server which guides citizens to specific sites of the institutions with more information on their work and their registers. Since sometimes applicants do not seek to obtain precise documents, but rather look for more general information, each institution has set up specific services to deal with such requests for information.

Specific rules on access to documents

The aim of the access regulation is to establish a 'framework law' on access to documents, but a number of Community legal acts contain specific provisions on the same subject matter. In order to prevent those rules from undermining the general system, article 18(3) of the access regulation obliges the Commission to examine their conformity with this regulation. However, the Commission has not identified any rules that are incompatible with those of the access regulation.

Article 2(6) of the access regulation clarifies that rights of public access to documents held by the institutions which follow from instruments of international law, or acts of the institutions implementing them, have priority in relation to this regulation. This provision may become pertinent after the adoption of a regulation on the application of the provisions of the Århus Convention on Access to Information, Public Participation in Decision-making and Access to Justice in Environmental Matters[41] to EC institutions and bodies. The Commission has presented a proposal to this effect[42], which provides for the extension of the system established by the access regulation to the other Community institutions and bodies as regards environmental information and obliges these institutions and bodies to actively collect and disseminate such information.

Summary and outlook

To sum up, it is not an exaggeration to say that enormous progress has been made since the issues of transparency and openness first appeared on the political agenda. A little more than ten years ago, there was no mention of these concepts in the treaties, there were no rules on access to documents, all Council meetings took place behind closed doors, and it was difficult for citizens to be informed about the positions their government representatives had taken within the Council and why. Today, openness and transparency are among the key concepts of the treaties, there is far-reaching transparency of the Council's legislative activities, and the widest possible access to documents is no longer an abstract concept, but has become a day-to-day reality for the institutions and, above all, for the citizens of the European Union. This has recently been recognised by the European Parliament which, in a resolution on public access to EU documents adopted unanimously on 25 September 2003, 'congratulates the institutions – and the people who work in them – on the progress achieved so far and at the same time wants to encourage them to continue the work; is pleased with the considerable increase in the documents now being placed at the disposal of the citizens, in particular by the Council...' (European Parliament, 2003).

This does not mean, of course, that everything is perfect. Reinforcing transparency and openness in the Union remains a continuous task and efforts to this effect are under way at various levels.

First, the draft constitutional treaty puts the concept of openness into the broader context of the democratic life of the Union. Article I-46(3) of the draft constitution states that every citizen shall have the right to participate in the democratic life of the Union and takes over the wording of article 1 of the Treaty on European Union, according to which decisions shall be taken as openly as possible and as closely as possible to the citizen. Along the same lines, article I-50(1) provides that, in order to promote good governance and ensure the participation of civil society, the Union institutions, bodies, offices and agencies shall conduct their work as openly as possible[43]. Pursuant to article I-46, the institutions shall give citizens and representative associations the opportunity to make known and publicly exchange their views in all areas of Union action and maintain an open, transparent and regular dialogue with representative associations and civil society[44]. It also obliges the Commission to carry out broad consultations with parties concerned in order to ensure that the Union's actions are coherent and transparent. All this conforms to the institutions' current practice, which is thereby provided a 'constitutional status'.

As for the openness of the Council's proceedings, experience to date has not confirmed fears that the Council's work may be paralysed by open debates or far-reaching access to documents relating to its legislative activities. Public debates neither caused any significant delays, nor did they have any noticeable influence on the preparedness of delegations to make compromises. As a logical step after the conclusions of the Seville European Council, the draft constitution consequently foresees that, like the European Parliament, the Council shall meet in public when considering and voting on a draft legislative act (article I-50(2) of the draft constitution) and obliges both institutions to ensure publication of the documents relating to the leg-

islative procedures (article III-399(2) of the draft constitution). Thus, with
the entry into force of the constitution, full openness of the legislative procedure will finally become reality.

Finally, articles I-50(3) and II-102 of the draft constitution extend the right
of access to documents of all Union institutions, bodies, offices and agencies[45], thus remedying a point which has often been criticised. Along the
same lines, the Commission has suggested that the benefit of the right of
access be extended to all natural and legal persons, irrespective of their
nationality or residence. As the access regulation has mainly benefited specialists, there is need for better information on how citizens can access the
information contained in documents, which requires enhanced cooperation
between all actors involved in EU communication and information activities. Also, in the light of further experience and case law, a number of issues
relating to the application of the access regulation may need to be
addressed, such as the definition of the concept of documents, the interface
between the institutions and member states as regards access to their respective documents, the interpretation of certain exceptions and the possibilities
for institutions to defend themselves against unfair, repetitive or clearly
unreasonable applications. Finally, although the public registers have
proved to be very effective in facilitating citizens' access to documents, there
is still room for improvement as regards their user-friendliness and the
number of documents which are directly accessible.

The current state of play as regards transparency and openness in the
Union has been eloquently summarized by Michael Cashman, MEP, in the
following terms: 'Everything I have said may imply that there is much to do.
Of course there is, because we aspire within the European Union to perhaps
defy our critics, to prove them wrong, to connect with our citizens and to
prove that the European Union project is one we should be proud of and
should celebrate. We have not got it right. Sadly, perfection often eludes us
in human endeavours, whether by politicians or anyone else. However, our
commitment to try is there within Regulation 1049/2001 and in the spirit of
those people who have worked to make access a reality' (European
Parliament, 2003b).

At the end of the day, valid assessments about the openness and transparency of the Council and the other EU institutions must take as their yardstick *not* a comparison with some abstract ideal of a polity, but with the
day-to-day practice and reality of openness in member states. By that
measure, the Council performs well. In the near future, a clearer definition
in the new constitution of what constitutes a legislative act will result in the
Council's legislative activity taking place almost entirely under the public
gaze. The logical concomitant is that the Council's non legislative work, as
in any collective 'cabinet' type function, be afforded the degree of confidentiality necessary for an effectively functioning executive. Difficulty in distinguishing these dual roles has been in part responsible for conveying the
impression that the Council has been dragged somewhat reluctantly down
the path of greater openness. Now that the Council has progressed much of
the way down that road, it is inevitable that it should shortly arrive at the
logical destination of full openness and transparency as far as its legislative
activity is concerned.

Chapter 21: The Council and the challenge of enlargement*,

by André Gillissen

The logic of internal reform

Historically, the process of enlargement has undoubtedly pressed Europe into further steps towards an 'ever closer Union'. Already at the time of the first enlargement, the need to deepen European integration as the Community was widening was recognised – and was in particular stressed by the 1969 summit in The Hague. The imperative of parallel progress in widening and deepening the Union has since been a recurrent theme, and many European Councils have emphasised the need to prepare the Union for enlargement by adapting its institutions.

Throughout the 1990s, as the prospect of the Union doubling in size became an immediate reality rather than a distant pipedream, the issue of institutional reform crept higher up the Union's agenda. The Union's institutions, conceived for six, and which were just about functioning with twelve, had indeed begun to creak under the weight of fifteen member states. To expand to twenty-five (and more) clearly required an overhaul of the Union's institutions in general, as well as of the Council in particular, if the Union were to continue to function.

However, the three intergovernmental conferences which were convened during the 1990s produced treaties which were either judged too ambitious (and whose ratification therefore became extremely difficult), or on the contrary deemed to fall well short of the challenges posed by enlargement. Deepening the Union in the light of its programmed enlargement seemed to be doomed – 'damned if you do, damned if you don't!'

This deadlock led to a series of attempts to improve where possible the functioning of the Council, whilst avoiding the heavy, and not necessarily productive, recourse to treaty reform. In particular, the European Council on two occasions commissioned reports on preparing the Council for enlargement from the secretary-general, and these were subsequently taken on board, at least in part, by the European Council at its meetings in Helsinki and Seville.

These efforts were largely focused on *internal* reforms – i.e., reforms which would not require changes to the treaties. The very nature of such reforms explains both their strength and their limits. They can easily be implemented; but they can just as easily be ignored. They can be seen as practical improvements to the functioning of the Council; but they can also be perceived as the first step towards more radical changes and thus immediately raise opposition of a quasi-ideological nature.

At the same time, the December 2001 Laeken European Council set into motion an ambitious attempt to reform the Union through an original method – the Convention on the Future of Europe, which was to pave the way to a 'last chance saloon' intergovernmental conference charged with properly preparing the Union for the challenges of the new century.

Enhancing the coordination role of the General Affairs Council

Historically, as the Community's competences expanded and the Council was accordingly fragmented into a growing number of different sectoral configurations, it fell upon the General Affairs Council[1] to ensure the coherence of the Community's action across the board of its different policies.

Although foreign ministers have certainly tried on several occasions to (re)assert their overall responsibility for overseeing and coordinating Union policies, their success has proven mixed. The innovations agreed at the 22 June 2002 Seville European Council may help strengthen the General Affairs Council, but, as ever, it requires the political will to translate rules and wishful thinking from paper to reality.

The limits to coordination

By 1975 a number of sectoral Council formations had been spawned, and foreign ministers felt the need to reflect on how best to ensure the general coordination of the Community's policies. At their meeting in Villa Marlia in October 1975 they accordingly stressed that whenever necessary they would hold joint meetings with other ministers (so-called 'jumbo Councils', due to the number of participants involved). They foresaw in particular the need to hold such meetings with finance ministers before the adoption of the Community's budget, as well as with agriculture ministers.

However, this procedure was not only relatively cumbersome, it also ran counter to the very reasons why the Council was fragmented into different formations, and consequently gradually fell into disuse.

Nowadays, even the Labour/Social Affairs and Ecofin Councils have ended what had become their traditional practice of holding jumbos to adopt the Joint Employment Report (now they meet separately to do so, which means that in practice the Council approves the report twice before submitting it to the European Council). As a sign of the demise of the jumbo, when in April 1999 NATO air strikes against Serbia were followed by a massive movement of refugees, rather than convening a joint meeting the presidency preferred to call for two separate Councils of justice/home affairs ministers and foreign ministers, held back-to-back. This new discipline was codified in the 1999 Helsinki guidelines, which state that 'Joint sessions of different Council formations shall no longer be convened, save in exceptional circumstances.'

Reports on the work of other Council configurations

In Villa Marlia it was also decided that foreign ministers would receive every month a report issued by the general secretariat describing the discussions being held in other Council configurations, so that the General Affairs Council could 'properly exercise its coordination function'. Very soon however this process was dropped altogether – until it was resurrected a quarter of a century later by the Belgian presidency in July 2001, in the form of a monthly 'report on the proceedings in other Council configurations'. This report gives a general overview of the main discussions held in other sectoral Councils, focusing in principle on those issues which should be of relevance to the General Affairs Council – e.g. progress on those legislative proposals that are part of the Lisbon strategy (and therefore are relevant to the preparation of the Spring European Councils); justice and home affairs issues having implications for external relations (such as the treatment of asylum-seekers); or economic dossiers with implications for international trade, such as the issue of state aid to the ship-building industry in South Korea. This standing item on the agenda of the General Affairs Council is meant to make the foreign ministers aware of such dossiers which may impact on their own work. It also provides foreign ministers with an opportunity to raise an issue primarily dealt with in a sectoral Council.

The device, however, has not proven to be much more successful than the defunct Villa Marlia procedure. On average, foreign ministers do not spend more than a few minutes on this agenda item. Coreper itself usually takes note of the report without any comment. When a delegation does comment, it is not clear to what end: as it is argued below, there are very few truly 'horizontal' dossiers which require coordination by the General Affairs Council, and it seems difficult to conceive of the foreign ministers appropriating for themselves a dossier already under discussion in a sectoral Council.

Furthermore, having such a standing item on the agenda of the General Affairs Council is procedurally debatable: if a point really is to be discussed in substance by the General Affairs Council, then a delegation should seek its inclusion on the agenda of that Council within the deadlines set in the Council's rules of procedure thereby allowing proper preparation of the discussion, or, alternatively, raise it under 'any other business'.

Organisation of the Council's agenda

Another procedural device aimed at facilitating the Council's coordinating role has been to separate more clearly its General Affairs and its External Relations functions. A first step was taken during the Austrian presidency of 1998, when the practice of formally dividing foreign ministers' agendas between horizontal issues and foreign policy issues was initiated.

Later on in Helsinki the European Council decided that: 'The General Affairs Council must be in a position to deal effectively with horizontal internal issues including overall policy coordination. The General Affairs Council agenda shall accordingly be divided into two distinct parts. Member States shall ensure that they are suitably represented at ministerial level at both parts of the session'.

Finally, in Seville it was decided that 'The current General Affairs Council configuration shall from now on be called the "General Affairs and External Relations Council". In order best to organise proceedings with regard to the two main areas of activity covered by this configuration, it will hold separate meetings (with separate agendas and possibly on different dates) and dealing, respectively, with:

(a)   preparation for and follow-up to the European Council (including the coordinating activities necessary to that end), institutional and administrative questions, horizontal dossiers which affect several of the Union's policies and any dossier entrusted to it, by the European Council, having regard to EMU operating rules;

(b)   the whole of the Union's external action, namely common foreign and security policy, European security and defence policy, foreign trade, development cooperation and humanitarian aid.'

The rationale was that by freeing up more time for foreign ministers to consider 'general affairs', a 'backbone', or a 'coordinating chain' made up of the European Council, the General Affairs Council and Coreper, would emerge to improve overall coordination of the Union. In practice this device has also had mixed results, for a number of reasons:

practical reasons, such as the difficulty of getting foreign ministers to spend the necessary time in Brussels, as well as an increasingly heavy workload in the field of external relations as the EU developed its CFSP and ESDP;

institutional reasons, such as the multiplication of parallel forums which also contribute to the preparation of the European Council (e.g. 'sherpas', or the Economic and Financial Committee-Ecofin *filière*);

domestic reasons: whatever procedures may be established, the fact remains that in the national context, it is far from obvious that the foreign minister would possess either the capacity or the authority to arbitrate between the diverging interests formulated by different governmental departments; in many national governments the finance minister wields more clout than the foreign minister.

For the General Affairs Council really to be a 'general affairs' Council, it would probably need to be composed of ministers for European affairs, who, rather than acting as mere stand-ins for the foreign affairs ministers, would need to have some degree of authority as ministers in their own right, possibly 'close' to prime ministers.

Coordination or arbitration?

While in general it is difficult for the General Affairs Council to exercise a genuine coordinating function , the one exception however would be those dossiers which are of such a horizontal nature that no sectoral Council formation could successfully deal with them. In recent years, it is on dossiers such as the Union's financial perspective (Agenda 2000) and enlargement that the General Affairs Council has been able to show itself in its best light.

If by 'coordination' one means 'arbitration', then clearly the body 'coordinating' with increasing frequency the developments in the Union's policies is the European Council. Indeed, the European Council has increasingly found itself getting into the details of sectoral policies. Any real coordination therefore performed by the General Affairs Council occurs in preparing meetings of the European Council.

The gate-keepers of the European Council

Both the Jürgen Trumpf and Javier Solana reports stressed the importance of enhancing the preparatory role of the General Affairs Council as a means of reversing the growing deficiencies in the organisation and running of the European Council. The Seville European Council put particular emphasis on the role of the General Affairs Council, which would come to act as a 'gate-keeper' to the European Council:

> 'European Council meetings shall be prepared by the General Affairs and External Relations Council, which shall coordinate all the preparatory work and draw up the agenda. Contributions by other configurations of the Council to the proceedings of the European Council shall be forwarded to the General Affairs and External Relations Council not later than two weeks before the European Council …On the eve of the European Council meeting the General Affairs and External Relations Council shall hold a final preparatory session and adopt the definitive agenda, to which no item may subsequently be added without the agreement of all delegations'.

This gate-keeping role was to express itself in practice through a 'draft annotated agenda' to be presented by the presidency to the Council a month before the meeting of the European Council, and a revised, more elaborate, version submitted to the Council meeting held on the 'eve' of the European Council.

'At a meeting held at least four weeks before the European Council, the General Affairs and External Relations Council, acting on a Presidency proposal, shall draw up an annotated draft agenda distinguishing between:

- items to be approved or endorsed without debate;
- items for discussion with a view to the definition of general political guidelines;
- items for discussion with a view to the adoption of decisions…
- items for discussion but not intended to be the subject of conclusions.'

So far, the establishment of the draft annotated agenda has proven to be a more successful procedural innovation than the other attempts described above.

Putting the annotated draft agenda to the test

The first post-Seville European Council was the one held in Brussels in October 2002. Two issues were on the agenda of the European Council – enlargement and problems connected to the particular status of the Russian enclave of Kaliningrad. As for enlargement, the Council meeting two days before the European Council was able to settle a number of important items by agreeing in advance of the European Council on the methodology for calculating net budgetary positions of the new member states as well as on the institutional aspects of enlargement – and thus avoided heads of government having to discuss these two complex and sensitive issues.

As far as the question of transit between Kaliningrad and the rest of Russia after Lithuania's accession to the EU was concerned, the Council defined the EU's position on the Russian requests, a position which was then simply endorsed by the European Council. More generally the Council also served as a way of testing the waters on the language to be included in the draft European Council conclusions.

The same judgement can apply to the Copenhagen European Council of December 2002. Although much negotiation took place in Copenhagen (both with the candidate countries and within the Union itself), the discussions held on the basis of the annotated draft agenda in the two previous meetings of the General Affairs Council (and in Coreper) allowed a progressive framing, through a series of approximations, of the parameters of what the final outcome was to be.

The Brussels and Copenhagen European Council meetings just referred to may well have been atypical in that they were focused on a limited number of issues – perhaps in part out of necessity, but this was also due to the authority of the presidency.

The specifics of the Spring European Councils, devoted to the broad agenda of the Lisbon Strategy (which encompasses practically all EU policies), were to provide a more arduous test for the annotated draft agenda. The presentation of the draft annotated agenda at the two General Affairs Council meetings prior to the March 2003 Brussels European Council did usefully allow delegations to flag particular concerns in advance, in a more transparent way than before, and thus helped the presidency in drawing up the draft European Council conclusions.

It is true, however, that at times the preparatory discussions in the General Affairs Council and Coreper tended to deteriorate into lengthy drafting sessions. Whilst all delegations recognised the need to maintain the 'strategic' nature of the conclusions of the European Council, few could resist the temptation to request the addition of a phrase or two on an issue of specific interest to them. This led one participant in Coreper to call for the annotated agenda to be both 'slimmed down' and 'fleshed out'! Although to a large extent the process in Coreper did help prevent such drafting work from taking place at the level of the European Council itself, one could conversely argue that the discussions in Coreper were at such a level that they in any case would not have detained heads for very long.

This process was taken to its extreme at the December 2003 Brussels European Council, since the presidency had decided that as many of the conclusions as possible should be agreed in advance in order to keep the

European Council as short as possible and allow the heads to focus their time and attention on the intergovernmental conference which also took place on that occasion. Coreper accordingly held marathon drafting sessions in the run-up to the European Council, allowing the presidency to submit to the European Council draft conclusions which were agreed, with only half a dozen amendments, in record time. There was however a cost to this process: because the presidency wanted to avoid any debate at the European Council, it was forced to take on board practically all the requests made by delegations in Coreper, and ended up with conclusions which were as long as the actual proceedings of the European Council were brief, covering a whole host of topics, many of which the heads of government never discussed.

In summary, the draft annotated agenda has played a useful role in:

- helping the presidency to limit the agenda from the outset to a limited number of issues;
- closing the agenda of the European Council before its meeting begins, and thus in principle avoiding additional points being added to the agenda of the European Council at the last minute, as used to be too often the case;
- clearing the agenda of the heads of state and government of a number of issues which will have been 'pre-agreed' by the Council;
- allowing drafting work to be conducted at the level of Coreper and Council, and thus allowing the heads to focus on the substance of the issues; and
- setting the parameters of the decisions to be taken by the heads.

From draft agenda to draft conclusions

If the annotated draft agenda were to deteriorate further into a pre-negotiation of the outcome of European Councils by Coreper, the European Council could run a real risk of losing all scope for meaningful discussions at its level. Conversely, it might end up drowning in excessive detail. On the one hand, as described above, if officials are tasked with drafting pre-agreed conclusions, it becomes difficult to keep the conclusions short and focussed on a limited number of issues on which the European Council is, in the words of the treaty, to 'provide the Union with the necessary impetus for its development and define the general political guidelines thereof'. The contents of the conclusions thus become increasingly detached from the substance of what the heads might actually discuss (to take one example, were the heads of state and government in December 2003 really aware of adopting conclusions on combating the impact of psychoactive substances use on road accidents?). In addition, there will be strong pressure to avoid any re-opening of the conclusions painstakingly approved by officials, thus depriving the European Council of the 'spontaneity' of its proceedings. Far from being the intimate 'fireside chat' envisaged at its creation, the European Council would turn into a set-piece drama whose actors simply read out their parts. The judgement recorded by one UK trade minister in his diaries on the quality of debates in the Council may soon be shared by members of the European Council:

'Not, really, that it makes the slightest difference to the conclusions of a meeting what ministers say at it. Everything is decided, horse-traded off, by officials at Coreper. The ministers arrive on the scene at the last minute, hot, tired, ill, or drunk (sometimes all of these together), read out their piece, and depart'. (Alan Clark, 2004)

On the other hand, the pre-negotiation of conclusions also raises the risk of submitting to the heads issues that cannot appropriately be addressed at that level. This was aptly demonstrated by the November 1981 London European Council, when the examination of the draft conclusions by officials actually led to an increase in the number of reservations on the text, and in the end prevented the conclusions being adopted. As was declared to the press by the then president of the European Council at the end of long discussions on agricultural and budgetary issues:

'We have examined [these issues] in fact section-by-section, in a very detailed manner, something which I had never witnessed in a European Council...It has been a very heavy European Council...The Heads of State and Government were very conscious of the fact that [they] have examined in detail questions which should have been left to specialists'.

The real answer to this dilemma would be for the European Council itself to approve a short document reflecting in straightforward, plain language what it has actually decided, rather than a lengthy paper which contains not only decisions, but sets out what the European Council thinks. The main problem is that the public impact of such long conclusions is much reduced, and indeed their nature makes it patently obvious that they have been drafted by officials for the benefit of officials, rather than by heads of government for press and public consumption.

Strengthening the presidency

Although the presidency of the Council is little more than a revolving *primus inter pares*, it is held responsible for the destiny of the Union. As such, it has attracted particular attention in the reflections on the reform of the Council. While delegations have agreed to a number of practical reforms, discussions on more ambitious changes stumbled in the on-going work in the Convention on the future of Europe.

Practical improvements

Whilst the proposals contained in the report by secretary-general Javier Solana on the European Council and the General Affairs Council were largely taken on board by the Seville European Council (see above), the reforms adopted in Seville as concerns the functioning of the rotating presidency were more limited.

Cooperation between presidencies

These reforms essentially consisted in enhancing cooperation between present and future presidencies: 'Where it is clear that a dossier will essentially be dealt with during the following six-month period, the representative of the Member State holding the Presidency during that six-month period may, during the current six-month period, chair meetings of committees (other than COREPER) and working parties at which the dossier is discussed. The practical implementation of this provision shall be the subject of an agreement between the two Presidencies concerned.'

In practice, so far, this has been limited to leaving it to the future (Italian) presidency to chair already during the first semester of 2003 the preparations of the 2004 budget, on which the final decisions were taken during its chairmanship.

Programming

The Seville European Council also called for more programming of the activities of the Council over a period longer than the six-month term of the presidency as a means of forcing more continuity, through the establishment of a one-year operational programme of activities as well as a three-year strategic programme.

In line with these decisions the Greek and Italian presidencies presented in December 2002 their programme for the whole of the year 2003 – which, however, did not deter them from presenting, as usual, their own six-month programmes. Though the presentation of this yearly programme did force delegations to reflect and discuss the priorities of the coming year, it is doubtful that this helped to overcome the 'permanent imbalance and infighting within the Union' described by Solana in his report as one of the negative side-effects of the rotating presidency.

In any case, it could be argued that in the legislative field the main programming effort lies in the hands of the Commission, which presents the proposals submitted to the Council, and that progress in the Council is also dependent on progress in the other branch of the legislative authority, i.e., the European Parliament.

In the Autumn of 2003 the six delegations which would hold the presidency in the coming three years presented a draft of the first multi-annual strategic programme. This programme emerged relatively unscathed from the discussions in Coreper and Council, and was only slightly amended before its adoption by the European Council in December 2003, demonstrating that the six future presidencies covered a sufficiently wide range of different interests. The six presidencies acted as a sort of 'laboratory of consensus', producing a programme globally acceptable to all delegations.

Fixed presidencies

At the moment the treaty provides that 'the office of President shall be held in turn by each Member State in the Council for a term of six months'. However, this has not prevented a number of committees or working parties from being given fixed presidencies. For instance, the economic and financial committee and the military committee elect their chair from amongst their ranks, and a number of groups are chaired by the general secretariat of the Council. This was extended by the Seville European Council, which decided to pass the chair of five additional groups to the general secretariat (working parties on electronic communications, on legal data processing, on the codification of legislation, on information and on new buildings) in addition to the two which were already chaired by the secretariat (the security committee and the lawyer-linguists working party).

Due to particular circumstances some ministerial meetings can also be chaired by the same person for a period longer than six months: during the last Danish presidency, owing to the Danish opt-out, meetings of defence ministers held in the framework of the General Affairs Council were chaired by the incoming presidency (Greece). And when the Ecofin Council is chaired by a member state whose currency is not the euro, meetings of the Eurogroup are chaired by the next presidency to chair the Eurogroup.

In Seville no decisions were taken on reforming the Council presidency, although 'a general readiness to examine the question [of the Presidency] further' was noted, with the proviso 'that any change in the present system of six-monthly rotation would in any event have to continue to observe the principle of equality between the Member States'. The Seville European Council accordingly remitted further work on this issue to the Danish presidency.

In the shadow of the IGC

Discussions were intensively pursued on improving the function of the presidency throughout the Danish presidency. But after six months the report presented to the Copenhagen European Council was quite blunt in stating that: 'A difference of views exists however on the need for change [to the presidency function] in view of enlargement. Some believe that it is possible to maintain the basic structure of the current rotating Presidency while others believe that it is necessary to consider more substantial reform.'

The only line of consensus seemed to consist in a number of very general 'key principles and objectives' – i.e., 'institutional balance; equality between Member States; strengthened continuity; improved efficiency; improved coordination, consistency and transparency in the Council's work'. The report went on to describe three different approaches raised in the discussions:

> an approach consisting in strengthening further the logic of cooperation between the present and incoming presidencies, possibly combined with a strengthening of the role of the high representative;
>
> an approach based on an 'institutional' (i.e., fixed) presidency for the Council's 'coordinating chain', while either introducing an elected presidency or maintaining the rotating presidency for most Council configurations;
>
> an approach based on the system of 'team presidency', while possibly retaining a six-monthly component for the 'coordinating chain' and adding an 'institutional' element for external relations,

These were in addition to the idea of an elected president of the European Council.

Very soon, it indeed appeared in the course of the discussions that it was difficult for some delegations to agree to proposals which they felt would anticipate on the outcome of the ongoing Convention on the future of Europe and of the forthcoming intergovernmental conference. Even the attempts to submit to the Copenhagen European Council reforms of a limited nature (so-called 'Seville plus' in reference to the very steps taken in Seville) foundered on the fear of some that the work in the Convention would thus be undermined.

In the end the Copenhagen European Council had to limit itself to merely taking note of the report on the presidency of the Union – which itself simply described the state of the discussions – and the discussions on the presidency within the Council were abandoned. In all truth, it could not have been much different considering that the European Council had one year before, in Laeken, entrusted to the Convention the task of reflecting inter alia on how to improve the efficiency of the Union.

Although the intergovernmental conference has not been able yet to conclude its work, a broad degree of agreement emerged relatively early in its proceedings on the establishment of a team presidency. The day the intergovernmental conference manages to reach an agreement, it is unlikely that its outcome regarding the future of the presidency will be very different from what was suggested in the last compromise proposal made by the Italian presidency – i.e., a team of three member states, collectively exercising the presidency over a period of 18 months. In such a system, the presidency of the General Affairs Council would continue to rotate every six months, but the presidency of the other Council formations (other than the Foreign Affairs Council, chaired by the new Union foreign minister) would be shared equally among those three member states throughout the 18 months. The Convention's proposal for an elected chair of the European Council remained untouched in the proposal of the Italian presidency.

Streamlining the Council – Council formations

In Helsinki the European Council noted that: 'Given the diversification of the Union's activities and broadening of the areas covered by the Treaties, it is important to prevent fragmentation of the Union's activities and decision-making by limiting the number of Council formations, and by avoiding artificial activities to fill up agendas. This will help focus the Union's action and improve overall policy coordination and consistency by the Council's preparatory bodies.' Subsequently, the number of Council formations was reduced to sixteen. In Seville it decided to cut their number down further to nine (see box 21.1).

Behind this apparently innocuous decision lay a few controversies. To take an example, a number of foreign ministers were very strongly opposed to the initially envisaged break-up of the GAC into two separate Council formations (General Affairs Council and External Relations Council), which they feared could weaken their position in their own cabinet, if another minister, especially if he were directly attached to the prime minister, were given the task of attending General Affairs Councils. As a consequence, the principle of a single Council formation was maintained (the General Affairs and External Relations Council), but it was stated in the rules of procedure that it 'shall hold separate meetings, with separate agendas and possibly on different dates'. Although initially the first presidency charged with implementing the Seville reforms did convene the General Affairs and External Relations sessions on separate days, very rapidly pressure from member states forced subsequent presidencies to hold both meetings in one day.

The decision to merge the Development Council into the General Affairs and External Relations Council was equally controversial, with some non-governmental organisations fearing that this would in fact marginalise the role and influence of development ministers. In reality, development ministers continue to meet twice a year (within the GAERC), albeit perhaps with less time at their disposal. At the same time, agendas are undeniably better focused. Furthermore, the merger into the GAERC has allowed a better integration of development issues in the Union's external policies (for example, trade and development, development and migration).

Having one Council nominally in charge of all external relations, including defence and development, as well as general affairs, may have enhanced the coherence of the Union's action. It has certainly contributed to many headaches for those in charge of ensuring the smooth running of Council meetings. Many officials still remember the violent outburst of one development minister who eventually stormed out of the Council's meeting room as the development items she had come to discuss were postponed later and later, as foreign ministers spent much more time than had been envisaged on their own business.

It should be noted that the Convention had pushed this logic of strengthening the General Affairs Council further, by proposing that a single Council formation (the Legislative and General Affairs Council) be tasked with legislation. In other words, all Council legislative business was to be conducted, or at least adopted, in this unique Council formation, leaving the External Affairs Council, and probably the Ecofin Council, to deal with 'executive' matters. This was one of the few proposals from the Convention to be the subject of a nearly unanimous view in the intergovernmental conference – that is, unanimously against it, since it was felt that it would be entirely artificial to squeeze the vast range of the Council's legislative work into a single Council formation and that, inevitably and very rapidly, the existing Council formations would de facto be recreated.

Council preparatory bodies

With the same logic the number of preparatory bodies of the Council has been reduced – the last such exercise brought the number down to around 150 working parties and committees. Examples of this restructuring effort included the merger of the working party on Central Europe and the working party on Southeast Europe (a logical consequence of the enlargement process) and the merger of the working party on the internal market and the working party on industry (a consequence of the creation of the Competitiveness Council).

Council working methods – the code of conduct

In March 2003 the Council set itself a 'code of conduct' aimed at improving the efficiency of the preparation and conduct of meetings. The code basically starts from the premise that whilst there will be an increased demand for speaking time (due to the presence of ten additional delegations), the supply of meeting time will remain static (due to the fact that the number of meeting rooms and interpreters remains physically limited). It went on to define sixteen 'rules', largely inspired from the procedures followed in parliamentary assemblies, which if respected could help alleviate this basic difficulty. Though voluntary, the code of conduct was subsequently 'upgraded' by being annexed to the Council's rules of procedures, in order to give it more visibility and enhance its enforceability.

The code of conduct lays great emphasis on the need to make better use of the time *between* meetings. This basically referred to the need to carry out more systematically some of the work outside of the meeting, for example by tasking a small group to study solutions to a particular stumbling block – it being clear that in any case their work would be reported back to the plenary group, which would fully retain its decision-making prerogatives. To some extent this codified existing practice.

Another solution advocated in the code was to substitute written exchanges for oral discussions. Thus, in advance of a meeting the presidency might circulate a proposal, on which delegations may exchange comments by e-mail, so that when the meeting is actually convened it can focus on the issues which will have been identified as problematic. Many complex dossiers were successfully dealt with in this manner in the Antici group during the 2003 Greek presidency.

The code also stressed that, with the forthcoming enlargement, a new threshold would have been crossed, and that a greater discipline would therefore be required from delegations if meetings were to achieve any results at all. Thus, certain meeting practices were to be banned (for example, no more items placed on the agenda of the Council for information only, and no more table rounds) and delegations were encouraged to make brief interventions, and where ever possible a 'spokesperson' could intervene on behalf of like-minded delegations.

Implementing the rules of the game

Many of these ideas would strike anyone familiar with the Council as having no novelty at all (one can find many of them in the Helsinki guidelines for reform, or in the Council's rules of procedure, for example). Some of them might even strike any normal citizen as sheer common sense. One may wonder why such rules would be applied now, whilst in the past they were ignored, despite having been given the highest political weight through their endorsement by European Councils; despite having been given legal weight by their inclusion in the Council's rules of procedure; and despite their obvious common sense. The optimistic answer would be found in a strengthened sense among the delegations that working methods simply had to improve if the Council is to carry out its essential role. In other words, the code of conduct constituted a last consolidation of well-known improvements to the Council's working methods, before the jump into the unknown which 1 May 2004 had come to represent.

Will the reforms stick?

The reform efforts described in this chapter are necessarily limited in scope given their very nature (as they must take place within the constraints set by the treaties) as well as due to the political context and the discussions in the intergovernmental conference. It is also true that these efforts are not new. Like the Loch Ness monster, the issue of Council reform seems regularly to turn up – often sighted, but never quite captured; over the years the Council has taken the same decisions on several occasions before relapsing into its bad habits. However, this particular package of internal reforms should not be discarded as a collection of mere stopgap measures, as it potentially will make quite a difference to the way in which the Council runs its business. The measures also present the advantage of being immediately applicable, without having to await the conclusion of cumbersome ratification procedures in twenty-five countries.

Sometimes, one has to sink to the bottom before being in a position to give a salutary kick back to the surface. In other words, it may well take the actual pressures of running effective meetings composed of twenty-five (soon twenty-seven or more!) delegations for all the measures and ideas described in this chapter to be implemented to their fullest potential.

Chapter 22: The Council in perspective

Over the past twenty years, the Council has evolved at extraordinary speed. This pace of change has been mirrored more widely in the Union as a whole. In slightly over two decades the Union has experienced four waves of enlargement – Greek, Iberian, Nordic/Austrian, and the 2004 'big bang' – which have successively extended the external frontiers of the Union out towards its geographical limits. The same period has seen a succession of no fewer than five revisions of the founding treaties; the advent of a single market and a single currency; the launching of EU-led civilian and military crisis management operations; the foundations of a common asylum and immigration policy; the adoption of a charter of fundamental rights; and, most recently, the drafting of a Constitution. Against the backdrop of the waning political appetite for, and public interest in, further constitutional change, the constitutional settlement reached in June 2004 is expected to be 'durable' (i.e., to last for at least a decade if not more). Further accessions are, however, already on the near horizon.

It would be rash to predict precisely how the changes foreseen as a result of the new Constitution and the latest waves of enlargement will affect the Council and its place in the Union's institutional set-up. As different chapters in this study have shown, the various component parts of the Council's decision-making apparatus have acknowledged the need for adaptation and change since the mid-1990s. Indeed, a number of significant adaptations and changes have already been carried through. But the new Constitution contains three innovations which can be expected to have a particular impact on the way the Council operates and also determine how effective it remains.

The first is the new structure of the Council presidency. While the six-monthly rotating element has largely been retained, in particular through the Coreper-General Affairs Council backbone, two innovations will render the six-monthly burden a more reasonable one to bear for member states, even those with small civil services to back up the effort. The injection of an element of permanency through the chairmanship of the Foreign Afairs Council by the Union's foreign minister should boost both overall consistency in the Union's external relations and improve the working of the Council. The logic of such an approach is that the minister's representatives in the Council secretariat should also chair the relevant preparatory bodies throughout the Council's structures. Given the monthly rhythm of Foreign Affairs Councils, their generally heavy agendas and the large number of meetings with third parties, this should somewhat alleviate the presidency burden. A further change in this context is the possibility for assistance to be given by other members of the presidential group in order to share out the presidential burden, if required, even through chairing Council sessions (as already happens in the budget context – see chapter 5.2).

The second innovation, following on from the fact that the Constitution now defines the Union's legislative work, is the creation of a genuinely "legislative" Council, not in the sense of a separate Council formation, but by ensuring that the legislative portion of Council agendas is clearly identified. This would allow the completion of the move to transparency in the Council's legislative work, placing it on a par with many national systems.

The third innovation is the creation of a permanent president of the European Council, elected to the position for a period of two and a half years (renewable once). This new form of presidency will clearly have major consequences for the political relationship between the European Council and the European Commission.

In addition to the Constitution's innovations, the Council is likely to see continued progressive incrementalism in refining and honing its working methods to cope with an ever larger Union. It is generally accepted that further rationalisation of the number of Council preparatory bodies is required. Behind this is recognition that more efficient use has to be made of scarce and costly meeting time, and this will inevitably place an increasing burden on the presidency and the secretariat. However, there is unlikely to be a revolution in this area. The Council has shown an ability to adapt incrementally, albeit in response to situations rather than pre-empting them. The process of incremental change will, therefore, continue.

It is beyond dispute that the Council will remain at the centre of EU decision-making. The question many analysts and scholars are likely to focus on in the coming years is whether the Union's constitutional settlement will reinforce the role and place of the Council/European Council as the Union's supreme political and executive authority. This is a question that goes beyond the scope of this study, since it raises broader questions about the role of the European Commission and the inter-relationship between the Council, the Commission and the European Parliament. It would be wrong, however, to portray the European Council and the European Commission as fierce rivals set to be locked in mortal combat: on the contrary, the two have long enjoyed a symbiotic relationship. The balance between the two may alter, but the fundamental relationship is likely to remain.

The Union is an entirely novel kind of political association with its own highly idiosyncratic constitutional system. Due care should be taken to nurture a mechanism which, over the years, has achieved so much. Many would argue that the onus is now on member state governments, the media and the general public to claim full ownership of the system. The Union is not some kind of super-state and nor is it evolving in that direction, but it is an integral part of the public and political life of the member states and of their peoples in every region and municipality. According to this view, 'the politicians' – that is, national members (ministers) of the Council and members of the European Parliament and the national parliaments, have a particular responsibility for anchoring the Union in the member states and conveying a sense that the European Union is "us" rather than some extraneous entity in a virtual 'Brussels', entirely divorced from reality in, for example, Edinburgh, Tampere, Naples, Pilsen, Coimbra, Valetta or Riga. The Council of the European Union is an integral part of, and focus for, that reality.

FOOTNOTES

PART I

Chapter 1

1 The treaties refer simply to 'the Council'. The designation 'Council of the European Union' was decided by the Council on 8 November 1993, following the entry into force of the Maastricht Treaty (see OJ L 281, 16.11.93, p. 18)

2 Italy had different, though similar, concerns. The Schuman declaration dealt a mortal blow to its plans for a Franco-Italian customs union, and thereafter it sought guarantees that it would enjoy equal status and powers with France and Germany. Like the Benelux countries, it was afraid that Schuman's initiative would result in a Franco-German steel cartel.

3 In the case of Italy he had to give in. Pleading the distance between Rome and Luxembourg, Italy insisted that its ambassador to Luxembourg could replace its minister in Special Council meetings.

4 See the new early warning procedure in article 7(1) TEU (as amended by the Treaty of Nice) for determining a serious breach by a member state of the fundamental principles on which the Union is founded.

Chapter 2

1 The decision of the representatives of the governments of the member states on 8 April 1965 on the provisional location of certain institutions of the Communities, and the conclusions of the December 1992 Edinburgh European Council, as consolidated by Council decision (OJ C 341, 23.12.94).

2 This was the name of a street that was done away with during the building work. Justus Lipsius, 1547-1606, was a 15th century Flemish humanist and, as some journalists insist on pointing out, a neo-stoic. He occupied variously the chair of history and philosophy at the University of Jena, in Germany, the chair of history and law at the new University of Leiden, and the chair of history and Latin at the University of Leuven.

3 Maltese is an official and working language of the Union. However, a temporary waiver from the requirement for all legislation to exist in Maltese has been applied since 1 May 2004 (for at least three years) pending the training an recruitment of sufficient numbers of Maltese translators.

4 The Council secretariat has, on occasion, received correspondence and replied in Irish. There are three Irish language translators employed by the Council for translating primary law (i.e. treaties) into Irish.

5 Using a relay language means that you do not have to provide for direct translation between, say, Latvian and Maltese, but that the text is first translated into English or French and then into the destination language. The two-way method refers to translations both into and from the native language of the translator. While translators normally work only into their native language, working into a foreign language should not result in any loss of quality given that the text is

generally always revised by a native speaker.

Chapter 3

1   For a detailed historical account of those rule changes, see the first and
second editions of this book.

PART II

Chapter 4

1   According to its own count, by the end of 2002 the Commission was accredited in 158 countries and international organisations and represented by 104 heads
of delegation in a total of 131 external diplomatic missions.
2   After the Brioni accords of June 1991, which ended the confrontation
between the federal Yugoslav government and Slovenia, Jacques Poos, the
Luxembourg foreign minister and then president-in-office of the Council, is
reported to have said 'this is the hour of Europe.' Within a year, however, much of
eastern Croatia had been devastated by war and a new conflict was underway in
Bosnia. Although perhaps intended as a call to assume responsibility rather than a
grand claim, the phrase came to symbolise the gulf between the EU's aspirations
and action.
3   The provisions on the CFSP were revised by the Amsterdam Treaty that
entered into force in 1999. Articles 11 to 28 of the Treaty on European Union are
devoted specifically to the CFSP.
4   A title popularised by the European press as 'Mr CFSP', 'Monsieur PESC',
or – in the breathless German acronym – 'Herr GASP'. Javier Solana took up the
post on 18 October 1999 for a period of five years (see chapter 19).
5   Article 17 (1) of the consolidated version of the TEU.
6   In addition to the participation of twelve member states and nine acceding
states, EUPM has had contributions from Bulgaria, Canada, Iceland, Norway,
Switzerland, Romania, Russia, Turkey and Ukraine.
7   The successful defusing of this crisis, that was heading towards a new war
in the Balkans, was a good illustration of how the new constellation of actors could
work together. High representative Solana was a central figure in the negotiation
of the Ohrid Agreement, alongside Nato secretary general Lord Robertson. A Nato
stabilisation force restored calm and helped in the process of disarmament. The
European Commission provided commercial and financial carrots through the
negotiation of a stabilisation and association agreement.
8   The large French contingent was supplemented by contributions from several EU member states together with elements from South Africa, Brazil and
Canada.
9   Although this was not the case when, in 2000, the Danish chief of defence
staff controversially cast what was rumoured to have been the decisive vote in
favour of a Finnish candidate for the chairmanship of the EU military committee.
This provoked vociferous complaints from the unsuccessful Italian candidate and a
subsequent apology from Copenhagen, together with an admission that no Danish
vote should have been cast.
10   The value of common strategies has not lived up to their promise. To date,

they have been too broadly defined in scope to be effective, often resembling inventories of existing policies rather than a strategic overview capable of driving operational prioritisation. Nor have they paved the way for the introduction of qualified majority voting in their implementation as had been hoped.

11   These obligations, though spelt out in the treaty, are of a political rather than a legal nature given the exclusion of the CFSP from the scope of jurisdiction of the Court of Justice.

12   The countries that are candidates for accession are also linked to the Council secretariat by a protected network.

13   To the bemusement of its international partners, the European Union insists that when acting together these four agents are referred to as the 'Troika'.

14   In doing so the member state risks considerable political criticism from its partners and from the EU institutions. When, at the press conference following the EU-Russia summit of 6 November 2003, prime minister Berlusconi departed from the well-established EU line on the issue of Chechnya, the Italian presidency was the subject of much criticism in the press, by the Commission and the European Parliament, and by other member states at the level of both working group and the ERC.

15   European Convention, Draft Treaty establishing a Constitution for Europe, 18 July 2003, art. I- 40 § 2.

16   IGC 2003 - Naples Ministerial Conclave: Presidency proposal, CIG 52/03 ADD1, 25 November 2003, Annex 17.

17   Presidency Conclusions, Brussels European Council, 12 December 2003, p. 23.

18   European Convention, Draft Treaty establishing a Constitution for Europe, 18 July 2003, art. I-40, § 6.

19   European Convention, Draft Treaty establishing a Constitution for Europe, 18 July 2003, art. I-40 § 3.

20   General Affairs and External Relations Council, 2541st session (External Relations), 17-18 November 2003, p. 11.

Chapter 5

1   Competence of national governments is largely general, while the Union can act only within the limits of the competencies conferred upon it by the member states (the principle of conferral). Exclusive competence implies that only the Union may act, while member states can act only if empowered to do so by the Union. For shared competencies, member states may exercise their competence to the extent that the Union does not. Also, competence may be restricted in the sense that decisions must comply with specific constraints.

2   These Treaty provisions have never been applied (which is not surprising given that cumbersome Community procedures cannot easily be reconciled with foreign exchange market realities). An informal practice has emerged, consistent with the above, according to which exchange rate interventions are a matter for the ECB in conjunction with the eurogroup.

3   Agreement has been achieved, inter alia, on directives on taxation of cross-border interest income, mergers, parent companies and subsidiaries and on a framework for excise duties on energy products.

4   Fiscal policy may be divided into a discretionary component and a part which represents automatic stabilisation. The latter reflects consequences of tax

(and income transfer) systems which occur without any (new) policy decisions. In particular, households and corporations pay less in tax in a recession because of reduced income, and the private sector correspondingly pays more taxes in a boom (as a consequence of favourable income developments). Such tax changes offset part of the fluctuations in private disposable income and thereby tend to stabilise private spending and total output (at the cost of changes in the government budget), hence the term 'automatic stabilisation'.

5   'Encomium to the budgeteer:
        There is no official label, yet there exists in the Community a race of men and women who alone possess the secret and recognise one another, like the Pleiades of Gobineau, without any introduction: in the Commission, the Commissioner responsible, a few members of his cabinet and his Directorate-General, one or two people near to Delors; in the Council, a few senior national civil servants, one or two ministers who have been in office for a sufficiently long time (which is rare), a few bureaucrats, who are blamed for everything that goes wrong but who at least have a memory; in the Parliament, a few coordinators, official or not, some civil servants in the political groups, the secretariat of the Committee on Budgets...' (Editor's translation). The Pleiades are clusters of seven stars in the constellation of Taurus. The name was used to describe a group of French poets in the second half of the sixteenth century.

6   The Council initiative was first launched in March 2001 under the Swedish presidency.

7   Thus it deliberates at one and the same meeting on the prospects for year N+1 and the lessons to be learnt from year N-2.

8   Because it does not receive 'proposals' but a 'preliminary draft'. The other exception is at the successful conclusion of conciliation in the co-decision procedure.

9   Historians may well, in retrospect, see this process in reverse if the Constitution texts were to be ratified: in that case, the current co-decision procedure would be transposed back into the budget procedure!

10   Very confusingly for the non-initiated, the Parliament may 'amend' non-compulsory expenditure, but has to propose 'modifications' to compulsory expenditure.

11   Very approximately 1% of the gross national income (GNI), as compared to a theoretical revenue availability of 1.24%. Also, it should be borne in mind that with the invention in 1988 of the '4th resource' (based on GNP) which is added sequentially to the product of the other resources, the budget is always balanced ex ante, subject to a re-balancing in year N+1.

12   Particularly when, as in 2002, the amount represents some 15% of resources called up!

13   Were the Constitution to be ratified, the difference between 'compulsory expenditure' (essentially EAGGF), on which the Council has the 'last word', and 'non-compulsory' expenditure on which Parliament has the last word, would disappear!

14   If expenditure on the structural funds (which is very largely pre-determined) is added, the proportion rises to some 80%.

15   Even the vote has a specific mode of calculation! (cf. article 205, § 2, indent 2 as revised for enlargement).

16   'In the specific case of the examination of the Community budget for a given financial year, meetings of Council preparatory bodies, other than Coreper,

dealing with the preparation of Council agenda items on the examination of the budget shall be chaired by a delegate of the Member State which will hold the Council Presidency during the second six-month period of the year prior to the financial year in question. The same shall apply, with the agreement of the other Presidency, to the chairing of Council meetings at the time when the said budget items are discussed. The Presidency concerned will consult on the practical arrangements.' (article 19(6)).

17   By contrast the Council and its preparatory bodies do spend a great deal of time on the management of those flows, i.e. the implementation rate.

18   Article 158(2).

19   Until the advent of the co-decision procedure in the Treaty on European Union, Council presidents appeared in the parliamentary committee, but not in plenaries, apart from the president of the General Affairs Council, who answered questions in plenary.

20   The budget committee meets anything from once to four times each week, whenever feasible; it also devotes much time to 'shadowing' work within the European Parliament. It can mutate effortlessly into the 'anti-fraud working party' whenever work on OLAF calls for this.

21   For a detailed account of the newest financial regulation (Council Regulation 1605/2002 of 25 June 2002, OJ L 248 of 16.9.2002) the reader could do no better than refer to an article that has the merits of having been written by officials closely and actively involved in the drafting of the regulation itself, F. Van Craeyenest and I. Saarilahti: 'Le nouveau règlement financier applicable au budget général de l'Union européenne: un maillon essentiel dans la réforme de la Commission', in: *Revue du Marché commun et de l'Union européenne*, No 474, janvier 2004. Perhaps the two changes that had the most immediate impact on the work of the Council's preparatory bodies were, on the one hand, the introduction (articles 22 and 47) of a limited autonomy for each institution to make internal transfers and alter its establishment plan (obviously decreasing the Council workload) and, on the other hand, introducing for the Commission the requirement to present its section of the budget under activity based budgeting (article 41) which meant for the delegations and the support staff alike an extremely rapid reform of ancient conceptual habits, and – it must be said – a certain unfortunate loss of transparency as regards overall administrative costs.

22   The first moves towards negotiating the financial framework for a period beyond 2006 will be being made as this book goes to press.

23   For an ample and complete history the reader need look no further than the European Commission's *European Union Public Finance*, Luxembourg, OPOCE, 2002.

24   In the 2000 budget for Kosovo; in the 2001 budget for Serbia; in the 2002 and 2003 budgets for structural actions; in the 2004 budget for Iraq. For the years 2000, 2001 and 2002 the full available amount of €200 million was called up.

25   OJ L 311 of 14.11.2002.

26   The previous version of this chapter tellingly described the 1988 interinstitutional agreement as 'the peace treaty of the ten years' war'; nine years further down the road, the description is still valid.

27   11 times in 2002; 11 times in 2003.

28   If the truth be known, this reduced and more businesslike format has proved to be a mixed blessing; ministers tend to leave the building before the vital vote is taken, robbing the Council of its quorum, meaning that the Council's

decision has to be formalised the following day by written procedure or as a so-called 'A item', an onerous and potentially accident-prone procedure!

29   The logistical reason behind this move is simply that, with the advent of a 25-member Council and for an equivalent Parliament delegation, a lunch of some 70 participants is in no way conducive to businesslike transactions.

30   Letter from President Chirac and the heads of government of Germany, Austria, Sweden, the Netherlands and the United Kingdom to President Prodi, dated 15 December 2003.

31   The presidents of the three institutions involved (Parliament, Council, Commission) were closely involved in defusing the crisis.

32   Except category 2 where the allocation in commitment appropriations is a spending target rather than a financial ceiling.

33   To the outsider, it would appear that the huge time and effort devoted annually to the CFSP line is in inverse proportion to its size (not even 0.1% of the EU budget). However, the underlying problem is institutional. At the risk of cari-cature, in the eyes of member states, 'information' quickly becomes 'prior informa-tion' which then quickly becomes 'consultation'.

34   It needs the tenacity of an archaeologist to unearth this agreement: it takes the form of a unilateral (!) Council resolution passed at the time of the long-since defunct Luxembourg treaty of 1970; the agreement is presumably kept alive by being referred to frequently by both institutions, a fact of life which would tend to give it an element of legal durability.

35   The implication of this arrangement can be vividly illustrated by a theoreti-cal situation which arose at the end of 2003 (but which did not happen): because of an unexpected salary adjustment, Parliament was thinking in terms of adjusting the budgets of all the institutions in a horizontal fashion at its second reading; it would not have adjusted the Council's budget, however, so the Council (alone) would have had to table its own 'amending budget' the following year.

36   Recent work within the Council bodies (but not the Ecofin Budget Council *filière*) to create, under article 28 TEU, an intergovernmental financial mechanism to finance the common costs of EU military operations ('ATHENA') of course consti-tutes a very significant step as such, in terms of the general history of EU finance, but it falls by definition outside the EU budget and budgetary process, and there-fore *a fortiori* outside the scope of this chapter.

The general secretariat of the Council has had two previous experiences of administering (either by the authorisation of staff or by their secondment) small budgets outside the general budget of the European Union as such:

a) the budget for the Schengen communication infrastructure (cf. Council Decision 2000/265/EC of 27 March 2000 on the establishment of a financial regula-tion governing the budgetary aspects of the management by the deputy secretary-general of the Council, of contracts concluded in his name, on behalf of certain member states, relating to the installation and the functioning of the communica-tion infrastructure for the Schengen environment, 'Sisnet' - OJ L 85 of 6.4.2000, p. 12), and

b) the financing of the convention on the future of the European Union, a somewhat convoluted construction under which the budget is agreed by the member states following the agreement of the European Parliament, Council and Commission (the actual contributors!). The Council budget *filière* as described in this chapter was thus, for all practical proposes, involved twice with each budget approval (and twice with each discharge). (Cf.: Decision 2002/176/EU of the

Representatives of the Governments of the Member States meeting within the
Council of 21 February 2002 setting up a Fund for the financing of the Convention
on the future of the European Union and laying down the financial rules for its
management – OJ L 60 of 1.3.2002, p 56 – Interinstitutional agreement on the
financing of the Convention on the future of the European Union – OJ C 54 of
1.3.2002, p. 1).

37   Council Decision 2001/80/CFSP of 22 January 2001 on the establishment of
the Military Staff of the European Union (OJ L 27 of 30.1.2001, p. 7). Council
Decision 2003/479/EC of 16 June 2003 concerning the rules applicable to national
experts and military staff on secondment to the General Secretariat of the Council
and repealing the Decisions of 25 June 1997 and 22 March 1999, Decision
2001/41/EC and Decision 2001/496/CFSP (OJ L 160 of 28.6.2003, p. 72).

38   Other than those mentioned above, the only other administrative/budget-
ary experiences that the general secretariat has ever undergone in fields not
directly related to its core traditional role as provider of support for meetings consisted, on the one hand, in the financing of a very small number of seconded
national experts in the JHA area and, on the other hand, in the (thankfully) short-
lived experiment (2001-2003) under which the administrative mini-budgets and
staff of all of the EU special representatives were transferred from the
Commission's section of the budget to that of the Council.

39   For example, the 2004 budget shows, within the Council's section, a title III
at 29.9 million euros (some 6% of the Council budget); previously, the Council's
budget had followed the simple traditional model common to other Institutions
with a title I representing salaries and allowances, and a title II representing infrastructure and running costs. Because the new military staff had a separate dedicated building and communications systems, and a separate emolument scheme, it
was relatively easy to construct a new title III.

40   Given that the whole raison d'être of the 'gentlemen's agreement' is that
Parliament and Council have only administrative expenditure, a symptom of this
malaise became especially visible when the European Parliament granted discharge to the Council for the 2001 financial year adding the term 'operational
expenditure' (OJ L 148 of 16.6.2003, p. 42). Cf also, as we are going to press, a
Parliament draft report on the 'guidelines for Section II...' (in the run-up to the 2005
exercise) which clearly states: '... continues to monitor the Council operational
budget, while respecting the gentlemen's agreement as regards the administrative
expenditure.'

Chapter 7

1   Décision du 12.5.1960 des représentants des gouvernements des Etats membres de la Communauté économique européenne réunis au sein du Conseil, concer-
nant l'accéléeration du rythme de réalisation des objectifs du traité (JO du
12.9.1960, p. 1217)

PART IV

Chapter 11

1   The standard text on Coreper and its development is Hayes-Renshaw et al, 1989, but three earlier works, Noël, 1966, Noël and Etienne, 1972, and De Zwaan, 1995, provide fascinating insights into Coreper's development and a wealth of insiders' detail. For a frank, Brussels-based view of Coreper's powers and role, see Barber, 1995.

2   This can be contrasted with one recent minister's colourful characterisation of the system:

'Not, really, that it makes the slightest difference to the conclusions of a meeting what Ministers say at it. Everything is decided, horse-traded off, by officials at Coreper, the Council [sic] of Permanent Representatives. The Ministers arrive on the scene at the last minute, hot, tired, ill, or drunk (sometimes all of these together), read out their piece, and depart. Strange, really, because the EC constitution is quite well drawn. The Council of Ministers is sovereign, and can/could boss Coreper around. But, as always in politics everywhere, democratic or autocratic, it's the chaps on the spot who call the shot' (Clark, 1994, p 139). And: 'A succession of meetings, but no possibility whatever of getting anything changed - not at my level anyway. Everything is fixed by officials in advance. Ministers shaking hands are just window dressing' (ibid., p 5).

PART V

Chapter 14

1   During the Nice IGC, one issue was what future configuration of the Union should be catered for in the negotiation. In the end, it was decided that account should be taken of all the candidate states with which the Union was in negotiation at that time (i.e. 12 states). Although Turkey was a candidate state, accession negotiations had not yet been opened.

Chapter 15

1   See, for example, Spain's attempts to block German unification unless quotas until 1996 in some European agricultural markets were reversed in Spence, 1991. Spain's attempts to hold the EFTA countries to ransom until adoptions to fisheries quotas were made as a spin-off to the enlargement negotiations in 1993-1994 is a further example. In this case a last-minute compromise in the Fisheries Council in December 1994 allowed agreement. Without it the Spanish government had been required by its Parliament not to ratify the accession treaties. (Granell, 1995).

Chapter 16

*   Chapter 16 is an adapted version of a piece which appeared as the keynote article in the *Journal of Common Market Studies* annual review Vol. 37, September

1999. David Galloway is grateful to Blackwell publishers for giving permission for this material to be reproduced.

1   It is worth noting that none of these countries objected to being net contributors as such nor sought a 'juste retour'. Their complaint was that they deemed they were contributing excessively in relation to their relative prosperity, with no safety net (except for the UK) to prevent further deterioration in their negative budgetary positions in future.

2   The friends of the presidency group is a group (involving all Council members) 'close' to Coreper composed of a mixture of ambassadors' assistants ('Anticis') and financial or political counsellors, under a single chair, although the composition of delegations varied depending on matters under discussion. Its main task was to carry out a detailed examination of various issues for Coreper and to remit more specific technical work on certain parts of the legislation to either the structural actions working party or the financial counsellors group. The group was particularly active during the UK and Austrian presidencies, when much of the work involved clarifying the content of the Commission's proposals by requesting and examining supplementary explanatory documents and background information from the Commission.

3   This also involved determining the nature and content of the report to be prepared for the Vienna European Council, in particular whether it should be a presidency or a Council (i.e. agreed) report, whether it should be issue-based or reflect delegations' views. On most of these points, the Council secretariat provided counsel and suggested language to the presidency at an early stage in their internal reflections as a basis on which the presidency could construct the line it wished to take.

4   While European Council conclusions are typically not negotiated in advance but only tabled on the second day of the summit meetings, Agenda 2000 constituted an exception to this well-established rule. Given the complexity and political sensitivity of the subject matter, where the inclusion or omission of single sentences, or even words, could cost individual member states hundreds of millions of euros, twenty-seven pages of densely-drafted conclusions could not be sprung on the European Council without prior scrutiny and familiarity with the overall structure and the language to be used. This method mirrored that used in the run-up to the Edinburgh European Council in December 1992 which sealed the Delors II package.

5   Text between square brackets may be used in negotiated texts as a working assumption or set out several options for solutions, with the use of square brackets indicating that the text is not yet agreed.

6   Presidency non-papers are texts prepared under the presidency's responsibility but without formally committing it, which are tabled to test the temperature by sounding out ideas, language and options so that the presidency can subsequently come forward with a more formal position based on its feeling for what the market will bear.

7   The Commission's initial approach involved reserving part of the margin (as a percentage of EU GNP) to cover part of the cost of enlargement. There was, however, a firm desire from all member states to include this cost in the financial perspective table in absolute amounts.

8   The margin for unforeseen expenditure in the indicative financial framework for EU-21 (i.e. taking account of the own resources available from six new member states) is 0.18 per cent in 2006.

9   While the guideline has remained unchanged, it now covers, in addition to the heading 1 ceiling, the amounts in heading 7 for the agricultural pre-accession instrument and the amounts set aside to cover the costs of agricultural expenditure after enlargement. In order to respond to concerns regarding the potential cost of enlargement in future, the European Council committed itself to review the guideline before enlargement, although without committing itself to any changes at this stage.

10   While the Commission had proposed an increase in objective 3 spending (development of human resources) which would apply in all regions of the Union outside objective 1 regions, some of the net budget contributors, who stood to 'benefit' from increased objective 3 funding, still preferred an across the board approach which contained structural expenditure, including objective 3, within acceptable financial limits, relying on side payments as part of the overall deal to improve their individual situation (see paragraph 44 of the Berlin summit conclusions). It is important to note that the concept of stabilisation by maintaining average per capita aid intensity levels under these three objectives was one used for determining the overall financial envelope for heading 2, and did not mean that each eligible area would receive the same amount as during the previous period. The actual allocation among eligible regions would depend on the programming process based on applying the relevant criteria laid down in the general regulation.

11   One of the stated objectives of pre-accession expenditure is to familiarise applicant countries with the procedures and methods used for implementing programmes within the Union.

12   Some of these additional payments included €500 million to Lisbon for objective 1 phasing out, €500 million for Northern Ireland, €550 million to Ireland under objective 1, €350 million for certain regions in Sweden, €100 million for East Berlin in objective 1 phasing out, €300 million for the Highlands and Islands of Scotland for objective 1 phasing-out (i.e. a similar allocation to what this region would have received if it had retained objective 1 status), payments to Greece, Ireland, Spain and Portugal to maintain the average level of per capita assistance reached in 1999, etc. For the complete list, refer to paragraph 44 of the Berlin European Council conclusions.

Chapter 17

1   Friday is the usual day. Before a meeting of the General Affairs Council (GAC), the meeting takes place on a Thursday. Similarly, Coreper II (permanent representatives) takes place on Thursdays as a rule, but on Wednesdays before a GAC.

2   The case for and against the view that German EU coordination is 'inadequate, incoherent and polyphonic' is argued by the former German permanent representative to the EU (and also former secretary-general of the Council of Ministers) Jürgen Trumpf in 'Reflections on Three German Presidencies – High Marks for the German Coordination Model, Low Marks for the Presidency System' in W. Wessels and E. Regelsberger (eds) op. cit.

PART VI

Chapter 18

1   One of the important 1977 provisions concerned the European
Community's representation in third countries. Not even the largest member states
are represented in all third countries, and the problem then arises as to how the
presidency can be represented where, in effect, it is absent. Under the ground rules
established in 1977, if the presidency is not present, it is represented by the next
member state following the order of rotation of the presidency. For example, in the
second half of 1995, of a list of 167 third countries, the Spanish presidency was able
to represent itself in 86. In the 81 other countries the presidency was represented
by other member states, principally one of the big four of Germany, France, Italy
and the United Kingdom.

2   The 'Three Wise Men' were Barend Biesheuvel, Edmund Dell, and Robert
Marjolin.

3   Leo Tindemans wondered aloud to the European Parliament 'Are we perhaps in the process of building up a library of forgotten reports? If I was one of the
mandarin class, I would propose writing a book entitled 'Remembrance of Past
Reports' or perhaps publishing a dictionary of wasted European ideas.' (European
Parliament Debates, N° 1-257, p 168, 18 June 1980) Roy Jenkins, then President of
the Commission, warned '...I do not think that in view of the scant respect with
which their reports have been treated we will find it easy to get figures of note to
do such work in the future.' Churchill Memorial Lecture, Luxembourg, 20
November 1980. Both are cited in Duff, 1981. But see Tindemans in Westlake (ed)
1998, for a more upbeat assessment.

4   In the case of the Single European Act and the economic and monetary
union side of the Maastricht Treaty, the draftsman's role was shared with the
Commission (Ludlow, 1985, p 152), but in the case of the political union side of the
Maastricht Treaty, the Presidency-Council general secretariat tandem worked
alone:

        'La présidence luxembourgeoise constitua, avec le Secrétaire Général du
Conseil, une équipe de rédaction composée de fonctionnaires du Secrétariat
Général du Conseil et de la Représentation Permanent du Luxembourg. C'est au
sein de ce groupe que les textes relatifs à l'Union politique furent rédigés.' (Cloos,
et al, 1993)

Chapter 19

1   The prejudices were fuelled by experiences such as the following. 'An
official from the Council's General Secretariat went to Vienna to a meeting of the
United Nations' Atomic Energy Agency. Armed with a press pass, he managed to
get into the meeting room, and then took a little sign out of his pocket which said
'Council of the European Atomic Energy Community', although the Treaty states
clearly that the EURATOM Commission is responsible for all necessary relations
with the institutions of the United Nations.' Mr. Sassen, a member of the
EURATOM Commission, to the European Parliament (Débats, 15 December 1958,
Nÿ 6, p 50, cited in Houben, 1964, p 155 – author's translation).

2   These are: the security committee, the working parties on information, legal

data processing, electronic communications, codification of legislation, new buildings and legal linguistic experts.

3   Case C-65/90, *European Parliament v. Council* [1992] ECR 7-1, p. 4593.

4   See the Order of the President of the Court of First Instance in Case T-
610/97 R, *Carlsen v. Council* [1998] ECR 3-4 II, p. 485.

5   e.g. Case C-41/95, *Council v. European Parliament* [1995] ECR 12-I, p. 4411, on
the latter's classification of certain items of expenditure as non-obligatory in the
budget for 1995.

6   Shortly thereafter, each of them implemented the code by a decision. On 20
December 1993, the Council adopted decision 93/731/EC on public access to
Council documents ('the 1993 Access Decision'), and on 8 February 1994 the
Commission adopted its decision 94/90/ECSC, EC, Euratom on public access to
Commission documents.

PART VII

Chapter 20

1 On 20 December 1993, the Council adopted decision 93/731/EC on public access
to Council documents ('the 1993 access decision') (OJ L 340 of 31.12.1993, p. 43), and
on 8 February 1994 the Commission adopted its decision 94/90/ECSC, EC, Euratom
on public access to Commission documents (OJ L 46 of 18.2.1994, p. 58).

2   In its judgment of 30 April 1996 in Case C-58/94, *Netherlands v. Council*, ECR
I-2186, the Court of Justice confirmed that Decision 93/731/EC had legal effects
vis-à-vis third parties and stated that 'so long as the Community legislature has not
adopted general rules on the right of public access to documents held by the
Community institutions, the institutions must take measures as to the processing of
such requests by virtue of their power of internal organization, which authorizes
them to take appropriate measures in order to ensure their internal operation in
conformity with the interests of good administration' (point 37).

3   Article 42 of the Charter of fundamental rights of the European Union (OJ C
364, 18.12.2000, p. 1) re-affirms this right in identical terms.

4   Council Decision 2000/527/EC of 14 August 2000 amending Decision
93/731/EC on public access to Council documents and Council Decision
2000/23/EC on the improvement of information on the Council's legislative activities and the public register of Council documents, OJ L 212 of 23.8.2000, p. 9.

5   OJ L 145 of 31.5.2001, p. 43.

6   Case C-260/01, *European Parliament v. Council* (OJ C 245 of 1.9.2001, p. 13).
As part of the compromise package which led to the conclusion of the interinstitutional agreement of 20 November 2002, the European Parliament decided to withdraw its action.

7   See Article 1 of Annex II of the Council's Rules of Procedure, Article 1 of the
Annex to the Commission's Rules of Procedure, as amended by Commission
Decision 2001/937/EC, ECSC, Euratom of 5 December 2001, OJ L 345 of 29.12.2001,
p. 94 and Rule 172(1) of the European Parliament's Rules of Procedure, as
amended by Decision of 13.11.2001, OJ C 140 E of 13.6.2002, p 116.

8   See judgment of 19 July 1999, Case T-14/98, *Hautala v. Council*, ECR II-2489,
and judgment of 6 December 2001, Case C-353/99 P, *Council v. Hautala*, ECR I-9594,
in which the fact that the applicant was a member of the European Parliament was

not an issue. See also the decision (document 14692/02) which is the subject of Case T-84/03, *Turco v. Council* (still pending), in which the Council treated the applicant, who was a member of the European Parliament, like any other applicant.

9   On 18 June and 22 July 2003, the Council adopted 15 regulations amending with effect from 1 October 2003 the constituent acts of Community agencies and bodies to make the access regulation applicable to documents held by these agencies and bodies and oblige their management committees to adopt, by 1 April 2004, practical arrangements to this effect. Furthermore, it was clarified that decisions taken by the agency or body refusing access to documents can be challenged before the Court of Justice or form the subject of a complaint to the Ombudsman (Regulations (EC) No. 1641-1655/2003, OJ L 245 of 29.9.2003, pp. 1-41). See also the Council Joint Actions of 20 July 2001 on the establishment of a European Union Institute for Security Studies (2001/554/CFSP, OJ L 200 of 25.7.2001, p. 1) and of a European Union Satellite Centre (2001/555/CFSP, OJ L 200 of 25.7.2001, p. 5) and Council Decision 2002/187/JHA of 28 February 2002 setting up Eurojust with a view to reinforcing the fight against serious crime (OJ L 63 of 6.3.2002, p. 1), which oblige these bodies to adopt rules on public access to their documents which take into account the principles and limits laid down in the access regulation. The Board of the Institute for Security Studies adopted such rules on 17 July 2002 (http://www.iss-eu.org), and the Board of the Satellite Centre adopted similar rules on 16 July 2003.

10   See the Rules on access to documents of the European Investment Bank, adopted by the management committee of the Bank (OJ C 292 of 27.11.2002, p. 10), the Committee of the Regions Decision No 64/2003 of 11 February 2003 on public access to Committee of the Regions documents (OJ L 160 of 28.6.2003, p. 96), the Decision 2003/603 of 1 July 2003 of the European Economic and Social Committee on public access to European Economic and Social Committee documents (OJ L 205 of 14.8.2003, p. 19) and the Decision ECB/2004/3 (2004/258/EC) of the European Central Bank of 4 March 2004 on public access to European Central Bank documents (OJ L 80 of 18.3.2004, p. 42). The Court of Justice and the Court of First Instance have not adopted any rules on access to their documents.

11   *Council v. Hautala*, Case C-353/99 P (quoted above), points 23 and 26.

12   Order of 27 October 1999, Case T-106/99, *Meyer v. Commission*, ECR II-3275, points 35 and 36.

13   Judgment of 25 June 2002, Case T-311/00, *British American Tobacco (Investments) Ltd. v. Commission*, ECR II-2784, point 35, and judgment of 12 October 2000, Case T-123/99, *JT's Corporation Ltd v. Commission*, ECR II-3269, point 58.

14   In order to avoid conflicting decisions by the three institutions covered by the access regulation and to ensure swift processing of applications for documents originating from one institution which are held by another institution, the services of the European Parliament, the Council and the Commission agreed on 9 July 2002 on a memorandum of understanding which provides for a mutual information and consultation procedure between specified contact points in each of the three institutions. Arrangements for consultation as regards third-party documents in general and the processing of requests for consultation received from other institutions are laid down in articles 2 and 3 of Annex II to the Council's rules of procedure.

15   See judgment of 17 September 2003, Case T-76/02, *Messina v. Commission*, points 40 and 55.

16   See Articles 9(2) and (3) of the access regulation. These provisions reflect two fundamental principles underlying the Council's security regulations: the 'need to know-principle' according to which access to classified information is authorized only to persons who need to take cognizance of it for the exercice of their functions and have undergone the appropriate security clearance, and the principle that any downgrading of the level of classification of a classified document, its declassification and its release requires the originator's consent.

17   See Article 9(4) of the access regulation. This provision codifies constant case law – see in particular the judgment of 5 March 1997, Case T-105/95, *WWF UK v. Commission*, ECR II-315, point 65.

18   Along the same lines, article 9(5) of the access regulation provides that 'Member States shall take appropriate measures to ensure that, when handling applications for sensitive documents, the principles in this Article and Article 4 are respected.'

19   Consistent case law since the judgment of 19 October 1995, Case T-194/94, *Carvel and Guardian Newspapers v. Council*, ECR II-2765, point 64.

20   See, in respect of Article 4(1) of the 1993 access decision, the Order of the President of the Court of First Instance of 3 March 1998, Case T-610/97 R, *Carlsen a.o. v. Council*, ECR II-485, point 48.

21   Judgment of 19 July 1999 in Case T-14/98, point 87, and judgment of 6 December 2001 in Case C-353/99 P, points 25 to 31 (both quoted above).

22   Judgment of 17 June 1998, case T–174/95, *Svenska Journalistförbundet v. Council* (ECRII–2289), points 121 and 122.

23   Case T-14/98, *Hautala v. Council*, see above, points 71 and 72.

24   Judgment of 12 July 2001, Case T-204/99, *Mattila v. Council* (ECRII–2265), point 65.

25   Judgment of 7 February 2002, Case T-211/00, *Kuijer (II) v. Council* (ECRII–488), points 60 to 68.

26   See in particular Regulation (EC) No. 45/2001 of the European Parliament and the Council of 18 December 2000 on the protection of individuals with regard to the processing of personal data by the Community institutions and bodies and on the free movement of such data (OJ L 8 of 12.1.2001, p. 1).

27   See the Ombudsman's decision on complaint 412/2003/GG against the Commission.

28   See the Commission's report on the implementation of the access regulation, point 3.4.5.

29   See in particular the Order of 3 March 1998, *Carlsen a.o. v. Council*, T-610/97 R, ECR II-485, the judgment of 8 November 2000, Case T-44/97, *Ghignone a.o. v. Council*, ECR IA-223, points 47 and 48, and the Order of 23 October 2002, Case C-445/00, *Austria v. Council*, point 12.

30   See the Ombudsman's Special Report relating to complaint 1542/2000(PB)SM and the draft recommendation of 27 March 2003 concerning complaint 1015/2002/(PB)IJH.

31   Case T-84/03, *Turco v. Council* (OJ C 112 of 10.5.2003, p. 38).

32   Judgment of 11 January 2000, *Netherlands and Van der Wal v. Commission*, C-174/98 P and C-189/98 P, ECR I-47.

33   Judgment of 7 December 1999, Case T-92/98, *Interporc v. Commission*, ECR II-3524, points 41 and 42.

34   Order of 3 April 2000, *Germany v. Parliament and Council*, C-376/98, ECR I-2247, point 10.

35		*Svenska Journalistförbundet v. Council* (see above), points 135 to 139.
36		See in particular *WWF UK v. Commission* (see above), points 62 to 64; judgment of 14 October 1999, *Bavarian Lager v. Commission*, T-309/97, ECR II-3217, points 40 to 47; judgment of 13 September 2000, *Denkavit v. Commission*, T-20/99, ECR II-3013, points 43 to 49; judgment of 11.12.2001, *Petrie a.o. v. Commission*, T–191/99, ECR II-3681, points 67 to 69.
37		At the adoption of the access regulation, the Commission made a statement to the minutes according to which it could agree, in a spirit of compromise, 'to infringement proceedings not being expressly include in the list of exceptions in Article 4(2) of the Regulation, as it considers that the text as worded does not affect current practice with regard to the protection of confidentiality for the purposes of its duties in monitoring compliance with Community law' (document 9204/01 ADD 1).
38		See the Council's reply to the letter sent by the European Ombudsman following a complaint (1641/2003/OV) made by Ms. Buitenweg, MEP (document 13142/03). A case in which the Council followed this approach is currently subject of courts proceedings (Case T-84/03, *Turco v. Council*, see above).
39		This fact is deplored by the Commission in its report on the implementation of the access regulation (point 4.3). Two cases in which the Commission refused to accede to particularly burdensome applications on grounds of the principles of proportionality and good administration are currently pending before the Court of First Instance (Case T-2/03, *Verein für Konsumenteninformation v. Commission*, and T-170/03, *British American Tobacco (Investments) Ltd v. Commission*).
40		Case T-211/00, *Kuijer (II) v. Council* (quoted above), point 69.
41		This UN/ECE Convention was signed by the Community and the member states on 25 June 1998, but has not yet been ratified by the Community.
42		COM(2003) 622 final of 24 October 2003.
43		See also Article III-398(1) of the draft Constitution, according to which 'in carrying out their missions, the institutions, bodies, offices and agencies of the Union shall have the support of an open, efficient and independent administration', and III-399(1) of the draft Constitution, which provides that 'the institutions, bodies, offices and agencies of the Union shall ensure transparency in their work and shall, pursuant to Article I-50, lay down in their rules of procedure the provisions for public access to documents.'
44		Pursuant to Article I-52(3) of the draft Constitution, this also applies to churches, religious associations or communities and philosophical and non-confessional organisations.
45		However, pursuant to Article III-399(1) of the draft Constitution, the Court of Justice of the European Union, the European Central Bank and the European Investment Bank are subject to the provisions of Article I-50(3) and to this article only when exercising their administrative tasks.

Chapter 21

*		This chapter is partially based on a paper first submitted at a seminar held at the University of Maastricht on 6 June 2003, part of the 'CONVEU 30' study led by the Stiftung Wissenschaft und Politik.
1		This chapter covers a period during which the Council composed of Foreign Ministers has been known under different names ('Foreign Affairs Council', then 'General and Foreign Affairs Council', later still 'General Affairs Council' and most

recently 'General Affairs and External Relations Council'). However, for the sake of simplicity, and given that this chapter is essentially concerned with the Foreign Ministers' general role in coordinating the EU's policies, it will refer throughout to the 'General Affairs Council'.

APPENDIX 1

Summits of EEC heads of state or government

Venue	Date	President	State holding the presidency
Paris	10-11.02.1961	Charles de Gaulle	France
Bonn	19-20.07.1961	Konrad Adenauer	Germany
Rome	29-30.05.1967	Aldo Moro	Italy
The Hague	01-02.12.1969	Petrus de Jong	The Netherlands
Paris	19-20.10.1972	Georges Pompidou	France
Copenhagen	14-15.12.1973	Anker Jorgensen	Denmark
Paris	14.09.1974	Valéry Giscard d'Estaing	France
Paris	09-10.12.1974	Valéry Giscard d'Estaing	France

European Council meetings

Venue	Date	President	State holding the presidency
Dublin	10-11.03.1975	Liam Cosgrave	Ireland
Brussels	16-17.07.1975	Aldo Moro	Italy
Rome	01-02.12.1975	Aldo Moro	Italy
Luxembourg	01-02.04.1976	Gaston Thorn	Italy
Brussels	12-13.07.1976	Joop Den Uyl	The Netherlands
The Hague	29-30.11.1976	Joop Den Uyl	The Netherlands
Rome	25-26.03.1977	James Callaghan	United Kingdom
London	29-30.06.1977	James Callaghan	United Kingdom
Brussels	05-06.12.1977	Leo Tindemans	Belgium
Copenhagen	07-08.04.1978	Anker Jorgensen	Denmark
Bremen	06-07.07.1978	Helmut Schmidt	Germany
Brussels	04-05.12.1978	Helmut Schmidt	Germany
Paris	12-13.03.1979	Valéry Giscard d'Estaing	France
Strasbourg	21-22.06.1979	Valéry Giscard d'Estaing	France
Dublin	29-30.11.1979	John Lynch	Ireland
Luxembourg	27-28.04.1980	Francesco Cossiga	Italy
Venice	12-13.06.1980	Francesco Cossiga	Italy
Luxembourg	01-02.12.1980	Pierre Werner	Luxembourg
Maastricht	23-24.03.1981	Andreas van Agt	The Netherlands
Luxembourg	29-30.06.1981	Andreas van Agt	The Netherlands
London	26-27.11.1981	Margaret Thatcher	United Kingdom
Brussels	29-30.03.1982	Wilfried Martens	Belgium

Venue	Date	President	State holding the presidency
Brussels	28-29.06.1982	Wilfried Martens	Belgium
Copenhagen	03-04.12.1982	Poul Schlüter	Denmark
Brussels	21-22.03.1983	Helmut Kohl	Germany
Stuttgart	17-19.06.1983	Helmut Kohl	Germany
Athens	04-06.12.1983	Andreas Papandreou	Greece
Brussels	19-20.03.1984	François Mitterrand	France
Fontainebleau	25-26.06.1984	François Mitterrand	France
Dublin	03-04.12.1984	Garrett Fitzgerald	Ireland
Brussels	29-30.03.1985	Bettino Craxi	Italy
Milan	28-29.06.1985	Bettino Craxi	Italy
Luxembourg	02-03.12.1985	Jacques Santer	Luxembourg
The Hague	26-27.06.1986	Ruud Lubbers	The Netherlands
London	05-06.12.1986	Margaret Thatcher	United Kingdom
Brussels	29-30.06.1987	Wilfried Martens	Belgium
Copenhagen	04-05.12.1987	Poul Schlüter	Denmark
Brussels	11-12.03.1988	Helmut Kohl	Germany
Hanover	27-28.06.1988	Helmut Kohl	Germany
Rhodes	02-03.12.1988	Andreas Papandreou	Greece
Madrid	26-27.06.1989	Felipe Gonzalez	Spain
Paris *	18.11.1989	François Mitterrand	France
Strasbourg	08-09.12.1989	François Mitterrand	France
Dublin	28-29.04.1990	Charles Haughey	Ireland
Dublin	25-26.06.1990	Charles Haughey	Ireland
Rome	27-28.10.1990	Giulio Andreotti	Italy
Rome	14-15.12.1990	Giulio Andreotti	Italy
Luxembourg *	08.04.1991	Jacques Santer	Luxembourg
Luxembourg	28-29.06.1991	Jacques Santer	Luxembourg
Maastricht	09-10.12.1991	Ruud Lubbers	The Netherlands
Lisbon	26-27.06.1992	Aníbal Cavaco Silva	Portugal
Birmingham	16.10.1992	John Major	United Kingdom
Edinburgh	11-12.12.1992	John Major	United Kingdom
Copenhagen	21-22.06.1993	Poul Nyrup Rasmussen	Denmark
Brussels	29.10.1993	Jean-Luc Dehaene	Belgium
Brussels	10-11.12.1993	Jean-Luc Dehaene	Belgium
Corfu	24-25.06.1994	Andreas Papandreou	Greece
Brussels	15.07.1994	Helmut Kohl	Germany
Essen	09-10.12.1994	Helmut Kohl	Germany
Cannes	26-27.06.1995	Jacques Chirac	France
Mallorca *	22-23.09.1995	Felipe Gonzalez	Spain
Madrid	15-16.12.1995	Felipe Gonzalez	Spain
Turin	29-30.03.1996	Lamberto Dini	Italy
Florence	21-22.06.1996	Romano Prodi	Italy
Dublin *	05.10.1996	John Bruton	Ireland
Dublin	13-14.12.1996	John Bruton	Ireland
Noordwijk *	23.05.1997	Wim Kok	The Netherlands
Amsterdam	16-17.06.1997	Wim Kok	The Netherlands

Venue	Date	President	State holding the presidency
Luxembourg	20-21.11.1997	Jean-Claude Juncker	Luxembourg
Luxembourg	12-13.12.1997	Jean-Claude Juncker	Luxembourg
Cardiff	15-16.06.1998	Tony Blair	United Kingdom
Pörtschach *	24-25.10.1998	Viktor Klima	Austria
Vienna	11-12.12.1998	Viktor Klima	Austria
Petersberg *	26.02.1999	Gerhard Schröder	Germany
Berlin	24-25.03.1999	Gerhard Schröder	Germany
Brussels *	14.04.1999	Gerhard Schröder	Germany
Cologne	03-04.06.1999	Gerhard Schröder	Germany
Tampere	15-13.10.1999	Paavo Lipponen	Finland
Helsinki	10-11.12.1999	Paavo Lipponen	Finland
Lisbon	23-24.03.2000	António Guterres	Portugal
Feira	19-20.06.2000	António Guterres	Portugal
Biarritz *	13-14.10.2000	Jacques Chirac	France
Nice	07-08.12.2000	Jacques Chirac	France
Stockholm	23-24.03.2001	Göran Persson	Sweden
Göteborg	15-16.06.2001	Göran Persson	Sweden
Brussels	21.09.2001	Guy Verhofstadt	Belgium
Ghent *	19.10.2001	Guy Verhofstadt	Belgium
Laeken	14-15.12.2001	Guy Verhofstadt	Belgium
Barcelona	15-16.03.2002	José-Maria Aznar	Spain
Seville	21-22.06.2002	José-Maria Aznar	Spain
Brussels	24-25.10.2002	Anders Fogh Rasmussen	Demark
Copenhagen	12-13.12.2002	Anders Fogh Rasmussen	Demark
Brussels	17.02.2003	Costas Simitis	Greece
Brussels	20-21.03.2003	Costas Simitis	Greece
Athens *	16.04.2003	Costas Simitis	Greece
Thessaloniki	19-20.06.2003	Costas Simitis	Greece
Brussels	16-17.10.2003	Silvio Berlusconi	Italy
Brussels	12-13.12.2003	Silvio Berlusconi	Italy
Brussels	25-26.03.2004	Bertie Ahern	Ireland
Brussels	17-18.06.2004	Bertie Ahern	Ireland
Brussels*	29.06.2004	Bertie Ahern	Ireland
Brussels	4-5.11.2004.	Jan Peter Balkenende	The Netherlands

* Denotes informal meetings without conclusions.

APPENDIX 2

Member states' permanent representatives and deputy permanent representatives since 1958

Permanent representatives	Dates	Deputy permanent representatives	Dates
Austria			
Manfred Scheich	1995-1999	Judith Gebetsroithner	1995-
Gregor Woschnagg	1999-		
Belgium			
J.C. Snoy d'Oppuers	1958-1959	M. Wendelen	1959-1961
Joseph Van der Meulen	1959-1979	Jean Doumont	1961-1973
Paul Noterdaeme	1979-1987	Hervé Robinet	1973-1979
Philippe de Schoutheete de	1987-1997	Marc Lepoivre	1979-1991
Tervarent		Lode Willems	1991-1992
Frans Van Daele	1997-2002	Jan de Bock	1992-1994
Jan de Bock	2002-	Luc Carbonnez	1994-1997
		Jean-Louis Six	1997-2002
		François Roux	2002-2004
		Geneviève Tuts	2004-
Cyprus			
Theophilous Theophilou	2004	Kornelios S. Korneliou	2004-
Nicolas Emiliou	2004		
Czech Republic			
Jan Kohout	2004-	Ludek Stavinoha	2004-
Denmark			
Niels Ersbøll	1973-1977	Otto E. Moeller	1973-1974
Gunnar Riberholdt	1977-1984	Ole Galthen Bech	1974-1977
Jakob Esper Larsen	1984-1989	Jakob Esper Larsen	1977-1980
Jakob Rytter	1990-1992	Flemming Hedegaard	1980-1983
Gunnar Riberholdt	1992-1994	Jakob Rytter	1983-1986
Poul Christoffersen	1995-2003	Torben Mailand Christensen	1986-1989
Claus Grube	2003-	Niels Henrik Sliben	1989-1995
		Niels Pultz	1995-2000
		Claus Grube	2000-2003
		Jeppe Tranholm Mikkelsen	2003-
Estonia			
Väino Reinart	2004-	Margus Rahuoja	2004-

Permanent representatives	Dates	Deputy permanent representatives	Dates
Finland			
Antti Satuli	1995-2001	Jan Store	1995-2000
Eikka Kosonen	2002-	Kare Halonen	2000-2004
		Nina Vaskunlahti	2004-
France			
Eric de Carbonnel	1958-1959	Jean Mille	1958-1961
Georges Gorse	1959-1961	Jean Pierre Brunet	1961-1965
Jean-Marc Boegner	1961-1972	Maurice Ulrich	1965-1968
Etienne Burin des Roziers	1972-1975	Emile Cazimajou	1968-1977
Jean-Marie Soutou	1975-1976	François Scheer	1977-1979
Luc de la Barre de Nanteuil	1977-1982	Jean Vidal	1979-1984
Jacques Leprette	1982-1984	Claude Martin	1984-1986
Luc de la Barre de Nanteuil	1984-1986	Jean Cadet	1986-1992
François Scheer	1986-1988	Pierre Sellal	1992-1997
Philippe Louet	1988-1989	Pierre Etienne	1997-2002
Jean Vidal	1989-1992	Christian Masset	2002-
François Scheer	1992-1993		
Pierre de Boissieu	1993-1999		
Pierre Vimont	1999-2002		
Pierre Sellal	2002-		
Germany			
Carl Friedrich Ophuels	1958-1961	Hans Albert Goers	1958-1959
Rolf Lahr	1961	Eberhard Boemke	1959-1976
Gunther Harkot	1961-1965	Walter Kittel	1976-1987
Hans-Georg Sachs	1965-1973	Jochen Grünhage	1987-2001
Ulrich Lebsanft	1973-1977	Peter Witt	2001-
Helmut Sigrist	1977-1979		
Gisbert Poensgen	1979-1985		
Werner Ungerer	1985-1989		
Jürgen Trumpf	1989-1993		
Dietrich Von Kyaw	1993-1999		
Wilhelm Schönfelder	1999-		
Greece			
Marco Economides	1981-1982	Antoine Exarchos	1981-1982
Nikos Dimadis	1982-1984	Alexandre Zaphiriou	1982-1984
Alexandre Zaphiriou	1985-1986	Elias Lymberopoulos	1985-1989
Constantinos Lyberopoulos	1986-1990	Haris Carabarbounis	1989-1991
Alexandre Vayenas	1990-1992	Jean Corantis	1991-1995
Leonides Evangelidis	1992-1993	Adamantios Vassilakis	1995-1999
Alexandre Zaphiriou	1993-1995	Dimitris Rallis	1999-
Pavlos Apostolides	1995-1998		
Loucas Tsilas	1998-2000		
Aristide Agathocles	2000-2003		
Vassilis Kaskarelis	2004-		

Permanent representatives	Dates	Deputy permanent representatives	Dates
Hungary			
Tibor Kiss	2004-	Egon Dienes-Oehm	2004-
Ireland			
Sean P. Kennan	1973	Edward J. Brennan	1973-1974
Brandan Dillon	1973-1981	Andrew O'Rourke	1974-1978
Andrew O'Rourke	1981-1986	Padraig Murphy	1978-1980
John H.F. Campbell	1986-1991	John Swift	1980-1985
Padraic MacKernan	1991-1995	Denis O'Leary	1985-1989
Denis O'Leary	1995-2001	Eammon Ryan	1990-1993
Anne Anderson	2001-	John F. Cogan	1993-1998
		James Brennan	1998-2002
		Peter Gunning	2002-
Italy			
Attilio Cattani	1958-1961	Giulio Pascucci-Righi	1958-1961
Antonio Venturini	1961-1967	Ugo Mosca	1961-1967
Giorgio Bombassei Frascani de Vector	1967-1976	Fernando Natale	1967-1969
		Enrico Macchia	1970-1976
Eugenio Plaja	1976-1979	Paolo Massimo Antici	1976-1978
Renato Ruggiero	1979-1984	Pietro Calamia	1978-1980
Pietro Calamia	1984-1990	Paolo Galli	1980-1986
Federico de Roberto	1990-1993	Enrico Pietromarchi	1986-1992
Enzo Perlot	1993-1995	Rocco Cangelosi	1992-1994
Luigi Cavalchini	1995-2000	Roberto Rossi	1994-1999
Silvio Fagiolo	2000-2001	Fabio Fabbri	1999-2002
Roberto Nigido	2001	Alessandro Pignatti	2002-
Umberto Vattani	2001-2004		
Rocco Cangelosi	2004-		
Latvia			
Andris Kesteris	2004-	Eduards Stiprais	2004-
Lithuania			
Oskaras Jusys	2004-	Romas Svedas	2004-
Luxembourg			
Lambert Schaus	1958-1959	Adrien Meisch	1958-1961
Albert Borschette	1960-1970	Jean Dondelinger	1961-1970
Jean Dondelinger	1970-1984	Jean Schleich	1970-1973
Joseph Weyland	1984-1991	Paul Peters	1973-1976
Jean-Jacques Kasel	1991-1998	Joseph Weyland	1976-1979
Nicolas Schmit	1998-2004	Jean Mischo	1979-1983
Martine Schommer	2004-	Jean Feyder	1983-1987
		Thierry Stoll	1987-1991
		Jim Cloos	1991-1993
		Jean-Marc Hoscheit	1993-1998

Permanent representatives	Dates	Deputy permanent representatives	Dates
Luxembourg (cont)			
		Marc Ungeheuer	1998-2002
		Christian Braun	2002-
Malta			
Richard Cachia Caruana	2004-	Chris Grima	2004-
Netherlands			
J. Linthorst Homan	1958-1962	J.I.M. Welsing	1958-1960
Dirk Spierenburg	1963-1970	Charles Rutten	1960-1969
E.M.J.A. Sassen	1971-1976	Jan Lubbers	1969-1973
Jan H. Lubbers	1977-1980	E.J. Korthals Altes	1973-1977
Charles Rutten	1980-1986	Rein van Swinderen	1977-1982
Peter C. Nieman	1986-1992	Henk Vijverberg	1982-1984
Bernard R. Bot	1992-2002	Ronald van Beuge	1984-1990
Thom de Bruijn	2003-	Ate Oostra	1990-1994
		Lambert J. Hanrath	1994-1998
		Jan de Jong	1998-2002
		Henne J.J. Schuwer	2002-
Poland			
Marek Grela	2004-	Ewa Synowiec	2004-
Portugal			
Fernando da Silva Marques	1986	Luís Roma de Albuquerque	1986
Leonardo Mathias	1986-1989	Pedro José Ribeiro de Menezes	1986-1988
Carlos Simões Coelho	1989-1990	Vasco Valente	1988-1993
José César Paulouro das Neves	1990-1994	João de Vallera	1993-1998
José Gregório Faria	1995-1997	Margarida Figueiredo	1998-2002
Vasco Valente	1997-2002	Domingos Fezas Vital	2002-
Álvaro Mendonça e Moura	2002-		
Slovakia			
Miroslav Adamis	2004	Juraj Nociar	2004-
Maros Sefcovic	2004		
Slovenia			
Ciril Stokelj	2004-	Marjeta Jager	2004-
Spain			
Carlos Westendorp y Cabeza	1986-1991	Francisco Javier Elorza Cavengt	1986-1991
Camilo Barcia Garcia-Villamil	1991-1994	Carlos Bastarreche Sagües	1991-1996
Francisco Javier Elorza Cavengt	1994-2000	Miguel Angel Navarro	1996-2003
Francisco Javier Conde de Saro	2000-2002	Cristóbal Gonzalez-Aller	2003-
Carlos Bastarreche Sagües	2002-		

Permanent representatives	Dates	Deputy permanent representatives	Dates
Sweden			
Frank Belfrage	1995-1999	Lars-Olof Lindgren	1995-2002
Gunnar Lund	1999-2002	Ingrid Hjelt af Trolle	2002-
Sven-Olof Petersson	2002-		
United Kingdom			
Sir Michael Palliser	1973-1975	Robert Goldsmith	1973-1977
Sir Donald Maitland	1975-1979	Sir William Nicoll	1977-1982
Sir Michael Butler	1979-1985	David Elliott	1982-1991
Sir David Hannay	1985-1990	David Durie	1991-1995
Sir John Kerr	1990-1995	David Bostock	1995-1999
Sir Stephen Wall	1995-2000	Bill Stow	1999-2003
Sir Nigel Sheinwald	2000-2003	Anne Lambert	2003-
John Grant	2003-		

APPENDIX 3

List of Council presidencies 1958-2006

Year	First half	Second half
1958	Belgium	Germany
1959	France	Italy
1960	Luxembourg	The Netherlands
1961	Belgium	Germany
1962	France	Italy
1963	Luxembourg	The Netherlands
1964	Belgium	Germany
1965	France	Italy
1966	Luxembourg	The Netherlands
1967	Belgium	Germany
1968	France	Italy
1969	Luxembourg	The Netherlands
1970	Belgium	Germany
1971	France	Italy
1972	Luxembourg	The Netherlands
1973	Belgium	Denmark
1974	Germany	France
1975	Ireland	Italy
1976	Luxembourg	The Netherlands
1977	United Kingdom	Belgium
1978	Denmark	Germany
1979	France	Ireland
1980	Italy	Luxembourg
1981	The Netherlands	United Kingdom
1982	Belgium	Denmark
1983	Germany	Greece
1984	France	Ireland
1985	Italy	Luxembourg
1986	The Netherlands	United Kingdom
1987	Belgium	Denmark
1988	Germany	Greece
1989	Spain	France
1990	Ireland	Italy
1991	Luxembourg	The Netherlands
1992	Portugal	United Kingdom
1993	Denmark	Belgium
1994	Greece	Germany
1995	France	Spain

Year	First half	Second half
1996	Italy	Ireland
1997	The Netherlands	Luxembourg
1998	United Kingdom	Austria
1999	Germany	Finland
2000	Portugal	France
2001	Sweden	Belgium
2002	Spain	Denmark
2003	Greece	Italy
2004	Ireland	The Netherlands
2005	Luxembourg	United Kingdom
2006	Austria	Finland

Bibliography

This bibliography lists only those works referred to in the text.

Allen, D., 2002, 'The United Kingdom,' in Hocking B., and Spence, D., *Foreign Ministries in the European Union; Integrating Diplomats*

Baldwin, R., Berglöf, E., Giavazzi, F., Widgrén, M., 2000, ´EU Reforms for tomorrow's Europe´, Discussion paper, No. 2623, Centre for Economic Policy Research, London, November

Balladur, E., 1994, *Le Monde*, 30 November

Barber, L.,1995, 'The Men Who Run Europe´, 1995, *Financial Times*, 11-12 March

Barnier, M., 2000, ´La grande illusion du droit de veto´, *Le Figaro*, 27 November

Barry, C., 1996, ´NATO's Combined Joint Task Forces in theory and practice´, *Survival*, No1.

Begg, I., Grimwade, N., 1998, *Paying for Europe*, Sheffield Academic Press

Best, E., 2000, ´The debate over the weighting of votes: the mis-presentation of representation? ´in E. Best, M. Gray and A. Stubb (eds.)

Best, E, Gray, M and Stubb, A. (eds.), 2000, *Rethinking the European Union – IGC 2000 and Beyond*, EIPA, Maastricht

Beyers, Jan, and Dierickx, Guido, 1998, 'The Working Groups of the Council of the European Union: Supranational or Intergovernmental Negotiations?' *Journal of Common Market Studies*, Vol. 36, N° 3, September

Bieber, R., 1992, *Das Verfahrensrecht von Verfassungsorganen. Ein beitrag zur Theorie das inner-und interorgangemeinschtlichen Rechtsetzung in der Europäischen Gemeinschaft, im Staatsrecht und Völkerrecht*, Nomos, Baden-Baden

Blondel, J., and Thiébault, J.-L. (eds), 1991, The Profession of Government Minister in Western Europe, Macmillan, London

Bostock, David, 2002, 'Coreper Visited,' *Journal of Common Market Studies*, Vol. 40, N° 2, June

Brandt, W., 1975, 'Rede vor der Organisation Française du Mouvement Européenne in Paris am 19 November 1974', *Europa Archiv*, (2)

Bulletin of the European Communities, 1992, 'Joint declaration of the Commission, the European Parliament and the Council,' 10

Bulletin Quotidien Europe, 1999, 7619, 1 December

Bulmer, S., and Wessels, W., 1987, *The European Council: Decision-Making in European Politics*, Macmillan, London

Bulmer, S., and Paterson, W., 1988, 'European Policy-Making in the Federal republic – Internal and External Limits to Leadership,' in *The Federal Republic of Germany and the EC: The Presidency and Beyond*, Europa Union Verlag, Bonn

Butler, M., 1986, *Europe: More than a Continent*, Heinemann, London

Central Policy Review Staff, 1977, *Review of Overseas Representation*, HMSO, London

Charter of fundamental rights of the European Union, in OJ C 364, 18.12.2000

Christiansen, T., 2002, ´Out of the Shadows: The General Secretariat of the Council of Ministers, in Van Schendelen, R., and Scully, R., (eds.)

Cichowski, R.A., 1999, 'Integrating the Environment: the European Court and the construction of supranational policy,' *Journal of European Public Policy*, Vol. 5 (3)

Clark, A., 1994, *Diaries*, Phoenix/Orion, London

Cornish, P., 1996, 'European Security: The End of Architecture and the New NATO', *International Affairs*, (4)

Cot, Jean-Pierre, 1988, 'Eloge du budgetaire,' *L'événement européen*, N°1, 317

Commission Decision 94/90/ECSC, EC, 1994, on public access to Commission documents, 8 February 1994, in OJ L 46 of 18.2.1994, pp. 58

Commission Decision 2001/844/EC, ECSC, Euratom, 2001, amending its internal Rules of Procedure, 29 November 2001, in OJ L 317 of 3.12.2001, pp. 1.

Council, 1993, Council Decision 93/662 EC of 6 December 1993 adopting the Council's Rules of procedure, OJ L 304, 10.12.1993, p. 1.

Council, 1995, Council's conclusions of 29 May 1995 on the transparency of the Council's proceedings, document 7481/95 (Presse 152).

Council, 1996, 'Commentary on the Council's rules of procedure', Council guide, Vol. II, General Secretariat of the Council.

Council, 1999a, 'Presidency conclusions', European Council, Berlin, 24-25 March

Council, 1999b,'Operation of the Council with an enlarged Union in prospect', Report by the Working Party set up by the Secretary-General of the Council, doc. SN 2139/99

Council, 2002a, 'Presidency report to the European Council on the use of languages in the context of an enlarged Union', (doc. 15089/02)

Council, 2002b, 'Administrative consequences of enlargement on the General Secretariat of the Council'

Council, 2002c, 'Seville European Council Presidency conclusions'

Council, 2003, Council's Annual report on access to documents for 2003

Council, 2003b,'Press release of the ECOCIN Council', 5 December 2003

Council, 2003c, 'Guide for producing documents for the Council and its preparatory bodies', Council Guide Vol. VI, General Secretariat of the Council

Council Decision 93/591/EC, 1993, concerning the name to be given to the Council following the entry into force of the Treaty on European Union, 8 November 1993, in OJ L 281, 16.11.93, pp. 18

Council Decision 93/662 EC, 1993, 1993 adopting the Council's rules of procedure, 6 December 1993, in OJ L 304, 10.12.1993, pp. 1

Council Decision 93/730/EC, 1993, Code of conduct concerning public access to Council and Commission documents, in OJ L 340 of 31.12.1993, pp. 41

Council 1995b, Document 10204/95 (Presse 271), pp. 15-18.

Council Decision 1999/64/Euratom, 1999, concerning the Fifth Framework Programme of the European Atomic Energy Community (Euratom) for research and training activities (1998 to 2002) in OJ L 26, 1.2.1999, pp. 34

Council Decision 2000/23/EC, 2000, on the improvement of information on the Council's legislative activities and the public register of Council documents, 6 December 1999, in OJ L 9 of 13.1.2000, pp. 22

Council Decision 2000/265/EC, 2000, on the establishment of a financial regulation governing the budgetary aspects of the management by the Deputy Secretary-General of the Council, 27 March 2000, in OJ L 85 of 6.4.2000, pp. 12

Council Decision 2000/527/EC, 2000, amending Decision 93/731/EC on public access to Council documents

Council Decision 2000/23/EC on the improvement of information on the Council's legislative activities and the public register of Council documents, 14 August 2000, in OJ L 212 of 23.8.2000, pp. 9.

Council Decision 2001/80/CFSP, 2001, on the establishment of the Military Staff of the European Union, 22 January 2001, in OJ L 27 of 30.1.2001, pp. 7.

Council Decision 2001/264/EC, 2001, adopting the Council's security regulations, 19 March 2001, OJ L 101 of 11.4.2001, pp. 1.

Council Decision 2001/320/EC, 2001, on making certain categories of Council documents available to the public, 9 April 2001, in OJ L 111 of 20.4.2001, pp. 29.

Council Decision 2001/840, 2001, amending the Council's Rules of Procedure, 29 November 2001, in OJ L 313 of 30.11.2001, pp. 40.

Council, 2001d, Decision 2001/C 189/01 of the Secretary-General of the Council/High Representative for Common and Foreign Security Policy of 25 June 2001 on a code of good administrative behaviour for the General Secretariat of the Council of the European Union and its staff in their professional relations with the public, OJ C 189 of 5.7.2001, p. 1.

Council Decision 2002/682/EC, Euratom, 2002, adopting the Council's Rules of Procedure, 22 July 2002, in OJ L 230 of 28.8.2002, pp. 7.

Council Decision 2003/479/EC, 2003, concerning the rules applicable to national experts and military staff on secondment to the General Secretariat of the Council and repealing the Decisions of 25 June 1997 and 22 March 1999, 16 June 2003, in OJ L 160 of 28.6.2003, pp. 72

Council Regulation (EEC, Euratom) No. 354/83, 1983, concerning the opening to the public of the historical archives of the European Community and the European Atomic Energy Community, 1 February 1983, in OJ L 43 of 15.2.1983, pp. 1.

Council Regulation (EC) No. 45/2001 of the European Parliament and the Council, 2001, on the protection of individuals with regard to the processing of personal data by the Community institutions and bodies and on the free movement of such data, 18 December 2000, in OJ L 8 of 12.1.2001, pp. 1.

Council Regulation (EC) No 1049/2001 of the European Parliament and of the Council, 2001, regarding public access to European Parliament, Council and Commission documents, 30 May 2001, in OJ L 145 of 31.5.2001, pp. 43.

Council Regulation 1605/2002, 2002, on the Financial Regulation applicable to the general budget of the European Communities, 25 June 2002, in OJ L 248 of 16.9.2002

Council Regulation (EC, Euratom) No. 354/83, 2003, concerning the opening to the public of the historical archives of the European Economic Community and the European Atomic Energy Community, in OJ L 243 of 27.9.2003, pp. 1.

Council Regulation (EC) No 1641/2003 of the European Parliament and of the Council, 2003, amending Council Regulation (EEC) No 1210/90 on the establishment of the European Environment Agency and the European Environment Information and Observation Network, 22 July 2003, in OJ L 245 of 29.9.2003, pp. 1-41.

Craeyenest, F. Van, and Saarilahti, I, 2004, 'Le nouveau règlement financier applicable au budget général de l'Union européenne: un maillon essentiel dans la réforme de la Commission', in: Revue du Marché commun et de l'Union européenne, 474, January

Dahrendorf, R., A third Europe?, Third Jean Monnet Lecture, Florence, 1979

Dashwood, A., 1996, 'The limits of European Community powers', European Law Review, Vol 1, (2), April

Debasch, C., 1987, Administrations nationales et intégration Européenne; CNRS, Paris

Decision of the Committee of the Regions No 64/2003, 2003, on public access to Committee of the Regions documents, 11 February 2003, in OJ L 160 of 28.6.2003, pp. 96.

Decision of EESC 2003/603, 2003, on public access to European Economic and Social Committee documents, 1 July 2003, OJ L 205 of 14.8.2003, pp. 19.

Decision 2001/C 189/01 of the Secretary-General of the Council/High Representative for Common and Foreign Security Policy of 25 June 2001 on a code of good administrative behaviour for the General Secretariat of the Council of the European Union and its staff in their professional relations with the public, in OJ C 189 of 5.7.2001, pp. 1.

Decision 2002/176/EU, 2002, of the Representatives of the Governments of the Member States meeting within the Council of 21 February 2002 setting up a Fund for the financing of the Convention on the future of the European Union, in OJ L 60 of 1.3.2002, pp. 56.

'Declaration of Heads of State and Government', 1994, NATO Council, 10-11 January.

De La Porte, C., and Pochet, P., 2002, *Building Social Europe through the Open Method of Co-ordination*, Interuniversitaires européennes press, Work and Society series, 34

De L'Ecotais, M.,1996,'La pondération des voix au Conseil des Ministres', *Revue du Marché Commun et de l'Union européenne*, 398, July

De L'Ecotais, M., 1997a, 'La pondération des voix au Conseil des Ministres', *Revue du Marché Commun et de l'Union européenne*, 401, July

De L'Ecotais, M., 1997b, 'La pondération des voix au Conseil des Ministres', *Revue du Marché Commun et de l'Union européenne*, 408, July

de Ruyt, J., 1987, *L'Acte Unique Européen*, Brussels Free University

Derycke, E., 1996, 'Belgium's contribution to the security in the Euro-Atlantic era', *Nato Review*, (6)

Dickie, J, 1992, *Inside the Foreign Office*, Chapmans, London.

Digneffe, T., 1999, 'The General Secretariat of the Council of the European Union: It's 'Power Base' in the EU Decision-Making Process,' MA thesis, College of Europe, Bruges

Draft Treaty establishing a Constitution for Europe, 2003, in OJ C 169 of 18.7.2003, pp. 1.

Duff, A., 1981, 'The Report of the Three Wise Men,' *Journal of Common Market Studies*, Vol. XIX (3), March

Duff, A., Pinder, J., and Pryce, R., (eds.), *Maastricht and Beyond. Building the European Union*, Routledge, London

EAEC Council Regulation No 3, 1958, Treaty establishing the European Atomic Energy Community, 1958, in OJ No. 17, 6.10.1958, p. 406

EC, 1993, Code of Conduct 93/730/EC of 6 December 1993 concerning public access to Council and Commission documents, OJ L 340 of 31.12.1993, p. 41.

EC, 2002, Interinstitutional Agreement 2002/C 298/01, OJ C 298 of 30.11.2002, p. 1.

Edwards, G., and Spence, D., 1995, *The European Commission* (2nd edition), Cartermill Publishing, London

Edwards, R.D., 1994, *True Brits: Inside the Foreign Office*, BBC Books, London

Egger, A., 1994, *Das Generalsekretariat des Rates der EU*, Nomos, Baden-Baden.

Eichener, V., 1992, 'Social Dumping or Innovative regulation? Process and Outcomes of European decision-making in the Sector of health and Safety at Work Harmonisation', Florence, EUI Working paper SPS 92/28

European Commission, 2004, Document COM(2004) 45 final of 30 January 2004 (Council document 5983/04).

European Council, 1992a, Joint declaration of the Commission, the European Parliament and the Council, *Bulletin of the European Communities (1992)*, No. 10, p. 9.

European Council, 1992b, Edinburgh European Council, Presidency conclusions, *Bulletin of the European Communities (1992)*, No. 12, p. 18.

European Parliament and Council Decision 182/1999/EC, 1999, concerning the fifth framework programme of the European Community for research, technological development and demonstration activities (1998 to 2002) in OJ L 26, 1.2.1999, pp.1.

European Parliament Decision 2003/410/EC, 2003, concerning discharge in respect of the implementation of the general budget of the European Union for the 2001 financial year - Section II – Council, 8 April 2003, in OJ L 148 of 16.6.2003, pp. 42

European Parliament, Resolution 2003/2022(INI) on public access to Parliament, Council and Commission documents (implementation of Regulation 1049/2001 in the year 2002).
European Parliament, 2003b, Verbatim report of proceedings of the European Parliament, sitting of 24 September 2003.
Everts, S., 2002, 'Foreign and security policy: from bystander to actor', *New Designs for Europe*, Centre for European Reform, October.

Fisher, R., and Brown, S., *Getting Together: Building a Relationship that Gets to Yes*, 1989, Hutchinson Business Books, London.
Fontaine, P., 1979, 'Le rôle de Jean Monnet dans la genèse du Conseil Européen,' *Revue du Marché Commun*, XXII
Forrest, A., 1998, 'The Politics of language in the European Union', *European Review*, Vol. 6(3)

Gehring, T., 1997, 'Governing in nested institutions: environmental policy in the EU and the case of packaging waste,' *Journal of European Public Policy*, Vol. 4 (3)
Golub, J., 1999, 'In the shadow of the vote? Decision making in the European Community', *Internal Organisation*, Vol. 53, Issue 4, Autumn 1999
Golub, J., 2000, 'Institutional reform and decision-making in the European Union', Paper for the Political Studies Association-UK 50th Annual Conference, London, 10-13 April
Granell, F., 1995, 'The European Union's Enlargement Negotiations with Austria, Finland, Norway and Sweden', *Journal of Common Market Studies*, Vol. 33(1), March
Grossir, J.-P., 2001, 'La procédure budgétaire pour 2001 : un long fleuve tranquille ?', *Revue du Marché commun et de l'Union européenne*, 449, June
Grossir, J.-P., 2002, 'La procédure budgétaire pour 2002 : la poursuite d'une entente cordiale entre les institutions, *Revue du Marché commun et de l'Union européenne*, 459, June
Grossir, J.-P., 2003, 'Le budget 2003: la fin d'une époque, *Revue du Marché commun et de l'Union européenne*, 471, September
Gross Stein, J., 1989, 'Getting to the table: The triggers, stages, functions and consequences of prenegotiation' in 'Getting to the Table"', *International Journal*, Vol XLIV(2), Spring
Guyomarch, A., Machin, H., and Ritchie, E., 1998, *France in the European Union*, Macmillan, London

Hayes-Renshaw, F., Lequesne, C., and Mayor-Lopez, P., 1989, 'The permanent representation of the member states of the European Communities,' *Journal of Common Market Studies*, XXVIII (2)
Heseltine, M., 1989, *The Challenge of Europe. Can Britain Win?*, Weidenfeld, London
Hocking, B., and Spence, D., 2002, *Foreign Ministries in the European Union; Integrating Diplomats*, Palgrave, London
Hoffman, S., 1995, 'Goodbye to a United Europe?', *The European Sisyphus*, Westview, Oxford
Hosli, M., 1996, 'Coalitions and Power: effects of qualified majority voting in the Council of the European Union', *Journal of Common Market Studies*, Vol. 34(2)
Houben, P.-H. J. M., 1964, *Les Conseils de Ministres des Communautés Européennes*, A.W. Sythoff, Leiden

IGC, 2003, Conference document CIG 57/1/03 REV.1 on defence
Interinstitutional agreement on the financing of the Convention on the future of the European Union, in OJ C 54 of 1.3.2002, pp. 1
Interinstitutional Agreement, 2002/C 298/01, 2002, between the European Parliament and the Council concerning access by the European Parliament to sensitive information of the Council in the field of security and defence policy, in OJ C 298 of 30.11.2002, pp. 1

Jackson, Sir G., 1981, *Concorde Diplomacy*, Hamish Hamilton, London

Jacqué, J.-P., and Simon, D., 1984, 'Le rôle constitutionnel et juridique du Conseil européen,' in *Le Conseil Européen 1974-1984: bila et perspectives*, Colloquium of the European Institute of Public Administration, Maastricht

Jeffrey, C., and Sturm, R., (eds.), 1993, *Federalism, Unification and European Integration*, Frank Cass, London

Jeffrey, C., 2000, 'Sub-National Mobilization and European Integration', *Journal of Common Market Studies*, Vol. 38 (1), March

Joint declaration relating to Regulation (EC) No 1049/2001 of the European Parliament and of the Council, 2001, regarding public access to European Parliament, Council and Commission documents, 30 May 2001, in OJ L 145 of 31.5.2001, pp. 5

Kendall, J., and Anheier, H.K., 1999, 'The Third Sector and the European Union Policy Process: An Initial Evaluation,' *Journal of European Public Policy*, 6(2), June

Kirchner, E.J.,1992, *Decision-making in the European Community. The Council Presidency and European Integration*, Manchester University Press, Manchester

Laffan, B., 1997, *The Finances of the European Union*, Macmillan Press, Houndsmill

Laffan, B., Shackleton, M., 2000, 'The Budget. Who Gets What, When, and How', in Wallace, H., and Wallace, W., (eds.), *Policy-making in the European Union*

Leonardy, U., 1993, 'Federation and Länder in German Foreign Relations: Power-Sharing in Treaty-Making and European Affairs', in C. Jeffrey and R. Sturm (eds.), *Federalism, Unification and European Integration*, Frank Cass, London

Lequesne, C., 1987, 'Coordonner la politique européenne de la France,' *Projet*, 206, July-August

Lequesne, C., 1988, 'France', *Jahrbuch der Europaischen Integration 1987/88*, Europa Union Verlag, Bonn

Lequesne, C., 1993, *Paris-Bruxelles: Comment se fait la politique européenne de la France*, Fondation Nationale des Science Politiques, Paris

Lequesne, C., 1996, 'French central government and the European political system: change and adaptation since the Single European Act,' in Mény, Y., Muller, P. and Quermonne, J.-L., *Adjusting to Europe: The Impact of the European Union on National Institutions and Policies*

Le Theule, F-G., Litvan, D., 1993, 'La Réforme de la PAC: analyse d'une négotiation communautaire', *Revue Française de Science Politique*, Vol. 43 (5), October

Lord, C., 1998, *Democracy in the European Union*, Sheffield Academic Press, Sheffield

Ludlow P. (ed.), 1995, *L'équilibre Européen. Etudes rassemblées et publiées en hommage à Niels Ersbøll*, General Secretariat of the Council, Brussels

Ludlow P., 1995, 'The Presidency of the Council: A new power in the European Union? ', in Ludlow P. (ed.), 1994, *L'équilibre Européen. Etudes rassemblées et publiées en hommage à Niels Ersbøll*

Majone, G., 1996, *Regulating Europe*, Routledge, London

Majone, G., 1996, 'The Commission as Regulator', in Majone, G., *Regulating Europe*

Mann, M., 1996, 'Why 60 hours of talking achieved almost nothing', in *European Voice* 4-10 July

Mazey, S., 1993, 'A European Policy Style?', in Mazey and Richardson, *Lobbying in the European Community*

Mazey, S. and Richardson, J., 1993, *Lobbying in the European Community*, Oxford University Press, Oxford

McDonagh, B., 1998, *Original sin in a brave new world – An account of the negotiation of the Treaty of Amsterdam*, Institute for European Affairs, Dublin

Mény, Y., Muller, P. and Quermonne, J.-L., 1996, *Adjusting to Europe: The Impact of the European Union on National Institutions and Policies*, Routledge, London

Metcalfe, L., 1994, 'European Policy Management as an Intergovernmental Process,' paper delivered to the Workshop on Multi-Organizational Partnerships: 'Working Across Organisational Boundaries,' EIASM, Brussels, 19-20 September

Metcalfe, L., 1997, 'Comparing Policy Coordination Systems: Do the Differences Matter?', paper delivered to the Fifth Erestein Colloquium, 30-31 October, Kerkrade

Metcalfe, L., and Zapico Goni, E., 1991, *Action or Reaction? The Role of National Administrations in European Policy-Making*, Sage, London

Michael Winkler, G., 1998, 'Coalition-Sensitive Voting Power in the Council of Ministers: The Case of Eastern Enlargement,' *Journal of Common Market Studies*, Vol. 36, N° 3, September

Moberg, Axel, 2002, 'The Nice Treaty and Voting Rules in the Council,' *Journal of Common Market Studies*, Vol. 40, N° 2, June

Monnet, J., 1976, *Mémoires*, Fayard, Paris

Monnet, J., 1978, *Mémoirs*, Collins, London.

Moravcsik, A., 1991, 'Negotiating the Single European Act´, in R. Keohane and S. Hoffmann, 'The New European Community': decision-making and institutional change*, Westview, Oxford

Moravcsik, A., 2003, 'The EU ain't broke´, *Prospect*, March

Morgan, R., and Bray, C., 1986, *Partners and Rivals in Western Europe: Britain, France and Germany*, PSI/Gower, London

Neyer, J., 2004, 'Explaining the unexpected: efficiency and effectiveness in European decision-making,' *Journal of European Public Policy*, Vol. 11 (1)

Nicoll, Sir W., 1994, 'Representing the States,` in Duff, A. et al, *Maastricht and Beyond*

Nicoll, Sir W. and Salmon, T., 1990, *Understanding the European Communities*, Philip Allan, London

Noël, E., 1966, 'The Committee of Permanent Representatives,' *Journal of Common Market Studies*, 3

Noël, E., and Etienne, H., 1969, 'Quelques aspects des rapports et de la collaboration entre le Conseil et la Commission,' in *La décision dans les Communautés européennes*, Brussels

Nugent, N., 1993, *The Government and Politics of the European Community*, (second edition), Macmillan, London

Nuttal, S., 1992, European Political Cooperation, Oxford University Press, Oxford

O'Keeffe, D. and Twomey, P. (eds.), 1999, *Legal Issues of the Amsterdam Treaty*, Hart, Oxford: Hart

OPOCE, 2002, *European Union Public Finance*, Luxembourg.

Page, E. and Wright, V., 1999, *Bureaucratic Elites in Western European States*, Oxford University Press, Oxford

Palliser, Sir M., 1985, Evidence to the Select Committee on the European Communities, *European Union*, London, HMSO 1985 p 215

Patten, C., 2000, 'Souveraineté et démocratie: Réflexions d'un britannique européen´, *Commentaires*, Paris

Petite, M., 2000, 'The IGC and the European Commission´ in E. Best, M. Gray and A. Stubb (eds.), *Rethinking the European Union – IGC 2000 and Beyond*, EIPA, Maastricht

Philippart, E. and Sie Dhian Ho, M.., 2000, 'The Pros and Cons of Closer Co-operation –

Argumentation and Recommendations', *Paper for the Netherlands Scientific Council for government policy*, The Hague, February

Putnam, R.D., 1988, 'Diplomacy and domestic politics: the logic of two-level games', *International Organisation*, 42 (3), Summer

Rees, G. W., 1998, *The Western European Union at the Crossroads*, Leicester, 1998

Rometsch, D., and Wessels, W., 1995, 'The Commission and the Council of the European Union,' in Edwards, G. and Spence, D., *The European Commission*

Rometsch, D., and Wessels, W., 1996, *The European Union and Member States: Towards Institutional Fusion?*, Manchester University Press, Manchester

Ross, G., 1995, 'Jacques Delors and European Integration', Blackwell/Polity, Oxford

Ruhl, L., 1999, 'Conditions and options for an autonomous common European Policy on Security and Defence', Discussion Paper, Centre for European Integration Studies, Bonn

Sanchez, Gonzalez, E., 1992, 'La Négociation des Décisions Communautaires par les Fonctionnaires Nationaux: les groupes de travail du Conseil', *Revue Française de l'Administration Publique*, No. 63

Scharpf, F.W., 1994, 'Community and autonomy : multi-level policy-making in the European Union,' *Journal of European Public Policy*, Vol. 1 (2)

Scharpf, F.W., 1997, 'The problem-solving capacity of multi-level governance,' *Journal of European Public Policy*, Vol. 4(4)

Schauble, W., and Lamers, W., 1994, *Reflections on European foreign policy*, Document of the CDU/CSU fraction in the German Bundestag, Bonn, September

Schloh, Bernhard, 1998, 'The Presidency of the Council of the European Union,' *Syracuse Journal of International Law and Commerce*, Vol. 25, Spring

Solana, Javier, 2001, 'Europe's place in the world', The Hague, February

Spence, D., 1991, Enlargement without Accession: the EC's response to German unification, RIIA discussion paper N° 36, Chatham House

Spence, D., 1993, 'The Role of the National Civil Service in European Lobbying: The British Case', in Mazey, S. and Richardson, J., *Lobbying in the European Community*

Stein, Gross, J., 1989, 'Getting to the table: The triggers, stages, functions and consequences of prenegotiation', in Getting to the Table, International Journal, Vol. XLIV (2), Spring

Stubb, A., 1998, 'Flexible integration and the Amsterdam Treaty: Negotiating differentiation in the 1996-1997 IGC' , PhD thesis (London: LSE)

Tarditi, S., K. Thomson, P. Pierani and E. Croci Angelini (eds.), 1989, *Agricultural Trade Liberalization and Economic Policy Perspectives in the EC*, Oxford University Press, Oxford

Teasdale, A, 1995, 'The Fouchet Plan: De Gaulle's Intergovernmental Design for Europe,' unpublished paper

Teasdale, A, 1999, 'The Luxembourg compromise', Westlake, M., *The Council of the European Union*, second edition, John Harper

'Three Wise Men', the, 1979, *Report on European Institutions*, presented by the Committee of the Three to the European Council, October

Tsebelis, G., 1990, *Nested Games; rational choice in comparative politics*, University of California, Berkeley

Tsebelis, George, and Yataganas, Xenophon, 2002, 'Veto Players and Decision-Making in the EU After Nice,' *Journal of Common Market Studies*, Vol. 40, N° 2, June

Thwaites, D., 1998, 'Has the Foreign and Commonwealth Office (FCO) been 'Europeanised'? The role of the FCO as an actor in national co-ordination end negotiation process in the European Union,' MA thesis, College of Europe, Bruges

Tindemans, L., 1975, 'European Union: Report by Mr. Leo Tindemans to the European Council,' December, in Nicoll, Sir W. and Salmon, T., Understanding the European Communities

Usher, J., 1994, 'The Commission and the Law', in Edwards, G., and Spence, D., *The European Commission*, Longmans, London

Van Eekelen, W., 1998, 'Debating European Security', 1949-1998, Brussels
Vasey, M., 1986, 'The 1985 Farm Price negotiations and the reform of the CAP', *Common Market Law Review*, 22
Van Schendelen, R., and Scully, R., (eds.), 2002, 'The Unseen Hand', Unelected EU Legislators, *The Journal of Legislative Studies*, Vol. 8 (4), Winter

Wallace, H., 1973, *National Governments and the European Communities*, Chatham House/PEP, London
Wallace, H. 1985, "Negotiations and Coalition Formation in the European Community", *Government and Opposition*, Vol 20 (4), Autumn
Wallace, H., 1986, 'Bilateral, Trilateral and Multilateral Negotiations in the European Community' in Morgan, R., and Bray, C., *Partners and Rivals in Western Europe: Britain, France and Germany*
Wallace, H., 1989, "The Best is the Enemy of the 'Could': Bargaining in the EC" in S. Tarditi et al "Agricultural Trade Liberalization and Economic Policy Perspectives in the EC", Oxford University Press, Oxford
Wallace, H., 1990, "Making multilateral negotiations work" in Wallace, W. (ed), *The Dynamics of European Integration*
Wallace, W., 1972, 'After Berill; Whitehall and the Management of British Diplomacy,' *International Affairs*, Vol. 54 (2), April
Wallace, W., (ed.), 1990, *The Dynamics of European Integration*, Pinter, London
Wallace, H., and Wallace, W., (eds.), 2000, *Policy-making in the European Union*, 4th Edition, Oxford University Press, Oxford
Weatherill, S., 1999, 'If I'd wanted you to understand I would have explained it better: what is the purpose of the provisions on close co-operation introduced by the Treaty of Amsterdam?', in O'Keeffe, D. and Twomey, P. (eds.), *Legal Issues of the Amsterday Treaty*, Hart, Oxford: Hart
Weiler, J.H.H., 1999, *The Constitution of Europe*, Cambridge University Press, Cambridge
Wessels, W., 1990, 'The Dynamics of Administrative Interaction; towards a European System of Cooperative States,' in Wallace, W., *the Dynamics of European Integration*
Wessels, W., and Rometsch, D., 1996, 'German administrative inter-action and the EU: the fusion of public policies,' in Mény, Y., Muller, P. and Quermonne, J.-L., *Adjusting to Europe: The Impact of the European Union on National Institutions and Policies*
Willocks, E., 2004, 'Enlargement of the European Union – the Council Process', in *A True European: Essays for Judge David Edward*, Hart, Oxford
Winham, G., 1977, "Negotiation as a Management Process", *World Politics*, Vol. XXX(1), October
Winkler, M., 1998, 'Coalition sensitive voting power in the Council of Ministers: the case of Eastern enlargement', *Journal of Common Market Studies*, Vol. 36 (3)

Newspaper articles

'A suitable rock to founder on', 1987, *The Economist*, November 28
'Britain is spying on EU Partners', 1998, *Guardian*, 2 January
'British to Block EC social policies', 1992, *Guardian*, 10 July
'EC out of touch - Thatcher', 1992, *Guardian*, 3 July
'European left accuses Hurd on social policy', 1992, *The Times*, 9 July
'Game, set and match to Britain', 1991, *Independent*, 11 December
'The UN loses a diplomatic bruiser', 1995, *Independent*, 28 July

Web sites referred to:

Council of the European Union: http://www.consilium.eu.int/en/summ.htm

The Web site of the Budget Directorate-General of the Commission:
http://europa.eu.int/comm/budget/infos/publications_en.htm

Index